For Reference

Not to be taken from this room

ENCYCLOPEDIA OF AMERICAN INDIAN ISSUES TODAY

ENCYCLOPEDIA OF AMERICAN INDIAN ISSUES TODAY

VOLUME 2

Russell M. Lawson, Editor

AN IMPRINT OF ABC-CLIO, LLC
Santa Barbara, California • Denver, Colorado • Oxford, England

Copyright 2013 by Russell M. Lawson

All rights reserved. No part of this publication may be reproduced, stored in a retrieval system, or transmitted, in any form or by any means, electronic, mechanical, photocopying, recording, or otherwise, except for the inclusion of brief quotations in a review, without prior permission in writing from the publisher.

Library of Congress Cataloging-in-Publication Data

Encyclopedia of American Indian issues today / Russell M. Lawson, editor.
   v.1— p. cm.
Includes bibliographical references and index.
ISBN 978–0–313–38144–7 (cloth : alk. paper) — ISBN 978–0–313–38145–4 (ebook)
1. Indians of North America—Encyclopedias. I. Lawson, Russell M., 1957–
E78.2.E64 2013
305.896—dc23   2012031756

ISBN: 978–0–313–38144–7
EISBN: 978–0–313–38145–4

17 16 15 14 13   1 2 3 4 5

This book is also available on the World Wide Web as an eBook.
Visit www.abc-clio.com for details.

Greenwood
An Imprint of ABC-CLIO, LLC

ABC-CLIO, LLC
130 Cremona Drive, P.O. Box 1911
Santa Barbara, California 93116-1911

This book is printed on acid-free paper ∞

Manufactured in the United States of America

This book is dedicated to the Students and Faculty of Bacone College

Contents

Introduction   xi
Russell M. Lawson

VOLUME 1

Section 1: People and Places

Borderlands: Change, Resistance, and Assimilation	3
Family: Traditional Kinship in the Modern World	8
Indian City Life	19
Indian Demographics: Definitions, Numbers, and Politics	28
Urban Indians: The Impact of Urbanization	36
Women: Changes in Identity and Power	46

Section 2: Economy and Work

Advertising and Indian Identity	57
American Indian Poverty in Urban Areas	67
American Indian Poverty on Reservations	75
Gaming and Casinos	85
Tourist Industry: Economic and Social Costs and Benefits	96
Tribal Economic Diversification	105
Unemployment	114

Section 3: Learning, Literacy, and Languages

Indian Colleges and Universities: Boarding Schools to Native American Studies	129
Indian Schools: History of Schooling Models	138
Literacy and Illiteracy	151
Native American Deaf	161
Public Education: Current Issues and Legislation	169
Red English: Language and American Indian English	180

Section 4: Health: Body and Mind, Private and Public

Domestic Abuse	189
Healthcare of American Indians	199
The Indian Child Welfare Act	209
Orphans	219
Psychological and Emotional Problems	228
Sexual Issues	242
Substance Abuse	249
Traditional Healing and Modern Medicine	260

Section 5: Ideas and Identity: Issues of Indian Identity, Spirituality, Traditional and Modern Thought

Cultural Preservation: Artifacts, Traditions, and Laws	273
Fake Indians: Modern Day Native American Identity	283
Historic Preservation: American Indian Inclusion and Contributions	292
Indian Mascots	301
Indian Ways of Knowing	311
Indians and Civilization: Shaping Society into the Future	318
Kennewick Man and the Controversy over Ownership of Indian Remains	328
Missionaries and the Translation of the Bible into Indigenous Languages	336
Modernization of American Indian Culture	345
National Museum of the American Indian: Contributing to American Culture	354
Native Spirituality and Christianity	364
Repatriation	376
Scientists: Supporting the Development of American Indians in Science	384
Stereotypes	393

VOLUME 2

Section 6: Sovereignty and Dependence: Rights, Reservations, Recognition

American Indian Athletes: Individual Contributions in the Face of Challenges	403
American Indian Smoke Shops: Struggles for Economic Independence	416
Bureau of Indian Affairs: A Historical and Contemporary Mission	426
Federal Recognition	434
Federal Reservations	444
Indian Civil Rights	454
Indian Sovereignty	464
Indians and the U.S. Constitution	476
Race Relations	484
Racism	493
Reservations and College Athletics: Identifying and Nurturing Talent	503
State Recognition	511

Section 7: Law, Politics, and Conflict

American Indians and the Military	521
Genocide	534
Grassroots Politics: Historical and Contemporary Activism	543
Indian Tribal Courts and the U.S. Court System	553
Indian Trust Lands Managed by the Federal Government	561
Indians and Congress	569
Law Enforcement in Indian Country	577
Leadership: Formal and Informal Leadership within Tribes	589
Political Activism: Examining the Issues	597
Prisons and Indians	606
Red Power: The American Indian Movement	615
Tribal Government: Local Decision-Making and Law Enforcement	626

Section 8: American Indian Expression

American Indian Art: Maintaining Culture, Tradition, and Identity	637
American Indian Theater and Performance: Political, Cultural, and Artistic Empowerment	648
Film Media about Indians: Representations and Misrepresentations	657

Film Media by Indians: Native Voices	665
Fraudulent Indian Art	673
Music: Vibrant Elements of American Indian Culture	681
Print Media by Indians: Words and Ideas of American Indians	691

Section 9: Environment

American Indians and Solid Waste	703
Climate Change	713
Environmental Racism	720
Nuclear Waste	726
Pollution	732
Preserving Habitats	743
Tribal Land Use	752

Section 10: Canadian Indians and Other Aboriginal Peoples

Aboriginal Peoples and the Canadian Government	769
Biocolonialism: Genetic Science and Aboriginal Peoples	780
Contemporary Issues of Aboriginal People in Canada	789
Human Rights of Indigenous People Worldwide	800
Missionaries to Canada's First Nations	811
Worldwide Indigenous Activism	820
About the Editor and Contributors	825
Index	829

INTRODUCTION

Russell M. Lawson

North American Indians in the twenty-first century face tests and challenges at the same time common to human experience and unique to indigenous peoples. All humans, including North Americans, experience war, conflict, and peace; good health and disease; family and community issues; social problems; issues of concern to local, state, and federal government; a fight for civil and human rights; educational and intellectual challenges; environmental concerns; religious, artistic, and cultural concerns; and regional and demographic challenges. North American Indians, because of unique historical and cultural experiences, face challenges that, while part of common human experience, are also specific to them. The *Encyclopedia of American Indian Issues Today* explores the legal, political, civil rights, human rights, economic, social, religious, educational, intellectual, psychological, cultural, artistic, demographic, property, environmental, urban, and regional issues facing American Indians. Essays describe theories, institutions, people, laws, customs, and forms of expression and behavior relevant to the particular issue. Sidebars give additional information on people and topics of particular interest as well as transcriptions of primary sources that provide firsthand, legal, governmental, and cultural evidence to document particular issues. In short, this is a reference tool that provides a complete survey of issues facing American Indians today in America.

The *Encyclopedia* is divided according to 10 sections of issues that feature 85 essays and 60 sidebars.

The first section, *People and Places*, provides a perspective on where Indians live and their numbers, and examines particular groups, such as women and the family—kinship patterns, marriage, intermarriage, and divorce. This section also describes issues related to urban Indians, the process of urbanization, the experience of living away from and not participating in reservation life, and the interaction of urban Indians with urban non-Indians; the disparate educational progress, mental and physical disabilities, and discrimination of Indian city life; the unique mestizo experience of the borderland between the United States and Mexico; and the demographic story of American Indians.

The second section, *Economy and Work*, examines unemployment on reservations and among Indians in urban areas; urban Indian poverty, including public housing and homelessness; the tourist industry and its challenge to Indian identity; topics involving casinos and gaming; the economic diversification of tribes; and issues in advertising in relation to Indian identity.

The third section, *Learning, Literacy, and Languages,* looks at issues related to higher education, the development of American Indian studies programs on college campuses, and the emergence of tribal colleges in America; topics related to public education such as the Indian Education Act and Office of Indian Education; issues related to reservation schools and other Indian schools, Indian Head Start, the Bureau of Indian Education, and the impact of No Child Left Behind on Indian education; and issues involving literacy and American Indian, or *red,* English, language reclamation, and language immersion.

The fourth section, *Health: Body and Mind, Private and Public*, examines healthcare topics such as self-determination in Indian healthcare, the Indian Health Service, immunizations, prevalent diseases such as diabetes, women's and children's particular health issues, and infant mortality; psychological issues, including emotional problems among Indians such as anxiety, phobias, and their treatment; mental illnesses such as depression, psychosis, schizophrenia, and bipolar disease, and their treatment; the prevalence of emotional and psychological problems on reservations; suicide; substance abuse, including drugs and alcohol; and traditional healing and modern medicine. This section also examines issues related to domestic violence, sexuality, orphans, and child welfare.

The fifth section, *Ideas and Identity: Issues of Indian Identity, Spirituality, Traditional and Modern Thought,* describes issues related to traditional spirituality and Christianity, such as the Native American Church, the use of peyote, and the American Indian Religious Freedom Act; also the question of the validity of the translation of the Bible into indigenous languages. This section also explores the American Indian identity, the Indian way of knowing, the preservation of Indian history and culture—the preservation of traditions, ceremonies, and languages that are essential to preserving the American Indian identity. As important is the status and interpretation of Indian cultural artificacts, the issue of repatriation, legislated in the Native American Grave Protection and Repatriation Act—the controversy over Kennewick Man is an example. Also significant are issues respecting the debate over historical interpretation of white-Indian relations; modernization—embracing modern culture and its assumptions, technology, and inherent materialism; and stereotypes and Indian mascots—traditional misconceptions of Indians, xenophobic language used against Indians, and ethnocentric attitude directed toward Indians.

The sixth section, *Sovereignty and Dependence: Rights, Reservations, Recognition*, focuses on human and civil rights topics that face American Indians today, including racism, which involves American Indians and hatred directed toward Indians; relations between Indians and other races in North America; Indian reservations and life on reservations today; the relationship between tribes and the Bureau of Indian Affairs; sovereign rights and challenges to tribal and individual sovereignty; and Indian civil rights and prejudice toward Indians in the workplace, school, and government. This section also examines the process of federal and state recognition of Indian tribes and its benefits, as well as the Office of Federal Acknowledgment. Also covered in this section are issues relating to Indian athletes.

The seventh section, *Laws, Politics, and Conflict*, focuses on political activism and grassroots politics—important events such as the occupation of Alcatraz and organizations such as the American Indian Movement (AIM)—that work to achieve recognition and rights for American Indians. Of great importance is the relationship between American Indians and the U.S. government, which involves the relationship between Indian tribes and Congress and the federal court system. This section also covers the various forms of Indian leadership, genocide, war, tribal government, law enforcement on reservations, and the Tribal Law and Order Act.

The eighth section, *American Indian Expression*, covers topics in Indian culture, arts, and media. This section examines stereotypes of Indians in literature and film as well as the American Indian voice in poetry, literature, music, theater, and art, including fraudulent Indian art. Issues of Indian perceptions occur in film and print media produced, performed, and written by American Indians. This section also examines film media that caricatures and misrepresents American Indians.

The ninth section, *Environment*, focuses on topics of tribal land use, including hunting, fishing, and hydroelectric power; the pollution of air, soil, and water on tribal lands; preserving habitats such as wetlands and floral and faunal species indigenous to tribal lands; climate change; the disposal of solid waste; and monitored storage of nuclear waste on tribal lands. Another issue is environmental racism, which involves governmental patronizing of tribal land use and whether tribes are independent in deciding environmental issues.

The tenth section, *Canadian Indians and Other Aboriginal Peoples*, examines significant issues involving the relations of Canada's First Nations with the Candian government; the validity of ongoing activities of Christian missionaries toward Canadian Indians; issues of indigenous education in Canada; indigenous movements worldwide working for political change and human rights; the UN declaration on behalf of indigenous peoples; and biocolonialism, which is the impact of genetic research on indigenous peoples.

These 10 sections provide a complete overview of issues facing American Indians in North America today. American Indians have been struggling and continue to struggle against centuries of discrimination, racism, colonialism, and oppression. In recent years, in the late twentieth century into the twenty-first century, the American and Canadian peoples, the U.S. and Canadian governments, have come to embrace more completely aboriginal peoples—their culture, language, arts, politics, and inherent rights—and have worked to ensure that aboriginal society and culture in North America will thrive and flourish in the years to come.

SECTION 6
Sovereignty and Dependence: Rights, Reservations, Recognition

American Indian Athletes: Individual Contributions in the Face of Challenges

G. Lola Worthington

American Indians represent a lasting presence in the history of athletics. Many Indian women and men compete in sports today, Although some male American Indian athletes made it into top sports organizations during the twentieth century, Indian athletes experienced several hindrances to achieve equality in sports. Even though in the past, female boarding school students were encouraged to compete in sports, the U.S. government, culturally and historically, discouraged women from continuing their athletic endeavors past school age, steering them instead toward domestic careers. The object of the boarding school was to help Indians assimilate into mainstream life. Athletic events were considered suitable for male athletes but were not an avenue for Indian women to pursue. School curriculum focused on women becoming housekeepers or domestics rather than athletes. Indian women remained athletic, but found few ways to compete due to this restricted cultural perspective. American Indian men were, however, sometimes encouraged to engage in sports. Common obstacles male athletes encountered included racial prejudice from players, management, and fans; inexperience in understanding official game rules and regulations; entering or signing contracts disadvantageous to their interests; and "quick buck" promoters who damaged athletic careers. Indian athletes established prominent celebrity for themselves in an abundance of American sports, the Olympics, and college athletics. Few, however, attained high-status employment as a head coach or team management in their dedicated sport after their acceptance into competitive athletic events in the nineteenth century.

HISTORICAL BACKGROUND

Early European explorers and colonial settlers in the sixteenth century were perplexed by the outstanding athletic abilities of American Indians. American Indians impressed explorers and settlers with their enigmatic ability to perform physically demanding feats. Hopi and Pueblo Indians could run long distances of 20 to 30 miles a day. Sixteenth-century Spanish explorers were astonished by Indians' ability to consistently cover these long distances. Southwestern Indians communicated important information between separate communities. Young men ran long distances of approximately 30 miles to deliver important information between Pueblos.

Europeans were stunned by the consistent physical abilities Indians displayed in daily tasks. Their concept of American Indians as a submissive, weak people differed after witnessing their athleticism. Precontact America did not contain large work animals, such as horses, oxen, or cows. The lack of large work animals forced American Indians to develop alternative means for communication and labor.

Early explorers witnessed Indian demonstrations of great physical prowess during team games. Lacrosse and chunky, both field ball games, demonstrated team deftness of physical quickness and organization. Many individuals' natural physical talents and abilities were demonstrated at public exhibitions. American Indian athletic skill and talent was further promoted by Indian boarding schools. Indian boarding schools built coeducational sports programs for their students. These schools encouraged students to participate in athletics. These programs alleviated the uninspiring school curriculum by representing an alternative for students. Boarding school administrators discovered student participation in physical sporting exercises, such as basketball, baseball, and track, showcased an excellence in athletics.

American Indian boarding school students were also inculcated, through sports, to learn "appropriate" Euro-Western behavior through the culture of American sport and games. Boarding schools intended for Indian students to develop a new "American" identity, since an inherent American Indian persona was unimportant to retain. American Indian students began assimilating mainstream social rules through learning typical American sports. As Indian students assimilated sport rules and regulations, they divested their old Indian identity.

The harsh and cruel circumstances within boarding schools allowed many Indian athletes to generate alternative systems to cope with forced family and community removals. Indians athletes frequently turned inward to combat the crippling environments and emotionally sterile boarding schools (Mills 2008). Billy Mills, 1964 Olympic 10,000-meter gold medalist, began running to escape the loneliness and negative atmosphere of his boarding school. Yet, boarding school administrators believed Indian student athletes demonstrated excellence in learning American games. Their athletic prowess assured administrators that Indians were learning appropriate American cultural forms and behaviors.

Appropriate team games and exhibitions allowed visitor-fans to witness non-Indians vie against Indian athletes. Public sporting exhibitions were popular for demonstrating how American Indians were learning American social and cultural skills. The boarding schools also used exhibition games to exploit Indian athletes for financial gain. School administrators created a pretext of public athletic exhibitions to pay for Indian student education. However, Congress allocated federal educational funds for all Indian students. Boarding schools instead used excess sports funds for administrative intentions. Public spectator money did not reward Indian student athletes directly. Indian athletes continued to live in poverty and want at boarding schools with poor food rations and in meager living conditions. Public funds raised from athletic exhibitions made no difference in daily student life.

TWENTIETH-CENTURY ATHLETES

Jim Thorpe, The World's Greatest Athlete

By the twentieth century, Indian boarding schools turned out many athletic American Indians. Extramural sports teams hired these outstanding athletes based

New York Giants right fielder Jim Thorpe at the Polo Grounds in New York City in 1913. Thorpe, an American Indian and one of the most gifted athletes in modern sports, excelled in football, baseball, and track. (Library of Congress)

on their promise of bringing teams success. The most famous American Indian athlete of the twentieth century was Jim Thorpe, Sac & Fox. Born in Indian Territory, now Oklahoma, on May 28, 1887, Jim Thorpe began his athletic prominence in 1904 while at the Carlisle Indian School in Pennsylvania. Thorpe excelled in football and running track at Carlisle. A natural athlete, he demonstrated excellent physical capabilities in athleticism alongside other Indian athletes on the Carlisle football team.

The Carlisle football team was considered equivalent to an intercollegiate high school team, not a typical college football team, because many members were under the age of 18 and Carlisle was classified as an Indian college. Many of these players nonetheless faced professional-level football players at public games for the school. The Carlisle Indian School football team excelled with Jim Thorpe playing. In 1912, Thorpe led the Carlisle intercollegiate football team to a national collegiate championship by scoring 25 touchdowns and 198 overall points (Botelho n.d.). Thorpe was named an All-American for his football abilities in 1908, 1909, and 1910. His athletic prowess on the Carlisle team financially benefitted other Indian students.

Jim Thorpe became a member on the official 1912 U.S. Olympic team that went to Stockholm, Sweden. He competed in the decathlon and pentathlon, and won both events. King Gustav V of Sweden honored Thorpe by personally presenting him with his two gold medals. As he presented the gold medals, the king said, "You, Sir, are the greatest athlete in the world" (quoted in Berontas 1992). Returning to the United States after the 1912 Olympics, Thorpe was proclaimed a national hero in a New York tickertape parade.

Upon his return, Thorpe began a career playing professional football and baseball. His natural athletic abilities earned him an accomplished reputation. Jim Thorpe was the most famous American athlete of his age in professional sports. In every sport he ever attempted, he excelled.

From 1913 to 1919, Thorpe played professional baseball. He was mainly an outfielder and occasionally pitched. He was one of only two men who ever played for the New York Giants in two different sports: football and baseball. Thorpe could play almost any sport he chose, but he preferred football (O'Hanlon-Lincoln 2006). In football, he was an outstanding running back and played for several teams. The team he most enjoyed playing with was the 1922/1923 all-Indian Oorang Indians.

Jim Thorpe earned numerous awards. In 1920, he was appointed as the first president of the American Professional Football Conference, now known as the National Football League (NFL). Some of his other notable accolades are his 1951 election to the College Football Hall of Fame, his All-American honors from 1908 to 1912, the National Press selection of Jim Thorpe as America's Greatest Football Player of the First Half-Century in 1950 along with their additional Most Outstanding Athlete of the First Half of the 20th Century award. In 2001,

ABC's Wide World of Sports named Jim Thorpe the Athlete of the Century. *Sport* magazine named Jim Thorpe in 1977 the Greatest American Football Player in History. The Professional Football Hall of Fame, the National Indian Hall of Fame, the National Track and Field Hall of Fame, and the Pennsylvania and the Oklahoma Halls of Fame, also enshrined Jim Thorpe.

Beyond athletic accolades, the United States honored Jim Thorpe in 1917 with U.S. citizenship. On January 30, 1998, the U.S. Postal Service honored Jim Thorpe on one of its commemorative Celebrate the Century Program stamps. The 106th Congress House of Representatives in 1998 passed a resolution designating James Francis Thorpe as America's Athlete of the Century (H.R. 198 May 27, 1999). Although Thorpe passed away on March 28, 1953, he remains the most recognized American Indian athlete of all time.

BILLY MILLS, 10,000-METER OLYMPIAN

Another notable American Indian athlete was Billy Mills, Oglala Lakota (June 30, 1938–). Mills won the 10,000-meter Olympic gold medal in Tokyo, Japan, in 1964. Mills grew up on the impoverished South Dakota Pine Ridge Reservation. His mother and father had both died by the time Mills was 12. An orphan, Mills had no legal guardians and was enrolled in the local boarding school on Pine Ridge Reservation. The federal government, as with all young Indians, believed school would protect and educate him until he was older. Mills's government teachers believed he demonstrated academic promise, and he was sent to the Haskell Institute, an Indian boarding school, in Kansas for an advantageous education. Mills began running to escape loneliness and isolation at Haskell.

Billy Mills earned a scholarship to the University of Kansas for running. A natural athlete, he became a three time NCAA All-American runner. As with many American Indians, Mills faced issues concerning his Indian heritage. Although he was a track success, his coach did not want him on the cross-country team. The University of Kansas coach erroneously believed Mills, because of his Indian heritage, would become a drinker. The coach inappropriately believed Mills's "natural Indian character" would ultimately emerge on the cross-country team. The coach's flawed belief about how other Indian athletes behaved led him not to invest time with Mills. Mills utilized the faulty beliefs of his cross-country coach to become a better athlete. Mills recalls he became determined to prove his coach's bigoted opinions were prejudicial and untrue. He recognized these demeaning prejudicial racial stereotypes about Indians were something he never would become but admitted it was difficult for him to overcome these judgments.

Mills joined the Marine Corps after graduating from Kansas. He trained alone to qualify for the U.S. Olympic Track and Field Team in the 10,000-meter and marathon events as a first lieutenant in the Corps Reserves. Mills qualified in both events for the 1964 Tokyo Olympics. Mills was a virtually unknown runner and not considered an actual challenger for either race.

Billy Mills entered the 10,000-meter race with a known group of runners, including the world record holder, Ron Clarke of Australia, and Mohammed Gammoudi of Tunisia. Mills experienced little support from the U.S. Olympic Track and Field Team in Tokyo. Running in borrowed shoes and with no official coaching, Mills remained an unnoticed competitor. During the event, Ron Clarke, as expected, set the pace, which did not change until the final stretch.

Mills's qualifying time was a full minute slower than Clarke's, and during the final lap, Mills, Clarke, and Gammoudi headed down the last stretch together. Mills was boxed in and eventually shoved twice out of his lane position. Gammoudi took the opportunity to surge past. Mills fell to fifth place, and in danger of not medaling at all. Trailing the other two runners, Mills surged passed both in lane 3, winning the 10,000-meter race.

Billy Mills set a new Olympic 10,000-meter record. His official time was a full 50 seconds faster than he had ever previously run. He remains the only American to win a gold medal in this Olympic event. Mills continued his Olympic experience in the marathon, finishing fourteenth.

After the Olympics, Billy Mills continued setting records in track and field and also dedicated his life to his personal charity, Running Strong for American Indian Youth, which assists young Indian people by focusing on health through sports activities. In 1965, he broke the world six-mile record, tying with Gerry Lindgren at 27:11:6 (USATF n.d.). The U.S. National Track and Field Hall of Fame inducted Mills in 1976, and the U.S. Olympic Hall of Fame welcomed him in 1984.

AMERICAN INDIANS IN BASEBALL

American Indians demonstrated major athletic promise in sports outside the Olympics. Baseball, more than football or any other American sport, recruited and promoted a multitude of American Indian athletes in the early twentieth century. American Indian achievements in baseball represent many well-known record holders.

The first renowned American Indian baseball player was Louis Francis Sockalexis, Penobscot (1871–1913). Sockalexis was a full-blood American Indian and a natural all-around athlete. Before entering professional sports, he attended both Notre Dame and the College of the Holy Cross in Massachusetts. Sockalexis was the first American Indian to play in Major League baseball. He played outfield for the National League Cleveland Spiders from April 22, 1897 until May 3, 1899.

Sockalexis was nicknamed Chief, Sock, and Sox. At the age of 25, he was 5 feet 11 inches tall and weighed 185 pounds. The National Baseball Hall of Fame enshrined Louis Sockalexis, its first American Indian inductee, when he was only 31. Detroit Tiger Hughie Jennings recalled Sockalexis's achievements, stating, "No other player, besides Louis Sockalexis, ever crowded so many remarkable accomplishments into such a short time" (Leavitt 1979). Sockalexis pitched three no-hitters and six shutouts, and he held batting averages of .436 and .444 in college (Leavitt 1979). One Boston newspaper commented on Sockalexis's debut in Cincinnati by writing, "His batting was wonderful, his fielding marvelous. His great speed permits him to steal bases at will" (Leavitt 1979). Sockalexis's prowess demonstrated the best of American Indian athletic talents to American fans.

Francis Sockalexis began his career playing for the Cleveland Spiders in 1897. He played in 66 games, batted .338, and stole 16 bases. He sadly exhibited only one brilliant major league season, in 1897. His baseball career quickly faded over the next few years. He played in only 21 games and batted only 67 times, with an average of only .224. During his last year of baseball, in 1899, he played in only seven games and batted only 22 times, averaging .273. Sockalexis vanished into obscurity after May 3, 1899. He died young, at the age of 42, in 1913. Sockalexis represented a brilliant burst of American Indian athleticism in major sports. The vast majority of American sports teams were closed to most ethnic groups. Sockalexis's presence allowed other American Indians to enter baseball.

A second notable American Indian figure in baseball history is Charles Albert Bender, Ojibwa (Chippewa) (1884–1954). Bender played baseball at the Carlisle Indian School in Carlisle, Pennsylvania. Bender attended Dickinson College before entering professional sports. He started as a major league pitcher with the Philadelphia Athletics on April 20, 1903 when he was 18, and stayed until the 1914 season. Bender was 6 feet 2 inches tall and weighed 185 pounds. He acquired the inappropriate but common nickname Chief, as most Indians do in sports.

Bender's personal outlook related to playing professional baseball was shrewdly direct. He told the *Chicago Daily News*, "The reason I went into baseball as a profession was that when I left school, baseball offered me the best opportunity both for money and achievement. I adopted it because I played baseball better than I could do anything else in life, and the game appealed to me, and because there was so little racial prejudice in the game. There has been scarcely a trace of sentiment against me on account of birth. I have been treated the same as other men" (quoted in Riess 1999).

Between 1910 and 1913, Bender won more than 20 games. Over his entire career, he held a 212–127 win-loss record with 1,711 strikeouts (National Baseball Hall of Fame n.d.). Bender also pitched in five World Series—in 1905, 1910, 1911, 1913, and 1914—with a 6–4 record. In Game 1 of the 1905 series, he shut out the Giants 3–0 on four hits, which was the only game the Philadelphia Athletics won in the series. In the 1910 Series, Bender pitched three no-hitters, and in the 1911 Series, he completed three games. His 1910 earned run average (ERA) was an incredible 1.58, placing him fifth in the league

Bender left the Athletics in 1915 and joined the Baltimore Terrapins in the short-lived Federal League. He returned to Philadelphia Athletics in 1916 and 1917 to play for the Phillies. Bender's last appearance in major league ball was in 1925 for a token one-inning appearance with the White Sox, where he also coached, when he was 42.

Charles Bender was exceptionally proud of his American Indian heritage. In 1910, he stated, "You ignorant ill-bred foreigners. If you don't like the way I'm doing things out there, why don't you just pack up and go back to your own countries" (quoted in Riess 1999). Bender routinely denied he encountered any personal discrimination when he played in the big leagues.

Charles Albert Bender was an impressive ball player. His athletic ability convinced other teams to recruit and sign other American Indian players to other teams (Powers-Beck 2004). His good sportsmanship, conduct, and impressive athletic skills influenced the careers of other up-and-coming players. Philadelphia Athletics owner Connie Mack was so pleased by Charles Bender's skillful performance that he allowed Louis Bruce, Mohawk, an opportunity to try out for the Athletics in 1904. Although the circumstance was opportune, Bruce was physically small, standing at 5 feet 5 inches and weighing only 145 pounds. Mack did not think Bruce was aggressive enough for the major leagues and sent him down to the minors for several years before his return to the majors (Thompson n.d.). Bender's recommendations allowed American Indians to play ball. In 1953, the Baseball Hall of Fame inducted Charles Bender before his death on May 22, 1954 in Philadelphia.

John Tortes Meyers, Cahuilla (1880–1971) is a third American Indian baseball star who played in the major leagues. He attended Riverside High School in Riverside, California. He also attended Dartmouth College in New Hampshire, which he described as instilling a spirit in you that lasts. He described college classmates as, "Dartmouth men are very, very close, all over the world. They'll never turn you down" (Ritter 1992). Meyers stood 5 feet 11 inches, weighed 194 pounds, and began as a star catcher with the New York Giants on April 16, 1909 when he was 28. Meyers played in over 100 games in six seasons. Between 1911 and 1913, the Giants won three division pennants but lost in all three World Series. In 1916, he was traded to Brooklyn and helped the team win a pennant. His record of 992 games over nine seasons with a .291 batting average remains impressive.

Known as the Ironman or Chief, Meyers dismissed the nicknames as stereotypical. He played ball for eight years until October 4, 1917, when he retired at the age of 37. Afterward, he worked for the U.S. Department of the Interior (DOI) as an American Indian supervisor. John Meyers died in San Bernardino, California, on July 25, 1971.

Allie Pierce Reynolds, Creek (1917–1994) is another major league baseball player of renown. Reynolds was born in Bethany, Oklahoma, and forbidden to play ball on Sundays because his father was a minister. As a result he missed out on gaining weekend sandlot game experience. Reynolds attended Capitol Hill High School in Oklahoma City and attended the Oklahoma Agricultural and Mechanical College (now Oklahoma State) on a track scholarship. Reynolds ran the 100- and 220-yard dashes and tossed the javelin on the OAMC track team. He also played three years of varsity football.

Clarence Gallagher, a coach for the Olympic team and the former wrestling coach at Oklahoma A & M, called Reynolds the greatest natural athlete he had ever seen (Thompson n.d.). Legendary Oklahoma basketball coach Hank Iba, also a Cleveland scout, approached Reynolds to play professional baseball as a pitcher. Iba aided Reynolds's 1939 contract negotiations and secured a $2,000 signing bonus.

Baseball offered Reynolds a professional career opportunity. He was 6 feet tall and weighed 195 pounds. He first played in the minors before entering the big leagues. At the age of 25, on September 17, 1942, he began playing for the Cleveland Indians as a starting pitcher. He astonished Cleveland fans by pitching five scoreless innings in two games. Reynolds played for four seasons with the Indians and was nicknamed Chief or Super-Chief.

Allie Reynolds left Cleveland in 1945 to join the New York Yankees. His trade genuinely helped both teams and was considered a blockbuster baseball deal at the time. Joe Gordon of the Yankees was traded to Cleveland to help win the 1948 pennant. Reynolds's trade to the Yankees gave him the highest winning percentage in the American League as a first season Yankee. He was their best pitcher, which allowed the Yankees to win five consecutive pennants from 1949 to 1953.

Reynolds became one of the most prominent American Indian players in post–World War II baseball. In 1952, he completed 24 of 29 his games, leading the league. In 28 games, he won 20 and lost only eight. Reynolds used to joke that his team relied on him like an ace left-hand seven-inning pitcher reliever who would come in to save the game (Thompson n.d.). Reynolds formally retired from baseball on September 25, 1954.

Allie Reynolds remarked that he did not face racial discrimination because he was too big to pick on. He weighed 210 pounds, and his size was an asset against further remarks. By the 1940s, baseball had seen American Indian players, and they were welcomed in the sport. Reynolds handled discriminatory pressure from others with self-confidence. His athletic fame and talent allowed him several post-game business opportunities, and he represented American League players with management from 1951 to 1953.

American Indian athletic success depended on each individual's proficiency in their sport. Some athletes handled mainstream sports with equanimity and a natural ability to embrace new situations. Others struggled, unsure of situations laced with overt racism and discrimination. Francis Sockalexis entered baseball with high athletic abilities and prestige but ultimately was unable to cope with external social pressures. The Sockalexis experience came to represent the unfortunate conditions the majority of American Indians faced in athletics. Sockalexis's death at the age of 42 in 1913 was brought on by the constant unpleasant encounters concerning his Indianness from predominant non-Indian spectators.

Francis Sockalexis came to baseball with much promise but was ultimately, as an American Indian, unable to sustain his potential as a major leaguer. Charles Bender and John Meyers represent a transitional era for Indian baseball players. Their careers were marked with achievements, including impressive personal statistics. Both emerged relatively unscathed in the sport regarding racism and discrimination. They exhibited magnificent athletic abilities on the field.

Some writers speculate the social world of the early 1940s, when Reynolds reached the majors, was somewhat more tolerant of minorities than the 1890s, when Sockalexis made his debut and racism and discrimination were more overt. Sadly, Reynolds's experience likely represents the exception of racial discrimination in professional sports and Sockalexis the rule.

Ethnic minorities often grow up in economically disadvantaged circumstances, doomed to a life of poverty or insufficient wages. A few, like Reynolds, handle sudden adulation with emotional and psychological equanimity. They take good advantage of athletic opportunities opened up to them versus negative instances concerning the misuse of alcohol or drug abuse that they are often exposed to in professional sports. Others cannot manage the pressure and are victims despite their athletic promise and success.

Baseball provided Reynolds, Meyers, Bender, and a handful of other Indian players with much self-esteem and dignity, but Louis Sockalexis and Jim Thorpe gave much more to the game. Stephen Thompson (n.d.) wrote that "the good conduct and performances by American Indian players helped other Indians reach the majors." Early Indian players affected managers and owners by bringing other tribal players to their attention. Within Indian communities, these players are hailed as heroes. For all Indians, tribal sports figures represent pride in being Indian, and show how one might have an athletic career.

OTHER INDIAN EVENTS

American Indian athletes participate in other sports outside of mainstream teams. One sport they are also involved with is professional wrestling. One of the most celebrated was Kit Fox, Delaware. Kit Fox began wrestling in the 1950s. Known as Chief, he was popular until the 1970s. Born in Anadarko, Oklahoma, Fox stood 6 feet 4 inches and wrestled at a weight of 234 pounds.

Trained by former wrestler Leroy McGurk, he was tag-team partnered with Chief Big Heart, an experienced and popular wrestler with an Indian persona. The pair alternately tagged each other in and out of the ring against their relentless opponents. Fox was burdened by stereotypical routines based on an American Indian act featuring characters and props, such as a tomahawk chop and carrying bow and arrows, which categorized his wrestling matches. He was known for displaying fancy key moves, including an intense airplane spin against opponents, which made him an audience favorite in the late 1950s. Fox was an unusual "Indian" wrestler, since unlike others wrestler professional portraying an Indian, he was a real American Indian.

Kit Fox reaching his highest popularity in 1957 in the Phoenix/Tucson area. Fox and his notorious opponent Tokyo Joe were known for wild and savage brawls. Fox was typecast in confronting a World War II enemy, and whenever the two faced off, their popularity skyrocketed. The two performed maniacal tomahawk chops and judo chops against each other in the ring.

Kit Fox and Chief Big Heart's talented wrestling careers ended with an unfortunate car accident. Fox broke his back and both legs in the accident, forcing him into early retirement. He moved to Las Vegas and became a card dealer. He also began to train other American Indians to perform stunt movie work. After he retired from this position, he advised Indian youth in athletic training. Kit Fox died in 1994 from heart bypass surgery complications at the age of 58.

Kit Fox inspired his nephew Rick Valentine to become a professional wrestler. Valentine converted himself in to the persona of Mustafa Sharmoot. Fox encouraged Valentine to enter the ring and become a professional. Valentine recalled his uncle showing him trick wrestling moves when he was young, which motivated him to engage in the sport.

American Indian athletes have always participated in athletic events. From early accounts, Indians were consistently involved in individual grueling athletic achievements and team sports. American Indian athletes are role models, heroes, and Olympians who contributed to prodigious records as Americans in sport. Indian boarding schools were principal locations for American Indians to perform in traditional American sports. Indian athletes showcasing themselves at school events brought income to their schools by demonstrating their athletic prowess to the public and recruiters. Indian athletes such as Jim Thorpe, Johnny Bench, Louis Sockalexis, and Billy Mills, profoundly contributed to American professional teams.

RECENT NOTABLE ATHLETES

Older Indians athletes encouraged more recent players to continue the long American Indian tradition to excel athletically. An example is Sam Bradford, who is a Cherokee and a National Football League quarterback with the St. Louis

Rams. Born in Oklahoma City, Bradford played football, basketball, and golf in high school. He attended the University of Oklahoma (OU) from 2007 to 2009. In his first year as a starter on the OU football team, Bradford broke the school record for passing yards (350) in a half. He also broke the NCAA record for consecutive pass completions and holds the record for the most touchdown passes in a season. In 2008, Bradford won the Heisman Trophy, the first American Indian to win the prestigious award. In 2008, the Associated Press named him the College Football Player of the Year.

In 2010, Sam Bradford signed with the Saint Louis Rams. His $78 million deal is the largest rookie agreement (Davis n.d.). In his first year with the Rams, Bradford completed 354 out of 590 passing attempts. Bradford was the first member of the Cherokee nation to start as a Division I university quarterback since Sonny Sixkiller, who played for the University of Washington between 1970 and 1972. Bradford's father, Kent Bradford, was a Sooner's offensive lineman from 1977 to 1978.

A recent development in American Indian athletics are the Indigenous Games, which commenced in 1990. These games are international offering, giving American Indians and indigenous peoples from other nations, such as Canada, Hawaii, Australia, Oceania, an opportunity to compete. In 2006, in conjunction with the Native American Sports Council (NASC), an offshoot of the U.S. Olympic Committee (USOC), the North American Indigenous Games was commenced. The NASC is dedicated to promoting community wellness through culturally appropriate youth-oriented sports programs. Founded on indigenous athletic traditions, the games teach young athletes from the regions of America, Hawaii, Alaska, and Canada life lessons found in traditional tribal competition. Commencing in 1990, these Games focus primarily on young athletes. They occur on a bi-yearly schedule and are hosted by several cities. The games generally offer individual and team sport competitions. Individual competitions are held in archery, boxing, canoeing, track and field, and golf. Team sports may include lacrosse, basketball, hockey, softball, and soccer. Game sponsorships originally operated under independent USOC sponsorship, but tribal-sponsored funding contributes to the international gathering. The North American Indigenous Games offer a unique opportunity to build future American Indian athletic talents.

The Alaskan Native Games existed prior to the North American Indigenous Games. These Games primarily emphasized traditional contests and recreational events. Native Alaskan students in grades 7 through 12 are selected to participate in games that instill personal confidence and self-esteem. Events require speed, stamina, ability, balance, agility, and power, and consist of various traditional Alaskan games. Competitions in the high kick, four-man carry, kneel jump, fish cutting, blanket toss, ear pulling, hand games, and so on focus not only on the abilities of competitors, but also on the fun of the events.

REFERENCES

Begay, Notah. Notah Begay website. Retrieved from http://notah.com/history.html

Berontas, Bob. *Jim Thorpe: Sac and Fox Athlete*. London: Chelsea House Publishers, 1992.

Botelho, Greg. "Roller-Coaster Life of Indian Icon, Sports' First Star." *CNN*, July 14, 2004. Retrieved from http://articles.cnn.com/2004-07-09/world/jim.thorpe_1_jim-thorpe-carlisle-indian-industrial-school-greatest-athlete?_s=PM:WORLD

Cohen, David, Richard Korch, and Rick Neft. *The Football Encyclopedia: Complete History of Professional Football from 1892 to the Present*. New York: St. Martin's Press, 1994.

Davis, Nate. *Rams QB Sam Bradford to Wear No. 8 as Homage to Troy Aikman*. USAToday. Retrieved from http://content.usatoday.com/communities/thehuddle/post/2010/04/rams-qb-sam-bradford-to-wear-no-8-as-homage-to-troy-aikman/1

Leavitt, Ralph Bud. "Louis Francis Sockalexis." *Bangor Daily News*, December 22, 1979.

Mills, Billy. *Interview*. Oklahoma City: 1964 Olympic 10,000 Gold Medalist, Tokyo Olympiad, 2008.

National Baseball Hall of Fame and Museum. Hall of Famer plaque. Cooperstown, NY.

Native American Sports Council. Available at http://www.nascsports.org/

Native Youth Olympics. "Native Youth Olympics: A History," August 16, 2006. Retrieved from http://www.ankn.uaf.edu/Curriculum/NativeGames/nyo.html

Nixon, Richard. "Proclamation 4209: Jim Thorpe Day." White House, Washington, DC, 1973.

O'Hanlon-Lincoln, Ceane. *Chronicles: A Vivid Collection of Fayette County Pennsylvania Histories II*. Fayette County, PA: Mechling Bookbindery, 2006.

Powers-Beck, Jeffrey. *The American Indian Integration of Baseball*. Lincoln: University of Nebraska Press, 2004.

Riess, Steven. *Touching Base: Professional Baseball and American Culture in the Progressive Era*. Urbana: University of Illinois Press, 1999.

Ritter, Lawrence. *The Glory of Their Times: The Story of the Early Days of Baseball Told by the Men Who Played It*. New York: Macmillan, 1992.

Seidel, Leroy. *Interview*. Philadelphia: Delaware Sports Authority, 2012.

Thompson, Scott. "The American Indian in the Major Leagues." Baseball Research Journal, Society for American Baseball Research. Retrieved from http://research.sabr.org/journals/the-american-indian-in-the-major-leagues

Trotter, Jake. "Sooners' Bradford Proves That He Belongs." NewsOk.com, September 2009. Retrieved from http://newsok.com/article/3121288 2008 Associated Press All-America Team." CBSSports.com, December 16, 2008. Retrieved from http://www.cbssports.com/collegefootball/story/11175822

United States 106th Congress, H.R. 198: Expressing the sense of the House of Representatives that James Francis Thorpe should be designated "American's Athlete of the Century." May 27, 1999, pp. 1–2.

USATF (United States of America Track Federation). "USA Outdoor Track and Field Champion Statistics: Billy Mills." Retrieved from http://www.usatf.org/Home.aspx

AMERICAN INDIAN SMOKE SHOPS: STRUGGLES FOR ECONOMIC INDEPENDENCE

Robert E. Sanderson

The struggle for economic independence has been a long journey with cultural resistance and misunderstanding coming from non-Indians who have sought to exploit native resources and rob Indians of their birthright. As America's indigenous people have made gains in their movement toward sovereignty, a few economic ventures have helped to provide some economic relief and give the people a sense of pride in their own unique entrepreneurship. One such enterprise stands as a symbol of success in Indian country—the Indian smoke shop. Although tobacco is a plant indigenous to the home of American Indians, its use has been largely expropriated by non-Indians who have profited greatly from its worldwide sale and distribution. From the early days of the "discovery" of this unique plant to the present multinational corporate domination of its economic power, Indians have been involved in the "tobacco industry" along with non-Indians. However, mainstream America has little knowledge of the role Indians play in this industry and even less understanding of Indian smoke shops. Indian smoke shops are also a visible symbol of Indian sovereignty.

EARLY NATIVE AMERICAN ECONOMIES

Perhaps the best-known means of exchange among Native Americans and early European colonists was wampum. Historical accounts suggest that Native American tribes manufactured wampum by collecting clamlike shells, drilling holes in them, and stringing them together as beads. Although primary producers of wampum such as the Narragansetts lived along Atlantic coastal areas, other groups further inland traded in this commodity of exchange. Iroquois Indians were described as being wealthy and powerful, in some measure, because of the quantity of wampum that they accrued through collecting tribute and trading with other tribes and colonists. Wampum was a convenient source of economic exchange, or money, because it also had an ornamental use. Beaded strings of shells were worn as necklaces or woven into belts, such as the now famous wampum belts of the Iroquois that are historical artifacts and record early treaties between tribal groups and European and American colonizers.

Early business ventures in the New World were involved in fur-trade. Whites on the frontier traded in furs and wampum with Indians, and they would "negotiate" for trapping fur-bearing animals on Indian lands with wampum and other desirable goods and tools. These negotiations also involved the ritual partaking of smoke from a plant indigenous to North America called tobacco. Tobacco was widely known and variously used by Native Americans prior to the arrival of Europeans, and Native Americans have continued their relationship with this herb up to the present day.

British colonists were imaginative in their efforts to make up for coinage shortages in the eighteenth-century American colonies. They used varied substitutes to conduct their commercial activities, including wampum, furs, and "cash crops." Legal tender in the colonies was practically anything that could be converted into pounds, shillings, and pence in the Royal British monetary system. Cash crops were referred to as Country Money, for example, rice, wheat, maize, and of course tobacco. Virginia used tobacco as money for nearly 200 years, twice as long as the gold standard in the United States (Davies 2002).

Paper money was another form that arrived later in colonial history, but the earliest form of paper currency used was the "tobacco note." Tobacco notes were scripts certifying that a quality and quantity of tobacco had been deposited in a public tobacco warehouse (Davies 2002). These certificates were used as money, which was much more convenient and transportable than a large bundle of tobacco being hauled around to conduct early commerce. During this time, tobacco was becoming one of the favorite exports from the colonies throughout Europe, especially in England. This helped to ensure stability of the plant as a viable cash crop form of currency for many years.

Although Europeans had developed a thriving economy, in part based on tobacco, the plant had entirely different uses and meanings for America's indigenous populations. Indigenous Americans used tobacco "in every conceivable form—drinking, licking, snuffing, chewing, and smoking" (Seig 1999, vii). Tobacco use among Native Americans was persistent and extensive throughout North America, long before the European discoveries of the New World and its exotic and tantalizing flora.

MEDICINAL, CEREMONIAL, AND RITUAL USE OF TOBACCO

Pre-Columbian America was home to cultivated tobacco plants that were used ritually by indigenous inhabitants on both continents of the Western hemisphere.

Early Native Americans regarded tobacco as a sacred plant with special powers that has been grown and cultivated in the Americas since around 6000 BCE. Some tribes believed that the sacredness of the tobacco plant required them to make sure that the gods were appeased and ritually thanked for the plant that was given them by the Creator. Medicine men were imbued with powers to heal and conjure spirits through the application of incantations and ceremonies that always involved tobacco as smoke, or some other variant, in their practice. Variations on the use of tobacco in the ancient Americas abounded. Perhaps the most enduring use of tobacco is that of being smoked in a pipe. In addition to being smoked, however, researchers have found evidence of tobacco being eaten, chewed, snorted (snuff), and in the case of Peruvian Aguaruna aboriginals, used ceremonially as a hallucinogenic enema (Borio 2001). For our purposes, though, we will consider smoking tobacco as the premiere form of and that preferred by Indians and non-Indians alike. For Native Americans, tobacco consumption goes hand-in-hand with its companion, the sacred pipe. Pipe-smoking has been an integral part of Native American ceremonial life since prehistoric times, and the evolution of the sacred pipe and the cultivation of tobacco have developed with all the attendant folklore and legends associated with any enduring ceremonial phenomenon. There are several individual origin myths relating to tobacco and the sacred pipe, but all have some similar themes that relate the origin of tobacco as a sacred gift from the Creator to humans for their enjoyment and celebration of their relationship to the cosmos and the Creator spirit.

> *A long canoe filled with medicine men passed near a river bank, where a loud voice had proclaimed to all the inhabitants to remain indoors, but some disobeying, died immediately. The next day the canoe was sought for and found, containing a strange being at each end, both fast asleep. A loud voice was then heard saying that the destroying of these creatures would result in a great blessing to the Indians. So they were decoyed into a neighboring council house where they were put to death and buried, and from their ashes rose the tobacco plant.*
>
> *—An Iroquois myth*

Another version given by the Huron, the "Tobacco tribe," and warring neighbors of the Iroquois tells that:

> *... in ancient times, when the land was barren and the people were starving, the Great Spirit sent forth a woman to save humanity. As she traveled over the world, everywhere her right hand touched the soil, there grew potatoes. And everywhere her left hand touched the soil, there grew corn. And when the world was rich and fertile, she sat down and rested. When she arose, there grew tobacco ...*

The sacred pipe has its own origin stories and legends associated with its place in Native American tribal lore. Perhaps the best known of these accounts is that of the Lakota myth of a feminine creature that first brought the sacred pipe to the people (Erdoes and Ortiz 1984).

Indian pipes come in a variety of shapes and sizes, and they are made from substances such as clay, wood, or reeds. The pipe bowls are often separate pieces of the pipe assembly molded from clay or carved out of soapstone, bone, wood, and red "pipestone" or Catlinite quarried from Pipestone, Minnesota, and other places. Pipes, especially those used for ceremonial events, are often ornate and depict an animal, a tool, or some symbol that has a special significance to the bearer. Pipes can also be less ornate and made in the form and shape of conventional tobacco pipes that are generally produced from burled briar wood or some other preferred hardwood. Jordan Paper (1988) has made a concise and comprehensive study of Indian tobacco pipes in his book *Offering Smoke*.

Numerous Native American tribes used tobacco for its "medicinal" qualities. In fact, it would be too cumbersome to list all the tribes and their particular etiologies for diseases or maladies and their subsequent medicinal therapies requiring tobacco. As an example, some of the ways in which tobacco was used as medicine may be seen in Cherokee practices. The Cherokee traditionally lived in an area that was conducive to growing some of the finest cultivated tobacco in the country. They used tobacco extensively in rituals by crushing the plant's leaves, stuffing them into pipes, and smoking them. Tobacco was also used among the Cherokee as a cathartic, and was usually smoked in pipes at night by those with the status and wealth to afford them. Otherwise, a person would simply roll the dry leaves tightly, light one end, and smoke it as a crude form of early cigar. Either way, the evidence suggests that tobacco was highly valued and used widely throughout the tribe. It was also a helpful antispasmodic that had a calming effect. The Cherokee used tobacco as a type of drug therapy for cramps and sharp pains, and as an antihelmintic in the treatment of parasitic worms. Poultices produced by beating the tobacco plant were applied to boils and insect bites or bee stings. In some cases, it was also used as a snake bite remedy. Tobacco has also been used as a diuretic and an emetic by several Native American tribes, including the Cherokee. Interestingly, the Cherokee sometimes used tobacco as a "miscellaneous" disease remedy, for such things as vertigo or even a toothache (Hamel and Chiltoskey, 1975).

Tribes in other areas of North America cultivated tobacco in similar fashion to the Cherokee and reportedly developed their own cornucopia medicinal uses. People of the Desert Archaic Culture raised "Indian tobacco," especially in large parts of California. The Kurok planted tobacco seeds and later harvested the leaves, stems, and seeds while never truly cultivating the ground. Instead, the Karok looked for the best garden areas around villages and would burn logs and brush to prepare the selected spots to plant the seeds each year. When the plants were grown, and while the stems were still green, they were harvested and all parts of the plant found some specific use among the Indians. For example, the stems were an inferior tobacco that was offered as a gift to the spirits during elaborate ceremonies and ritual offerings. As medicine, desert Indians would smoke tobacco mixed with sage as a cure for colds. Often the leaves were steamed or ground into a poultice to reduce swollen throats or some forms of rheumatism. Like the Cherokee, desert Indians also used tobacco for miscellaneous maladies such as toothaches, insect and snake bites, and to prevent infections in open cuts. Clearly, in the pharmacology of American Indians peoples, tobacco was a valued substance and held a prestigious place in the ritual and practice of medicine.

Most references to tobacco use among Native Americans include some mention of its ceremonial and ritual significance. It was an almost universal substance that was drunk, chewed, snuffed, or smoked in purification ceremonies. Whether being used as an herbal drink during Aztec human sacrifices or to seal a pact at the signing of a treaty, tobacco has been accompanying Native Americans in their ceremonies and rituals since long before the appearance of Europeans on the shores of the New World. Partly out of reverence to the Great Spirit, and partly because of its mysterious powers on the minds and bodies of its users, tobacco has enjoyed a preferred and honorable status among Native Americans. Many researchers believe that it became popularized as a "drug of choice" among American Indians only as an afterthought because of the pleasure derived from smoking and that tobacco was first seen as a special herb with ceremonial and sacred importance. Hence, the health problems associated with today's cigarette smoking pandemic did not present issues among early Native American users.

INDIAN TOBACCO ENTREPRENEURSHIP

Elias C. Boudinot (Cherokee), the son of the founding editor of the *Cherokee Phoenix*, had an interesting and historically significant career in the tobacco industry. After their military exploits as officers in the Confederate States of America (CSA) during the Civil War, Boudinot and his uncle, Stand Watie, purchased a tobacco factory in Missouri and then moved it to Indian Territory. In this new location, the factory produced leaf, pipe, and chewing tobacco as well as snuff. The mainstay of the business was a tobacco "plug," produced with native grapes and tobacco. After the Civil War, tobacco plugs were used as money in the cash-strapped economy.

The Cherokee Treaty of 1866 stated that Cherokee manufacturers were not subject to federal excise taxes. As a result, Watie and Boudinot were able to undersell the competition and thereby profit significantly from the stipulations of the new treaty. However, rival tobacco dealers outside Indian Territory complained that the Indians were underselling them and thus ruining their business. Watie and Boudinot were arrested for evading excise taxes on their products, which resulted in an important Supreme Court case called the Cherokee Tobacco Case. In 1870, the Supreme Court ruled against them. Even though there was no revenue collection district that included Cherokee lands, the Supreme Court ruled that the Cherokee were within the jurisdiction of the United States, that the treaty had been repealed by the Revenue Act (despite the fact that there is no language in the act to that effect), and therefore the Cherokee must pay the tax. This was an important case in that it seriously undermined the treaty-making process between the United States and Indian tribes. In fact, the following year Congress passed the Indian Appropriation Act of March 3, 1871, which contained a rider essentially giving Congress plenary power in all decisions involving any and all tribal rights previously granted by treaty. This also marked a period when non-Indian businesses used their clout and connections in the U.S. government to capitalize on the displacement of legitimate American Indian tobacco industries for the remainder of the nineteenth and twentieth centuries. As a result, American (non-Indian) tobacco companies became some of the largest and most profitable businesses in the world.

SMOKE SHOPS AND TRIBAL SOVEREIGNTY

Taking advantage of a little-known piece of congressional tax legislation, the Jenkins Act of 1949, Indian tribes have been able to sell tobacco products without notifying a state's tax department of any taxable transactions. In essence, Indian tobacco outlets have operated in several states and are able to sell tobacco products at a significantly reduced rate since they are exempted from paying state tobacco taxes.

Throughout the twentieth and into the twenty-first century, a person traveling anywhere throughout Indian Country comes upon "Indian smoke shops." These small tobacco stores are perhaps some of the most visible reminders of tribal sovereignty and Native American entrepreneurship in the modern era. However, these businesses have operated under duress and some of the most blatant attacks on tribal sovereignty has been experienced in the tentative relations between tribes that seek economic independence and individual states that seek revenues for state treasuries. Often, there is confusion, mistrust, and resulting misunderstandings between tribes and states because of the complexity of tax agreements between tribal and state governments in states that have sovereign tribal lands. In attempts to resolve their differences, state and tribal governments have examined contested tax issues together, negotiated for their particular interests, and generally agree to cooperate for their mutual benefit. These negotiations may result in profit sharing or compact agreements that help to ensure that both parties benefit from retail sales of tobacco products sold on trust land or Indian reservations. Regardless of how

Narragansett Indian chief Sachem Matthew Thomas looks off during a blessing of the circle ceremony in front of the Narragansett Indian Smoke Shop in Charlestown, Rhode Island, on July 14, 2004. An attorney for the tribe argued in front of the U.S. Circuit Court of Appeals that the tribe had a right to sell cigarettes at a smoke shop on its land without charging the Rhode Island tax. (AP Photo/Victoria Arocho)

amenable the agreements are between these governmental bodies, there are forces that continue to erode the relations between tribes and states; some are philosophical, and others are purely economical.

In 2009, the U.S. House of Representatives passed the Prevent All Cigarette Trafficking Act, or the PACT Act, which amends the Jenkins Act to revise provisions governing the collection of taxes on, and trafficking in, cigarettes and smokeless tobacco. Many Indian tribes were concerned over how this new act would impact them and their smoke shop businesses and whether it would repeal the state tax exemptions that they enjoyed because of their sovereign status. However, the act is intended to halt the sale and distribution of contraband or counterfeit tobacco products, particularly to minors, through illegal Internet sales of cigarettes and smokeless tobacco. Such practices have become lucrative for criminal organizations seeking tax-free profits by avoiding state tax regulations.

The vast majority of Native American outlets in the United States sell cigarettes through legitimate smoke shops, where tobacco sales occur through personal transactions with consumers. Smoke shops sell tobacco products responsibly and within the requirements of the laws and compacts that govern their operations. The few Indian tribes that operate Internet outlets are subject to federal law and are not subject to state laws regarding sales of any tobacco products apart from specific agreements or compacts enacted between state and tribal governments.

While federally recognized American Indian tribes are sovereign relative to any particular *state government*, they are not sovereign relative to the *federal government*, nor are they exempt from *federal law*. The PACT Act of course is a *federal requirement*. Nevertheless, state governments continue to assail Indian tribes, arguing that American Indians enjoy "special privileges" that give them unique advantages over non-Indian owned businesses. Most states working on behalf of private corporate interests seek to eliminate the governmental "privileges" that Native Americans rightfully claim because of treaties between sovereign tribal nations and the federal government. States argue that Native Americans avoid paying sales taxes on everything from cigarettes to gasoline and operate in markets that stifle competition from non-Indian businesses that have to pay such taxes. In reality, no such special privileges exist. Rosales (1998) reports that in *Tax Commission vs. Citizen Band Potawatomi Indian Tribe of Oklahoma* (1991) the U.S. Supreme Court reiterated that "the doctrine of tribal sovereign immunity does not prevent a State from requiring Indian retailers doing business on tribal reservations to collect a state-imposed cigarette tax on their sales to nonmembers of the Tribe." The Court also concluded that the doctrine of sovereign immunity effectively prevents states from directly suing a tribe to compel the payment of any state sales taxes on tribal businesses. At first glance, it appears that states have no recourse but to accept any revenue loss that is legitimately owed them on tobacco sales to nontribal members. To remedy this dilemma, the Court's decision included a provision that states may of course collect the sales tax from cigarette wholesalers, either by seizing unstamped cigarettes off the reservation, or by assessing wholesalers who supplied unstamped cigarettes to the tribal stores. States may also enter into compacts or agreements with the tribes to adopt a mutually satisfactory system for the collection of this sort of tax.

Ironically, states exist on lands that were originally inhabited by tribal people. And now, tribes are allowed by treaty to have only a small portion of their former lands. Most tribes occupy lands that are remote and inhospitable, and they lack the resources to become economically independent and prosperous. Tribal people quite often experience extreme poverty and what few enterprises they have do not begin to compare with the economic benefits that states enjoy, quite often through ill-gotten gains at the expense of Native Americans. Billions of dollars have been lost by Indian tribes through thievery, manipulation, and even murder by state entities and private citizens who have all but eradicated Indian tribes throughout the country. And while billions of dollars are collected by state governments each year through income, sales, and property taxes, Native Americans cannot collect even a penny on property taxes alone. Ironically, these same states and the federal government as well, did not voice any complaint as Native Americans were robbed of their land, water, minerals and other natural resources over the centuries leading to the present era. In fact, the assault on tribal sovereignty has almost become a national pastime, especially during the periodic election cycles when aspiring politicians in states with Indian tribes seek to satisfy their constituents' implacable and insatiable hunger for another dollar or another acre of land.

However, the American Indian smoke shop has stood as a symbol of the resourcefulness and steadfast resolve of America's indigenous peoples to survive, thrive, and prosper in spite of centuries of assault, immeasurable losses, and austere social and economic neglect under the rule of the dominant social order. And as these small institutions are absorbed by or displaced in deference to other institutions such as casinos, Native Americans can look back with pride and reverence to a sacred weed that has helped them sustain their culture and stave off their extinction, even into the modern era. Tobacco, as many elders have sought to remind us, is not simply a substance for personal enjoyment or source of economic prosperity, but it is a sacred medicine whether it winds up at the end of a sacred pipe or in a pack of cigarettes at a tribal smoke shop.

REFERENCES

Bonnie, R. J., K. Stratton, and R. B. Wallace. *Ending the Tobacco Problem: A Blueprint for the Nation*. Washington, DC: National Academies Press, 2007. Retrieved from http://www.nap.edu/catalog.php?record_id=11795 on December 16, 2010.

Borio, Gene. "The Tobacco Timeline," 2001. Retrieved from http://www.tobacco.org/resources/history/Tobacco_History.html on December 16, 2010.

Brown, Joseph Epes (Ed.). *The Sacred Pipe: Black Elk's Account of the Seven Rites of the Oglala Sioux*. Norman: University of Oklahoma Press, 1953.

Davies, Glyn. A *History of Money from Ancient Times to the Present Day* (3rd ed.). Cardiff: University of Wales Press, 2002.

Erdoes, Richard and Alfonzo Ortiz. *American Indian Myths and Legends*. New York: Pantheon Books, 1984.

Hamel, Paul B. and Mary U. Chiltoskey. *Cherokee Plants and Their Uses: A 400 Year History*. Sylva, NC: Herald Publishing, 1975.

Morgan, Lewis H. *Ancient Society*. London: MacMillan & Company, 1877.

Paper, Jordan. *Offering Smoke*. Moscow: University of Idaho Press, 1988.

Parins, James W. *Elias Cornelius Boudinot: A Life on the Cherokee Border*. Lincoln: University of Nebraska Press, 2006.

"Prevent All Cigarette Trafficking Act or PACT Act Update," *NCAI Sentinel*, Summer Edition (2003): 14. Retrieved from www.ncai.org/ncai/resource/documents/sentinel.pdf on December 16, 2010.

Rosales, Jon. "Contemporary Threats to Tribal Sovereignty from the Courts." *American Indian Policy Center*, 1998. Retrieved from http://www.americanindianpolicycenter.org/research/st98cont_courts.html on December 18, 2010.

Seig, Louis. *Tobacco, Peace Pipes, and Indians*. Palmer Lake, CO: Filter Press, 1999.

U.S. General Accounting Office (GAO). *Internet Cigarette Sales: Limited Compliance and Enforcement of the Jenkins Act Result in Loss of State Tax Revenue*. Washington, DC: Author, 2002. Retrieved from http://www.gao.gov/new.items/d03714t.pdf on December 16, 2010.

Bureau of Indian Affairs: A Historical and Contemporary Mission

Ralph Hartsock

The Bureau of Indian Affairs (BIA), the oldest bureau in the U.S. Department of the Interior (DOI), administers services to 1.9 million Native Americans in 565 recognized tribes. Its mission is to "enhance the quality of life, to promote economic opportunity, and to carry out the responsibility to protect and improve the trust assets of American Indians, Indian tribes, and Alaska Natives" (DOI n.d.). Today, the BIA is involved in a plethora of issues relevant to American Indians, ranging from land and water use to education, from gaming to justice. The BIA has, however, a long and checkered history, at least regarding how the federal government has dealt with the rights and sovereignty of American Indian tribes

The concept of a department to manage interactions between European settlers and Native Americans began prior to the ratification of the U.S. Constitution. The Continental Congress organized a Committee on Indian Affairs in 1775, chaired by Benjamin Franklin. Article IX of the Articles of Confederation authorized Congress to regulate trade and manage Indian affairs. Secretary of War Henry Knox took over as chair of the committee in 1786. Policy in the colonial period reflected the English attitude of superiority in three activities: (1) removal of Indians to an Indian country and separation of Indians from non-Indians; (2) assimilation of Indians into European oriented society, including education and training; and (3) assigning Indians to reservations to eliminate conflict with white settlers.

The Bureau of Indian Affairs was founded, without congressional authorization, on March 11, 1824. In his letter of appointment to the first administrator, Thomas L. McKenney, Secretary of War John C. Calhoun used the term *Bureau*. McKenney served from 1824 to 1830 and was succeeded by Samuel S. Hamilton from 1830 to 1831. On July 9, 1832, Congress authorized President Andrew Jackson to appoint a Commissioner of Indian Affairs, who would report to the Secretary of War. Elbert Herring served as the first commissioner in this agency, called the Office of Indian Affairs. Even before the formation of a congressionally sanctioned Office of Indian Affairs, Congress passed the Indian Removal Act of 1830, authorizing forcible relocation of American Indians from the eastern regions of the United States. Noteworthy among these were tribes that ceded their lands to federal agents for nominal monetary compensation, including the Shawnee (1831), Menominee (1831), Winnebago (1832), and Potawatomi (1832). Many were sent to an area called Indian country, which later became the state of Oklahoma.

In 1832, the government's health services began when Congress authorized the distribution of smallpox vaccines to selected tribes. For 15 years (1835–1850) the federal government invested funds originally intended to benefit Indian tribes into various states' bonds. Some states later failed to pay interest, and these funds earned little.

On March 3, 1849, the Office of Indian Affairs was transferred to civilian control, inside the Department of the Interior, to manage public land, Indian land, and Indian affairs. It operated as a side division, not a primary division of the department. Not until the late twentieth century did the Bureau of Indian Affairs become a full division, headed by the Assistant Secretary for Indian Affairs. The division continued its policy of assimilation. George W. Manypenny, who served during the presidency of Franklin Pierce (1853–1857), was one of the first to suggest that Indians were wards. This idea was advanced further by Interior Secretary Caleb B. Smith in 1862, and subsequently by Ely Parker.

Ely Samuel Parker (1828–1895), of the Seneca tribe, was the first American Indian to serve as Commissioner of Indian Affairs. Appointed by Ulysses S. Grant in 1869, he helped the president institute a Peace Policy, which rendered control of Indian agencies to Christian denominations. During his tenure, he prohibited mining on Indian lands, a point of contention with many corporations. He also chaired a Board of Indian Commissioners to fight the corruption that had grown from within the Grant administration. Parker also perpetuated the concept that Indian tribes were wards of the federal government, ineligible to make treaties. After a final treaty in 1868, a three-year extension of the change in this policy ended the treaty-making process at about 650 treaties in 1871. The Supreme Court, in *United States vs. Kagama* (1886), concurred that members of Indian tribes were wards. The Court also stated that the government was obligated to protect these tribes and their members.

Education of American Indian children occurred in mission schools operated by various Christian denominations. Mission schools grew from the early nineteenth century, providing vocational and literary education. Two types emerged. The day school allowed students to return to their families nearby at the conclusion of the school day. Boarding schools were developed at distances too far to travel on a daily basis. These institutions received federal funds, and in 1897 Congress stipulated that no further expenditures be made to these sectarian schools, a policy that took effect in 1900.

In 1879, the Office of Indian Affairs created the first off-reservation school, in Carlisle, Pennsylvania, a trend of remote education that continued into the mid-twentieth century. Founded by Captain Richard H. Pratt, the Carlisle Indian School served as a model for assimilation by education. By 1887, over 10,000 students were in boarding schools, located in Oregon, New Mexico, Colorado, Kansas, Nebraska, and Oklahoma. By the end of the nineteenth century, over 25 schools existed. More vocational training was emphasized, such as blacksmithing and tailoring for males, and sewing for females. The Carlisle School ceased operating in 1918.

Historically, boarding schools have garnered a sizable portion of the BIA budget. From 1900 to 1970, these schools drew over half of the bureau's budget. The Office of Indian Education Programs was renamed in 2006 as the Bureau of Indian Education (BIE). Its director reports to the Assistant Secretary–Indian Affairs in the Department of the Interior. By 2009, one hundred eighty-three elementary and secondary schools, located on 64 reservations in 23 states, served 41,000 students. Included in these numbers are 52 boarding schools, and only seven of these boarding schools are not on reservations. BIE also funds 31 tribal colleges and technical schools.

ASSIMILATION, AND THE DAWES ACT

In 1881, ethnographer Alice Cunningham Fletcher (1838–1923) spent several months residing on tribal and reservation lands of the Omaha Indians in Nebraska, and the Sioux in Dakota Territory. She went to Washington, DC, to lobby in support of the Omaha remaining in their original land and not being transferred to Indian Territory (today's Oklahoma). After Congress passed a special act for the Omahas, Fletcher was appointed as a special agent in the Bureau of Indian Affairs. She opposed the agency model in which Native Americans were confined to reservations. In this effort, she later helped write and lobby for the General Allotment Act (1887), also known as the Dawes Severalty Act.

Introduced by Senator Henry Laurens Dawes, the General Allotment Act promoted the philosophy of assimilation. It allowed the federal government to divide reservations into plots of 160 acres each. Fletcher believed this would provide Indians with land, education, and citizenship. She was then employed to implement this law with the Winnebagos (Ho-Chunk) in the Midwest (1887–1889) and Nez Perce in the Northwest (1889–1890). But by 1898, she realized that the allotment program was flawed; many tribal lands west of the Mississippi River went into the possession of non-Indians. Various other allotment acts followed. This transfer of tribal lands to non-Indians was due to the fact that after 25 years, this land could be purchased by non-Indians. The Burke Act of 1906 extended this period an additional 25 years. Over the 50 years following the Dawes Act, Indian holdings dwindled from 136 million acres to less than 50 million acres.

Even before Prohibition took effect for white Americans, American Indians were prohibited from transporting, using, selling, or bartering beer or wine via the Intoxication in Indian Country Act of 1892 and the Indian Liquor Act of 1897. Since the Snyder Act of 1921, policy in the BIA has trended away from acculturation and assimilation and toward self-determination, both in governance and education. This was enhanced by the Indian Reorganization Act of 1934, and the Indian Self-Determination and Education Assistance Act of 1975.

The era of assimilation continued from 1871 until 1928 and the presidency of Herbert Hoover. In 1928, Lewis Meriam issued *The Problem of Indian Administration*, also known as the Meriam Report. This became a prelude to the end of the allotment era, and began a period of greater concern for reinstituting the reservation system and enacting further protections of Indian rights and cultural heritage. The report was highly critical of the General Allotment Act and the policy of forced assimilation.

NEW DEAL BRINGS MORE CHANGE

Changes in attitude continued when Charles J. Rhoads became the commissioner of the OIA in 1929. He was the son of James E. Rhoads, a reformer of Indian policy and one of the original members of the Indian Rights Association. James Rhoads served as president of the Indian Rights Association for nine years. Charles Rhoads, influenced by his own Quaker roots, was appointed by president Herbert Hoover. Serving from 1929 to 1933, he worked toward the eventual passage of the Indian Reorganization Act of 1934, which resulted in increased autonomy for tribal councils. After 1932, he spoke in favor of assimilation for American Indians.

Franklin Roosevelt continued the trend of assimilation in 1933, as he appointed Harold L. Ickes as Secretary of the Interior, and John Collier as Commissioner of Indian Affairs. Collier sought to "protect Indian rights and lands and to bring greater cultural understanding of American Indians to the larger American population" and Pritzker. The Indian Reorganization Act of 1934 (the Wheeler-Howard Act), a vast improvement over and contrast to the General Allotment Act of 1887, created tribal governments, allowed for purchase of additional land for Native Americans, and extended the trust on Indian lands, a reversal from the activities of the late 1910s (Taylor 1984, 21). But the fallacy of the Indian Reorganization

Act, particularly in Title I, the section governing tribal self-determination, required approval by the Secretary of the Department of the Interior.

Based on his review of the Meriam Report, Collier advocated that the Office of Indian Affairs transfer some of its law enforcement, health, and educational activities to tribal, state, county, or city governments. His recommendations resulted in the formation of a county-Indian hospital in Albuquerque, New Mexico, in 1950. By 1955, the Indian Health Service was transferred to the Public Health Service and resides today within the Department of Health and Human Services. Also spawned by the Meriam Report was Collier's recommendation of bilingual education for American Indians. Although this effort was interrupted by World War II, during the 1940s, educators in the BIA collaborated with Pueblo, Sioux, and Navajo tribes to develop the *Indian Life Readers*. These books, either fictional stories or history, were written in both English and a specific American Indian language. The books served to further bilingual education.

During his tenure as commissioner, Charles J. Rhoads proposed an Indian Claims Commission to govern Indian land claims between 1946 and 1978; the Indian Claims Commission Act was finally enacted in 1946. Although a part of the termination movement, this commission benefited American Indians. By 1978, the commission had resolved over 500 claims and dispersed $800 million.

On June 19, 1947, the Department of the Interior changed the name of the Office of Indian Affairs to the Bureau of Indian Affairs. Even then, the agency was not fully responsive to Native Americans' needs. After World War II, termination policy sought to free American Indians from the reservation system and to further assimilate them into mainstream society. Its intent was to eventually liquidate the BIA and absolve the federal government of its trust responsibility to Native Americans, which would allow the government to withdraw federal services and funds previously obligated in treaties and other legal agreements. Tribal status, including the tax-exempt status of tribes, would also cease.

Termination policy affected over 70 tribes, mostly in the period from 1954 to 1958. Noteworthy examples are the Klamath Termination Act, and the Menominee Termination Act, both passed in 1954. The Menominee Restoration Act of 1973 repealed the Menominee Termination Act of 1954, returned most of the reservation land to that tribe, and recognized the Menominee as a tribe.

ERA OF INDIAN REPRESENTATION AT BIA

Forty-five men have served as the Commissioner of Indian Affairs. Six of these have been Native Americans, beginning with Ely S. Parker (1869–1871). The next time this occurred was during the administration of Lyndon B. Johnson, under the leadership of Secretary of the Interior Stewart Udall. Robert L. Bennett, of the Oneida tribe, regarded the BIA as an advocate for Native American causes.

Neither he nor his predecessor Philleo Nash (1961–1966) mentioned termination; rather, they emphasized economic, social, and civic development of tribes.

Although the Indian Reorganization Act of 1934 validated the preference for hiring American Indians for employment in the BIA, they were limited to lower-level positions for several years. But during the 1970s, Interior Secretary Rogers C. B. Morton and commissioner Louis R. Bruce, of the Mohawk-Oglala Sioux tribe (1969–1973), applied this concept to all positions. The courts concurred. In 1950, American Indians constituted a majority of the BIA staff. By 1982, they were 75 percent of the bureau.

During the Nixon and Ford administrations, commissioner Louis R. Bruce was succeeded by Morris Thompson, of the Athabascan tribe (1973–1976). Additional laws promoted self-determination, such as the Alaska Native Claims Settlement Act (1971) and the Indian Financing Act of 1974.

In 1972, the American Indian Movement (AIM) occupied the BIA building in Washington, DC. Due to the Trail of Broken Treaties in 1972, the bureau was decentralized. The Menominee Restoration Act of 1973 restored previously withheld federal services to the tribe from Wisconsin. These policies rejected those of termination. With passage of the Indian Self-Determination and Education Assistance Act of 1975, the BIA was transformed from a direct manager of Indian affairs to an agency that awarded contracts and grants.

The final two commissioners in the pre-1977 arrangement of BIA were Benjamin Reifel, Sioux (1976–1977) and William E. Hallett, Red Lake Chippewa (1979–1981). In 1977, the position of Assistant Secretary for Indian Affairs (AS-IA) was created in the Department of the Interior. The first to serve in this post was Forrest Gerard, of the Blackfoot tribe. In 1981, the BIA eliminated the position of commissioner and developed a Principal Deputy Assistant Secretary, who reported to the AS-IA. He or she would be supported by two deputies and two division directors, one each for BIA and BIE. One deputy counseled the agency on finances, information, environment and culture. The second deputy managed the Office of Indian Energy and Economic Development, along with Indian Gaming, and the implementation of policies related to Indians throughout the federal government.

Subsequent occupants of the position of AS-IA were Thomas W. Fredericks, Mandan-Hidatsa (1981); Kenneth L. Smith, Wasco (1981–1984); Ross O. Swimmer, Cherokee (1985–1989); Eddie F. Brown, Tohono O'odham-Yaqui (1989–1993); Ada E. Deer, Menominee (1993–1997); Kevin Gover, Pawnee (1997–2001); Neal McCaleb, Chickasaw (2001–2002); David W. Anderson, Lac Courte Oreilles Chippewa-Choctaw (2004–2005); Carl J. Artman, Oneida Tribe of Wisconsin (2007–2008); and Larry Echo Hawk, Pawnee Nation of Oklahoma (2009–).

In recent years, there has been more of a shift toward employing American Indians as the Assistant Secretary of the Department of the Interior for Indian

Affairs. This has given American Indians a resident voice in policy decisions. Termination and other failed policies are being discarded. Fewer off-reservation boarding schools are used than a century ago. American Indians are also learning their languages, cultures, ceremonies, artifacts, and traditions. On August 29, 2006, the Office of Indian Education Programs was renamed the Bureau of Indian Education (BIE), to manage education.

The BIA collaborates with the National Interagency Fire Center (NIFC), a division within the Bureau of Land Management, in Boise, Idaho, to distribute news via the quarterly newsletter *Smoke Signals*. The periodical actively works to prevent and reduce wildfires and the damage they cause to humans, their dwellings, animals, plants, ecosystems, watersheds, and landscapes. Included are methods to preserve Indian lands from erosion and floods.

Also within BIA, the Office of Facilities, Environmental and Cultural Resources (OFECR) manages facilities, construction, environmental factors, and safety; at also administers cultural resource management programs. Within this division is the Office of Facilities Management and Construction, headquartered in Albuquerque, New Mexico. Its major focus includes architectural planning, design, construction, environmental safety in the facilities, and their condition. To this end, the OFMC surveyed 181 of the schools in 2010. Some required no repairs, while many were classified as poor, with some poor schools needing $10 to $15 million in renovations. Also within the OFECR is the Division of Environmental and Cultural Resources Management, a group that assists the AS-IA to implement environmental and cultural resources laws that apply to or might affect Indian trust lands. These laws include the National Environmental Policy Act, National Historic Preservation Act, Archeological Resources Protection Act of 1979, and the Native American Graves Protection and Repatriation Act of 1990. This division also manages the Museum Property Program.

REFERENCES

Castagno, Angelina E. and Bryan McKinley Jones Brayboy. "Culturally Responsive Schooling for Indigenous Youth: A Review of the Literature." *Review of Educational Research* 78 (2008): 941–993.

Champagne, Duane. *Chronology of Native North American History: From Pre-Columbian Times to the Present*. Detroit: Gale Research, 1994.

Daily, David W. *Battle for the BIA: G.E.E. Lindquist and the Missionary Crusade against John Collier*. Tucson: University of Arizona Press, 2004.

Gover, Kevin. "An Indian Trust for the Twenty-First Century." *Natural Resources Journal* 46 (2006): 317–374.

Grossman, Mark. *The ABC-CLIO Companion to the Native American Rights Movement*. Santa Barbara, CA: ABC-CLIO, 1996.

Jackson, Curtis E. and Marcia J. Galli. *A History of the Bureau of Indian Affairs and Its Activities among Indians*. San Francisco: R & E Research Associates, 1977.

Johansen, Bruce E. and Barry M. Pritzker (Eds.). *Encyclopedia of American Indian History*. Santa Barbara, CA: ABC-CLIO, 2008.

Lomawaima, K. Tsianina and Teresa L. McCarty. "When Tribal Sovereignty Challenges Democracy: American Indian Education and the Democratic Ideal." *American Educational Research Journal* 39 (2002): 279–305.

Meriam, Lewis (Ed.). *The Problem of Indian Administration*. Baltimore, MD: Institute for Government Research, Studies in Administration, 1928.

Stuart, Paul. *The Indian Office: Growth and Development of an American Institution, 1865–1900*. Ann Arbor, MI: University Microfilms International (UMI) Research Press, 1979.

Taylor, Theodore W. *The Bureau of Indian Affairs*. Boulder, CO: Westview Press, 1984.

U.S. Department of the Interior (DOI). *BIA Profile: The Bureau of Indian Affairs and American Indians*. Washington, DC: U.S. Governmental Printing Office, 1981.

U.S. Department of the Interior (DOI). "Indian Affairs." Retrieved from http://www.bia.gov/ in May 2011.

Federal Recognition

Debra Buchholtz

There are 565 federally recognized tribal bodies, the most recent being the Shinnecock tribe. Inclusion on this all-important list does not create a tribe; rather, it recognizes tribal sovereignty, or a government-to-government relationship with the United States. It thereby acknowledges the immunities, privileges, responsibilities, powers, limitations, and obligations the tribe has by virtue of sovereignty. Sovereignty confirms a tribe's eligibility for Bureau of Indian Affairs (BIA) oversight, funding, and services. It also enables a tribe to have its lands held in trust by the federal government, exempting lands from state and local taxation. This special status has many other important consequences for American Indian groups and for local, state, and federal jurisdiction over their affairs.

Federal recognition of American Indian tribes depends on the history of interaction between the tribe and the federal government. Tribes that attracted attention before the twentieth century by being perceived as a threat to white Americans or by possessing desirable lands or resources have generally achieved federal recognition. Tribes deemed inconsequential by Anglo-Americans have generally not been recognized. Of the latter were many tribes east of the Appalachian Mountains that had by the late eighteenth century suffered such catastrophic population loss and disruption to traditional culture as to render them insignificant to the federal government.

Current American Indian tribes that wish to attain recognition must seek congressional or presidential action, or navigate their way through the cumbersome federal recognition process. Success is by no means assured and, as in the case of the Mashpee, can take many years to achieve. Between 1978 and 2008, the Office of Federal Acknowledgment (OFA) received 82 completed petitions for

Tribal chairman Randy King, center, outside of the courthouse in Central Islip, New York, on June 15, 2005, where he filed papers claiming tribal ownership of 3,600 acres of land in Southampton, New York. Members of the small Indian tribe on New York's Long Island were celebrating with prayers and song after receiving notification from the Federal Bureau of Indian Affairs that it had been formally recognized as a tribe. (AP Photo/Ed Betz)

recognition. Of the 66 that were resolved, 23 resulted in federal recognition and two in restoration of previously rescinded recognition. During that same interval, OFA received more than 250 other letters of intent or partially completed petitions, most of which are still pending or have been dropped. Some tribes, like the Lumbee of North Carolina, are recognized by the state in which they reside yet do not have federal recognition.

BENEFITS OF RECOGNITION

Groups like the Houma of Louisiana and the Lumbee realize that federal acknowledgment can strengthen their sense of shared identity; the primary reasons for seeking recognition are for the political, economic, and other rights, benefits, and protections that accrue from the government-to-government relationship and federal recognition of tribal sovereignty. Federal recognition exempts tribes from state and local taxation, limits state and local jurisdiction over tribal lands held in trust by the federal government, and increases self-governance. The Bureau of

> ## OFFICE OF FEDERAL ACKNOWLEDGMENT
>
> The Office of Federal Acknowledgment determines whether a tribe gains federal recognition. The U.S. Department of the Interior, Indian Affairs, provides an overview on its website, which is reproduced in part here.
>
> The Office of Federal Acknowledgment (OFA) within the Office of the Assistant Secretary–Indian Affairs of the Department of the Interior (Department) implements Part 83 of Title 25 of the Code of Federal Regulations (25 CFR Part 83), *Procedures for Establishing that an American Indian Group Exists as an Indian Tribe*. The acknowledgment process is the Department's administrative process by which petitioning groups that meet the criteria are given Federal "acknowledgment" as Indian tribes and by which they become eligible to receive services provided to members of Indian tribes. . . .
>
> By applying anthropological, genealogical, and historical research methods, OFA reviews, verifies, and evaluates groups' petitions for Federal acknowledgment as Indian tribes. OFA makes recommendations for proposed findings and final determinations to the AS-IA, consults with petitioners and third parties, provides copies of 25 CFR Part 83 and its guidelines, prepares technical assistance review letters, maintains petitions and administrative correspondence files, and conducts special research projects for the Department. OFA also performs other administrative duties that include maintaining lists of petitioners and responding to appeals, litigation, and Freedom of Information Act requests.
>
> Since 1978, 350 groups have stated their intent to seek acknowledgment through the administrative process. Of this number, 265 groups have submitted only letters of intent or partially documented petitions, and are not ready for evaluation. The remaining 84 have submitted completed petitions. Of this number, the Department has resolved 52 and 19 have been resolved by Congress or through other means; the current OFA workload consists of 9 petitions under active consideration, while 4 petitions are ready and waiting for active consideration. Two resolved decisions are in litigation in Federal court and one before the Interior Board of Indian Appeals.
>
> *Source*: Office of Federal Acknowledgment. Retrieved from http://www.bia.gov/WhoWeAre/AS-IA/OFA/index.htm

Indian Affairs administers a range of federally funded contracts, services, and programs worth billions of dollars. Most of the funds are earmarked for federally recognized tribes. Some address community needs like law enforcement, criminal justice, education, sanitation, highway maintenance, and social welfare, which parallel services normally provided by state and local agencies. Federally recognized tribes are also eligible for special assistance programs that target economic development, job training and employment, education, healthcare (including mental health), agriculture, natural resource management, and improvements to tribal infrastructure. Recognized tribes can also establish their own courts and law enforcement agencies, regulate business, and levy taxes within their reservation borders. The basis for and nature of these entitlements and exemptions are complicated and poorly understood by non-Indians, who often object to what they perceive as the unwarranted special privileges enjoyed by American Indian tribes at the federal taxpayer's expense.

Perhaps most enticingly and controversially, federal recognition and the quasisovereign status it entails also enable tribes to enter into gaming compacts with the states where they are located and open bingo parlors and casinos. Such ventures, if successful, provide badly needed jobs and income, sometimes in great abundance. Tribes use their gaming profits in different ways. How they do so can prove highly divisive, with different elements within the tribe having different ideas about how the money can best be used. Some, like the Mille Lacs Band of Ojibwe (Chippewa) in Minnesota, use their profits to build schools, museums, and recreational facilities. Others redistribute at least a portion in per capita payments to tribal members, a practice that can raise thorny questions pertaining to membership criteria and eligibility for payments. Sometimes the prospects of per capita payouts lead nontribal members to seek inclusion on the tribal roll. Members already eligible to receive payments may suspect the newcomers' motives and resist what they perceive as an attempt by the undeserving to cash in on casino profits. The implication of this is clear: as more people get a cut of the financial pie, the slices will get smaller. In many cases, tribal leaders have been pressed to revise the criteria for tribal membership, which are often based on blood quanta and descent. Sometimes they have been asked to tighten them so that fewer people reap more benefits from tribal membership. In other cases, there is pressure to loosen the criteria so more people can benefit.

Critics of the federal recognition system, as well as some tribal leaders, argue that entities without legitimate tribal claims are now seeking federal recognition so that they can open and profit from their own casinos. An example recently in the spotlight is the Native Hawaiian bid for recognition as an American Indian tribe through the vehicle of the Akaka Bill. American Indian critics, in particular, fear that widening the circle of federal recognition in this way would weaken arguments based on American Indian heritage and sovereignty. They also worry that it would pull gaming traffic, and hence revenues, away from casinos run by legitimate tribal bodies. States have concerns regarding their ability to regulate reservation gaming and reap benefits from the profits, and non-Indians living in proximity to the casinos worry about the impact of gambling on their communities. In reality, many newly recognize tribes do open bingo halls and casinos as a means of generating the revenue needed to cover the high costs of their bid for recognition.

> ## SHINNECOCK TRIBE
>
> The Shinnecock Indian nation is the most recent tribe to achieve federal recognition. The following abridged news release, from the U.S. Department of the Interior, provides details.
>
> > Acting Principal Deputy Assistant Secretary–Indian Affairs George T. Skibine on June 13, 2010, issued a final determination... to acknowledge the Shinnecock Indian Nation (Petitioner #4) as an Indian tribe. This petitioner, located in Southampton, Suffolk County, N.Y., has 1,292 members.
> >
> > The evidence in the record for the proposed finding demonstrated that the petitioner met all seven of the mandatory criteria for Federal acknowledgment....
> >
> > The Shinnecock petitioner meets the seven criteria and affirms the proposed finding as follows:
> >
> > Criterion 83.7(a) requires that external observers have identified the petitioner as an American Indian entity on a substantially continuous basis since 1900....
> >
> > Criterion 83.7(b) requires that a predominant portion of the petitioning group has comprised a distinct community since historical times....
> >
> > Criterion 83.7(c) requires that the petitioning group has maintained political influence over its members as an autonomous entity since historical times. The proposed finding determined that because the group's three elected trustees have allocated and managed the reservation's lands and resources since 1792, it demonstrated it meets this criterion using —"high evidence" described at 83.7(c)(2)(i). This final determination affirms those findings....
> >
> > Criterion 83.7(e) requires that the petitioner's members descend from a historical Indian tribe.
> >
> > The evidence in the record shows that at least 97 percent of the 1,292 members descend from the historical 1789 Shinnecock tribe, as determined by their descent from the 1865 reservation residents listed in the New York State census. Thus, this final determination affirms the proposed finding—but with a revised membership total and percentage of descent—that the petitioner meets this criterion.
>
> *Source*: Bureau of Indian Affairs. Retrieved from http://www.bia.gov/idc/groups/public/documents/text/idc009906.pdf

RECOGNITION AND TERMINATION

Over time, tribes have achieved federal recognition through a variety of mechanisms. Most tribes automatically attained federal recognition in the eighteenth or nineteenth centuries when they signed treaties with the U.S. government or accepted settlement on reservations. Treaties, by definition, are agreements forged between sovereign nations, and therein lays the origins of American Indian sovereignty and all that it entails. In many cases, however, tribes signed treaties but did not get federal recognition because Congress failed to ratify the treaties. Other groups have acquired recognition through congressional or administrative action, or by presidential proclamation. After Congress formally ended the treaty-making period with a rider attached to an 1871 appropriations bill, those were the only avenues left open to groups seeking federal recognition.

Recognition became increasingly important with the 1934 passage of the Indian Reorganization Act (IRA), which specified that only federally recognized tribes could organize tribal governments and reap the benefits and exemptions of recognition. The question then became how unrecognized groups could attain necessary recognition. The "landless" tribes of western Washington State, which include the Duwamish, Cowlitz, and Chinook, seized the opportunity and tried to organize tribal governments under the IRA and thereby attain recognition. For various reasons stemming from fine-grained legal interpretations of each group's history of interactions with the federal government, most efforts were unsuccessful. For several decades after the passage of the IRA, the BIA and the solicitor of the Department of the Interior assumed responsibility for recognizing tribes.

In 1953, in an attempt to end federal responsibility for recognized tribes, House Concurrent Resolution 108 introduced what came to be known as the termination policy. It paved the way for the enactment of legislation that terminated the special status of those tribes deemed self-sufficient enough to no longer warrant federal oversight. Termination would withdraw federal recognition and all the rights, benefits, and powers that come with it. Despite opposition from most of the tribes involved, Congress terminated 109 tribal entities between 1953 and 1964, including the Menominee and the Klamath. In most cases, termination had disastrous consequences for the people affected and often for their neighbors as well. Almost overnight, many of the counties in which reservations of terminated tribes were located joined the ranks of the most impoverished counties in the nation. Thousands of American Indians lost access to education, healthcare, and other services upon which they had depended. Nearly as many were left destitute as their tribes lost federal funding for economic development, employment, housing, and social welfare programs. Subject to taxes from which they previously had been exempt and now could not afford to pay, many tribal members also lost their lands through tax forfeiture. Out of desperation, people left their home communities to seek work in distant cities, where the jobs they found were often among the lowest paying available.

After long struggles, several terminated tribes, including the Menominee, Klamath, and Catawba, succeeded in having their federal recognition restored. That, too, required legislative action. While most American Indian tribes, organizations, and individuals have supported the restoration of federal recognition to terminated tribes, there are those who have objected. Some have argued that many tribes willingly accepted termination in exchange for economic considerations and should, therefore, live with the consequences of their decisions. Others have voiced self-interested fears that restoration of federal recognition would increase the number of tribes drawing on the limited federal funds earmarked for tribal use and thus decrease the amount available to each tribe. Non-Indians have also opposed the reinstatement of what they perceive as the preferential treatment enjoyed by their Indian neighbors.

There are also many American Indian groups that, like the Houma, Narragansett, and Mohican, have never been federally recognized but have nonetheless maintained their distinctive cultural identities. Many of them have long wanted to reap the benefits and privileges of recognition. Such groups have faced widespread opposition from non-Indians because such acknowledgement would expand the list of sovereign tribes eligible for federal programs and funding, and thus add to the taxpayer burden. Members of recognized tribes have also opposed the recognition of heretofore unrecognized groups. In some cases (mainly those involving groups in the South and East), they have questioned the legitimacy of asserted claims to American Indian heritage. Key to this is an assumption rooted in a confusion of biology (i.e., descent or genetics) and culture (i.e., cultural identity or "Indian-ness") and commonly expressed in the idiom of blood. These individuals allege that some of the groups seeking recognition are of mixed African American, American Indian, and European American heritage. As such, they are "tri-racial isolates" rather than American Indian and are, therefore, ineligible for recognition as a tribe. The flawed logic of blood has also underpinned federal Indian policy determinations of eligibility for services and benefits as well as the blood quantum requirements most tribal constitutions set for tribal membership. This has relevance for other issues arising from federal recognition, including who can and cannot benefit from tribal programs and gaming profits. As in the case of restoration of recognition to terminated tribes, some American Indians have expressed concerns over the impact a growing number of recognized tribes would have on the services and funding available to each tribe. Such objections, along with concerns regarding their eligibility criteria for tribal membership, have dogged the 55,000-strong Lumbee tribe's bid for federal recognition.

Conflict also arises over the demarcation of tribal entities and lands for the purposes of federal recognition. The Diné (Navajo), for example, resisted the San Juan Paiute's successful bid for federal recognition, arguing that the small group is really Diné. At stake was the possible loss of a strip of ancestral Paiute land within the Navajo reservation. The federally recognized Mille Lacs Band of Objiwe, along with other members of the Minnesota Chippewa tribe, similarly resisted restoration of federal recognition to the Sandy Land band, which was placed under the auspices of the Mille Lac band in 1934. The Sandy Lake band believes that resistance stems from the added competition for federal funding, programs, and economic development that would result from their recognition. Outside observers, however, link the Mille Lac band's resistance to casino revenues. Restored recognition would enable the Sandy Lake band to negotiate a gaming compact with the state and open a casino of its own, which could impact the Mille Lac band's gaming revenues.

FEDERAL ACKNOWLEDGEMENT PROCESS

Despite the voicing of objections, the influential 1961 American Indian Chicago Conference called for the recognition of all tribes that can demonstrate they have maintained their identity and tribal organization over time. By the 1970s, increasing numbers of groups were seeking federal recognition along with the benefits and opportunities it affords. By then, frustrated American Indian leaders were pressing for an overhaul of what they saw as a chaotic, arbitrary, and unfair process. In 1978, the procedure was standardized with the introduction of the Federal Acknowledgement Process. It established the Branch of Acknowledgement and Research (BAR) within the BIA through which American Indian groups could petition for federal recognition. The process was further refined and clarified in 1994. Four years later, the Department of the Interior issued its Official Guidelines for the Acknowledgement Process, which some legal experts argue makes the procedure seem unrealistically straightforward.

But it is not at all straightforward. Many American Indians believe the procedure is designed to limit expansion of the number of federally recognized tribes. Regulations laid out in 2001 specify seven mandatory conditions an American Indian group must satisfy to qualify for federal recognition. Although the document provides detailed guidelines for how those conditions can be met, a heavy burden of proof falls upon the petitioner (i.e., the tribal body seeking recognition).

First, the petitioner must prove that it has existed continuously as an identifiable American Indian group since 1900.

Second, the tribe must demonstrate that since historical times, its members have continuously constituted a distinct community.

Third, it must show that, acting as an autonomous entity, it has continuously exerted political control or authority over its members, again from historical times to the present.

Fourth, it must be able to document or describe its membership criteria and procedures for governance.

Fifth, it must show that its membership consists of individuals descended from a single historical tribe or from more than one tribe that came together to function as a single autonomous political body.

Sixth, most of the members must not already be members of a federally recognized tribe.

Seventh, the petitioner cannot have been denied federal recognition in the past or had its recognition rescinded. Breaks in the continuity of the group as a distinct and identifiable political entity or failure to meet any of these criteria results in denial of federal recognition.

Compiling the evidence needed to prove that a tribal body meets all of these conditions is a massive undertaking that usually requires extensive research by a team of tribal leaders, lawyers, historians, anthropologists, archaeologists, and other experts. Those involved claim that building a case for recognition is further complicated by shifting federal expectations and continual demands for additional evidence. Another complicating factor is that most tribal groups have traditionally relied on oral history and culturally specific techniques to record their pasts rather than on the written documentation preferred by American legal and political bodies. Moreover, traditional forms of social organization, leadership, and governance are not easily reconciled with the criteria laid out in the regulations. Consequently, recognition inevitably proves a costly, frustrating, and drawn-out process. In the majority of cases decided to date, the petitioner has had its request for federal recognition denied.

The Duwamish experience is particularly telling. They were granted federal recognition by President Clinton in the closing days of his administration only to have it suspended when President George W. Bush took over. Shortly thereafter, it was rescinded altogether on the grounds that the Duwamish did not satisfy all of the conditions for federal recognition.

Dissatisfaction with the federal recognition process remains widespread among tribal leaders and other American Indians. In the fall of 2009, the U.S. Senate Indian Affairs Committee convened an Oversight Hearing on Fixing the Federal Recognition Process. The committee took testimony from legal experts and tribal leaders like Frank Ettawageshik cochair of the National Congress of American Indians (NCAI) Federal Acknowledgement Task Force. They described their experiences with the process, outlined what they see as its shortcomings and failures, and called for specific changes. Ettawageshik reported that his people, the Odawa, eventually gave up on the federal recognition process altogether and successfully pursued their bid for recognition in the legislative arena. He described the process as "broken" and as "an active cause of injustice in the relationship between the federal government and the sovereign tribes throughout the country." Among the problems he highlighted are demands for evidence, a disjuncture between of the types of evidence required and the cultural realities of American Indian peoples, and the length of time it takes to receive a final decision. He also observed that the process itself provokes conflict within and between tribes. Speaking on behalf of the NCAI, Ettawageshik called for future judgments to be based on reasonable evidence that the group has maintained its tribal identity since historic times; for the process to be conducted in a timely, transparent, and fair manner; and that the process take into consideration the specific cultural and historical factors that shaped each group's relationship with the federal government.

REFERENCES

Blu, Karen. "Region and Recognition: Southern Indians, Anthropologists, and Presumed Biology." In Rachel A. Bonney and J. Anthony Paredes (Eds.), *Anthropologists and Indians in the New South*. Tuscaloosa: University of Alabama Press, 2001.

Cramer, Reneé Ann. *Cash, Color, and Colonialism: The Politics of Tribal Acknowledgement*. Norman: University of Oklahoma Press, 2005.

Goodner, Lindsay. "The Potential Passage of Proposed Senate Bill 147 and Its Implication on Native Hawaiians and Gaming." *American Indian Law Review* 31, no. 1 (2006/2007): 111–130.

"H.R 31 Lumbee Recognition Act." *Legislative Digest*, June 3, 2009. Retrieved from http://www.gop.gov/bill/111/1/hr31

Hughes, Jennifer P. "Primer on Federal Recognition and Current Issues Affecting the Process, Updated February 21, 2001," Retrieved from http://www.msaj.com/papers/fedrecnov.htm

Miller, Mark. *Forgotten Tribes: Unrecognized Indians and the Federal Acknowledgement Process*. Lincoln: University of Nebraska Press, 2004.

Porter, Frank W., III. "In Search of Recognition: Federal Indian Policy and the Landless Tribes of Western Washington." *American Indian Quarterly* 14, no. 2 (1990): 113–132.

Quinn, William W., Jr. "Federal Acknowledgement of Indian Tribes: The Historical Development of a Legal Concept." *America Journal of Legal History* 34 (1990): 331–364.

Turner, Allen C. and Robert C. Euler. "A Brief History of the San Juan Paiute Indians of Northern Arizona." *Journal of California and Great Basin Anthropology* 5, no. 1/2 (1983): 199–207. Retrieved from http://www.escholarship.org/uc/item/447601ts in December 2009.

U.S. Senate Committee on Indian Affairs. "Oversight Hearing on Fixing the Acknowledgement Process," November 4, 2009. Retrieved from http://indian.senate.gov/public/index.cfm?FuseAction=Hearings.Hearing&Hearing_ID=b79b3f0e-ba45-4fde-a122-9f788fc5afc0 in December 2009.

U.S. Senate Committee on Indian Affairs. "Testimony of the National Congress of American Indians on Fixing the Federal Acknowledgement Process," November 4, 2009. Retrieved from http://indian.senate.gov/public/_files/FrankEttawageshiktestimony.pdf in December 2009.

Federal Reservations

William P. Kladky

A federal Indian reservation is an area of land reserved for a tribe or tribes as a permanent tribal homeland under treaty or some other agreement with the United States, such as an executive order, federal statute, or administrative action. The federal government holds title to the land in trust on behalf of the tribe. The word *reservation* derives from tribes' former status as independent sovereigns in the 1780s. Early treaties identified land parcels that the tribes "reserved" to themselves, and the parcels eventually were termed *reservations*. Reservations in America are often places of despair, while at the same time they help to maintain Indian tradition and culture.

An Indian reservation is managed by a legally recognized Indian (or Native American) tribe under the Bureau of Indian Affairs (BIA) of the U.S. Department of the Interior (DOI). The 310 current reservations vary considerably. Some reservations' residents are from one tribe, some have many. Some reservations' land is divided into tribal, individual, and privately owned parcels. Reservations can include pueblos, rancherias, missions, villages, and communities. Some reservations are a small portion of a tribe's original land. Others were created by the federal government for resettling Indians, usually forcibly, from their original homelands.

Reservations total 55.7 million acres, which is 2.3 percent of the United States. Twelve reservations are larger than the state of Rhode Island; nine are larger than Delaware. The largest—the Navajo Nation Reservation in Arizona, New Mexico, and Utah—is roughly the size of West Virginia. The smallest is the California location of the Pit River tribe's 1.32-acre cemetery. Many small reservations are less than 1,000 acres. Most reservations are west of the Mississippi River.

Indian treaties have the same recognition under federal law as national treaties with foreign governments. Because tribes have sovereignty, albeit limited, laws on tribal lands vary from those enforced in the surrounding area. These laws can permit legal casinos on reservations, for example, which attract tourists. The tribal council, not the local or federal government, has jurisdiction over reservations. Different reservations have different systems of government, which may or may not replicate the forms of government found outside the reservation. Most Indian reservations were established by the federal government; a limited number, mainly in the East, were established by individual states.

HISTORICAL BACKGROUND

Indian reservations date from the early seventeenth century under English treaties establishing small land reservations in exchange for a monetary payment and the Indians' lands. The English law was based on the right of discovery, a concept originally promulgated by Spanish monarchs regarding Columbus's expeditions and the Dutch conscience-based "buying" of lands from the Indians. The Dutch legally required a landowner to have purchased title from the Indians. In taking power from its American colonies over Indian affairs in 1755, the British recognized the tribes as sovereign nations but also claimed the right to land purchase. The British Proclamation Act of 1763 established the Appalachian Mountains watershed as the boundary between tribes and white settlements. British authorities considered these reservations as temporary; they would be adjusted according to settlers' needs.

This policy was continued by the American government after independence. Initially, the tribes were given the status of sovereign nations. The Delaware and the Cherokee, for example, were given the option of becoming states. An 1802 law declared that federal law ruled in Indian lands, and land transfers were allowed only by treaty with a tribe. But as white settlers continued to move with the Louisiana Purchase in 1803 and after the War of 1812, the boundary was pushed farther westward. Adopting Thomas Jefferson's land exchange idea, it was hoped that the tribes would settle in the west, abandon their nomadic life, and become respectable settlers.

The push westward was set back temporarily when an 1822 federally commissioned study recommended that Indians be given the Northwest Territory (between the Ohio Valley and the Great Lakes) to eventually become a state of the union. Indian rights were strengthened further in 1823 when the U.S. Supreme Court gave its bedrock Marshall Trilogy decisions, declaring the Cherokee nation was a "state," a "domestic dependent nation," and possessing of rights. However, President Andrew Jackson (1767–1845), the seventh president of the United States (1829–1837) and the first born west of the Appalachians, refused to enforce this. Some Indians were shifted in the 1820s, with the major removals after the 1830 Indian Removal Act.

In 1849, the Bureau of Indian Affairs recommended that tribes be placed in areas of "limited extent and well-defined boundaries," that is, reservations. The Bureau (or Office) of Indian Affairs was created in 1851 to supervise reservations. By the 1850s, the demarcation line was shifted west of Kansas and Nebraska due to white settlers' continuing pressure for land. Tribal reservations were set up on lands occupied by nonpacified tribes, leading to conflict somewhat policed by the U.S. Army. The 1851 Indian Appropriations Act ended the federal government's recognition of tribes as independent nations, converting Indians to clients of the BIA. Subsequent reservation treaties occasionally included a grant of parcels and goods to a tribe, but the lands were small and often infertile, and if white settlers complained, the parcels' sizes were reduced. Because many tribes had to be forced onto the parcels, the Army then limited tribes' movements, resulting in massacres and wars such as the Sioux War's Battle of Little Bighorn. In 1871, Congress ended the treaty system with the Indian Appropriation Act.

In 1880, most Indians were living on 100 reservations. The purpose of the reservations was to isolate Indians but also to keep settlers from bothering Indians. The BIA enforced federal law on reservations, in violation of most treaties' recognition of self-government. This included tribal courts to enforce the law but also to penalize those who continued in banned tribal ways such as ceremonies. The 1886 *United States vs. Kagama* U.S. Supreme Court case demoted the status of tribal governments from being sovereign to that similar to a state.

During this time, Ulysses S. Grant (1822–1885), the eighteenth president of the United States (1869–1877), tried his "peace policy," with reservations trusted to five Protestant denominations for assimilation. The policy failed. The well-meaning but infamous 1887 Dawes Act, or General Allotment (Severalty) Act, replaced the policy of granting lands to tribes by giving to individual tribal members. White reformers held that reservations segregated Indians and postponed their eventual assimilation to become independent and self-reliant. The results of the act satisfied its timber industry and large cattle rancher backers: tribes lost 60 percent of their territory, and the best lands were allocated by the BIA to whites.

This downward trend was reversed somewhat after 1924's Indian Citizenship Act in recognition of the 8,000 to 10,000 Indians who fought in World War I. After the Indians' deplorable state was documented by the Brookings Institution's Rockefeller-funded Meriam Report in 1928, some improvements were made. The Indian Reorganization Act of 1934 (called the Indian New Deal) created new rights, corrected some BIA abuses, overturned privatization of tribal properties, and supported tribal sovereignty on the reservations. After this, the federal government developed better reservation infrastructure, healthcare, and education. The 1946 congressional establishment of the Indian Claims Commission continued this liberal trend, giving Indians the right to make reparation claims for lands taken from them.

In 1953, this liberal policy changed as the federal government pursued a "withdrawal program," or "termination" of its responsibility. Termination of the tribe's federal trust status meant that the federal government no longer would provide protection or services. Numerous tribes were either terminated or lost their federal recognition, many individual Indians were relocated to cities, and most federal development programs ended. By 1960, approximately 40 percent of Indians lived in cities. However, spurred by more skillful Indian activism (e.g., the American Indian Movement [AIM]), national attention to the plight of Indians reversed this neglect in the 1960s, culminating in the 1975 Indian Self-Determination and Education Assistance Act. Tribal governments gained significant rights, development programs were restored, and the BIA lost authority.

REZ LIFE

Novelist, English professor, and Ojibwa David Treuer's book *Rez Life: An Indian's Journey through Reservation Life* (2012) describes his experiences growing up on the Leech Lake Reservation in Minnesota and his assessment of what life on a reservation is like. Contrary to the general belief that reservation life is restricted to poverty, drug abuse, and despair, Treuer argues that reservations are places of joy and hope as well. In an interview on National Public Radio's *Talk of the Nation*, Treuer said, "The truth to me seems to be that reservations are places of surplus. There's more of everything. There might be more hardship, but there's joy. There might be more pain, but there's more opportunity. There's more of everything, and that's reality—that was a great surprise to me."

Treuer journeys as well through the historical experience of Indian reservations. He notes that "it's good to remember . . . that reservations are . . . remnants of our homelands that have been reserved for our use and for us to live on. So these weren't given to us. These are the miniaturized portions of land that has always been ours."

Treuer writes that reservation life is engendering in Indians a new form of activism different than the other-directed activism of the past, such as that of the American Indian Movement. Rather, Indians are developing an activism that is inner-directed toward the reservation itself. It is an attempt to resurrect culture, to stave off "cultural death," to engender again the love for tribal traditions, tribal laws and government, and tribal languages. And, yes, to engender love for what has often been an object of hatred—the reservation.

Sources: "Ojibwe Writer Celebrates the Beauty of 'Rez Life'," *NPR: Talk of the Nation*, February 20, 2012.

David Treuer. *Rez Life: An Indian's Journey through Reservation Life*. New York: Atlantic Monthly Press, 2012.

SOVEREIGN IMMUNITY

Today, federal law recognizes a special kind of Indian sovereign authority to govern themselves, subject to overriding federal authority. Sovereign immunity is a legal doctrine that the sovereign or state cannot commit a legal wrong and is immune from civil suit or criminal prosecution. The U.S. government has sovereign immunity and may not be sued unless it has waived its immunity or consented to a suit. Indian sovereignty is complicated because Indian tribes are considered by federal law to be domestic, dependent nations. This sovereign authority includes Indian tribal courts, which solely judge Indian cases.

Tribal governments thus have a form of governmental immunity roughly like states, local governments, and the federal government. Like the federal government, tribes have limited immunity to protect government funds and other activities. Tribes provide for insurance and limited waivers of their sovereign immunity, and have legal responsibility for their tribal employees. Many tribes have developed risk management systems, and work with insurance companies and their own tribal courts to create a fair, equitable system for anyone injured by the tribe.

Sovereignty is a controversial issue to Indians because the level of tribal sovereignty steadily has diminished. Public Law 280 (1953) reduced a tribe's level of tribal sovereignty in Indian country to roughly the same as counties. (*Indian country* is a legal and common term to describe self-governing Indian communities, and is legally a technical term for Indian reservations, communities, and trust lands.) County and municipal authorities have claimed authority over reservations in various states. The battle is between tribal sovereignty and congressional power to legislate regarding Indian affairs, as well as a legal conflict between tribal rights and individual rights.

RESERVATION GOVERNANCE AND LAND RIGHTS

Reservations today are subject to three forms of governance: federal, state and/or local, and tribal. Legal authority varies considerably. Numerous federal statutes deal with Indian rights and governance, such as the Indian Reorganization Act (1934) and 1968's Indian Civil Rights Act (the Indian Bill of Rights). This somewhat complicated legal standing makes it difficult for tribes to effectively manage their reservations. Additionally, some reservation boundaries overlap local and county government jurisdictional lines. Complex legal battles are commonplace. For instance, in a legal contest between the Devils Lake Sioux and North Dakota, it was found that non-Indians actually owned more reservation land than the tribe, although more Indians lived there. The court's 1990 decision found the tribe did not have legal jurisdiction over land held by non-Indians. In response, some tribes (e.g., the Yakama Indians) have divided their reservations into open and closed areas: open for non-Indian landownership and residence, and closed solely for tribal residence and use.

Today, tribes are legal entities that operate like any other corporation. They control land use (planning and zoning), can negotiate (with the oversight of the Bureau of Indian Affairs) leases for timber harvesting and mining, and pursue economic development (e.g., ranching, agriculture, tourism, and casinos). Tribes may hire their own members, other Indians, and non-Indians. Tribes may run tribal stores, gas stations, and museums. Their members can utilize resources owned by the tribe, such as a range for animal grazing and land for agricultural cultivation. They may build homes on tribal lands. Tribal members living on the reservation are common tenants, a situation similar to communal tenure, and the tribe can change tenant in-common practices.

Of the many churches on reservations, most occupy land by tribal or federal consent. BIA offices, hospitals, schools, and other facilities usually are on federal parcels within reservations. Many reservations include one or more sections (approximately 640 acres) of school lands, which were granted to states at the time of statehood. Such lands may sit idle or be grazed by tribal ranchers. The federal Indian Gaming Regulatory Act of 1988 made the state a part of any tribal contractual or statutory agreement that is made (e.g., regarding a casino).

Major legal disagreements continue concerning how Indians can and cannot use their land.

WATER RIGHTS

There recently have been numerous battles between reservations and non-Indian communities and states over water rights. The issue is critical because over 70 percent of Indians and 50 percent of reservations lie in arid or semiarid lands. Reservations rely on water sources for self-sufficiency, and rivers and streams for agriculture. Reservations also need the rights to what is in the water (e.g., to fish the water). For the other communities, lack of water is forcing limitations on expanding metropolitan areas.

Water battles also have arisen because the water needs of tribes and reservations have consistently been ignored in treaties and actions. This violation of reservation water rights has continued with the rapid development of Southwestern cities and irrigated agricultural farming. To meet the growing need, huge canal systems were constructed to import the needed water from faraway river basins, as was the Central Arizona Water Project, which tapped the Colorado River.

The legal problem over water rights is a contrast of two ways to determine rights. Under the Riparian water system right, utilized primarily in the eastern United States, the landowner bordering the source of water is entitled to the water. In

Western states, however, water ownership rights are accorded via an appropriative system that gives water rights to the first user who beneficially uses the water, as long as he or she continues putting the water to good use. The federal reserved water rights doctrine was established by the U.S. Supreme Court in 1908 in *Winters vs. United States* when it found that a reservation (the Fort Belknap) may reserve water for its future use. The resulting landmark Winters Doctrine was the first time the federal government varied from regarding water law as a state matter.

Since then, court decisions mostly have limited Indian water rights. The 1952 McCarren Amendment gave water management power back to the states. Today, federal reserved water rights include just enough water to meet the primary purpose for the reservation. Most current legal battles are over the quantification of Indian water rights.

LAW AND ORDER RIGHTS

Indian reservations' administration of justice, law, and order is a function that tribes have as sovereign nations. Today, tribes retain the authority to determine the legal structure to use to administer justice and the type of relationship they maintain with county, state, and federal governments. The structures differ significantly. Many reservations have a dual justice system: one based on the modern American justice tradition, and the other based on Indian custom and tradition. Others have a hybrid of the two. The Indian system—which guides family and community forums as well as traditional courts—is holistic, and is based on shared and balanced power and responsibility. It is nonadversarial and involves discussion to promote problem resolution and to restore ongoing relationships.

The specifics of law enforcement vary considerably among reservations. Some have their own tribal police funded or operated with tribal and federal funding. Others have federal police provided completely or partially by the BIA, the Federal Bureau of Investigation (FBI) for felony investigations, and the U.S. Marshals. Some are under state or county criminal jurisdiction. As of 1996, sixty percent of tribal law enforcement departments were operated by the tribes themselves as a result of the Indian Self-Determination Act. On the reservation, tribal officials are the first responders in most crime situations, including those over which the tribal court does not have jurisdiction. Tribal courts have jurisdiction over most situations on reservations, but federal law—under the Indian Civil Rights Act—has limited tribes' jurisdiction over non-Indians and over sentencing power in criminal cases.

Unfortunately, a U.S. Commission on Civil Rights study in 2003 found that all three parts of law enforcement—policing, justice, and corrections—were poor on reservations compared with the rest of the nation. Most tribal law enforcement departments are small, are in rural locations, and cover large geographic areas.

They usually cannot operate specialized crime units, and officers are poorly trained. As a result, the lack of adequate law enforcement hurts victim protection and safety. Indians are twice as likely as any other racial or ethnic group to be victims of crime. Indians have long held that tribal court systems have not been funded sufficiently or consistently, and per capita spending on law enforcement in Indian communities is 60 percent of the national average. Jail facilities are more overcrowded than the most crowded state or federal prisons. As a result of these problems, studies have found, many Indians have lost faith in the justice system because of perceived bias, as well as proportionately higher Indian incarceration rates due to unfair treatment (e.g., racial profiling, prosecution bias, and little legal representation).

There have been some improvements. Tribes throughout Indian country have instituted new or adapted existing peacekeeping, justice, and law and order systems to keep up with the ever-changing needs of their citizens, historical factors, society, and modern technologies. Information sharing between tribes and surrounding jurisdictions is becoming more prevalent because the need is growing. Information sharing is necessary when there are multijurisdictional crime locations, to get tribal members' crime history information, and to get information about nonmembers both for criminal and noncriminal purposes. Indian country law enforcement funding increased almost 85 percent between 1998 and 2003. However, since then there has been a downward trend in funding that, if continued, will severely compromise the already low level of public safety in Indian communities.

EDUCATION RIGHTS

The right of reservation Indians to the same educational opportunities as all Americans has been mostly neglected. However, the education aspect of the Indian Self-Determination and Education Assistance Act 1975 gave tribes control over BIA-operated schools; enhanced federal-state or territory cooperation and funding in Indian education; and created advisory boards made up of parents of Indian children for schools that get federal funds.

The first time the U.S. Department of Justice ever enforced the laws related to the right of education Indians was in 1994 when it sued a Utah school district for not having a high school in the Navajo Mountain community. The Navajo and Paiute high school students had to travel over 90 miles and live in dormitories or with relatives and attend boarding schools operated by the BIA. The school district, which had high schools in areas where non-Indians lived, argued that reservation Indians did not have the right to a public school built and operated by the district. The court disagreed, stating that reservation Indians do have the right to receive the same state and county government services as other citizens, and it required the district to build a new high school to serve the Indian community.

FISHING AND HUNTING RIGHTS

When Indian tribes were forced to move to reservations, the federal government gave them the right to hunt and fish on their reservations and on their former lands that were sold to and settled by whites. However, white hunters and fishers protested against Indians having such rights off their reservations, and were joined by some state agencies that noted the impact on conservation efforts. Despite these objections, in *United States vs. Winans* (1905), the U.S. Supreme Court upheld the off-reservation right and established the Reserved Rights Doctrine that treaties are not rights granted to the Indians, but rather "a reservation by the Indians of rights already possessed and not granted away by them."

In the early 1960s, several states ignored the Reserved Rights Doctrine. The largest amount of opposition and resentment toward Indians' fishing and hunting rights is in the Pacific Northwest. To stop Indians from fishing and hunting, state enforcement officials made numerous arrests, and confiscated boats and fishing equipment. Some Indians fought back, ignoring the new state restrictions. In Washington, Indians were supported by such celebrities as Marlon Brando, Jane Fonda, and Dick Gregory.

The struggle was strengthened greatly by the 1970 formation of the Native American Rights Fund (NARF), a nonprofit organization that uses laws and treaties to compel state governments and the national government to abide by their legal obligations. Probably NARF's most important case resulted in the 1974 Boldt decision, when a U.S. district judge ruled that the state of Washington must respect tribal treaty rights, namely the right of most of the tribes to continue their salmon fishing. The dispute arose because the state blamed declining fish catches on Indian netting and lawlessness, as the Indians did not follow state-mandated seasons, get licenses, or abide by catch limits. Aware that non-Indian commercial fishers caught salmon in millions of tons in the area, the tribes felt the real problems were commercial fishing, dam-building, and logging. This was confirmed after much research in the following decades.

Reservations in America have a mixed record. On the one hand, they are some of the most impoverished places in America. For example, Pine Ridge Reservation in South Dakota has extremely high unemployment and poverty rates. There are few jobs on the reservation, and those who work must travel long distances to their jobs. Only about 20 percent of the residents are employed, almost seven in 10 live below the federal poverty line, and family income and resources are often negligible. Healthcare is terrible, and many simply do not have it. Overcrowded housing is the norm, and many people are homeless. On the other hand, some reservations, such as Leech Lake Reservation in Minnesota, despite economic and social problems, still maintain a sense of the value of the Indian experience. Indians feel at home, feel a strong sense of community, and feel secure. Reservations like Leech Lake are places of hope, of regenerating Indian life, culture, and traditions.

REFERENCES

American Indian Relief Council. "Reservations: South Dakota: Pine Ridge Reservation." Retrieved from http://www.nrcprograms.org/site/PageServer?pagename=airc_res_sd_pineridge

College of Law, University of Oklahoma. "American Indian Legal Resources," 2011. Retrieved from http://www.law.ou.edu/native/ailegal.shtml

Frantz, Klaus. *Indian Reservations in the United States*. Chicago: University of Chicago Press, 1999.

Page, Jake. *In the Hands of the Great Spirit: The 20,000-Year History of American Indians*. New York: Free Press, 2003.

Schultz, Jeffrey D. *Encyclopedia of Minorities in American Politics*. Westport, CT: Greenwood Publishing Group, 2000.

Treuer, David. *Rez Life: An Indian's Journey through Reservation Life*. New York: Atlantic Monthly Press, 2012.

Indian Civil Rights

John H. Barnhill

Although American Indians were granted citizenship in 1924, the civil rights of Indians have not always been granted and guaranteed. The establishment of civil rights for American Indians has been piecemeal and remains far from complete. Indians are disadvantaged in the same ways as other minorities, but often to a greater extent. Social and economic discrimination produce unusually high unemployment, infant mortality, and poverty as well as low rates of high school completion.

Civil rights in the United States are guaranteed by the Bill of Rights as well as the Fourteenth Amendment to the Constitution and subsequent federal law. Civil rights include due process, freedom from discrimination, equal protection, and freedom of religion, speech, press, and assembly. American citizens also have guarantees against unreasonable search and seizure, a right to a speedy trial with advice of the charges and confrontation of witnesses, the right to an attorney, protections against self-incrimination, and no excessive bail or cruel and unusual punishment, or double jeopardy. No law will be enforced against an action taken legally prior to its enactment, that is, there will be no ex post facto law.

HISTORICAL BACKGROUND

Before the civil rights era of the 1950s and 1960s, it was not uncommon in some states to find Indians segregated in the same way as African Americans, with separate water fountains and separate seats in theaters. From the 1950s through the 1970s, a civil rights movement sought to make constitutional guarantees real, first for black Americans and subsequently for other minorities, including Native Americans. Since the civil rights laws of the mid-1960s, Native Americans have

INDIAN CIVIL RIGHTS ACT OF 1968
(THE INDIAN BILL OF RIGHTS)

The Indian Civil Rights Act, or the Indian Bill of Rights, passed by Congress in 1968, extended in general the Bill of Rights, the first 10 amendments of the Constitution, to American Indians. This allowed individual Indians more freedoms and rights when dealing with tribes. Parts of the text of the Indian Bill of Rights are reproduced here.

No Indian tribe in exercising powers of self-government shall—

1. make or enforce any law prohibiting the free exercise of religion, or abridging the freedom of speech, or of the press, or the right of the people peaceably to assemble and to petition for a redress of grievances;
2. violate the right of the people to be secure in their persons, houses, papers, and effects against unreasonable search and seizures, nor issue warrants, but upon probable cause . . . ;
3. subject any person for the same offense to be twice put in jeopardy;
4. compel any person in any criminal case to be a witness against himself;
5. take any private property for a public use without just compensation;
6. deny to any person in a criminal proceeding the right to a speedy and public trial, to be informed of the nature and cause of the accusation, to be confronted with the witnesses against him, to have compulsory process for obtaining witnesses in his favor, and at his own expense to have the assistance of counsel for his defense;
7. require excessive bail, impose excessive fines, inflict cruel and unusual punishments, and in no event impose for conviction of any one offense any penalty or punishment greater than imprisonment for a term of one year and [1] a fine of $5,000, or both;
8. deny to any person within its jurisdiction the equal protection of its laws or deprive any person of liberty or property without due process of law;
9. pass any bill of attainder or ex post facto law; or
10. deny to any person accused of an offense punishable by imprisonment the right, upon request, to a trial by jury of not less than six persons.

Source: Indian Civil Rights Act of 1968 (the Indian Bill of Rights). Retrieved from http://www.tribal-institute.org/lists/icra1968.htm

been covered by the laws that prohibit discrimination due to race, color, or national origin. The Indian Civil Rights Act of 1968 (the Indian Bill of Rights) guarantees civil rights by, in effect, applying the Bill of Rights to Native Americans.

CITIZENSHIP

Citizenship came piecemeal in the nineteenth century to some Indians for abandoning the reservation or service in the military, and to all in 1924. With citizenship came the right to vote, except in states that argued that Indians were not residents. Colorado in 1936 blocked Indians from voting because they were not citizens. Reservations by this logic were not part of the state, and an Indian who wanted to vote had to move from the reservation to the state. Nonpayment of state taxes was another excuse to deny the vote, as was incompetence (ward of the state) or illiteracy in English. The Voting Rights Act of 1965 ended these practices, as did the Nationality Act of 1940. Since 1965, there have been 74 cases under the Voting Rights Act or Fourteenth and Fifteenth Amendments against states and municipalities that try to disfranchise Indians. The cases are predominantly from states with large Indian populations.

Civil rights are customarily regarded as individual rights. In the case of Native Americans, however, they can be collective (i.e., tribal) rights. As domestic dependent nations, tribes retain their sovereignty. By right, they govern themselves, define who is a member, manage their property and business, and determine domestic relations. Their relationship with the federal government is government to government. The government has trust obligations to protect tribal lands, resources, and rights to self-government. The government also has an obligation to provide services that will encourage survival and advancement of the tribe.

Native Americans became citizens in 1924, but they had civil rights before then independent of their status as American citizens. There are over 550 tribes with recognized governments, and about 300 reservations with governing bodies that function similar to state governments. Reservation tribes have their own police forces, courts, and departments of justice. Relations with the federal government are in accord with treaties, recognized in law as the same as treaties with foreign states. Some reservations are larger than some states, for example, the Navajo reservation is over twice the size of Massachusetts, 14 million to 5.28 million acres, and larger than nine states. At the same time, the 1.89 million acres of the Wind River, Wyoming, reservation is more land than Rhode Island, a state of only 777,000 acres. Indians are members of tribal nations, and they have a special relationship, a dual citizenship. They have rights as members of sovereign entities and as American citizens.

COMPETING JURISDICTIONS

Sovereignty and treaty rights have always been a major part of the struggle to establish civil rights. Sovereignty disputes with the various states pertain to gaming, hunting, and fishing. The case *Menominee Tribe vs. United States* (1968) stated that establishment of a reservation included the rights to hunt and fish on said reservation without regulation by the state. Indians as citizens, however, must observe all U.S. laws. *United States vs. Winans* authorized Indians to hunt and fish on all their old grounds, even those that they no longer own, public or private. Hunting and fishing are particularly sensitive issues in the Northwest and Alaska.

Sovereignty was sacrificed to civil rights when on April 30, 2009, in Washington State nine Snoqualmie members won habeas corpus in their attempt to overturn their banishment by the tribal government. The court ruled the tribe had violated the due process provision of the Indian Civil Rights Act of 1968 (ICRA). In a related matter, the petitioners' previous open-ended social banishment was reduced to 90 days, after which they could return to tribal land for tribal events. This was the first federal case dealing with tribal banishment in the context of the ICRA. Banishment is becoming increasingly popular as a tribal tool for discipline and control, and the new willingness of the federal courts to intervene should cause tribes to be more cautious.

Native Americans seek civil rights redress in many areas, including elimination of mascots that reflect unfavorable stereotypes and promote racism, as well as establishment of their own civil rights organizations to fight police misconduct and discrimination in the justice system. And, because many Native Americans have no telephone access, there is an increasing digital divide that makes it harder for them to get jobs, education, and the other benefits of information technology (IT). Equal employment and education are keys to solving many Native American problems.

Many Native Americans in South Dakota have major doubts about the equitability of that state's criminal justice system as well as the federal system, regarding both as racist. They believe that justice depends on race, with differential enforcement of laws and different judicial outcomes. To substantiate their charge, they cite the large disparities in the numbers of unsolved murders and those reported to the Federal Bureau of Investigation (FBI). They also believe that violence involving Native Americans is treated differently than that involving whites, with crimes of whites against Indians prosecuted with less diligence than those perpetrated by Indians against whites. In August 2003, state troopers and Narragansett members had a confrontation that provoked civil rights groups to ask Governor Dan Carcieri to explain why the troopers did not withdraw when they encountered resistance as the governor had instructed them. The groups alleged that it was clear from reports of the incident that the police were prepared for a confrontation and continued their pressure once the conflict started.

Indians also suffer from underrepresentation at all levels of state and federal government, including justice institutions. This problem applies in many localities as well. Without equal representation, they suffer neglect and lack of equal access to training, technical aid, and funding for tribal law and court systems. Native Americans lack equal access to attorneys, and when they do have representation, it is often through the public defender programs, noted for inexperienced and indifferent attorneys as well as serious underfunding. Native Americans need stronger hate crime laws and tribal civil rights agencies to assist them in pursuing redress for civil rights violations.

CULTURAL AND RELIGIOUS RIGHTS

Another area in which civil rights are jeopardized is cultural matters. This includes the right to pass on language, social customs, and religion. As late as 1935, Native Americans faced fines and imprisonment for practicing their traditional religion. Religious freedom has been under attack by government in areas of access to religious sites, restrictions on traditional and ceremonial worship, and banning of sacred objects. In the past, whites denied Indians the right to use herbs in religious ceremonies and rituals such as the Sun Dance. Indian children were Christianized in white boarding schools. During the twentieth century, in *Lyng vs. Northwest Indian Cemetery Protection Association* (1988), the U.S. Forest Service was allowed to build a road through a site that several tribes regarded as sacred. The U.S. Supreme Court ruled that the road did not violate Indians' First Amendment rights. *In Employment Division of Oregon vs. Smith* (1991), the Supreme Court removed the previous state and city requirement to show a "compelling governmental interest" before restricting religious exercise.

The American Indian Religious Freedom Act of 1978 allowed religious freedom but limited ceremonial items such as endangered American eagles and peyote. Peyote use was discouraged as early as 1949 as addictive. It became a forbidden psychedelic under the Drug Abuse Control Act of 1965 but was allowed for religion. State law varied, with some outlawing it. Of the 17 states that outlawed it in 1970, only five allowed a religious exemption. Two Oregon men were refused unemployment benefits because they took peyote as part of a Native American Church (NAC) rite. Religious bodies throughout the United States protested this weakening of religious freedom. And in 1993, after President Bill Clinton signed the Religious Freedom Restoration Act (RFRA) that would have overturned *Oregon vs. Smith* by restoring the compelling interest standard, the Supreme Court in *City of Boerne vs. Flores* ruled RFRA unconstitutional. Clinton was successful in 1994 in enacting a law that exempted from state and federal controlled substance laws the use of peyote for religious purposes.

In another example of religious rights, in May 1999, California's attorney general sued to allow the repatriation of Ishi's remains from a dedicated cemetery. Several tribes believed Ishi to be the last of the Yahi Indians. His remains were at the Smithsonian and in a California cemetery. In April 2000, the court ordered that the remains be given to the Native Americans for interment in accord with California Indian tradition.

EDUCATION

One area of discrimination is education, as Indian schools are underfunded. The U.S. Civil Rights Commission noted that less than two thirds of Indians between the ages of 18 and 24 are high school graduates, and under a tenth of those over 25 have college degrees. Native American children score lowest in reading, math, and history, and are 3 percent of national high school dropouts despite being 1 percent of students. The National Indian Education Association came into being in 1969 to fight discrimination in education. American Indians also fought for native rights to own their own media and the right of their journalists to be free from persecution. This goal was attained only through appeal to the United Nations.

When Navajo and Paiute high school age students at Navajo Mountain, Utah, had no school closer than 90 miles from home and had to live with relatives or in dormitories operated by the Bureau of Indian Affairs (BIA), the Department of Justice sued the nearby school district. The district contended that because the Indians were on a reservation, they had no right to access to a nonreservation school. The court ruled that Indians have the same right to state and county government services as all other citizens. Thus, the district had to build a school in the community. The 1997 case was the first time the civil rights division had ever enforced education law for Native Americans. The suit was originally brought by the students and their parents, and the Navajo tribe and United States joined the suit.

Discrimination in schools is not restricted to institutional practices. In some cases, the system allows individuals to violate Native Americans' civil rights. Some individual violations are tacitly accepted by the school systems.

South Dakota's American Civil Liberties Union (ACLU) has for years received many complaints about school mistreatment of Native American students. The Education Department's civil rights office began investigating Winner, South Dakota, schools in 1997. In 2000, the office ordered the district to change its practices and take measures to end racial harassment. The department closed the case, citing district compliance, in 2004. According to the ACLU, the district manipulated its records to show no racial disparities when in fact school records showed that the 14 percent of Native Americans were involved in 85 percent of in school suspensions and 59 percent of out-of-school suspensions in 2002 and 2003. Taunting, name-calling, bullying, and other civil rights violations by white students continued, with school officials doing nothing other than punishing Native Americans who retaliated. Native Americans who were denied their right to an education dropped out, transferred, or ended up in juvenile facilities.

In June 2005, the federal Education Department received a complaint from 14 Native American families, the ACLU, and the Rosebud Sioux attorney general. The complaint alleged that Winner, South Dakota, schools discriminated against

Native American children in the way it enforced discipline and that it prevented the students from receiving equal education. The ACLU alleged that Winner's disciplinary practices forced Indian students out of school and into the juvenile justice system.

The ACLU attributed the harsh discipline to a general trend toward get tough policies against student misconduct; the new policies emphasized suspension and the use of police to deal with minor school problems. Statistics showed that this trend, the school to prison pipeline, was more likely to affect minorities than whites. The ACLU noted that the Winner situation was replicated around the nation, with discrimination and educational disadvantage common.

STEREOTYPICAL SYMBOLS

The civil rights movement of the 1960s was a catalyst for the elimination of many of the derogatory and offensive symbols and images targeting blacks. At the same time, the use of derogatory stereotypes of Native Americans continued among secondary schools, colleges, and professional sports teams. This persisted despite Native American leaders and groups' efforts since the 1970s to indicate that many mascots and team names trivialize and mock the Native American culture and religion. The U.S. Commission on Civil Rights in 2001 noted that schools utilizing Native American imagery in their sports programs were particularly inappropriate because one of the purposes of education is to teach students respect and understanding of other cultures. Stereotyping promotes a hostile and intimidating environment, adding to the already dismal Native American graduation and college attendance and graduation rates. Official stereotypes send a message to impressionable youth that such stereotyping is acceptable. Schools should not provide this erroneous message to a captive audience (even in college, cost, proximity to potentially insensitive classmates, and availability of financial aid restrict the ability of an offended student to remove himself or herself from an unpleasant environment).

Schools contend that they are honoring Native American culture and stimulating interest in it. They ignore strong opposition statements by Native American and Indian-sympathizing leaders, groups, and religious and civil rights organizations. Even positive images distort the past, and distorted and romanticized images block non-Indians from learning the real history and culture of their Native American co-citizens. Contemporary Indians also suffer from bias and prejudice from people more interested and admiring of the mythical Indian.

On April 13, 2001, the U.S. Commission on Civil Rights requested that nonnative schools discontinue their use of Native American names and images for sports teams. Although the First Amendment allows such expression, it is insensitive at best and not to be encouraged. According to some civil rights and Native

American groups, the mascots may be discriminatory and thus in violation of the law. It is certain that they are disrespectful and offensive given the long history of forced assimilation. The commission encouraged voluntary elimination of the mascots and team names but had no means of forcing its recommendations.

In 2009, after 17 years of litigation, the Washington Redskins won against Native American plaintiffs who argued that the team's mascot and logo were racially offensive. Dodging the issue of racism, the court ruled that the plaintiffs had waited too long to start the lawsuit. The Redskin trademark dates to 1967. An earlier court had ruled that the suit was too late, but an appeals court remanded the case after noting that the youngest plaintiff, at one year of age in 1967, could not have sued at the time. The next decision was that the youngest plaintiff turned 18 in 1984 and should have sued then, not eight years later. The Redskins cited millions of dollars of economic loss should the organization lose the brand. Still, a new group of Native Americans, between the ages of 18 and 24, were preparing to sue, hoping to get a ruling on the merits, not a technicality.

MUCH REMAINS TO BE DONE

Indian travel was once restricted by the federal government since Indians were considered wards of the state (before they became citizens in 1924). Agents issued passes, and when Indians overstayed their leave, the Army routinely pursued them and returned them to the reservation. With the arrival of the railroads in the 1890s, Indians were denied seats but instead got rights to ride the undercarriage, the roof, or in a vacant car in return for tribal granting of right of way to the railroads. Indian agents disliked their loss of control. The right of free movement came with citizenship.

Another civil right is the unrestricted use of one's land. In 2007, the New York Seneca nation claimed a stretch of Interstate 90 by revoking a 1954 agreement that allowed right of way for the highway. The move was in retaliation for New York's attempt to collect taxes on Seneca land. The state claimed immunity, and the Seneca lost.

Indicative of the reality that much remains undone is the situation at Farmington, New Mexico. In April 1974, two Navajo men were found dead, partially burned and bludgeoned. A week after the first two, a third was found. Three high school students at Farmington High School were charged with murder, and later the crime came to be seen as another instance of "Indian rolling," abuse by mostly teenagers of inebriated Navajo street people. The crimes led to protests of racism and bigotry that caused the white community to rethink its historical indifference to the Native American community. Whites were confused, afraid, and unprepared to deal with Indian outrage. The state sent an investigative committee to the town, and the committee reported that many elected officials and community leaders had failed to promote positive relationships among the various populations. Health, jobs, police behavior, and social services all needed improvement. The community lacked an apparatus for dealing with civil rights claims. The police hired too few Indians, had an ineffective community relations program, and had no sensitivity training. The higher crime rate for Navajos than for whites was primarily due to arrests for alcoholism. Once in court, Navajos were disadvantaged by proceedings not in their native language. Hospitals were reportedly reluctant to serve Navajos, and the contract medical program was inadequate. Indian jobs were mostly low wage and low skill, and public sector employment was too low. In the economy, the Navajo-white relationship was one of subordinate to superior rather than of equals.

Thirty years later, despite progress in provision of services, hiring of Native American police officers (only 8 percent while Navajos constitute 17 percent of the population), and creation of a civil rights entity, Native Americans were still targets of police profiling that led to conviction and incarceration in disproportion to their percentage of the population. Alcohol abuse remained a major problem, harassment still occurred, and Native Americans were underrepresented in government.

Over three decades, Indian law has developed as a specialty resting on statutes and case law. Among the organizations fighting for civil rights is the Native American Rights Fund (NARF), which provides legal assistance and representation to organizations, tribes, and individuals. NARF is a nonprofit organization that offers technical and legal assistance to tribes, organizations, and individuals who otherwise lack access to the justice system. Over 29 years, it has established a positive reputation with those who are responsible for preparing laws. It works with other organizations—religious, civil rights, Native American—to safeguard civil and religious rights. It uses current law and treaties to keep federal and state governments in compliance with their obligations. Its board of directors has 13 Native American members from through the United States. Its staff of 15 attorneys includes many Native Americans. It works with religious, Native American, and civil rights organizations to advocate for additional laws related to civil and religious rights. Cases involve sovereignty; tribal recognition; preservation of traditional rights to hunt, fish, and otherwise use water; religious rights; and return of remains and artifacts for reburial. Most important, the NARF works to protect Native American voting rights.

NARF selects cases that have the breadth and potential to set precedent. Commonly, NARF handles 50 cases at a time. These cases can take several years to reach conclusion. The 1970s and early 1980s were years when the courts were generally receptive. After that, however, the courts shifted to a more conservative stance and Indian rights cases became more difficult to win. Also, the costs of litigation in time and money are extensive, so the focus is on negotiating to reach consensus and settle without going to court. With NARF aid, tribes in all states are better equipped to develop their governments, economies, and natural resources and social services.

REFERENCES

ACLU.org. "South Dakota Schools Discriminating against Native American Students, Charge ACLU and Tribe," June 23, 2005. Retrieved from http://www.aclu.org/racialjustice/edu/15917prs20050623.html

California Attorney General. "Repatriation of Native American Remains." Retrieved from http://ag.ca.gov/civilrights/sections/remains.php

"Civil Rights Groups Seek Explanation Concerning Confrontation between Native Americans and State Police in RI." *Boston Globe*, August 6, 2003. Retrieved from http://pluralism.org/news/article.php?id=4722 in November 2009.

Guedel, Greg. "Redskins 1, Dignity 0? Native Americans Lose Offensive Mascot Lawsuit." *Native American Legal Update*. May 15, 2009. Retrieved from http://www.nativelegalupdate.com/2009/05/articles/redskins-1-dignity-0-native-americans-lose-offensive-mascot-lawsuit

Guedel, Greg. "Snoqualmie Members Overturn Banishment in Federal Court." *Native American Legal Update*, May 1, 2009. Retrieved from http://www.nativelegalupdate.com/

Johnson, Troy. "Farmington Report on Civil Rights: 30 Years After." Retrieved from www.usccr.gov/pubs/122705_FarmingtonReport.pdf

Johnson, Troy. *Red Power: The Native American Civil Rights Movement*. New York: Chelsea House, 2007.

Leadership Conference on Civil Rights Education Fund 2001. *Native Americans*. Retrieved from www.civilrights.org/resources/civilrights101/native.html in October 2009.

Native American Rights Fund. *About NARF*. Retrieved from http://www.narf.org/about/about_whatwedo.html in November 2009.

Ross, Luana. *Inventing the Savage*. Austin: University of Texas Press, 1998.

U.S. Commission on Civil Rights. "Commission Statement on the Use of Native American Images and Nicknames as Sports Symbols," April 13, 2001. Retrieved from http://aimsupport.org/civil-rights.htm

U.S. Department of Justice. "Civil Rights and Native Americans: Policy Almanac." Retrieved from http://www.policyalmanac.org/culture/archive/native_americans.shtml in October 2009.

INDIAN SOVEREIGNTY

Patti Jo King and John H. Barnhill

Sovereignty is the internationally recognized power of a nation to govern itself. Among American Indian communities, it is the conceptual foundation upon which native self-determination rests. American Indians are not simply members of a collective ethnic minority group; each Indian is also a member of a specific political group or tribe. Tribal members hold dual citizenship as members of tribes and as citizens of the United States. The issue of sovereignty has been and continues to be complex and controversial in federal, state, and tribal relations.

All peoples under international law have rights of self-determination. They are sovereign, which refers to the right of a group or nation to exercise sole control, to be the final authority. Sovereignty includes complete independence from foreign control as well as the power over laws, accounting to no other power. Other sovereign powers include the collection of taxes as well as the making war and treaties. Individuals subject to a sovereign power have no higher recourse because by definition, sovereign means supreme. American Indians argue that tribes are sovereign nations. Like much else in tribal life, sovereignty is inseparable from culture, law, and the entire life of the people. However artificial, it becomes apparent that sovereignty is a vital, perhaps dominant, element of tribal being, something that dates from the first European exposures, something essential to preserving a traditional community under unrelenting pressure from the assertive society that surrounds it.

HISTORICAL BACKGROUND

Although today the United States recognizes Indian tribes as having a special relationship with the federal government, their legal status as sovereign nations

U.S. DEPARTMENT OF JUSTICE STATEMENT ON TRIBAL SOVEREIGNTY

The U.S. Department of Justice during the Clinton administration published a statement of policy regarding tribal sovereignty, portions of which are reproduced here.

THE EXECUTIVE MEMORANDUM ON GOVERNMENT-TO-GOVERNMENT RELATIONS BETWEEN THE UNITED STATES AND INDIAN TRIBES
On April 29, 1994, at a historic meeting with the heads of tribal governments, President Clinton reaffirmed the United States' "unique legal relationship with Native American tribal governments" and issued a directive to all executive departments and agencies of the Federal Government that:

As executive departments and agencies undertake activities affecting Native American tribal rights or trust resources, such activities should be implemented in a knowledgeable, sensitive manner respectful of tribal sovereignty.

President Clinton's directive requires that in all activities relating to or affecting the government or treaty rights of Indian tribes, the executive branch shall:

1) operate within a government-to-government relationship with federally recognized Indian tribes;
2) consult, to the greatest extent practicable and permitted by law, with Indian tribal governments before taking actions that affect federally recognized Indian tribes;
3) assess the impact of agency activities on tribal trust resources and assure that tribal interests are considered before the activities are undertaken;
4) remove procedural impediments to working directly with tribal governments on activities that affect trust property or governmental rights of the tribes; and
5) work cooperatively with other agencies to accomplish these goals established by the President.

The Department of Justice is reviewing programs and procedures to ensure that we adhere to principles of respect for Indian tribal governments and honor our Nation's trust responsibility to Indian tribes. Within the Department, the Office of Tribal Justice has been formed to coordinate policy towards Indian tribes both within the Department and with other agencies of the Federal Government, and to assist Indian tribes as domestic dependent nations within the federal system.

Source: U.S. Department of Justice Statement on Tribal Sovereignty. Retrieved from http://www.justice.gov/ag/readingroom/sovereignty.htm

has not always been clear. The tribes that exist today evolved from early, self-governing native kinship bands and extended families. When first contact occurred in North America, Europeans considered the indigenous tribes they encountered to be nations.

European contact defined sovereignty. In 1493, the papal bull Inter Caetera granted to Spain all the lands and peoples discovered by Columbus. Even earlier, Romanus Pontifex in 1455 established Christian rule over pagans, including enslavement and the taking of pagan property without consent. The legal basis for U.S. sovereignty over American Indians is Christian discovery. When John Marshall wanted justification for state power over indigenous people, he cited these precedents, as in *Johnson vs. M'Intosh* (1823), which noted that the Europeans, desirous of taking for themselves the vast lands of the New World, rationalized their expropriation by claiming that they were giving the Indians civilization and Christianity in return. Europeans denied Indians rights because they were pagan. Although Marshall knew that the doctrine of Christian discovery was in conflict with natural rights doctrine, he still maintained that it was the law. Marshall also knew that the law did not enforce itself. Force, conflict, and war backed it.

During the first few centuries of Euro-Indian relations, representatives from countries such as England and France acknowledged Indian sovereignty by entering into treaty agreements. Early treaties served as formal recognition of the special nation-to-nation relationships shared by European countries and native tribes. Since that time, both the U.S. Constitution and the U.S. Supreme Court have attributed certain powers and rights of sovereign nations to Indian tribes. In Article 1, Section 8 of the Constitution states that "Congress shall regulate commerce with and enter into treaties with foreign nations and Indian tribes." The fact that tribes existed as self-governing entities long before Europeans set foot on this continent bolsters their claim of sovereign status. Yet because Europeans claimed dominion over all of North America, uncertainty has consistently clouded the legal definition of tribes as fully sovereign nations.

EROSION OF SOVEREIGNTY

Indian sovereign rights have been eroding since the 1820s, when three pivotal Supreme Court decisions attempted to redefine the sovereign status of Indian tribes. These decisions, referred to as the Marshall Trilogy or the Cherokee Trilogy cases, remain the foundation of all Indian law and policy to this day.

In 1823, the case *Johnson vs. M'Intosh* questioned the validity of land sales by tribal members to private persons. In this case, the Court held that Indian tribes had no power to grant or sell lands to anyone other than the federal government. Then, in 1831, in the case *Cherokee Nation vs. Georgia*, the Cherokee nation requested an injunction against the Georgia to stop its efforts to remove the tribe from their southern homeland. The Court's decision described Indians as neither U.S. citizens, nor independent nations. Instead, Chief Justice Marshall argued that tribes were "domestic dependent nations" whose relationship to the United States "resembles that of a ward to his guardian." This decision upheld the responsibility of the federal government to protect tribes from non-Indian interference. Finally, in *Worcester vs. Georgia* (1832), a missionary living and working in Cherokee territory brought suit against the Georgia for arresting and trying to remove him from the tribe's land. He claimed the state had no authority to act within the boundaries of the Cherokee nation. The Court ruled in Worcester's favor and held that state laws did not extend to Indian country. Although the decisions in these important cases were not enforced and the Cherokees were ultimately compelled to leave their homelands, the Worcester case established three important legal points: (1) tribes do not lose their sovereign status by subjecting themselves to the powers of the United States, (2) only Congress has full and complete plenary power over Indian affairs, and (3) states do not have legal jurisdiction in Indian country. The immense significance of these three cases and the inclination of states to challenge them motivated renowned tribal law professor Frank Pommersheim to refer to Marshall's decisions as "the crucible of sovereignty" (Pommersheim 1995, 61, 191–193).

Over the years, Congress has enacted dozens of laws and policies that have continuously chipped away at the sovereign power of tribes, leading to further debate and redefinitions of the nation-to-nation relationship. As a result, there are many examples of federal statutes that limit tribal sovereignty, such as the assimilation campaign during the allotment era. Two distinct phases of the program existed, both characterized by changing assumptions. Initially, white reformers saw assimilation as a means of uplifting Indians while at the same time assuaging guilt over the unfair treatment of individual Indians and tribes. Conservatives later replaced these ideas, however, with negative assumptions about the inability of Indians to improve, as federal policymakers abandoned the idea of individual equality for native people. Thus, by 1920, the promise of the uplifting objective of assimilation was merely an empty slogan. The constant debate over the concept of sovereignty mired Indians in a state of powerlessness.

President Franklin Roosevelt's New Deal policies brought the concept of tribal sovereignty into sharper focus during his administration. One of the most important reform measures of that era is the Indian Reorganization Act of 1934 (IRA). This law reversed earlier federal policies that stripped tribes of their right of self-governance and control of their own resources and assets. By relying on tribal sovereignty as a foundational principle, the IRA established a new standardized political framework for self-governance that still exists today in the form of elected tribal councils. Tribal councils had powers sufficient to maintain order on the reservation but nothing beyond the confines. IRA sovereignty did not extend to the point of allowing tribal lawsuits in federal court against states (a provision to that effect was cut out of the reform legislation). The councils established under the IRA remain a source of claims to bona fide sovereignty. When co-opted or bribed, these councils are also often avenues through which dissenters and governments work around the wishes of the majority.

INDIAN REORGANIZATION ACT

The Indian Reorganization Act of 1934, or the Indian New Deal, was landmark legislation during Franklin Delano Roosevelt's New Deal. The Indian New Deal reversed the Dawes Act, in which the federal government divided up Indian lands, and returned these lands to Indian ownership. The Indian New Deal offered tribes the chance to form new constitutions to govern their own sovereign affairs. The opening sections of the Indian Reorganization Act are reproduced here.

The Indian Reorganization Act
(W'heeler-Howard Act)
June 18, 1934
—An Act to conserve and develop Indian lands and resources; to extend to Indians the right to form business and other organizations; to establish a credit system for Indians; to grant certain rights of home rule to Indians; to provide for vocational education for Indians; and for other purposes.BE IT ENACTED by the Senate and House of Representatives of the United States of America in Congress assembled, That hereafter no land of any Indian reservation, created or set apart by treaty or agreement with the Indians, Act of Congress, Executive order, purchase, or otherwise, shall be allotted in severalty to any Indian.

Section 2. The existing periods of trust placed upon any Indian lands and any restriction on alienation thereof are hereby extended and continued until otherwise directed by Congress.

Section 3. The Secretary of the Interior, if he shall find it to be in the public interest, is hereby authorized to restore to tribal ownership the remaining surplus lands of any Indian reservation heretofore opened, or authorized to be opened, to sale, or any other form of disposal by Presidential proclamation, or by any of the public land laws of the United States; Provided, however, That valid rights or claims of any persons to any lands so withdrawn existing on the date of the withdrawal shall not be affected by this Act: Provided further, That this section shall not apply to lands within any reclamation project heretofore authorized in any Indian reservation: Provided further, That this section shall not apply to lands within any reclamation project heretofore authorized in any Indian reservation.

Source: Indian Reorganization Act. Retrieved from http://www.cskt.org/gov/file/reorganizationact.pdf

Other limitations to tribal sovereignty included the 1973 court case *United States vs. Blackfeet Tribe*, in which the district court for Montana ruled in a case where the Blackfeet business council authorized gambling on the reservation and slot machine licensure. The Federal Bureau of Investigation (FBI) seized four slots, and the Blackfeet court issued a restraining order against removal of the machines from the reservation. The FBI removed the machines anyway, and the tribal court ordered the U.S. attorney, who had advised the agent who removed the machines, to show cause why he was not in contempt. The attorney sought a federal injunction blocking the citations. The tribal court argued that it was an arm of a sovereign entity, and the contempt citations were within its powers. The federal court ruled that the tribes had at one time been sovereign, were sometimes referred to as sovereign, but in fact their sovereignty depended on federal definitions. Their status as independent nations with treaty-making power ended in 1871 with enactment of a law banning treaty making. Subsequent decisions upheld the law. Because Congress prohibits interference with a federal officer in performance of his or her duties, and because a tribe has no power to issue contradictory ordinances, the U.S. attorney and FBI agent were not subject to the ruling of the tribal court. The basis lies in the U.S. claim to plenary power, to tend to wards of the state—and it applies to taxes, land ownership, and virtually everything else. The status of inferior sovereignty destroys claims to true sovereignty.

In every generation, federal Indian policy shifts, alternating between liberal paternal centralization and conservative laissez-faire delegation of power to the states. The former is exemplified by Democrats, who encourage self-determination while providing limited-strings-attached federal support. Republicans are antitribal and antisovereignty, delegating Indian policy to the states while the federal government washes its hands. For example, during Reagan's administration, Congress passed the Indian Gaming Regulatory Act of 1988, in which the federal government allowed the states to take greater responsibility and to have greater oversight and control. Forcing Indians to deal with the states was a blow to Indian sovereignty and an insult to their status. But the change did not occur overnight. Sovereignty was under attack on the Oglala reservation at Wounded Knee before 1973, and the American Indian Movement (AIM) takeover was in part a fight for redress of grievances and treaty violations. It was not a complaint about federal or state neglect of a constituent group but rather a grievance against a sovereign nation, the United States, that had failed to abide by its treaty obligations to another, the Oglala Sioux. Thus, AIM attempted to take the Wounded Knee case to the United Nations, asking if gaming and border enforcement were rights of legal and sovereign states, the American Indians, and whether Indians were immune to state and federal laws. In 1978, the Bureau of Indian Affairs (BIA) established a regulatory process that currently entails petitioning and demonstrating conformance to seven criteria, including historical and continuous identity as American

Indians in a distinct community. Since 1960, only 8 percent of federally recognized tribes have earned recognition through the administrative process. If a tribe is not recognized, its members and the tribe itself are not entitled to sovereign immunity.

SOVEREIGNTY AND LAW

The tenets of sovereignty in federal Indian law are based on the native "right of occupancy," a legal theory that replaced the colonial-era theological belief in divine right with the supreme power of the U.S. government. In the earliest treaties, the United States regarded Indian nations as having a "conditional" sovereignty contingent upon this right. Although they were denied absolute sovereignty as independent nations in these agreements, the United States regarded tribes as possessing "tribal sovereignty," or the power of authority over their own affairs.

The courts have also sometimes referred to sovereignty as a "backdrop," a legal concept to be used solely for analyzing treaties and statutes rather than viewing at it as a special status for judging all Indian political and economic power. The Institute for Development of Indian Law, a public interest law firm and research training center on federal Indian law, however, defines sovereignty as the supreme power from which all specific political powers derive.

Scholar Vine Deloria, Jr. argued in the late 1970s that the courts fluctuated between completely subjugating native sovereignty and hailing it as a third type of sovereignty—a special privilege granted to tribes by the federal government that existed behind national and state sovereignty.

Tribal sovereignty, however, does not emanate from the U.S. government or from congressional acts, executive orders, treaties, or any other source outside of the tribe.

Native Americans argue that sovereignty is not a gift but an inherent right of a free and autonomous people. In the early 1990s, the Supreme Court acquiesced, ruling that Indian tribes share the same status as foreign sovereign nations. Sovereign immunity means that U.S. citizens cannot sue American Indians without specific congressional authorization or unless the tribe waives immunity. Sovereign immunity has been under attack for decades. But as late as 1991, in *Oklahoma Tax Commission vs. Citizen Band Potawatomi Indian Tribe*, Supreme Court Justices Rehnquist and Stevens ruled that domestic dependent nations retain inherent sovereignty over their territory and members, and can be sued only if the tribe waives immunity or Congress overrules in a specific instance.

In recent years, the U.S. Supreme Court has ruled on issues of tribal sovereignty and state control. In *Wagnon vs. Prairie Band*, for example, the Court ruled that the Kansas state fuel tax can be collected from nonmember distributors off the reservation. The controversy began in 1995 when Kansas changed its motor fuel tax law and collected taxes for fuel distributed to Indian lands. The Prairie Band

Potawatomi Nation sued, arguing that even though the tax was levied on the nonmember distributor, the cost eventually fell on the Indian retailer selling gas on the reservation through a tribally owned station. Customers were mostly nonmember patrons of the tribal casino. The law, said the tribe, pre-empted federal law and infringed on tribal rights of self government (sovereignty). The district court found for the state, but the Tenth Circuit Court of Appeals reversed the lower court's decision, finding that state taxation was a violation of law. On appeal, the Supreme Court reversed the verdict.

The Supreme Court at the time made no firm demarcation between state jurisdiction and state sovereignty. It did grant that tribes were sovereign based on their treaties and the commerce clause, and that they were independent of the states while subject to federal law. This is the quasisovereign status Marshall enunciated in *Worcester vs. Georgia*. The Court enunciated in *Williams vs. Lee* that a state could act if there was no federal law or policy and if the state act did not infringe on tribal sovereignty. A decade after *Williams vs. Lee*, federal policy turned toward promoting self-sufficiency and economic development, which led to increased interaction between tribes, states, and nonmembers as tribes began developing on-reservation resources, developing businesses, and constructing facilities on reservation (including casinos and gas stations). One of the advantages the tribes touted was their tax-exempt status. The rise of tax-exempt businesses led to *White Mountain Apache Tribe vs. Bracker*. Both sovereignty and federal law were barriers to state action, and the Bracker interest balancing test required inquiry as to whether a specific state action violates federal law. Sovereignty was no longer the primary basis for deciding. Rather, decisions would be taken with sovereignty as part of the context. This was the prevailing standard up to Wagnon, and increasingly the Court allowed state action, as in *Cotton Petroleum Corp. vs. New Mexico* and *Oklahoma Tax Commission vs. Chickasaw*, the latter of which enunciated the "legal incidence test." Under this test, if a tax falls on the tribe or a member, it is a violation; if it falls on a nonmember, the matter is more ambiguous. After Kansas changed its law to clearly tax the non-Indian distributor, the Wagnon case ensued.

The Shakopee Mdewakanton Sioux acknowledges that it is subject to the federal government but denies authority to state, county, or city governments. States are empowered only to the extent that Congress says they are. Congress alone regulates Indian affairs. The Sioux analogize their status to that of Canada, which the state of Minnesota would never consider subject to its authority. Although they can voluntarily pay cities and counties for the services these governments provide, the Shakopee and all other federally recognized tribes are exempt from state taxes, rules, and dictates. And it is permissible and appropriate for the sovereign Shakopee to work with neighboring governments on common benefits such as roads and sewers. Over a 24-year period, the Shakopee have established more than 70 such agreements. The Shakopee Mdewakanton Sioux community, the tribal government, uses gaming and nongaming revenues to take care of the community, the nation, and the members of the tribe on the reservation. It regulates all land use and conforms to federal environmental rules. It buys and develops infrastructure including housing, water, wastewater and sewer, and roads, and it takes care of social well-being through health and welfare as well as educational services.

PINE RIDGE AND SOVEREIGNTY

John H. Barnhill

On the Pine Ridge Reservation in South Dakota, Alex White Plume and his family played by the rules of reservation life, planting alfalfa, barley, and corn on the poor soil and raising horses and buffalo. Even though none of their efforts succeeded beyond subsistence and dependence on government aid, the family persisted in keeping with Lakota traditions of self-sufficiency. After much research, Alex and his family planted industrial hemp, the relative of marijuana for which there was a booming worldwide demand. The Pine Ridge Tribal Government (in Shannon County, South Dakota, which is the poorest county in the United States), facing 85 percent unemployment, authorized growing of hemp while specifically excluding marijuana. Growing was legal under U.S. law, but selling was not. Alex assumed that hemp growing and selling were protected under tribal sovereignty, the same as casinos. White Plume and other Lakota cite the 1851 Treaty of Ft. Laramie that acknowledges their sovereignty and authorizes the Pine Ridge Lakota to grow any food or fiber crop. The Oglala Sioux Tribe enacted an ordinance in 1998 permitting the growing of low-THC (tetrahydrocannabinol) hemp on the reservation but clearly differentiating it from marijuana.

The U.S. government promoted hemp growing during World War II. Used in paper and wood products, the plant grows quickly—with a 120-day cycle—and is environmentally friendly with no need for chemicals. But once planted, it is nearly impossible to eradicate. With world forests shrinking, wood is more expensive and hemp is a highly attractive alternative, that is, an appealing cash crop. And industrial hemp does not contain the psychoactive THC; in fact, it dilutes marijuana that is growing nearby. The U.S. Drug Enforcement Administration (DEA) acknowledges that industrial hemp is virtually free of the psychoactive component that is in marijuana, but federal law makes no distinction. Hemp is perfect for the near-desert climate of the county, and it offers potential nutritional and economic benefits to the hard-hit county. White Plume saw a good deal, and in 2000 his family planted their first hemp crop. White Plume was the first to grow industrial hemp in the

United States in over 40 years. Armed federal agents attacked the field at 6:00 a.m. on August 24, 2000, using weed whackers as they do against marijuana. They cited White Plume for eight civil violations.

The tribal government that authorized White Plume's crop contends that its sovereignty is absolute because the Fort Laramie Treaty of 1868 recognized the Lakota as an independent nation. The Bureau of Indian Affairs (BIA) says sovereignty is only limited. In 2000 and every year since, White Plume has grown industrial hemp. In 2000 and every year since, the DEA has confiscated the crop at a total expense to taxpayers of over $1 million. The tribe contends that by treaty, it has the right to use reservation land any way it sees fit. Other Lakota are sensitive because of a history that includes Wounded Knee, both in 1890 and 1973, as well as a long string of broken treaties. And it does not help that a once self-sufficient and proud nation now has high rates of alcoholism, suicide, poverty, and disease exacerbated by overcrowding on a reservation short up to 2,000 housing units. The reservation residents resent the DEA action just a year after Clinton visited to celebrate the designation of Pine Ridge as an empowerment zone (a congressional designation of a rural area that receives federal benefits such as tax breaks and grants). A federal court of appeals ruled against White Plume in 2006, the year of the documentary film *Standing Silent Nation* about the White Plumes.

This situation raises issues of various sorts, including the question of what crimes warrant the overriding of tribal sovereignty. For the Pine Ridge Lakota, sovereignty is a last defense after long years of abuse of their rights.

Sources: Broydo, Leora. "The Drug Wars Come to the Rez: Growing a Little Industrial Hemp Might Get You Busted at Pine Ridge." *Native Press*. Retrieved from http://www.thenativepress.com/business/hemp.html in October 2009.

"POLL: Native Americans Growing Hemp: Sovereignty Collides with Government." *Industrial Hemp News*, June 27, 2007. Retrieved from http://www.420magazine.com/forums/industrial-hemp-news/66226-poll-native-americans-growing-hemp-sovereignty-collides-government.html

INDIAN GAMING

Sovereignty is vital to sustainable economic development on Indian reservations. Such development succeeds when tribes address their own problems and create their own solutions. Every sustainable economic development created on a reservation has involved the exertion of tribal sovereignty at some level. Tribes effectively exercise sovereignty in a variety of ways, from tribal control over resource management and tribally designed economic development strategies, to tribal administration of healthcare and other social services.

Perhaps no other issue in Indian country generates as much controversy and awareness about tribal sovereignty as the pursuit of economic development through Indian gaming. In 1988, Congress passed the Indian Gaming Regulatory Act (IGRA) to regulate tribal gaming operations. Although only about one third of all tribes in the United States have gaming operations, the IGRA mandates that states must negotiate in good faith with tribes in forming gaming agreements or compacts. These compacts define the terms of the games offered to the public as well as their limits. Although a tribe always has final say in its gaming enterprises, some tribes manage their casinos themselves while others contract with experienced outside management companies to conduct their business.

Indian gaming is subject to more stringent security and legal controls than commercial gaming. The major difference between tribal gaming operations and regular commercial casinos is the way in which tribes may utilize their profits. The main purpose of tribal gaming profits is to benefit the operation of the tribal government, finance reservation infrastructure, and improve services such as health, education, and welfare for tribal members. Under the auspices of IGRA, a multilevel plan of checks and balances ensures the integrity of tribal gaming enterprises. Each tribe has its own Tribal Gaming Commission that oversees operation of the tribe's gaming enterprise, making sure the operation complies with the law. Next, state compliance officers regularly review the operation through their tribal-state compacts. Finally, the National Indian Gaming Commission monitors the operations on a federal level through agencies such as the Justice Department, the Treasury Department, and the Department of the Interior.

CONCLUSION

The concept of Indian sovereignty, regardless of its convoluted or contradictory nature, remains a critical part of federal Indian law. Tribal councils established under the IRA act as self-governments, although federal funding and authority often place limits on them. The federal government must protect and defend native hunting and fishing rights against state and local regulation, although ultimate authority exists outside the realm of tribal sovereignty. Legal sovereignty made economic development through gaming possible, but federal restrictions placed on tribal gaming operations are further examples of limited sovereignty. Finally, federal Indian law regards Indian nations as having legal immunity under the doctrine of sovereign immunity, yet tribal power over nontribal members within their territory is limited. The persistence and survival of the concept of tribal sovereignty into the twenty-first century has bolstered a new idea that the people themselves are the ultimate source of their own authority. Embraced by Native Americans across the United States, this reassertion of sovereignty holds that the essence of tribal sovereignty is the ability to self-govern and to protect the health, safety, and well-being of tribal members within their own territory. Although states and the federal government may continue to try to diminish or redefine tribal sovereignty, Native Americans across the country will continue to fight to preserve sovereignty and culture as the unique qualities that define them as a people.

REFERENCES

Bauu Institute. "The Sovereign Status of Native American Indigenous People's Nations in the United States." Retrieved from http://www.bauuinstitute.com/Articles/NativeAmerican SovereignNations.html (last updated January 2008).

Cohen, Felix S. "The Erosion of Indian Rights, 1950–53: A Case Study in Bureaucracy." *Yale Law Journal* 62, no. 3 (1953): 348–390.

Cohen, Felix S. "The Scope of Tribal Self-Government." *Handbook of Federal Indian Law*. Washington, DC: U.S. Printing Office (1945), 122–150.

Corntassel, Jeff and Richard C. Witmer II. *Forced Federalism*. Norman: University of Oklahoma Press, 2008.

"The Court's Struggle to Define Indian Sovereignty." *Rutgers Law Review*. Retrieved from http://pegasus.rutgers.edu/~review/content/Sample3.pdf.

Deloria, Vine Jr. *Of Utmost Good Faith*. New York: Bantam Books, 1971.

d'Errico, Peter. "Sovereignty: A Brief History in the Context of Indian Law." In Jeffrey D. Schultz, Kerry L. Haynie, Anne M. McCulloch, and Andrew Aoki (Eds.), *The Encyclopedia of Minorities in American Politics*. Phoenix: Oryx Press, 2000.

Debo, Angie. *A History of the Indians of the United States*. Norman: University of Oklahoma Press, 1970.

Determination Era," *Political Research Quarterly* 57, no. 2 (June 2004): 295–303.

Frickey, Philip P. "Tribal Sovereignty." *Harvard Law Review* 119, no. 2 (December 2005): 445.

Hoxie, Frederick E. *The Final Promise: The Campaign to Assimilate the Indians, 1880–1920*. Lincoln: University of Nebraska Press, 2001.

Jarding, Lilias Jones. "Tribal State Relations Involving Land and Resources in the Self-Determination Era," *Political Research Quarterly* 57:2 (June 2004): 295–303.

Johnson, F. William. "Legalized Gambling: Economic Sovereignty for Native Americans." *Word & World* 15, no. 2 (1995). Retrieved from http://www.luthersem.edu/word& world/Archives/15-2_Revelation/15-2_Face_to_Face.pdf

Office of the Attorney General. *Department of Justice Policy on Indian Sovereignty and Government-to-Government Relationships with Indian Tribes* (1995). Retrieved from http://www.justice.gov/ag/readingroom/sovereignty.htm

Pommersheim, Frank. *Braid of Feathers*. Berkeley: University of California Press, 1995.

Prucha, Francis Paul. *The Great Father: The United States Government and the Indians*. Lincoln: University of Nebraska Press, 1986.

Shkopee Mdewakanton Sioux Community. "Sovereignty." Retrieved from http://www .ccsmdc.org/sover.html in September 2009.

Wright, Douglas R. "Sovereignty: Indian Sovereignty and Tribal Immunity from Suit." *American Indian Law Review* 8, no. 2 (1980): 401–418.

Wunder, John R. *Native American Sovereignty*. New York: Routledge, 1999.

Indians and the U.S. Constitution

Lindsey Hanson

The relationship between American Indians and the Constitution of the United States is complex. Many scholars argue that the U.S. Constitution was itself modeled after the constitutions of American Indian tribes, the Iroquois in particular. The U.S. Constitution directly addresses American Indians in two locations, and implicitly addresses American Indian treaty rights. However, the U.S. Constitution does not directly apply to American Indians on federally recognized American Indian reservations as sovereign domestic dependent nations. As a result, the Indian Civil Rights Act of 1968, although controversial in its limitation of tribal sovereignty, was meant to address what many felt were injustices and rights violations taking place on reservations. The Indian Civil Rights Act applied most portions of the Bill of Rights to tribal governments. It did not, however, apply every portion of the Bill of Rights, and since its passage there have been questions about the degree of enforcement and the manner in which it should be enforced.

TRIBAL CONSTITUTIONS AS MODELS FOR THE U.S. CONSTITUTION

The Iroquois nation, which includes tribes such as the Mohawk, Oneida, and Seneca who were historically in the Great Lakes region who speak the Iroquoian language, had a constitution called the Great Law of Peace, which Benjamin Franklin, one of the founding fathers, utilized as a model for establishing the U.S. Constitution. Franklin became familiar with the document when he printed the minutes of the Iroquois nation's meetings while acting in his official capacity as the printer for the state of Pennsylvania. The Iroquois constitution, which was developed sometime between 1000 and 1400 CE, included clauses that provided for freedom of expression and religion as well as the election of representatives. The Iroquois document also provided the framers of the U.S. Constitution with the model for the federalist system that made room for both state and federal governments, and the model for a two-house legislative body. Unlike the British system, which the framers were familiar with, the Iroquois system required members to be silent while another member was speaking. The U.S. government also adopted this practice. The Iroquois constitution also provided for a commander-in-chief and an annual state of the union address. Interestingly, the Iroquois constitution provided for more participation of females than does the U.S. Constitution.

REFERENCES TO AMERICAN INDIANS IN THE U.S. CONSTITUTION

The U.S. Constitution makes overt or implied reference to American Indians in three locations. The first reference is Article 1, Section 2, in which American Indians are not counted as citizens of the United States for the purposes of taxation and representation. Indians were considered citizens of sovereign American Indian nations. Even after the Civil War when the Fourteenth Amendment extended citizenship rights to former slaves and "persons born or naturalized in the United States," American Indians were not considered citizens. Most American Indians were not citizens of the United States until the passage of the 1924 Indian Citizenship Act, also known as the Snyder Act.

The second reference to Indians in the Constitution is the Commerce Clause at Article I, Section 8, Clause 3, in which the Constitution gives Congress the power "To regulate Commerce with foreign Nations, and among the several States, and with the Indian Tribes." Under the Articles of Confederation—the first government of the United States (1777–1789), which preceded the Constitution—Congress also had the power to regulate and manage relations with American Indian tribes. Under the Articles of Confederation, Congress signed eight treaties with various American Indian tribes. However, under the Articles of the Confederation, Congress was not able to maintain exclusive relations with American Indian tribes; independent states also maintained relations with American Indian tribes. Wars broke out, for example, between tribes and the states of Georgia and South Carolina because of the relations between those states and the tribes. To prevent situations such as these, the new U.S. Constitution granted the power to regulate affairs with the tribes exclusively to the federal government. Article VI states that all treaties entered into by the federal government must abide by the "supreme Law of the Land," that is, the Constitution. At the time, treaties with American Indian tribes outnumbered treaties with other countries, so this provision was meant largely to regulate relations with American Indian tribes. Within the first five weeks after the Congress convened under the new Constitution, it passed four laws dealing with relations with tribes. In 1790, Congress actually passed a law, still in effect today, that prohibits states and private citizens from buying land owned by American Indian tribes and from carrying out official relationships with those tribes.

Notwithstanding federal control of Indian affairs, in recent years state governments have become increasingly involved in tribal relations. The legal foundation for such state interaction with tribes is found in the Tenth Amendment's reservation of powers clause, which reserves for the states those powers not delegated to the federal government. While the federal government is generally recognized as having plenary power over relations with tribes, it has delegated some of these powers to the states. Thus, where federal law does not conflict with state law regarding tribal relations, state law is enforceable.

APPLICATION OF THE U.S. CONSTITUTION TO AMERICAN INDIAN NATIONS

The U.S. Constitution does not directly apply to American Indian tribes, which are domestic dependent nations with certain sovereignty rights. The U.S. Supreme Court established these sovereignty rights in *Cherokee Nation vs. Georgia* (1831). In *Barron vs. Baltimore* (1833), the Supreme Court established that the Bill of Rights did not apply to state governments, only to the federal government. Beginning in the 1890s, however, the Supreme Court issued a series of decisions that incorporated most sections of the Bill of Rights and applied them to states.

The Supreme Court did not, however, apply the Bill of Rights to American Indian tribes as domestic dependent sovereign nations. This was solidified in the 1896 decision of the Supreme Court in *Talton vs. Mayes*. The case was brought by a Cherokee by the name of Bob Talton who had been convicted of the murder of another Cherokee man and sentenced to death. Talton argued that his conviction violated the Fifth and Fourteenth Amendments of the U.S. Constitution. He alleged that his conviction was in violation of the Fifth Amendment because the Fifth Amendment requires a grand jury indictment, U.S. law required more than five members on a grand jury, and his indictment was issued by a jury of less than five. He further alleged that he was subject to federal law because the Fourteenth Amendment provided for equal protection under the law for all citizens, and that because he had been born and raised in the United States he was entitled to that equal protection. The Court, however, did not agree with Talton's arguments and held that because of the unique status of American Indian tribes as domestic dependent nations under *Cherokee Nation vs. Georgia*, the protections of the Fifth Amendment do not apply to American Indians on American Indian reservations. Likewise, the Tenth Circuit, in *Native American Church vs. Navajo Tribal Council* (1959), held that the First Amendment did not require the Navajo nation to allow members of the Native American Church (NAC) to use peyote in its rituals. The Constitution and the Bill of Rights, then, do not apply to sovereign federally recognized American Indian tribes as domestic dependent nations.

THE INDIAN CIVIL RIGHTS ACT OF 1968

The decision in *Talton vs. Mayes* and later decisions in line with *Talton* led to the passage of the Indian Civil Rights Act of 1968 (ICRA), which applied certain provisions of the Bill of Rights to federally recognized American Indian tribes. While the Court in *Talton vs. Mayes* held that the Fifth Amendment did not apply to American Indian tribes, it also held that the tribal rights of self-governance were subject to federal legislation, and that Congress had plenary power to, "limit, modify or eliminate the powers of local self-government which the tribes otherwise possess." This established the legal precedent necessary for the passage of ICRA.

The political will for the passage of ICRA was established by stories of corrupt tribal officials and injustice on reservations. One major impetus for the passage of ICRA was the *Colliflower vs. Garland* (1965) case. In that case, the Gros Ventre tribal court had sentenced a woman to five days in jail without providing her with an attorney, or giving her the opportunity to confront witnesses, after she failed to remove cattle from land that had been leased to another individual. Due to these civil rights violations, the Ninth Circuit stepped in and took jurisdiction despite the fact that the incident took place on a reservation and concerned tribal members. Hearing this and similar stories, in the 1960s, Congress surveyed numerous individuals and held hearings on abuses of justice and individual rights on American Indian reservations. This led to the ICRA, which has its supporters and critics both on and off reservations. Proponents of the act tout its important role in protecting vulnerable persons on reservations, including women and children. Opponents view ICRA as an infringement by the federal government on tribal sovereignty.

ICRA applies certain provisions of the Bill of Rights to American Indian tribes. ICRA provides for freedom of religion, speech, press, and assembly on American Indian reservations. Although some tribal leaders argued against the inclusion of free speech rights in ICRA because of the close-knit nature of tribes and the disruption caused by certain types of speech, Congress chose to include this protection. ICRA also provides for protections against unreasonable search and seizure as well as double jeopardy, and for the Fifth Amendment right against self-incrimination. It further requires that if private property is taken for public use, the owner must be given just compensation. ICRA requires speedy and public trials in criminal proceedings, the right to confront witnesses, and the right to counsel at the expense of the accused. It prohibits excessive bails or fines, and cruel and unusual punishment. ICRA also provides for equal protection under the law, forbids bills of attainder or ex post facto laws, and provides for the right to a jury trial for crimes punishable by imprisonment, as well as for writs of habeas corpus.

ICRA also provides for due process of law. Due process does not require procedures identical to state and federal court systems; however, many tribal courts have chosen to adopt rules of evidence and other rules of civil procedure similar to state and federal courts. This adoption has been in part to increase the perceived validity of tribal courts, and in part to create a system with which attorneys are familiar. ICRA does invalidate some previous tribal codes that, in accordance with regulations of the Secretary of the Interior prior to 1961, prohibited professional attorneys from appearing before the tribal court. However, even under ICRA, tribes have the power to reasonably regulate attorneys who practice in tribal courts. Many tribal courts require familiarity with tribal law for the admission of attorneys or lay advocates.

ICRA does not apply all of the constitutional protections of the Bill of Rights to American Indian tribes. It does not include establishment clause language that requires the separation of church and state, because Congress did not want to disrupt the traditional Pueblo system, which was theocratic. ICRA also does not guarantee a republican form of government. Later court interpretations of ICRA have held that it does not require tribal officials to be democratically elected. Tribal elections are not covered by the Constitution or federal voting laws, but tribal elections are covered by the equal protection and due process clauses of ICRA.

ICRA does not require a jury trial in civil cases and does not provide for the right to bear arms. The Third Amendment protection against quartering troops in private homes and the Tenth Amendment reservation of unenumerated powers to the states are excluded because they are not relevant to American Indian tribes. ICRA also does not require the appointment of defense counsel for indigent defendants. Congress chose not to require court-appointed attorneys because of the scarcity of attorneys on some reservations. Even where attorneys are available, tribes may not have the funds available to pay for their appointment. Additionally, under the original version of ICRA, which has since been amended, tribes were authorized to impose only small fines and short prison terms for which indigent defendants would not have been entitled to counsel even in the federal system or in most state systems.

The Tribal Law and Order Act of 2010 amended ICRA and allows tribes to impose higher fines and longer prison terms, but it also requires the appointment of counsel in more serious cases. The amendments instituted by the Tribal Law and Order Act increase tribal authority for sentencing in criminal cases. Previously under ICRA, tribes could not imprison defendants for over a year or fine individuals over $5,000. Under the amendments, tribes can impose fines of up to $15,000 and prison terms of up to three years for criminal offenses if the defendant has been previously convicted of the same or a comparable offense by any U.S.

jurisdiction or if the offense, or a comparable offense, would be punishable by more than a year of imprisonment in the federal or any state court system.

In cases where the defendant is subject to more than a year of imprisonment, defendants are entitled to effective assistance of counsel at least equal to that guaranteed by the U.S. Constitution, and tribes must provide indigent defendants with counsel at the tribe's expense. Additionally, in cases where the defendant is subject to more than a year of imprisonment, the presiding judge must have sufficient legal training and be licensed to practice law in any U.S. jurisdiction. In such cases, the tribe is also required to make publicly available its criminal laws and regulations, and its rules of evidence and procedure. The tribal court must also maintain a record of criminal proceedings, including an audio or other recording. Under the Tribal Law and Order Act amendments, tribal courts can require the defendant to serve his or her sentence in an approved tribal correction center, a federal facility, a state- or local government–approved detention or correctional center, or in an alternative rehabilitation center owned by the tribe. Tribes can also sentence defendants to alternative punishments allowed for under tribal law.

AFTER THE INDIAN CIVIL RIGHTS ACT

The Indian Civil Rights Act was limited, 10 years after its passage, by the U.S. Supreme Court's decision in *Santa Clara Pueblo vs. Martinez*. That case involved a plaintiff who wanted to stop the tribe's practice of denying membership to children born to female members who had married outside the tribe. The tribe was not denying membership to children born to male members who had married outside the tribe. The plaintiff argued that such sex discrimination was in violation of equal protection rights under ICRA, but the Court held that the tribe was immune from suit based on common law sovereign immunity. The Court's decision meant that while tribes are required to comply with ICRA, federal courts will not oversee compliance with the law except in unusual cases or in habeas corpus proceedings. Thus, ICRA violations can be pursued only within tribal court systems in most cases.

When tribal appellate procedures do not exist or are not adequate, a defendant may seek release by applying for a writ of habeas corpus outside the tribal court system. The only remedy available to an individual tribal member under ICRA is a writ of habeas corpus if he or she is in custody, unless the tribe waives its sovereign immunity rights. Due to this fact, in the ICRA context habeas corpus proceedings have been extended to cases where the individual is not strictly in custody. In *Poodry vs. Tonawanda Band of Seneca Indians*, five Seneca tribal members questioned tribal council finances and were found guilty of treason. As punishment, they were stripped of membership rights and banished from the reservation. The court held that banishment was such a severe punishment and that it so constricted the defendants' liberty that it amounted to detention, and the habeas corpus provision of ICRA thus applied, allowing the federal court system to monitor ICRA compliance. In a similar vein, in *U.S. vs. Wadena* (1998), the Eighth Circuit went so far as to criminalize ICRA and held that tribal officials who engaged in election fraud were subject to state criminal jurisdiction in cases where the tribal government was no longer operating legitimately because a conspiracy to commit election fraud amounted to a violation of ICRA.

Application of the U.S. Constitution to American Indian tribes is also mitigated by the fact that a tribal court's interpretation of the provisions of ICRA may vary from the manner in which U.S. courts have interpreted the various provisions of the Bill of Rights. However, scholars who have studied the topic have argued that in fact tribal courts are much more likely to utilize established state and federal precedent to interpret and apply ICRA provisions than to develop their own unique tribal interpretations.

There are also concerns and questions about the degree to which ICRA is actually being enforced in tribal courts. One commonly cited problem with enforcement is a lack of funding, which results in insufficient staffing and high turnover rates in existing tribal court staff. Other issues with enforcement include a lack of qualified attorneys to bring ICRA violation cases. There has also been concern about the likelihood that tribes would waive sovereign immunity to allow ICRA violation suits to go forward. Individuals cannot sue a tribal government for monetary damages, or even an injunction, which is a court order demanding that some action be stopped, unless the tribe waives its sovereign immunity. Without such waiver, the provisions of ICRA are limited in their application.

While the Iroquois constitution may have served as a model for the U.S. Constitution, and the Constitution addresses some aspects of the treatment of American Indians, the relationship between American Indian tribes and the Constitution is by no means simple. The Constitution applies to American Indians, sovereign domestic dependent nations on federally recognized reservations, only through the Indian Civil Rights Act of 1968. The degree and manner of enforcement of that act, and even the act itself, has been subject to a great deal of controversy since its passage in 1968. The passage of the Tribal Law and Order Act in 2010 and its amendments to the ICRA, which expand tribal sovereignty in the area of criminal law, will undoubtedly lead to further controversies and complexities to be worked out as the court system continues to determine the precise relationship between American Indian tribes and the U.S. Constitution.

RESOURCES

Byram, Jennifer S., *Civil Rights on Reservations: The Indian Civil Rights Act and Tribal Sovereignty*, 25 Okla. City U.L. Rev. 491, 2000.

Fenton, William N. *The Great Law and the Longhouse: A Political History of the Iroquois Confederacy*. Norman: University of Oklahoma Press, 1998.

Fletcher, Matthew L. M. *Tribal Courts, the Indian Civil Rights Act, and Customary Law: Preliminary Data*. MSU Legal Studies Research Paper No. 06-05, 2008.

Hearing before the U.S. Commission on Civil Rights: Enforcement of the Indian Civil Rights Act, March 31, 1988. Available at http://www.law.umaryland.edu/marshall/usccr/documents/cr18in25z.pdf

"Indian Bill of Rights and the Constitutional Status of Tribal Governments." *Harvard Law Review* 82, no. 6 (1968): 1343–1373.

Iroquois Great Law of Peace (full text). Available at http://www.iroquoisdemocracy.pdx.edu/html/greatlaw.html

Kennedy, Gary D. "Tribal Elections: An Appraisal after the Indian Civil Rights Act." *American Indian Law Review* 3, no. 2 (1975): 497–508.

Oren, Lyons. *Exiled in the Land of the Free: Democracy, Indian Nations, and the U.S. Constitution*. Santa Fe, NM: Clear Light Books, 1992.

Poodry vs. Tonawanda Band of Seneca Indians, 85 F.3d 874 (1st Cir. 1996).

Sommer, Melanie. *Broken Trust: Civil Rights in Indian Country*. Minnesota Public Radio, April 2001. Retrieved from http://news.minnesota.publicradio.org/projects/2001/04/brokentrust/history/history_intro.shtml

Talton vs. Mayes, 163 U.S. 376 (1898). Available at http://supreme.justia.com/us/163/376/case.html

Text of Indian Civil Rights Act of 1968; U.S.C. Title 25, sections 1301–1303.

U.S. Commission on Civil Rights. *The Indian Civil Rights Act: A Report of the United States Commission on Civil Rights* (SuDoc CR 1.2:IN 2/8).

U.S. Commission on Civil Rights. *American Indian Civil Rights Handbook*, March 1972. Retrieved from http://www.law.umaryland.edu/marshall/usccr/documents/cr11033.pdf

Wilkins, David E. and K. Tsianina Lomawaima. *Uneven Ground: American Indian Sovereignty and Federal Law*. Norman: University of Oklahoma Press, 2001.

Wunder, John R. *"Retained by the People": A History of American Indians and the Bill of Rights*. New York: Oxford University Press, 1994.

Race Relations

Lindsey Hanson

The U.S. Declaration of Independence describes American Indians as "[T]he merciless Indian Savages whose known rule of warfare, is an undistinguished destruction of all ages, sexes and conditions." This summary of the colonists' view of American Indians forms part of the backdrop upon which racial relations between American Indians and other racial and ethnic groups takes place today. This understanding, along with the prior and subsequent takings of land, Indian removal and relocation acts, forced boarding schools, and the modern federal government's mismanagement of assets held in trust, creates a historical and contemporary background that has resulted in, at times, tense race relations between American Indians and other racial and ethnic groups, particularly white or Caucasian Americans.

Contributing to problems with race relations is the fact that some American Indians feel invisible and as if they, as a group, have been left out of the national discussion on race and race relations. The portrayal of American Indians in the media and the use of American Indian mascots and imagery, in sports in particular, has also been the source of racial tension. The racial tensions between American Indians and other racial and ethnic groups is evidenced by the disproportionally high number of interracial violent crimes committed against American Indians and the disproportionately high number of hate crimes committed against American Indians.

The state of race relations in two American towns, one in the Southwest, and one in the Midwest, will be discussed to provide real-life examples of the status of race relations between American Indians and other racial and ethnic groups. An overview of the racial tensions that ensued after the murder of three Navajo men in the 1970s in the town of Farmington, New Mexico, and the efforts to combat those racial tensions will be discussed. A study of the racial perceptions and attitudes of both American Indians and white Americans in one off-reservation community located between three American Indian reservations will also be presented as a case study on race relations. Despite some of the tensions identified by this data, and in these two towns in particular, community members and activists remain hopeful that the future will bring improved relations between American Indians and other racial and ethnic groups.

INVISIBLE INDIANS

Despite racial tensions, American Indians have often been left out of the discussion on race relations in the United States. For example, in 1998, American Indians protested the President's Race Commission because of none of its seven members were American Indian. The commission had set up forums with panelists in various locations throughout the country to lead a discussion on race. In Denver, Colorado, when the panelists began their presentations a group of American Indians shouted in protest and demanded to know why an American Indian representative was not among the group. The forum allowed individuals to come forward to speak but eventually continued as planned, without an American Indian representative. The event became so heated that one of the panelists left in frustration. During the second day of the event, American Indian activists carried on their protest outside and were joined by a handful of individuals from other racial and ethnic groups.

American Indians also cite the lack of inclusion of Native Americans in advertisements, even in local advertisements in areas with high American Indian populations, as evidence of the population's invisibility. The invisibility felt by some within the community is further amplified by the underrepresentation of American Indians in local, state, and federal positions of power and leadership. Activists also point out that while K–12 educational curricula often include African American history, there is a lack of inclusion when it comes to American Indian history. The feeling that the nation as a whole not only fails to understand American Indian history and culture, but as a result also fails to grasp the historical trauma of removal, boarding schools, relocation, and the mismanagement of land and other resources held in trust by the federal government, adds to the feeling of invisibility felt by some within the community.

DEPICTIONS OF AMERICAN INDIANS IN CULTURE, MEDIA, AND SPORTS

In addition to the relative invisibility of the problem of race relations with American Indians, activists cite depictions of American Indians in the media, and in particular in sports, as contributing to an environment that is not conducive to healthy race relations. American Indian scholars point out numerous instances where racially insensitive comments or imagery directed at other racial or ethnic groups has led to the removal of products from stores, or the end of high-profile careers. They also point out that this same standard does not seem to apply to derogatory comments and images directed at American Indians. Teams like the Washington Redskins, Atlanta Braves, Cleveland Indians, and Kansas City Chiefs continue to use American Indian names and imagery as mascots. Scholars and activists point out that the Washington Redskins continue to use the word *Redskins*, which many consider to be the equivalent of the *N* word for American Indians. They also argue that the Cleveland Indians' mascot is the equivalent of Little Black Sambo, which would never be tolerated as a mascot today.

Sports teams are not the only organizations that utilize American Indian imagery and mascots, and activists also take issue with some non-Indian companies that use American Indian logos to advertise their products. Activists further point out that words like *squaw* and phrases like *Indian maiden* present offensive or overly romanticized portrayals of American Indian culture that are not appropriate in modern society. Some within the American Indian community also took offensive that the code name used for Osama bin Laden during the military operation that eventually led to his death was Geronimo. Geronimo was an Apache leader who fought against Mexico and the United States to protect tribal lands during the Apache wars of the nineteenth century. Many American Indians consider him a hero. The use of Geronimo as a code name for an American enemy, and the use of American Indian names and imagery in manners considered offensive to many within the American Indian community, contribute to an environment that is not conducive to healthy race relations, according to some scholars and activists.

CRIMES AGAINST AMERICAN INDIANS

American Indians are more likely than other racial or ethnic groups to be victims of violent crimes where offenders are non-native. On average, between 1992 and 2001, victimization of American Indians accounted for 1.3 percent of all violent crimes despite the fact that American Indians made up only 0.5 percent of the population used to calculate the rate of victimization. The U.S. Department of Justice estimates that one out of every 10 American Indians has been the victim of a violent crime. That rate is 2.5 times higher than for whites, four times higher than for Asian Americans, and twice as high as it is for blacks. Although American Indian men are more likely to be victims of violent crime than American Indian women, American Indian women are still twice as likely to be victims of violent crime as women of other racial or ethnic groups.

According to a 1999 study by the Bureau of Justice Statistics, 70 percent of violent crimes against American Indians are committed by someone who is not American Indian, which makes American Indians the population most likely to experience victimization by someone outside of their own race. In a study of crimes committed between 1992 and 2001, eighty-eight percent of violent crimes against American Indians were committed by black or white offenders, and 13 percent were committed by offenders classified as Asian American or American Indian. When American Indians were asked what race their offender belonged to, 57 percent of the offenders were reported to be white, 34 percent other, and 9 percent black. This is a higher interracial victimization rate than reported by blacks or whites. white victims of violent crimes reported that 70 percent of their offenders were also white, and black victims of violent crimes reported that 80 percent of their offenders were also black. In cases of rape American Indians reported that almost four of five offenders were white, and one in ten was black. For robbery 57 percent of offenders against American Indians were described as white, and 17 percent were described as black. Fifty-eight percent of aggravated assault offenders against American Indians were described as white, and 10 percent were described as black. For cases of simple assault 55 percent of offenders against American Indians were described as white, and 9 percent were described as black. Interestingly, the less serious the offense the more likely the American Indian victim was to describe the offender as belonging to a race other than white or black.

American Indians are more likely than other races to be the victims of violent crimes committed by strangers; forty-two percent of violent crimes committed against American Indians are committed by strangers. American Indians are also more likely to be victimized by individuals who have ingested alcohol prior to the incident, and who use a weapon. In forty-percent of the incident involving the victimization of American Indians the offender consumed alcohol prior to the offense; this was most likely to be the case in domestic violence offenses.

American Indians were less likely than all other races to be murdered by someone of their own race. Between 1976 and 1999, eighty-six percent of white homicide victims were murdered by someone of their own race, 94 percent of black murder victims were murdered by someone of their own race, and 60 percent of Asian American murder victims were murdered by someone of their own race. By comparison, 58 percent of the murders of American Indians were committed by other American Indians; 32 percent of the murders of American Indians were committed by a white offender, 10 percent by a black offender, and 1 percent by an Asian offender.

Between 1997 and 1999, there were 48 hate crimes reported against American Indians. This number represented 2.6 percent of all hate crimes, a disproportionate amount for the number of American Indians in the general population. In 1999, the Department of Justice reported 64 incidents that were motivated by racial bias against American Indians, 84 offenses during those incidents (offenses are crimes such as arson, manslaughter, assault, rape, and theft), and 87 victims of racially motivated crime. Given that this data was based on reports from only 17 states, most of which did not have relatively significant American Indian populations, there is reason to believe that the actual number of hate crimes committed against American Indians nationwide was much higher that year. In 2001, the Department of Justice estimated that one in 10 racially motivated hate crimes was committed against an American Indian. According to data gathered by the Federal Bureau of Investigation (FBI) in 2005, two percent of hate crimes committed that year were against American Indians; American Indians make up only 1 percent of the population, so American Indians experience hate crimes at a disproportionate rate. In both 2006 and 2007, there were 75 hate crimes committed against American Indians. While the number of hate crimes overall dropped from 2006 to 2007, the number of hate crimes committed against American Indians did not. Furthermore, some scholars estimate that actual numbers are probably higher since only about 10 percent of hate crimes committed against American Indians are reported to authorities. Scholars suggest that low rates of report may be due to victims' perceptions that the police will not take the crime against them seriously, or that the police cannot be trusted. The fact that American Indians are more likely to be victims of racially motivated hate crimes and are more likely to be victims of interracial violent crime suggests tension in race relations between the American Indian community and other racial and ethnic groups.

RACIAL RELATIONS IN CRISIS: FARMINGTON, NEW MEXICO

In the town of Farmington, New Mexico, in 1974 three Navajo men were murdered. White high school students were charged with the murders, and there were allegations that the murders had taken place while the students were "Indian rolling." In the town of Farmington, abusing inebriated Navajo street people was known as Indian rolling. The incident sparked severe racial tensions in the town, to the point that the U.S. Commission on Civil Rights was called in. The advisory committee to the commission found that community leaders did not feel a great deal of responsibility for maintaining healthy race relations, that there was no process for making discrimination complaints, that there were disproportionally low numbers of American Indians in local government and in the police department, and that the police department had no requirement for diversity training. It also found that healthcare and employment for the local American Indian community were in a state of crisis.

A follow-up study in 2004 revealed that while problems still existed, both sides felt that there had been substantial progress since the racial unrest in the mid-1970s. Still, American Indians in the community reported being discriminated against by law enforcement officials and employers. There were also continuing reports of racially motivated harassment, particularly by youths. Despite the commission's finding of substantial progress in the area of race relations in the community, shortly after it released its report, there was another high-profile killing of a Navajo man, suggesting that race relations in the community were still in need of improvement.

A CASE STUDY: RACIAL RELATIONS BETWEEN AMERICAN INDIANS AND WHITE RESIDENTS IN BEMIDJI, MINNESOTA

While there has not been a great deal of scholarship on the current status of race relations between white residents and American Indian residents in Indian country, at least one community has looked closely at the issue in recent years. The town of Bemidji, Minnesota, is an off-reservation town of 13,431 that is located between the Red Lake and Leech Lake reservations, and within a little more than an hour of the White Earth reservation. The small town is located in Beltrami County, one of the poorest in the state. As of the 2012 census, the population within the city limits was 80.5 percent white, and a 10.9 percent American Indian.

The researchers randomly surveyed residents, allowed residents to opt-in to the survey, and conducted focus groups on the three nearby reservations as well as with American Indians living within the city limits. The study found that most respondents felt that race relations in the area were fair. However, American Indian respondents were much more likely to view race relations in the area as poor. Twenty percent of white respondents rated race relations in the area as poor, while 55 percent of American Indians living in the Bemidji area, and 71 percent of American Indians living on nearby reservations, rated race relations as poor. Forty-two percent of American Indians living on nearby reservations reported being discriminated against on a very regular basis, 35 percent of American Indians living in the Bemidji area itself reported being discriminated against on a very regular basis, and 7 percent of white respondents reported being discriminated against on a very regular basis.

Three out of every four American Indian respondents felt that housing discrimination was an issue in the area, and half said that they had experienced this kind of discrimination in the last year. When it came to employment discrimination, two out of three white respondents felt there was equal employment opportunity, while only one out of four American Indian respondents felt there was equal employment opportunity. Almost half of American Indian participants reported experiencing employment discrimination in the past year. White participants and American Indian participants who live in Bemidji agreed that there were equal educational opportunities in the area, but American Indians on the nearby reservations were more likely to disagree with this statement. Almost three out of four white participants agreed that people are treated fairly within the educational system, while one out of five American Indian participants living in Bemidji, and less than one out of five American Indian participants living on a nearby reservation agreed. Half of American Indian participants reported being discriminated against in the area of education in the last year. Over half of the American Indian participants also reported being discriminated against in the healthcare system in the last year, and less than two thirds reported being satisfied with their healthcare access. Conversely, over four fifths of white respondents were satisfied with their access to healthcare. More than two thirds of American Indian participants reported being discriminated against by law enforcement in the last year, and 25 percent reported that this happened regularly. Over two thirds of white respondents felt that people of different races were being stopped equally by law enforcement, while only one quarter of American Indian respondents agreed.

Most respondents of both races felt that race relations had not changed much in last five years, but American Indian participants were more likely to feel that things had gotten worse in that time period. Respondents of both races felt that race relations were not likely to change much for the worse or the better in the next five years. Most respondents of both races agreed that generations of racism and discrimination made it more difficult for minorities to achieve goals, although American Indians, particularly those on reservations, were more likely to agree with this statement. Three fifths of white participants agreed that their race gave them certain advantages. American Indians were also less likely than white participants to feel that community leaders were addressing diversity issues. Nearly 50 percent of participants in the study felt that race relations should be a top priority in the community, and most participants said they would like to know people of other cultures and races better. Study participants felt that that the best way to begin to address issues related to discrimination and race relations in the community was through employment and the accompanying income, education, legal system access, and civic and social engagement. Both white and American Indian respondents ranked these as the most important issues; the only major area of difference was that American Indians were more likely to rank access to the justice system as highly important.

IMPROVING RACE RELATIONS

The researchers who conducted the Bemidji case study as well as other scholars and activists have recommended actions that might improve race relations between American Indian communities and other racial and ethnic groups. Suggestions include dealing with the root causes of racism by addressing historical injustices and stereotypes. Scholars, researchers, and activists suggest that educating communities, and particularly youth, about these issues will contribute to improved race relations in the future. Educational efforts, they suggest, could come from both within and outside the school system. Curricula might include learning about different racial and ethnic groups, discussions of race and racism, and teachings about American Indian history and culture. Others suggest building collaborative relationships with law enforcement, setting up meetings with law enforcement, and providing diversity education for police officers. Still others suggest providing opportunities for individuals of different races to meet and interact, and encouraging community leaders and organizations to provide venues for discussion about race relations within the community. Researchers, activists, and scholars also suggest that including more American Indians in leadership groups and in leadership roles within communities would improve the status of race relations. Further involving the media, religious organizations, and other social and civic organizations has also been suggested by individuals working to reform racial relations.

These individuals hope that reform efforts will make the problem of race relations with the American Indian community more visible to the nation as a whole. In turn, the hope of these activists is that with increased attention to the concerns of the American Indian community, images of American Indians seen in the media, and in sports in particular, will change. Activists also hope for a decrease in hate crimes and interracial violent crimes against American Indians. The expectation is that with reform efforts like those outlined earlier, race relations in communities like Farmington, New Mexico, and Bemidji, Minnesota, will be marked by less tension and more understanding in the future.

REFERENCES

Baca, Lawrence R. "Native Image in Schools and Racially Hostile Environment." University of Texas. Retrieved from http://www.cwrl.utexas.edu/~bacon/Archives/Mascot/Native%20Images%20in%20School%20and%20the%20Racially%20Hostile%20Environment.pdf

Buchanan, Susy. "Indian Blood." *Intelligence Report* 124 (Winter 2006). Retrieved from http://www.splcenter.org/get-informed/intelligence-report/browse-all-issues/2006/winter/indian-blood?page=0,0

Buchanan, Susy. "Malign Neglect." *Intelligence Report* 124 (Winter 2006). Retrieved from http://www.splcenter.org/get-informed/intelligence-report/browse-all-issues/2006/winter/indian-blood/malign-neglect

Forbes, Jack D. *Africans and Native Americans: The Language of Race and the Evolution of Red-Black Peoples*. Champaign: University Press of Illinois, 1983.

New Mexico Advisory Committee to the U.S. Commission on Civil Rights. "The Farmington Report: Civil Rights for Native Americans 30 Years Later," 2005. Retrieved from http://www.usccr.gov/pubs/122705_FarmingtonReport.pdf

Perry, Barbara. *Silent Victims: Hate Crimes against Native Americans*. Tucson: University Press of Arizona, 2008.

Perry, Steven W. "American Indians and Crime: A BJS Statistical Profile, 1992–2002." U.S. Department of Justice, Office of Justice Programs, Bureau of Justice Statistics,

December 2004. Retrieved from http://www.justice.gov/otj/pdf/american_indians_and_crime.pdf

Shared Vision. "Bemidji Area Study on Race Relations: An Exploration of Current Race Relations between American Indian and White Residents," February 2009. Retrieved from http://www.hrdc.org/html/documents/FINAL-SHARED-VISION-REPORT.pdf

U.S. Department of Justice, "Hate Crime Statistics 2009: Incidents, Offenses, Victims, and Known Offenders by Bias Motivation," 2009. Retrieved from http://www2.fbi.gov/ucr/hc2009/data/table_01.html

Racism

John H. Barnhill

Racism is a belief that a person's skin color or other surface characteristic associated with "race" (a scientifically debunked classification based on superficial group characteristics such as skin color) defines that person, that some races are superior to others, and that individuals of supposedly inferior races should be looked down on and discriminated against by members of superior races regardless of individual characteristics. Racism against Indians has long been understood as comparable to racism against blacks. Thus scholars have focused on hallmarks, widespread and commonly understood methods of differentiation, of white-black racism. Use of blood quantum (a proportion based on the number of ancestors of one racial category or another) is a marker of racism. Contrarily, the lack of a hallmark, the prohibition of interracial marriage that under the label miscegenation characterized white-black racism until relatively recently, is also a marker. These are individual aspects, and racism against Indians has historically been directed at the tribe, the "owner" of the asset sought by whites, while at the same time whites sought to flatter the individual by defining him or her as capable of leaving the inferior tribal society for the superior "civilized" white one. American racism has consistently been stronger during times of assimilation. By targeting the Indian community and not individual Indians, it denies Indian groups their status as political entities with governmental status.

Racism promotes alcohol and drug abuse as a means of dealing with it. Suicide rates are high too, as are incarceration rates. Racism historically has also included assimilation by churches and schools as well as loss of land and customs. Racism also includes the use of stereotypes in media, as sports mascots, and in the military. Institutional racism persists, particularly in a legal system that discriminates against Native Americans and other minorities. An additional concern is the economic racism that has traditionally seen the reservation as a place for exploitation, a dumping ground for the refuse of American industry. Antiracists are increasingly confronting individual racism based on ignorance, but they are also taking on institutions and industries that persist in traditionally accepted practices that are no longer appropriate.

HISTORICAL RACISM

Racism was common in the settlement of the New World. It included massacre, relocation through forced march, Indian wars, starvation, and disease. In the twentieth century, these exploits would fall under the rubric of genocide or ethnic cleansing. During the colonial era, these practices were legal under laws of discovery or conquest, or the empty land doctrine. A papal bull in the fifteenth century justified war against non-Christians everywhere and called for conquest, colonization, and exploitation. Another established Christian domination over the new world and called for subjugation of natives and native territories, with shared responsibility between Spain and Portugal. The Treaty of Tordesillas adjusted the lines, and Brazil became Portuguese. The bulls remain in effect despite requests from indigenous peoples that the Vatican revoke them. Evolved into the law of nations and then international law, the doctrines of discovery are the basis for Christian claims to terra nullus, or heathen and pagan lands. Those who lived there, the Native Americans, became wards of the state or dependent nations. The government had the power to revoke their status at any time. Many contemporary Native Americans contend that this is discriminatory because native land title, claim to ownership, is not equal to ordinary title. Native American claims to their land are inferior legally because of a racist doctrine dating back 500 years.

From shortly after first contact until late in the nineteenth century, the white approach to dealing with Indians was to destroy them, either physically or culturally. The assumption was that Native Americans were inferior and had nothing to contribute. Eventually, superior numbers and firepower prevailed, and the surviving Indians were institutionalized, isolated, and marginalized. The intent was to make them white, assimilate, and slowly disappear as a distinct culture. The United States broke up communal holdings under the Dawes Severalty Act and removed young Native Americans to residential schools to erase language, religion, and culture through ridicule and coercion, banning native language speaking, clothing and hairstyles, and customs. Violation earned harsh punishment. Some schools attempted to block contact with family. Some told potential runaways that their parents were dead or their homes destroyed. Physical and sexual abuse were extensive in the isolated boarding schools. Indian boarding schools remained in use well into the late twentieth century.

STEREOTYPES AND SLURS

Longstanding negative stereotypes include those related to the redskin and squaw. These expressions of hate and inequality are justifications for keeping Indians out of workplaces, out of neighborhoods, out of good schools, on reservations, and in urban ghettos. Symbols send powerful messages. Mascots such as Chief Wahoo are as detrimental to Indians as are cigar store Indians, Tonto, the make-believe Indians in Thanksgiving pageants and parades, and all those savages in innumerable western movies. Defenders contend that mascots are a way of indicating respect and admiration. Native Americans do not see it that way; in fact, they do not see themselves in any of these images at all. Racial stereotyping is inappropriate in a country that prides itself on its inclusiveness, and cartoonish figures are an insult to Native Americans as well as all other Americans. Dignity and equality go by the wayside when the mascots of Cleveland, Atlanta, Washington, and other sports teams caricature Native Americans, thus insulting Native American cultures. Despite the increasing multiculturalism of American society, racist stereotypes remind us that the American people are far from understanding or accepting the legitimacy of racial and ethnic difference. The committee for Native American rights of the American Indian Movement (AIM) and other organizations have for years sought to eliminate the offensive mascots. In the late 1990s, protesters burned Chief Wahoo in effigy. When asked to meet with representatives of native organizations, owners of the offending teams responded with press releases, sensitivity sessions, and business as usual. In 2000, Cleveland area Native American groups joined in protest of Chief Wahoo. The group resolution against Chief Wahoo denounced any team or organization's use of "offensive racist logos" because they demean and diminish by portraying Native Americans as less than human. These images hamper development of self-esteem and make the struggles of young Native Americans more severe. They promote isolation and confusion that leads to dysfunctional behavior, including dropping out of school, suicide, and alcoholism.

In February 2009, the small town of Carpentiria, California, became the scene of mascot outrage. In April 2008, the school board voted to remove the offensive Warrior mascot, a stereotypical stoic Plains Indian, after an Indian student protested. A local newspaper published an ad attacking the student by name, and he and his family received death threats. Backers of the mascot ousted the school board and installed one sympathetic to their goal. Many Native American families moved away, while others kept quiet due to fear of violence against them.

Eli Cordero decided to fight, and his efforts drew support: "Individuals and organizations have formed CARE (Coalition Against Racism in Education) to support his cause. A sampling of its 27 members includes the American Civil Liberties Union of Santa Barbara, American Indian Movement West, Black

Student Union of Santa Barbara City College, El *Congreso* Students Association of UCSB, and the Fund for Santa Barbara" (Murillo, 2009).

Racism in modern America is more subtle than it was half a century ago. This is not to say that there are no longer racist assaults and insults of the blatant old style. In the 1970s, the reservations boycotted Bemidji, Minnesota, businesses after a local radio personality used a racial slur on air. Racism against Indians is more blatant in the Midwest. Native American and white justice are distinctly different, with only token investigation of crimes against Indians, including murder, and aggressive prosecution of crimes by Indians against whites. Native Americans are still routinely refused service in eating establishments and subject to racial slurs. Racism is ongoing. Native Americans are increasingly challenging these practices. In January 2001, the Bemidji McDonald's had an incident in which a Red Lake woman said a white woman hit her grandson and attacked her verbally. The woman filed a complaint with the state human rights agency alleging mishandling of the incident by McDonald's and the Bemidji Police Department, and the Red Lake Tribal Council resolved to support her, as did at least one member of the Anishinaabe coalition.

In January 2009, an Iron River, Michigan, complainant to the state civil rights agency alleged that the West Iron County Public Schools discriminated against his son, a Native American, in elementary school. The complaint alleged that a white teacher grabbed the student, something the teacher had done more than once before, without any action by the school district. The complainant noted that his son was written up for conflicts with white students, but the white students were not disciplined. It seemed the district was trying to force the student out of school. The Michigan AIM director backed the complainant, noting that the second-grade student had been beaten up and otherwise harassed by other students since kindergarten, and the administration did nothing. The complaint to the state commission came after attempts to deal with the school system were fruitless and the county prosecutor declined to press charges.

A 2002 survey of a university campus with a large Native American population revealed that racial incidents were common, with a fourth of respondents indicating they were victims of ethnoracism, usually not violent but rather slurs and insults, intimidation and slights. Perpetrators were commonly white males, but faculty accounted for 10 to 15 percent of reports. Indians were generally moved to the margins, ignored, and deprived of equal access, as in other aspects of daily life (Perry 2002).

RACIST VIOLENCE

In 2007 around Thanksgiving, three episodes of violence against Native Americans occurred around Cortez, Colorado, one by two Hispanic males, the others by white males. Racist violence and prejudice had long characterized the city of Cortez and the Four Corners area. The Southwest Intertribal Voice's (SWIV) founder declared that Montezuma County had tolerated this problem far too long. The SWIV hosted a meeting that included 45 residents and representatives from the Colorado Commission of Indian Affairs and the Denver Anti-Discrimination Office. Solutions included cultural education in the public schools, which led one participant to note that when he wanted to buy a house, he was shown an inferior dwelling; for him, cultural education in the schools was no solution. When the issue of racism was community-wide and affected broader aspects of life such as home ownership, then a school-based solution was inadequate. A Navajo noted that the previous summer, white youths beat an American Indian and in Farmington, New Mexico, a police officer killed a Native American. Local police in Cortez said their pursuit of criminals was color blind, leading a Ute woman to point out that the police did nothing when her son was beaten two years before. The police chief countered that one of the assailants was prosecuted, and he had not heard any complaints before. Another Ute noted that Indian-on-Indian discrimination was a problem, as well as Indian discrimination against Hispanics and whites.

INSTITUTIONAL RACISM

The 2.5 million Native Americans have approximately 300 reservations and 550 tribal governments. Key concerns for all are the preservation of tribal sovereignty, the right to self-governance, defining membership, and taking care of property, business, and domestic affairs. Treaty rights are key to preservation of sovereignty. The U.S. government is responsible for safeguarding Native Americans within the context of treaty obligations. It defines Native Americans as a minority, and minorities in the United States face discrimination. Before the civil rights movement, some states maintained three drinking fountains and sectioned off movie theaters: white, colored, and Indian.

South Dakota may be the worst offender. Indians there believe that both state and federal justice systems are racist, biased, and anti-Indian. Crime against Indians is more likely to go unreported or uninvestigated, as is shown by major differences in the numbers of unsolved murders and murders reported to the Federal Bureau of Investigation (FBI). The perception is that Native American victims are less likely to have vigorous prosecution of their cases than are white victims of Native American crimes.

Discrimination and racism have led to Native American economic and social disadvantage, the same as with other groups that face discrimination. They suffer poverty and unemployment at high levels, go to jail at rates out of line with their numbers, have problems with education, and are too often left behind in the struggle to realize the "American dream." To counter their despair and degradation, they attempt to retain or revive their traditions in religion, language, and customs. These rights to traditional practices are under pressure as governments deny access to holy sites and use of sacred objects, including drugs. Pressure was particularly severe in the 1990s, with federal actions restricting religious practices and access to holy sites.

During the 1950s, federal policy was to encourage assimilation by terminating Indian tribes, breaking up their reservations, and moving over 100,000 Indians to cities. Some adjusted, but many found themselves confused by the urban culture, lost without traditional structures and supports, and enduring culture shock that either caused them to return to the reservation or adapt to an urban life of poverty and discrimination. Urban poverty promotes inferior education, which is a human rights issue. The environment is apartheid, and the educational approach is old-style rote memorization, reminiscent of the nineteenth-century Indian boarding schools and alien now as then to Indian customs. The reason for this toxic situation is white racism, and the result is reinforcement of the white-minority disparity, with one group learning confidence and life skills and the other learning that it belongs at the bottom of a system beyond its competence, a system that does not value it enough to provide decent schools, teachers, or equipment. Poverty is not color blind—it affects 12.5 percent of white children but 39.8 percent of black, 32.2 percent of Hispanic, 17 percent of Asian, and 38.8 percent of Native American children. Performance, documented on standard tests, lags, and in the fourth grade 40 percent of whites can read competently, while less than 20 percent of blacks, Hispanics, and Native Americans are competent. Similar results can be seen in math (Campbell n.d.).

ENVIRONMENTAL RACISM

Another form of racism is environmental. The "nuclear sacrifice zones" of the Southwest have adversely impacted Nevadans and Utahans for decades, but it is Native Americans who take the brunt of the blow. The Goshute reservation in Utah was a target when Private Fuel Storage wanted to store 40,000 tons of commercial high-level radioactive waste next to the two dozen residents of the Skull Valley band's reservation. Both the federal government and the commercial nuclear industry have targeted Native Americans for years. The Office of the Nuclear Waste Negotiator opened in 1987 and asked every federally recognized tribe in the country to consider hosting dumps. Hundreds of thousands, sometimes millions of dollars were offered. Finally, the list narrowed to about two dozen tribal councils. Native American antidump activists fought back. The Nuclear Waste Negotiator's last target was the Mescalero Apache reservation in New Mexico, and the reservation council seemed amenable to accepting the dump site. Reservation community resistance blocked the council and negotiator from reaching a deal. The office dissolved in 1994. Commercial nuclear power interests took over but were unable to convert the Mescalero. Thus, attention turned to Skull

Valley, another site on the negotiator's list. Industry money flowed to Washington, DC, as several proposals for temporary and permanent dump sites, including Yucca Mountain, rose and fell between 1995 and 2000. The Clinton administration blocked Yucca Mountain, and the industry turned to the Skull Valley band, which had 25 members on the reservation and 100 or so in surrounding towns. The reservation is already surrounded by Magnesium Corporation's chlorine gas and hydrochloric acid clouds, Envirocare's low-level nuclear dump, Dugway Proving Grounds where nerve gas tests in 1968 killed 6,400 Skull Valley sheep, an army chemical weapons stockpile, and Hill Air Force Base. With this environment, the county has no alternative sources of jobs or money. The tribal chair answered critics that development must be consistent with what was already there. He signed a lease agreement with Private Fuel Storage (PFS), the dump management company, without consulting the tribal council. The U.S. Nuclear Regulatory Commission (NRC) ruled that the generous lease fee made the dump fair, not a violation of environmental justice. Among tribal members unhappy with the agreement, rumors swirled that the council took a payoff between $60 and 200 million. Activists fought back, citing both traditional home and spiritual values as well as the risk to tribal sovereignty if it could be sold to the highest bidder.

In March 2006, the UN Independent Committee on the Elimination of Racial Discrimination alleged that the United States had violated Indian land rights in violation of an international antiracism treaty. The violation dealt with U.S. actions on land of the Western Shoshone (Snake or Newe), particularly the effort to establish commercial mining on their land. The United States claimed ownership of 90 percent of Shoshone's 60 million acres in Nevada, Idaho, Utah, and California. The applicable treaty is the Treaty of Ruby Valley (1863), along with a 1979 Supreme Court ruling that awarded the federal government trusteeship. The federal government argued that tribal members had abandoned their traditional tenure and practices. Further, nontribal interests had encroached, so the federal government had made the land federal territory. The Western Shoshone argued to the United Nations that the gradual encroachment was due to federal policy, an attempt to steal their land—that is, racism. The UN panel investigating the Shoshone claim asked for a federal response but got none. The UN panel then ruled that the federal government and state legislature's attempt to privatize, give land to mining and energy companies, and open a nuclear waste site (Yucca Mountain), were a violation of contemporary norms, as were federal intimidation of natives through arrest, hunting and fishing restrictions, and grazing fees.

Similar findings were made by the Organization of American States' (OAS') Inter-American Commission on Human Rights in 2003. The United States countered that in 2004, the majority of the 10,000 Western Shoshone had accepted the Claims Distribution Act of 2004 that gave the Shoshone $145 million for the land. Western Shoshone dissenters claimed the deal for sale at 1872 prices was unacceptable and a violation of the treaty. Some of the most polluted areas of the United States are native lands. Waste trading efforts are ongoing, and only grassroots efforts have stalled the majority of efforts to dump waste on reservation lands in what Native Americans refer to as radioactive colonialism, development genocide, or toxic invasion. Over 100 proposals for dumps have included attempts to establish 16 nuclear waste dumps on reservations, and 77 sacred sites have been disturbed or desecrated by developers and mining. The most visible proposal was the Yucca Mountain dump. Radioactive colonialism seems viable because of the chronic problems of sovereign Indian nations whose economic infrastructure is inadequate to deal with inferior education and healthcare, high unemployment, poverty, and assorted other social problems.

Led by Johnnie Bobb, third from left, members of the Western Shoshone tribe take part in a ceremony near the gates of the Nevada Test Site, in background, and the proposed Yucca Mountain nuclear waste dump in Mercury, Nevada, on May 11, 2002. Nine runners from the tribe travelled about 250 miles from near their reservation in central Nevada to the gates of the test site where they were joined by about 100 protesters opposed to the nuclear waste facility. The Western Shoshone claim that Yucca Mountain is a sacred site. (AP Photo/Joe Cavaretta)

The Eastern Navajo blocked a proposal to mine uranium in New Mexico in 1999. Other successful defenses have occurred among the California Mohave, the Idaho Skull Valley Goshutes, and the Nevada Western Shoshone.

FIGHTING BACK

Fighting for rights and against racism involves seeking voting rights; ending use of offensive mascots; fighting police misconduct and discrimination in the justice system; gaining equal representation in the federal, state, and local law and justice systems; working for better training and participation in electoral participation; and seeking better legal resources and funding for tribal legal and law enforcement systems. Without all this, Native Americans who have been discriminated against have problems getting redress. The insufficiency of hate crime laws means that racial bigotry remains a factor in too many crimes against Indians.

The Native American Rights Fund (NARF) is a nonprofit organization that legally represents tribes, other organizations, and individuals. Aside from working to preserve sovereignty and get recognition for many tribes, the NARF works to regain religious rights, return artifacts and remains, and restore fishing, hunting, and voting rights.

Native Americans in Bemidji, Minnesota, began meeting in August 2001 as the Anishinaabe Coalition for Peace and Justice. Native Americans in the area felt discriminated against in areas related to work, housing, shopping, and dining. The discrimination was nearly invisible, not blatant, a feeling just under the surface rather than a slur or shove or other overt act, more noticeable than racism elsewhere. The coalition was a spiritually oriented group, and it was prepared to go forth with or without white support. Bemidji is surrounded by reservations: White Earth, Red Lake, and Leech Lake. This type of coalition is not new; comparable groups have come and gone over the years. The one that has persevered is the Bemidji Area Race Relations Council, which dealt with over a dozen complaints in a year. The council membership is white and Indian, and some Indians claim it is ineffective and elitist. The council counters that life for Indians is better than it was a generation before, and business leaders and officials are more culturally sensitive. At least one council member acknowledges, however, that the racism remains. The coalition wants a community-wide racism treatment program so that everybody understands the nature and causes of racism instead of just handling the symptoms as they arise. Among the problems is stereotyping of Indians as well as reflexive rather than reflective perception of the other.

Racism against Native Americans, as against other minorities, remains a problem. It promotes poverty, disease, and shortened life expectancy as it denies its victims the economic opportunity that allows them to afford adequate schools, healthcare services, and other elements of the American way of life. In their stead, racism brings alcoholism, drug abuse, depression and suicide, and other forms of societal malfunction.

REFERENCES

American Indian Movement (AIM) West. *Racism and Intimidation in Carpinteria*. Retrieved from http://www.indybay.org/newsitems/2009/02/04/18568094.php in October 2009.

Berger, Bethany. *Red: Racism and the American Indian*. UCLA Law Review 59 (2009). Retrieved from http://papers.ssrn.com/sol3/papers.cfm?abstract_id=1269527#

Bullard, Robert D. "Poverty, Pollution and Environmental Racism: Strategies for Building Healthy and Sustainable Communities." Environmental Justice Resource Center. Retrieved from http://www.ejrc.cau.edu/PovpolEj.html in October 2009.

Campbell, Duane. *Racism and the Crisis of Urban Education*. Retrieved from http://www.dsausa.org/antiracism/editorials/editorials.html in September 2009.

Chawkins, Steve. "Carpinteria Board Votes to Retain Native American Images as Part of School Regalia." *Los Angeles Times*, March 17, 2009. Retrieved from http://latimesblogs.latimes.com/lanow/2009/03/carpinteria-boa.html

Crane, John. "Indians Address Racism." *Electricbrave's Tribal Storytime*, January 13, 2007. Retrieved from http://people.tribe.net/electricbrave/blog/61ae1f0c-74f9-44b0-9be8-57abbeb6707d

Fixico, Donald Lee. *The Urban Indian Experience in America*. Albuquerque: University of New Mexico Press, 2000.

Kamps, Kevin. "High-Level Atomic Waste Dump Targeted at Skull Valley Goshute Indian Reservation in Utah." Nuclear Information Resource Service, February 15, 2001. Retrieved from http://www.nirs.org/factsheets/pfsejfactsheet.htm

Martin, Phillip W. D. "Nicknames Such as Indians, Braves Retain Limited Sentiment but Have Lots of Sting." *Boston Globe*, April 19, 1998. Retrieved from http://ishgooda.org/racial/ohwah3.htm

Murillo, Cathy. "Carpinteria School Board to Decide Mascot Issue: The War over the Warrior." *Santa Barbara Independent*, March 12, 2009. Retrieved from http://www.independent.com/news/2009/mar/12/carpinteria-school-board-decide-mascot-issue/

Perry, Barbara. "American Indian Victims of Campus Ethnoviolence." *Journal of American Indian Education* 41, no. 1 (2002). Retrieved from http://jaie.asu.edu/v41/V41I1A3.pdf

Rizvi, Haider. "U.S. Found in Violation of Native Americans' Rights, Anti-Racism Treaty." *OneWorld.net*, March 11, 2006. Retrieved from http://www.commondreams.org/headlines06/0311-07.htm

World Conference against Racism. "'Doctrines of Dispossession': Racism against Indigenous Peoples." Retrieved from http://www.un.org/WCAR/e-kit/indigenous.htm in October 2009.

Younk, Nikki. "Civil Rights Accusation Made against West Iron." *Iron Mountain Daily News*, January 31, 2009. Retrieved from http://www.ironmountaindailynews.com/page/content.detail/id/505812.html?nav=5002

Reservations and College Athletics: Identifying and Nurturing Talent

Stan C. Weeber

For years, college coaches felt little need to look to American Indian reservations as a source of college-level athletic talent. Few Native American youth appeared to be going to college and even fewer showed an interest in intercollegiate athletics. Only a handful of Native Americans became standout athletes who could serve as role models for young people. Further, the stories that coaches heard from mentors and predecessors suggested that coaches would be hard pressed to find healthy adolescents on the reservation, much less potential college athletic talent. They were told that talented Indian youth had to flee the reservation to attend high school elsewhere, and only by leaving home could they find success. So coaches' discovery of Indian talent was essentially the same as for athletes of any ethnicity—through site visits to major high schools with long track records for producing highly ranked recruits within their respective sports. Coaches did not view this narrative as prejudicial because there were sets of objective observations about reservation life that supported it.

Now that reservations are becoming better off due to the adoption of economic development strategies, the traditional narrative about the relationship between college athletics and the reservation is giving way to a newer, emerging one. This newer narrative suggests that reservations should not be overlooked as sources of college-level athletic talent. The new narrative has also poked some holes in the older stories passed down from coach-mentors, and boldly challenged the older views as being prejudicial and unduly influenced by stereotypes held by the dominant culture about American Indians. It also suggests that there were many Native American star athletes in the past that chose for a variety of reasons not to highlight or emphasize their ethnicity. Thus with the newer narrative, there is some rewriting or revisionist thinking with respect to the older narrative. The new narrative is both political and critical; the role of broader structural issues such as poverty and subsequent lack of opportunities as inhibiting factors in Native American athletic success move up to the front of the story.

THE TRADITIONAL NARRATIVE

Coaches could learn simply from a day's research in the local library that American Indians have been the nation's poorest minority group according to major socioeconomic indicators. In 1970, with unemployment among Indians six times the national average, 30 percent of the Native American population lived below the poverty line, living essentially in Third World conditions. Life expectancy was less than that of the typical American, and death rates for certain illnesses were much higher than among the whole U.S. population. Adolescent health indicators were also subpar, and as late as 2000, it was known that Native American and Alaska Native youth fared poorly on several well-being indicators. For instance, among American Indian teens, there were higher than average rates of high school dropouts (ages 16–19); higher rates of not attending school and not working (ages 16–19); and higher rates of teen deaths by accident and homicide. Indian adolescents were more likely to be living with parents without full-time, year-round employment; and they were more likely to be living in families with children headed by a single parent. These kinds of results persisted in spite of the introduction of gaming on Indian reservations along with other kinds of economic development that were designed to lift residents out of poverty and out of the kinds of health and well-being problems that have been documented. Further studies have shown that American Indian and Alaska Native adolescents reported high rates of sexual abuse as well as high rates of psychiatric disorders. Risk taking and health compromising behaviors were overrepresented among young Native Americans, and suicide was the second leading cause of death. Compared with non-Indian young people, Indian youth reported high rates of drug use. Coaches inferred from the totality of this information that youth on reservations, and Native American youth in general, would not produce a rich pool of potential college talent.

These objective observations of poor health among Native American youth unfortunately fed into stereotypes that non-Indians held about Native Americans, and coaches were no different than other educators who may have been susceptible to these kinds of thought processes. Over the years, Native Americans have been regarded as shiftless, untrustworthy, incompetent, lazy, and poor decision makers. For coaches at colleges where character issues play a role in recruitment, these false images based on stereotypical ways of thinking were black marks against potential Native American recruits. Coaches also conceded that it might take extra work to mold a Native American recruit into a star. The effort might not pay off, as the recruit was likely to succumb to the temptations that college life provides and end up not fulfilling the requirements of the scholarship. Unlike inner-city youth looking for a way out of a troublesome life, Native American youth seem strangely attracted back to the comfort zone of the reservation, dysfunctional as that environment may appear to those on the outside.

Prejudicial ways of thinking about Native Americans also made their way into the English language. The lives of Indians and whites have been closely interwoven for centuries, and because of that, a certain amount of unflattering verbiage made its way into language. College coaches, being for the most part drawn from mainstream culture, were as susceptible as any privileged person might be to being swayed or affected by these harsh negative words. This kind of biased language was another source feeding false stereotypes and reinforcing coaches' belief that few, if any, Native American recruits would develop into standout college athletes. Unfortunately, buying into these stereotypical ways of thinking amounted to a form of prejudgment that directed coaches away from reservations as recruiting grounds.

Ultimately, it was the paucity of examples of successful Native American athletes who had come from reservations that was a determining factor that swayed coaches' opinions against recruiting Indians. What little Native American success they could find among college athletes tended to be by youth that fled the reservation for environments more conducive to athletics. For example, Olympic champion Billy Mills, an Ogallala Sioux, was sent away from his reservation after the death of his father. With no one to provide for his needs, Mills ended up at Haskell Institute in Lawrence, Kansas. Mills came to the attention of Kansas University coaches after he won the state two-mile cross country championship. The Indian school's proximity to the university, also located in Lawrence, was important in Mills being discovered.

Marine Lt. Billy Mills of Coffeyville, Kansas, throws his arms into the air as he hits the finish line to win a gold medal for the United States in the Olympic 10,000-meter run in Tokyo on October 14, 1964. Mills, who was considered far out of his class in the event against one of the best fields ever assembled, outsprinted world record holder Ron Clarke of Australia, to win in a time of 28 minutes, 24.4 seconds. It was the first time an American ever won this Olympic event. (AP Photo)

Ben Nighthorse Campbell endured a similarly difficult childhood, getting into trouble often and dropping out of high school after his junior year. Though not raised on a reservation, he kept in touch with relatives living there. It was during a stint with the U.S. Air Force that he finally gained a solid sense of structure in his life. He continued to work on the sport of judo, which had been taught him by Japanese youth he met while picking fruit in Sacramento County, California. In the Air Force, he completed his GED and then used his GI bill to enter San Jose State University, where he was an All-American in judo.

Jim Thorpe developed his athletic skills away from the reservation as well. Like Billy Mills, Thorpe attended Haskell Institute in Lawrence, Kansas. Thorpe schooled there for three years, leaving in the summer of 1901. In 1904, Thorpe attended Carlisle Indian Industrial School, the first off-reservation school for American Indians to be established in the United States. He was selected as a third-team All American in football in 1908 and first team in 1911 and 1912 as a halfback. It was widely acknowledged that the Carlisle team would have been greatly limited and less successful had it not been for Thorpe. An Olympic champion in the decathlon and pentathlon, Thorpe's prowess was such that some of his relatives believed he was the reincarnation of the great Chief Black Hawk. Today, some view him as the world's greatest athlete of the twentieth century.

THE NEWER NARRATIVE

The older narrative was controlled by the dominant culture's definition of success as participation in Division I college athletics together with a very high level of accomplishment in postcollegiate sports such as the Olympics. Such success was personified by people such as Jim Thorpe who had earned iconic or near iconic reputations in their sport of choice. The older narrative, furthermore, was controlled by mostly white newspaper and book editors who set the bar high when it came to success—almost too high for Native American athletes to realistically achieve. The older narrative additionally failed to consider that Native Americans' inability to live up to the white's definition of excellence was linked to sociocultural and political factors that inhibited the progression of Native American athletes to Division I athletics.

First of all, white editors failed to note that American Indian high school teams and individual participants repeatedly won state championships and excelled in sports such as basketball, lacrosse, cross country and hockey. It could be that because some of these are perceived to be "minor" sports, they did not resonate with editors as being accomplishments worthy of note. Also, news from such isolated places as reservations may not help sell newspapers in urban areas. Finally, editors might have noticed that Native Americans adapted some of the games played by the dominant culture according to their own indigenous cultural traditions, which meant that their sports were not real sports but "Indian games," at least in the mind of the editors.

Second, editors might have sensed a measure of cultural resistance or pushback in some tribes toward the whole idea of high school athletes reaching out for athletic excellence at the next level. To do so, the youngsters would have to separate themselves from the wishes of community elders who were advising them not to stand out from the communal culture of the reservation. A college education often meant adopting Western ways of knowing, which in many ways conflicted with Indian ways of knowing and with Indian notions of spirituality. The community pressure, then, was not to go to college or to achieve success in athletics. Thus, young people who entered college with scholarships were known to sabotage their educational or athletic careers by flunking out of school and running back to the friendly confines of the reservation.

The new narrative that emerged in the 1990s was fully cognizant of broader structural factors that made it difficult for the economic development of tribes to go forward, and along with that, some cultural space for youngsters to pursue athletic visions if they wished. By 1975, there was some recognition that the marginalization and isolation of the reservations had created more social and economic problems than it solved, and that a certain amount of self-determinate power needed to be restored to reservations. The Indian Self-Determination and Education Assistance Act of 1975 was passed by Congress with the intention of fostering Indian self-reliance, and it was hoped that this new law would reverse forever some of the deleterious effects of prior legislation such as the General Allotment Act and the Indian Reorganization Act. Still, even after 1975, tribes faced external and internal barriers to economic development. They had limited access to land resources, including those theoretically owned by tribes. To gain control over these resources, tribes often had to go to court to fight for their rights. State governments interfered also, claiming that casinos on sovereign Indian land led to underpayment of taxes and as a result hurt the interests of the states where they were located. Internally, tribes had to find the proper political mechanisms to enable and use whatever rights and privileges they did have access to. In particular, tribes had to have a leadership style that fit their cultural traditions as well as economic goals.

In the 1970s, tribes turned to gaming as the potential new single source that would clothe and feed the Indian people. Though it fell well short of that lofty goal, gaming is believed to be the most successful economic venture ever to occur consistently across a wide range of American Indian reservations. For example, gaming monies helped ease poverty on Indian reservations in the years from 1990 to 2000. Per capita income rose, and good paying jobs were created. Gaming revenues built critical infrastructure, and they had a lasting impact on education. Among Indians, there was an 80 percent increase in postsecondary school enrollment during the years from 1984 to 2004. Some tribes built colleges—there are currently at least 39 tribal colleges nationwide—and funded education trust funds and scholarships.

With self-determinate power came a measure of freedom for tribes to develop their own information sources related to a range of issues, including sports. Additionally, a new generation of journalists sensitive to the discrimination and structural barriers faced by Native Americans were more likely to be amenable to a definition of success less stringent than was evident under the older narrative. For example, such journalists were more likely to find instances from the past where much prowess was shown but the accomplishments were painfully obscure. The newer narrative recognized American Indian athletic success by less than iconic stars, including some lesser stories previously ignored, such as Franklin P. Mount Pleasant, a football player and track and field athlete. He was at the school where Jim Thorpe starred, but because his record was less prominent than Thorpe's, it sailed underneath the radar of many sports historians. Mount Pleasant played football at Carlisle and later became an Olympian like Thorpe. While still in college, Mount Pleasant tried out for the Olympics and became the first Carlisle student ever to qualify. At the 1908 Olympics in London, Mount Pleasant finished sixth in both the long jump and the triple jump. After returning home from the Olympics, Mount Pleasant was the first Native American to graduate from Dickinson College. After that, Mount Pleasant went on to be a respected coach at Indiana Normal School.

One of the oldest stories recognized under the new narrative is that of Louis Sockalexis, who began playing baseball at Holy Cross College in 1895. Transferring to Notre Dame to finish his college career, he then signed with the Cleveland Spiders, where he made his major league debut in 1897. Sockalexis was not the first Native American to play in the majors, but he was among the first to feel the sting of prejudice from fans. Opposing fans wore Indian headdresses and started screaming whenever Sockalexis came to the plate. On July 4 of his rookie year, he was hitting .335 but unfortunately was injured that day in an off-field incident. In the following days, his fielding deteriorated and he spent most of the rest of 1897 riding the bench. Over the next two seasons, he played in only 28 games and left the majors for good at the end of his third season.

Another early Indian athletic story is that of Charles Albert Bender, born a Chippewa in 1884 in Crow Wing County, Minnesota. Sent at age eight to a mission boarding school near Philadelphia, he did not see his family again for five years. Upon his return to the reservation, he was disappointed in how conditions there had deteriorated, and he ran away to Carlisle Indian School. From 1898 to 1901, he played football and baseball at Carlisle and then enrolled at Dickinson College. Bender needed money to pay for his college tuition, so he played semiprofessional baseball and was known to baseball crowds as Charles Albert. Albert eventually signed with the Philadelphia Athletics in 1903 and ended up winning

212 major league games, including six World Series games in a career that spanned from 1903 to 1925. In baseball's record books, he is known as Chief Bender, though he signed his autographs Charles. Bender was elected to the Baseball Hall of Fame in 1953.

Yet another Indian whose accomplishments remained unrecognized for many years was Robert Gawboy. Born a Chippewa in the summer of 1932 on the Vermillion Lake Indian Reservation in Minnesota, he became such a talented swimmer that he entered Purdue University hoping to swim competitively and earn a degree. Gawboy placed first in the 150-yard individual medley at the 1950 collegiate East-West Meet; he was second in the 150-yard individual medley at the 1952 National Collegiate Athletic Association (NCAA) Championships; and he was the gold medalist in the 220-yard breaststroke at the 1955 Indoor National Amateur Athletic Union (AAU) Aquatic Meet, setting a new world record of 2:38.0

More recently, there has been a continuation of the tradition of excellence in baseball. Joba Chamberlain (University of Nebraska and New York Yankees) and Jacoby Ellsbury (Oregon State University and Boston Red Sox) have been two of the most talented players in the game. Jayhawk Owens (Middle Tennessee State University) was one of the original players on the Colorado Rockies roster when the team began major league play in 1993. In other sports, Native American stars have burst on to the scene such as Notah Begay (Stanford University) on the Professional Golf Association (PGA) tour and Tahnee Robinson (University of Nevada), drafted by the Women's National Basketball Association (WNBA) Connecticut Sun. The newer narrative also continues to identify players from the past who due to the anticipation of discrimination chose not to highlight their ethnicity during their playing days. Thornton Lee (California Polytechnic–San Luis Obispo and Cleveland Indians) and Bob Harrison (University of Michigan and Minneapolis Lakers) serve as examples.

For Native American high school athletes today, there are more venues that provide opportunities to be seen by college coaches than was the case in the past. The Jim Thorpe Classic, for example, is an all-star game that brings talented Native American football players together for friendship, competition, and opportunities to be interviewed by college scouts.

Still, some major problems remain in the relationship between collegiate sports and reservations. According to Sports Illustrated reporter Selena Roberts, only 310 American Indians were among the 70,856 college athletes in Division I who received athletic aid in the 1998 to 1999 school year. As of 2000, American Indians made up 1 percent of the country's population, but they accounted for only 0.4 percent of the scholarship athletes at the major college level. Recent numbers are equally discouraging: during the 2010 to 2011 season, only 126 American Indian men and women played college basketball out of 33,208 total basketball players at NCAA institutions. Thus, it appears that high school standouts continue to have trouble coming to the attention of college coaches. For instance, on the Navajo reservation in Arizona, the boys and girls basketball teams from Tuba City were among the state's elite teams in Class AAA from 2002 to 2003. However, the boys basketball coach from Tuba City was never contacted by a Division I or Division II coach during that stretch, despite Northern Arizona University being located close by. In spite of a number of promising native teams in New Mexico, former University of New Mexico basketball coach Fran Fraschilla confessed that he never made a recruiting trip to any of the reservations. Moreover, few head coaches in Division I sports have much knowledge of reservations. Northern Arizona University football coach Jerome Souers is believed to be the only American Indian head coach in Division I college football.

Sports law specialist Jeff Miller suggests that facilitating the movement of skilled athletes from the reservations to colleges and beyond will require a major commitment by a broad coalition of tribal and nontribal leaders. They must be thoroughly dedicated to ensuring that athletic visions of individual athletes come to fruition. Gaming monies could assist in this process. It is estimated that if even a small proportion of the billions reaped by Indian gaming could be earmarked to support Native American sports programs, it would be a meaningful start in enabling non-Indian and Native American athletes to compete equally. As a corollary move, the development of information technology infrastructures on reservations that would allow student athletes to market themselves directly to college coaches via Twitter, Facebook, MySpace, and other web 2.0 tools could also assist in leveling the playing field for the Native American athlete.

REFERENCES

Blum, Robert, Brian Harmon, Linda Harris, Lois Bergeisen, and Michael Resnick. "American Indian–Alaska Native Youth Health." *Journal of the American Medical Association* 267 (1992): 1637–1644.

Goodluck, Charlotte and Angela Willeto. *Native American Kids 2001: Indian Children's Well Being Indicators Data Book.* Portland, OR: National Indian Child Welfare Association, 2001.

Hendrickson, Brian. "Dream Catcher: Tribal Colleges Plant Seed of Hope Through a Game Woven Into the Culture of American Indians." NCAA.org. Available online: http://www.ncaa.org/wps/wcm/connect/public/NCAA/Champion+Features/dream+catcher (accessed September 14, 2012).

Miller, Jeff. "Native American Athletes: Why Gambling on the Future Is a Sure Bet." *Virginia Sports and Entertainment Law Journal* 4 (2005): 239–265.

Oliphant, Emmerentie and Sharon B. Templeman. "If We Show Them Will They Come? Attitudes of Native American Youth Towards Higher Education." *First Peoples Child and Family Review* 4 (2009): 99–105.

Roberts, Selena. "In the Shadows: A Special Report: Off-Field Hurdles Stymie Indian Athletes." *New York Times*, June 17, 2001, p. 1.

STATE RECOGNITION

Lindsey Hanson

Certain American Indian tribes are recognized by the federal government, some by state governments, and some by neither. When a tribe is "recognized," the government recognizing the tribe agrees that it exists and that there is a government-to-government relationship between the tribe and the recognizing government. The legal rights of an American Indian tribe are impacted by whether they are recognized and whether it is the federal government or a state government that recognizes that tribe. Federal recognition can be achieved in three ways, which will be discussed later in this essay. State recognition procedures vary by state. State recognition is usually conferred by a state agency or the state legislature but can also be conferred by an act of the state executive branch. Not every state recognizes tribes at the state level. In fact, fewer than half of the states have any state-recognized tribes. For states that do recognize tribes, the rights of those tribes vary from state to state. Like federal recognition, state recognition of tribes is controversial, with some supporting it and others not.

To understand what it means to be a state-recognized tribe, it is necessary to have some background understanding of what it means to be a federally recognized tribe, and where the legal basis for both federal and state tribal relations comes from. With this background in mind, it will be possible to undertake an overview of state processes for recognition of tribes. It will also be possible to understand the controversy over whether states should recognize tribes or whether recognition should be left to the federal government alone.

BACKGROUND: WHAT IT MEANS TO BE A FEDERALLY RECOGNIZED TRIBE

When the federal government recognizes a tribe, it acknowledges that the tribe is a sovereign nation and finds that the tribe existed, or is a successor of a tribe that existed, at the time of original contact between settlers and tribes. Federally recognized tribes have certain rights to govern themselves and also rights to particular federal protections, services, and benefits. Many of these tribes have their own tribal councils, constitutions, and court systems.

The process to gain federal recognition is a difficult one that can be accomplished in one of three ways. A tribe can go through a complex and lengthy administrative process with the Bureau of Indian Affairs (BIA) in which it produces genealogical records that evidence its continuous existence since the time of first contact between settlers and American Indian tribes. This process can take decades and hundreds of thousands of dollars to complete. Tribes can also gain federal recognition through an act of Congress, although this can often be difficult due to the politics involved with Indian gaming.

Finally, tribes can gain federal recognition through the court system. If a tribe seeks court recognition under BIA regulations, the BIA first gets an opportunity to make an administrative decision as to whether the tribe qualifies for federal recognition before the court reviews that decision. When the court reviews that decision, great deference will be given to the BIA's administrative decision. Tribes can also gain federal common law recognition through the court system. This type of federal recognition is easier to achieve, but it conveys only limited benefits, mostly involving federal court jurisdiction. Given that the process to receive full statutory federal recognition is so lengthy and complex, it is not surprising that some tribes that seek federal recognition do not succeed in gaining that recognition despite decades of efforts. In fact, some tribes that are recognized by their respective state governments have made unsuccessful bids for federal recognition.

Some of these tribes simply lack the genealogical records necessary to prove their continuous existence since colonial times. In Virginia, for example, these records were destroyed pursuant to the State's Racial Integrity Act of 1924, which changed birth records for Native Americans to state that they were simply "colored" rather than American Indian. As of October 2010, Virginia had no federally recognized tribes, despite evidence of a historical American Indian presence in the area. The process for gaining federal recognition is long and arduous. Every year, only one or two tribes are added to the list of tribes seeking federal recognition, and that list contains over 100 tribes attempting to make their way to the next step in the process of gaining federal recognition.

OVERVIEW: WHAT IT MEANS TO BE A STATE-RECOGNIZED TRIBE

As of 2008, there were only 62 state-recognized tribes. Most of these tribes are concentrated on the East Coast. State recognition confers different benefits depending on the state doing the recognizing. Twenty-one states have some plan for providing tribes with state recognition. Those states include: Alabama, California, Connecticut, Delaware, Georgia, Hawaii, Louisiana, Massachusetts, Montana, New Jersey, New York, North Carolina, Ohio, South Carolina, Vermont, and Virginia. Kansas, Kentucky, Michigan, Missouri and Oklahoma are also included on that list, although as of 2008 they did not actually provide state recognition to any tribe. State recognition in states such as Connecticut, New York, and Virginia stems from the period of colonization and actually predates the U.S. federal government.

Twelve of these 16 states have recognized at least one tribe via passage of a state law. Delaware was the first to do so, in 1881, and Vermont was the most recent state to do so, in 2006. Six states—California, Georgia, Louisiana, New Jersey, Ohio, and Virginia—provide for state recognition based on a resolution from both houses of the state legislature. Unlike the passage of a state law, these resolutions are not signed by the governor and consequently do not hold the full force of law. Alabama, Massachusetts, and South Carolina provide administrative processes for tribes to go through to gain state recognition. Finally, Connecticut, Montana, New York, and Virginia have recognized tribes through their executive branches either by executive order, proclamation, or historical treaty. Michigan is unique in that it does not formally recognize tribes, but it does have an "eligible for state services and state funding" status that tribes can apply to obtain. Hawaii is also a unique case because there is no official state recognition, but there is a long history of state relations with tribes in that state. Tennessee, Maryland, and Florida have all considered developing a state recognition process but do not currently have such a process in place.

Today, state recognition generally confers fewer benefits than does federal recognition. The benefits created by state recognition vary depending on the law in the particular state that has recognized a tribe. State recognition also confers some limited federal benefits. For example, state recognition allows tribes to exhibit as Native American artists under the Indian Arts and Crafts Act of 1990, which is a federal act. Members of state-recognized tribes are also eligible to receive scholarships in the medical field under the Indian Health Care Act, and are eligible for community service block grants and certain other federal grants.

HISTORICAL ROLE OF THE FEDERAL GOVERNMENT AND STATES IN UNITED STATES–AMERICAN INDIAN RELATIONS

With the advent of the federal government and the ratification of the U.S. Constitution, the establishment of relationships with tribes came to be recognized as being largely within the purview of the federal government rather than the states. The Commerce Clause, which grants to Congress the power "To regulate Commerce with foreign Nations, and among the several States, and with the Indian Tribes..." is often quoted in support of this notion. The Indian Nonintercourse Act of 1790 also placed substantial power to govern relations with tribes with the federal government by prohibiting states and individuals from signing land contracts with tribes without the approval of the federal government.

There were also three decisions that came down from the U.S. Supreme Court during the Marshall era (the time period between 1801 and 1835 during which John Marshall was Chief Justice) that placed the responsibility for regulation of relationships with tribes in the hands of the federal government. Those decisions included *Worcester vs. Georgia* (1832), *Cherokee Nation vs. Georgia* (1831), and *Johnson vs. M'Intosh* (1823). This set of decisions established tribes as "domestic dependent nations" subordinate to the federal government as the "discovering" nation. The Marshall court also established the doctrine of Indian title to land, that is, only the federal government, not state governments or individuals, could purchase land and resources from tribes.

While tribal-government relations have long been dominated by the federal government, the years since the civil rights movement have seen an increasing role for state governments. The legal foundation for such state interaction with tribes is found in the Tenth Amendment's reservation of powers clause, which reserves for the states those powers not delegated to the federal government. While the federal government is generally recognized as having plenary, or complete, power over relations with tribes, it has delegated some of these powers to the states. Thus, where federal law does not conflict with state law regarding tribal relations, state law is enforceable.

A SURVEY OF STATE-RECOGNIZED TRIBES AND THEIR RIGHTS

Each state that recognizes tribes confers different rights on those tribes and recognizes the tribes through a slightly different process. Alabama recognizes nine tribes. All nine were originally recognized in the 1970s through passage of a state law. Today, the Alabama Indian Affairs Commission is responsible for carrying out state relations with these tribes and for administering a process through which new tribes can be recognized within the state. Tribes must show a membership of at least 500, show a shared tribal ancestry going back 200 years, provide a document containing a statement of tribal history, and swear that none of the petitioning members already belong to a tribe recognized by a state or the federal government.

In California, two tribes have state recognition. Both tribes were recognized in the 1990s through a legislative resolution. The state does not have set criteria for recognition, but rather makes the decision on a case-by-case basis. Neither of these tribes have reservations, and relations with the tribes are carried out through legislative committees. Connecticut has provided recognition to three tribes. Each of these tribes was recognized by a state law. Two of these state-recognized tribes actually had federal recognition for a brief time period, but that recognition was later reversed. The Connecticut Office of American Indian Affairs, within the Environmental Protection Department, carries out the state's relations with the tribes. Connecticut state law requires the governor to enter into agreements with tribes defining the powers and duties of the tribes. Tribes recognized by the state have the right to determine who lives on reservation land and the right to lease reservation land. The law also provides for a housing authority for each tribe if requested by the tribal council, although laws that apply to a state housing authority also apply to these tribal housing authorities.

Georgia, which contains no federally recognized tribes, recognizes four tribes. Recognition was accomplished through passage of a state law. However, Georgia law does not provide statutory criteria for recognition; rather, it grants recognition powers to the legislature so that future recognition may come through resolutions of that body. State recognition in Georgia does not convey substantial benefits on tribes. Most of the benefits of recognition deal with Indian burial grounds. Louisiana, which contains no reservations, recognizes nine tribes. Recognition was completed through resolutions of the legislature. The State Office of Indian Affairs carries out relations. State recognition in Louisiana does not convey upon tribes any state benefits.

Ohio recognizes one tribe and did so through legislative resolution. Delaware recognizes only one tribe, and did so through passage of a state law in 1881. Massachusetts recognizes six tribes. The Commonwealth of Massachusetts Commission on Indian Affairs is responsible for carrying out state-tribal relations and for creating criteria through which state recognition can be administratively conferred. Montana recognizes one tribe which was accomplished through both state court decisions and executive branch declarations. Legislation in the state has since confirmed the recognition. New Jersey, which provides recognition through state law and has provided recognition through legislative resolutions, recognizes three tribes. As of 2002, any future recognition will have to be established through passage of a state law. The New Jersey Department of State Commission on Native American Affairs handles state-tribal relations. New York recognizes two state tribes. The tribes were originally recognized through the passage of state laws, but legislative resolutions have since further defined the relationships between the tribes and the state. New York's recognition of these tribes is based on the historical relationship between the state and these tribes, and New York does not have a process in place to allow for the recognition of additional tribes. The New York State Office of Children and Family Services' Native American Services carries out tribal-state relations.

North Carolina recognizes seven tribes, and did so through the passage of state laws. Criteria for recognition is established by North Carolina's Department of Administration's Commission on Indian Affairs. To be recognized, tribes must be able to trace their tribal ancestry back prior to 1790. The tribe must also be able to do at least five of the following: show continuity in their ancestry; list family names among the petitioning members that are commonly identified as traditional North Carolina American Indian names; detail any kin relation to any other recognized tribes; submit documentation of any prior relationship between the tribe and the state or federal government; provide any documents identifying the group as American Indian; document any past or current relationship with another recognized tribe; submit any documented traditions, customs, or legends; or signify the tribe's American Indian heritage and grant participation in programs designed for American Indians. North Carolina also recognizes and provides certain benefits for urban Indians.

South Carolina has recognized five tribes, two Indian groups, and one state Indian organization. The state has shifted from a state law recognition process to an administrative process. The State Commission for Minority Affairs is the agency responsible for tribal recognition. Tribes seeking state recognition must show that they are indigenous to the state, that they have been in the state for the past 100 years, and that they are organized for the purpose of preserving native culture and meeting certain needs of American Indian people. Claims for recognition must be supported by official records, documentation of kinship with other recognized tribes, and customs and traditions. The tribe must also show at least 100 living descendants who can trace their ancestry linearly, meaning that all 100 must be direct descendants of an individual considered the "founder" of the line. Indian groups must establish the same criteria, except they are not required to show documentation of customs and traditions. To be recognized as an Indian organization, a group must show a 100-year presence, that it is indigenous to the state, and that it is organized for the purpose of preserving culture and meeting the needs of American Indian peoples. Tribes in South Carolina are still subject to civil, criminal, and regulatory control by the state, and cannot engage in Indian gaming.

Vermont recognizes certain tribes within the Abenaki people group, which is composed of numerous tribes. The law, however, confers no additional rights on the Abenaki. The Vermont Commission on Native American Affairs carries out the state's relations with the Abenaki. Virginia recognizes eight tribes and has done so through executive and legislative processes, as well as through state law. Currently, the state has a detailed process through which tribes can apply to be recognized through the passage of a state law. The Virginia Council on Indians carries out state-tribal relations and establishes criteria for recognition. Currently, that criteria includes showing Indian identity over time, showing descent from an historical Indian tribe within Virginia at the time of colonization, and continued existence within the state. Tribes must also provide a genealogy of current members, show that the group has been "socially distinct" from other cultural groups since at least the twentieth century, and show evidence of a current formal organization.

THE CONTROVERSY OVER STATE RECOGNITION OF TRIBES

Not everyone believes that states should provide recognition for tribes. While some are against state recognition because of the federal government's exclusive plenary power over relations with tribes, as previously discussed, controversy may also derive from Indian gaming as well as from allegations that the recognition of false tribes distorts American Indian culture and identity.

The Cherokee nation is one group that believes recognition should come from the federal government only. While the Cherokee nation emphasizes the plenary power of the federal government to regulate relations with tribes, it also argues that since many state regulations for recognition are less stringent than federal standards, fraudulent groups are gaining recognition. The Cherokee nation goes so far as to allege that some of these groups have been created with a criminal purpose in mind. It argues that false tribes are distorting Indian history and identity, and diverting resources from legitimate tribes. The Cherokee nation identifies legitimate tribes as those with a continuous history as a government and alleges that most legitimate tribes have treaties with the U.S. government. It argues that at least 22 agencies at both the federal and state levels provide services or other benefits to tribes that do not have federal recognition. By Cherokee nation calculations, at least 6 million dollars in grants were given to these tribes over a five-year period. The Cherokee nation also alleges that false tribes seeking these benefits infringe upon the names and trademarks of legitimate tribes, allow false tribes to gain profits by selling arts and crafts falsely marketed as Native American, and also engage in illegal activity that reflects poorly on legitimate tribes.

Conversely, others believe that federally recognized tribes are opposed to state recognition for other tribes due to possible competition in the area of Indian gaming, not from any real belief that the tribes are illegitimate. Supporters of this viewpoint point out the highly complex and congested federal system for recognition and the need for another form of recognition. They also argue that tribes were applying for state recognition well before the advent of Indian gaming, so Indian gaming is not the real motivation for an application for state recognition.

Despite this controversy, it is likely safe to say that state recognition of tribes and the debate over what benefits state recognition should confer will continue as long as the process for federal recognition remains complicated, financially burdensome, and time-consuming. The future will tell whether more states will engage in state recognition, or whether states will shy away from engaging in a process that, historically at least, was primarily carried out by the federal government.

REFERENCES

Cherokee Nation. *Sovereignty at Risk: Identity Theft, Revisionism, and the Creation of False Tribes*. Retrieved from http://tribalrecognition.cherokee.org/taskforce.cherokee.org/SovereigntyatRisk/tabid/123/Default.aspx on March 27, 2011.

Cherokee Nation vs. Georgia, S. 1 (1831).

Johnson vs. M'Intosh, 21 U.S. 543 (1823).

Koenig, Alexa and Jonathan Stein. *Federalism and the State Recognition of Native American Tribes: A Survey of State-Recognized Tribes and State Recognition Processes across the United States. University of Santa Clara Law Review* 48 (2007). Retrieved from http://works.bepress.com/alexa_koenig/2/ on March 27, 2011.

Native American Rights Fund. *Resources by Topic: Federal Recognition and State Recognition*. Retrieved from http://www.narf.org/nill/resources/recog.htm on March 27, 2010.

Virginia Council of Indians. *State Recognition of Indian Tribes*. Retrieved from http://indians.vipnet.org/stateRecognition.cfm on March 27, 2011.

Worcester vs. Georgia, 31 U.S. 515 (1832).

SECTION 7
Law, Politics, and Conflict

American Indians and the Military

Robert E. Sanderson

Native America has always responded to the call of its country, and countless American Indian men and women have served in America's armed forces. The warrior tradition is strong and an honored custom among many tribes today. In fact, whenever there is a conflict involving U.S. combat units, you will find an American Indian serving his or her country, tribe, and community with the same dedication and commitment as his or her forebears who fought and bled to protect the land of their birth. Although the United States is ethnically diverse and its indigenous population represents one of the lowest in actual numbers, the percentage of American Indian participation in military service is higher than any other ethnic group in the country. And although seldom recognized and often overlooked, American Indians have distinguished themselves on the battlefield and have significantly contributed to America's military successes.

AMERICAN REVOLUTIONARY WAR (1775–1783)

Most historians concede that America's struggle for independence from Great Britain was a complex venture that included the involvement of Native American tribes. Many tribal communities east of the Mississippi River were divided in their support of and participation in the revolutionary struggle of the emerging United States, but they could not escape the impact of the war and its effects on tribal life. Although a few tribal people served with the Americans, most enlisted to fight for the British since native lands were increasingly being threatened by expanding American settlement. The Iroquois Confederacy had the largest representation of Native American groups that fought for the British (Boatner 1966). The Seneca supported the British perhaps more than any other tribe in the Northeast. Even so, not all members of the Confederacy joined the British, and some suggest that this contributed to the political weakening of the Iroquois Confederacy, already in disintegration years before the Revolutionary War (Merrell 1991).

The Americans and the British continuously sought support from Native American tribes throughout the American Revolution. In fact, tribes along the Canadian border and west of the Appalachian Mountains were part of the "Indian War." Both Great Britain and America were seeking Indians to side with their cause or at least stay neutral. And often there was a shifting of loyalties because Indians had their own interests at stake and really never wanted either of these two groups on their land. The warfare was brutal and fought in the fields, villages, and homes of both the American frontier people and Native Americans, especially in New York. The Seneca were the most tragic recipients of American wrath and savagery. During the summer of 1779, the Sullivan Expedition conducted a retaliatory "scorched earth" campaign against the Seneca and other British-supporting Iroquois that resulted in the attack on 40 Iroquois villages in upstate New York. Every Indian man, woman, and child was a potential casualty of the expedition. The attacks resulted in an intolerable winter for the Iroquois and renewed attacks on Americans in the following spring. One thing became obvious to the Americans during the Revolutionary war: Indians were a formidable opponent (Spicer 1969).

George Washington once commented about his Indian troops, "I think they [Indians] can be made of excellent use, as scouts and light troops" (Meadows 2003, 12). Their courage, determination, and fighting ferocity were impressive, and it was not long before the new republic of the United States was engaging its indigenous citizens in other wars and contests requiring military intervention, only this time they were fighting as American armed forces.

WAR OF 1812

One of the most successful Native American leaders to emerge during this period was Tecumseh, the Shawnee most credited with attempting to rally disparate Native American tribes in a mutual defense of their lands. Tecumseh and his brother Tenskwatawa, also known as The Prophet, were adamant in their rejection of the ways of the whites and losing any more lands to the United States. Tecumseh did not confront the United States with military action directly; rather, he worked diligently to confront other tribes who were selling off lands that he believed were under the common ownership of all Indian tribes and not for sale. He was successful in rallying some support, and in the South the Creek became allies, their struggle culminating in the Creek war. While Tecumseh was in the South, Governor of the Indiana Territory, William Henry Harrison moved against Tenskwatawa outside of Prophet's Town (Greenville) and engaged in the Battle of

Tippecanoe. The Americans were victorious and burnt the town to the ground. When Tecumseh returned to Greenville, he was ready for war. In the War of 1812, Tecumseh sided with the British and fought as its ally against the United States until his death in 1813 (Spicer 1969).

Today in Canada, he is revered as a national hero and a brilliant war chief. Many Canadians believe he is responsible for halting the U.S. invasion of their country, although tragically, he could not save his own people. He has earned a place on the list The Greatest Canadians, which commemorates the accomplishments of Canada's most revered citizens. "A more ... gallant Warrior does not, I believe, exist," proclaimed Major-General Sir Isaac Brock (Tupper 1847, 253).

THE AMERICAN CIVIL WAR (1861–1865)

The Civil War saw for the first time the active participation of Native Americans in uniformed combat on the field of battle. During the Civil War, Native Americans fought for both the Union and Confederate Armies. Both sides had some special Indian units, but many served in regular army units.

Choosing sides in Indian country was determined in much the same way as it was in other states, by location. For the most part, though, Indian tribes preferred to remain neutral. The general consensus was that this was a "white man's war" (Debo 1970, 168).

But the white man's war was certain to involve the Civilized Tribes because while few Indian leaders were slave owners, many were steadfast Southerners. Although some members of the Five Civilized Tribes lent their support to the Confederacy, tribal affiliation alone was not a clear determinant of allegiance. Often, tribes were sharply divided in their support and choice of alliance. For example, the Cherokee had their own civil discontent going back to the removal period and the divisions created by the actions of John Ridge and his Treaty Party against the majority of Cherokee who denounced the signing of the Treaty of New Echota. The principle opponent of the Ridge party and legitimate leader of the Cherokee, Chief John Ross, was a leader in the struggle to convince other tribes to remain neutral in the whites' civil war. On the other hand, Stand Watie became a brigadier general of the Confederate States of America and led Cherokee and other Indian troops in the fray. The Confederacy also recruited Creek, Choctaw, Chickasaw, and Seminole, who formed smaller units that were attached to other regiments (Debo 1970).

Two other notable Indian leaders who served with some distinction in the Union Army were Seneca Indians Isaac Newton and Ely Parker. A sachem of the Seneca nation, adjutant to Ulysses S. Grant during the Civil War, and a political and cultural intermediary, Ely Samuel Parker was a pivotal figure in the Seneca nation during the second quarter of the nineteenth century. "In 1857, Parker was hired to assist in the construction of the new custom house in Galena, Ill., where he befriended a relatively obscure army officer, Ulysses S. Grant. The Grant connection would serve Parker well. Although Parker's attempts to join the army at the outbreak of the Civil War were repeatedly rebuffed, first because of his engineering obligations and later because he was an Indian, he finally succeeded in securing a commission as Captain of Engineers in 1863. By the end of that year, he was assigned to duty on Grant's staff. Following Grant from Chattanooga to Virginia, Parker was given the honor at Appomattox of writing down the terms of surrender for the Army of Northern Virginia, and was brevetted Brigadier General for his services in 1865" (*Ely Samuel Parker Papers*, 2006).

WORLD WAR I (1917–1918)

It was of some consequence that American Indians were not citizens of the United States during the Great War (World War I), but they served along with white citizens on the battlefields of Europe without regard for their less than equal status. America was a segregated society during this period, and debate ensued over how to utilize the Indian troops: should they be placed in segregated "Indian" units or integrated into white regiments? Some segregationists proposed offering Indians a certificate of citizenry in the United States for their service in all-Indian units. Even the Board of Indian Commissioners was in favor of all-Indian regiments because it would reduce unemployment on reservations and equip Indians with the education and skills necessary to improve their economic lot. It was assumed that many Indians preferred to serve in all-Indian companies, although no one polled Indians about their preferences.

Integrationists proffered their reasons for mixing Indian troops with whites on the basis of the general goals of assimilation. Commissioner of Indian Affairs Cato Sells was an ardent opponent of all-Indian units throughout his tenure. The Secretary of War was opposed to segregating and creating all-Indian regiments because of his concern with military efficiency. But perhaps the most strident supporter of Indian troop integration was Richard Henry Pratt. As the founder of the Carlisle Indian School, an institution developed on a model of military discipline and organization, Pratt knew that Indians could adapt to the rigors of regimental life and perform well as soldiers. Several had served with him as scouts between 1867 and 1875, and others had become members of Indian police units during the troubling days of the Ghost Dance movement (Tate 1986, 427).

The exact number of Native Americans that served in the military in World War I is difficult to determine. However, conservative estimates put the number of Indian servicemen at around 17,000. Of course, not all American Indians who served in the military during the Great War went to France, but those that did were assigned duties in all branches of the Army. Some served as engineers, medical personnel, and military police, as well as in other military occupational specialties. Also, reputations earned from previous campaigns that American Indians had been involved in resulted in several troops being assigned scouting duties with infantry units. Many Indians sought the prestige and adventure of military aviation, as did many whites who were preferred as aviator candidates over all other ethnic groups (Camurat 1996).

Also noteworthy is the fact that American Indian women served in various noncombatant capacities during the war, with only a few enlisting as nurses. Whether serving as Red Cross volunteers, buying bonds, or enlisting in armed service auxiliary units, Indian women were enthusiastic about doing their part during World War I. However, many Indian women were poorly educated, and the training that many received at Indian boarding schools was focused on turning out domestic servants; nursing curricula and other professional educational programs were late in being included at these institutions.

Indian boarding schools were the best recruitment camps for the newly "Americanized" Native Americans. Nearly every male student attending an Indian boarding school volunteered to serve in some branch of the armed forces. Some estimates run as high as 90 percent volunteerism rates from the various boarding schools, thus indicating that a significantly high number of Indian servicemen were educated. Also, it must be remembered that boarding schools were modeled, in part, after military training academies, and the discipline and regimental structure of these schools made it easy for Indians to adapt to military life. Another consequence of boarding school education was that the curricula was geared toward instilling patriotism, good physical fitness, and some military training in students. From its inception, Superintendent Pratt ran the off-reservation boarding school at Carlisle like a military base. He favored uniformed, disciplined, and militarily fit students under his supervision, as several accounts of life at Carlisle have suggested. Hence, American Indian boarding school attendees got a head start in the process of making soldiers out of civilians. Regardless of circumstance, the Native American contribution to winning World War I was impressive.

WORLD WAR II (1941–1945)

Having proved themselves as capable soldiers, sailors, and marines in World War I, American Indians were eager to demonstrate their patriotic zeal in defending their homeland after the attack at Pearl Harbor. By this time, however, tribal people were citizens of the United States after Congress passed the Indian Citizenship Act on June 7, 1924, and issued certificates of citizenship to all Indians born within the United States. Of course, several American Indians had already become U.S. citizens as part of an agreement with the federal government that they be offered citizenship in return for having served in the armed forces during World War I (Prucha 2000). Citizenship entitled Indians to all the rights and privileges every other citizen enjoyed, including being draft eligible when the World War II broke out. Most Indian men, however, did not wait to be drafted; rather, they signed on to serve in every branch of the armed services within the first few months of the war. At the time, Commissioner of Indian Affairs John Collier believed that Indians volunteered for the armed forces in larger proportion than any other group in the country.

Some of those that were not eligible for armed service, men and women, went to work in the war production industry that quickly materialized during the early months of America's effort to mobilize for war.

When the Japanese forces struck Pearl Harbor, more than 5,000 Native Americans were already serving in the U.S. armed forces. But, according the Selective Service records in January 1942, 99 percent of all eligible Native Americans had registered for the draft. In tribal communities across the country, American Indians were preparing to go to war or help in the war effort in any way they could. And by July of 1942, the Iroquois Six Nations Confederacy enacted its own declaration of war, as they did against Germany in 1917, only this time it was against the Axis powers. In fact, the Iroquois Confederacy had never made peace with Germany after World War I, so they automatically resumed fighting their former enemy. The Navajo were so eager to go to war that many showed up at their local recruiters' offices with their own rifles, only to be told that the Army would supply them with everything they needed to go into battle. At Fort Defiance, Arizona, which was almost in the shadow of their former adversary Colonel Christopher "Kit" Carson's old headquarters, Navajo Indians stood patiently in line during winter snows to register for the draft. By the end of February 1942, approximately 8,000 Navajo were registered for selective service, a record-breaking number that was the result of an intense registration campaign conducted by the Navajo tribal council.

WORLD WAR II: CODE TALKERS

Several tribal groups were involved in intelligence and communication programs during World War II because of the uniqueness of their unwritten native languages. Because Indian languages had been used so successfully during World War I, the Army decided to continue the program. During World War II, then, the Army recruited members from the Comanche, Choctaw, Kiowa, Winnebago, Seminols, Navajo, Hopi, Cherokee, and other tribes. There was some concern, however, since both Germany and Japan had sent students to the United States prior to World War II to study Native American languages. Some felt that Indian languages would be less secure because of these students' access to the language and culture of America's indigenous tribes. Nonetheless, the Army was successfully able to use tribal code talkers for several operations, and British cryptographers had also cracked the German Enigma code, which greatly enhanced British and American intelligence operations throughout the war.

During World War II, the Marine Corps developed its own secure communications system using a special group of Navajo called the Navajo Code Talkers. They refined and expanded the Army work and perfected it into an elite security outfit. The Marines felt the Navajo language would be more secure for several reasons: the language was virtually unknown outside the Navajo nation, it was unwritten, and the complex syntax and complicated tonal qualities made it difficult to learn as an adult. The Code Talkers used a special code they themselves had created based on the unwritten Navajo language to transmit messages, making it futile for the Japanese to decipher American battle messages about the time and place of attack.

NAVAJO CODE TALKERS

American Indians served in World War II in a variety of ways, most particularly as an important means of communicating messages by code, the Navajo language, during battle. The website of the U.S. National Security Agency provides details on the Navajo Code Talkers, and the leadership of Navajo Philip Johnston, who had the idea of a military code based on the Navajo tongue. He convinced the Marine Corps to give the idea a try with an initial demonstration. Some of these details are presented here.

The Navajos involved in the demonstration had clearly shown that they could take messages from a variety of sources in English, translate and transmit them in Navajo, and then send them back in English. Due to the success of the trial run, those who had witnessed the testing initially lobbied for the recruitment and training of over 200 "Code Talkers." In the end, a total of only 30 men would be approved for the first group; however by VJ Day, over 400 Navajos would work in the program....

After their primary skills had been honed, Johnston and his compatriots began putting into place the system that would protect critical Marine battlefield communications for the duration of the war. At first glance, it would seem that the language itself would be enough to provide the required level of security. However, the Marine Corps realized they could make the system virtually unbreakable by further encoding the language through word substitution. In addition, because the Navajo language contained no words to describe the modem implements of war, the trainees took familiar words from their language and applied them to items such as tanks (turtles) and planes (birds). Finally, in order to protect the code from falling into enemy hands, the aforementioned system was committed to memory. This intense training regimen achieved the desired goal of making the code undecipherable to everyone but the Code Talkers....

During the first 48 hours on Iwo Jima, 6 Code Talkers working 24-hour shifts sent and received over 800 messages, all without error. "Were it not for the Navajos, the Marines would have never taken the island."

Source: Origins of the Navajo Code Talkers. Retrieved from http://www.nsa.gov/about/_files/cryptologic_heritage/publications/wwii/navajo_codetalkers.pdf

WOMEN IN UNIFORM

American Indian women served in noncombatant capacities during World War II just as they had in World War I. Like other American women, many native women worked in fields and factories across America to help bolster the war effort at home. War production plants hired hundreds of American Indian women to work as riveters, chemists, sheet metal workers, and machinists. They worked on farms and ranches, and in Indian forests to help provide agricultural products for the war industry and the rest of the country. But this time, many Indian women had enlisted in women's auxiliary organizations in all branches of the armed force.

As World War II drew to a close, most Native Americans were once again about to pass into obscurity on the American landscape. Some of the returning warriors, however, made that an unlikely prospect for themselves and their people. They had proven themselves on the battlefields of the Pacific and other fronts to which America sent troops, and they were not about to lose their struggles for their native rights here at home. Like their non-Indian counterparts, these veterans returned home with a new vision and an invigorated sense of purpose as Native American. And although the United States had helped to quench the fires of World War II and signed what was hoped to be a lasting peace, there were the eerie beginnings of the Cold War.

KOREAN WAR (1950–1953)

Although the Korean War, often called America's first police action, is fast becoming a footnote in history, there was a noticeable presence of American Indians serving in the armed forces during the three years of fierce fighting that ended in a stalemate. Battle-seasoned veterans, joined by new recruits seeking to carry on the warrior tradition, fought with distinction in America's first conflict of the Cold War. Known today as the Forgotten War, Korea was anything but forgotten by American Indians who served in combat. At a time when many Americans were busy trying to reap the harvest of an unparalleled period of economic growth, and the postwar baby boom was well underway, American Indians were once again struggling to survive the U.S. government's failing Indian policies that governed all aspects of native life; their participation as warriors in the Korean War was no exception. Although Indians had proven themselves worthy as sailors, soldiers, and Marines in fighting to defend America's way of life in two world wars, they were still not enjoying the rewards of their sacrifice and service, and were largely forgotten by the country they had fought and died for. There were some notable exceptions, however, of American Indians who were doing well. It was these exceptions that fueled the drafting of the termination and relocation policies of the early 1950s, policies that were clearly designed to get the remaining Indian lands and destroy Indian country once and for all. Native American Korean War veterans returned to reservations that were being terminated and the residents being "encouraged" to move to urban areas to "complete their assimilation" into American society (Fixico 1986; Momaday 1999).

VIETNAM WAR (1962–1973)

Among the annals and stories of the Vietnam War are many references to Indian country, a term given by American troops to describe the territory held by their enemy, the Viet Cong. As a term, Indian country conjures images of the unfamiliar terrain inhabited by bloodthirsty, heathen savages of American western folklore, reminiscent of the war-whooping raiders of the Great Plains tribes, circling the covered wagons and the charge of the U.S. Cavalry. Ironically, however, in Vietnam there were no Indian war parties, no attacks on covered wagons, and when the U.S. Cavalry charged into battle, it had the support of Native Americans whose ancestors were the targets of former U.S. policies in another series of conflicts known as the Indian Wars. The Vietnam War brought about some profound changes. Gone were the old myths about the revival of a pre-Columbian Native America. Gone, too, were the old myths about vanquished Indians being left to vanish on federal Indian reservations. A new portrait of Native Americans began to emerge during the Vietnam era. This new American Indian was more independent and autonomous, and possessed a greater awareness of his or her place in American history and modem society. The Vietnam War presented this emergent Native American with new opportunities.

After years of bearing the yoke of dependency, created in part by the misguided policies of a seemingly indifferent government, Native Americans began to emerge as a more visible and active U.S. minority. It was during this time, when Native Americans were facing problems related to adjusting to contemporary life, that the Vietnam War was gaining momentum. For many Native Americans, the Vietnam War presented a way out of the cycle of poverty experienced on government reservations. For others, it was a way of demonstrating patriotic pride and following the warrior's path through active military service. Regardless of individual reasons, approximately 42,000 Native Americans served in the military during the Vietnam War era.

Tales of American Indian heroism and courage in Vietnam abound. Most of them are about combat soldiers and Marines who were involved in some of the fiercest fighting of the war. Names like Khe Sanh, Tet, and Hamburger Hill have made it into popular media and have tantalized the American public with stories of intense warfare, bloodshed, and American bravery. In those and other places and events, American Indians were steeped in the daily trials of guerrilla warfare, and many were wounded and died during violent clashes with a relentless enemy.

American Indian servicemen performed valiantly in most cases, and their peers were often amazed at their dedication and perseverance under fire. Several received accolades from their comrades and citations from their superiors for their often extraordinary valor in performing their duty.

WARS OF THE MIDDLE EAST

American Indians have exhibited a continuous presence in U.S. armed forces, their record of service dating back to the founding of this nation. And although many fought against the United States during the Indian Wars, their descendants have worn the uniform of every military branch of service, and they have fought in every war involving the United States of America.

Native Americans were engaged in U.S. combat operations throughout the 1980s and 1990s in such places as Grenada, Panama, the Persian Gulf, and Somalia. From September 11, 2001, to the present, American Indian Marines, soldiers, sailors, and airmen are answering the call to arms in the Iraq and Afghanistan campaigns as part of America's War on Terrorism. Most Native Americans serving in the U.S. armed forces consider themselves warriors and extensions of the centuries-old warrior culture. As warriors, they serve as guardians of their people, not simply uniformed personnel in a modern, technologically sophisticated armed force. These modern warriors have noted that the code of the U.S. Army is similar to their Native American warrior code. For them, fighting wherever they are ordered to serve requires a disciplined adherence to the warrior code and a commitment to protect the larger community from which they come. Native Americans maintain that they are fighting for the land and the people, not the government, nor some abstract principles, nor any political ideology. The mission of the Native American warrior has been the same since pre-Columbian times—a warrior is a protector of his people.

As protectors of the people, Native Americans continue these traditions well into the twenty-first century. Although Native Americans serve in every branch of the armed services, most tend to join the combat infantry units of the Marine Corps and the U.S. Army. Regardless of their mode of service, Native Americans honor their warrior traditions with a sense of pride and willingness to offer the ultimate sacrifice for their community, their tribe, and their country as America's first warriors.

Tribal warriors enter the armed forces from different communities from all across America. Each community has its own culture, its unique religious orientation, and social mores. Also, most tribal communities have rituals and ceremonies that reflect their support for the well-being of their warriors. They are honored members of their communities, and they wear their uniforms proudly as symbols of their willingness to protect the people and the land, and if necessary, to pay the ultimate cost of giving their life.

Native American warriors do not receive any special powers that make them "supermen," nor are they imbued with spiritual gifts that make them impervious to the traumas and horrors of combat. They experience fear, confusion, anxiety, and hypervigilance like non-native men and women. They scream when they are in pain, they shudder when assaulted, and they bleed when wounded. In fact, the primary distinction for Native Americans comes from their communities, not from their race. Tribal communities accept and support them when they leave for war and when they return. This community support is an essential component of native warriors, and without that community bond many would experience alienation and loss of identity after enduring combat. To assuage the anxiety and self-doubt that often accompany young recruits entering military service, tribal communities have ceremonies that help prepare the warrior for combat and the traumas he or she will experience in the work of death and destruction. They also have prayers, rituals, and ceremonies for those that return and need healing and transition back into the life of the tribe. After returning from combat, veterans are always honored at tribal ceremonies and powwows, and some tribes even award their veterans with tokens or symbols that signify their accomplishments while in service. One such ceremony is the awarding of eagle feathers to celebrate the warrior role, like the Red Feather awarded to wounded veterans among the Lakota people. Not all tribes use feathers or other visible indicators of military service, but rarely does any tribal ceremony begin without the traditional color guard and acknowledgement of those in service, their veteran brothers and sisters, and those that have fallen on the battlefield. Debra American Horse Wilson, Oglala Lakota Sioux Marine Corps veteran, from a long line of Lakota veterans, proclaims, "Let's remember we are a great nation because of what our veterans have done" (Chavez 2010).

Whether fighting in the treacherous mountain regions of Afghanistan or training recruits in Iraq, Native Americans will be in the ranks of our nation's armed services alongside their non-Indian counterparts, doing what their forefathers did before them—protecting the people and defending the land.

REFERENCES

Abel, Annie Heloise. *The American Indian as Participant in the Civil War*. Lincoln: University of Nebraska Press, 1992.

Adams, David Wallace. *Education for Extinction: American Indians and the Boarding School Experience, 1875–1928*. Lawrence: University Press of Kansas, 1995.

"American Indians in World War II." Native American Indian Heritage Month. Retrieved from http://www.defenselink.mil/specials/nativeamerican01/wwii.html on June 19, 2006.

Boatner, Mark Mayo, III. *Encyclopedia of the American Revolution*. New York: McKay, 1966 (rev. 1974).

Bradley, James with Ron Powers. *Flags of Our Fathers*. New York: Bantam Books, 2000.

Broker, Claudia G. "Indian Women in the War." In *The Oglala Light*. Pine Ridge, SD: Printing Department of the Oglala Indian Training School 19, no. 9 (May 1918).

Camurat, Diane. *The American Indian in the Great War: Real and Imagined*. Master's thesis submitted in 1993 to the Institute Charles V of the University of Paris VII, Master's Thesis, 1996. Retrieved from http://www.lib.byu.edu/~rdh/wwi/comment/camurat1.html on June 8, 2006.

Chavez, Will, Sr. "CN Honors Native Veterans." *Cherokee Phoenix*, December 2010, 1, 8

Code Talkers Exhibit, National Security Agency/Central Security Service. Retrieved from http://www.nsa.gov/museum/museu00010.cfm on June 19, 2006.

Cunningham, Frank. *General Stand Watie's Confederate Indians*. San Antonio: Naylor Co., 1959 (paperback reprint 1998 by University of Oklahoma Press).

Davis, Julie. "American Indian Boarding School Experiences: Recent Studies from Native Perspectives." *Organization of American Historians Magazine of History* 15, no. 2 (Winter 2001): 20–22.

Debo, Angie. *A History of the Indians of the United States*. Norman: University of Oklahoma Press, 1970.

Ely Samuel Parker Papers, American Philosophical Society. Retrieved from http://www.amphilsoc.org/library/mole/p/parker.htm#bibliography on June 14, 2006.

Fixico, Donald L. *Termination and Relocation: Federal Indian Policy, 1945–1960*. Albuquerque: University of New Mexico Press, 1986.

Griffin, Benjamin. "Lt. David Moniac, Creek Indian: First Minority Graduate of West Point." *Alabama Historical Quarterly* 2 (Summer 1981): 99–110.

Henri, Florette. *The Southern Indians and Benjamin Hawkins, 1796–1816*. Norman: University of Oklahoma Press, 1986.

Hirschfelder, Arlene and Martha Kreipe de Montano. *The Native American Almanac: A Portrait of Native America Today*. New York: Prentice Hall General Reference, 1993.

Holm, Tom. *Strong Hearts, Wounded Souls: Native American Veterans of the Vietnam War*. Austin: University of Texas Press, 1996.

Hoxie, Frederick E., (Ed.). *Talking Back to Civilization: Indian Voices from the Progressive Era*. Boston: Bedford/St. Martin's, 2001.

LaFarge, Peter. *The Ballad of Ira Hayes*, recorded by Johnny Cash for Legacy Recordings on March 5, 1964.

Lapahie, Harrison Jr. *Diné Bizaad Yee Atah Naayéé' Yik'eh Deesdlíí' (The Navajo language assisted the military forces to defeat the enemy)*. Retrieved from http://www.lapahie.com/NavajoCodeTalker.cfm on June 18, 2010.

Louisiana State Museum. "The Battle of New Orleans," *The Cabildo: Two Hundred Years of Louisiana History: Colonization through Reconstruction*, Retrieved from http://lsm.crt.state.la.us/cabildo/cabildo.htm on June 20, 2010.

Meadows, William C. *The Comanche Code Talkers of World War II*. Austin: University of Texas Press, 2003.

Merrell, James H. "Indians and the New Republic." In Jack P. Greene and J. R. Pole (Eds.), *The Blackwell Encyclopedia of the American Revolution*. Malden, MA: Blackwell, 1991.

Momaday, N. Scott. *House Made of Dawn*. New York: HarperCollins, 1999.

Nelson, Guy. *Thunderbird: A History of the 45th Infantry Division*. Oklahoma City: 45th Infantry Division Association, 1970.

Office of the Clerk, U.S. Capitol. "Congressional Gold Medal Recipients." Retrieved from http://clerk.house.gov/index.html on July 10, 2006.

Oswalt, Wendell H. *This Land Was Theirs: A Study of Native Americans* (7th ed.). Boston: McGraw-Hill, 2002.

Parker, Arthur C. *The Life of General Ely S. Parker: Last Grand Sachem of the Iroquois and General Grant's Military Secretary*. Buffalo, NY: Buffalo Historical Society, 1919.

Prucha, Francis Paul (Ed.). *Documents of United States Indian Policy* (3rd ed.). Lincoln: University of Nebraska Press, 2000.

Spicer, Edward H. *A Short History of the Indians of the United States*. Malabar, FL: Krieger, 1969.

Tate, Michael L. "From Scout to Doughboy: The National Debate over Integrating American Indians into the Military, 1991–1918." *Western Historical Quarterly* 17, no. 4 (October 1986): 417–437.

Tupper, Ferdinand Brock. *The Life and Correspondence of Major-General Sir Isaac Brock, K.B.* (2nd ed.). London: Simpkin, Marshall & Co., 1847.

U.S. Department of the Interior, Office of Indian Affairs. *Indians at Work* 9, no. 5 (January 1942).

U.S. Department of the Interior, Office of Indian Affairs. *Indians at Work* 9, no. 6 (February 1942).

U.S. Department of the Interior, Office of Indian Affairs. *Indians at Work* 9, no. 7 (March 1942).

U.S. Department of the Interior, Office of Indian Affairs. *Indians at Work* 9, no. 9/10 (May–June 1942).

U.S. Department of the Interior, Office of Indian Affairs. *Indians at Work* 11, no. 2 (July–August 1943).

U.S. Department of the Interior, Office of Indian Affairs. *Indians at Work* 11, no. 3 (September–October 1943).

U.S. Department of the Interior, Office of Indian Affairs. *Indians at Work* 11, no. 6 (March 1944).

U.S. Department of the Interior, Office of Indian Affairs. *Indians at Work* 12, no. 2 (July–August 1944).

U.S. Department of the Interior, Office of Indian Affairs. *Indians at Work* 12, no. 4 (November–December 1944).

U.S. Department of the Interior, Office of Indian Affairs. *Indians in the War*. Chicago: Haskell Printing Department, November 1945.

White, Christine Schultz and Benton R. White. *Now the Wolf Has Come: The Creek Nation in the Civil War*. College Station: Texas A&M University Press, 1996.

GENOCIDE

Debra Buchholtz

The 1992 quincentenary of Christopher Columbus's first voyage to the Americas focused attention on the devastation Europeans wrought upon the indigenous peoples of the New World. Few people today would deny that the conquest and colonization of the Americas resulted in hemisphere-wide suffering and depopulation. But disagreement remains over just how many people were in the Americas at first contact, the causes and extent of the population collapse set in motion by the Conquest, how best to describe it, and whether it constitutes genocide or was merely a tragic outcome of unstoppable but nongenocidal processes.

STRUGGLE OVER TERMINOLOGY

Native American and other historically oriented scholars increasingly describe the catastrophic population decline that began with Columbus's 1492 landfall and continued for the next 400 years as genocide. Some even call it a holocaust. Rather than acquiesce to such passive metaphors as the *vanishing American*, which depict the indigenous population loss as an unfortunate but natural consequence of structural changes, they attribute it to the actions of agents of European imperialism and colonialism. In contrast, many Holocaust scholars insist that the term *holocaust* applies uniquely to the Nazi's World War II Judeocide and that the indigenous American experience, as horrific as it was, does not properly constitute genocide. They hold that the genocide label requires clear evidence of intent to exterminate a group in its entirety. Since the depopulation of the Americas resulted from disease and structures of domination and oppression over a long period of time rather than from the intentional actions of specific agents, it does not constitute genocide (Barkan 2003). What those who pose such arguments often neglect to mention is that the Holocaust itself was not an exclusively Jewish experience; the Nazis also targeted Gypsies, homosexuals, and the Slavic peoples for extermination.

Yehuda Bauer (1991), a historian and Holocaust scholar, concedes that genocide has occurred throughout history. He believes that every instance of genocide is unique because its causes, mechanisms, and consequences are unique. Nonetheless, he distinguishes between genocide, something that aims to eliminate a national or ethnic group, and holocaust, something that seeks to totally annihilate such a group. He envisions the two terms as constituting the pole ends of a continuum along which the genocides of history can be hierarchically arranged with the Jewish experience alone constituting the holocaust pole. This reflects and attempts to resolve the tension between those like himself who see the Holocaust as a uniquely Jewish experience and those who would universalize the term and the type of atrocity it describes. Other scholars caution that overuse of words like *holocaust* and *genocide* erode their descriptive utility and water down their moral and emotive force. They ask that writers exercise great care in using them.

Advocates of these varied positions usually begin with the definition of genocide laid out in the 1948 United Nations Convention on Genocide. Some expand it to make it more inclusive. Others tighten it to exclude, for example, cultural genocide (or *ethnocide*), which they deplore but nonetheless see as something altogether different because it involves cultural assimilation rather than physical extermination. A few argue that to constitute genocide, a sufficiently large number of people must have died or that the deaths had to have been deliberately inflicted through direct means, like the Nazi's firing squads and gas chambers. Still other people, writing specifically about the indigenous American experience, find it politically useful to earmark specific types of assaults on Native American peoples as genocidal (i.e., "tending toward genocide"). This can be seen in their use of terms like *environmental genocide* or *ecological genocide* and *spiritual genocide*. All sides dig through the more than 500 years of original documents, analysis, and research data pertaining to demography, warfare, slavery and forced labor, disease, murder, and intent in search of evidence to support their arguments and to undermine those they disagree with.

DEFINITIONS AND CLARIFICATIONS

Estimates of the indigenous population of North America when Europeans first arrived range widely. Most scholars consider anthropologist James Mooney's 1910 estimate of just over 1 million too low. Russell Thornton, a Cherokee sociologist and historical demographer, has suggested a figure of about 7 million, which enjoys relatively wide acceptance. Few scholars lend much credence to

> ## UN CONVENTION ON GENOCIDE
>
> In 1948, the General Assembly of the United Nations embraced resolution 260A(III), the Convention on the Punishment and Prevention of the Crime of Genocide, which is reproduced in part here.
>
> The Convention, a major pillar in the evolving framework of international humanitarian rules, declares genocide a crime under international law. It condemns genocide, whether committed in time of peace or in time of war, and provides a definition of this crime. Moreover, the prescribed punishment is not subject to the limitations of time and place.
>
> The Convention defines genocide as any of a number of acts committed with the intent to destroy, in whole or in part, a national, ethnic, racial or religious group: killing members of the group; causing serious bodily or mental harm to members of the group; deliberately inflicting on the group conditions of life calculated to bring about its physical destruction in whole or in part; imposing measures intended to prevent births within the group, and forcibly transferring children of the group to another group.
>
> The Convention also declares that there shall be no immunity. Persons committing this crime shall be punished, whether they are constitutionally responsible rulers, public officials or private individuals.
>
> Furthermore, the Convention stipulates that persons charged with genocide shall be tried by a competent tribunal of the State in the territory in which the act was committed or by such international penal tribunal as may have jurisdiction with respect to the Contracting Parties....
>
> Unlike other human rights treaties, the Genocide Convention does not establish a specific monitoring body or expert committee. It stipulates that any Contracting Party may call upon the competent organs of the United Nations to take such action under the United Nations Charter, which they consider appropriate for the prevention and suppression of acts of genocide. Thus, the matter may be brought before the International Court of Justice which may order interim measures of protection.
>
> *Source*: UN Convention on Genocide. Retrieved from http://www.un.org/millennium/law/iv-1.htm

anthropologist Henry Dobyn's high-end estimate of 18 million (which includes northern Mexico). Other estimates come in higher still, and at least one historian dismisses them all as guesswork because the data to support them simply do not exist. Regardless of the numerical starting point, the depopulation that ensued was unprecedented, with the native North American population reaching its low point of about 375,000 at the end of the nineteenth century. By then, many indigenous peoples had been completely wiped out. Most others had seen their populations fall by as much as 90 to 95 percent and in some cases even more. After the turn of the century, the populations of those that had survived began to slowly recover. For low-counters and high-counters alike, what happened between 1492 and 1900 represents an alarming rate of depopulation. But does it constitute genocide? If it is genocide, is that genocidal tendency ongoing? And is it best described as a single hemisphere-wide genocide or many different genocides perpetrated by many different agents? The answers to those questions depend largely on how one chooses to define genocide and interpret the historical data.

The term *genocide* derives from the Greek word *genos* ("race" or "tribe") and the Latin word *cide* ("killing"). Horrified by the atrocities of World War II, Rafaël Lemkin, a Polish lawyer of Jewish descent, coined the term in 1944 to describe the destruction of a nation or ethnic group (Lemkin 2002). As he envisioned it, genocide does not necessarily entail the direct physical destruction of a group but could be the outcome of an attack on the sociocultural foundations of group life aimed at bringing about the group's demise, if not the actual death of its members. Moreover, he argued, genocide has two phases: destruction of the oppressed group's culture followed by imposition of the oppressor group's culture. The indigenous peoples of the Americas have suffered both, and many continue to do so today.

Lemkin campaigned vigorously to have genocide recognized and prosecuted as a crime. In 1948, the General Assembly of the United Nations adopted resolution 260A(III), the Convention on the Punishment and Prevention of the Crime of Genocide (UN 2002). It went into force in 1951. Article 3 of the convention defines genocide as any of a series of acts committed with the "intent to destroy, in whole or in part, a national, ethnical, racial, or religious group." It identifies five acts as genocidal: "(a) Killing members of the group; (b) Causing serious bodily or mental harm to members of the group; (c) Deliberately inflicting on the group conditions of life calculated to bring about its physical destruction in whole or in part; (d) Imposing measures intended to prevent births within the group; (e) Forcibly transferring children of the group to another group." Omitted from this list, but present in Lemkin's original formulation, is the destruction of a group's culture, or what is often referred to as cultural genocide. After much debate, the United States finally ratified the convention in 1988. Canada did so in 1952 but limited its applicability to First Nations peoples.

Most scholars acknowledge the UN Convention on Genocide as an important first step, but many feel that it does not recognize the full range of genocidal acts that have been and continue to be perpetrated against Native American and other peoples. To rectify this, Ward Churchill, a Creek/Cherokee/Métis scholar and activist, has proposed a "functional definition" of genocide comprised of four degrees that parallel the degrees of murder in American criminal law (Churchill 1995). In his typology, Genocide in the First Degree would include those instances in which the intent to commit genocide is clear, as in the case of the Nazi's slaughter of European Jews. Genocide in the Second Degree would cover cases where intent is not clear, but the perpetrator committed genocide while engaging in a criminal act such as conducting an illegal war or appropriating American Indian lands. Genocide in the Third Degree would include those instances wherein intent was absent and no criminal act was committed, but genocide occurred due to insensitivity or recklessness. Churchill lists as examples of this form of genocide the flooding of the James Bay Cree's homeland by a hydrological project and the forced relocation of thousands of Diné (Navajo) from Black Mesa so that coal could be extracted from beneath their homes. In both instances, forced relocation broke up communities and dispersed their members. Genocide in the Fourth Degree would be genocide resulting from poor judgment, as in the case of U.S. federal Indian policies like assimilation and termination, which sought to undermine the sense of collective identity or community often referred to by outsiders as tribalism. Churchill's expansion of the definition of genocide and the examples he offers are controversial. Nonetheless, his degrees of genocide usefully highlight what many people see as shortcomings in the Convention on Genocide and, in particular, its lack of attention to cultural genocide as a multifaceted and ongoing practice.

GENOCIDE OR REGRETTABLE TRAGEDY?

While Congress debated ratification of the UN Convention on Genocide in the 1980s, debate over the proposed U.S. Holocaust Memorial Museum heated up as its planners grappled with issues of content and inclusiveness. Like Bauer, most of them saw the Holocaust as a singularly Jewish moment in history. Some, however, bowing to pressure from the White House, suggested that as a national museum situated on the Washington Mall, it needed a universal message and should address the Armenian, Native American, and other genocides. During that same period, Native American activists were beginning to maneuver in the international arena and were looking for more compelling language to use in talking about their pasts and in framing their political arguments. A universalizing sense of genocide and holocaust expressed their feeling of victimhood and served their political purposes well, particularly in the context of the much belated ratification of the UN convention by the United States and the rapidly approaching Columbian quincentenary, both of which focused media attention on such issues.

Native American and other scholars began to analyze the depopulation of the Americas and the human suffering that accompanied it as genocide. Thornton (1987) published a carefully documented analysis of the Native North American population decline and recovery since 1492. In it, he attributes the population collapse, or what he calls the American Indian holocaust, to genocide resulting from virgin soil epidemics, murder, warfare, slavery and forced work regimes, starvation, disrupted fertility and reproduction, government policies, and social, political, cultural and economic upheaval. While describing these factors as interlinked, he notes that a high percentage of deaths resulted from introduced European diseases like smallpox, measles, and influenza. The aboriginal population had never been exposed to them and, because they lacked acquired immunity, the resulting death toll was massive.

Historian David Stannard (1994) has described the European newcomers' brutality and the hemisphere-wide upheaval, suffering, and loss of life that followed their arrival. He, too, labels the outcome a holocaust. But his main contribution has been to trace the roots of the genocidal practices noted to early Christian theology, which he argues dehumanized the indigenous peoples and provided Europeans with ideological justification for exploiting their labor, taking their lands, and even killing them. He also cites evidence showing that many of the newcomers viewed the horrendous levels of death from disease that they witnessed among the Indians as a matter of divine intervention on their behalf. Some even encouraged the spread of disease by sending persons known to be ill into indigenous communities or by distributing smallpox-infected blankets. Few took steps to stem the rapidly mounting death toll; most just watched and waited.

Stannard also describes instances from the East Coast across the Great Plains to the gold fields of California in which the European newcomers—and then the Americans in turn—deliberately destroyed Indian villages, food stores, and crops. That impacted the residents' ability to feed and care for themselves and their sick, and resulted in starvation, lowered resistance to disease, and—ultimately—mass death. This, according to Stannard, constitutes genocide.

Churchill (1999) agrees with Stannard and argues that many of the genocidal practices noted by Stannard and Thornton are still happening. He pays particular attention to cultural genocide, as evidenced, for example, by government policies that force assimilation or promote acculturation, and environmental or ecological genocide, such as that seen in the radioactive contamination of Diné, Pueblo, Lakota, Shoshone, Paiute, Yakima, and other Native American lands. All three writers base their arguments on the more encompassing definition of genocide first suggested by Lemkin.

Not so Stephen Katz (2009), an academic specializing in Holocaust and Jewish studies. Resisting what he perceives as attempts to co-opt and misuse the terms *genocide* and *holocaust*, and thereby undermine what they stand for, Katz has narrowed the UN definition even further to exclude all acts except those explicitly aimed at the physical destruction of a racial, ethnic, religious, or national group. He views the Holocaust as unique in history and singularly Jewish. Never before or since, he argues, has a state set out to systematically exterminate an entire people. Thus, the Holocaust serves for him as the prototype against which all other genocides are to be matched. What, to him, distinguishes the Native American experience of mass death from the Holocaust is the role played by disease as opposed to state-sponsored bureaucratically organized mass murder, a position similar to that taken by some historians. This, of course, ignores the fact that a great many Holocaust victims actually died from disease and not in the gas chambers. By Katz's calculation, only about 3.7 percent of the indigenous population loss between 1775 and 1890 and less than 1 percent of the loss before then is attributable to some form of murder. Population loss of that magnitude, he argues, contravened the self-interested wishes of the colonizers. They did not intend for it to happen and were powerless to stop it. And that, to him, is the critical point: the Native American population collapse was not intentional but accidental. Consequently, neither the mass death precipitated by the Columbian Encounter nor any of those caused by the many colonial encounters that followed constitute genocide. Katz used the Pequot War as the example upon which to build his case.

Writing about the Native American situation more generally, Barkan (2003, 135) notes that regardless of whether the newcomers deliberately introduced disease among the indigenous peoples they encountered, they clearly intended for them to vanish by one means or another. If that is true, he suggests, arguments about intent such as that posed by Katz are little more than academic quibbles.

Michael Freeman (1995), another historian, has responded directly to Katz's argument as developed in the context of the Pequot War. At issue for him is whether the 1637 to 1638 bloody conflict between the Puritans and the Pequot culminated in genocide, which has proven to be a matter of how one defines the term and interprets the historical evidence. Citing both Lemkin's and the UN's definition of genocide, and much of the same evidence Katz uses, Freeman argues that the Pequot War does constitute genocide. Stannard (1994, 112–115) also interprets the Pequot War as genocide and provides evidence of intent. But Katz (1991; 1995), brandishing his more restrictive definition of genocide, insists that because the Puritans' aggression against the Pequot was not racial but a response to a perceived threat to their own survival, it was defensive and hence not genocide. This has led Freeman to criticize him for assuming that defensive wars cannot be genocidal and for using the Holocaust as a yardstick against which to measure all other genocides. Throughout history, Freeman observes, perpetrators have justified genocide as a defensive act, but the outcome has been genocide nonetheless.

To recognize the Pequot War as a genocide is not to equate the English with the Nazis but to recognize the Pequot War for what it was: a specific instance in which nation-building entailed nation-destroying. Both Stannard and Freeman disagree with Katz's interpretation of the historical evidence and definition of genocide. And unlike Katz, who distinguishes cultural genocide from physical genocide, they join Churchill and Thornton in recognizing cultural and physical genocide as different ways of achieving the same end: the destruction of a people.

THE STAKES

Much is at stake in this argument. Holocaust uniqueness proponents like Bauer perceive the Holocaust as a sacred memory that binds survivors and their descendants in shared victimhood. It gives Jews a sense of commonality and community despite their dispersal. Bauer, Katz, and others locate the Holocaust's uniqueness in the Nazi's plan to totally exterminate the Jewish people and in the ideology that underpinned it. Many construe any attempt to universalize it as Holocaust denial and anti-Semitic because it de-Judaizes the Holocaust and thereby dilutes its meaning and diminishes its impact and emotive force (Bauer 1980). It also deflects attention from continuing attacks on Jews worldwide.

Many Native Americans, while not denying the Holocaust or the deep and multifaceted meaning it holds for Jews, interpret as racist any opposition to analyses of the depopulation of the Americas as genocide or a holocaust, a population loss they describe as unprecedented. Adopting the rhetoric of their Jewish counterparts, they label such stances *genocide (or holocaust) denial* and argue that they naturalize and thereby excuse the exploitation, suffering, and mass death that plagued their ancestors and still threaten indigenous peoples today. They understand arguments like those advanced by Katz as participating in what Barkan calls a passive discourse of vanishing peoples in which there are no agents to hold accountable, just the inevitable march of progress. M. Annette Jaimes (1992), a Juaneño/Yaqui scholar and activist, believes that such discourses deflect responsibility and pose barriers to positive change.

Jaimes detects many parallels between the Nazi genocide of the Jews, Gypsies, and Slavic peoples, and the American genocide of its indigenous peoples as exemplified by the Sand Creek massacre. They include similarities in worldview, motivation, objectives, and method. The main distinction she sees derives from the technological advances that enabled the Nazis to commit their crime with greater efficiency. To dismiss Native American deaths by disease and starvation ignores their root causes and suggests that such deaths were a natural outcome of civilizing progress. It also overlooks the fact that a great many of the deaths in the Jewish Holocaust resulted from the same causes. Moreover, it glosses over what Jaimes sees as the most critical point: in both cases, the progress of the nation was built on such atrocities.

REFERENCES

American Indian Holocaust. Available at http://www.unitednativeamerica.com/aiholocaust.html

Barkan, Elazar. "Genocide of Indigenous Peoples: Rhetoric of Human Rights." In Robert Gellately and Ben Kiernan (Eds.), *The Specter of Genocide: Mass Murder in Historical Perspective*. Cambridge: Cambridge University Press, 2003, 117–140.

Bauer, Yehuda. "Whose Holocaust?" *Midstream* 26, no. 9 (1980): 42–46.

Bauer, Yehuda. "Holocaust and Genocide: Some Comparisons." In Peter Hayes (Ed.), *Lessons and Legacies: The Meaning of the Holocaust in the Changing World*. Evanston, IL: Northwestern University Press, 1991, 36–46.

Churchill, Ward. "Genocide: Towards a Functional Definition." In *Since Predator Came: Notes from the Struggle for American Indian Liberation*. Littleton, CO: Aigis Publications, 1995, 75–107.

Churchill, Ward. *A Little Matter of Genocide: Holocaust and Denial in the Americas, 1492 to the Present*. San Francisco: City Lights Books, 1997.

Churchill, Ward. "A Breach of Trust: The Radioactive Colonization of Native North America." *American Indian Culture and Research Journal* 23, no. 4 (1999): 23–69.

Freeman, Michael. "Puritans and Pequots: The Question of Genocide." *New England Quarterly* 68, no. 2 (1995): 278–293.

Jaimes, M. Annette. "Sand Creek: The Morning After." In M. Annette Jaimes (Ed.), *The State of Native America: Genocide, Colonization, and Resistance*. Boston: Southend Press, 1992, 1–12.

Katz, Stephen. "The Pequot War Reconsidered." *New England Quarterly* 64, no. 2 (1991): 206–224.

Katz, Stephen. "Pequots and the Question of Genocide: A Reply to Michael Freeman." *New England Quarterly* 68, no. 4 (1995): 641–649.

Katz, Stephen. "The Uniqueness of the Holocaust: The Historical Dimension." In Alan S. Rosenbaum (Ed.), *Is the Holocaust Unique? Perspectives on Comparative Genocide* (3rd ed.). Boulder, CO: Westview Press, 2009, 55–74.

Lemkin, Rafaël. "Genocide." Reprinted in Alexander Laban Hinton (Ed.), *Genocide: An Anthropological Reader*. Oxford: Blackwell Publishers, 2002, 27–42.

Rosenbaum, Alan S. (Ed.). *Is the Holocaust Unique?: Perspectives on Comparative Genocide* (3rd ed.). Boulder, CO: Westview Press. Available at http://www.scribd.com/doc/13496380/Is-the-Holocaust-Unique

Stannard, David E. *American Holocaust: The Conquest of the New World*. Oxford: Oxford University Press, 1994.

Thornton, Russell. *American Indian Holocaust and Survival: A Population History since 1492*. Norman: University of Oklahoma Press, 1987.

United Nations. "Text of the UN Genocide Convention." Reprinted in Alexander Laban Hinton (Ed.), *Genocide: An Anthropological Reader*. Oxford: Blackwell Publishers, 2002, 43–47.

University of Minnesota, Center for Holocaust and Genocide Studies. Available at http://chgs.umn.edu/webBib/

Grassroots Politics: Historical and Contemporary Activism

Amy L. Fletcher

Grassroots activism refers to political pressure on government institutions and elites that starts at the local level, often at the initiative of a few dedicated citizens. It is a key driver of political change in the United States, given that the founding fathers—James Madison in particular—established a system of divided and pluralist government that empowered organized groups of citizens to pursue competing interests and claims in the public sphere. Key tactics of grassroots activism include civil disobedience, strikes, class action lawsuits, and skillful use of the mass media to raise the visibility of previously hidden or local issues.

The United States is also a capitalist country in which power often accrues to those who command large industries and/or have private fortunes. While grassroots activism is rarely easy, it can serve as an important check on the concentration of political power among only the economically privileged. Indeed, some of the most important changes in American law and policy, such as desegregation in the American South and voting rights for African Americans and women, began with ordinary citizens mobilizing to draw the nation's attention to moral, legal, and political injustices. The remainder of this essay focuses on grassroots activism as a key tool in the advancement of Native American rights, identity, and culture in the United States.

NATIVE AMERICAN ACTIVISM BEFORE WORLD WAR II

Grassroots activism is a phenomenon often associated with the twentieth century, and especially with the post–World War II period when groups ranging from African Americans to women to the disabled to older adults began to actively use legislation and the courts to obtain both procedural and substantive equality.

Native American grassroots activism also flourished in the 1960s and 1970s; however, many key advances for Native American rights were achieved in the nineteenth and early twentieth centuries. While in retrospect some of these changes may seem modest, it is crucial to remember that these early instances provide a foundation for the vast expansion of Native American activism that occurred in the post–World War II period.

In the eighteenth and nineteenth centuries, the U.S. government's actions toward Native Americans ranged from at best paternalistic (with Native Americans treated as wards of the national government) to at worst negligent, corrupt, or cruel. The American Continental Congress created three departments of Indian Affairs (Northern, Central, and Southern) in 1775, primarily to negotiate treaties with tribes and to obtain tribal neutrality in the imminent Revolutionary War. In 1824, Secretary of War John C. Calhoun created the Bureau of Indian Affairs (BIA), which was transferred to the Department of the Interior (DOI) in 1849, where it remains today. The BIA initially distributed food and medical aid to Native American communities. While well-meaning doctors and nurses sought to use the BIA to improve Indian health and welfare, the Native American recipients of this aid had virtually no power or autonomy in relationship to the federal government. Moreover, by the 1850s, some of the medical and welfare workers employed by the BIA began to complain about the rampant corruption that plagued the food distribution network.

Corruption within the BIA dovetailed in time with a series of Indian rebellions and wars in the West that prompted Congress to initiate a Joint Special Committee investigation into the conditions and dynamics of U.S.-Native American relations (Joint Resolution of Congress, March 3, 1865). The Joint Committee released its report (referred to as the Doolittle Report) in 1867. The Doolittle Report recommended a major policy change via its advocacy of the establishment of Indian reservations to replace the ongoing wars and brutality. While this initiative, in context, may have meant well, the report also expected the reservation system to assimilate Native Americans into the farming practices, culture, and norms of settler society. For later generations of activists, this assumption that Native Americans had to assimilate into white culture to survive constitutes one of the most serious grievances against the United States and provides a platform for widespread protest and direct action to reassert indigenous and tribal identities. Nevertheless, despite its flaws, the Doolittle Report was an important milestone in establishing the factual basis of some Native American grievances. In particular, the report documented that one of the events that had initially sparked the investigation—the 1864 Sand Creek Massacre of Cheyenne and Arapaho Indians by the Third Regiment of Colorado Volunteers under the leadership of Colonel John Milton Chivington—was not a brave victory against aggressive Indian warriors as originally reported, but a stealth attack on a sleeping village that resulted in the deaths of unarmed women and children.

After the turn of the twentieth century, the release of the Meriam Report (1928) was one of the most important events pertaining to official acknowledgement of Native American grievances. Initiated at the request of the Secretary of the Interior, the 847-page report clearly documented serious failures and corruption within the reservation system. The authors, having visited 95 jurisdictions and investigated conditions at reservations, hospitals, and schools, found widespread and severe Indian poverty, serious overcrowding, chronic underfunding of the health and food aid systems, the destruction of the Native American economic base via policies imposed by the federal and state governments (as well as the extermination of the buffalo), and extremely high levels (compared to the general population) of tuberculosis and trachoma. The report was especially scathing about the boarding school system, concluding that "the survey staff finds itself obliged to say frankly and unequivocally that the provisions for the care of Indian children in boarding schools are grossly inadequate" (Meriam 1928, 11). As with the earlier Doolittle Report, much of the Meriam Report's language can seem paternalistic and antiquated to modern readers. Nevertheless, it was a major step forward in the documentation of systematic abuses of Native Americans, and it attributed blame for the dismal conditions found on the reservations not to an assumed Native American "inferiority" but to specific and intentional policies of the U.S. government. The report concludes that the early chapters in the relationship between the federal government and the Indians "contains little of which the country may be proud" (Meriam 1928, 51).

INDIVIDUAL AMERICAN INDIAN ACTIVISTS

Lindsey Hanson

A number of American Indian Movement (AIM) members and other American Indian activists played, and continue to play, important roles in the fight for American Indian rights. Leonard Peltier, an AIM member, is one of those individuals. Peltier is currently serving time in a federal penitentiary for aiding and abetting the murder of two Federal Bureau of Investigation (FBI) agents. Peltier was raised on the Turtle Mountain Reservation in North Dakota and received only a ninth grade education. He became involved in the Pine Ridge Reservation corruption scandal that led to the incident at Wounded Knee and later returned to the Pine Ridge Reservation because of the continued violence after the incident. In the summer of 1975, two FBI agents were murdered while investigating an assault and robbery on the reservation. Peltier was arrested and charged with the murders on the basis of information provided by a woman named Myrtle Poor Bear. Poor Bear alleged that she was his girlfriend at the time of the incident, and that she had witnessed the murders. Peltier, however, alleged that he did not know Poor Bear. Poor Bear was known to have serious mental health issues, and later stated that she had confessed under pressure from FBI agents,, and did not actually know Peltier. At Peltier's trial, her testimony was barred for lack of competence. While Peltier's conviction has been upheld on appeal, both Amnesty International and Archbishop Desmond Tutu, as well as numerous American Indian activists, have called for his release. Peltier was denied parole in 2009 and will not be up for parole again until 2024. His projected release date is October 2040.

Early leaders of the AIM movement—Dennis Banks, Clyde Bellecourt, and Russell Means—also became well known for their activism. Banks was born on the Leech Lake Reservation in northwestern Minnesota. He participated in the Alcatraz Island takeover, the Trail of Broken Treaties, and the 1973 incident at Wounded Knee. Bellecourt was born on the White Earth Reservation in Minnesota and then moved to Minneapolis. He currently serves as a coordinator for the National Coalition on Racism in Sports and the Media. Means was born on the Pine Ridge Reservation in South Dakota, but his family later moved to California. Means (who died in October 2012) was a member of AIM and once served as the group's director. Means participated in the Alcatraz takeover and was involved in indigenous rights activism with the United Nations.

Annie Mae Aquash, an influential female figure in the AIM movement despite having been born in Canada, was involved in the Trail of Broken Treaties protest. She was murdered on the Pine Ridge Indian Reservation in the late seventies. There has been a great deal of speculation as to why Aquash was murdered. Some believe that she was killed because she is alleged to have heard Leonard Peltier bragging about the murder of two FBI agents. Arlo Looking Cloud and John Graham have been convicted for her murder.

Two individuals from the White Earth Reservation in Northwestern Minnesota who play active roles in contemporary activism efforts are Gerald Vizenor and Winona LaDuke. Vizenor is a professor, journalist, and writer of fiction and nonfiction. He is a former director of the American Indian Employment and Guidance Center in Minneapolis. LaDuke, current director of the White Earth Land Recovery Project, is best known as the 1996 and 2000 vice-presidential candidate for the Green Party. LaDuke, who is Ojibwa, was born in California and raised in Oregon. She is a graduate of Harvard University, an author, former high school principal, and land rights activist.

Sources: Peltier, Leonard. "Statement from Leonard Peltier." AIM Movement, January 31, 2009. Retrieved from http://www.aimovement.org/peltier/index.html

Peltier, Leonard. *Prison Writings: My Life Is My Sun Dance*. New York: St. Martin's, 1999.

Means, Russell. *Where White Men Fear to Tread: The Autobiography of Russell Means*. New York: St. Martin's, 1995.

NATIVE AMERICAN ACTIVISM AFTER WORLD WAR II

Following World War II, the United States began to experience a momentous shift in its application of civil rights to minority groups and women that culminated in a renaissance of grassroots activism in the 1960s and 1970s. Native Americans, women, African Americans, and many other groups had worked hard and sacrificed to help the United States defeat the Axis powers and emerge as the uncontested victor of World War II (1941–1945). For example, like many African American men, many Native American men voluntarily enlisted to fight in Europe and the Pacific in the 1940s, in the name of both American security and the liberation of those oppressed by the totalitarian Nazi and Japanese regimes. These soldiers, who had fought for the ideal of freedom abroad, returned to an America that continued to withhold the full rights and dignity of citizenship from them. This discrepancy between the ideal of freedom and the reality of discrimination—in combination with the rising numbers of young Native Americans achieving college educations and, hence, the tools for direct challenges to the law and public policies—was one of the major factors that prompted a new generation of activists to begin the slow process of securing full recognition of Native Americans. While the Doolittle Report and the Meriam Report, however sympathetic to Native American grievances and conditions, had been initiated and implemented by white elites, this new grassroots activism emerged from within Native American communities and was led by Native American activists such as Vine Deloria, Jr., Buffy Sainte-Marie, Wilma Mankiller, and Clyde Bellecourt.

By the 1950s, the civil rights struggles of African Americans had moved to the forefront of the national consciousness, both politically and in terms of media coverage. African Americans faced de jure segregation in the South, and de facto segregation in most other regions of the United States. Led by activists such as Martin Luther King, Jr., and Medgar Evers, thousands of citizens, both black and white, mobilized into various interest groups (such as the Southern Christian Leadership Conference and the Congress for Racial Equality) to force the United States to respect, uphold, and enforce such basic rights as the right to vote and to assemble, and to have equal opportunity in employment, health, and housing. During this time frame, Native Americans also pursued political and cultural change through institutional and organizational channels such as the National Congress of American Indians (established in 1944) and the Indian Historical Society (1964). In a portent of more radical activism to come, the National Indian Youth Council, established in 1961, began openly to use the phrase *Red Power*.

The African American civil rights movement was long and faced often violent and lethal resistance directed against leaders, protestors, and student activists. Many Native American tribes recognized and sympathized with the civil rights struggles of African Americans, as well as with those of other groups, such as farm laborers, who also began to mobilize and assert their rights in this time period. However, it is crucial to recognize, as many Native American activists continue to emphasize, that the Native American struggle differs in a significant way from the struggles of other minority groups in the United States. Their main political imperative is *not* to secure the civil rights and civil liberties inherent in U.S. citizenship. Instead, the focus is on having Native American sovereignty recognized, based on tribal indigenous status as the first peoples of North America. This goal, considered radical, controversial, and/or impractical by many critics, does not automatically translate into a desire to overthrow or even fight with the U.S. government. There is also wide disagreement and debate within native communities and tribes on what sovereignty means, which groups can claim it, and how it can best be achieved. Nevertheless, the general goal of establishing sovereign and recognized Indian nations that coexist with the United States is significantly different from the goal of integration into mainstream U.S. society. By the late 1960s, when activism often took on a more confrontational and even violent character compared to the earlier era of civil disobedience, the fundamental difference between Native American indigeneity—and its attendant goal of tribal sovereignty—and the claims of minority/immigrant groups could produce misunderstanding and tension. For example, Vine Deloria, Jr., recounts in his seminal book *We Talk, You Listen* (1972) the story of a Sioux elder who, after listening to impassioned speeches from Black Power activists about killing "pigs" (1960s slang for police) and the coming race war, noted dryly that he might support the "overthrow of the establishment" after "we get paid for the Black Hills" (Deloria 1972, 14).

THE AMERICAN INDIAN MOVEMENT AND THE OCCUPATION OF ALCATRAZ ISLAND

Based on the earlier efforts of individuals and tribes across a 500-year struggle, the grassroots activists who led the fight in the 1960s and 1970s heralded a renaissance in the assertion of Native American culture and identity. The American Indian Movement (AIM) emerged as one of the most significant organizations devoted to securing Native American rights and sovereignty. Initially formed to protect urban Indians' civil rights, one of its earliest actions occurred in Minnesota in 1968 when it created the Minneapolis AIM Patrol to protest and draw attention to widespread police brutality against Native Americans in that city. AIM was also a major participant in perhaps the most famous and iconic Native American protest in this time frame—the 19-month occupation of Alcatraz Island.

In 1969, Native American activists reclaimed Alcatraz Island, which had been used as a federal prison from 1934 to 1963. The penitentiary's notoriety was partially based on the fact that no prisoner had ever successfully escaped (though many had tried). From a Native American viewpoint, however, the island was also important because the Treaty of Fort Laramie (1868) between the United States and the Sioux ostensibly required the federal government to return to Indians all abandoned federal lands as a matter of national policy. Therefore, when the government in 1963 declared Alcatraz Prison—and the island—surplus federal property upon the prison's closure in 1963, Red Power activists decided to re-take the land as both a significant protest action and a test case. In March 1964, a few Sioux managed to claim the island for a few hours. Then, beginning November 20, 1969, AIM, among other organizations and individuals led by the United Indians of All Tribes, occupied the island until June 11, 1971, in the name of human rights and in an effort to restore the pride and dignity of the more than 554 recognized American Indian tribes in the United States at that time. Spokespeople for the protest, in an ironic mimicry of colonial and settler duplicity toward Native Americans, offered to purchase the island from the federal government for "24 dollars in glass beads and red cloth." The Alcatraz Proclamation to the Great White Father and his People (1969) also caustically delineated the similarities between Alcatraz Island and the reservations, including lack of sanitation and adequate roads, the absence of healthcare and educational facilities, the lack of oil and mineral rights, and high unemployment (Native Village n.d.).

The occupation of Alcatraz Island—which ended when protestors were finally forced from the island by government officers—raised the media and political profile of Native American grievances tremendously, and forced Native American issues into the mainstream spotlight. Following Alcatraz, for example, AIM became a multitribal protest organization that organized such seminal events as the 1970 Thanksgiving Day protest, in which activists painted Plymouth Rock red and seized the *Mayflower II* replica in Plymouth, Massachusetts. Based in Minneapolis, AIM also filed numerous lawsuits against the federal government, articulated and pursued a policy of Native American self-determination, and tried to balance the cultural diversity of Indian tribes against the common grievances and set of interests that united indigenous Americans and provided a basis for collective political power. AIM remains highly controversial today, due primarily to the Pine Ridge Indian Reservation confrontation between members of the organization and agents of the Federal Bureau of Investigation (FBI) in 1975. Activist Leonard Peltier was convicted of the murder of two FBI agents and remains in federal prison serving two life sentences. Peltier's supporters continue to argue that he is a political prisoner, being held unjustly, while the FBI routinely opposes his appeals for parole. Various FBI files about the American Indian Movement, released under the Freedom of Information Act, can be found online at http://vault.fbi.gov/reading-room-index#N (accessed September 22, 2012).

American Indian Leonard Peltier, who is serving two life sentences for the 1975 murder of two FBI agents, is shown in prison in February 1986. (AP Photo/Cliff Schiappa)

CONTEMPORARY NATIVE AMERICAN ACTIVISM

Following the momentum created by the Alcatraz occupation, the federal government initiated a series of policy changes sought by activists. Congress, in 1970 and 1971, passed 52 legislative proposals regarding tribal self-rule. President Richard M. Nixon, in cooperation with the legislature, increased the BIA budget by 225 percent, doubled funding for Indian healthcare, and established the Office of Indian Water Rights. President Nixon also quietly ended the policy of termination (initiated during the Eisenhower administration in an attempt to divest the federal government of responsibility for reservations) and replaced it with the first significant executive recognition of the policy of Native American self-determination. Though this change did not receive substantial media attention, in certain respects this shift to the language of self-determination remains one of the most crucial achievements of this period of grassroots activism.

Important political actions and achievements continued throughout the 1970s. In 1970, for example, AIM assisted the Lac Court Orieles Ojibwa (Wisconsin) in taking over a dam controlled by the North States Power Company. Construction of the dam had required flooding of significant amounts of reservation land; following the protest, government officials supported a settlement that required North States Power to return more than 25,000 acres of land to the tribe. The Alcatraz–Red Power Movement (ARPM), which demanded full inclusion in American institutions as well as retention of Native American cultural identity, initiated the Trail of Broken Treaties in 1972, which also included participation by AIM, the Native American Rights Fund, the National Indian Youth Council, the National Council on Indian Work, National Indian Leadership Training, the American Indian Committee on Alcohol and Drug Abuse, and the National Indian Brotherhood (a Canadian organization). Participants wrote the famous 20-Point Position Paper, which asserted Native American sovereignty (AIM 1972). Wounded Knee '73, initiated by Lakota elders who had contacted AIM regarding both BIA corruption and Tribal Council corruption, led to a 71-day standoff between activists and federal agents. An 8-month trial started in 1974, culminating in a decision by U.S. District Court Judge Fred Nichol to dismiss all charges against the activists. Judge Nichol found that government misconduct "formed a pattern throughout the course of the trial" and that the "waters of justice have been polluted" (*U.S. vs. Dennis Banks and Russell Means* 1974).

The 1960s and 1970s were a period of fervent grassroots activism in the United States, much of it coalescing around the social and economic changes following World War II, and the intense domestic conflict over the legality and morality of the Vietnam War. For those who lived through it, the activism of this period can seem both romantic and unprecedented in terms of what it achieved and the overriding sense of collective empowerment among the previously disenfranchised. Nevertheless, while the 1980s proved in many ways much less glamorous and exciting in terms of grassroots activism in general, Native American activists continued to achieve significant advances. Building on the policy of self-determination, activists began slowly but inexorably to wrest control over education, cultural issues, health, and tribal politics from political elites as well as federal and state governments, and to return it to tribal communities. An especially important milestone in this time frame concerned passage of the Native American Graves and Repatriation Act, a federal law passed in 1990 that provided mechanisms and requirements by which museums and other institutions had to repatriate sacred and funerary items, as well as human remains, to tribes from which they had been stolen in the eighteenth and nineteenth centuries (see http://www.nps.gov/history/nagpra/). Native Americans were also crucial participants in the global indigenous resistance to the original Human Genome Diversity Project (HGDP), arguing that as initially conceived by government officials, the project simply repeated bioethical mistakes of the settler era despite being dressed up in the guise of modern genetic and health-related research.

At the beginning of the twenty-first century, numerous complicated issues remain to be resolved between Native Americans and federal and state governments. Environmental issues in Indian communities, in particular—such as coal mining, water depletion and pollution, expropriation of jobs and resources, corruption, and health risks—remain central to the activist agenda today. Despite these many challenges, however, the ideal—if not always the reality—of Native American self-determination now provides the foundation for the incremental realization of cultural and political autonomy.

REFERENCES

American Indian Movement (AIM). "Trail of Broken Treaties Twenty Point Position Paper," October 1972. Retrieved from http://www.aimovement.org/archives/index.html on December 12, 2010.

Cobb, Daniel M. *Native Activism in Cold War America: The Struggle for Sovereignty.* Lawrence: University Press of Kansas, 2008.

Deloria, Vine Jr. *We Talk, You Listen.* New York: Delacorte Press, 1972.

Doolittle, James Rood. *Condition of the Indian Tribes: Report of the Joint Special Committee Appointed Under Joint Resolution of March 3, 1865.* Washington, DC: Government Printing Office, 1867.

Durrett, Deanne. *Unsung Heroes of World War II: The Story of the Navaho Code Talkers.* Lincoln: University of Nebraska Press, 1998.

Henson, C. L. "From War to Self-Determination: A History of the Bureau of Indian Affairs." *American Studies Today Online*, 2009. Retrieved from http://www.americansc.org.uk/Online/indians.htm on September 1, 2010.

Johnson, Troy. *Indian Self-Determination and the Rise of Indian Activism: The Occupation of Alcatraz Island.* Urbana-Champaign: Board of Trustees of the University of Illinois, 1996.

Kelsey, Harry. "The Doolittle Report of 1867: Its Preparation and Shortcomings." *Arizona and the West* 17, no. 2 (1975): 107–120.

Lewis, David Rich. "Still Native: The Significance of Native Americans in the History of the Twentieth-Century West." *Western Historical Quarterly* 24, no. 2 (1994): 203–227.

Meriam, Lewis. *The Problem of Indian Administration: Report of a Survey Made at the Request of Honorable Hubert Work, Secretary of the Interior, and Submitted to Him, February 21, 1928.* Baltimore, MD: Institute for Government Research. Available at http://www.alaskool.org/native_ed/research_reports/IndianAdmin/Indian_Admin_Problms.html

Native Village. "1969 Occupation of Alcatraz Island." Retrieved from http://www.nativevillage.org/Inspiration-/Occupation%20of%20Alcatraz%20and%20the%20Alcatraz%20Proclamation%20alcatraz_proclamation.htm on December 12, 2010.

Peltier, Leonard. *Prison Writings: My Life Is My Sundance.* New York: St. Martin's Press, 1999.

Indian Tribal Courts and the U.S. Court System

Iris Hahn-Santoro

To understand the current relationship between Indians and the U.S. justice system, it is important first to understand the unique role that Indian tribes have been assigned by the Constitution of the United States, the ways this status was interpreted and further defined by landmark Supreme Court rulings, and how the tribal court systems work.

Many state courts within in the United States are reluctant to honor orders from tribal courts because they are not always sure how the tribal court system works and whether it complies with the legal standards of the United States. To alleviate some of the problems that go along with this lack of understanding, many states have established trial-state court forums. These forums allow for interaction and dialogue between the two systems and seek better understanding between state courts and tribal courts. The participants are usually judges from both systems.

The Bureau of Indian Affairs (BIA) uses the term *federally acknowledged tribal entity* for various indigenous groups that have a political relationship with the federal government. Groups included under this designation include tribal nations, pueblos, bands, villages, and Alaskan Inuits and Aleuts. Tribes are politically independent nations located within the boundaries of the United States, located on sovereign land. Roughly 2 percent of lands within the United States are governed by Native American tribal governments. This land is referred to as Indian country.

TRIBES AND THE FEDERAL GOVERNMENT

Tribes' unique, or rather extraconstitutional, status derives from the Commerce Clause of the U.S. Constitution. Article 1, Section 8, Clause 3 empowers Congress "to regulate Commerce with foreign Nations . . . States, and with the Indian Tribes." This provision explicitly gives Congress, rather than states, the power to act as the primary agent in relationships with tribes. This clause does not grant Congress the power to regulate Indian affairs, however. The legal standing of Native Americans in the United States is not the result of a planned, organized development of legal principles, but rather the accumulation of policies from different treaties, agreements, and rulings over time. U.S. Indian policy became further defined by three landmark Supreme Court decisions, namely *Johnson vs. M'Intosh* (21 U.S. 543; 1823), *Cherokee Nation vs. Georgia* (30 U.S. 1; 1831), and *Worcester vs. Georgia* (31 U.S. 515; 1832). In *Johnson*, the Court ruled that private citizens may not purchase land from Indians because the federal government had the sole power to negotiate with the nations and to dispense with their land. *Cherokee Nation* ruled that because the tribes were dependent nations within the United States, they should be considered wards of the federal government. Further, because they were dependent nations, not foreign nations, they lacked the standing to challenge state actions in federal court. Collectively, these decisions meant that tribes were nations essentially free of state controls, while their status as dependent nations meant that the United States was responsible for Indian health and welfare.

Worcester further clarified and revised the relationship between tribes and the federal and state governments. Samuel Worcester was a missionary living on Cherokee land. Georgia had passed a law that all non-Indians living on Indian land could live there only with a state-issued license. Worcester was arrested and sentenced to military service for not having obtained this permit. He appealed his conviction to the Supreme Court, arguing that the state had no authority over sovereign Indian land. The Supreme Court ruled in his favor and confirmed the political independence of Indian tribes. More importantly, the Supreme Court expressly rejected the idea that the states had any jurisdiction over Indian tribes within their borders.

In sharp contrast to these decisions stands *Lone Wolf vs. Hitchcock* (187 U.S. 553), a 1903 case that granted Congress plenary (i.e., absolute) power over Indian peoples. This meant that Congress now could change treaties and end specific rights without the consent of the affected tribes. Congress now had the power to unilaterally dispose of originally treaty-protected Indian land. Since the trust responsibility was still in effect, however, this absolute power was to be used only when it was deemed beneficial to the Indian peoples. Even though this decision has been widely discredited, it has not to date been overruled.

The years between 1830 and 1860 were marked by the removal policy, starting with the forcible removal of the Five Civilized Tribes (Cherokee, Chickasaw, Chocktaw, Creek, and Seminole) from the Southeastern United States to the newly created Indian Territory. Subsequently, the continued westward push of white settlers resulted in the reservation system and introduced the period of forced cultural assimilation. In 1887, Congress passed the General Allotment Act, authorizing the BIA to divide all reservation land into smaller parcels and then assign these parcels to Indian families and single adults over 18 years of age. Every Native American receiving an allotment also received U.S. citizenship. The intent was to persuade Indians to adopt the U.S. farming lifestyle. All land left over after the parcels were assigned was declared surplus and sold by the United States. This policy was an economic disaster for Indian tribes because the parceled land was often unproductive desert, and owners often were unable to pay the necessary property taxes or feed their families with crop yields. Many had to sell off their allotments or had them foreclosed on.

The relationship between Indians and the United States became even more complicated in 1924, when the Indian Citizenship Act made all Indians U.S. citizens. This resulted in Indians having multiple citizenship—their tribal citizenship and now American citizenship. While in *Standing Bear vs. Crook* (1879) a federal court decided that Indians had the right to withdraw from their respective tribe, there was no similar court decision after 1924 that would make it possible for Indians to decline to become U.S. citizens. Indians now were allowed to vote and hold state offices, but they were not subject to state law while on Indian land. However, the Bill of Rights, specifically the amendments referring to legal rights like due process, freedom from self-incrimination, the right to a speedy and public trial, trial by a jury in civil cases, freedom from excessive bail, and freedom from cruel and unusual punishments, did not apply to Native Americans, who were therefore not protected from tribal governments as they were from federal and state actions.

When the effects of the Allotment Act became apparent, federal policy toward Native Americans reverted to tribal sovereignty. The Indian Reorganization Act, which encouraged tribes to adopt U.S.-style constitutions and form tribal governments, was passed in 1934. Many tribes chose to adopt these constitutions. A number of tribes drafted and ratified constitutions closely modeled on the U.S. Constitution; others, though a smaller number, modeled their constitutions more on their tribe's traditional way of governance. In this period, tribes were also permitted to establish their own criminal justice regulations and operate their own court systems that enforced tribal laws. As part of this continuing process, some organizations, for example, the Navajo Tribal Court and the Mille Lacs Band of Chippewa Indians in Minnesota, are incorporating more traditional ways of settling disputes like Peacemaking and Sentencing Circles. The Navajo Peacemaking Program is a fixed part of its tribal court system and entails regulated discussion about disputes as a way of resolving them, while the Mille Lacs Band uses Sentencing Circles to deal with juvenile delinquents. Both the victim and the offender are present, together with their support groups and representatives of legal and social services; cases are decided by consensus on what the offender has to do in order to restore the peace.

TRIBAL COURTS

Many factors are involved in determining which party—tribe, local or state government, or federal government—has jurisdiction in cases, and thus in which court system a case will be tried. Among these factors are the severity of the crime; which parties were involved; whether either the perpetrator, victim, or both, are tribal members; whether it was a victimless crime; and whether the crime occurred on tribal land but neither the perpetrator nor the victim are tribal members.

In some states, tribes do not operate court systems or their courts may be limited such that they are permitted to hear only certain types of cases, like violations of hunting and fishing laws on the reservation or child welfare cases. These limitations go back to Public Law 83-280. This law was passed in 1953, expanding state jurisdiction onto tribal lands in six states—Minnesota, Wisconsin, California, Nebraska, Oregon, and later Alaska—due to the perceived lack of law enforcement and court system on certain reservations. This law further decreased tribal sovereignty in those states. Before Public Law 280 was enacted, states had no jurisdiction in civil or criminal matters involving Indians in Indian country; the Indian tribal courts and the federal government shared jurisdiction over such matters. In the states affected by Public Law 280, state courts could now prosecute all persons, Indian and non-Indian, who commit crimes on tribal land. Further, state courts could hear all private disputes, such as divorce, contract disputes, and personal injury cases.

On reservations in other states, the tribal justice system often evolved from courts that the BIA set up on reservations. These courts were an early attempt to assimilate native peoples into the U.S. legal system. These courts date back to a case occurring in the 1880s on what is now the Rosebud reservation in South Dakota. Crow Dog, a Lakota, allegedly killed another Lakota, Spotted Tail. The Lakota utilized their traditional methods of resolving such disputes, and Crow Dog had to pay restitution to Spotted Tail's family. The U.S. government deemed that this case did not meet acceptable standards of law enforcement and justice in Indian country, and brought Indians who had committed serious crimes under federal authority by enacting the Major Crimes Act in 1885. Further, they established Courts of Indian Offenses on the reservations, which were empowered to handle lesser offenses and disputes. Often the judges in these courts were superintendents of the local BIA office. There are still about 20 Courts of Indian Offenses active in the United States; because they operate under federal regulations contained in Volume 25 of the Code of Federal Regulations (CFR), they are often referred to as CFR Courts.

The roughly 150 tribal courts are operated by the tribes under their own laws. While they often receive funding from the Department of Interior (DOI), most tribes supplement their court systems using their own resources. While many provisions of the Bill of Rights were extended to Indian peoples via the 1968 Indian Civil Rights Act (25 USC 1302), including free speech protections, free exercise of religion, and due process, notable exceptions include the right to a jury trial in civil cases and free legal counsel for the poor, neither of which were covered by that act. Since Indian tribal courts are not mentioned in the U.S. Constitution, questions as to their authority and the degree of respect they are entitled from other courts often arises, particularly with regard to whether tribal court judgments are to be honored by other courts under the full faith and credit clause. This clause means that one court system must honor and enforce decisions from other court systems, meaning that the U.S. Constitution compels state courts to honor each other's court decisions. One settled matter concerns cases that fall under the Indian Child Welfare Act, which explicitly requires state courts to grant full faith and credit to tribal court child custody orders.

In *Oliphant vs. Suquamish Tribe* (435 U.S. 191; 1978), the Supreme Court ruled that Indian tribal courts cannot prosecute crimes committed by non-Indians on Indian reservations. Mark David Oliphant was a non-Indian living as a permanent resident on the Suquamish reservation in northwest Washington. Oliphant was charged with assaulting a tribal officer and resisting arrest. Oliphant then applied for a writ of habeas corpus in federal court, meaning that he challenged the tribe's right to detain and prosecute him. This application was rejected by the lower courts, which held that the authority to prosecute such crimes was an important attribute of tribal sovereignty. The Supreme Court, however, overruled the lower courts in a 6–2 decision (with one abstention). The Court's principal argument was that legal jurisdiction over non-Indians is not an inherent right and therefore can be invested only by an explicit congressional act or treaty. In 1990, the Supreme Court extended this decision by ruling that tribes also lack jurisdiction over Indians of other tribes. Within six months, however, Congress passed legislation reversing the Court's ruling and amending the Indian Civil Rights Act to specifically state that tribes have jurisdiction over nonmember Indians.

Tribal courts procedures are similar to those of state and federal courts. Tribal judges are either appointed or elected by the governing body of the specific tribe to serve a certain term. Some tribes require a bar exam for their attorneys but, since most tribes allow both attorneys and tribal members who have become knowledgeable in tribal law to practice in the court system, counsel eligibility is often limited to paying a fee. Tribal courts use sworn testimony, keep a record of all court proceedings, and use a judge and jury system to come to decisions. The primary difference between tribal and state or federal courts is not procedural, but rather, as already stated, the limitations on the court's authority. All criminal cases involving a non-Indian perpetrator must be prosecuted outside the tribal court system, even if the crime was committed against a member of the tribe. If the victim was

Indian, the case will be prosecuted in federal court, whereas all cases involving a crime against a non-Indian are tried in state court, as are all victimless crimes.

Tribal courts are also limited in the kinds of sentences they can impose on Indians convicted of offenses. The Indian Civil Rights Act prohibits tribal courts from imposing a jail sentence in excess of one year or a fine in excess of $5,000 for any single offense. Because of this limitation, most tribes prefer not to prosecute felonies such as murder, rape, and aggravated assault; they turn these cases over to the federal courts. Tribal jails often resemble holding cells in a police station and frequently are not equipped for long-term incarceration. In many cases, tribes have established contracts with local city or county facilities, or sometimes with a neighboring tribe, for housing their offenders.

Some offenders can be tried in both tribal and federal or state courts. *United States vs. Wheeler* (254 U.S. 281; 1978) declared it permissible to prosecute some crimes in both federal and tribal courts. Anthony Robert Wheeler was a member of the Diné (Navajo) tribe who was convicted in tribal court of disorderly conduct and contributing to the delinquency of a minor. He was subsequently indicted by a federal grand jury for statutory rape arising from the same criminal act. Initially, the federal district court in Arizona dismissed this case on the grounds that Wheeler had already been convicted of the crime. On appeal, the Supreme Court held that the Diné tribe had acted as an independent sovereign in punishing Wheeler for violating Navajo tribal law. The tribal court was not to be understood as an arm of the federal government, which meant that a subsequent federal prosecution for a crime arising from the same criminal incident is not barred by the double jeopardy clause.

In accordance with the Indian Civil Rights Act, any person charged with crimes in tribal court has the right to remain silent, to be read the charges against him or her, to confront and call witnesses, to reasonable bail, and to a jury trial when facing a possible jail sentence. Unlike federal courts, however, which guarantee trial before a panel of 12 jurors in any case where a potential jail sentence exceeds six months, a defendant in a tribal court has the right to a six-person jury. Further, tribal courts are not required to provide free counsel for someone charged in tribal court; although every person has the right to representation, the court is not obligated to appoint and pay for an attorney when the defendant cannot afford one. Most tribes, however, have systems to assist indigent tribal defendants, such as special grants for which defendants may apply to hire counsel. On the other side, some tribes employ a tribal prosecutor or employ counsel specifically for certain crimes, like domestic violence.

Congress has given Indian tribes some influence over cases tried in federal courts when the crime was committed on a reservation. One example of this influence is that the death penalty may not be sought against those standing trial for a murder committed on a reservation if the tribe in question has not passed a tribal resolution permitting that punishment. By the same token, three-strikes rules for repeat offenders may apply only if the tribe permits it; likewise, an affirmative tribal resolution is necessary to try juveniles under the age of 13 as adults. A convicted defendant may appeal to federal court in order to challenge his or her conviction after he or she has exhausted the tribal court system's appeals process. In this case, however, the appellant must show that the original trial violated some provision of the Indian Civil Rights Act.

CIVIL CASES

Tribal courts have broader authority when prosecuting civil cases. A civil case is a legal dispute between two or more parties, for example, divorce or cases arising from a debt. In *Williams vs. Lee* (358 U.S. 217; 1959), the Supreme Court ruled that all civil disputes involving an Indian on a reservation may be brought only in tribal court and cannot be passed on to a state court. This is so even if one of the parties to the dispute is a non-Indian. Hugh Lee was a non-Indian running a general goods store on the Diné reservation where Paul Williams, a Diné Indian, and his wife Lorena purchased merchandize on credit. Lee filed a claim against the Williams couple in state court to collect on the debt. The lower court filed in Lee's favor, allowing Lee to acquire the Williams's sheep herd, thus taking away their only means of earning a living. Williams and his wife appealed, arguing that the Diné tribe had a legal system sufficient to handle the case. The Supreme Court ruled in favor of the appellants, confirming and strengthening Indian sovereignty in civil disputes.

If a non-Indian enters into a relationship with a tribe, either through marriage to a tribal member or by signing a contract to perform work on tribal land, the tribal court can hear and decide all disputes that may arise from this relationship. Tribal courts can also exercise authority over non-Indians when an event occurs on tribal land that seriously impacts the tribe and its members' health, such as domestic violence cases or the pollution of reservation waters. In these cases, while the tribal court has the authority to issue orders to prevent further pollution or violence, it nevertheless is restricted from prosecuting the non-Indians in these cases in tribal court. Tribal courts are further barred from hearing bankruptcy cases or law suits against the U.S. government. These cases must be heard in a federal court.

Tribal court procedures in civil cases often mirror those in state and federal courts. A judge will decide the case after listening to the arguments and evidence brought forward by the parties involved. Some tribes permit a jury trial in cases involving a large amount of money. The tribal courts will also sometimes decide cases in accordance with the tribe's custom law, which is often not defined in the tribe's legal code. In custody disputes or neglect cases, for example, many tribal courts will place Indian children with their grandmothers because grandparents traditionally were in charge of raising children. It is also still customary that everyone, especially elders, has the right to be heard in court. These testimonies are allowed to take a long time and often go, seemingly, off-topic. It is considered respectful and necessary to hear all parties out and listen to their concerns to the end.

REFERENCES

Henson, Eric C. et al. *The State of the Native Nations: Conditions Under U.S. Policies of Self-Determination*. New York: Oxford University Press, 2008.

O'Brien, Sharon. *American Indian Tribal Governments*. Norman: University of Oklahoma Press, 1989.

Tribal Court Clearinghouse. Available at http://www.tribal-institute.org/

Wilkins, David E. *American Indian Sovereignty and the U.S. Supreme Court*. Austin: University of Texas Press, 1997.

Wilkinson, Charles F. *American Indians, Times, and the Law: Native Societies in a Modern Constitutional Democracy*. New Haven, CT: Yale University Press, 1987.

Indian Trust Lands Managed by the Federal Government

Lindsey Hanson

The U.S. government holds almost 60 million acres of land on and off reservations in trust for American Indian tribes and individual American Indians. This land is referred to as tribal trust land, or individual trust land, respectively. The federal government's management of this trust land through the Department of the Interior (DOI) has been subject to numerous litigated and unlitigated claims of trust mismanagement. To understand these allegations, it is first necessary to understand the history of Indian trust land, or how it is that the land came to be held in trust by the U.S. government in the first place. It is also necessary to understand how trusts work and the duties the manager of a trust owes to the beneficiary of a trust. With this background, it will be possible to understand the accusations of mismanagement as well as past and ongoing efforts to reform how Indian trust land is managed by the federal government.

THE HISTORY OF INDIAN TRUST LAND

Prior to European colonization of the land that is now the United States, the land was occupied by American Indian tribes. As early as 1790, the U.S. Congress passed the first Indian Intercourse Act, which prohibited American Indian tribes from selling land to any person or entity other than the federal government. By U.S. Supreme Court order in *Johnson vs. M'Intosh* (1823), land occupied by American Indian tribes was said to be held in "Indian title." A tribe had a right to occupancy of land held in Indian title, but as the discoverer, the U.S. government had "ultimate dominion" of the land. Practically, this meant that tribes could pass good title to land only to the U.S. government, not to another tribe, a state, or private individuals. As the only available purchaser, the U.S. government entered into a series of treaties with American Indian tribes that resulted in much of the land previously occupied by tribes being ceded to the federal government for settlement. The smaller areas of land that remained occupied by American Indian tribes became known as reservations.

The General Allotment Act of 1887, also known as the Dawes Act, fragmented tribal control of these reservations and gave portions of land within the reservations to individual American Indians. Each allotment was held in trust by the U.S. government for individual American Indians for 25 years. After the allotment process took place on a reservation, the federal government then generally made agreements with the tribe about which lands were to be held and which could be opened for settlement by non-Indians. The result was extensive loss of land for American Indians. For example, after the allotment process, American Indians on the Leech Lake Reservation in Minnesota owned only 4 percent of their own reservation. In addition to the land that was lost outright, the allotment process resulted in much confusion of title; even today, many tracts of land on reservations have such clouded title that they cannot be legally sold.

Under the Burke Act of 1906, land allotted to individual American Indians was to be taken out of trust with the U.S. government and given to the individual in fee simple. When land is held in fee simple, the title-holder has absolute ownership and can use and sell the land freely. A fee simple owner is also subject to taxes. Often, allotments were taken out of trust without the individual American Indian allottee knowing that this had happened or being aware that taxes were owed on the land. The result was unpaid taxes and the land later being sold at a tax sale to pay for those taxes.

The Indian Reorganization Act of 1934 reversed most of this allotment policy. The act disallowed additional allotments and required that the land be held in trust not for 25 years, but for an indefinite period of time. Land on reservations that had not been allotted was restored to American Indian tribes, and the U.S. Secretary of the Interior was authorized to purchase additional lands to hold in trust for American Indians. This land is still being held in trust for American Indians by the U.S. Secretary of the Interior.

HOW TRUSTS WORK: THE DUTIES OF A TRUSTEE AND THE RIGHTS OF A BENEFICIARY

As the entity holding assets in trust, the U.S. government is a trustee. As a trustee, the federal government owes certain duties to beneficiaries of the trust. A beneficiary is the original owner of a trust asset when it is placed in trust. In this case, individual American Indians or tribes are the beneficiaries.

As a trustee, the U.S. government owes fiduciary duties to the American Indian beneficiaries of the trust land. A trustee owes a beneficiary the duty of loyalty, which means the trustee cannot take advantage of the trust assets for its own benefit, but must act in the best interests of the beneficiary. Trustees also have certain duties to inform beneficiaries about the trust and administration of the trust.

As holder of beneficial title, individual American Indians and tribes have the right to occupy and use the land; any profits from the land belong to these tribes or individuals. The land held in trust may generate profit in a number of ways. It may be leased out for grazing, or for coal production, oil production, or timber harvesting. The profits are then disbursed to the holders of beneficial title through Individual Indian Money (IIM) accounts, which are interest-bearing accounts managed by the Department of the Interior (DOI).

Beneficial title can be passed on by will, sold, or inherited. However, tribal code may place limits on whether non-Indians, or Indians not enrolled in the same tribe, can hold beneficial title to particular Indian trust land. Land held in trust by the United States for American Indians is subject to neither state or local taxation, nor regulation.

Despite the duties the federal government owes to American Indian beneficiaries, there has been widespread recognition that the government has not been living up to its duties as a trustee. In fact, there has never been a full accounting of trust assets to any American Indian tribe. As a result, the federal government's trust management has been the source of much litigation and many reform efforts.

THE AMERICAN INDIAN TRUST FUND MANAGEMENT REFORM ACT OF 1994

One such reform effort was the American Indian Trust Management Reform Act of 1994. This act recognized the responsibility of the Secretary of the Interior to account for balances of Indian trust funds on a daily and annual basis, and required the Secretary to provide a statement of performance to tribes and individuals within 20 business days of the close of each calendar quarter. These periodic statements are to include "(1) the source, type, and status of the funds; (2) the beginning balance; (3) the gains and losses; (4) receipts and disbursements; and (5) the ending balance" (25 USC 42 Sec. 4011(b)) (l).

The act also required an annual audit of all funds held in trust for American Indian tribes or individuals. Additionally, it allowed tribes greater control over tribal funds currently held in trust and gave tribes the opportunity to submit a plan to withdraw trust funds. It also provided for the Secretary of the Interior to supply technical assistance to tribes undertaking the management of trust funds, and developed a grant program to award grants to tribes for the purpose of developing and implementing plans for the use of trust funds.

Finally, the act established the Office of the Special Trustee for American Indians (OST) within the Department of Interior to improve trust management.

The OST is charged with collecting funds for the trust, investing funds, disbursing funds, appraising property within the trust, and improving trust management through reform. The Bureau of Indian Affairs (BIA) has the responsibility of managing resources within the trust, including managing permits, rights-of-way, and leases of property. However, despite this reform effort, controversy and mismanagement continued.

LITIGATED ACCUSATIONS OF TRUST MISMANAGEMENT: *COBELL VS. SALAZAR* AND OTHERS

In 1996, Native American Rights Fund (NARF) attorneys filed suit in the largest ever class-action lawsuit involving American Indians against the U.S. government. The NARF attorneys alleged that the federal government had failed to account for assets in individual Indian trusts, making it impossible to tell whether funds had been properly disbursed to individual beneficiaries. The lead plaintiff in the suit was Elouise Cobell, a member of the Blackfoot reservation in Montana. Although the U.S. government held land that was being used for farming and oil drilling in trust for Cobell's family, the family was never paid regularly for the use of the land.

NARF's objective in filing the suit was twofold:

1. To require the federal government to create and maintain an adequate system to properly manage and accurately account for the trust assets of individual Indians
2. To require the federal government to provide a full and accurate accounting to individual Indian trust beneficiaries, and to restate IIM account balances accordingly

The trial was bifurcated to deal with these two issues separately. In December 1999, the U.S. District Court for the District of Columbia ruled on the first phase of the trial and held that the U.S. government had breached its responsibility to individual Indian trust beneficiaries. The federal government was ordered to reform its system for managing individual Indian trusts. The U.S. government appealed this ruling to the U.S. Court of Appeals for the District of Columbia, but the ruling was unanimously upheld.

In December 2009, the U.S. government reached a $3.4 billion settlement with the plaintiffs in the case, which by this time was known as *Cobell v. Salazar*. Under the terms of the settlement, only $1.4 billion, minus attorneys' fees, which could run as high as $100 million, will go to the individual plaintiffs. Some of the funds will go to create a trust to provide higher education opportunities for American Indians. Two billion dollars will go to the Department of the Interior, which is charged with buying more land to create larger and more profitable holdings for tribal trusts. As part of the settlement, the Department of the Interior also agreed to reform its management of trust accounts to make the accounts more effective.

The settlement terms were signed, and funding was authorized by President Obama on December 8, 2010. The terms of the settlement were given preliminary approval by the District Court on December 21, 2010. In late January 2011, possible beneficiaries of the settlement began to be notified, and in June 2011, a fairness hearing on the settlement terms was held.

While the settlement was widely lauded, many American Indians remain skeptical. The skepticism of many comes partially from the fact that even accountants for the U.S. government believe that it is $8 to $40 billion that is actually owed to American Indians and tribes for trust mismanagement. In fact, by the plaintiff's calculations, the government may have owed as much as $47 billion, and the plaintiffs had rejected an $8 billion settlement offer in October 2006. Despite these large numbers, under the settlement terms, each individual American Indian affected will likely receive less than $2,000. Given the Interior Department's prior mismanagement, many American Indians also have doubts about the provision entrusting $2 billion to the department to buy more land and create more profitable holdings. Some are concerned that the money may revert to the U.S. government if there are not enough individuals willing to sell their land to an agency that has garnered such distrust.

Despite its notoriety, *Cobell* is not the only lawsuit that alleged mismanagement of Indian trusts by the U.S. government. As of February 2010, there were approximately 95 cases before federal courts in which American Indian plaintiffs were alleging trust mismanagement. In one such case, the heirs of Andrew Oenga, a member of the Inupiat in Alaska, were recently awarded $4.924 million. A lease of Oenga's land to oil giant BP was drafted by the BIA in 1989 for Oenga, who could not speak or read English. Despite requests from the Oenga family to take action, the BIA allowed BP to use the land in violation of the lease for 16 years. Lease violations included the production of oil from unauthorized areas and unauthorized subletting of the land to other oil producers. No further fees were collected from BP for these additional and unauthorized uses. The Oenga family may also be awarded additional funds, from $7 to $12 million, for payments due from authorized uses of the land. It is not yet known whether the federal government will appeal the $4.924 million judgment.

INDIAN TRUST REFORM

As part of the *Cobell* case, the federal government was ordered to develop a trust reform plan. The DOI released a roadmap for trust reform in January 2002. The agency contracted by the DOI to study and assess the reform efforts identified challenging issues unique to Indian trust management. Among the unique factors identified were the sheer amount of land under management, that the trust was established by the government trustee rather than a trustor, that the cultural heritage of particular portions of land may exceed the monetary value, that some individual accounts are very small, that there is no requirement to generate a profit and no service charge, that investments are limited to government or government-backed securities, and that agreements or documents do not exist for every account between the government and the beneficiary to give specific guidance on trust management.

The investigation into trust reform also found that reform had "lacked a vision or strategy," and that there was no comprehensive strategy for meeting fiduciary duties like accounting for trust assets, preparing reports for account holders, assuring account accuracy, or managing resources on trust lands. The contracted assessor also found that trust beneficiaries were not receiving the level of service customary in commercial trust relationships, that a number of inefficiencies in trust management existed, and that there was a lack of resources available for trust management. The roadmap focused reform efforts on bringing the federal government into compliance with its fiduciary duties. These fiduciary duties include acting as a prudent investor exercising reasonable care, skill, and caution and meeting the duties of loyalty and impartiality while accounting for trust assets and managing trust resources.

The National Congress of American Indians (NCAI) also advanced its own priorities for trust reform. Among those priorities, the NCAI did not want reform and reorganization to result in a centralized bureaucracy. Instead, it wanted to see individuals working in various regions and on different reservations addressing unique regional and tribal issues with trust management. NCAI was also concerned that overall funding for Indian programs and services would drop as a result of increased funding for the central office to undertake trust reform efforts. NCAI also supported laws that would encourage the consolidation of trust lands and make administration and management of the trusts easier. It did not want to see the trust responsibility of the Department of the Interior lessened; rather, it wanted to encourage settlement of trust mismanagement suits and reform of the trust management system. Finally, the NCAI emphasized the importance of continued support for tribal self-determination and the role of the federal government as trustee in protecting the long-term self-determination of tribes. To this end, the NCAI advocated for future trust management that involves increased tribal control over the land and resources, with technical assistance and oversight coming from the U.S. government.

According to the 2008 OST report to Congress, the government's reform efforts have been largely successful. The OST reports that early on it started utilizing the Trust Funds Accounting System (TFAS), the same software utilized by major commercial trust institutions. This software allows for automated collections and disbursements, allows account holders access to daily balances, and schedules periodic statements of performance for account holders. The TFAS also assists in the reconciling of investment holdings with custodians and the reconciling of daily activity with the Treasury. Among other reforms, the OST reports that it has implemented a lockbox system for secure, centralized processing and depositing of payments, and a system that allows beneficiaries to receive payments through a debit card or direct deposit. The OST also reports that it has been providing account holders with statements for trust assets since 2000. In 2004, the OST implemented a centralized call center to answer beneficiary questions. In 2008, the OST employed an additional 52 fiduciary trust officers (FTOs) to serve as local contact points for beneficiaries and to engage in community outreach. Six regional trust administrators (RTAs) also serve as points of contact. Additionally, independent annual audits of trust funds have been completed each year since 1995.

Despite these changes, however, the OST also identified a number of remaining challenges in trust management. Among those challenges is the issue of fractionation, or numerous interests in one tract of land. This fractionation makes maintaining title, and managing probate and trust property in an effective manner difficult. The OST predicts that if the fractionation issue were resolved, there would be fewer accounts to manage, property could be managed to generate more income, and less money would be spent on account management. If this issue were resolved, beneficiaries could also take on a greater role in managing the assets. The OST also identified the need to create a long-term commitment to trust reform even without the impetuous created by pending litigation or controversy. Other challenges identified by the OST include ensuring that staff utilizes new systems, standardizing procedures across tribes and agencies, and transitioning to a paperless system. Additional challenges faced by the OST include efficiently responding to ongoing trust related litigation and dealing with the ongoing problem of resolving historical accounting issues to improve public perception of the program.

The National Congress of American Indians addressed the issue of trust reform in December 2010 at the White House Tribal Nations Summit. At that summit, the NCAI commended the government for the settlement of *Cobell* and urged similar settlements for other related ongoing litigation, and continued efforts at reform of the trust management system. It recommended that the U.S. government consult with tribes on trust reform to increase efficiency of the trust administration and improve trust returns. Like the OST, the NCAI recognized fractional interests as a continued area of concern for trust management. It encouraged immediate consultation with tribes to identify land that could be acquired and consolidated. The NCAI also advocated for increased self-determination for tribes, including the removal of the requirement for the Secretary of the Interior's approval of all leasing decisions made by tribes.

It remains to be seen what reforms in Indian trust will occur as we enter further into the era of tribal self-determination. There will undoubtedly be disagreements between American Indian tribes and the federal government about what the future of Indian trusts should be. However, there is at least agreement that past management of Indian trusts fell short of the duties of the federal government as trustee, and recognition that continued efforts at reform remain necessary.

REFERENCES

American Indian Trust Fund Management Reform. 25 U.S.C. 42 Sec. 4011(b) http://www.law.cornell.edu/uscode/text/25/4011

Capriccioso, Rob. "Cobell's Final Toll." *Indian Country Today*, January 17, 2011. Retrieved from http://indiancountrytodaymedianetwork.com/2011/01/cobells-final-toll/ on February 13, 2011.

Echohawk, John. "Individual Indian Money (IIM) Accounts *Cobell v. Kempthorne*: Fact Sheet for IIM Account Holders and Other Individual Indian Trust Beneficiaries." *NARF*. Retrieved from http://www.narf.org/cases/iimgeninfo.htm on February 13, 2011.

Indian Trust Settlement. Available at http://www.cobellsettlement.com/

McCoy, Melody L. "Tribal Trust Funds Accounting & Mismanagement Litigation," February 11–12, 2010. Retrieved from http://www.law.ku.edu/academics/triballaw/pdfs/McCoy_CLE.pdf on February 13, 2011.

McNeel, Jack. "Oegna Family Awarded $4.924 Million." *Indian Country Today*, February 11, 2011. Retrieved from http://indiancountrytodaymedianetwork.com/2011/02/oenga-family-awarded-4-924-million/ on February 13, 2011.

National Congress of American Indians. "Trust Reform," December 2010. Retrieved from http://www.ncai.org/fileadmin/ncai_events/2010_WH_Summit/1d_-_Trust_reform_-_FINAL.pdf on February 13, 2011.

National Congress of American Indians. "Trust Reorganization." Retrieved from http://www.ncai.org/ncai/resource/documents/governance/trust-ncai_statement_on_trust_reorganization.pdf on February 13, 2011.

Office of Special Trustee for American Indians. "Individual Indian Money Account Information." Retrieved from http://www.bia.gov/idc/groups/mywcsp/documents/collection/idc010124.pdf on February 13, 2011.

Office of the Special Trustee for American Indians. "Meeting the Challenge: 2008 Annual Report to Congress." Retrieved from http://www.doi.gov/ost/press_room/publications/annualreports/OST_2008_Annual_Report_to_Congress.pdf on February 13, 2011.

Reis, Patrick. "Obama Admin Strikes $3.4B Deal in Indian Trust Lawsuit." *New York Times*, December 8, 2009. Retrieved from http://www.nytimes.com/gwire/2009/12/08/08greenwire-obama-admin-strikes-34b-deal-in-indian-trust-l-92369.html on February 13, 2011.

Treuer, Anton. *People in Minnesota: Ojibwe in Minnesota*. St. Paul: Minnesota Historical Society Press, 2010.

U.S. Department of the Interior. "Trust Reform Final Report and Roadmap," January 24, 2002. Retrieved from http://www.doi.gov/indiantrust/pdf/roadmap.pdf on February 13, 2011.

INDIANS AND CONGRESS

Amy L. Fletcher

As the lawmaking branch of America's divided system of government, Congress wields extensive power and influence with respect to the norms and laws that govern the relationship between Native American tribes and the federal government. The history of congressional–Native American relations is long and complex, and involves treaties, citizenship, land and property, and the recent commitment to reconciliation between the United States and the indigenous peoples of America.

HISTORICAL BACKGROUND

During the Revolutionary War, the Continental Congress—comprising delegates from the 13 colonies that fought for independence—wanted to discourage Native American tribes from joining the British in their disputes with the colonies. The Continental Congress worked with the tribes on a diplomatic basis, signing, for example, a treaty with the Delaware tribe in 1778. Following the Revolutionary War (1775–1783), the newly independent United States agreed to govern itself via the Articles of Confederation. Because each individual state wanted to assert power and sovereignty, the Articles of Confederation were weak from a federal point of view. Each state could print its own money and regulate its own commerce. The number of treaties between the United States and Indian tribes, including important agreements with the Iroquois Confederacy, the Cherokee tribe and the Shawnee tribe.

The Constitutional Convention of 1787 was originally convened in Philadelphia to amend the Articles of Confederation. However, convinced that the new and fragile American government faced imminent collapse due to both wartime debt and lack of a strong central government, major figures at the convention such as Alexander Hamilton and James Madison decided to discard the Articles of Confederation and start anew. The resulting Constitution of the United States, along with the Bill of Rights (the first 10 amendments to the Constitution) was ratified by all American states by 1791. Article I of the Constitution, which enumerates the powers of the House and the Senate, specifically vested the "power to regulate commerce with the Indian tribes" in the U.S. Congress. Though Native American relationships with state governments remain important, particularly in areas such as water rights and environmental issues, the federal authority of Congress is supreme in this regard. Reflecting the importance of Native American relations to the new government, the First Congress (1789–1791) enacted four statutes relating to Indian affairs within its first five weeks. Specifically, it delegated responsibility for Indian affairs to the Department of War and set aside money to negotiate treaties.

The initial period of relative harmony between the newly independent citizens of the United States and the indigenous tribes began to deteriorate rapidly during the period of westward expansion. In 1787, the Congress passed the Northwest Ordinance, which essentially opened up the area that would later become Ohio, Michigan, Wisconsin, and Illinois to settlers and economic development. The Northwest Ordinance symbolized and accelerated the American push west. While the ordinance excluded slavery in the new states, the effect of westward expansion was devastating to Native American tribes. The reservation system began at this time, as the U.S. government often promised protection from white settlers to those tribes that peacefully forfeited their traditional lands and moved onto smaller settlements. These promises were often not kept, and horrific levels of violence characterized many of the battles between Native Americans and settlers. Following the Civil War (1861–1865), the federal government essentially adopted a policy of Native American assimilation, seeking to absorb Native American tribes into the larger society. To contemporary eyes, this policy seems ill advised from the outset, and certainly it often resulted in the harsh oppression of native cultures, languages, religions, and mores. However, it is important to remember that many reformers and liberals of the era supported the assimilation policy because they thought it was the only realistic way to keep Native Americans from vanishing as a people under the onslaught of modernity. To aid assimilation, and to extend American control over western territories, Congress in 1871 forbade the President from negotiating any more formal treaties with tribes and also declared that it would no longer treat tribes as distinct nations within the United States.

It is within this political context that the General Allotment Act of 1887 (also known as the Dawes Act, after its principal sponsor, Congressman Henry Dawes) passed Congress. The Dawes Act was notable for its overt belief in the "civilizing power" of private property. The main goal of the act was to break up land held communally by tribes and convert the land into a system of privately held allotments. The bill's sponsors believed that owning private property would give individual Indians a stake in westward expansion and economic development, and would hasten the assimilation of tribes into the now-dominant white/settler society. Essentially, the U.S. government would hold land in trust for 25 years, for, as the bill states, "the sole use and benefit of the Indian to whom such an allotment shall have been made," and then would transfer the property deed outright, and at no cost, to the Indian title owner. Each allotment was approximately 160 acres, and, as an added inducement, American citizenship was extended to all Indians with property allotments and to those Native Americans who "voluntarily" decided to live apart from any Indian tribe and to adopt "the habits of civilized life." "Surplus land" not distributed through the allotment system was opened up to settlers; thus, the Dawes Act also furthered settlers' goals of westward expansion and economic development.

NATIVE AMERICANS AND CONGRESS IN THE TWENTIETH CENTURY

One unintended effect of the Dawes Act was that the question of Native American citizenship became extremely complex. Indians at this time were barred from the normal naturalization processes open to immigrants from foreign countries. Moreover, and partially as a result of the Dawes Act, some Native Americans had citizenship due to ownership of allotments, while others had citizenship because of marrying a white person, military service, or through special treaties. Finally, in June 1924, Congress passed the Indian Citizenship Act, which granted citizenship to all Native Americans and sought to absorb Indians into mainstream American civic life. Supporters of the act emphasized the dedication of Native American soldiers who fought in World War I and argued that Indians had clearly earned citizenship due to their willingness to fight totalitarianism in Europe. (There were no segregated Native American units in the U.S. military in World War I, in contrast to the segregated units that existed for African American men.)

Following World War I, the United States entered a period of intense economic development and social upheaval. Particularly influential in this timeframe were the "progressives," a loose band of social reformers, conservatives, feminists, socialists, and liberals who sought to improve the lot of the urban poor, increase legal and political rights for women, improve higher education, and build "fitter families" through advances in social engineering, hygiene, and modern medicine. Progressives could be found on all sides of the political spectrum, and in retrospect many of their policies seem paternalistic at best and racist at worst. Within their own time frame, however, most progressives sincerely sought to improve health, welfare, and educational outcomes for various groups in American society. It is against the progressive-era backdrop that the Meriam Report of 1928 was released. Congress requested the report in 1926, authorizing the Institute for Government Research (now known as the Brookings Institution) to study Native American economic and social conditions. The report concluded that the Dawes Act policy of allotments was failing, both practically and morally, and that incompetence and corruption plagued the underfunded Office of Indian Affairs. (The Office of Indian Affairs was transferred from the War Department to the Department of the Interior in 1849 and renamed the Bureau of Indian Affairs in 1947.)

Despite the stock market crash of 1929, supporters of the Meriam Report instituted several policy initiatives—often referred to collectively as the Indian New Deal—to address the most serious failings of nineteenth century policies of assimilation. John Collier, Commissioner of the Office of Indian Affairs (1933–1945), used the report as the basis to push for substantial funding increases from Congress. Collier also sought to reverse the idea of total assimilation, pushing instead for recognition and preservation of indigenous cultures. The most important legislative victory in this time frame is the Indian Reorganization Act of 1934. Also known as the Wheeler-Howard Act, the law ended the Dawes allotment system, reinstituted tribal self-government, and resulted in approximately 2 million acres of land being returned to communal tribal holdings.

Following the Great Depression and the Japanese attack on Pearl Harbor in 1941, the United States quickly mobilized for World War II. As in World War I, many Native Americans fought valiantly against the fascist and dictatorial regimes in Europe. As the war ended, and the United States emerged as the single Western country capable of balancing the power of the Communist Soviet Union, a period of sustained economic growth and prosperity followed. During the 1950s, the federal government abandoned both the nineteenth century policies of assimilation and the reforms advanced by the Meriam Report, and began to implement a policy known today as termination. In 1953, for example, Congress passed House Concurrent Resolution 108 (also known as the Termination Act). This legislation sought to end the trust relationship between the U.S. government and tribes and also to end Native Americans' status as dual citizens. Critics noted that the practical effects of the Termination Act would be assimilation by other means since, if implemented fully, those tribes chosen for termination would have their status as tribal governments nullified, which in turn would render funding and/or protection from the federal government, as promised in treaties, null and void.

The Menominee tribe of Wisconsin was one of the most prominent tribes chosen for termination. Based on the assumption that lucrative profits from forestry conducted on the Menominee reservation would continue even in the absence of a trust relationship, the federal government formally terminated relations with the tribe in 1961. By the mid-1960s, however, it was obvious that the termination policy had failed the Menominee, due to the complexities of property taxes and the significant financial effects of trying to keep tribal social programs operating. Partially due to grassroots efforts, Congress was finally persuaded in 1972 to pass the Menominee Restoration Bill, reestablishing the Menominee as a tribe and reconstituting the trust relationship. Several other tribes experienced similar ill effects of the termination policy, which by the early 1970s quietly began to lapse due to congressional inactivity. In January 1983, President Ronald Reagan issued a statement formally repudiating the termination policy.

CONGRESSIONAL APOLOGY TO AMERICAN INDIANS

In 2010, Congress issued a formal apology to American Indians for unjust practices committed by the United States against Indians over the course of American history. The abridged text of the resolution follows.

IN THE SENATE OF THE UNITED STATES
April 30, 2009
JOINT RESOLUTION
To acknowledge a long history of official depredations and ill-conceived policies by the Federal Government regarding Indian tribes and offer an apology to all Native Peoples on behalf of the United States.
RESOLUTION OF APOLOGY TO NATIVE PEOPLES OF THE UNITED STATES.

(a) Acknowledgment and Apology- The United States, acting through Congress—

(1) recognizes the special legal and political relationship Indian tribes have with the United States and the solemn covenant with the land we share;

(2) commends and honors Native Peoples for the thousands of years that they have stewarded and protected this land;

(3) recognizes that there have been years of official depredations, ill-conceived policies, and the breaking of covenants by the Federal Government regarding Indian tribes;

(4) apologizes on behalf of the people of the United States to all Native Peoples for the many instances of violence, maltreatment, and neglect inflicted on Native Peoples by citizens of the United States;

(5) expresses its regret for the ramifications of former wrongs and its commitment to build on the positive relationships of the past and present to move toward a brighter future where all the people of this land live reconciled as brothers and sisters, and harmoniously steward and protect this land together;

> (6) urges the President to acknowledge the wrongs of the United States against Indian tribes in the history of the United States in order to bring healing to this land; and
>
> (7) commends the State governments that have begun reconciliation efforts with recognized Indian tribes located in their boundaries and encourages all State governments similarly to work toward reconciling relationships with Indian tribes within their boundaries.
>
> *Source*: Congressional Apology to American Indians. Retrieved from http://thomas.loc.gov/cgi-bin/query/z?c111:S.J.RES.14:

ACTIVISM

During the 1950s and 1960s, the civil rights struggles of African Americans tended to receive the majority of media and political attention, due in part to the violence meted out against activists by those who sought to preserve segregation. By the middle of the decade, the Vietnam War had become the political flashpoint, dividing American society seemingly into two opposed, and increasingly antagonistic, camps. However, by the late 1960s, and against the general backdrop of significant advances in civil rights for African Americans, women, and people with disabilities, Native American grievances against the federal government became more visible to the general public. The occupation of Alcatraz, from November 20, 1969 to June 11, 1971, was perhaps the most famous organized protest by Native Americans, but it precipitated an era of activism that sought neither assimilation nor termination, but renewal of Native American cultures, languages, and tribal rights. Key to this cultural renaissance was a different, and more equal, relationship between Native American tribes and Congress.

The Native American Graves Protection and Repatriation Act (NAGPRA), passed by Congress in 1990, is one of the most significant legislative victories in this new era of activism. NAGPRA sought to provide legal and responsible channels for the repatriation of Native American artifacts, skeletons, and funerary objects from museums, university collections, and libraries to Native American descendents and tribes. (The Smithsonian Institution is not covered by NAGPRA, but by different legislation.) Well into the twentieth century, museums and academic institutions paid little attention to the customs of the Native American tribes from which they essentially stole cultural and religious items. Prior to NAGPRA, which also seeks to address previous instances of graverobbing and burial desecration, Native American tribes had to rely on tort doctrines to seek redress, and could move forward with a case only when the remains in question were not on federal land. NAGPRA does attempt to strike a balance between Native American rights and the advancement of science by including a clause that allows for scientific study of remains or objects deemed "indispensable" to science or of "major benefit to the United States." The conflict between science and religion has resulted in controversies such as the Kennewick Man case, in which eight anthropologists sued to have a skeleton found in Washington reserved for scientific study, over the objection of tribes who sought immediate repatriation and burial of the remains. However, while it cannot completely resolve the tensions between scientific inquiry and indigenous spirituality, NAGPRA represents a major congressional acknowledgement of past wrongs committed in the name of science against Native Americans, and is generally considered an important civil rights victory for tribes.

This push toward self-determination continues as the United States enters the twenty-first century. Particularly significant is the recent resolution of a class action lawsuit filed by Elouise Cobell against the Interior and Treasury Departments in 1996 on behalf of Native American beneficiaries of trusts held for them by the federal government. These trusts date to the Dawes Act, when the federal government kept mineral and oil rights exempt from the general allotment policy, and continued to hold these rights "on behalf of" tribes rather than move them into individual ownership. In 1996, Senators John McCain and Bryron Dorgan, leaders of the Senate Indian Affairs Committee, introduced the first of several legislative attempts to calculate some form of fair compensation for the Native Americans affected (approximately 500,000 people) and to settle the lawsuit. However, both Treasury and the Interior proved resistant to settlements, and the inquiries seemed to stall until 2010, when Congress passed (and President Obama signed) a law mandating $3.4 billion in compensation to trust beneficiaries. The settlement is complex, as are the procedures for receiving compensation. Nevertheless, settlement of the *Cobell* lawsuit reflects a major admission of wrongdoing on behalf of the federal government, and a major victory in the fight for reconciliation and self-determination. In that same congressional session, Congress also approved four water rights settlements worth more than $1 billion to provide clean drinking water to tribes in New Mexico, Arizona, and Montana.

One of the most controversial issues currently facing Native Americans and the federal government is the question of Native Hawaiian sovereignty. Unlike Alaska Natives and the tribes of the continental United States, indigenous Hawaiians do not have the same government-to-government status as a sovereign people. The Kingdom of Hawaii was overthrown in 1893 and was annexed by the United States in 1898. (Hawaii became a U.S. state in 1959.) Indigenous Hawaiians did receive a formal apology from the U.S. government in 1993, but the state and indigenous groups are currently divided politically on whether to push for tribal recognition (similar to Native American and Alaskan tribes) or to attempt to achieve complete Hawaiian sovereignty (which would imply formal succession from the United States). The Native Hawaiian Government Reorganization

Act, introduced by Senator Daniel Akaka (D-Hawaii) in 2009 (and in previous legislative sessions) would provide a process for tribal recognition of Native Hawaiian groups. However, the bill is currently opposed both by Hawaiian indigenous groups who want to press for full sovereignty, and by some members of Congress who argue that passage of the bill would result in an unconstitutional race-based government in Hawaii.

Perhaps the most important symbolic legislative act of recent times is the passage of a joint congressional resolution apologizing to Native Americans for "ill-conceived policies" and "acts of violence" committed by the federal government. Senator Sam Brownback (R-Kansas) and other senators had been pushing for the resolution since 2004. In 2009, both chambers of Congress finally passed the resolution, which was signed in December 2009 by President Obama. In May 2010, Senator Brownback and Senator Jim McDermott (D-Washington) were joined by representatives of the Cherokee, Choctaw, Muscogee (Creek), Sisseton Wahpeton Oyate, and Pawnee nations for a reading of the apology at the Congressional Cemetery in Washington, DC.

REFERENCES

Cryne, Julia A. "NAGPRA Revisited: A Twenty-Year Review of Repatriation Efforts." *American Indian Law Review* 34, no. 1 (2009/2010): 9–122.

The Dawes Act of 1887. Available at http://www.pbs.org/weta/thewest/resources/archives/eight/dawes.htm

Deloria, Vine Jr. (Ed.). *The Indian Reorganization Act: Congress and Bills*. Norman: University of Oklahoma Press, 2002.

Fine-Dare, Kathleen S. *Grave Injustice: The American Indian Repatriation Movement and NAGPRA*. Omaha: University of Nebraska Press, 2002.

The Meriam Report of 1928. Retrieved from http://library.nau.edu/speccoll/exhibits/indigenous_voices/merriam_report.html

Rusco, Elmer R. "John Collier: Architect of Sovereignty or Assimilation?" *American Indian Quarterly* 15, no. 1 (1991): 49–54.

Wilkins, David E. and K. Tsianina Lomawaima. *Uneven Ground: American Indian Sovereignty and Federal Law*. Norman: University of Oklahoma Press, 2001.

LAW ENFORCEMENT IN INDIAN COUNTRY

Claudette Robertson

On September 7, 1783, concerned that unethical land speculators and dishonest traders would instigate Indian hostilities, President George Washington issued a policy restricting individual land and trade dealings with Indians. During the same month, the Continental Congress issued a proclamation declaring that Congress had the "sole and exclusive" right and power to regulate trade and manage Indian affairs. These policies birthed what came to be known as the federal Indian trust responsibility and laid the foundation for the United States to be legally obligated and morally responsible for all dealings with U.S. Indian tribes. Several years later, these policies were established as the law of the land when they were included in the ratification of the U.S. Constitution. Since 1789, this trust doctrine has been examined in numerous supreme court cases, congressional acts, and executive orders, and has been proven to be inadequate to provide protection for the welfare of Indian people. This essay on law enforcement illustrates the historic and contemporary issues that deter progress and protection for Indian populations within Indian country.

HISTORICAL BACKGROUND

In 1869, President Ulysses S. Grant authorized a Board of Indian Commissioners to serve as unpaid advisors to the Secretary of the Interior. These commissioners examined the policies of Indian affairs and conditions on reservations and then recommended reforms that addressed the problems of civil and criminal behavior within Indian country.

Commissioner John Q. Smith's 1876 annual report outlined the cumbersome methods of policing the various tribes under the reservation policy. Smith proposed that civil and criminal activities amongst the tribes be legislatively assigned to the jurisdiction of U.S. courts so that Indians would "occupy the same relation to law that a white man does" (Prucha 1990, 3) Smith was not the first to propose the idea of non-Indian law enforcement jurisdiction within Indian country.

The basic precepts of the first law enforcement program in the United States were established in 1850 when the California legislature enacted laws giving local non-Indian judges jurisdiction over all criminal and civil cases involving Indians. These laws included regulating child adoptions, contracts, and restrictions on Indian slavery. In addition, selling liquor to Indians was forbidden, and Indians who committed crimes such as stealing or loitering could be whipped or fined. Jury trials could be requested by both Indians and non-Indians within Indian country, and a white man could post bail for an Indian, but a white man could not be convicted of a crime on the testimony of an Indian.

In 1869, twenty years after the creation of the Department of the Interior, Thomas Lightfoot, an agent for the United States, established the first Indian police force with the Iowa and the Sac and Fox tribes in Nebraska. Although the War Department opposed an Indian police force, in 1872, General O. O. Howard assigned 130 Navajo soldiers to police the reservation with authority to arrest thieves and recover stolen property and stock. Two years later, the San Carlos reservation agent, John Clum, hired four Apache to serve as police officers at a salary of $15 per month. The force was later expanded by another 21 officers. Using Indians to police the reservations proved to be so successful that Commissioner Ezra A. Hayt, in his 1877 *Annual Report to Congress*, recommended that an Indian police force be formed to serve on other reservations. The following year, Congress authorized funding to support 430 privates and 50 officers, and in 1879, Congress raised the amount to cover 800 privates and 100 officers.

Four constitutional provisions serve as the foundation for all subsequent changes in law enforcement within Indian country. The first is based on the Commerce clause (Article I, Section 8, Clause 3), which gives Congress the power to regulate commerce with Indian tribes. The second is the Property clause (Article IV, Section 3, Clause 2), which gives Congress the power to dispose of, and to make rules and regulations respecting, the territory or property of the United States. The Necessary and Proper clause (Article I, Section 8, Clause 18), which allows Congress to legislate new laws that were not authorized under the enumerated powers. Finally, the Supremacy clause (Article VI, Clause 2) established all treaties as the supreme law of the land; therefore, all judicial authorities are bound to this law.

FEDERAL STATUS AND SELF-GOVERNANCE

Law and order on Indian reservations and within Indian country is codified under Title 25, Subchapter B, Part 11 in the *Code of Federal Regulations*, and in Title 18 *U.S. Code* (USC). Title 25 also delineates the process of tribal reorganization under the *1934 Indian Reorganization Act* (IRA). Successive legislation has opened up more opportunities for tribes to become self-governing sovereign nations. This status of self-determination allows tribes to provide programs and services, such as law enforcement, that were previously administered by either a state or the Bureau of Indian Affairs.

The General Crimes Act Title 18 USC 1152 was passed in 1885 to prosecute perpetrators of crimes that were committed within the United States but exclusive of Indians within Indian country. Later that year, Congress passed the Major Crimes Act, Title 18 USC 1153, which extended the General Crimes Act to include Indians in Indian country. The Assimilative Crimes Act, codified by Section 13 of Title 18, USC in 1948, allows for the U.S. District Court to prosecute Indians for crimes that are not defined in Title 18 but that are "assimilated" from the laws of the surrounding state jurisdictions (Strickland 1982, 162). The Indian Crimes Act of 1976 extended the original list of murder, manslaughter, kidnapping, rape, incest, burglary, and robbery in the Major Crimes Act to include arson, maiming, larceny, assault, and several other related offenses.

Less serious criminal offenses defined by the 1935 Bureau of Indian Affairs code and by different tribal codes are the same as many of the lesser offenses identified by federal, state, and local law enforcement agencies. Major criminal offenses such as murder and drug trafficking are prosecuted by the federal government under the Major Crimes Act or the Assimilated Crimes Act, or they may fall under state jurisdiction if the crime is committed in a Public Law 83-280 state.

Public Law 83-280, usually referred to as "280," is the primary legislative act that determines which government entity will have jurisdiction within Indian country. Public Law 83-280 was passed by Congress in 1953 to give state courts civil and criminal jurisdiction over American Indians on reservations. When 280 was passed, the Major Crimes Act and the General Crimes Act as they apply to Indians were suspended in those states where 280 was implemented. However, the law did not grant the states jurisdiction over hunting, fishing, trapping, or other resources where lands were held in trust by the federal government. Nor could states encumber, alienate, or tax any lands held in trust. States may retrocede their police authority under 280 at any time. Table 1 lists the states that operate under the directive of Public Law 83-280 and the year they assumed jurisdiction.

Table 1 Public Law 83-280 States (USC 18, 1162)

States/Reservations	Date
California; Minnesota, excepting Red Lake Reservation; Nebraska; Oregon, excepting Warm Springs Reservation; Wisconsin, excepting Menominee Reservation	1953
Nevada	1955
Alaska	1958
South Dakota, Washington	1957–1963
Florida	1961
Idaho, Montana, North Dakota, required tribal consent	1963
Arizona, Iowa	1967
Utah	1971

JURISDICTION AND CROSS DEPUTIZATION

Jurisdiction generally applies to a government entity exercising legal authority over certain criminal and civil laws within a geographical area. There are basically three law enforcement jurisdictions: tribal, federal, and state. The police authority is determined by the nature of the crime, the location, the citizenship of the victim and the perpetrator, and the legislative authority under which the jurisdiction falls. In some districts the Bureau of Indian Affairs (BIA) may have jurisdiction over every tribe that resides within that district that is not a self-governing tribe. But if a murder is committed, then the Federal Bureau of Investigation (FBI) will be called in. In districts where there are self-governing tribes, the BIA may have a presence but not have law enforcement or judicial jurisdiction. For example, the BIA has an office in the territory of the Muscogee (Creek) Nation but their law enforcement jurisdiction is limited because the Creek nation is self-governing, and has its own law enforcement agency and court system. In 280 states, tribal or BIA police are authorized to enforce the law only if they are cross-deputized with the local police. The Hoopa Valley reservation, in a remote region of northern California, is the traditional territory of the Hoopa Valley Tribe. However, since California is a Public Law 83-280 state, the Hoopa Valley tribal police must be cross-deputized with the Humboldt County Sheriff's Office to enforce criminal and civil violations within their tribal boundaries.

With subsequent legislation and case law, some states have been forced to retrocede their police authority, and some have negotiated memorandums of understanding (MOU) with tribal governments to voluntarily retrocede their authority. For example, in 1958, the Metlakatla Indian Community was granted concurrent jurisdiction with the state of Alaska. When MOUs are negotiated, tribal and state police officers are often cross-deputized. Each agency will then have law enforcement powers on or off the reservation.

New police officers must understand the concept of Public Law 83-280 and how it applies to their patrol area in order to know the limits of their police powers. Criminal jurisdiction is probably the most complicated and confusing element of law enforcement and crime within Indian country. The laws of the federal, state, and local agencies are all applicable to the Indian citizen. However, within the boundaries of Indian country, only federal and tribal police may apprehend Indian citizens, unless it is a 280 state, in which case the state has criminal and civil jurisdiction even within Indian Country. To resolve the issue of jurisdiction, police must answer basic questions of place and citizenship.

TRIBAL COURTS, COURTS OF INDIAN OFFENSES

Today there are tribal courts, administrated by self-governing tribes with federally recognized tribal codes, and there are BIA Courts of Indian Offense (CIO), which were established in 1883 by the BIA in an effort to restrict the power of tribal chiefs. These courts administrate and represent court business on behalf of all the tribes within a certain jurisdiction. In 1935, the Collier Commission revised the Code of Indian Tribal Offenses and with the IRA, permitted the tribes to supplant the Court of Indian Offenses.

LAW ENFORCEMENT OPERATIONS

Indian Law Enforcement services fall under the portfolio of the Office of Indian Affairs. The Division of Law Enforcement Operations is divided into six regional districts with 208 bureau and tribal law enforcement programs. Of the 208 programs, 43 are operated by the BIA. Operations involve telecommunications, uniformed police officers, and criminal investigations. The main office for Indian Law Enforcement is in Albuquerque, New Mexico, with district offices located in Aberdeen, South Dakota; Muskogee, Oklahoma; Phoenix, Arizona; Albuquerque, New Mexico; Billings, Montana; and Nashville, Tennessee).

Prior to 1968, training opportunities for Indian police were limited to state police or Federal Bureau of Investigation academies where BIA and tribal law enforcement personnel were put on multiyear waiting lists. The delay forced police officers to learn their skills on the job with an occasional in-service training session. This method was inadequate for police protection and investigations. The need for training Indian police was finally settled in 1968 when the U.S. Indian Police Academy was established at Roswell, New Mexico. Within a few years, specialized training programs were offered to meet the need for training supervisors, prison personnel, juvenile officers, and criminal investigators.

In 1973, the police academy and the Division of Law and Order, Research and Statistical Unit, from Pierre, South Dakota, were both relocated to the Inter-tribal School campus in Brigham City, Utah, and renamed the Center for United States Indian Police Training and Research. After several years, the Research and Statistical Unit was separated from the academy and relocated to the Office of Technical Assistance and Training. Five years later, in 1984, the Division of Law Enforcement was moved again, this time to to Marana, Arizona, where it was renamed the Indian Police Academy, Federal Law Enforcement Training Center (FLETC) until 1993, when it was moved to its present location in Artesia, New Mexico. Today, the center is known as the Bureau of Indian Affairs–United States Indian Police Academy and the Department of Homeland Security at the Federal Law Enforcement Training Center.

At the academy, cadets are put through a rigorous training schedule. They are required to pass certification exams in physical training, weapons safety and use, self-defense tactics, first responder procedures, defensive driving, and felony car stops. Cadets must also pass written exams covering treaties, executive orders, and federal statutes that apply to jurisdictions, sovereignty issues, investigation techniques, crime scene processing, and human behavior. Advanced training courses are offered in specialized crime activity such as child abuse, terrorism, gang activity, gaming, cultural resource protection, supervisory techniques, jail procedures, and dispatcher training. Each program is designed to meet standards equal to that of the FBI and Homeland Security and is conducted by a faculty of experts, many of whom have earned bachelors, masters, and doctorate degrees in their respective fields.

OBSTACLES TO EFFECTIVE LAW ENFORCEMENT

Over the years, two Supreme Court cases have challenged tribal jurisdiction and sovereignty while hindering law enforcement efforts to reduce crime in Indian country. In *Oliphant vs. Suquamish Indian Tribe* (1978), the Court ruled that tribal police had no authority to arrest Mark Oliphant, a non-Indian resident of the Port Madison Reservation in Washington, for assaulting a tribal police officer. As a result, the question of authority arises each time an arrest is made in Indian country. More recently, a 2001 Supreme Court decision, *Nevada vs. Hicks*, determined that tribal courts are not courts of "general jurisdiction" with concurrent authority. Tribal police now face multiple restrictions when attempting to execute warrants off the reservation, but the ruling does not prohibit state police from entering Indian country to investigate or prosecute violations. The Court also moved that tribal jurisdiction over non-Indians extended only as far as the tribe's legislative jurisdiction.

The ruling has broadly impacted Indian police efforts to maintain safety. Non-Indian offenders easily avoid arrest, and criminals who know the limitations of tribal police authority are often repeat offenders. Other obstacles to effective policing include gaps in coordination at the federal level, delayed implementation of programs due to grant funding issues, and conflict between tribes and the Bureau of Indian Affairs. Furthermore, correctional facilities often operate on policies that vary within the judicial and criminal systems. Finally, whether the police are state or tribal, the response time is usually slow given the size of the area some agencies must cover.

LAW ENFORCEMENT STATISTICS

During the 1990s, violent crimes within Indian country occurred at twice the rate as similar crimes in any other ethnic group in non-Indian jurisdictions. These statistics and the *Nevada vs. Hicks* ruling served as the impetus for a 2001 Tribal Law Enforcement Summit to recommend ways in which crime in Indian country could be alleviated. Summit participants agreed on six areas of concern: jurisdictional issues, resources, training, coordination and cooperation amongst agencies, victim services, and crime prevention. One central recommendation was that Congress should consider legislation dealing with the *Oliphant* case as soon as possible to ameliorate the anticipated conflict in jurisdictions arising from the *Nevada* decision.

The Justice Department issued the first comprehensive survey on Indian law enforcement in 2002. Of the 314 federally recognized tribes that responded to the survey for the years indicated, 188 administered some form of a tribal justice system. Criminal and civil cases were adjudicated through 80 juvenile courts, 51 family courts, 174 general jurisdiction tribal courts, and 91 appellate courts. At least 165 respondents to the survey employed one full-time officer, while 71 maintained a detention facility. Of these 314 agencies, 84 percent adjudicated misdemeanor cases and offered services to over 60 percent of their victims while another 60 percent networked with local agencies to provide detention services.

The situation of Indian police departments can be characterized as having large jurisdictions patrolled by small departments. There are 75 medium-size departments with between 10 and 50 officers that patrol 50 percent of reservation lands under the prevue of a tribe or the Bureau of Indian Affairs. Some reservations have fewer than 12 officers patrolling areas as large as Connecticut. In other cases, an area the size of Delaware with a population of 10,000 may have a police force of three or fewer. Where in New York City or Baltimore the ratio of police to citizens may average 5.25:1,000, on tribal lands, the ratio is 2:1,000.

The latest BIA statistics indicate approximately 1,894 law enforcement officers worked in Indian country in 2002, but inadequate resources were still a major obstacle to effective policing. The BIA estimated another 4,300 officers were needed to service the reservations. Although Indian policing may have more available resources than a local non-Indian agency, the rate of crime within Indian country is two or three times higher than the national average.

Only 13 percent of Indian police officers speak their native language, and there are fewer native speakers on some reservations than on others. Approximately

33 percent of the police in Indian country are non-Indians. Of that number, more are Hispanic than Caucasian, and 12 percent of the officers are women. Indian police are usually high school graduates who have attended certified law enforcement academies. Recruiting and training Indian police is the most serious administrative problem a department faces due to negative background checks and a lack of training opportunities.

CRIMES WITHIN INDIAN COUNTRY

Some of the more heinous crimes in Indian country include murders committed in Oklahoma, South Dakota, and New Mexico. In the spring of 1921, Anna Brown, an Osage Indian, was taken to a remote region of the Osage reservation in northern Oklahoma and shot in the head. Over the next eight years, more than 20 Osage citizens, all related to Anna, were murdered. The BIA did not have police jurisdiction, so the FBI was called in. By 1929, the FBI had uncovered an elaborate conspiracy in which William K. Hale planned to rob the Osage of their tribal inheritance. Hale, Ernest Burkhart, Kelsey Morrison, and John Ramsey all received life sentences for the murders.

In December 1975, Anna Mae Picout-Aquash, a high-level member of the American Indian Movement (AIM) and a Mi'kmaq tribal member from Nova Scotia, was raped and beaten then taken to a remote canyon on the Pine Ridge Reservation in South Dakota, where she was executed. Her body was found two months later. In 2004, Arlo Looking Cloud, a fellow AIM member, was convicted of her murder.

Navajo country covers 27,000 square miles where 270 Navajo police are called out on as many as 235,000 cases annually Many times, police rush from one call to another. One such case involved Kiara Harvey, a two-year-old Navajo girl, who was found dead in her mother's bed in 2008 at her family home in Window Rock, Arizona. The police arrived more than an hour after they had been called. The first response officer's report noted the bruises and burn marks on Kiara's body but claimed he saw no signs of foul play. The disparity between the officer's report and the medical

Photo of Arlo Looking Cloud in 1998, provided by the Denver Police Department. Looking Cloud was convicted in 2004 of first-degree murder for his role in the 1975 shooting death of an American Indian Movement activist. His federal prison sentence was reduced from life to 20 years. (AP Photo/Denver Police Department, File)

examiner's report, which indicated repeated abuse, is part of the problem in Indian country. No witnesses have come forward in this case and since a major crime is within the jurisdiction of the FBI, which has refused to pursue the case, no arrests had been made as of June 2011.

The Department of Justice (DOJ) declines to prosecute cases when it believes the evidence is weak, when there are reluctant witnesses due to their relationship with the victim or the suspect, or if there are questionable jurisdiction issues. Often the U.S. attorney's office is inadequately staffed, and former prosecutors have testified that reservation cases were not a priority. Other reasons the DOJ declines to prosecute include lack of evidence of a federal offense, or a crime not serious enough to be a federal crime. In 2010, the DOJ declined to prosecute 37 criminal cases in the Navajo nation, but across the United States, almost half of all federal cases on Indian land were declined. In South Dakota, prosecutors declined 61 percent of the 2,414 cases sent to them. In Arizona, 12 tribes requested assistance with 2,538 cases; 38 percent were declined. Former Senate Indian Affairs Committee Senator Byron Dorgan of North Dakota reported that reservation crime is "a full-blown scandal ... If you report a rape, a cop might show up the next day" (Daly 2010).

TRIBAL LAW ENFORCEMENT FUNDING IN 2010

Generally tribal law enforcement programs are administered through grants and contracts negotiated with the federal government. Tribes that do not have contracting status are served by the Bureau of Indian Affairs. Currently, there are 565 federally recognized American Indian tribes and Alaska Native groups with over 3 million American Indians and Alaska Natives. Across the United States, many tribes receive federal funding to assist with crime prevention, intervention, apprehension, and adjudication services. In 2010, twenty-nine states received 285 awards totaling $123,287,438. California had the most programs, with 33 receiving $10,971,473. Washington, with 32 programs, received the most funding ($14,005,272). Utah, with one program, received the least amount of funding ($150,000).

CONCLUSION

The National Institute of Justice has found that the number of crimes such as stalking, rape, and domestic violence against Native American women have risen. Many of the tribal strategies such as the Violence against Women Act of 1994 have served as a temporary stop-gap to crime but have not provided long-term solutions to violence in Indian country. Evaluations have determined the primary weakness is the absence of culturally relevant strategies.

The Tribal Law and Order Act of 2010 (TLOA) was passed by Congress as Title II of Public Law 111-211 on July 29, 2010. This law authorizes increasing the number of federal law enforcement officers, requires federal agencies to collect data on criminal activity in Indian country, and requires the Justice Department to maintain criminal data on cases the department has declined to prosecute.

Crime, of course, exists in Indian country, especially on reservations, to a greater degree than in non-Indian society, but hard data on how much exists, and whether it is increasing or declining, is difficult to come by. As one exasperated observer recently said, "You're in the dark, trying to make policy in the dark.... Without any crime data, it's very difficult to gauge just what's happening in Indian Country and just how to address issues" (Whitehurst 2010).

THE TRIBAL LAW AND ORDER ACT

The Tribal Law and Order Act, which became law in 2010, aimed to give tribes more control over law enforcement. The following summary is reproduced from the website of the United States Senate Committee on Indian Affairs.

The bill generally seeks to bring greater local control to tribal law enforcement agencies to combat reservation crime, and establish accountability measures for federal agencies responsible for providing public safety in Indian Country.

Title I of the bill would require the Department of Justice to file declination reports to tribal justice officials to coordinate the prosecution of reservation crimes. . . .

Title II of the bill would permit Tribes to call on the United States to assist State governments in the prosecution of major crimes where the States have the authority, but lack the resources to address reservation crimes. . . .

Title III would provide tools to tribal justice officials to fight crime in their own communities. This Title would expand on a program to authorize tribal police [to] make arrests for all crimes committed on Indian lands. . . .

Section 304 of the bill would increase the sentencing authority of tribal courts to three years for any single offense (up from 1-year limitation under current law). . . .

Title IV would reauthorize and amend existing programs to better serve tribal communities. The programs to be reauthorized include the BIA and DOJ tribal courts laws, the DOJ Jails statute, tribal juvenile justice laws, and the Indian Alcohol and Substance Abuse Act. . . .

Title VI includes provisions to address the epidemic of domestic violence and sexual assault in Indian Country. Section 601 would require federal officials to notify tribal justice officials when a sex offender is released from federal custody into Indian Country. . . . Section 602 requires law enforcement officers and prosecutors to receive specialized family violence training to enhance the prosecution of crimes of sexual violence in Indian Country.

Source: The Tribal Law and Order Act. Retrieved from http://www.indian.senate.gov/public/_files/TLOonepagerMar2009.pdf

REFERENCES

Bureau of Indian Affairs (BIA). Available at http://www.bia.gov

Bureau of Indian Affairs (BIA). Retrieved from http://www.bia.gov/WhoWeAre/BIA/Office of Justice Services/Division of Law Enforcement. September 17, 2012.

Daly, Matthew. "Banner Year for American Indians on Capitol Hill." Associated Press, December 29, 2010. Retrieved from http://www.cnsnews.com

Grim, Charles W. *Making Medicine*. Oklahoma City: Oklahoma Supreme Court Sovereignty Symposium XX, 2007.

Hurtado, Albert L. and Peter Iverson (Eds.). "Statutes of California: 1850." In *Major Problems in American Indian History* (2nd ed.). Boston: Houghton Mifflin, 2001.

International Association of Chiefs of Police (IACP). "Improving Safety in Indian Country: Recommendations from the IACP Summit: Executive Summary," October 2001. Retrieved from http://www.theiacp.org

Law Enforcement within Indian Nations: Introductory Course Manual, Marana, Arizona. Glynco, GA: Federal Law Enforcement Training Center, 1985

Perry, Steven W. "Census of Tribal Justice Agencies in Indian Country." Washington, DC: Bureau of Justice Statistics, U.S. Department of Justice, 2005. Available at http://bjs.ojp.usdoj.gov/content/pub/pdf/ctjaic02.pdf

Prucha, Francis Paul (Ed.). *Documents of United States Indian Policy* (2nd ed.). Lincoln: University of Nebraska Press. 1990.

Public Law 94-297 (PL). Act of May 29, 1976.

Rennison, Callie. *Violent Victimization and Race, 1993–1998*. (National Criminal Justice Bulletin #176354). Washington, DC: Bureau of Justice Statistics, U.S. Department of Justice, March 2001.

Strickland, Rennard (Ed.). *F. Cohen's Handbook of Federal Indian Law*. Charlottesville, VA: Michie Company, 1982.

Tribal Law and Order Resource Center. "Tribal Law and Order Act of 2010 (TLOA)." *National Congress of American Indians*. Retrieved from http://tloa.ncai.org/ on May 31, 2011.

U.S. Census. Available at www.census.gov

U.S. Code (USC). Title 18. S1323.

U.S. Code (USC). Title 18. S1162.

U.S. Code (USC). Title 25. The Indian Reorganization Act, June 18, 1934. [461 et seq. 473a, 476, 477, 503.] (1991). Public Law 92-203. Alaska Native Claims Settlement Act, 1971. Public Law 93-638. "The Indian Self-determination and Education Assistance Act of 1975." Including amendments from 1976 to 1988. Public Law 100-472. "Indian Self-Determination Act Amendments of 1988." Public Law 102-184: "Tribal Self-Governance Demonstration Project Act." 1991. Public Law 103-413. "The Self-Governance Act of 1994."

U.S. Department of Justice (DOJ). "Coordinated Tribal Assistance Award List." Retrieved from http://www.tribaljusticeandsafety.gov on September 15, 2010.

U.S. Department of Justice (DOJ). Available at http://bjs.ojp.usdoj.gov

Wakeling, Stewart, Miriam Jorgensen, Susan Michaelson, and Manley Begay. "Policing on American Indian Reservations." Washington, DC: U.S. Department of Justice, 2000. Retrieved from http://www.ncjrs.gov/pdffiles1/nij/188095.pdf on July 23, 2011.

Whitehurst, Lindsay. "New Program Tracks Crime on Indian Reservations," November 9. 2010. Retrieved from http://public.shns.com/content/new-program-tracks-crime-indian-reservations

Leadership: Formal and Informal Leadership within Tribes

Linda Sue Warner

Traditional beliefs can work to create a vibrant tribal organization linking the problems of contemporary American Indian tribes to the culture and languages that have sustained them for over 500 years. Formal leadership for American Indian tribes is a result of the 1934 Indian Reorganization Act, which established formal councils for representative voices throughout Indian country. As a result, the federally recognized tribes have elected tribal councils and leadership positions, such as chairman or chief. The type of formal leadership within a tribe is determined by the tribe itself, and variations can be found in the numbers and types of positions that hold formal leadership largely because tribes have wide variances in populations and services.

For many traditional American Indian communities, leadership is designated as a skill open to anyone who can persuade others to do something they would not have otherwise done. The different forms of leadership rest in different forms of persuasion, not in different formal positions more commonly associated with Western models of leadership. Within tribes, formal and informal leadership is found, and cultural expectations are connected to both.

Much of the early work on leadership within American Indian commmunities, such as it was, explored the issues through a Western cultural lens that may have been distinctly unhelpful and incapable of understanding that what counted as leadership was, in essence, different between the Western and American Indian traditions. In traditional Western approaches, leadership is identified with an individual leader whose traits propel him (and sometimes her) to positions of authority over an organization or community. Such models tend to rest in hierarchies of authority where power and responsibility increase with movement up the hierarchy. American Indian traditions, on the other hand, tend to be more related to the requirements of the community, to be much more dispersed throughout that community, and to be rooted in situations rather than individuals. Thus, one could argue that American Indian traditions of leadership are more akin to heterarchies than hierarchies—flexible and changing patterns of authority rather than rigidly embedded in a fixed and formal bureaucracy. Because Indian leadership involves heterarchies representing a high level of diversity among and within American Indian nations, conceptions regarding the "American Indian way" should be treated with great caution and skepticism. In practical terms, these two alternative approaches have inhibited mutual understanding and compounded the difficulties faced by American Indian "leaders," whose different approach to leadership has often been interpreted as an inability to lead rather than a different ability to lead.

This is not to say that American Indian traditions are ethically superior to traditional Western models, or indeed that there is one American Indian model of leadership that should replace the one Western model. There are enough examples of atrocities organized by hierarchic nonindigenous leaders and heterarchic Indian leaders to negate any claim that the latter were essentially ethically superior to the former.

HISTORICAL BACKGROUND

In purely pragmatic terms, the failure of Indian nations to unite under one leader in the face of nonindigenous incursions condemned the American Indians to defeat in the long term. For example, after 1783, the British tried to facilitate an Indian confederacy, less to help the American Indians than to construct a block on American ambitions north of the Ohio River. Nevertheless, a confederacy would have strengthened the American Indian position against incursion if it had not foundered on their eventual betrayal by the British desire of the tribes to remain independent of each other, despite the best efforts of the Shawnee and Miami tribes. Fifty years later, in the 1830s, the Cherokee nation sought the protection of the Supreme Court from attempts by Georgia to deport them from their traditional lands but, despite ruling in favor of the Cherokee in 1832, by 1833 Georgia announced a public lottery of Cherokee land and property. By 1834, the once unified Cherokee nation split into two camps, with John Ridge leading the smaller acquiescent group who signed away the Cherokee land at New Echota and promptly left. This left John Ross leading the larger group of resisters who ignored the treaty and stayed put. By 1838, after the U.S. Senate had ratified the New Echota Treaty, the U.S. Army deployed 7,000 troops to move the 18,000 Cherokee resisters out. By the end of their 6-month forced march, over 4,000 Cherokee had died on the infamous Trail of Tears. The point being made here, therefore, is not that of displacing one imperialist leadership model with another but rather of denying the viability of any imperialist claim to ethical, pragmatic, or cultural superiority. "Western-like" hierarchical leadership, in that it might have controlled tribal division, may have been helpful to extending Indian survival or, actually, putting off the inevitable for some time.

Scholars now believe that prior to contact with Europeans, American Indian people had complex, dynamic, and diverse methods for developing, assigning, or asserting leadership within tribal cultures (see Mihesuah 1996). Accurate historical evidence is difficult to determine and may have been initially confused by the tendency of the recorders to equate and conflate governance with leadership. In many of the nearly distinct prewhite societies, women held positions of leadership. The Iroquois, for example, had a society approximately 400 years ago which has been described as most nearly a true matriarchy as has ever existed in modern or ancient time.

On the one hand, governance was often reduced to the institutions that the nonindigenous settlers developed in response to their new situation, in particular the U.S. Constitution and the separation of powers between the judicial, executive, and legislative branches. The assumption that governance means the same thing to different people also encouraged the U.S. government to insist that American Indian governance structures replicate its normative ideal of constitutional, elected republics. Since 1934, American Indian tribes have been required to base their governmental structure on that of the U.S. Congress. However, while the formal structures mirrored what the government required, other governance and leadership structures (indigenous ones) were often maintained at the reservation level. Indeed, one such misunderstanding was that the governance of the United States was itself derived and conceived from American Indian influence. In fact, the people of the Six Nations (also known as the Iroquois Confederacy) called themselves the Haudenosaunee, meaning people building a long house, and did have a system of governance that included the separation of power. However, it is not clear to what extent the framers of the U.S. Constitution used this as a blueprint. On the contrary, the U.S. government tried to enforce this model on the American Indians and in some cases, for example the Cherokee in 1828, was successful. Similarly, the Navajo tribe (like the Iroquois Confederacy) was matriarchal. After 1934 when the Indian Reorganization Act required the tribes to create protypical congressional councils, men dominated the seats even in matriarchal tribes at least until the late 1980s.

On the other hand, leadership was often reduced to the assumption that each organization and institution could have only one individual leader. For instance, in 1851, conflict between American Indians and the U.S. government over opening up the Oregon Trail was, in part, rooted in the false assumption made by the latter that the Sioux nation could be bound by the word of a single leader—chosen by the Superintendent of Indian Affairs—when the Sioux themselves insisted that no single person could make such a decision. In contrast to many Western assumptions about leadership, Freisen and Lynn's early work (1970) on leadership in southern Alberta's native communities suggests a high regard for individual rights, underlying regard for cooperation, family cohesiveness, and tolerance. The study focused on Indian culture and education, and compared variables from Indian and non-Indian communities. Their research found that each Indian tribe operated under the leadership of a chief and council, with membership on the councils based on some success in the community. Some Siouan bands represented their systems of governments with peace chiefs, war chiefs, and ceremonial leaders.

In a later study, the Yaquai world-view of leadership was contextualized differently, with time playing a far more critical role than in the Siouan bands described earlier. In particular, the Yaquai existed within two realities of time, that is, a circular, primeval timeline and a linear time development in the historical European time conception (Chilocott 1985). This study was an ethnography designed to determine examples of cultural dissonance that affected decision making in the Yaqui community. The multiple realities created by the two understandings of time still impact the leadership within this community. As an example, linear time development regulates formal leadership appointment, as in the election of tribal council members to specific four-year terms. In a circular, indigenous timeline, leadership would rely on effectiveness and performance. It would start and end with an event, not a specific calendar date. For example, leadership would transfer upon the death of the current leader.

VARYING LEADERSHIP STYLES

With over 550 federally recognized tribes in the United States, each with unique cultures and languages, it is not surprising to find that leadership traditions and styles also vary. Tribal leadership prior to white contact was often hereditary and followed matriarchal or patriarchal lineage. In 1934, upon passage of the Indian Reorganization Act, Congress required tribes who expected to enter into a relationship with the federal government to create forms of tribal leadership to replace those traditional practices. One example of this can be found in the Navajo nation, a traditionally matriarchal society. It created an elected tribal council made up of geographically located chapter houses and for decades, there were no female elected members in the formal leadership of this tribe. Other tribes had similar experiences.

The practice of leadership and the formal "face" of leadership divided in these tribes, but there is evidence that the traditional forms of decision making and leadership have not disappeared. Historical accounts of leadership in battle, whether it be armed conflict or congressional debate, point to the same agenda in contemporary affairs—the defense of sovereign nations to self-determine their traditions, lifestyle, language, and economy. Today's tribal leadership works in an era of self-determination implementation, more accurately called self-actualization.

In recent decades, the study of American Indian leadership in education has centered on research and practice developed at Pennsylvania State University. The American Indian Leadership Program was founded in 1970 and is the oldest and most successful programs of its kind in the United States. One of the objectives of the program is to develop individual leadership that will be able to support intellectual development, create positive change, function in complex environments, and help to define and shape the future of American Indians and Alaska Natives and their communities. The program has a 95 percent matriculation rate. The program is housed in the College of Education, Department of Education Policy Studies. This formal leadership training is linked directly to educational programs; leadership training for economic and health benefits for tribes has formal, as well as informal, venues as well.

LEADERSHIP IN ECONOMICS

Indigenous leaders share the responsibility of economic well-being for their tribes. Tribal leaders stress the responsibility for establishing a sound economic base for tribes as they enter the twenty-first century. Economic health is imperative for tribes in an era of declining resources. Tribal economic security is linked to cultural integrity; leaders are responsible for maintaining and developing a tribal identity while supporting policies that reinforce economic development. Conflicts between culture and economic activity can arise; leaders who understand the cultural integrity of their tribes' resources can link economic development to contemporary enterprises.

Within many tribes is the notion of seven generations as a focus for decision making. This concept supports a reflection of the past seven generations when making decisions for the next seven generations. Most tribal leaders also propose that formal education, supported by knowledge of tribal traditions, creates leadership. These components link to Arthur Blazer's (Mescalero Apache serving as deputy under secretary for Natural Resources and Environment in the USDA) call for the creation of a trial executive leadership academy (Harvard Project 2008). Leadership issues for tribes continue to be affected by the mobility of tribal members from designated reservation land or Indian communities to urban areas. Urban Indians represent a substantial number of tribal members in the twenty-first century as tribal leaders respond to the needs of their communities. Tribal leaders of a newer global economy link the resilience of tribal communities to the future economic well-being of those communities through interaction with other nations. Formal leadership activities include the stabilization of local economies from diversified enterprises to the training of future tribal leaders using elder role models.

LEADERSHIP IN HEALTH AND SOCIAL WELFARE

Nationally, leadership in health and social welfare is provided by the Indian Health Service (HIS) through their 12 regional offices and augmented by such national organizations as the National Indian Health Board (www.nihb.org). Leadership activities at the national level represent the diversity of tribal values and opinions. The goal of working collaboratively with the federal government in services to federally recognized tribes is to provide advocacy, policy formation and analysis, legislative and regulatory tracking, research, and project management. The National Indian Health Board was established in 1972 and currently advocates on behalf of 565 federally recognized tribes in the development of national Indian health policy.

Regional healthcare preparation programs at colleges may include tribal culture and language in the preparation of health professionals. In Denver, four Indian nurse leaders developed a curriculum for training native nurses that includes nine modules, including Being a Leader in the Indian Way, Indian Nursing and Tribal Sovereignty, and Indian Nursing and Indian Health Programs ("Developing Nurse Leaders" n.d.). The program was developed based on interviews with Indian leaders and personal experiences of the Indian nurses in the program. This program began in 1997 and represents one example of the various regional programs for both nurses and health administrators.

Tribal priorities for Indian health reflect a wide array of issues, including advocacy, budget development, resource management, partnership possibilities, and urban Indian healthcare. The Developing Nurse Leaders' Program identified training needs to address the characteristics for future Indian leaders in healthcare that include negotiating skills, fiscal management knowledge, knowledge of the federal system, fundraising, networking ability, public relations skills, cultural sensitivity, flexibility, patience, and creativity.

LEADERSHIP FOR YOUTH

Leadership training for youth in Indian country can be found regionally and nationally. In December 2011, the White House honored Champions of Change by recognizing programs highlighting American Indian youth. This recognition allowed tribal youth to share stories about their perspectives on local issues. Nationally, the United National Indian Tribe Youth (UNITY) organization has 211 youth councils operating in 34 states and Canada. The National Congress of American Indians (NCAI) sponsors a Youth Commission designed for students who are interested in tribal and governmental affairs as well as legislation. The Bureau of Indian Education sponsors a national leadership conference each year at Haskell Indian Nations University. The American Indian Higher Education

Consortium (AIHEC) sponsors tribal college leadership initiatives each spring at its annual meeting. In additional to national intertribal efforts, many tribes have leadership development locally that links tribal elders to tribal youth and fosters intergenerational leadership development.

RESEARCH PERSPECTIVES ON LEADERSHIP AND SACRED PLACE

A review of the literature on the research of leadership and indigenous place within the context of the sacred merges leadership with the concepts, sacred place and home. The question became "Where is this place that imbues a native leader with the strength to lead, or how do leaders acknowledge a place as sacred?" Hawaiian activist Peter Apo's definition of place is "located space." Indigenous leaders identify located space that is tribally specific and in specific case studies of leadership, there is often a direct link to this located space, or tribal place (Apo 2006).

Connecting indigenous leadership to place allows us to explore the collective memory of the place within a tribal nation. By linking the research and practice of leadership, spirituality, and place, the evidence needed for contemporary policymakers can be highlighted, paving the way for an honest discussion about next steps. Indigenous leadership, framed in native ways of knowing, provides alternatives for reflection on the study of leadership.

In 2006, using Tahdooahnippah Leadership Variables, Warner and Grint proposed that traditional leadership was characterized in roles of observation, narration, experience, and tradition (Tuboopv Puni Wapv, Sootitekwa, Pvbvetv, and Mahimiawapv) to create the leader as "he who speaks for all of us." The roles linked to researcher, author, elder, and role model in native communities. The study of cultures informs the research on leadership practice, and we know that the study of the language of leadership, particularly metaphors, informs the research on leadership practice. For American Indian tribes, this language includes an understanding of patrilineal and matrilineal relationships. The informal nature of leadership in many indigenous communities connects spirituality with place and links decision making that reflects a holistic perspective of the tribal community. The language of leadership in tribal cultures blends native traditions with assimilated practice in the twenty-first century.

REFERENCES

Anderson, Owanah. *Charting New Directions. Words of Today's American Indian Women*. Washington, DC: U.S. Department of Education, 1981.

Apo, P. "What Does 'Sense of Place' Mean to You?" *Hawaii Magazine*, March–April, 2006, 8–9.

Chilocott, John H. "Yaqui World View and the School: Conflict and Accommodation." *Journal of American Indian Education* 24 (1985): 21–32.

"Developing Nurse Leaders in the Indian Way." Retrieved from http://www.minoritynurse.com/print/567

Friesen, J. D. and Lyon, L. C. (May 1970). "The Progress of Southern Alberta Native Peoples." *The Journal for American Indian Education* 9(3): 15–23.

Harvard Project on American Indian Economic Development. *The State of the Native Nations: Conditions under U.S. Policies of Self-Determination*. New York: Oxford University Press, 2008.

Mihesuah, D. A. "Commonality of Difference: American Indian Women and History." *American Indian Quarterly* 20, no. 1 (1996): 15. Retrieved from http://www.ed.psu.edu/ailp/

Warner, L. S. and Grint, K. "American Indian Ways of Leading and Knowing." *Leadership* 2 (2006): 225–244.

Political Activism: Examining the Issues

Patti Jo King

When discussing American Indian political activism, the 1960s and 1970s, marches and protest rallies, direct and sometimes violent demonstrations, clenched fists, and Red Power slogans commonly come to mind. Long before the rise of the confrontational politics of the 1960s, however, Native Americans were engaged in a persistent struggle against Euro-American attempts at social, political, and economic domination over the North American continent and its respective native nations. Indian protest dates back to the beginning of the colonial period. Then, just as now, Indian people desired to be treated with the kind of respect that is due citizens of sovereign nations—a respect that has been frequently denied them. In 1773, Gieschenatsi, a Shawnee chief, spoke of the matter this way: "The whites tell us of their enlightened understanding, and the wisdom they have from Heaven, at the same time, they cheat us to their hearts' content.... We are as fools in their eyes, and they say among themselves, the Indians know nothing. The Indians understand nothing...." (De Schweinitz 1870, 391).

Throughout the eighteenth and nineteenth centuries, native rights were trampled again and again by encroaching settlers and aggressive, nascent states. It became evident that the federal government either could not or would not control the intruders, nor could it protect the tribes from invasion, as it had sworn to do through solemn treaties. Federal authorities stood idly by during these decades and watched while territory after territory pushed its Indian inhabitants out, making room for American settlements, and eventually embracing statehood. Gold rushes, railroad intrusion, and industrialization were further causes for marginalization, as hundreds of thousands of Native Americans were forced onto small, strictly organized reservations. Land and water issues, hunting and fishing rights, criminal and civil jurisdiction, and religious freedom all became issues of concern and contention. By the end of the century, the disturbing policy of forced assimilation had also taken a heavy toll on native communities everywhere, and Indian people were engaged in a desperate fight for survival. Realizing that military resistance was futile, they turned to political resistance as the most effective strategy for challenging subjugation and uneven Indian policies.

At the turn of the twentieth century, Indian activists began to remonstrate against intrusive and inflexible governmental control over all aspects of native life. As legal scholar Frederick Hoxie (2001) points out, "[Charles] Eastman and other Native Americans ... criticized the actions of the Indian Office and its authoritarian bureaucrats. They proposed alternatives to the government's boarding schools and to its regimented programs for bringing Indians to 'civilization' " (3). Then, in the mid-1920s, federal Indian policies were condemned in a remarkable assessment issued as the Meriam Report. The 1928 report severely criticized the education, health, and social services administered to Indians and tribes. The report also addressed the policy of forced assimilation, suggesting that cultural understanding and tolerance might be more appropriate policies. When in 1934 Commissioner of Indian Affairs John Collier convinced Congress to pass the Indian Reorganization Act (IRA), many of the Meriam Report's recommendations were implemented, including efforts to preserve native culture, rather than trying to destroy it.

CULTURAL REVITALIZATION

Perhaps most importantly, these concerned men and women began to identify the inherent differences that existed between American and native values, and to defend Indian culture, rather than quietly accept demoralizing mainstream criticisms and reforms. Modern Indian political resistance began with cultural and spiritual revitalization—a reintroduction and return to native traditions of the past that had been lost or taken away, to enhance and enrich contemporary social conditions. For years, American reformers had viewed native culture as an impediment to Indian assimilation and independent thinking. Revitalization efforts included the rejuvenation of native languages that were once forbidden in state-sanctioned boarding schools, as well as a reintroduction of dances, foods, ceremonies, arts, and crafts. Vine Deloria described this new era of cultural revitalization in his pivotal 1969 book *Custer Died for Your Sins:* "In so many ways, Indian people are re-examining themselves in an effort to redefine a new social structure for their people. Tribes are reordering their priorities to account for the obvious discrepancies between their goals and the goals whites have defined for them" (2). Through a renewed embrace of culture and native identity, Indian people strengthened themselves for the confrontations that lay ahead.

ENVIRONMENTAL ISSUES AND LAND USE

By the beginning of the twentieth century, reservation lands had been drastically altered by agriculture, stock grazing, and resource exploitation. Upon creation of the reservation system, federal Bureau of Indian Affairs (BIA) agents were placed in charge of the regulation and management of tribal lands. These agents coerced the tribes into signing low-rate, long-term leases that kept them in a state of economic depression and effectively limited tribal access to their own natural resources. Furthermore, reservations were initially established for the purpose of encouraging Indians to take up agriculture, yet some tribes, particularly those in the Southwest, found that water for irrigation was routinely diverted by authority of surrounding states to non-Indian users before it reached tribal lands. In addition, the construction of hydroelectric dams along optimal fishing sites, recreational sport fishing, and commercial harvesting of fish before they reached the reservation lands severely limited tribal access to native "secured" fishing rights guaranteed by treaty law. Even after their rights to fish and hunt were reassured by modern legal decisions, however, these treaty guarantees frequently went unenforced, motivating grassroots community organizers to take matters into their own hands.

FISH-INS

One of the earliest twentieth century issues native political activists addressed was the unfair competition they faced from sport and commercial fishers. The tribes of the Pacific Northwest were hit especially hard. Public Law 280 (1953) transferred jurisdiction over civil and criminal matters of tribes within certain states from the federal government to the state. This created a one-sided imposition of state-sanctioned rules and regulations on Indian nations that failed to recognize tribal sovereignty, self-determination, or treaty rights. Although Washington was not initially included in the law, the state adopted regulations based on the law in 1957 and began placing restrictions on tribal fishing within the state, claiming the move as a means of conservation. An anti-treaty movement began to grow in the Pacific Northwest, with members of Oregon tribes who fished along the tributaries of the Columbia and Snake Rivers being arrested for engaging in subsistence fishing. Consequently, a grassroots fishing rights movement emerged when these local tribes began drawing attention to the violation of their rights through civil disobedience. These activists masterminded a unique form of protest they called the fish-in to call attention to the injustice. Robert Satiacum (Puyallup) initiated a test case by net fishing in the Puyallup River. Then a Swinomish tribal member was convicted of fishing in the Washington state–restricted waters of the Skagit River. In Oregon, three members of the Confederated Tribes of the Umatilla were arrested for fishing in the Blue Mountains.

As arrests, convictions, and violence rose, Billy Frank, Jr., Robert Satiacum, and Don Matheson established the Survival of the American Indian Association (SAIA), an intertribal organization dedicated to preserving and asserting tribal fishing rights. The group, assisted by Indian activists from many tribal nations, staged fish-ins on rivers in the Pacific Northwest in support of subsistence fishing tribes such as the Yakima, the Makah, the Puyallup, and the Muckleshoot. In 1965, violent confrontations between Indian fishermen and state wardens began to attract nationwide interest in the controversy. Celebrities, including Marlon Brando, traveled north to join the fish-ins, as well as well-established civil rights organizations such as the National Association for the Advancement of Colored People (NAACP), the American Civil Liberties Union (ACLU), and the American Friends Service Committee. After years of struggle, the fish-in strategy paid off—the SAIA achieved its objective, and fishing rights were restored to tribes in the Northwest.

FEDERAL RECOGNITION

A decade after the passage of the Indian Reorganization Act, a conservative turn in the federal government ushered in another era of assimilation. This period (1946–1970) was characterized by implementing new Indian policies to end government responsibilities to tribes through the termination of federal tribal recognition. In 1953, House Concurrent Resolution 108 aimed to end the government's trust relationship with tribes. As a result, federal protection and economic assistance ended for terminated tribes. One of the most celebrated cases of tribal termination began on June 17, 1954, when President Dwight Eisenhower signed the Menominee Termination Act, making the Menominee Nation one of the first tribes marked for dismantling. The procedures leading up to termination were so expensive that the tribe's treasury holdings were almost entirely depleted long before the process was near finalization. Subsequently, the lack of funds created a series of crises for the tribe. Forced closing of the tribe's healthcare facility exacerbated the problem of tuberculosis among the Menominee people. Babies born after the date of the tribe's termination could not be legally recognized as Indians. Educated tribal members began to leave for employment in cities, creating a paucity of skilled leaders. When the process of termination was complete in 1961, the new Menominee County emerged as the poorest district in the state of Wisconsin. The disastrous results were the catalyst for the formation of the grassroots organization Determination of Rights and Unity for Menominee Shareholders (DRUMS) in 1970. The organization was founded by a younger generation of educated, politically astute Menominee who brought with them a new sense of pride in their culture and heritage.

In seeking an end to termination and a restoration of federal recognition for the tribe, DRUMS engaged in a well-organized campaign of direct, political, and legal actions. The group, led by Ada Deer, James White, Silvia Wilbur, Shirley Daly, and others, formed a three-chapter coalition of supporters to achieve their objectives. Together, they publicly confronted tribal leaders who consented to sell the tribe's waterfront property to non-Indians and coordinated a series of highly publicized protest demonstrations to discourage such sales. At the same time, they criticized Wisconsin's policies, disrupting public meetings, and lobbied strenuously in Washington, DC. In April 1972, the Menominee Restoration Bill was introduced in the House and Senate. The bill passed in the House in October 1973 and in the Senate two months later. President Richard Nixon signed the Menominee Restoration Act into law December 22, 1973. The success of the DRUMS activists can be attributed not only to their fearless persistence, but also to their dedication to the principals of sovereignty and self-determination. Between 1953 and 1964, over 100 tribes were terminated, some 13,000 tribal members lost their legal status as Indians, and nearly 1.5 million acres of tribal lands were opened to non-Indian settlement. The policy of termination helped inspire the native political activism of the 1960s and 1970s.

ALCATRAZ

In July 1963, an out-of-court settlement touched off the most explosive and influential native political activism of the decade. The longstanding controversy over Indian land claims in California came to an abrupt end after the Indian Claims Commission promised $29.1 million as compensation for approximately 64 million acres of land illegally taken from California tribes. Considering the settlement a travesty, five Sioux Indians, living in California as part of the federal Urban Indian Relocation program, decided to use the terms of an older Sioux treaty to dramatize the inequitable outcome of the settlement. The island had been the site of one of the nation's most notorious maximum-security prisons, but the institution had been closed in March 1963 and was sitting dormant on its rocky perch in the middle of the San Francisco Bay. The 1868 Treaty of Fort Laramie stated that abandoned federal lands could be reclaimed by the Sioux. Armed with that assurance, on March 8, 1964, these five men, a handful of supporters, their attorney, and invited members of the press, landed on Alcatraz Island. The men, dressed in tribal regalia, declared that they were claiming Alcatraz as Indian land, and they also offered to sell it back for $0.47 an acre—an approximate equivalent of the California land settlement. The group's takeover was a symbolic gesture, and the Indians left the island after doing a victory dance.

On November 20, 1969, however, a much larger group of young American Indians of both college and working class backgrounds, led by a Mohawk college student from San Francisco State University named Richard Oakes, took over the island again. This time, they came to stay. From its beginning, the Occupation of Alcatraz was a peaceful demonstration of native self-determination. Secretary of

A group of American Indians, part of Indians of All Tribes Inc., occupies the former prison at Alcatraz Island, San Francisco Bay, California, November 25, 1969. The occupiers were demanding a visit by the secretary of the interior to discuss possession of the property. (AP Photo)

the Interior Walter Joseph Hickel immediately denounced the invasion and stated adamantly that there would be no consideration of Indian demands until the group had vacated the island. The event was widely covered by the international media, however, and the public overwhelmingly sympathized with the occupiers. Consequently, the group received magnanimous support from the local community as well as from thousands of people across the country who watched daily reports of the occupation on television newscasts. In December, the group began a radio program, "Radio Free Alcatraz," which was broadcast daily on Berkeley's

KPFA-FM radio station, on Los Angeles' KPFX-FM station, and on New York City's WBAI-FM. Radio coverage delivered the group's message to more than 100,000 listeners. Indians from hundreds of tribes around the United States and Canada began to flock to Alcatraz. Some came for a weekend just to be able to say they were a part of the movement; others came as occupiers. Although the occupation ended on June 11, 1971, when the last Indians were removed from the island by federal marshals, the occupation had been an incredible success. Alcatraz had become a dramatic rallying cry and international symbol of Native American solidarity, renewed resistance, and Red Power.

THE AMERICAN INDIAN CHICAGO CONFERENCE

In June 1961, a week-long conference, which was attended by approximately 500 Native Americans from 90 different tribal communities, began in Chicago. The American Indian Chicago Conference had been organized by Sol Tax and Nancy Lurie, anthropologists who wanted to start a dialogue about the state of Indian affairs. During the conference, the assembly drafted a policy statement, asking the federal government to end the policy of termination, increase educational and healthcare opportunities for Indians, provide better protection and management of tribal natural resources, and reconsider plans to build the Kinzua Dam. The controversial plans to build the dam would condemn 10,000 acres of the Allegheny Reservation set aside for the Seneca in the 1794 Treaty of Canandaigua and would result in the forced relocation of approximately 600 Seneca tribal members. Federal recognition of many of the tribes terminated in previous years had not been restored as had the status of the Menominee; many others, such as in California, had never been recognized at all. The conference was a first opportunity for many of these non–federally recognized tribes to participate in the ongoing debates. It also ignited the spark for a movement for federal recognition.

NATIONAL INDIAN YOUTH COUNCIL

One of the oldest national Indian organizations in the United States, the National Indian Youth Council (NIYC), was established in 1961 in Albuquerque, New Mexico, by an intertribal group of Indian students. The organization was borne out of the experiences of several students who attended the 1961 American Indian Chicago Conference. At the conference, Shirley Hill Witt, Mel Thom, and Clyde Warrior, along with other students, formed an ad hoc youth committee to compose and present a declaration on Indian peoples' inherent right to self-government. The conference adopted the declaration, which became the philosophical foundation for the National Indian Youth Council. It was an outright rejection of paternalism and an embrace of traditional Indian values.

A subsequent follow-up meeting was called when the group returned to Albuquerque and adopted a constitution and bylaws. The group emerged alongside the civil rights movement and employed acts of protest and civil disobedience to achieve its objectives. National Indian Youth Council members took part in high profile actions (e.g., fish-ins in the Northwest, freedom rides in the South), and they coordinated the Indian segment of the Poor People's Campaign in 1968. In the following decades, the NIYC turned its attention to environmental issues, cultural and spiritual exploitation, Native American political participation, and employment opportunities for Indian people.

AMERICAN INDIAN MOVEMENT

Perhaps the most well-known group of Indian activists is the American Indian Movement (AIM). Established as a community watch group (AIM Patrol) in Minneapolis in 1968, the organization, which initially formed to put an end to abusive police practices toward urban Indians, went on to become the most celebrated Indian rights organization in U.S. history. Largely masterminded by urban Indians, through persistent, aggressive direct action, AIM began to attract the attention of an international audience to the ongoing problems of native peoples. By the 1970s, they were responsible for staging hundreds of well-publicized, sensational demonstrations, such as the Trail of Broken Treaties (1972), the Occupation of Wounded Knee (1973), and the Longest Walk (1978). A number of spinoff organizations emerged from AIM activism, including Women of All Red Nations (WARN), formed in 1974 by AIM members Lorelei DeCora Means, Madonna Thunderhawk, Phyllis Young, and Janet McCloud; the International Indian Treaty Council (IITC), founded at an AIM gathering held at Standing Rock, South Dakota, attended by more than 5,000 representatives of 98 indigenous nations; and the National Coalition on Racism in Sports and Media (NCRSM), established in 1991 at a meeting at Augsburg College in Minneapolis, Minnesota. NCRSM is best known for its demonstrations at sports stadiums across the United States to raise awareness of the issue of racial stereotyping.

There can be no doubt that the political activism of the twenty-first century had a great influence on Congress as it began to enact more informed, progressive legislation and Indian policies. Much credit for improvements in the relationship between the government and tribes, particularly new opportunities for Indian political participation, must be given to the pioneering organizing efforts of these remarkable native activists.

REFERENCES

Banks, Dennis. *Ojibwa Warrior: Dennis Banks and the Rise of the American Indian Movement*. Norman: University of Oklahoma Press, 2005.

Cobb, Daniel. *Native Activism in Cold War America: The Struggle for Sovereignty*. Lawrence: University of Kansas Press, 2010.

Cornell, Stephen. *The Return of the Native: American Indian Political Resurgence*. New York: Oxford University Press, 1988.

Deloria, Vine Jr. *Behind the Trail of Broken Treaties: An Indian Declaration of Independence*. New York: Dell, 1973.

Deloria, Vine, Jr. *We Talk, You Listen*. New York: Macmillan, 1970.

Deloria, Vine, Jr. *Custer Died for Your Sins: An Indian Manifesto*. New York: Macmillan, 1969.

De Luca, Richard. "'We Hold the Rock!' The Indian Attempt to Reclaim Alcatraz Island." *California History* 62, no.1 (Spring 1983), 14.

De Schweinitz, Edmund. *The Life and Times of David Zeisberger: The Western Pioneer and Apostle of the Indians*. Philadelphia: J.B. Lippincott and Company, 1870.

Hauptman, Laurence. "The Voice of Eastern Indians: The American Indian Chicago Conference of 1961 and the Movement for Federal Recognition." *Proceedings of the American Philosophical Society* 132 (1988): 316.

Hoxie, Frederick E. *Talking Back to Civilization: Indian Voices from the Progressive Era*. New York: Bedford/St. Martin's, 2001.

Johnson, Troy. *The American Indian Occupation of Alcatraz Island: Red Power and Self Determination*. Lincoln: University of Nebraska Press, 2008.

Johnson, Troy, JoAnne Nagel, and Duane Champagne. *American Indian Activism: Alcatraz to the Longest Walk*. Urbana: University of Illinois Press, 1997.

Josephy, Alvin M. *Now That the Buffalo's Gone: A Study of Today's American Indians*. Norman: University of Oklahoma Press, 1984.

Means Russell. *Where White Men Fear to Tread: The Autobiography of Russell Means*. New York: St. Martin's, 1995.

Matthiessen, Peter. *In the Spirit of Crazy Horse*. New York: Penguin Books, 1992.

Nagel, JoAnne. *American Indian Ethnic Renewal: Red Power and the Resurgence of Identity and Culture*. New York: Oxford University Press, 1996.

Nesper, Larry. *The Walleye War: The Struggle for Ojibwe Spearfishing and Treaty Rights*. Lincoln: University of Nebraska Press, 2002.

Peroff, Nicholas C. *Menominee DRUMS: Tribal Termination and Restoration, 1954–1974*. Norman: University of Oklahoma Press, 1982.

Prisons and Indians

Wendell Johnson

The crime rate for American Indians is much higher than for other racial groups in America. The Department of Justice, for example, reports that "American Indians experienced a per capita rate of violence twice that of the U.S. resident population" (Perry 2004, iv). As a result, the rate of incarceration for American Indians is higher than for non-Indians. Poverty, ignorance, reservation conditions, and inequity in the justice system are in part responsible for these trends.

Prior to the arrival of Europeans on the American continent, many Indian tribes had established codes of conduct to deal with crime. Traditionally, justice in Native American communities was reconciliatory rather than retributive. When an individual violated the rights of another, penalties were culturally prescribed. After restitution was made to the injured party, the matter was closed. Other penalties included spiritual disenfranchisement, exclusion from tribal ceremonies, and the ultimate sanction, temporary banishment from the community. Individual tribal members were taught to become personally responsible for their conduct, which represented the values of the entire culture. Prisoners captured in intertribal warfare were frequently adopted into the tribe or ritually killed.

Indian prisoners were often treated harshly by their European captors. Following a revolt against authorities in 1598, for example, the Spanish killed 800 Indians and cut off one foot of all surviving Acoma Indian males over 25 years of age. Men and women of the tribe were sentenced to 20 years of slavery and children placed in missions. Prisoners captured by the British in the Pequot War (1634–1638) and Second Powhatan War (1644–1648) were sentenced to slavery in the Caribbean (Cave 1996).

Prior to King Philip's War (or Metacom's War, a conflict between Native Americans and English colonists in southern New England; 1675–1676), Indians in Massachusetts were given some autonomy in how to punish crime. In Natick, hereditary leaders were responsible for the administration of justice. The duties of the Indian constable, or tithing man, were modeled after colonial English law. The constable was obligated to apprehend criminals and convey them to prison. Indian jurors were empanelled for murder and rape trials involving other Indians. Among the crimes that Indians were likely to commit were polygamy, incest, Sabbath-breaking, counterfeiting, murder, burglary, theft, and assault. Then, as now, alcohol was considered a contributing factor to Indian crime (Schultz and Tougias 1999).

The westward expansion of the United States brought many tribes into conflict with federal authorities. The effects of becoming a prisoner of the federal government were severe. During the Minnesota Uprising (1862), over 300 Dakota Indians were sentenced to be hanged. President Abraham Lincoln commuted the sentences of many, but 38 were executed on December 26, 1862 (Graves and Ebbott 2006). During the Texas Indian Wars, commanders adopted a no prisoners policy. However, after the Civil War, army leaders discovered that capturing a band's women and children provided leverage that forced warriors onto reservations. At the end of the Apache Wars (1860–1886), Geronimo and the Chiricahua and Warm Springs Apache were shipped from Arizona to Florida for confinement.

LEGISLATION

Congress passed the General Crimes Act in 1854, which gave federal courts jurisdiction over criminal acts committed on tribal lands. Two key exceptions to the General Crimes Act should be noted: crimes between Indians and crimes where offenders were punished under tribal law. In one precedent-setting incident, Crow Dog, a member of the Brule Sioux tribe in the Dakota Territory, killed Spotted Tail (also a member of the Brule tribe) in a personal dispute in 1881. Following traditional Sioux law, Crow Dog's family paid restitution to Spotted Tail's family in the form of $600 cash, eight horses, and a blanket. Federal authorities decided that the tribal punishment was too light. They arrested Crow Dog for murder, and he was tried in Dakota territorial court, where he was found guilty and sentenced to death. Crow Dog appealed, claiming that federal courts had no jurisdiction over crimes committed by one Indian against another. In *Ex Parte Crow Dog* (1883), the Supreme Court reversed Crow Dog's conviction. Justice Matthews wrote that federal treaties and statues dictate that crimes committed by Indians against other Indians had to be prosecuted by Indians themselves: "To uphold the jurisdiction exercised in this case, would be to reverse in this instance the general policy of the government towards [Indians], as declared in many statutes and treaties and recognized in many decisions of this court. To justify such a departure requires a clear expression of the intention of Congress..." (Ex Parte Crow Dog, 109 U.S. 556, [1883]). Surprised by the Supreme Court's ruling, Congress followed instructions, passing The Major Crimes Act of 1885. This legislation listed seven crimes, including murder, which, if committed on Indian land, would fall under the jurisdiction of federal courts. Two other Supreme Court cases bear mention. In *Oliphant vs. Suquamish Indian Tribe* (1978), the court held that tribal courts did not have jurisdiction over non-Indians accused of crimes on Indian land. *Duro vs. Reina* (1990) further maintained that tribes do not have legal jurisdiction over Indians who do not reside in the land where a crime occurred (Mikula and Mabunda 1999).

JAILS IN INDIAN COUNTRY

As of 2008, there were 92 correctional facilities, including jails and detention centers, in Indian country (self-governing native America communities) holding a total of 2,135 inmates. The 10 largest jails in Indian country, with their respective custody population, are Gila River Department of Corrections and Rehabilitation (Arizona, 161); Tohono O'odham Detention Center (Arizona, 121); White Mountain Apache Police Department (Arizona, 91); Pine Ridge Correctional Facility (South Dakota, 77); Hopi Rehabilitation Center (Arizona, 75); Salt River Department of Corrections (Arizona, 68); Warm Springs Detention Center (Oregon, 48); Peach Springs Detention Center (Arizona, 46); Rosebud Sioux Tribe Law Enforcement (South Dakota, 44); and Menominee Tribal Jail (Wisconsin, 44) (Minton 2011).

Jurisdiction over crimes in Indian country depends on the severity and location of the crime. Tribal jurisdiction generally extends to property crimes committed by Indians in Indian country. Sentences are limited to one year of imprisonment, a $5,000 fine, or both (25 U.S.C. §1302 [7]). Federal jurisdiction includes crimes listed in the Major Crimes Act, and state jurisdiction includes other crimes on tribal lands specified under Public Law 280 (18 U.S.C. § 1162).

Indian country jails were operating at 64 percent capacity in 2008. The 12 smallest jails, rated to hold fewer than 10 inmates, were operating at 20 percent of their rated capacity. Larger jails, rated with a capacity of 50 or more inmates, had 50 percent of their bed space occupied on an average day in June 2008 (the latest year that statistics are available). Indian country jails rated to hold 25 to 49 inmates were operating at near full capacity (97 percent) in 2008. About 40 percent of Indian country jails were operating above rated capacity on an average day. Thirteen Indian country jails are under consent decree. Four facilities were ordered to limit the number of inmates incarcerated in their respective facilities. Of the other nine, five facilities were ordered to house inmates under more humane conditions, two were ordered to cease housing juveniles, one was ordered to separate adults from juveniles and males from females, and one was ordered to limit detoxification detention for any individual prisoner to eight hours per offense (Minton 2011).

INDIAN CRIME STATISTICS

The following data was collected by the Department of Justice and published in the report, *American Indians and Crime*.

- On average, American Indians experienced an estimated 1 violent crime for every 10 residents age 12 or older.
- From 1976 to 2001 an estimated 3,738 American Indians were murdered.
- After 1995 the annual American Indian murder rate decreased about 45% from 6.6 to 3.6 murders per 100,000 residents in 2001.
- From 1976 to 1999, 7 in 10 American Indian juvenile murder victims were killed by another American Indian.
- The violent crime rate in every age group below age 35 was significantly higher for American Indians than for all persons.
- The rate of violent victimization among American Indian women was more than double that among all women.
- American Indian victims of violence were more likely than all victims to report an offender who was under the influence of alcohol at the time of the crime.
- Compared to all murder victims, American Indian victims of homicide were more likely to have been killed by a rifle/shotgun or a knife.
- The arrest rate among American Indians for alcohol violations ... was higher than the rate among all races.
- American Indians were arrested for driving under the influence (DUI) at a rate of 479 per 100,000 residents, compared to 332 for all races.
- The U.S. attorney's office is the principal prosecutor of criminal cases for violation of Federal laws in Indian country.
- Within 3 years of their release from State prison in 1994, an estimated 3 in 5 American Indians were arrested for a new crime. ...
- Nearly 15% (11) of 75 American Indians released from prison in 1994 for a past homicide were arrested for another murder within 36 months.

Source: American Indians and Crime. U.S. Department of Justice. Retrieved from http://www.justice.gov/otj/pdf/american_indians_and_crime.pdf

MEDICAL FACILITIES IN INDIAN COUNTRY JAILS

Most Indian country jails provide medical services to inmates. Thirty-seven jails offer medical services off-site through the Indian Health Service (IHS), a subsidiary of the U.S. Department of Health and Human Services. Thirteen Indian country jails contract with private medical services, and nine facilities use on-site physicians. Thirty-five jails test inmates for HIV, and 38 facilities test for tuberculosis. Some jails also test inmates for hepatitis and infectious diseases.

American Indians have unique mental health needs. Twenty-seven Indian country jails screen inmates for mental health disorders, and 20 jails provide 24-hour mental health care. All facilities have suicide prevention measures in place and provide staff training in risk assessment and suicide prevention. In addition, many facilities (33) offer alcohol dependency and drug awareness programs.

OTHER PROGRAMS

Fourteen jails in Indian country offer classes in parenting and children rearing. Eleven provide training in life skills and community adjustment (personal finance and conflict resolution). Half of the institutions make educational programs available to the inmates. These programs include GED (General Education Development) classes and special education classes. Six jails offer college-level courses. Vocational training is offered at nine facilities, and 31 jails offer work assignment, including road maintenance and agricultural work.

AMERICAN INDIANS UNDER CORRECTION

The incarceration rate for American Indians in 2008 was 921 per 100,000 residents (based on an estimated 28,400 American Indians in prison or jail). This rate is 21 percent higher than the national overall incarceration rate of 759 per 100,000 persons. Correctional authorities supervised 71,400 American Indians in 2008 (up from 71,300 the previous year—see Table 2). Between 2000 and 2008, the number of American Indians in jails and prisons grew by an average of 4 percent annually. Of American Indians under correctional supervision in 2008, most (62 percent or approximately 47,000) were on probation or parole. The Plains states of Montana, Nebraska, North Dakota, Oklahoma, South Dakota, Minnesota, and Wyoming have the highest total number of Indians under correction. In the Southwestern United States, Arizona and New Mexico have relatively high numbers of Indian inmates, while Idaho and Washington have high numbers in the Northwest. Alaska has the largest percentage of Indian prisoners—over 30 percent.

Table 2 American Indians and Alaska Natives in Custody, 2007–2008

	2007	2008	% Change
Total	71,300	71,400	5.8
In Custody	27,000	28,400	2.5
Local jails	8,600	9,000	4.7
Jails in Indian country	2,163	2,135	−1.3
State prisons	13,956	14,264	2.2
Federal prisons	2,955	2,989	1.2

Source: T.D. Minton, *Jails in Indian Country*.

American Indian inmates differ from other inmates in certain demographic and other characteristics. American Indians are more likely than other detainees to:

- Be older
- Have more children
- Be either unemployed or underemployed
- Have more alcohol-related charges
- Have been arrested more often
- Have served more time in jail
- Have been hospitalized more often for alcohol-related problems
- Used correctional services for emotion and mental health issues

AMERICAN INDIANS AND CRIME

American Indians not only have a higher rate of incarceration than the population at large, they experience a per capita rate of violence twice that of the U. S. resident population. They experience one violent crime for every 10 residents ages 12 or older. The violent crime rate for every age group below 35 is significant higher for American Indians than for other groups. American Indians aged 25 to 34 have a rate of violent crime victimization more than 250 percent that of all persons the same age. Indian victims of violence are more likely than other victims to report that the offender was under the influence of alcohol (62 percent for American Indians, 42 percent for the national average) (Perry 2004).

According to the National Crime Victimization Survey (DOJ 2000), the annual average violent crime rate among American Indians is twice as high as that for African Americans, 2.5 times higher than that for whites, and 4.5 times than that for Asians. American Indians experience a per capital rate of violence victimization of one for every 24 residents, compared to one violence victimization for every 20 African Americans, one for every 25 whites, and one for every 45 Asian Americans. In five states (Alaska, Minnesota, North Carolina, Oregon, and

Table 3 Number of Victimizations per 1,000 Persons Age 12 and Older

	All Races	American Indians
Violent victimizations	41	101
Rape	5	2
Robbery	5	8
Aggravated assault	25	9
Simple assault	26	51

Source: Steven W. Perry, "American Indians and Crime."

Washington), the proportion of murder victims who were American Indians exceeded their proportion of each state's resident population (see Table 3).

INDIANS AND ALCOHOL

In alcohol-related arrests, American Indians have a rate of 479 per 100,000 for driving under the influence (DUI) as compared to 332 per 100,000 for all races. (Criminal Justice Collective 2009). Some studies show that the majority of homicides and assaults committed by Indians are the result of alcohol abuse. Other studies have indicated that Indians with alcohol dependence have more interaction with the penal system than with alcohol treatment programs. Indian inmates often continue substance abuse while in prison, sometimes producing moonshine. In Nebraska, for example, 40 percent of Indian inmates admit to substance abuse while in custody. Many Indians continue to struggle with substance dependence while on parole, indicating the failure of rehabilitation services in the prisons.

JUVENILE DETENTION

The Indian Child Welfare Act (1978) requires that a tribe be notified when an Indian child is brought into state court in a matter of abuse or neglect. The tribe has the option of requesting transfer of jurisdiction to a tribal court. Ten jails in Indian country have been designated as juvenile facilities. According to the recent federal statistics, these facilities supervised180 juveniles. The juvenile facilities were rated to hold 321 inmates and were operating at 54 percent capacity. As in all Indian country jails, the majority of offenders in juvenile facilities (62 percent) were being held for misdemeanors. Approximately 10 percent of the juveniles were being held for felonies, and the remainder for other offenses, including status offenses (truancy, curfew violations, possession of alcohol) and court orders. The average officer to inmate ratio for juvenile jails was 1:1, and several tribes had more officers than juvenile inmates (Perry 2004).

INDIANS, CAPITAL PUNISHMENT, AND DEATH ROW

Federal law limits the circumstances under which Indians are subject to capital punishment. A capital offense that is committed on a reservation must be prosecuted by the governing tribal authority. Indians remain subject to capital punishment for murder committed outside of Indian Territory. As of July 1, 2009, thirty-seven Indians resided on death row in state and federal prisons. Since 1961, fifteen Indians have been executed, 13 for killing whites and 2 for killing fellow Indians. For the period from 1639 to 2006, four hundred sixty-four Indians were executed in the United States, 150 by the military, 132 by the states (Massachusetts has executed the most Indians, at 79), 65 by the federal government, 52 by territorial courts, and 33 by Indian tribunals. The other 32 capital cases cannot be accounted for (Perry 2004).

RECIDIVISM

The Bureau of Justice Statistics (BJS) studied recidivism rates for American Indians for the period from 1992 to 2002 (Perry 2004). BJS reports state that recidivism rates for American Indians were similar to those for all offenders. Within three years of release from state prison, an estimated 60 percent of American Indians were arrested for a felony or serious misdemeanor. Of the American Indians released from prison during this time, 46 percent were convicted of a new crime within three years, and 21 percent of these individuals were sentenced to prison for the new offense. Indian offenders who were returned to prison amounted to 36 percent because of a technical violation of their parole or probation. Nearly 15 percent of American Indians released from prison for a past homicide were arrested for another murder within 36 months.

CHALLENGES

American Indians under correctional custody face unique religious challenges. Historically, only Christian beliefs have been endorsed by prison officials, and as a result, Indian prisoners struggle to uphold their traditional rituals and spirituality. Many corrections officials do not understand native ceremonies. Native American prisoners are often denied sacred objects such as pipes, eagle feathers, and herbs. Many Indians need the smoke from their pipes to carry their prayers to the spiritual world and so are unable to worship without them. Cultural sensitivity is also lacking related to Indians' hair. Many Native Americans keep long hair as a living extension of their prayers. Compulsory haircuts affect an inmate's spiritual practice.

In 2003, a group of American Indian inmates sued the Maine State Prison over a three-year-old smoking ban they argued violated their religious freedom. In the lawsuit, the 14 inmates contended prison officials denied them the right to build a sweat lodge, seized religious items, and temporarily confiscated a bowl used in their weekly smudging ceremony, where sweetgrass is burned to produce smoke and the residue is "smudged" or rubbed over an inmate in order to cleanse the body (in 2000, based on health concerns, the Maine Department of Corrections banned smoking). Many federal judges do not want to interfere with prison officials' control over security issues. At present, only half of the states permit Native American sweat lodge ceremonies in prisons. Organizations such as Native American Prison Support fought to ensure the religious rights of Native American prisoners. As a result, sweat lodges, talking circles, sacred pipes, and other rituals became more prevalent in correctional institutions (Grobsmith 1994).

REFERENCES

Cave, A. *The Pequot War*. Amherst: University of Massachusetts Press, 1996.

Criminal Justice Collective. *Investigating Difference: Human and Cultural Relations in Criminal Justice*. Upper Saddle River, NJ: Pearson Prentice Hall, 2009.

Graves, K. and E. Ebbot. *Indians in Minnesota* (5th ed.). Minneapolis: University of Minnesota Press, 2006.

Grobsmith, E. "Prisons and Prisoners." In Mary B. Davis (Ed.), *Native America in the Twentieth Century: An Encyclopedia*. New York: Garland Publishing, 1994.

Mikula, M. and Mabunda, L. (Eds.). *Great American Court Cases*. Detroit: The Gale Group, 1999.

Minton, T. D. *Jails in Indian Country*. Washington, DC: Office of Justice Programs, 2011.

Perry, Steven W. "American Indians and Crime: A BJS Statistical Profile, 1992–2002," 2004. Retrieved from http://www.justice.gov/otj/pdf/american_indians_and_crime.pdf

Schultz, E. and Tougias, M. *King Philip's War: The History and Legacy of America's Forgotten Conflict*. Woodstock, VT: Country Man Press, 1999.

U.S. Department of Justice (DOJ). Bureau of Justice Statistics. *National Crime Victimization Survey*, 2000. doi:10.3886/ICPSR22921.v1

Red Power: The American Indian Movement

John H. Barnhill

Red Power, like Black Power, was a label taken by members of a minority group to express newfound pride and to refuse to accept degradation any longer or to wait patiently while the civil rights movement slowly brought about piecemeal change. Red Power is most commonly identified with the American Indian Movement (AIM) because AIM was the most radical of the Indian organizations of the 1960s and 1970s. The term, however, predates AIM and its original use belongs more accurately to the more moderate National Indian Youth Council (NIYC).

PRECURSORS

In 1970, Native American unemployment was 10 times the national average, and 40 percent of Indians were poor. The group's life expectancy of 44 years was a third less than the national average. In Arizona on the Navajo reservation, birthrates were high, at third-world levels, and purchasing power was low. Average educational attainment was the fifth grade, and only one-sixth of adults had finished high school. These conditions were nothing new for American Indians. Long before the late 1960s, they were the poorest of any minority group. Commonly, reservation homes lacked telephones, and Indians relied on outhouses and wood burning stoves. Half a million Indians lived in shanties or abandoned automobiles. Their death rate was a third higher than the American average. For specific diseases, death rates could be as high as 60 times the norm.

Native Americans by no means passively accepted their plight, even in the early twentieth century. Long before the Red Power movement, some Indians protested their miserable conditions, with increasing activity during periods of adverse governmental activity. But their radicalism was muted. Founded in 1911, the Society of American Indians (SAI) was Christian and assimilationist, and its impact was minimal. Society of American Indians members were mostly professionals, well educated and advocating assimilation to end poverty by ending reservation life. Also assimilationist and Christian was the 1934 American Indian Federation. The SAI provided a foundation for later reform groups by engaging during the 1920s and 1930s in lobbying and debating national issues such as Indian citizenship and the Indian New Deal.

The first long-lasting intertribal Indian organization came into being during World War II in an attempt to counter a government attempt to assimilate Native Americans. The National Congress of American Indians (NCAI) formed in 1944 as a lobby and litigation group that, like the individual tribes and the National Association for the Advancement of Colored People (NAACP), sought legal redress, in the case of the NCAI a return of land and treaty rights as well as improved education. When Congress enacted termination in the early 1950s and gave states legal jurisdiction over reservations regardless of tribal consent, the NCAI opposed both measures, without success.

Under termination between 1952 and 1960, the Bureau of Indian Affairs (BIA) relocated 35,000 Indians to cities such as San Francisco, Phoenix, Denver, and Los Angeles. A third returned after failing to find jobs or adequate housing. Those who stayed in the cities became lonely and dependent on federal aid, but they regarded their urban plight as better than that on the reservation, where life expectancy for the average male was less than 45 years. As termination forced growth of urban communities, Indians began to develop support structures and methods of preserving their culture and traditions. And Indians throughout the United States began comparing notes on the failures of termination

Even though the NCAI was a national organization, during the 1950s, most activism was local. Over 20 major localized, nonviolent demonstrations occurred during the 1950s. The Iroquois League used both passive resistance and militancy to prevent New York state projects such as the Kinzua Dam that would have displaced Indians and flooded their land. The effort succeeded in keeping part of the reservation from becoming a reservoir. The goals of the individual tribal efforts were to prevent additional loss of their land base, reduce white brutality and insensitivity, and reverse termination. At this point, the effort was primarily tribal, and American Indians lacked any strong sense of pan-Indianism.

NIYC

Then in 1961, the National Indian Youth Council (NIYC) formed. It was the first Indian organization to call for Red Power. NIYC challenged the old guard NCAI, which opposed demonstrations. NIYC formed in reaction to socioeconomic changes after World War II, the civil rights movement and the Cold War. Termination was also a concern. NIYC called for sovereignty, traditional culture, self-determination, and treaty rights. NIYC led demonstrations, marches, and most famously fish-ins to protest state violation of federal treaty rights to fish.

College and university students in New Mexico had been working in the Regional Indian Youth Council (RIYC) since 1957. The RIYC brought individual young Indians to its sessions so that they could develop a broader awareness of Indian-ness. The RIYC was a white-sponsored, white-dominated, campus-level organization that generated weak self-image among attendees and tended to blame Indians for their own problems. When Clyde Warrior of Oklahoma became head of the RIYC in 1961, he provided the spark that moved the RIYC into a national organization emphasizing Indian pride and activism.

Clyde Warrior of the NIYC in the early 1960s became a spokesperson for self-determination as the only way to end poverty and dismal conditions. Indians should be in charge of their own destiny, designing and managing their own programs based on their own experience and needs. The War on Poverty was not the answer. Warrior was among the new activist Red Power Indians, Vietnam veterans going to college on the GI Bill as well as BIA relocates.

Shortly after Warrior took over, the RIYC became one of the organizations at the American Indian Chicago Conference, which involved 500 attendees from 90 tribes and bands. The conference generated the Declaration of Indian Purpose and furthered the development of activism and pan-Indian awareness. It also provoked the RIYC under Warrior to become an Indian organization, the NIYC.

The most radical NIYC effort was the fish-in movement in the Pacific Northwest, but the NIYC was unable to bring it to a successful conclusion on its own. The state of Washington in the mid-1950s began restricting Indian access to areas off the reservation, citing conservation and equity with white fishermen. Indians argued that they had customary usage since the 1850s, and in 1963 they won a federal case that the state ignored. When the state closed the fishing areas to Indians, the Survival of American Indians Association (SAIA) formed in protest. The fish-ins began when tribal members fished in waters that state and local laws barred to them despite federal treaty guarantees. NIYC intervened, but SAIA was successful in keeping off-reservation fishing rights.

Warrior died in 1968 and the NIYC lost its radicalism, which had been an uneasy fit for the moderate-leaning organization anyway.

ALCATRAZ

Meanwhile, individual tribal and local activities continued. The Native American Rights Fund litigated against states that took land or abolished hunting, fishing, or water rights guaranteed by treaty. Other tribal actions included suits against strip mining or the spraying of pesticides. In 1964, San Francisco Bay–area Indians formed the Indian Historical Society, dedicated to history from the Native American perspective.

The invasion of Alcatraz in 1964 by 40 Indians was a protest that used Indian culture to raise public awareness. The invaders wore traditional costume while engaging in a symbolic act of reclaiming what had been taken from Native Americans. It was an act of theater, a four-hour performance, that ended peacefully with the Indians being escorted off the island and their images planted in the world mind thanks to the evening news and newspapers. In one act of theater, the Indians overcame decades of frustrating struggles with the red tape of the BIA. Indians had public attention and public sympathy, so the next step was to get the government to feel the pressure and bring about change.

By the late 1960s over half of all Indians were urban, a trend begun during World War II as industrial jobs opened, the federal government pushed urbanization of Indians, and America in general urbanized. Indians in cities perceived the federal government as failing them. In San Francisco, Indian parents and youth alike also saw college as a route to better life. Urban Indians organized; urban Indian youth enrolled in college. In college, disillusioned youth, urban and talking to one another, began demanding reform, what would come to be called Red Power. In 1969, Red Power was raging, and when the Indians of All Tribes took over Alcatraz, it was more than a media event. The mostly young and college-educated progressive Indians who led the movement were charismatic and devoted to building a pan-Indian consciousness, self-awareness, and pride. They were the next step in a historical progression of Indian resistance and social movements.

Rather than four hours, the length of the first occupation of Alcatraz, the second occupation lasted 19 months. The Alcatraz seizure of November 1969 involved about 200 Indians. They held it for 19 months in an effort to bring attention to the plight of the reservations. Like the reservation, Indians said, Alcatraz was without running water, decent sanitation, and jobs. It had high unemployment, no healthcare, and rocky soil. They offered the government $24 in trinkets for the island.

AIM

In the 1960s, centuries of political, economic, and cultural repression and abject Indian poverty both on and off the reservations became intolerable to the new generation. The collective struggle of diverse groups, from mainstream and moderate to far left radical, was for individual and community Indian self-determination and autonomy: Red Power.

Red Power activists tended to be younger, more impatient, and more avid for change. To promote pan-Indianism, they formed national organizations of, by, and for Native Americans, among them the American Indian Movement (AIM).

The most noticed, most notorious, most aggressive of the Red Power groups was AIM, formed in Minneapolis in 1966 by Chippewa to protest police brutality. AIM activists were younger, urban, better educated, and more liberal than the general Indian population. They were not willing to accept the slow improvement that the civil rights movement was bringing, but they were dedicated to improving their communities. They grew up on the reservations but had been to college where they encountered the campus activism of the 1960s. Although angry, they were not violent. Like young whites and blacks, young Indian activists had different values than their elders. They were part of the generation gap of the 1960s and 1970s.

AIM was pivotal in winning support for Red Power from urban Indian charitable organizations, churches, and other social groups. The powwow circuit and kinship ties helped to network the Red Power.

AIM leaders were also effective in getting media attention. On Thanksgiving of 1970, AIM painted Plymouth Rock red and seized the replica *Mayflower* in Plymouth, Massachusetts. Also on this Thanksgiving Day, a group of Wampanoag Indians held a national day of mourning at Plymouth, and another group of Indians established a settlement at Mount Rushmore to assert Indian claims to the Black Hills. These were visible acts, strong evidence of the growth of Red Power in the late 1960s and early 1970s.

INDIAN AWARENESS

The Red Power movement was not unique in calling for an end to suppression, deprivation, and injustice. By the 1960s, Native Americans had a long history of successful social protest, mostly tribal and focused on treaty or land issues but some multitribal (such as the NCAI) or in coalitions for temporary issues. Red Power leaders moved beyond legal issues to create a new Indian awareness, a new self-image, pride, and activism based on the Indian heritage.

Red Power after Alcatraz was different from earlier Indian social protest movements that were willing to sacrifice culture for inclusion or inclusion for cultural autonomy; activists demanded cultural identity as well as inclusion within the mainstream culture. Red Power evoked history to inspire and organize their memberships for new struggles. Historical Indian resisters such as Geronimo were also used as symbols.

Between Alcatraz in 1969 and the Longest Walk in 1978, the Red Power movement protested government failure to honor treaty obligations, demanding that the government give Indians promised resources to ease poverty and provide adequate education, healthcare, and housing.

Red Power sought federal funds to rectify centuries of cultural repression by creating Indian colleges and Native American studies programs as well as museums and cultural centers. In 1969, the Third World Liberation Front, a student movement demanding ethnic studies in San Francisco area universities, included Indians when it struck for relevant courses, Indian instructors, and equality. The strike failed but did mobilize young Indians.

The Red Power movement wanted reform and inclusion with preservation of Indian cultural identity. Inclusion without assimilation helped to define multiculturalism. The Red Power movement took property seizure, used sparingly in the past, to new extremes. It also was adamantly supratribal, seeking an Indian-ness beyond the temporary multitribalism of those who, for instance, fought termination. The Red Power movement was new in bringing Indian issues to national awareness and visibility.

Their principal tactic was the seizure of property they claimed was taken wrongly from their ancestors. The occupation of Alcatraz encouraged AIM to begin seizing other national government facilities. The seizure of Alcatraz was a major success, emulated to a lesser extent during the subsequent 74 takeovers of federal facilities. The Alcatraz takeover brought Indian concerns to the attention of the public and the federal government. It also altered Native American perceptions of themselves, their culture, and their right of self-determination. After Alcatraz, the federal government reversed termination policies and replaced them with self-determination. Congress passed 52 acts dealing with Indian self-rule between 1970 and 1971. The BIA budget increased by 225 percent, and healthcare funds doubled. The Nixon administration also established a water rights office and increased Indian scholarship funds by $848,000. From the Office of Equal Opportunity came increased funding for economic development, drug and alcohol recovery, housing, and other on-reservation programs.

THE LONGEST WALK

Lindsey Hanson

The Longest Walk, a march between San Francisco and the District of Columbia, took place from February to July of 1978. The march was meant to symbolize the forced removal of Native Americans. The protestors also wanted to draw national attention to treaty rights issues and the poverty and other social ills the community was faced with. Although then President Jimmy Carter refused to meet with leaders of the march, the American Indian Religious Freedom Act, which protects and preserves traditional American Indian religion and culture, was passed during the protest. In 2008, activists organized a Longest Walk II to commemorate the thirtieth anniversary of the original walk. The 2008 marchers highlighted environmental concerns as well as the importance of tribal sovereignty.

GOVERNMENT ASSISTANCE

Militancy got results. Although there is disagreement over whether AIM radicalism was popularly supported within the Native American community, there is evidence that the guerrilla theater was effective in getting positive results. Changes in Indian policy and legislation, including the Indian Self-Determination and Education Act of 1975, came about at least in part due to the pressure of public opinion, pressure created by AIM's success in evoking public sympathy with the Indians' cause.

The Indian Education Act of 1972 gave parents more control over schools. The 1976 Indian Health Care Act and the 1978 Indian Child Welfare Act gave tribes more resources and control to correct longstanding abuses.

From 1959, the Supreme Court ruled in favor of Indians in sovereignty and self-government cases. By the 1970s, tribes were suing to regain illegally taken land, and in 1980 the Penobscot and Passamaquoddy of Maine got $81.5 million, and the South Dakota Sioux $105 million. Courts also ruled that tribes had rights to run casinos and gas stations, levy taxes, and sell tax-free cigarettes. And Indian population numbers turned around; by 1990, there were over 2 million, more than five times the 1950 number. Half were on reservations and half in urban settings. Many were newly self-identified now that Indian-ness was fashionable.

RADICALISM

After Alcatraz, AIM led most of the protest actions. The organization led the Trail of Broken Treaties in 1972. In 1973, when it led 200 armed Indians in the takeover of Wounded Knee, AIM became labeled a terrorist organization. Indian demands were self-determination and reform of the BIA; they were preservationists rather than assimilationists. They opposed termination and advocated museums, educational programs, and other efforts to preserve their culture within the broader U.S. institutional structure.

Aside from Indian influences, the Red Power Movement also took from the Black Power movement that began with the radicalization of the Student Non-Violent Coordinating Committee and the formation of Students for a Democratic Society. The New Left radicalized students during a time when the civil rights movement seemed too slow and the Vietnam War seemed too wrongheaded and racist. Black Power fed into La Raza, Red Power, and feminism, as student demonstrations seemed everywhere—sit-ins, sleep-ins, lockouts, teach-ins.

At Alcatraz and elsewhere, Red Power dominated, forcing awareness, creating street theater, and dramatizing the Indian plight and demands through the early 1970s. Takeovers of federal property ended in 1972, and the movement shifted to AIM radicalism. Indian rights shifted to Indian protest.

Like other protest movements, as time passed and frustration grew, violence increased. When the 1972 Trial of Broken Treaties caravan arrived in Washington, DC, the groups found that the Department of the Interior (DOI) had failed to provide promised logistical support. AIM reacted by taking over BIA headquarters, taking Indian Health Service (IHS) and BIA files, and causing damage totaling $2.2 million. In return for AIM ending the occupation, the administration gave the protesters $66,000 to buy transportation out of town.

AIM was not universally accepted. It was a progressive urban organization, and when it entered reservations, it encountered traditionalist opposition. It was a young movement, and it encountered opposition from older generations. It was an outside organization, and it encountered opposition from tribal leadership. As AIM protests became angrier during the 1970s, tensions between AIM and anti-AIM camps intensified. The ultimate expression of the tensions came at Wounded Knee on the Pine Ridge Reservation.

Meanwhile, the urban protests moved to the reservations, increasing friction between traditional and assimilated Indians. The culminating event was the 10-week siege of the Pine Ridge Reservation at Wounded Knee, South Dakota, after AIM and many traditional leaders sought to oust the allegedly corrupt tribal chairman. Forces for and against the chairman armed themselves, and eventually the matter included media, philanthropic organizations, federal agents, and the military. The ouster effort failed, with two Indians dead and two federal agents wounded, and the chairman still in power, but reservation protests became common during the next few years.

In 1978, between February and July, several hundred Indians marched from San Francisco to Washington, DC, as a symbolic protest of the forced removals of the past and the continuing problems on reservations. The march also sought to counter a backlash against treaty rights that was growing in Congress. The walk ended peacefully.

DECLINE

During the 1970s, Federal Bureau of Investigation (FBI) infiltration and repression through the Counterintelligence Program (COINTELPRO) led to the decline of the Red Power movement as well as other dissenting groups. In the three years after Wounded Knee II (the first Wounded Knee being the late nineteenth-century massacre), 69 AIM supporters died violently on reservations, and almost 350 others were assaulted with no resultant convictions; in some cases of assault, there was no investigation at all. AIM leaders went to jail, and the movement split between urban activists and national activists. Seizure of federal property became unpopular with activists after 1978, and the Red Power movement waned.

Red Power peaked in the late 1960s and early 1970s. Like so many other minority rights groups of the time, it radicalized itself to the point of creating a major

THE TRAIL OF BROKEN TREATIES AND THE INCIDENT AT WOUNDED KNEE

Lindsey Hanson

AIM was one of the organizations behind the Trail of Broken Treaties march on Washington, DC, in 1972. Organizers of the march drafted a 20-point position paper outlining their concerns and the reasons for the protest. Foremost among the protesters' concerns were treaty rights, but protestors also wanted relations between tribes and the federal government to be restructured. In addition, the organizers demanded changes in the way crime on reservations is treated, immunity from taxation, protection of native religion and culture, and improved housing, education, employment, and economic development for American Indians. With these demands, the activists caravanned from the West Coast to the East, where in protest they took over the BIA for a week in early November. The protestors took confidential files and caused an estimated $2.2 million in damages. The Nixon administration, which had just taken office, agreed to address their concerns within the month in order to end the takeover.

In 1973, AIM took over the town of Wounded Knee, South Dakota, on the Pine Ridge Indian Reservation, for over two months in what became known as the Wounded Knee incident. The AIM takeover was intended to address corruption within the BIA and the Pine Ridge Tribal Council. During the takeover, AIM activists, federal marshals, and Federal Bureau of Investigation (FBI) agents exchanged gunfire. The incident left two American Indians dead and 12 people wounded. Twelve-hundred individuals were arrested before both sides agreed to disarmament in early May 1973. After a federal trial that lasted eight months, AIM leaders were acquitted of any wrongdoing.

white backlash in the 1970s. The mood of the times shifted, and Red Power as an aggressive activist force faded, in part because the old radical leadership disappeared—sometimes violently, sometimes into the establishment—as happened with the Black Power, Chicano power, and radical feminist leadership. Although tamed, Red Power by no means disappeared.

Rather, Red Power matured. Grown up, it took on new forms, more mainstream and less confrontational. AIM, NCAI, and NIYC remained active and viable in 2012, still promoting betterment of the Indian community. As their websites show, they are no longer in opposition to government; rather, they are more willing to tie themselves to the bureaucracy in return for financial benefits and access as pressure groups. Having gained the attention of the people and the government by going to extremes, the Red Power movement abandoned its sixties radicalism, moved into the mainstream, and found alternative methods of attaining the same goals.

Radical Red Power may have diminished or disappeared, but by the early 1980s over 100 Indian studies programs were in operation, many tribes had museums, and the United Nations recognized Indian rights. AIM persisted in targeting Indian mascots, seeking recovery of land and grazing rights, and working to retrieve sacred objects taken from Native American land. Since 1975, Indians gather at Alcatraz on Un-Thanksgiving Day.

The old problems of inferior education, inadequate healthcare, insufficient jobs, and the dismal state of the reservation persist, but largely due to the Red Power movement. Indians are not passively accepting but are working to improve their lot within the system while preserving their unique culture and identity as citizens, not wards.

Many more Americans are choosing to identify as Native American. In 1950, before Red Power and widespread activism in general, the Native American population was under half a million. Forty years later, after Indians became fashionable in part due to the media attention given to Red Power activism, the population exceeded 2 million, a number well in excess of what could be attributed to decreased death rates and increased birth rates or even immigration. The federal government's allowing people to self-identify as Indians also swelled the rolls, as did the possibility of getting a piece of the federal pie. Joane Nagel's *American Indian Ethnic Renewal* documents and explains the rise, which is similar to the rise of ethnic pride movements in general. Superficial Indians, however, are not always accepted by true Indians struggling to hold reservations and cultures together.

Meanwhile, the old-time Red Power organizations continue on, having shifted their emphasis from radicalism to community improvement, particularly assisting their constituencies, whether reservation tribal or urban pan-Indian, to collect grants from private and government sources, to litigate against corporations and governments, to safeguard their rights and their heritage. Radicalism is dead; Red Power is a movement for the long haul. And Native Americans remain the most desperately poor of American citizens.

REFERENCES

AIM homepage. Available at http://www.aimovement.org/

"Alcatraz Is not an Island." Pbs.org, 2002. Retrieved from http://www.pbs.org/itvs/alcatrazisnotanisland/activism.html

Digitalhistory. "America in Ferment: The Tumultuous 1960s: The Native American Power Movement." Retrieved from http://www.digitalhistory.uh.edu/database/article_display.cfm?HHID=387 in December 2011.

Gudzune, Jeffrey R. "Red Power." American Indian Movement. Retrieved from http://jeffreygudzune.suite101.com/red-power-a1874#ixzz1YPP6ZweE

Johnson, Troy R. *Red Power Movement, History and the Headlines*. Available at http://www.historyandtheheadlines.abc-clio.com/ContentPages/ContentPage.aspx?entryId=1171695&currentSection=1161468&productid=5

Nagel, Joane. *American Indian Ethnic Renewal: Red Power and the Resurgence of Identity and Culture*. New York: Oxford University Press, 1997.

NCAI homepage. Available at http://www.ncai.org/

NIYC homepage. Available at http://www.niyc-alb.org/

Rios, Kelly. "The Efficacy of the Red Power Movement." Retrieved from http://www.calstatela.edu/centers/perspectives/Volume%2035/Rios.pdf in December 2011.

Shreve, Bradley G. *Red Power Rising: The National Indian Youth Council and the Origins of Native Activism*. Norman: University of Oklahoma Press, 2011.

Tribal Government: Local Decision-Making and Law Enforcement

Terry Ahlstedt

Tribal governments provide law enforcement and government services for 56 million acres of land, an area larger than the 10 states of West Virginia, Maryland, Vermont, New Hampshire, Massachusetts, New Jersey, Hawaii, Connecticut, Delaware, and Rhode Island. In the administration of 2 percent of the United States, tribal governments face many of the same issues encountered by federal and state governments. But a key difference is that the federal government has committed itself to a trust responsibility intended to protect tribal communities and tribal lands while providing services. Under the current policy of tribal self-determination, tribal governments make local level decisions and provide many services, while the federal government retains its trust responsibility (National Congress n.d.).

HISTORY

The development of modern tribal government owes much to changes brought about by the introduction of European peoples to the continent. The first major change came as a result of the treaty-making era. Traditionally, tribal governments incorporated safeguards against the concentration of power by individuals. This was done out of a perceived need among the tribes to preserve the values of freedom, respect, and harmony. Tribal decisions came through the approval of leaders among several bands, with the position of the band leader being based on the consensus of band members.

This broad consensus form of government was exasperating to federal negotiators impatient to gain quick resolution of treaty negotiations. To simplify and speed up the process, they pressured tribes to centralize their governments. In addition to external pressure, tribes experienced internal pressures to centralize based on a need to defend against "divide and conquer" strategies used by U.S. negotiators and the need to prevent land cessions by weak, malleable leaders.

When the focus of U.S. policies changed from making treaties to assimilation during the land allotment era, it became the aim of the federal government to weaken and reduce the power of tribal governments, sometimes to the extent of eliminating them. By the 1930s, traditional tribal government had ceased to exist in over half of all reservations, with the Bureau of Indian Affairs (BIA) gaining control of resource distribution, land allocation, and tribal judicial and law enforcement systems. This loss of tribal sovereignty was abruptly changed with the appointment of BIA commissioner John Collier, who was Commissioner of Indian Affairs from 1933 to 1945.

Collier's time as Indian commissioner saw the creation of the Indian Reorganization Act (1934). With this act, Collier sought to reconstitute Indian health care and allow for a system of Indian self-government that reorganized half of all federally recognized tribes. Under this act, native tribes organized their governments with constitutions similar to state constitutions. The late 1940s and early 1950s would see a new effort by the federal government to assimilate Indians through efforts to terminate governmental responsibilities to the tribes and the integration of Indians into white communities. The passage of the 1975 Indian Self-Determination and Educational Assistance Act ended these efforts, denouncing termination and pledging federal resources to strengthen Indian autonomy without endangering Indian communities. This act allows federal authorities to contract directly with tribal governments in administering BIA or Indian Health Service (IHS) programs, meaning that tribal governments now manage much of their own internal affairs.

While many tribes have adopted state-styled constitutions, other tribes like the Pueblo groups, the Onondaga and Tonawanda Seneca of New York, most native groups in Alaska, and many small bands in California maintain traditional forms of government. Other tribes like the Crow and Yakima adopted governments according to rules and procedures unique to individual tribal resolutions.

The 1960s and 1970s were a critical period for the survival of nativism in tribal governments. The need for progress in housing, health, and economics meant that tribal members needed to be more acculturated into the ways of mainstream white society. American Indians sought to achieve parity with the general standards of living in the United States. This resulted in internal and external pressures for both tribal members and tribal governments, which further resulted in a need for effective leadership and competition among leaders for executive positions. As a result, there was a pressure among tribal governments to be ultra-efficient in order to represent their people and communities in dealing with the outside mainstream world. Tribal governments become like business corporations resulting in modern alliances or collations shaped by common regional interests.

THE STRUCTURE AND FUNCTION OF TRIBAL GOVERNMENTS

Tribal leadership has learned to negotiate the way between tribal life and the mainstream. In doing this, leaders maintain a fine balance between outside and inside politics. While change has been good for the tribes, this transition always comes at the risk of the loss of cultural traditions. Change seems to be accelerating as tribal governments are forced to develop and make critical decisions at an even faster pace.

While they may resemble state governments in some ways, tribal governments are different than state administrations. Unlike the states, they are not the product of the U.S. Constitution; rather, tribal governments came from authority that existed before that document was considered. Tribal governments were recognized as sovereign nations by the Spanish, French, Dutch, and English colonists who negotiated treaties with these longstanding entities. Native tribes were recognized as having executive, legislative, and judicial powers of their own. Although the structure and laws of these governments have changed over the years, their purpose remains the same: to meet the social, physical, and cultural needs of their people.

There are three facts to consider in regards to indigenous communities. First, the preexisting status of these communities as separate and sovereign peoples means that tribal governments have original and unencumbered claims (free of prior debts) to territory and sovereignty that have been both recognized and disputed by European governments. Second, is the historical development of unique political, legal, economic, cultural, and moral rights and powers exercised by tribal nations; rights that the United States tried to change to acquire tribal resources and assimilate native Americans. Third, there is a constant fluctuation on the part of the federal government and the American people in regards their perception and treatment of indigenous nations.

This ambivalence is reflected by the fact that the federal government supports the rights of tribes to self-determined sovereignty and promotes policies and laws that affirm their rights as separate yet connected nations, but the federal government has produced numerous laws and policies that have often weakened and upset the sovereignty of tribes, something that often left them in an inferior position in relation to the federal government and the states.

Tribal governments exercise a myriad of government powers, including a variable mixture of civil and criminal jurisdiction over their own members, nonmember Indians, and—to a lesser extent—non-Indians. They hold the power to define membership criteria; administer justice via their own court systems; regulate domestic and family relations like marriage, divorce, and child welfare; regulate zones, exchange, purchase, and sell property; exclude nontribal members from tribal lands; regulate hunting, fishing, and gathering rights; regulate all economic activities and tax; negotiate with other governments; and provide social, health, housing, and educational services for tribal and nontribal citizens. Tribal governments also hold the power of extradition.

But these powers are complicated and often contested from within and without. There are two essential characteristics that need to be considered related to the values of Indian political culture. The two characteristics are the politics of scarcity and the politics of interference. The politics of scarcity refers to the fact that Indian tribes remain among the most disadvantaged and impoverished groups in American society. The extreme social problems of economic poverty, combined with a decided loyalty on reservations to the social group, shape the political behavior of tribal leaders. Tribal leaders, feeling pressure to relieve poverty, have historically sought outside support and funds. Reliance on outside help leads to acquiescence to outside regulations and acceptance of other forms of interference.

Interference can be sociocultural, that is, coming from within tribal membership. Interference can also come from the outside, that is, from government or corporate entities. Internal interference is based on the reality that for many Indians, the primary allegiance is to family, clan, village, or a social group with which they share values, lands, religious views, and language. This sort of loyalty often does extend to the reservation-wide tribal government, which theoretically represents all groups and sometimes different tribes. Outside interests may include Congress; the Department of the Interior and its key agency, the Bureau of Indian Affairs; other federal agencies; state and local governments; and corporate interests.

FREEDMEN CONTROVERSY

Russell Lawson

The Cherokee Freedmen controversy involves the descendants of freed African slaves and the Cherokee nation of Oklahoma. The Cherokee held slaves in what had been Indian Territory until the end of the Civil War, when the Thirteenth Amendment freed all slaves in America. The Dawes Commission enrollment of Indians in the 1890s became the subsequent basis for Cherokee citizenship. Those who did not enroll, that is, those who could not prove Indian blood (including many Cherokee Freedmen), were not included in tribal rolls and granted tribal citizenship. In the twentieth century, Indian citizenship has been determined by the Certificate of Degree of Indian

Blood (CDIB) and blood quantum, which has been used by the Cherokee nation to disenfranchise Freedmen.

The issue of the Cherokee Freedmen has been extremely controversial in recent years. In 1985, Chief Wilma Mankiller issued an executive order requiring a CDIB for citizenship. But in 2004, the case *Allen vs. Cherokee Nation Tribal Council* led the Cherokee Nation Judicial Appeals Tribunal to overturn the former restrictions on Freedman citizenship. In response, Chief Chad Smith led an effort to amend the Cherokee Constitution to deny citizenship to Freedmen, which was successful in 2007. In 2011 and 2012, there have been numerous court cases and responses from the Cherokee nation that have granted and denied citizenship. According to Reuters, "On Aug. 22, 2011, the Cherokee Nation Supreme Court ruled in Nash v. CN Registrar that a March 2007 constitutional amendment that was approved by Cherokee voters and prevented Freedmen descendants without Indian blood from being C[herokee] N[ation] [CN] citizens was valid and that the CN may deny Freedmen citizenship rights." In response, "attorneys for the Freedmen filed an injunction on Sept. 2 in the U.S. District Court to regain Cherokee Freedmen rights, including voting rights. Following yesterday's agreement, the court ordered today [September 21] that the 1,200 Freedmen registered to vote be allowed to vote in the Sept. 24 election 'in the same manner as all other Cherokee citizens, without intimidation or harassment, and to have their votes counted on the same basis as all other Cherokee citizens.'" According to the *Cherokee Phoenix*, "Acting Principal Chief Joe Crittenden, who attended, . . . [the] hearing in Washington, D.C., said he has been concerned about federal funding [being] withheld from the CN, and he hoped the agreement would allow the recently withheld $33 million in Housing and Urban Development funds to be released." The Department of Housing and Urban Development had threatened to withhold the money unless the rights of Freedmen were respected. The controversy is hardly over, however, and will likely continue for some time.

Sources: Chavez, Will. "Freedmen Descendants Have Citizenship Restored and May Vote Sept. 24." CherokeePhoenix.org, September 21, 2011. Retrieved from http://www.cherokeephoenix.org/Article/Index/5516

"Into the Nations: Native Peoples of Arkansas and Oklahoma," Fourth Annual Fort Smith Regional History Conference, Fort Smith, Arkansas, 2012.

Olafson, Steve. "Controversial Chief Loses Re-election Bid." *Reuters*. Available at: http://www.reuters.com/article/2011/10/12/us-cherokees-election-idUSTRE79B0NU20111012

ISSUES

Along with loyalty conflicts, tribal governments, as well as Native Americans in the larger society, face struggles amid poverty to maintain a stable quality of life. These include a variety of health issues, some of which involve nutrition and access to healthcare. Native American communities have high rates of alcoholism. Though numerous tribal governments have prohibited the sale of alcohol on reservations, it is easy for residents to obtain alcohol form nearby border towns. The U.S. Commission on Civil Rights states that "It has long been recognized that Native Americans are dying of diabetes, alcoholism, tuberculosis, suicide, and other health conditions at shocking rates. Beyond disturbingly high mortality rates, Native Americans also suffer a significantly lower health status and disproportionate rates of disease compared with all other Americans." In answer to these problems, an increasing number of American Indians are entering the fields of community health and medicine. Agencies working with Native American communities are seeking to form partnerships, and establish representatives on policy and program boards. Many communities seek to establish ways to learn and respect tribal traditions while integrating within their society the benefits of Western medicine (U.S. Commission on Civil Rights 2004, 2).

On reservations, a significant number of resident families receive welfare support and live at or below the poverty level. They are usually reported at the bottom of national income statistics and have high unemployment. There are an inadequate number of Indian enterprises, and many reservations lack the resource diversity necessary to support more than a small number of residents. One major source of employment is in administrative and supervisory roles within tribal government, with some residents working in administration directly as elected or appointed officials and others working in tribal planning, housing, health services and other related fields. Many tribal governments realize that their reservations are too limited and lacking in resources to support large populations. With that in mind, they recognize a need for greater use of high technology. But this means that tribal survival requires tribal governments to develop a better educated and professional population. This goal is helped by a larger number of Indians completing high school and entering college.

Tribal governments face a lack of capital and business expertise. Because of this lack of expertise, many tribal governments lease out much of their land, including properties with timber and other natural resources. Tribes with large energy resources have formed the Council of Energy Resource Tribes (CERT), which seeks to prudently develop energy resources. Use of tribal lands suffers from a legacy of shifting federal land policies that have often created a checkerboard of conflicting ownership and trustee situations that make resource development difficult. The BIA administers many of the existing leases and has frequently been faulted for collecting incomes that are six to nine times lower than those of the standard market.

While Congress mandated in 1975 greater self-determination to "plan conduct, and administer programs" independent of the BIA, many tribes still depend on federal funds, and few tribes have rapidly embraced self-determination because many fear that acting too boldly might lead to a return of the termination policies of the 1950s. Thus, federal officials still make basic decisions and policy. Duane Champagne states that critics fault this as "a tactical shift in the fundamental commitment of society to bring Indians into the mainstream, not a permanent movement toward true recognition on permanent rights to exist" (Champagne 1994, 222–223).

Critics also state that the federal bureaucracy has increased paperwork and been accused of interfering with growth programs. Even though the 1975 Self-Determination and Education Assistance Act was designed to contract BIA service to tribal government and Indian organizations, the BIA has expanded its operations and budget. Indians' drive for self-determination is contradicted by the "seeds of dependency" (Champagne 1994, 222–223). Many critics contend that tribes can never have political self-determination without economic self-determination. But this is hindered by their need for federal funds

A major issue facing tribal governments is the large number of American Indians who live outside the reservation. After World War II, termination and relocation polices were designed to encourage Indians to leave the reservation and seek jobs in urban areas. By 1990, only 22 percent of the nation's Indian population lived on reservations. Today, three out of four Native Americans live outside a reservation. Urban migration has changed the notion of Indian country, the idea of tribes as rural and isolated. Today in the largest cities like Los Angeles and New York, one will encounter the most urban Indians. In Albuquerque, New Mexico, the growth of the city has turned several pueblos into bedroom communities. Many tribes have attempted to extend sovereignty beyond their reservations, but maintaining tribal bonds is difficult for urban Indians who live amidst a variety of cultures. A third of urban Indians return to reservations, where they find family support and encouragement, and another third move back and forth between the city and the reservation to seek employment and a better way of life. Many fear that urbanization is eroding the distinctiveness of Native American culture. Urbanization has reduced tribal unity. In the 2000 census, 26 percent of the urban Indian population expresses little or no tribal affiliation. Large numbers of urban Indians are marrying non-Indians. It is estimated that by 2080, only 8 percent of the Indian population will be more than one-half Indian by birth.

But the urban Indian is as much an Indian as the reservation Indian. Most of those who have migrated to the city have not severed their tribal ties. Federal trust responsibilities, created to preserve and protect both Native Americans and their resources, make no distinction between reservation and urban Indians. While urbanization has been a "process of struggle, loss and hope, combined with a longing to go and a determination to stay," it has resulted in new social adaptations. Some have gone down the path of assimilation, but many urban Indians have found ways to preserve old ways and live in a bicultural world. Urbanization has been key to a current rebirth of native spirit and Indian activism, resulting in groups like the American Indian Movement (AIM). Many urban political leaders have returned to their tribes to continue their leadership careers (Champagne 1994, 611–619).

In 1988, Congress passed the Indian Gaming Regulatory Act, which recognizes Indian gaming rights. Today, the National Indian Gaming Commission states that there are over 400 Indian gaming operations in 29 states (U.S. Department of the Interior n.d., 7). Advocates state that gaming offers tribes, who were formerly dependent on government programs, a new choice of direction in their economic development. It represents a form of economic clout that brings tribal members together and connects individual interests to larger national issues. Gaming elevates the standing of tribes and helps them mobilize as an effective political force. It also provides a training ground for younger leaders to develop their skills to effectively interact with non-Indians.

But critics state that gaming has numerous negative impacts. First, it contributes to increased drug and alcohol abuse, crime, neglect, abuse of children and spouses, missed workdays, and increased numbers of compulsive gamblers. Second, due to the nature of the business (i.e., primarily cash), there are opportunities for theft, embezzlement, and the introduction of criminal influences. Third, the enormous profit potential of Indian gaming may lead to the weakening of cultural integrity, as the success of gaming has resulted in numerous people with dubious claims alleging tribal membership, which leads to disputes over who is entitled to control the tribe's operations and receive income. Fourth, gaming increases the inequality of wealth between urban and rural tribes, and gaming and nongaming tribes. Fifth, a majority of casino jobs are low-wage, high-turnover positions. The few high-paying professional and technical jobs require college education. Unless the tribe offers job training to members, these jobs tend to go to outsiders. Finally, gaming often draws money away from other businesses.

Many tribes have benefited from the recent development of gaming, but tribal leaders recognize that the gaming boom may be short lived due to market saturation and forces aligned to confront Indian gaming. Because poverty remains deeply rooted in tribal communities, there is a great desire among the gaming tribes to secure capital and diversify their economies as much as possible to prepare for the time when gaming incomes may decrease or cease all together.

CONCLUSION

Going into the early twenty-first century, tribal governments are reacting to Native American communities that exhibit continuing growth and revival while increasing participation in the American economy. Native communities have needed to modify their governments to administer services such as firefighting, natural resource management, social programs, housing, and law enforcement. Today, most American Indian communities have responded to the need to establish court systems to arbitrate concerns involving matters related to local ordinances. Many tribal governments are attempting to rely on various forms of moral and social authority, such as forms of restorative justice, a form of justice that relies on the tribal nation's traditional culture. To address Native American housing needs, Congress passed the Native American Housing and Self-Determination Act (NAHASDA) in 1992. This legislation was designed to replace public housing built by older BIA and Housing Act programs, and it is directed toward tribal run Indian housing authorities that provide housing for those with low incomes. It is designed to give Indian tribal governments more autonomy over the administration of block grant funds for tribes to develop their own housing.

REFERENCES

Champagne, Duane (Ed.). *The Native American Almanac*. Detroit: Gale Research, 1994.

Fixico, Donald. *Daily Life of Native Americans in the Twentieth Century*. Westport, CT: Greenwood Press, 2006.

Johnson, Troy R. *Contemporary Native American Political Issues*. Walnut Creek, CA: AltaMira Press, 1999.

Lopach, James J. Margery Hunter Brown, and Richard L. Clow. *Tribal Government Today: Politics on Montana Indian Reservations* (rev. ed.). Niwot: University Press of Colorado, 1998.

National Congress of American Indians. "Policy Issues." Retrieved from http://www.ncai.org/policy-issues in November 2011.

O'Brien, Sharon. *American Indian Tribal Governments*. Norman: University of Oklahoma Press, 1989.

U.S. Commission on Civil Rights. "Broken Promises: Evaluating the Native American Health Care System," September 2004. Retrieved from http://www.usccr.gov/pubs/nahealth/nabroken.pdf

United States Department of the Interior, Budget Justifications and Performance Information: Fiscal Year 2013, "Executive Study: National Indian Gaming Commission." http://www.doi.gov/budget/appropriations/2013/upload/FY2013_NIGC_Greenbook.pdf

Wilkins, David E. *American Indian Politics and the American Political System*. Lanham, MD: Rowman and Littlefield, 2007.

SECTION 8
AMERICAN INDIAN EXPRESSION

American Indian Art: Maintaining Culture, Tradition, and Identity

Dylan A. T. Miner

American Indian art, as well as Arts of the Americas, are common names given to the material and visual expressions produced by indigenous artists and artisans in the United States. Art is the means by which the deepest emotions and experiences of a people are expressed. Art is an important issue among Indians because it is a means of collective identity, a means of maintaining culture and traditions, a means of asserting what it means to be Indian.

Recent international developments have created an interest in a collective discussion of indigenous art. Because of the vast cultural diversity within Indian country, not to mention the creative practices of native people throughout the world, the history of American Indian art is likewise varied. Contemporarily, American Indian art ranges from the production of pre-European contact quotidian and ceremonial objects to the creation of avant-garde and contemporary art by visual artists who happen to be indigenous. Because of pre- and post-contact migrations (including forced migration and relocation), certain tribes may be culturally part of one geographic region, but live in an entirely different region. One famous migration example is the Trail of Tears, which forced the Five Civilized Tribes (Cherokee, Choctaw, Chickasaw, Creek, and Muscogee) from the Southeast into Indian Territory, which is present-day Oklahoma.

Among these multiple indigenous traditions, art historians and anthropologists commonly categorize aboriginal objects into a classificatory system based on the similarities of style and materiality among objects created in a region. American Indian art is grouped in the following geographic fashion: East, West, North, Southwest, and Northwest Coast. While the U.S.–Canada border is often transgressed to include First Nations art history within the common legacy of North

American Indian art, most discussions of American Indian art do not likewise incorporate Native traditions from Mexico. This anti-Mexican bias is problematic for many reasons, especially since most indigenous peoples have never recognized the colonial imposition of national borders on indigenous territories. Moreover, contemporary indigenous cultures continue to share cultural practices and political institutions across both the U.S.–Canada and U.S.–Mexico borders. The Tohono O'odham reservation, for instance, crosses the U.S.–Mexico border, while Akwesasne extends on both sides of the U.S.–Canada demarcation line. In turn, any substantial discussion of American Indian art must incorporate a discussion of the native arts of Mexico, in addition to the United States and Canada.

As such, the main categories of indigenous art include:

1. North (including the Artic and Subartic)
2. East (including Mississippian, Northeast and Woodlands, Great Lakes, and Southeast)
3. Northwest Coast
4. West (including Plains and California)
5. Southwest (including Ancient Puebloan art, Pueblos, Navajos, Tohono O'odham, and Apache)
6. Mexico (including Central Mexico, Oaxaca, and Maya)

NORTH

The North consists of the areas in Alaska and northern Canada, incorporating both Artic and Subarctic areas where Indian artisans are most known for their intricate crafting of cold-weather clothing, many of which are constructed from waterproof animal intestines. Historically, Arctic peoples were migratory, following the seasonal travels of local game animals. During the 1950s and 1960s, U.S. and Canadian governmental policy formed permanent settlements for tribal peoples as a way to exert political control. Because of the centrality of hunting as the primary mode of acquiring food, shamanistic practices are common within the Arctic and can be seen in the creation of art.

In the mid-nineteenth century, Anglophone missionaries amassed large collections of ivory carving and masks. Moreover, due to capitalist and settler encroachment during the time of fur trade and the gold rush, Indian artisans also began producing objects for the tourist and market trade. Because the region is vast with inclement weather, European contact transpired over many centuries, beginning in the late sixteenth century. In response to the varied colonial development, the usage of Western materials and styles likewise varies. Métis artists in the Subartic, particularly in the Canadian provinces of Manitoba, Saskatchewan, and Alberta, are known for making extraordinary beadwork, drawing heavily on flower patterns learned from Catholic nuns.

Baffin Island, Qikiqtaaluk in the Inuktitut language, has become the the center for the production of contemporary Inuit arts, particularly printmaking in and around Cape Dorset. Much of the artwork is produced and marketed through indigenous artist-run cooperatives. These cooperatives, chiefly producing stonecuts, operate on a more egalitarian basis than do traditional art galleries (which commonly keep 40 percent of the sale price of an artwork). Between 1959 and 1965, over 20 Inuit artist co-operatives were established.

The stonecut is a relief printing technique similar to the woodcut in which artists cut into a locally found stone. It has become synonymous with Inuit visual art. As a technique, stonecutting was first introduced to aboriginal artists in 1957 by James Houston, a Canadian artist and government administrator working in the North, who also established a national and international market for Inuit artwork. Kenojuak Ashevak, the matriarch of modern Inuit art, is featured in a 1963 National Film Board (NFB) of Canada–released documentary.

EAST

Traversing the entire U.S. and Canadian seaboard from Florida to the Maritimes and west into the Great Lakes, the East may be divided into three very different cultural subregions, first, the Northeast or Woodlands (mainly consisting of the Iroquois Confederacy); second, the Southeast (Seminole, Muscogee, Choctaw, Creek, Chickasaw, eastern Cherokee); and third, the Great Lakes (predominantly the Anishinaabeg [Odawa, Ojibwa, and Potawatomi] and Huron).

Historically, the eastern region was populated with ancient mound-building societies. During the Middle Woodland Period (1 to 350 CE), Hopewell people built mounds, while centuries later, during the Mississippian period (800 to 1500 CE), the Mississippi people also constructed mounds. The Hopewell cultures were centered around the Ohio River valley, while the Mississippian sites are farther to the south, usually located in the Mississippi River valley. Major Mississippian sites include Spiro (Oklahoma), Moundville (Alabama), Etowah (Tennessee), and Cahokia (Illinois), which is located just outside St. Louis. Since many Mississippian objects share a stylistic and aesthetic likeness to those produced in Mesoamerica, some scholars have discussed the possibility of complex trade networks throughout the entirety of North America.

After European contact, the Northeast and Great Lakes established a recognized aesthetic integration of beadwork, a commodity-based adaptation of the indigenous tradition of quillwork. Quillwork, which is still practiced throughout North America, is the process in which artists use dyed porcupine quills "woven" into leather or fabric. The Métis, a group of mixed-blood indigenous people with communities throughout the Great Lakes and Subarctic regions, are commonly known as the Flower Beadwork People due to their near exclusive use of floral patterning in their beadwork. Other tribes, such as the Anishinaabeg, also use floral patterning in their beadwork, while many other communities use geometric patterns.

Much like the pre-contact Mississippian cultures, many Southeastern tribes produce a style of art that is aesthetically similar to Mesoamerican visuality, even though they, after contact with Europeans, adopted materials and techniques from both Anglo-American and African American art. An example of this would be the traditional Seminole patchwork clothing, possibly adopted from techniques used by African slaves. In addition to their wonderful patchwork, Southeastern tribal artists are also recognized for their skill in basketry.

NORTHWEST COAST

Long known for large-scale crests (often called totem poles), as well as intricate black and red designs known as the formline, the Northwest Coast, much like the other regions, includes a diversity of objects, styles, and iconography within its material culture. At one time, the region was home to 45 languages belonging to 13 language families. Unlike the agriculturally based lifestyle of Mesoamerica, the pre-contact Northwest Coast was densely populated, yet did not actively engage in subsistence agriculture. Its art and iconography reflects its ways of life based primarily on hunting and fishing.

Bill Holm, in his 1965 book *Northwest Coast Indian Art*, analyzed the development of the formline style and its three main styles of representation, as well as three design principals. Because of the way artists have been able to complexly work with two-dimensional form, the Northwest style has become iconic within mainstream Anglo-America. Most prominent are the use of crests, usually a vertical pole that includes both human and animal beings, symbolic of the moiety or clan relation. Contemporary fashion designer Dorothy Grant uses traditional Northwest coast motifs, iconography, and materials in her line of clothing.

WEST

The West begins in the plains and prairies to the east, extends south into Texas, across the intermountain West, and further west to California's coastal areas. Much like the Arctic and Subarctic, the immense size of this region allowed for different Indian nations to have contact with European settlers throughout in history. In turn, different peoples have vastly distinct relations to Anglo-American and Spanish Mexican society. There has always been intense intertribal trade and cultural sharing in the West—certain elements of Mississippian cosmology can be found amongst the buffalo hunting societies on the northern prairies in present-day Canada.

Plains artists have been historically adept at producing painted leatherwork, but also engaged in the production of both quillwork and beadwork. During the late nineteenth century, many Cheyenne and Kiowa warriors created drawings while imprisoned in Fort Marion, Florida. These books are known as ledger art because they were written in the lined pages of ledger books. Wohaw, an imprisoned Kiowa warrior, created a self-portrait entitled (by subsequent art historians) *Between Two Worlds*. This important image is commonly described as a depiction of an aboriginal male figure caught between two competing ways of life: the traditional migratory ways of the buffalo hunter and the sedentary life of a farmer. This type of imagery marks a transition in the way of life for many Plains Indians.

On the northern prairies along the present-day U.S.–Canada border, the Métis, who had communities in the Great Lakes as well as on the prairies, produced heavily beaded European-style clothing that incorporated European and aboriginal materials. Unlike other tribal peoples, the Métis serve as a unique example of a "hybrid" people, often as represented through clothing and other cultural production. Métis artists produced an impressive array of leatherwork that included mittens and gauntlets, as well as the L'Assomption sash and cariole decorations. The sash serves as the national symbol of the Métis people. Even amongst Plains groups, iconographic and visual distinctions mark tribal groups.

Further West, California tribes are most regarded for their skill in basketry. The Pomo, a group of approximately six dozen villages north of San Francisco, incorporate feathers, shells, and other objects into their coiled and twined designs. The Washoe, living in western Nevada and the Great Basin of California, are also known for their production of baskets. During the late nineteenth century until the 1940s, Washoe women made baskets for the capitalist marketplace. One of the most prominent basketmakers of this period is Louisa Keyser, who created a basket style known as the *degikup*. This style had no precedent in premarket Washoe baskets.

SOUTHWEST

The Southwest includes Colorado, Utah, Arizona, New Mexico, west Texas, and parts of northern Mexico. As a region, the Southwest encompasses a variety of ecological zones and is commonly connected by the commonalities among its Indian peoples of having continuously lived in the region for 3,000 years. The spiritual and cultural focus on corn is also shared with their Mesoamerican counterparts.

The main tribal groups in the Southwest include the Diné (Navajo), Pueblo (Tewa-, Tiwa-, Towa-, and Keres-speaking peoples of the Rio Grande valley), Apache, and Tohono O'odham. This region has the most fully developed American Indian art market, centered in Santa Fe, New Mexico. The region became the economic center for the American Indian art market with the founding of the

Santa Fe Indian Market in 1922. Since its founding, the Indian Market is held annually and attracts hundreds of artists, as well as thousands of collectors, to New Mexico.

There are three primary ancient cultures in the Southwest: the Hohokam (300 to 1400 CE) in what is now in southern Arizona and Chihuahua, Mexico; the Mimbres (a subdivision of the Mogollon; 600 to 1150 CE) in what is presently southwestern New Mexico; and the Anasazi (500 to 1300 CE), where the state borders of Utah, Colorado, New Mexico, and Arizona meet. These three groups were all sedentary agricultural tribes that developed the "three sisters": corn, beans, and squash. Each respective group was also involved in a vast trade network extending to the Pacific Ocean, well into central Mexico, and into the prairies. Certain Mesoamerican spiritual or religious traits were also seen among these Southwestern societies. Some contemporary artists evoke the architectural and ceramic traditions of these influential tribes.

Hohokam developed around 200 CE and shared certain cultural and spiritual traits with Mesoamerican cultures, particularly the presence of a ball court. Its size also rivaled the large and complex societies to the south, with as many as 400,000 living within the Hohokam society. The Anasazi are the ancestors of the contemporary Pueblo peoples, yet have architectural sites on the lands of the Navajo nation. Important Anasazi sites include Canyon de Chelly and Chaco Canyon. The Anasazi ceramic tradition developed polychromatic pottery that primarily used geometric patterns. The Mimbres, one group of the greater Mogollon culture, primarily produced handcoiled pots that integrated geometric forms and abstract animal motifs surrounding a central axis in the middle of the pot.

Of all American Indian art, Southwest pottery has possibly received the most attention from both scholars and collectors. Presently, there is an expansive corpus of research on pre-contact Southwestern American Indian material culture, as well as a post-contact visual art, especially Pueblo ceramics. María Martínez is perhaps the most important American Indian artist. She is from San Ildefonso Pueblo and, along with her husband Julián, Martínez is known for reviving black-on-black pottery, a complex technique that oxidizes the pottery by eliminating oxygen during the firing process. Roxanne Swentzell, another important Pueblo potter, produces clay figures of the *koyemshi*—the Puebloan sacred clown character, popular in Southwest ceremonies. Diego Romero currently creates ceramics that merge comic book–based imagery with traditional ceramic techniques.

The Diné are recognized for producing ephemeral sand paintings, which are usually made by male "chanters" as part of spiritual or medicinal ceremonies that last several nights. Although the ephemeral nature of these paintings is an aspect of the objects' importance, the market economy has established a collector base for sand paintings on canvas. Diné artists are also well known for their weavings, usually categorized based on their colors, patterns, and compositions. "Navajo Chief" blankets also have an immense market base, depending on the quality of the weaving.

MESOAMERICA

Monte Albán, in contemporary Oaxaca, was the first urban site in Mesoamerica and was established in approximately 500 BCE. A millennium later, by 500 CE, the city of Teotihuacan (present-day Mexico City) had an established and hierarchical population of 200,000. The size and scope of Mesoamerican societies, like those of the pre-Contact Southwest, were enabled by the development of corn and aboriginal agricultural practices. Mesoamerican architecture is characterized by its expansive scale and use of pyramidal structures, as seen in the pyramids of the sun and the moon at Teotihuacan. It is also characterized by the inclusion of ball courts (also seen in the Southwest), which were used for ceremonial purposes.

Moreover, cities were commonly constructed using a North–South axis, while architects would frequently insert chambers within the hearts of buildings. Since Mesoamerican society was metonymic, even the structure of the buildings represented the general structure of society. Most Mesoamerican societies incorporated the concepts of duality, with all energies and ideas having polar opposites. This dualistic tension, an idea that parallels Hegelian dialectics, was reinforced within Mesoamerican cosmology through the real daily need to feed the sun and moon to ensure continued rebirth.

Within the material culture of Mesoamerican societies, turquoise, obsidian, jade, and other semiprecious stones were used for personal adornment and regularly incorporated into small- and large-scale sculpture. Moreover, the Nahua tribe developed artworks by using colored feathers to create tactile paintings. Mixtec, Maya, and Nahua societies all produced painted manuscripts, called *amoxtli* in Nahuatl, on either *amate* paper (an indigenous paper used in rituals) or deerskin. Following the arrival of the Spanish, these books were still created, although they were more frequently painted on large cloths held within communities as historic documentation. These cloths, known as *lienzos*, were commonly used within colonial Spanish courts to prove the land rights of tribal communities.

Today, indigenous artisans are known for continuing to produce textiles (such as *huipiles* or blouses) and ceramics. As for their U.S. and Canadian contemporaries, the tourist trade serves to fund the development and expansion of some American Indian material culture. For instance, the Mexican state of Oaxaca has produced a large number of indigenous artists who work in contemporary styles, with Francisco Toledo being the most accomplished. The establishment of an indigenous arts infrastructure, commonly based on women's cooperatives, has proven successful for many American Indian artists and communities.

HISTORY, THEORY, AND METHODS OF AMERICAN INDIAN ART HISTORY

In North America, the academic study of American Indian art can be traced to nineteenth-century Anglo-American anthropology, although earlier studies were conducted in Mexico. During the nineteenth century, anthropologists, as well as governmental officials and non–American Indian artists, collected objects for posterity, believing American Indian people and their respective ways of life were on the verge of extinction. During this period, museums such as the Smithsonian Institution and Harvard's Peabody Museum were created throughout the United States and Canada. In an attempt to save the cultural heritage of the "vanishing Indigene," anthropologically based natural history museums amassed large collections of "Primitive art" that they housed under the category Arts of Africa, Oceania, and the Americas. Presently, many museums continue to categorize non-Western artworks into a single curatorial unit, ignoring the immense distinctions between indigenous and postcolonial art practices around the world.

Using what Marcia Crosby calls the salvage paradigm, or what Renato Rosaldo names imperialist nostalgia, Anglo-American intellectuals attempted to "save" the

Dr. JoAllyn Archambault, of the Sioux tribe, and director of the American Indian program at the Smithsonian Institution's Department of Anthropology, holds up an Ojibwa model *tikanagan*, or cradle, and a Sioux buckskin shirt, June 16, 2004. The British Museum in London had just announced the acquisition of the unique Native American collection. (AP Photo/Richard Lewis)

history of the dying Indian in a Eurocentric progression that had horrendous implications on American Indian peoples and their ways of life, but it also greatly impacted the method by which American Indian objects have become canonized and studied. This was all transpiring during the late nineteenth century and early twentieth century, a period of immense social and cultural change for both indigenous and non–American Indian peoples alike. Subsequently, the artworks of this period have become the measuring stick for what is considered traditional, ignoring the temporal specificity of "traditional" American Indian art.

Figures such as Franz Boas, Franklin Hamilton Cushing, and Stewart Cullin were fundamental in establishing an academic field of study that laid the foundation for how contemporary scholars (both native and non-native) interpret and understand American Indian art. During this period, merchants and traders also played a central role in the collection and promotion of indigenous art within a non–American Indian consumer marketplace, establishing American Indian art as a capitalist market commodity. Recent indigenous-centric publications challenge the anthropological stranglehold established by non–American Indian thinkers. Cherokee art historian Aaron Fry believes that to properly understand American Indian art, we must incorporate tribal knowledge and history. Likewise, Choctaw/Chickasaw art historian Heather Ahtone argues that the use-value and tribal importance of an object need to be better integrated into how American Indian art history is written. From these tribal points of view, traditional historic and anthropological perspectives of indigenous art do not allow for a culturally relevant reading and must be expanded. Since even American Indian art historians come only from their own cultural milieu, a fully developed analysis of American Indian art becomes difficult. Organizations such as the Native American Arts Studies Association, Aboriginal Curatorial Collective, and Native American and Indigenous Studies Association, not to mention tribal and mainstream institutions (such as the National Museum of the American Indian), are attempting to redirect how American Indian art is understood.

MODERN AND CONTEMPORARY ART

Modern and contemporary indigenous artistic practices emerged out of the tourist trade, beginning in the nineteenth century and expanding through the early twentieth century. The establishment of the Institute for American Indian Arts in 1962 has helped train generations of indigenous artists working in both traditional and contemporary modes of production. As American Indian people became embedded in the capitalist economy, so too did their artistic practices grow increasingly connected to market economies. Moreover, because of forced assimilation, through mandated practices such as residential schools, younger American Indian artists began to be trained in Western institutions and styles. This training allowed many younger artists to integrate their tribal aesthetics into modernist (and postmodernist) artistic styles.

One of the most exciting aspects of American Indian artistic production is the diversity and scope of modern and contemporary artists. For instance, some artists continue to work in tribal modes, styles, and media, primarily evoking tribal iconography and cosmology within their work. Inversely, other American Indian artists work exclusively using Western media and iconography. Somewhere in the middle exists a range of American Indian artists who combine elements from indigenous, Western, and contemporary experiences into a complex system usually known as contemporary American Indian art. This segment of the artistic world is growing, characterized by the Institute of American Indian Arts (IAIA) recently changing the name of its Santa Fe museum to the Museum of Contemporary Native Art. Born in the atrocities of the colonial experience, these postmodernist artistic approaches challenge both traditionalist and assimilationalist narratives.

Many American Indian artists in New Mexico and Oklahoma were trained in important academic institutions that arose during the 1920s and 1930s. At the Santa Fe Indian School, Anglo-American teacher Dorothy Dunn established a formal training program in 1932. Important Indian artists such as Allen Houser (Haozous), Harrison Begay, Pablita Velarde, Eva Mirabel, and Oscar Howe (Mazuha Hokshina) were trained in Santa Fe under Dunn. Dunn's training taught a particular auto-ethnographic style in which paintings were illustrated in a pictorially flat fashion. Similarly, at the University of Oklahoma, a parallel flat and decorative modernist style emerged under Swedish professor Oscar B. Jacobson. Under his tutelage, a small group of Plains artists, including Spencer Asah, James Auchiah, Jack Hokeah, Stephen Mopope, and Monroe Tsakoke, became known as the Kiowa Five. Fellow artist Lois Smokey never reached the same level of fame, possibly due to gender discrimination during the period.

When modern American Indian art history began is the subject of a complex and nuanced debate. For instance, art historian W. Jackson Rushing places the origins of modern American Indian art in the early twentieth century when Api Begay (Diné) produced works on paper for non–American Indian audiences. Berlo and Phillips place the origins earlier and farther to the east with the early-nineteenth-century watercolor paintings of Tuscarora artist Dennis Cusick. Other art historians recognize art being produced in the Southwest at an even earlier date as operating within the framework of "modern" art. In Mexico, one could find additional origin dates by investigating the art made by mixed-blood or American Indian artists. Regardless of when and where one chooses to place the origins of contemporary American Indian art, it is paramount to acknowledge that American Indian artists have always engaged with contemporary trends and experiences, and must not be relegated to a "prehistoric" and outdated past.

The founding of IAIA in Santa Fe, New Mexico, serves as another watershed and quickly became the training ground for new generations of American Indian artists. Its initial faculty included Oscar Howe (Yanktonai Dakota) and Luiseño painter Fritz Scholder. Scholder's work, as with that of his former student T. C. Cannon, has become canonical in its use of gestural markings and evocation of Western art styles, as well as his integration of popular culture.

In 1990, the Department of the Interior (DOI) began prosecuting non-Indian artisans and stores for falsely selling non–American Indian artworks as "authentic" Indian art. While well intentioned, the Indian Arts and Crafts Act of 1990 has had unintended consequences on nonenrolled American Indian artists who are commonly unable to exhibit or sell their work within "Indian" markets or events. For instance, Cherokee artist Jimmie Durham has seen the brunt of this legislation, living and working in Europe so to avoid prosecution.

In Canada, there is an important network of indigenous curators, many of whom are artists and art historians themselves, known as the Aboriginal Curatorial Collective. In 2009, IAIA began the Vision Project, which intends to better document the history of contemporary American Indian art by having indigenous art historians and critics write its history.

REFERENCES

Ahtone, Heather. "Designed to Last: Striving toward an Indigenous American Aesthetic." *The Journal of the Arts in Society* 4, no. 2 (2009): 373–385.

Anthes, Bill. *Native Moderns: American Indian Painting, 1940–1960*. Durham, NC: Duke University, 2006.

Berlo, Janet C. (Ed.) *The Early Years of Native American Art History: The Politics of Scholarship and Collecting*. Seattle: University of Washington, 1992.

Berlo, Janet C. and Ruth B. Phillips. *Native North American Art*. New York: Oxford University Press, 1998.

Brody, J. J. *Indian Painters and White Patrons*. Albuquerque: University of New Mexico Press, 1971.

Fields, Virginia and Victor Zamudio-Taylor (Eds.). *Road to Aztlán: Art from a Mythic Homeland*. Albuquerque: University of New Mexico Press, 2001.

Fry, Aaron. "Local Knowledge and Art Historical Methodology: A New Perspective on Awa Tsireh and the San Ildefonso Easel Painting Movement." *Hemisphere: Visual Cultures of the Americas* 1 (Spring 2008): 46–61.

Krinsky, Carol Herselle. *Contemporary Native American Architecture: Cultural Regeneration and Creativity*. New York: Oxford University Press, 1996.

American Indian Theater and Performance: Political, Cultural, and Artistic Empowerment

Courtney Elkin Mohler

Despite centuries of political obstacles, restrictive policies, and U.S. cultural imperialism, a robust and vibrant American Indian theater exists today. There are multiple definitions of what comprises American Indian theater, drama, and performance, stemming from multiple historical, political, and traditional perspectives; contemporary dramatists and performers grapple with these ranging definitions and perspectives through their plays and productions. Some of the current cultural, political, and artistic issues associated with American Indian theater include topics such as representation, authenticity, cultural empowerment, and practical production concerns.

DEFINING THE GENRE

Multiple issues surround the genre of American Indian theater and its history; the boundaries and limits of the form are unstable and often contested by Indian and non-Indian theater specialists alike. Some theater historians include as Indian theater plays by non-Indian writers that represent Indians, while others define the genre as plays written by American Indian playwrights, performed by American Indian actors, for American Indian audiences. There are similar debates over periodization. Some scholars feel that traditional performance practices that were indispensable to American Indian cultural life and predate European contact should be included in, or even, define the genre, while others focus on plays derived through hybrid cultural experience, placing American Indian theater within the twentieth and twenty-first centuries. Such debates link to larger cultural, political, and artistic concerns over identity, ethnicity, representation, and cultural sovereignty. American Indian dramatists and performers often negotiate these debates and concerns through their art.

SURVIVAL OF TRADITIONS

There was a great deal of cultural diversity in preconquest America; most of these societies had distinct religious beliefs and practices, moiety systems, political structures, and art and performance influenced by centuries of oral cultural transmission, intersocietal negotiations, and relationships with the specific climate, geography, and flora and fauna of their traditional homelands. Performance was integrated into many aspects of native cultural life well before Europeans invaded the Americas. American Indians performed ceremonies for well-being and protection, and to celebrate, revere, and mourn life cycles. These ceremonies included storytelling, song, dance, costumes, and sometimes even lighting techniques, all used to create emotional and spiritual impact. Despite the great cultural diversity in preconquest America, all American Indian societies transmitted knowledge, history, and culture orally. Storytelling, song, dance, and drumming remain significant aspects of traditional native life.

Resilient American Indian tribes withstood repressive U.S. government policies in the 1800s and 1900s designed to educate Indian children according to European American standards. Children were forced to leave their families to attend boarding schools where students were forbidden to speak tribal languages or practice traditional religious ceremonies, dancing, music, and storytelling. Sacred and secular performance within and across tribal communities continued, however, especially after American Indians were officially allowed religious freedom and cultural expression in 1934. Today, many American Indian playwrights and performers draw upon traditional tribal performance practices, stories, and characters to inform their dramatic work. An example of the survival of traditions, ceremonial practices, and performing arts include the Navajo Chantways. These performance-based ceremonies involve the extended family and friends of a sick, injured, or imbalanced person gathering together for days to witness a trained singer/shaman sing ceremonial songs and recite creation stories and dialogue in order to restore balance to the ailing. Another example of a traditional native performance that survived are the Ojibwa bear ceremonials, the Zuni rain dance, and the various Plains medicine bundle rituals.

THE TRICKSTER CHARACTER IN AMERICAN INDIAN DRAMA

The most ubiquitous character in native orature, literature, and drama is the Trickster, a shape-shifter who can switch genders and change between human and animal form within the course of the story. The Trickster often appears as

Raven in stories from Arctic and Northwest societies, and as Coyote in stories from the West. In his or her many manifestations, the Trickster is a mischievous jokester, and is often depicted as prone to human temptations, greed, laziness, and lust. Traditionally, Trickster stories function to show the pitfalls of human behavior, providing valuable lessons for individuals and groups to live in balance with each other and the natural world. Contemporary native playwrights such as Tompson Highway, Hanay Geiogamah, Marie Clements, and many others have used Tricksters as comic, witty troublemakers who dramaturgically push the action forward. They provide insight and humor to stir up relationships or solve problems presented in the plays.

NATIVE WORLDVIEW IN LITERATURE AND DRAMA

In addition to traditional characters and stories, contemporary American Indian theater and performance is also greatly influenced by traditional ways of seeing and understanding the world that are dissimilar to the Western worldview. American Indian drama, for example, brings the performers, participants, and audience to a place of balance and a feeling of unity with each other and the universe. This goal is often achieved through the theatrical use of cyclical time and infinite space; many American Indian plays weave stories, layering traditional myths with historical events, biographies, performers' autobiographies, and fictional elements to dramatize the links between the past, present, and future. The stage can also represent multiple spaces within the course of one play and sometimes will illustrate movement between the metaphysical world and earthly locations. Critics who are unfamiliar with the native worldview and corresponding aesthetics often misunderstand American Indian performances that dramatize dynamic notions of time, space, and characterization.

A LEGACY OF REPRESENTING "INDIAN"

From the beginning of their contact with American Indians, Euro-Americans conceived of contradictory notions about America's indigenous peoples. Early American literature and theater grappled with dichotomous representations of Indians as either savage, ruthless heathens or as childlike, innocent "natural men" in need of European and Euro-American leadership. Seeking to create a distinct national identity, Euro-American novelists, playwrights, and artists conceived of romanticized stories and images of American Indians. Although arguably sympathetic to the American Indian plight, authors such as Lewis Henry Morgan, James Fenimore Cooper, and Washington Irving contributed to the national legacy of imagining Indians as a doomed and vanishing race. Some critics have argued that works such as Cooper's *The Last of the Mohicans* influenced the American cultural imagination in two interconnected ways: first, they promoted the idea that all American Indians were dying off due to the genetic, political, and military superiority of white America, justifying Manifest Destiny and Indian removal policies. Second, such rhetoric established a unique American myth of origins that began with uncivilized, pagan disorder and ended with Euro-American modernity and civilization.

Images of Indians in the nineteenth century vacillated between pitiable and frightening but nearly always depicted the American Indian as a "historical relic," stuck in an imagined precolonial time. Characterizations of noble and ruthless savages as well as submissive Indian princesses filled the American stage between 1829 and the turn of the twentieth century. These Indian plays ranged from farces to melodramas and usually featured a sachem or chief fighting the loss of his homeland at the face of evil European colonists. *Metamora; or the Last of the Wampanoags*, written by Euro-American playwright John Augustus Stone and first produced in 1829, offers an infamous example of the Noble Savage character and the nineteenth-century American cultural fascination with romanticized depictions of American Indians as fallen victims of history. This play was commissioned by American actor Edwin Forrest as a star vehicle for himself and was produced with great regularly from 1829 until 1872, when Forrest died. In the role of the booming, majestic, half-naked Wampanoag sachem, Forrest helped circulate the image of the Noble Savage and added to the popular belief that Indians were inevitable victims. Forrest's red-faced portrayal of Metamora as the last of a dying people had lasting consequences on the American psyche. In 1976, the Wampanoags of Mashpee filed a suit to reclaim lands taken over by the town in 1869. They lost the case on grounds that the Wampanoag tribe had been exterminated in King Philip's War 300 years before. Even though anthropologists and ethnohistorians testified to the contrary, the Mashpee Wampanoags were told by the courts that they did not exist. Many American Indian artists today directly address issues of presence, asserting present-day identities and community concerns in their works.

Following the onslaught of Indian plays, all of which were written by non-Indians, came the next major genre of Indian representation: Wild West Shows. The most famous and longest running of these spectacles, "Buffalo Bill's Wild West Show," ran from 1883 to 1913. These shows romanticized the wild nature of the newly acquired Western frontier and played mainly to the expectations, fears, and excitement of their audiences in the American East. "Buffalo Bill's Wild West Show" employed massive casts of hundreds of performers, including cowboys, Mexicans, American Indians, Texas long-horns, and buffalo. Usually they featured an elaborate equestrian parade, staged gunfights, a buffalo hunt, and other rodeo-type events. Significantly, these shows also featured historical reenactments of Indian-white conflicts, which characterized American Indians as ruthless, bloodthirsty savages. Such performances popularized the Noble Savage/Ruthless

Savage binary in white imagination. Unfortunately, representations of the vanishing (or vanished) Indian have continued in American films and television shows of the twentieth and twenty-first centuries.

From the 1960s on, American Indian activists, artists, and scholars have admonished representations of the Noble Savage, the Ruthless Savage and the Indian Princess because these stereotypes help enforce the notion that American Indians are victims of past colonial atrocities and are no longer part of the present day American population. Additionally, many feel that the continual reproduction of the historical Indian, regardless of the representation, is sympathetic to the colonized or the colonizers, and obscures the real cultural, political, and economic issues of contemporary native peoples. Professional native theater artists work to correct such misrepresentation and ingrained stereotypes by telling stories from the American Indian point of view, often drawing on oral history and personal narratives in their work. Plays often weave aspects of native ceremony, storytelling, and performance traditions with current community concerns to illustrate the interconnectedness of past, present, and future American Indian issues.

AMERICAN INDIAN THEATER FROM THE 1930s TO THE PRESENT

Lynn Riggs, a biracial enrolled member of the Cherokee nation, was the first American Indian playwright of note. Riggs wrote several notable Broadway dramas, including 1931's *Green Grows the Lilacs*, upon which musical theater moguls Rodgers and Hammerstein based their musical *Oklahoma!* Although its 1932 premiere production was not met with critical success, Riggs's *Cherokee Night* is now considered to be the first and one of the most influential examples of modern American Indian theater and dramaturgy. *Cherokee Night* explores issues concerning the Cherokee people such as the extreme racism inflicted upon full and mixed-blood Cherokee in Oklahoma, the displacement of American Indians from their ancestral lands, the desperation and economic hardship felt during the transformation of Indian Territory to Oklahoma's statehood, the eradication of native traditions and languages, and infighting and prejudice experienced among Cherokee with varying degrees of Indian ancestry. Although Riggs's work predated the American Indian Movement (AIM, or the Red Power movement) by several decades, many of its themes foreshadowed the concerns American Indian playwrights would later explore in the 1960s.

American Indian performance practices endured and transformed between the eighteenth and twentieth centuries even as tribal communities suffered tremendous losses in population, removal, and Americanization policies. It was not until the Red Power movement of the 1960s, however, that many of these performance traditions, transformations, and innovations gained national attention and established a place within the political and ethnic American theater scene. Pan-tribal theater collectives formed, espousing radical political activism, renewed cultural awareness, and community empowerment for native peoples. The plays developed during the Red Power movement had political goals distinct from those of other ethnic groups at this time, most of which fought for civil rights and increased social equality; many American Indian artists and activists during the 1960s and 1970s advocated instead for increased independence, treaty rights, and political and cultural sovereignty.

In 1962, the Institute of American Indian Arts (IAIA) was founded in Sante Fe, New Mexico. The school developed several native arts training programs, including an influential professional theater program. Under the direction of Dr. Rolland Meinholz, the theater program brought together many talented professional theater teaching artists, drawing on multiple American Indian performance traditions to train formally young native performers. In 1969, the director of the IAIA, Cherokee Lloyd Kiva New, wrote the "Credo for American Indian Theater," which stated that a new era of American Indian theater "can be evolved out of the framework of Indian traditions" and "will come only as the result of an educational process in which Indian artists are created who can then make their own statements" (New 1990, 3). Several key native theater artists were trained at IAIA, including playwrights Bruce King and Terry Gomez.

By the 1970s, AIM had gained considerable momentum, partially through their creative public protests, which demanded national attention. Two significant protests, notable for their performative nature, were the AIM occupation of Alcatraz Island in 1969 and the AIM siege at Wounded Knee in 1973. In both cases, AIM protesters mobilized to publicly trespass and occupy U.S. property that held symbolic significance. During this radical time of American Indian political protest and cultural rebirth, Kiowa director and playwright Hanay Gieogamah founded the American Indian Theater Ensemble (AITE), which would later change its name to the Native American Theater Ensemble (NATE). Co-sponsored by Ellen Stewart of La MaMa Experimental Theater Club, AITE was established during the New York City avant-garde theater scene in 1972. AITE/NATE developed and toured important political shows such as Geiogamah's *Body Indian* (1972), *Foghorn* (1973), and *49* (1975). Additionally, NATE served as a theatrical incubator, launching the careers of several notable native actors and playwrights such as Aleut actor Jane Lind, and Navajo playwright and actor Geraldine Keams.

Other theater groups that formed during the 1970s were also influential in the development of contemporary American Indian performance. Two of these groups, Thunderbird Theater and Spiderwoman Theater, continue to create and perform theatrical work today. Thunderbird Theater was founded in Kansas at the Haskell Indian Nations University in 1974, under the artistic direction of Pat Melody. According to the university's website, Thunderbird Theater was founded as a non-profit student organization with the mission "to provide Native American theater to both Native and non-Native audiences; to explore and expand the direction and form of Native American theater and; to initiate the training of Native American theater professionals." Over the past three decades many prominent theater professionals have worked in Thunderbird Theater as either teaching artists or students. Perhaps the best known of these artists is Bruce King, a member of the Turtle clan of the Haudenosaunee-Oneida nation. King has worked extensively at Thunderbird Theater, IAIA, Indian Time Theater, and the Echo-Hawk Theater Ensemble as a playwright, director, and artistic director. The American Indian Studies Center at the University of California–Los Angeles, has included King's works in two of their major anthologies, and it published a collection of King's plays in 2007. In addition to Bruce King, students in Haskell's theater company have also had the opportunity to learn from playwrights Marcie Rendon, Dianne Yeahquo Reynor, and playwright and director Julie Pierson-Little Thunder. Reynor and several other alumnae of Thunderbird Theater went on to open the American Indian Repertory theater in 2006 in Lawrence, Kansas.

Founded in 1976 by sisters Muriel Miguel, Gloria Miguel, and Lisa Mayo (Kuna/Rappahannock), Spiderwoman Theater is now noted as the oldest continually running feminist theater group in North America. Spiderwoman originally focused on radical, multicultural feminist politics and included a diverse group of women ranging in ages, sexual orientation, and races; but by 1979, the three sisters split with the other women in the company to concentrate more expressly on issues pertaining to the Native American and native women's communities. Spiderwoman Theater is known for creating theatrical pastiche, as the three core members weave elements of their autobiography, traditional stories, contemporary events, community issues, satire, politics, humor, song, and dance to create multivocal, original plays. Often considered their signature piece, *Sun, Moon and Feather* (1981) exemplifies Spiderwoman's collaborative, patchwork approach to their work. This style, known as storyweaving, has had a tremendous impact on Native American theater at large.

In 1999, Randy Reinholz and Jean Bruce-Scott established Native Voices at the Autry Museum of the Southwest as an organization "devoted to developing and producing new works for the stage by Native American playwrights" (Autry Website). Reinholz and Scott began their efforts to cultivate new Native American plays in 1993 at Illinois State University, where they were teaching at the time. After an official call for new Native American plays in the development stage, they organized a series of workshops called *Native Voices: A Festival of Native Plays*. Among the first playwrights selected to workshop their scripts were Drew Haden Taylor, William S. Yellowrobe Bruce King, Joseph A. Dandurnd, and Marie Clements, who have all gone on to contribute significant work to the field of Native American drama. In later years, Native Voices at the Autry has helped develop and produce works by Joy Harjo, Diane Glancy, Darrell Dennis, Larissa Fasthorse, Terry Gomez, Aragon Star, and James Lujan.

While its programming has increased steadily throughout the past two decades, Native Voices continues to host a workshop and festival each year. The company usually workshops three new works that have not been professionally produced or published. The company connects the playwright with a professional dramaturge and director to provide feedback during the rewriting process, and, in a week-long retreat, produces staged readings of the works in progress, read by professional actors. The company usually selects one play from the Annual Playwrights Retreat & Festival of Plays to produce fully at the Autry under Equity contract. In 2013, Native Voices at the Autry is an important resource for Native American playwrights, actors, and directors, and produces significant new native works.

The field of American Indian theater continues to grow and transform with increased interest from natives and non-natives alike. Unfortunately, contemporary artists and producers are faced with several practical challenges. Casting American Indian professional productions often proves to be difficult because of the relative lack of trained Indian actors. The challenge of casting is compounded because many American Indian playwrights feel strongly that their plays be performed by American Indian actors, sometimes specifying the characters' tribal affiliations within the character breakdowns. Funding and marketing can present additional challenges to the American Indian theater community, as its audience is a distinct niche. Yet the numbers of native plays written and produced are increasing despite these material challenges. Additionally, the field has recently garnered increased academic interest, evidenced by several anthologies of American Indian plays and collections of critical articles on the genre. Ongoing conversations and debates about theatrical aesthetics, representation, funding, and intertribal and multicultural theatrical endeavors promise that that the field of American Indian theater will continue to expand in the twenty-first century.

REFERENCES

Allen, Paula Gunn. *The Sacred Hoop: Recovering the Feminine in American Indian Traditions*. Boston: Beacon, 1986.

Autry National Center of the American West. "Theatre, Native Voices at the Autry: Mission Statement." Retrieved from http://theautry.org/whats-here/theater-native-voices on June 10, 2010.

Bird, S. Elizabeth. *Dressing in Feathers: The Construction of the Indian in American Popular Culture*. Boulder, CO: Westview Press, 1996.

Darby, Jaye T. "Broadway (Un) Bound: Lynn Riggs' *The Cherokee Night*." *Baylor Journal of Theatre and Performance* 4, no. 1 Special ed. *Nations Speaking: Indigenous Performances across the Americas* (2007): 7–23.

Deloria, Philip J. *Playing Indian*. New Haven, CT: Yale University Press, 1998.

Geiogamah, Hanay, and Darby, Jaye T. *American Indian Theatre in Performance: A Reader.* Los Angeles: UCLA American Indian Studies Center, 2000.

Grose, B. Donald. "Edwin Forrest, 'Metamora,' and the Indian Removal Act of 1830," *Theatre Journal* 37, no. 2 (May 1985): 181–191.

Haskell Indian Nations University. "Thuderbird Theatre." Retrieved from http://www.haskell.edu/theatre/index.html on September 5, 2012.

King, Bruce. *An Evening at the Warbonnet and Other Plays.* Los Angeles: UCLA American Indian Studies Center, 2007.

New, Lloyd Kiva. "Credo for American Indian Theatre." In Hanay Geiogamah et al. (Eds.), *American Indian Theatre in Performance: A Reader.* Los Angeles: UCLA American Indian Studies Center, 1990.

Spiderwoman Theater. "Spiderwoman Theater: About Us." Retrieved from http://www.spiderwomantheater.org/SpiderwomanAboutUs.htm on June 10, 2010.

Stanlake, Christy. *Native American Drama: A Critical Perspective.* New York: Cambridge University Press, 2009.

Film Media about Indians: Representations and Misrepresentations

Renae Watchman

The misrepresentation and distortion of American Indians in the United States and of First Nations in Canada by filmmakers has a long and well-documented history, with its roots in late nineteenth and early twentieth century media. Inaccuracies and negative stereotypes abound in film and other visual representations of Indians, and North American indigenous actors, directors, writers, and scholars have taken an active role to reclaim and reframe these distortions. Misrepresentations of Indian-ness in film has informed contemporary film scholarship, which serves as the springboard to this essay.

Reservation Reelism (2010) is Michelle H. Raheja's "attempt to see an alternate vision of Native American representation and spectatorship as products of a complicated and sometimes discomfiting history with a vibrant, equally complex future rather than only as abject repositories of the victimized" (xi). Raheja offers a critical scholarly contribution to the study of film media and not only highlights Indigenous actors and directors since the inception of film, but also offers a tripartite theoretical model for film studies and American Indian studies. Raheja acknowledges that both Native and non-Native actors have engaged in "redfacing," which misrepresents and distorts the subjects being depicted. The second part to her theoretical model looks at the site of the "virtual reservation . . . [which] is a more creative, kinetic, open space where Indigenous artists collectively and individually employ technologies and knowledges to rethink the relationship between media and Indigenous communities" (150). Finally, Raheja tackles the concept of "visual sovereignty" by encouraging indigenous self-identification and representation as well as working toward cultural sensitivity vis-à-vis indigenous cinematic hermeneutics.

Film media, since the era of silent films, has depicted "Indians" at odds with mainstream society, without regard to the diversity that makes up disparate Native Nations in the United States and Canada. Indians were deemed either a threat to progress or a dying, vanishing race. Since European contact and the establishment of the United States and Canada, both governments legislated and instituted numerous policies designed to rid the Western hemisphere of Indians.

Thomas Edison captured a kinetescopic record of dance and culture from 1894 to 1898 as part of saving the ostensible vanishing Indian (Raheja 2010, 35). Edison's 1898 production of several shorts (Kilpatrick 1999, 17), including *Sioux Ghost Dance* and *Buffalo Dance*, are the earliest moving pictures and can be viewed at YouTube.com. The plots of a great majority of silent films of the early twentieth century embraced the pre-reservation Indian (buckskin, feathers, and the ubiquitous Plains warrior and maiden). Silent era films featured Native and non-Native actors, and the Library of Congress offers an extensive collection of Edison kinetoscope motion pictures as well as a comprehensive listing of American Indians in silent film by Karen C. Lund.

Two of the silent era's successful Indigenous directors, actors, screenwriters, and filmmakers were Edwin Carewe (born Jay Fox, Chickasaw, 1883–1940) and J. Younger Johnston, stage name James Gordon Young Deer (Ho-Chunk. d. 1946). Both Carewe and Young Deer made over 200 films during the silent film era. The content of their individual works was diverse, and their careers as American Indians in the Hollywood film scene have recently received critical attention.

Hollywood Westerns flourished after the silent film era. Sound opened up a new world for filmmakers. Talkies, as they are dubbed, rampantly depicted negative and hateful images of Indians in films, yet such films, like those directed by Cecil B. DeMille and John Ford, also brought Native places and faces to the silver screen. Hollywood actors as well as famed Indian fighters and haters like Marion Morrison, better known as John Wayne, made famous stereotypes and issues like racism, miscegenation, savagery, and misogyny. Angela Aleiss and Michelle Raheja critically discuss Hollywood Westerns and the history of misrepresentation of Indians in film media in their respective works *Making the White Man's Indian* (2005) and *Reservation Reelism*.

A handful of black and white films appeared at mid-century. One of them, *The Exiles* (1961) by non-Native filmmaker Kent MacKenzie, is a snapshot of a night in Los Angeles (a prominent relocation city) and of urban Indians who struggle to make this city home. Unlike the majority of mid-century films, *The Exiles* does not force its Native actors to play pre-reservation, stereotyped Indians in buckskin and feathers; however, stereotypes abound in the form of alcoholism, dysfunction, and the urban plight.

Despite Indians' growing agitation about the Hollywood Indian, Hollywood continued throughout the twentieth century to release films that caricatured Indians.

Hundreds of blockbuster films were produced and released from a non-indigenous lens until *Smoke Signals* (1998), which was directed by Chris Eyre (Cheyenne and Arapaho). The screenplay was written by award-winning author Sherman Alexie (Spokane/Coeur d'Alene), and the movie features several prominent American Indian and First Nations actors. In 2001, the movie *Atanarjuat: The Fast Runner*, directed by Zacharias Kunuk (Inuit), was released as a feature-length film in the Inuktitut language. *Atanarjuat* is an award-winning indigenous film that successfully depicts Inuit life through Inuit eyes. The success of this film and its overwhelmingly positive reception prompted the filmmakers to continue their storytelling and teachings via film media by bringing the "virtual reservation" to a worldwide audience.

Movie director Chris Eyre poses in Santa Fe, New Mexico, August 17, 2002. "It's the 'Rolling Rez' Tour. We're taking 'Skins' on the road coast to coast for free screenings for Indians across the country," said Eyre, who directed both *Skins* and *Skinwalkers* and also made *Smoke Signals*. Many Indian reservations have no movie theaters, and without the rolling tour, many Indians might never see *Skins* in a theater. (AP Photo/Jeff Geissler)

KEY FIGURES

Redfacing is a term that Raheja used to describe how actors of any era and ethnicity donned Plains garb and often painted their faces to play Indian. *Reel Injun: On The Trail of the Hollywood Indian* (2009), by award-winning filmmaker Neil Diamond (Cree), highlights several A-list, Hollywood actors who painted up in redface. Notable actor and director Clint Eastwood, said. "I remember once we were on a set, the director said 'I want a real native, upfront. I want to see the real thing.' We couldn't find one!" Until the late 1970s, redfacing was commonly practiced in the film industry, primarily by non-Natives, but also by some Natives. Hollywood film media and visual representations required all actors to fit one mold of what constituted an Indian based on negative and highly inaccurate stereotypes: the war-whooping brave, the wise shaman, the noble sidekick, the fair-skinned "half-breed," the alcoholic, the downtrodden maiden, the voluptuous savior-princess, and anyone from a pre-reservation Plains tribe. Many American Indians actors did not come from pre-reservation Native Nations, yet they were required to play such roles; they were required to participate in redfacing. Some noteworthy actors include Luther Standing Bear (Lakota, 1868–1939); Minnie Devereaux, stage name Minnie Ha Ha (Cheyenne, 1891–1984); Ray Mala (Inupiaq, 1906–1952); Mary Alice Nelson, stage name Molly Spotted Elk (Penobscot, 1903–1977); Harold J. Smith, stage name Jay Silverheels (Mohawk, 1912–1980); Lillian St. Cyr, stage name Princess Red Wing (Ho-Chunk, 1873–1974); Charles "Charlie" Stevens (Apache, 1893–1964); and Nipo T. Strongheart (Yakima, 1891–1966). Molly Spotted Elk was featured along with other Native actors in *The Silent Enemy* (1930), which "actively engaged in the creation of representations of Native Americans and were able to, at least for the duration of the film shoot, participate in the cultural activities that had been banned by the government" (Raheja 2010, 91–92).

Native women have, since European contact, been grossly misrepresented and under-represented. Disney's Pocahontas is, perhaps, the silver screen's most famous Indian woman. She is outspoken and beautiful, but this was not the filmic norm for depictions of Native women. Violence toward Native women, women as drudges, silenced women, and Native woman known only as the *s*-word, have dominated film media. The misrepresentation of women in film media has, until recently, been ignored. M. Elise Marubbio addressed this grave oversight in her study *Killing the Indian Maiden: Images of Native American Women in Film* (2006). She identifies three commonly depicted Indian women: "the celluloid princess," "the sexualized maiden," and "the hybrid celluloid maiden." These types of Hollywood depictions of Native women, with few exceptions, abound in cinematic portrayals from the silent film era until today. The topic of misrepresentations of Native women is a vast and flourishing field, and is beyond the scope of this essay, but it does not deserve to be ignored. Several contemporary documentaries have been released—and some motion pictures have been produced and directed—that star indigenous women and that have allowed North American indigenous women to make positive steps toward reclaiming and redefining what it means to be an Indian woman, which is not a catch-all phrase. Noteworthy films and documentaries with gender and identity as focal points include Tracey Deer's *Mohawk Girls* (2005), which began as a documentary and is now a series featured on Canada's Aboriginal People's Television Network; Shelley Niro's *Honey Moccasin* (1998); and Billy Luther's (Diné) *Miss Navajo* (2007), which works to combat misrepresentations of pageantry.

STATE OF AFFAIRS

Prior to the turn of the twenty-first century, scores of Hollywood pictures engaged the theme of "the Indian," and the database of such films is well documented, yet Native screenwriters, directors, producers, and actors continue to work toward Hollywood inclusion. Furthermore, there is an active agenda toward decolonizing the lens and indigenizing various film genres, and challenging the stereotype of the Hollywood Indian. The Screen Actors Guild recently released a 10-minute video that highlights twenty-first-century actors who reflect on the Indian stereotype.

Indigenous filmmakers are steadily increasing in number and presence, and their works reflect their Native Nation's politics, histories, stories, and issues, while others do not. Examples of feature filmmakers and a sampling of their recent and notable works include Blackhorse Lowe (Diné), *The 5th World* (2005); Chris Eyre, *Imprint* (2007); Shelley Niro (Mohawk), *Kissed by Lightning* (2009); and Randy Redroad (Cherokee), *The Doe Boy* (2001).

Documentary filmmaking is a rapidly growing genre, and many indigenous documentaries are housed online. Michigan State University keeps an updated list. A sample of documentary filmmakers and their works include Alanis Obomsawin (Abenaki), *Rocks at Whiskey Trench* (2000); John Blackbird (Cree), *Indianer* (2001); Tracey Deer (Mohawk), *Club Native: How Thick Is Your Blood?* (2008); Bennie Klain (Diné), founder of Trickster Films (Lewis 50-61), *Weaving Worlds* (2007); Steffany Suttle (Lummi), *Fry Bread Babes* (2007); and Victor Masayesva, Jr. (Hopi), *Imagining Indians* (1992).

Youth are a critical demographic in terms of the impact film media has on communities as well as on combating negative stereotypes and misrepresentations. *Native Networks*, available through the Smithsonian's National Museum of the American Indian's website, offers resources for youth media makers. Klee Benally is a Diné artist, activist, and documentary filmmaker, and in addition to his documentaries, he aims to inspire and encourage Native youth, which he does through two organizations: Indigenous Action Media and Outta Your Backpack Media.

Currently, Canada is paving the way in indigenous film media outlets and resources. Among the many resources, two prominent national broadcasting networks are the Aboriginal Peoples Television Network (APTN) and Inuit Broadcasting Corporation (IBC). Since 1999, APTN's presence in Canadian households and across the globe through the Internet has worked to correct misrepresentations in the media. Their website exclaims: "... for the first time in broadcast history, First Nations, Inuit and Métis Peoples have the opportunity to share their stories with all of Canada through a national television network dedicated to Aboriginal programming. Through documentaries, news magazines, dramas, entertainment specials, children's series, cooking shows and education programs, APTN offers all Canadians a window into the remarkably diverse worlds of Indigenous Peoples in Canada and throughout the world" (www.Aptn.ca). APTN has maintained its foothold in the Canadian context and is the subject of recent scholarship, *Indigenous Screen Cultures in Canada* (2010), which looks at the power of media and its impact due to globalization.

The IBC and Isuma TV both focus on Inuit and Indigenous issues of today and yesterday, with a vision for tomorrow. IBC is Canadian province, Nunavut's, public broadcaster, and Isuma TV is an activist and pedagogic web resource, streaming in over 30 languages. Additionally, the National Film Board of Canada (NFB) streams a wealth of films that span various genres while not being strictly Native-focused.

The United States does not have a national broadcaster like APTN in Canada; however, there are several online resources that are outlined in the References section of this essay. The National Museum of the American Indian (NMAI) has an extensive website devoted to Native media made in the Americas, called *Native Networks*. Their resource list allows for easy interconnectivity to websites that focus on indigenous organizations in the areas of film and video, radio, distributors, and festivals and awards. *Native Networks* also devotes a site to Native Youth Media Makers, which is an area that is seeing rapid growth.

Through the Public Broadcasting System (PBS), and depending on one's local station, television viewers have access to Native media, and a listing of programs can be found at the Native American Public Telecommunications website. The Internet has a wealth of information and resources. Most of the online sources are indigenous owned and operated, and reflect views that cater to cross-cultural understanding and educating viewers about Native American culture, language, history, stories, and contemporary situations.

Native filmmakers are recognized at annual national and international awards ceremonies, including the American Indian Film Festival (San Francisco, California), Dreamspeakers (Edmonton, Alberta), imagineNative (Toronto, Ontario), and Indianer Inuit: North American Native Film Festival (Stuttgart, Germany). *Native Networks* provides links to a plethora of community and local film festivals that recognize and award Nation-specific films and filmmakers.

OUTLOOK FOR THE FUTURE

Because of the well-documented misrepresentation and distortion of Native culture in the (Hollywood) mediascape, indigenous filmmakers are actively seeking to overturn commonly held misconceptions and stereotypes. Film media about Indians should not be limited to the Americas, and presently work is being done in all parts of the globe where indigenous people are active agents in all things filmic. Projects abound that range from shorts, documentaries, feature-length films, and music videos to impromptu videos uploaded to YouTube. Because of the ease of uploading to the Internet, there is an increasing amount of visual media by and about Native people. YouTube is the premier gateway for both amateur and professional videographers and filmmakers.

Landscape, as a featured actor in most films depicting Natives, often goes overlooked by mainstream viewers and critics. Director Chris Eyre, however, highlights and focuses on land and landscape. The relationship between Indians and land usually goes hand-in-hand in terms of identity formation and self-representation. Some recent films, however, have used Native landscapes, landmarks, and homelands to depict "other" areas. John Ford began using Native landscapes, namely Monument Valley, in his earliest films, like *The Searchers* (1956), in which Monument Valley was staged as Texas. Shiprock in northern New Mexico is a Diné reservation town and a geological rock formation, yet is touted as Iraq in the major motion picture *Transformers* (2007). Walt Disney Pictures produced *John Carter of Mars* (2012), and depicts Shiprock (Mars) as "a world away." Conversely, "Indian films," made a world away from Indian Country, namely in Europe, had a positive reception from its viewers and were widely popular. Winnetou, an Apache hero of European Westerns, was a fictionalized, romanticized Indian concocted by author Karl May of Radebeul, Germany, in the nineteenth century. The popularity of these dime novels resulted in Hollywood-style Westerns, without "real" Indians in the cast. Winnetou was not the sole hero of European Westerns, yet he is the most enduring. European filmic images of Indians tended to reinforce the stereotype of the Plains Indian, while also relating a political message. Edward Buscombe's *"Injuns!" Native Americans in the Movies*, devotes a thorough chapter to the history, role, and reception of European Westerns, while highlighting Hollywood Westerns in general. Today one can find "real" Indians in Europe, living, working, thriving, and also playing Indian, and indigenous people are not limited to being depicted on the silver screen or through a dime novel.

Film media about Indians is an emerging field of study and will continue to grow. From the earliest modes of moving images to the modern-day cyberspace frenzy, capturing images of "Indians" is done with ease. What differs is the intended message: American Indians and indigenous peoples continue to reclaim and redefine what it means to be an Indian, and one way this is being done is through the medium of film. Many are carving out a space that clashes with mainstream notions and misunderstandings of what it means to "be Indian," while also reclaiming individual, sometimes Nation-specific, lifeways, languages, cultures, and histories—none of which can be nicely packaged under the misnomer of "Indian."

REFERENCES

Books

Aleiss, Angela. *Making the White Man's Indian: Native Americans and Hollywood Movies*. Westport, CT: Praeger, 2005.

Buscombe, Edward. *"Injuns!": Native Americans in the Movies*. London: Reaktion Books, 2006.

Hafsteinsson, Sigurjón Baldur and Bredin, Marian (Eds.). *Indigenous Screen Cultures in Canada*. Winnipeg: University of Manitoba Press, 2010.

Kilpatrick, Jacquelyn. *Celluloid Indians: Native Americans and Film*. Lincoln and London: University of Nebraska Press, 1999.

Lewis, Randolph. "The New Navajo Cinema: Cinema and Nation in the Indigenous Southwest." *The Velvet Light Trap: A Critical Journal of Film and Television* 66 (2010): 50–61.

Marubbio, M. Elise. *Killing the Indian Maiden: Images of Native American Women in Film*. Lexington: University Press of Kentucky, 2006.

Raheja, Michelle H. *Reservation Reelism: Redfacing, Visual Sovereignty, and Representations of Native Americans in Film*. Lincoln and London: University of Nebraska Press, 2010.

Singer, Beverly R. *Wiping the War Paint off the Lens: Native American Film and Video*. Minneapolis: University of Minnesota Press, 2001.

BROADCASTERS AND WEBSITES

Aboriginal Media Lab. Available at http://www.aboriginalmedialab.com
Aboriginal Peoples Television (APTN). Available at http://www.aptn.ca/
Indigenous Action Media. Available at http://www.indigenousaction.org
Inuit Broadcasting Corporation (IBC). Available at http://www.inuitbroadcasting.ca/
Isuma TV. Available at www.isuma.tv
The National Film Board of Canada. Available at http://www.nfb.ca/
Native American Public Telecommunications. Available at http://www.nativetelecom.org/
Native American TV. Available at http://www.natv.org/
Native American Tube. Available at http://natube.magnify.net/
Native Networks. Available at http://www.nativenetworks.si.edu/frameset_html.html
Outta Your Backpack Media: Native American Youth Media Workshops. Available at http://oybm.org/
Rezolution Pictures. Available at http://www.rezolutionpictures.com/
Television Northern Canada. Available at http://www.tvnc.ca/
Trickster Films. Available at http://www.tricksterfilms.com/

FILM FESTIVALS

American Indian Film Festival. Available at http://www.aifisf.com/
Dreamspeakers. Available at http://dreamspeakers.org/
imagineNative. Available at http://www.imaginenative.org/
Indianer Inuit: North American Native Film Festival. Available at http://www.nordamerika-filmfestival.com/en/index.html
Native Networks Festivals and Awards. Available at http://www.nativenetworks.si.edu/eng/yellow/festivals.htm

Film Media by Indians: Native Voices

Lindsey Hanson

The relationship between American Indian culture and film has often been one of tension. Many prominent mainstream films depicting American Indians have been criticized for their stereotypical portrayal of American Indians. The frustration with the portrayal of American Indians in film took the national stage at the forty-fifth Academy Awards in 1973. At the awards ceremony, Native American activist Sacheen Littlefeather, at Marlon Brando's request, declined the Best Actor Award for Brando's role in *The Godfather*. Brando wanted to protest the treatment of American Indians in film and television, and wanted to highlight the American Indian Movement (AIM) protest in the town of Wounded Knee, South Dakota. There, AIM protestors had staged a takeover of the town to address corruption within the tribal council and the Bureau of Indian Affairs (BIA).

Although Littlefeather was not able to present Brando's intended speech because of time constraints imposed by the Academy, it was released to the press afterward. In the speech, Brando lamented the film industry's depiction of American Indians. From romanticized portrayals of American Indians to depictions of American Indians as bloodthirsty savages, the native voice has often been missing from films that deal with American Indian culture.

However, particularly since the mid-1990s, the native voice in film has been gaining strength through the films of directors such as Chris Eyre, Rodrick Pocowatchit, Tvli Jacob, and Steve Judd, as well as the work of organizations such as the American Indian Film Institute and Native American Public Telecommunications. The films created by these directors and promoted by these organizations portray Native Americans and their culture from the native perspective. They deal with issues like reservation life, cultural tension, injustice, native history, and prominent native individuals. Some seek simply to entertain while portraying Native American characters and Native American cultural settings in a new light.

NATIVE AMERICAN DIRECTOR CHRIS EYRE AND HIS PREDECESSORS

Chris Eyre is credited with being the first Native American film director in the United States to reach mainstream audiences. Eyre's film *Smoke Signals* won the 1998 Sundance Film Festival Filmmakers Trophy and the Sundance Audience Award. It also drew significant attention to Native American film. Eyre, who was born and raised in Oregon, is a member of the Cheyenne and Arapaho tribes. He holds a bachelor's degree in media arts from the University of Arizona, and continued his studies at New York University's Graduate Film Program. Eyre's short film *Tenacity*, about two teens on a reservation who have a tragic run in with "rednecks," was screened at the 1995 Sundance Film Festival and garnered him numerous awards.

He then went on to direct the critically acclaimed film *Smoke Signals*, which is based on the short stories of Native American author Sherman Alexie. The film follows two young Native American men on a bus ride to retrieve the ashes of the father of one of the men. The two men have very different memories of the man whose ashes they are on their way to collect. The son remembers his father as an abusive and alcoholic man who abandoned him. The second young man remembers him as a hero who saved his life.

Eyre went on to produce the 2001 film *The Doe Boy*, a coming of age story about a half-Caucasian, half-native boy who suffers from hemophilia. Eyre's second feature film, *Skins* (2002), takes place on the Lakota reservation. The film is about a native police officer and his alcoholic brother. In the film, driven by his frustration with his brother and the prevalence of alcoholism on the reservation, the officer flies into a rage of vigilante justice. That same year, Eyre went on to direct *Skinwalkers* for public television, a murder mystery that takes place in the Navajo nation. Eyre's 2003 film *Edge of America*, about an out-of-town teacher and basketball coach's attempt to fit in on a reservation in Utah, was screened on the opening night of the Sundance Film Festival and received numerous awards, including the Director's Guild of America's award for outstanding directorial achievement.

In 2004, Eyre directed *Thief of Time*, a mystery film about investigators' pursuit of an archeologist suspected of selling Anasazi pottery on the black market. His 2005 film, *A Thousand Roads*, follows an Inupiat girl, a Navajo boy, a Mohawk stockbroker, and a Quechua healer throughout a single day in each of their lives. Eyre also produced the 2007 thriller *Imprint*, about a Native American attorney who returns to the reservation to visit her dying father and begins receiving messages from the spirit world.

In 2007 and 2008, Eyre directed *We Shall Remain*, a five-part documentary that is part of the public television *American Experience* series. Each episode addresses a specific topic or incident in Native American history. The first episode, *After the Mayflower*, deals with the interactions between Pilgrims and Native Americans. *Tecumseh's Vision*, the second episode, addresses the interaction between Native Americans and settlers moving westward. The third episode, *Trail of Tears*, tells the story of the forced removal of the Cherokee, and the fourth episode, *Geronimo*, details Geronimo's resistance against settlers' expansion into Apache lands. The fifth and final episode, *Wounded Knee*, chronicles the 1973 American Indian Movement protest at Wounded Knee. Eyre's most recent release, *Hide Away* (originally entitled *A Year in Mooring*), was released in 2011. As of July 2012 his film *Dead River* was in preproduction.

While Eyre reached mainstream audiences in a way previous native directors had not, he was not the first Native American director. Native American directors like James Young Deer and Edwin Carewe were involved in the film industry as far back as the silent movie era. Hopi director Victor Masayesva, Jr. was directing in the 1980s. Masayesva is the director of the 1985 film *Itam Hakim, Hopiit*, in which a Hopi elder tells about his personal history and the history of his culture as he tells of the Pueblo revolt, the Hopi emergence, and other stories. Masayesva also directed the 1988 film *Ritual Clowns*, which explores Hopi sacred clowns from various angles. Masayesva continues to direct. His 2007 film *Paatuwaqatsi: Water, Land & Life* follows Hopi and Navajo activists as they join a 200-mile run to Mexico City for the World Water Forum. The activists ran to bring attention to water and indigenous issues, and were ultimately successful in stopping certain coal-mining practices that jeopardized the safety of drinking water. Also prior to Eyre's arrival on the scene, Arlene Bowman, who is Navajo, directed the 1986 40-minute film *Navajo Talking Picture*. In the film, she goes back to her reservation to document her grandmother's traditional practices.

Eyre is also not the only contemporary native director. Many have followed in his footsteps. Up and coming directors Steve Judd (Kiowa and Choctaw) and his business partner, filmmaker Tvli Jacob (Choctaw), directed the 2003 film *American Indian Grafitti: This Thing Life*. The film interweaves the life stories of four Native Americans. There is Stephanie, who recently graduated from high school but has not been accepted at the colleges she wants to attend and has also recently learned that her mother wanted to abort her. Then there is Rachel, Stephanie's once close friend who is trying to deal with the death of her mother and brother. Steve is a well-known artist who suddenly feels confused and frustrated creatively, and finally there is Barry, who lives with the guilt of having killed two individuals while driving drunk. Judd and Jacob are also the writers of the film *Shouting Secrets* (2011), which deals with father-son relationships and life on the reservation.

Another notable contemporary native director is Rodrick Pocowatchit of the Pawnee, Shawnee, and Comanche tribes. He directed *Dancing on the Moon* (2003) about three friends who get stranded on the way to a powwow, and *Sleepdancer* (2005) about the mystery of a mute native man who dances in his sleep to escape a tragic past. Pocowatchit also directed a video documentary short entitled *Happy Birthday, Grandma*, and a short called *A Momentary Lapse of Brilliance*. In his latest film, *The Dead Can't Dance* (2010), he makes a foray into the comedic horror genre. Native directors such as these continue to make inroads for the native film artists of tomorrow in a variety of genres.

FILM, RESERVATION LIFE, AND A CULTURE IN TENSION

Many films from Native American directors address the difficulties of reservation life, and the feelings of tension many Native Americans have between traditional cultural practices and modern mainstream American culture. *The Yup'ik Way* is a documentary feature from director Beth Edwards that addresses just these cultural challenges as they are experienced by the Yup'ik village in Alaska. The village is composed mostly of young people on government assistance who know that if they leave to pursue an education, they will not be able to return to their home to practice their profession because of a lack of opportunity in the area. The film explores these issues by following the lives of Joy, a young high school mother with two children; Shaun, who makes his money brewing illegal alcohol; and sisters Neva and Helen, elders who reflect on the young people in their village.

Many other films explore the challenges young Native Americans face on reservations. *Changes*, a short film directed by Greybuck Espinoza, tells of the struggles of a young tribe member facing the difficulties of reservation life while trying to follow his dream of becoming a musical performer. The 2005 film *5th World*, directed by Blackhorse Lowe of the Navajo nation, is about a young romance and tribal culture. Lowe explores similar themes in his short film *B. Dreams*. Janessa Starkey of the United Auburn Indian community and Jack Kohler of the Hupa, Yurok, and Karuk tribes of Northern California directed the 2010 film *Behind the Door of a Secret Girl*. The film follows Sammy, a teenage girl who lives with her meth-addicted mother in a trailer on the Indian Ridge Reservation. Sammy struggles with cutting herself and finds an escape in her best friend David, who is a foster kid. Sammy, David, and a group of homeless youth take on the reservation drug lords, including the boyfriend of Sammy's mother. While the film was Starkey's first, Kohler is also the director of *Three Tales of Choices*, a 2010 animated short that introduces children to Native American stories in an effort to encourage them to avoid drug and alcohol use.

Like *Three Tales of Choices*, *The Legend of Secret Pass* from Steve Trenbirth, is a film for children that seeks to familiarize them with Native American culture and mythology. The computer-animated fantasy film is about the Thunderbirds, which play a prominent role in Native American mythology, and the story of Manu, a Native American boy who lives in the mountains with his grandfather who must fight for the survival of his family.

Four Sheets to the Wind is a film about a native family in a small town in Oklahoma. At the opening of the film, Cufe discovers that his father has committed suicide. He buries him in the pond as his father had long requested, and only then does he tell his mother about the tragedy. What ensues is a story about a family learning to communicate and love again, as well as an exploration of life for Native Americans on and off the reservation.

Hearing Radmilla, from director Angela Webb, is a documentary feature about the 1997 Miss Navajo Nation, Radmilla Cody. The film explores the issue of cultural tension in a unique way. Cody was the first biracial Miss Navajo, which sparked debate within the community about what it means to be Navajo. Cody, who grew up on the reservation with her grandmother, was eventually recognized as one of the most well-liked Miss Navajos and went on to record a popular album of traditional Navajo songs. Cody became involved with an abusive male who was involved in drug trafficking, was indicted in 2002 for failing to report his criminal activities, and spent almost two years in federal prison. Since her release, Cody has continued to record her music, is attending college, and is now an activist who speaks out against domestic violence. Webb's film chronicles these transformations.

In exploring the cultural tension many films from native directors deal with, Native Americans who have left the reservation return for one reason or another and must come to grips with their reservation childhood. One such film is Sherman Alexie's *The Business of Fancydancing*. Alexie, who may be better known for his work as a writer, both wrote and directed this 2002 film. The film is about a reunion that takes place between two friends who grew up on the Spokane Reservation together. The two meet up at a funeral 16 years after their graduation from high school. One of the young men is a successful gay poet whose reunion forces him to come to terms with his growing-up years on the reservation. *The Reawakening* (2004) uses this plot device as well. Director and writer Diane Fraher of the Osage tribe tells the story of a New York attorney who returns to his reservation to defend his childhood friend on murder charges and to represent a client who wants to build a casino. Each of these films, like Eyre's *Smoke Signals*, explores both the challenges and triumphs of reservation life, life as a Native American, and the tension between traditional native culture and mainstream American culture.

PORTRAITS OF NATIVE AMERICAN LIVES IN FILM

Like Arlene Bowman's *Navajo Talking Picture,* many more recent films from native directors present portraits of individual Native Americans whose life stories present a way to explore what it means to be native. *Spirit of the Wind*, from director Ralph Liddle, is a film that does just this. This feature-length biography is about the life of George Attla, a member of the Athabascan tribe. The film is set in Alaska and follows the life of the man known for his championship dog-sled racing. *Two Spirits*, a documentary feature directed by Lydia Nibley, interlaces the story of a mother who has lost her son and a discussion of the changing role of gender in Native American culture, including the special place of honor once held within the culture for those who identified as neither fully male or fully female. *Silent Thunder* is a short documentary from Angelique Midthunder, and it tells Stanford Addison's story. Addison is an elder and quadriplegic, spiritual leader, and a tamer of horses.

Directors Lynn Salt and David Mueller are behind the documentary feature *A Good Day to Die*, which explores the life of American Indian Movement cofounder Dennis Banks. The film, which won the 2010 American Indian Film Festival Best Documentary Feature award, looks at Banks's life from his early days in boarding schools to his stint in the military in Japan, and time spent in Stillwater State Prison. It also explores his role in founding AIM. *Manitou Api, Where the Sun Rises* is a documentary from director Cindy Pickard about an Anishinabe elder curious about the placement of Anishinabe symbols on a legislative building in Winnipeg, Manitoba. The elder meets with architectural scholar Frank Albo, and the two form a relationship as they explore the architecture and symbolism of the building as well as Anishinabe culture. The directors of these films explore native culture as it plays out in the lives of individuals.

DOCUMENTARY FILM AS ACTIVISM AND HISTORY TELLING

Many documentary films from Native American directors explore injustices faced by the Native American community, and in bringing to light these injustices thus serve, in their own way, as a form of activism. Other documentary films make a place for the story of Native Americans in history. One film with a more activist bent is the documentary *Don't Get Sick After June: American Indian Healthcare* from director Chip Richie. This documentary explores the creation of Indian Health Services (IHS), its ongoing role in the lives of Native Americans, and the current health crisis facing the Native American community.

A documentary with a more historical bent is the feature *Choctaw Code Talkers*, directed by Valerie Red-Horse, which explores the important role of Choctaw soldiers in World War I. The soldiers, who in 1918 were not even United States citizens, used their Choctaw language to develop a code that German forces could not break. Director Sonya Rosario is responsible for the historical documentary *Idaho's Forgotten War*, which tells the story of the 1974 war declared by the Kootenai tribe against the U.S. government.

FILM AS ENTERTAINMENT

Other films from native directors simply seek to entertain while incorporating Native American culture and Native American characters. *The Dead Can't Dance* by director Rodrick Pocowatchit is a feature-length comedic horror film that seeks to do just that. It is a story about Native American family members who find themselves somehow immune from whatever is turning everyone around them into zombies. *Christmas in the Clouds* is a comedy of mistaken identity written and directed by Kate Montgomery. The film takes place at a tribal ski lodge where Joe Clouds on Fire, a retired chief, exchanges love letters with a widow named Tina. Tina and Joe mistakenly assume they are the same age, but when Tina arrives at the ski lodge the same weekend an important critic is visiting, she mistakes Joe's son Ray, who runs the lodge, for Joe. The comedy of mistaken identity unfolds while the important critic goes unnoticed.

FESTIVALS AND GROUPS FOCUSED ON NATIVE AMERICAN FILM

There are a number of organizations and festivals dedicated to the advancement of Native American film. One such organization is the American Indian Film Institute (AIFI), which was officially founded in 1979 but has roots as far back as 1975. The group's mission is two-fold: to counter common media stereotypes of American Indians by promoting an understanding of Native American culture through the use of film, and to expand the native voice in media. To that end, AIFI holds an annual American Indian Film Festival in San Francisco, maintains a film library, has a Tribal Touring Program that takes films out into the community, and also provides workshops for youth.

The Native American Film + Video Festival, founded in 1979, is held annually by the Film and Video Center (FVC) of the National Museum of the American Indian. The festival includes not only American Indian artists, but indigenous artists from all over the world. The First Nations Film and Video Festival also screens films by native directors. The Native Arts Circle, which is based in Minneapolis, Minnesota, partners with the Walker Art Center to hold the Two Rivers Native Film and Video Festival to do the same.

Native American Public Telecommunications (NAPT) provides education, promotion, and distribution services to share native stories through public television and radio. Other organizations that seek to promote native artists include The Native American Producers Alliance, Pacific Islanders in Communications, SKC-TV, and the Native American Program of the Sundance Institute.

Each of these organizations and the directors, producers, and writers they promote expand the Native American voice in the film industry and thus work to dispel stereotypical portrayals of American Indians in film. As they explore the lives of prominent Native Americans and issues like reservation life, cultural tension, injustice, and native history and culture, or even as they show Native American characters in positive roles in films meant simply to entertain, they break down the misconceptions and stereotypes created by the portrayal of American Indians as savage and bloodthirsty, or romantic and vanishing.

REFERENCES

American Indian Film Institute. Available at http://www.aifisf.com/

Index of Native American Movie Resources on the Internet. Available at http://www.hanksville.org/NAresources/indices/NAmovie.html

National Museum of American Indian Art: Film Collection. Available at http://www.nmai.si.edu/subpage.cfm?subpage=collections&second=film

Native American Public Telecommunications. Available at http://www.nativetelecom.org

Raheja, Michelle H. *Reservation Reelism: Redfacing, Visual Sovereignty, and Representations of Native Americans in Film.* Lincoln: University Press of Nebraska, 2001.

Rollins, Peter C. and John E. Connor. *Hollywood's Indian: The Portrayal of the Native American in Film.* Lexington: University Press of Kentucky, 2003.

Singer, Beverly R. *Wiping the War Paint off the Lens: Native American Film and Video.* Minneapolis: University of Minnesota Press, 2001.

Website of director Chris Eyre. Available at http://www.chriseyre.org/

Fraudulent Indian Art

Rodney G. Thomas

Fraudulent Indian art is art that is falsely purported to have been made by an American Indian according to traditional methods. Indians consider the fraudulent reproduction and sale of items advertised as *authentic* as a continuance of cultural destruction started long ago, similar to the theft of historic artifacts from old settlement sites.

In the midst the Great Depression, the seventy-fourth U.S. Congress passed Public Law 355, The Indian Arts and Crafts Board and Act of 1935. The law established a program for American Indian artisans and craftspeople to realize more of the commercial potential of their work. Indian arts and crafts were defined in a legal sense and a board, now known as the Indian Arts and Crafts Board (IACB), was established in the Department of the Interior (DOI). The hard economic realities of the Great Depression severely impacted the reservations on which America's indigenous population resided. This law not only defined such artisanship but also provided for methodologies by which the IACB could help protect Indian-made goods and engage in marketing venues outside the reservations and tourist stops. The impetus behind this law was simple: economic support. Fake Indian art, while it existed, was not the economic or culturally destructive force it would become several decades later.

By the 1980s, several forces combined to eventually led to a new law being passed in 1990. While economics was still a consideration, renewed tribal concerns about cultural theft and destruction led to a more stringent set of laws. The Indian Arts and Crafts Act of 1990 (Public Law 101-644) significantly restricted advertising goods as "Indian made" if not made by any Indian, Indian tribe, or Indian arts and crafts organization on the list of federally or state-recognized tribes.

The law covers all Indian art in any form—traditional and contemporary—made after 1935. To some who worked in museums, cultural studies, and with tribal history and cultural organizations, the 1990 law did not go far enough. Norman Feder, one of the earliest students of traditional Indian arts and crafts, developed his "double standard," which is now widely accepted and used in defining and identifying traditional cultural items. For an item to be both traditional and Indian, it must be made in the traditional fashion and by an Indian trained in the tradition (Feest 2001).

Despite the stringent new law, the commercialization of the Internet in the 1990s provided a new outlet for faked items: eBay became the place of business for many fraudulent dealers. In 1935, it was easy for most people, even those not familiar with Indian-produced goods, to tell fake from authentic. By 1990, even Indian artisans themselves found it difficult to determine authenticity. Along with increased places to market faked items came increased access to information and knowledge that dramatically made details about cultural construction and materials readily available to everyone, including fakers. Fabricators began turning to manufacturing capabilities overseas, and with detailed construction knowledge available, fake products flooded markets. Products and replicas made in China, Thailand, India, Mexico, and even Pakistan now adorn online sales and auction site as well as art and crafts shows across the country. Several states have enacted more stringent laws against the practice, and state inspection agencies, aided by tribal organizations, now watch for fraud. Producing and making fraudulent Indian items was not a twentieth-century development; the practice started not long after European travelers visited the American Plains in search of vanishing indigenous civilizations.

HISTORICAL BACKGROUND

George Catlin's paintings and drawings of the American West from the 1830s are some of the most famous portrayals of people and landscapes at a time before the great Western immigrations started. Catlin, like many educated people in the eastern United States, considered the Indians to be "vanishing" from the continent, so he took on a mission to artistically capture the people of the Plains before that happened. While others came before him, such as Swiss artist Karl Bodmer who accompanied German Prince Maximilian of Wied-Nuewied in 1832 and 1834, Catlin was one of the first if not the first to portray people and events from several different tribes. He also produced some buffalo hide paintings and warrior shirts made to look like Indian work. Scholarship in the last few decades has shown several such pieces are held by public collections (Horse Capture and Tyler 1992; Taylor 1998.)

Halcyon Days, a painting by George Catlin, depicts Sioux Indians in a peaceful scene where women tan buffalo skins and dry meat. (AP Photo/Museum of Natural History)

The German artist Balduin Mollhausen traveled the Plains in the early 1850s and befriended several Indians. Like the Indians, he made paintings on buffalo hides and sold them to collectors. While none of his forgeries have been identified in any collection, most experts think they are present (Graf 1991).

Moving forward into the twentieth century, a 1989 imitation buffalo hide painting showing war exploits of a Plains warrior was commissioned from a well-known replicator for a private collection. Sometime later it was sold to another collector and once it was showcased, many leading scholars took it as a genuine and significant artifact. It was subsequently featured in a credible piece of analysis in 2001 that attempted to identify some of the figures portrayed as well as the Plains tribe to which the warrior-artist belonged. Once the research was published, the replicator read the book and notified both owners and the scholar of the spurious nature of the painting. Known as the Fisher Robe, the fake painting has come down in history as authentic, as most researchers do not know of the follow-on piece published by the original author exposing the fake.

These three examples of fake traditional Indian artifacts demonstrate the cultural destruction felt by tribal members. They also demonstrate the ease with which fake items can be introduced into collections meant to portray a people's heritage. Despite years of study, people diligently working with tribal historians and artisans may misidentify and misinterpret such items. Attribution of such items confounds the historical record for everyone concerned. The sophisticated creation of the Fisher Robe was possible in the late 1980s due to readily available information, and it demonstrated the skill of those who create such replicas.

Even more destructive from both a cultural and an economic view is the faking of almost all aspects of Indian culture, traditional and contemporary. Fake religious items, jewelry, baskets, parfleches or tanned leather containers, weapons, and clothing are readily available in almost any venue where commerce is conducted. The financial loss is substantial, but the loss of tribal control over artistic expressions of culture is perhaps the biggest loss. The demand for these items remains high. The reasons for the high demand go back to the early days of the Republic.

As the eighteenth century ended and the nineteenth century began, a growing belief that Indian civilizations were disappearing solidified in the New England gentry and intelligentsia. Religious and literary leaders promoted this view and developed a perspective regarding the Indian as the "noble savage." This characterization is seen in the writings of James Fenimore Cooper and others of his era. This belief, translated into white religious and social policy and action, began a long process of Indian culture and identity being defined by non-Indian immigrants with the resultant loss of Indian voices in creating such identity. Non-Indian views imposed on Indian societies helped focus the belief about Indians' disappearance. Well into the twentieth century, well-meaning and well-intentioned non-Indian leaders worked diligently to preserve as much of Indian culture as they found attractive. Despite the almost constant state of war between the U.S. government and the tribes, first in the East and then west of the Mississippi as the tribes were relegated to living on smaller and smaller portions of the land, those individuals and groups played a role in developing the market for Indian things. Not fully acculturated to white agriculture and industry, these now reservation-bound groups found making cultural items, such as leather goods, beaded items, and other art items a small beginning to a lucrative trade.

At first, trading for Indian-produced items made possible the collection for some future remembrance. Later, after the cultural destruction of entire villages during the Plains wars was underway, items made for a prior lifestyle no longer had the same utility. Decorated hides that wrapped around the interior of a Plains tipi helped interior living conditions and were no longer needed as the tipis were replaced by log cabins. Those hides, known as liners, were often decorated with vignettes of warrior prowess in war, hunting, and horse raiding. Once ensconced in log cabins on reservations, Indian inhabitants hung unbleached muslin on interior cabin wall to cut down on drafts and falling chinking or mud and moss stuffed between the log walls. They were also painted with liner-style vignettes until the old warriors passed away and no new deeds were possible.

By the late nineteenth and early twentieth centuries, as more Americans acquired wealth and nicer living quarters, a phenomenon known as the Indian Room caught on. This was a room or space in larger homes that was filled with as many Indian items as the owner could obtain. Items often made for traveling "wild west" shows would end up in these collections, as would items made to be sold to tourists or to be given as gifts to reservation visitors. There are also stories of entire villages being tricked into providing as many of their possessions as possible for such collections. At the same time, a small group of scholars began to take on a more serious approach to understanding Indian culture. These original ethnologists, again meaning well, represented a natural growth of the philosophy developed by authors such as Cooper and Thoreau, and artists like Catlin. They refined white definitions of Indian but then started a new approach as they talked with tribal members about Indian culture.

At this same time, large numbers of civic organizations, authors, artists, and performers spread Indian lore in various ways. By the 1920s, most Americans lived in cities and along with this came a desire for open spaces and what many perceived to be a cleaner, healthier, more meaningful lifestyle—that is, an Indian lifestyle. Along with this desire to get back to nature was the continuing need to save Indians from disappearing. Out of all this came the Camp Fire Girls, a resurgence in the Internal Order of Red Men originally founded during the American Revolution; the Boy Scouts; and a myriad of performers, local organizations, songs, school programs, and of course, the need for more Indian "things." Of all these groups and organizations, one of the most famous and long-lasting Indian lore "interpretive" acts was that of Reginald and Gladys Laubin. In 1947, this couple was once described by Crow leader Bird Horse as "...nothing but a white man but he looks more real more like the early days, than you young fellows do" (Ellis 2008, 21). The Laubins were adopted by One Bull, nephew of the Hunkpapa leader Sitting Bull, in 1934. He thought the Laubins had been sent by the Great Spirit to represent the Lakota people throughout the United States.

By 1935 when the original Indian Arts and Crafts Act was passed, serious study with tribal leaders, historians, and artisans had captured significant details on some aspects of life before the reservations. Some aspects were never discussed with non-Indian researchers and remain closed to this day to nontribal members. Most of this early work was published in limited quantities of annual reports by sponsoring organizations such as the Smithsonian Institute, the American Anthropological Association, and some of the larger museums. Until digitization of these documents was started in the 1990s, access to and even awareness about them was limited to specialized students and scholars. Once digitized and placed in online collections, the details of materials and construction were available to all who wished to read them. More importantly, as the twentieth century proceeded, the desire for Indian Room material never waned. By the mid-1950s and early 1960s, the desire for Indian Room materials had increased, as had the types of non-Indian groups who wanted to own or use the items.

NON-INDIAN ARTISTS

One of these groups was, and remains today, known as hobbyists. These are non-Indian artisans who diligently study, recreate, replicate, and even restore Indian artifacts and customs. They are so skilled at traditional methods and materials used by pre-reservation Indian artisans that usually some of them uncover fakes. They replicate but do not sell. They teach and learn at the same time. They often wear and use the items they create in a serious effort to understand the nature of the items. Their ranks are filled with people from all walks of life and include professional scholars, curators, and others with legitimate and respectful interests. They include people who participate as "living historians" and re-enactors both at historic celebrations and in films. They also include people who participate in the growth of tribal powwows as dance groups travel across the country to participate in these traditional celebrations. They should not be confused with a group that has been termed wannabes or a group known as fakers.

Non-Indians categorized as wannabes have assumed what they consider to be an Indian lifestyle, and almost all have assumed the lifestyle they believe was practiced on the Great Plains before the 1880s. Tribal leaders have expressed displeasure and disgust at these groups that pervert tribal religious and philosophical beliefs as well as fuel the demand for faked cultural items. While religion is not an "artifact," the erroneous practice of an Indian belief system by non-Indian people is just as fraudulent as selling a fake dance shield. Some believe wannabes are even more destructive, especially when participation or admission fees are charged to their events.

The third group of non-Indian people discussed here are known in art and cultural circles as the fakers. These people either make or cause to be made fake items, also known as artifakes, for either sale or passing off as authentic for some serious purpose such as acquisition by a museum or even a tribe. They have succeeded in maintaining and in some cases increasing prices for what appear to be authentic items from pre-reservation days. While the Indian Room fad has passed away, there remains the desire to possess an item that at best represents a romantic version of that long-ago lifestyle. It is the remnant of the noble savage concept and is lucrative for those who are adept at fraudulent recreations. All this continues to encourage the fabrication of a non–Indian defined lifestyle.

The 1990 law recognized the increased skill and locations of people who were manufacturing of Indian arts and crafts. The dramatic shift in quality noted earlier is causing increased loss of revenue, not to mention the continuing assault on Indian culture. This fraud has now reached beyond Plains Indian warrior accoutrement. Serious reproducers have extensively researched techniques, materials, styles, and convincing aging processes. Stones and minerals used in traditional items such as pipe bowls used in ancient Southern U.S. cultures are now being mined again, making detection of a fake extremely difficult. Shell masks, gorgets and necklaces, grooved stone axes, and well-used carving knives are now offered for sale as authentic. The results of aging and long-term use effects processes are such that determination as a fake can now be done only by expensive testing and analysis. Increasing numbers of people enter this business, and their demand for sellable stock fuels production at overseas locations (Berner 2004).

From a tribal view, such fakery continues to allow their societies to be defined by non-Indians. It certainly is illegal, according to the law of the land, but more importantly, it lessens the economic well-being of those working at maintaining traditional ways. Sellers of fake art respond to the continuing demand while at times passing off frauds to serious organizations, which pollutes the historical record and especially the peoples' understanding of their own past. Interest in Indian cultures has not waned, nor has the demand for cultural artifacts. Despite a rather significant federal law, along with state laws and agencies, reducing the quantity of fake items for sale remains a battle.

REFERENCES

Berner, John F. "Artifact or Artifake?" *Central States Archaeological Journal* 52, no. 4 (2004), 56.

Brownstone, Arni. "Anatomy of a Fake." *American Indian Workshop Newsletter*, no. 59 as part of *Native American Studies* 16, no. 2 (2002), 55.

Catalogue Raisonne Scholars Association Guidelines for Issuing Scholarly Opinions about Authenticity. Available at http://catalogueraisonne.org/

Dyar, Jennifer. "Fatal Attraction: The White Obsession with 'Indianness.'" *Historian* 65, no. 4 (2003): 817–826.

Ellis, Clyde. "More Real Than the Indians Themselves: The Early Years of the Indian Lore Movement in the United States." *Montana: the Magazine of Western History* 58, no. 3 (Autumn 2008): 3–22.

Feest, C. F. (Ed.). *Studies in American Indian Art: A Memorial to Norman Feder*. Seattle: University of Washington Press, 2001.

Graf, Andreas. *The Death of the Wolf: The Adventures and Momentous Life of Novelist and American Traveler Bauldin Mollhausen (1825–1904)*. Berlin: Duncker & Humblot, 1991.

Holm, Bill. "Four Bears' Shirt: Some Problems with the Smithsonian Catlin Collection." In G. P. Horse Capture and S. G. Tyler (Eds.), *Artifacts/Artifakes: The Proceedings of the 1984 Plains Indian Seminar*. Cody, WY: Buffalo Bill Historical Center, 1992.

Indian Arts and Crafts Act of 1990. Available at http://www.doi.gov/iacb/act.html

Miller, Preston E. and Carolyn Corey. *The New Four Winds Guide to Indian Weaponry, Trade Goods, and Replicas*. Atglen, PA: 2007, 139–158.

National Powwow. Available at http://www.whisperingwind.com

Taylor, Colin F. *Catlin's Glee-pa: Mandan Culture and Ceremonial. The George Catlin O-pa Manuscripts in the British Museum*. Foreword by W. Raymond Wood. Wyk, Germany: Verlag fur Amerikanistik (Publisher of American Studies) D. Kruegler, 1998.

Music: Vibrant Elements of American Indian Culture

Susan M. Taffe Reed

Music is a living, vibrant element of American Indian culture that is interconnected with many facets of life, from birth to death and all the significant and mundane points in between. Music plays a role in artistic expression, ceremony and prayer, greeting foreign nations, war, treaty making, honoring others, socializing, childrearing, and courtship. The U.S. and Canadian governments banned American Indian music and other cultural activities from the late nineteenth century into the twentieth century. Despite attempts to suppress and eventually eradicate Native American music and dance, it survived and continues to thrive. But removal from traditional homelands, children being sent to boarding schools, and centuries of colonization took their toll on American Indian traditions. Erosion of American Indian culture led to loss of music, dances, and ceremonies. Retention and revitalization of music are goals of many contemporary American Indian communities, who see music as vital to the sustenance and endurance of their cultures.

MUSICAL ELEMENTS

The diversity of American Indian music has historically been ignored. Each nation possessed unique music and dances. These traditions might be shared with visitors or neighboring tribes. There are similarities in musical form, rhythm, technique, and aesthetics such as timbre—the quality of musical tone—and vocal effects in American Indian music from common geographical areas. A rich variety of musical traditions are represented across native North America. Songs of the Eastern Woodlands, for example, are markedly different from the Northwest Coast, as are those from the Southwest.

In the past, most traditional American Indian music was monophonic. Monophony means music with a single melody. When individuals sang, they did so in unison, meaning they produced the same pitch. Polyphony, music with more than one part, is esteemed in European music. Because American Indian music was monophonic, it was stigmatized by Europeans as simple and unsophisticated. Their cultural bias is seen by the fact that they only considered pitched parts in analyzing native music, thereby ignoring complex rhythms in the vocal line and supporting instruments such as drum and rattle. Today, some contemporary Native American artists are using Western instruments and harmony in their music.

A common misconception is that all American Indian music is improvised, that is, made up on the spot. In fact, very little music is improvised. The most common example of improvisation is by Native American flute players. Music is passed down from elders to youngsters through oral tradition. Certain Haudenosaunee singers, for example, grow to be expert culture bearers and cultural specialists. They may know hundreds or thousands of songs and their proper uses. The six nations that are members of the Haudenosaunee, or Iroquois, Confederacy—Mohawk, Oneida, Onondaga, Cayuga, Tuscarora, and Seneca—share many of the same social dance songs, so there is overlap in song repertoire and slight variations in the way songs are sung between communities. Many songs have been passed down for generations, and some ancient songs may be centuries old.

Song lyrics come in several varieties. Some songs are made entirely of vocables, syllables with sounds such as wey, hey, ya, ho, we, ney, ha. Other songs, particularly those referred to as '49 songs, may incorporate English words. There are also songs that incorporate a native language or are sung exclusively in that language. In general, ceremonial songs are more likely to incorporate native language. Today, songs are playing a supportive role in language revitalization, with teachers composing songs that incorporate native language for their students. Powwow drum groups have interest in incorporating their indigenous language into their songs, and some communities with few speakers of their language would like to reintroduce it into their ceremonies and sacred songs.

American Indian musical genres have been categorized with terms like *traditional* or *contemporary*. Labeling Native American music can be complicated because of the influences of other kinds of music and debate over what constitutes traditional music. Some scholars and native people argue that classification of music is artificial and problematic. Controversy also exists over what features constitute American Indian music and how it should be defined. Does the musician, lyrics, instruments, melody, or a special combination of these elements make music American Indian? Is classical music by an American Indian artist that weaves Native American melodies into a polyphonic composition American Indian music? Is a blues song by an American Indian performer with lyrics related to native issues

American Indian music? Commercial music sales are an indication of what native and non-native listeners want to hear, but only American Indians themselves can define what constitutes American Indian music. Their answer is ever evolving and varies from region to region, community to community, and probably even from person to person.

ACADEMIC SCHOLARSHIP, INSTITUTIONS, AND REPATRIATION

Anthropologists and ethnomusicologists have studied American Indian music from cultural, musical, and historical perspectives. Since the advent of audio recording technology, scholars have made millions of American Indian recordings, many of which are now held in museum and university collections around the world. Jesse Walter Fewkes (1850–1930), employed by the Peabody Museum of Archeology and Ethnology at Harvard University, was the first anthropologist to use mechanical recording equipment for ethnological research in 1890. Other notable figures who made early recordings of Native American music include Frances Densmore (1867–1957), an American ethnographer and ethnomusicologist who worked for the Smithsonian Institution's Bureau of American Ethnology and recorded songs from a number of tribes on wax cylinders; George Herzog (1901–1983), a musicologist, ethnomusicologist, and anthropologist born in Hungary who worked on defining stylistic musical areas of Native North America; and Frank Speck (1881–1950), an American anthropologist who specialized in Iroquoian and Algonquin peoples of the Eastern Woodlands. Contemporary scholars studying American Indian music include ethnomusicologists such as Beverly Diamond, Jason Jackson, Victoria Lindsay Levine, and Tara Browner.

There are traditional protocols that need to be respected when researching Native American music, whether in the field or in institutional collections. Some tribes do not want certain ceremonial music to be recorded. Some feel that recordings made in the past are not intended to be listened to by the uninitiated or that certain songs should be performed only at specific times of the year or for particular events.

Today, institutions are repatriating music and music-related artifacts. A prime example is the Federal Cylinder Project, organized in 1979 by the American Folklife Center (AFC) and the Library of Congress in relation with the Smithsonian Institution, the Bureau of Indian Affairs (BIA), and other federal agencies, which began disseminating recordings to their communities of origin in 1985. Repatriation has also been spurred by a federal law passed in 1990 called the Native American Graves Protection and Repatriation Act (NAGPRA). Section C of this act addresses the repatriation of cultural patrimony, which includes information such as musical knowledge and ceremonial objects such as musical instruments. Ceremonial instruments like drums, rattles, and whistles, and accompanying ceremonial objects such as masks, were collected or even stolen from communities or from graves.

POWWOWS

Powwows range in size from small events attended by a couple hundred people to massive intertribal gatherings attracting thousands of participants and spectators. The word *powwow* comes from an Algonquin word that refers to an assembly of medicine people, but the formation of contemporary powwows is a Plains custom that has been adopted by tribes across North America. The drum, referred to as the "heartbeat of Mother Earth" is the most central element of the powwow. Like the dance arena, Mother Earth, the Sun, and the Moon, the drum is in the shape of a circle, a symbol that holds great meaning to American Indian people for its representation of life, cyclical continuity, and unity. Although powwows are social events, many participants feel a spiritual connection to the dance circle and to the drum.

Powwows are places where people celebrate life through dance, shop for gifts and supplies, eat traditional foods, and honor those who deserve acknowledgment. In reconnecting with old friends, social engagement and community building take place. People talk about current issues, reminisce about the past, laugh at jokes, and give gifts. The unity developed at powwows has helped to instill pride in many American Indians about their unique culture and history. Powwows promote cultural awareness as well as education of participants and spectators, and they help shape American Indian social identity. Powwow culture is alive and constantly being redefined. Powwow fashions change from year to year: dancers devise new ways of making outfits flashier and more noticeable to the judges by incorporating brightly colored ribbons, shiny sequins, or intricate beadwork in traditional designs; there are new ways of constructing outfits to fit more seamlessly, be lighter, or move more freely with use of materials such as Velcro, elastic, and new fabrics and new dance steps are invented.

People from hundreds of indigenous nations and all ages participate in powwows. Alcohol and drugs are not allowed on the powwow premises. Intertribal social networks of people on the powwow circuit have known one another for several generations. Young people find powwows appealing because they offer an opportunity to meet other native people their age. Fast dance styles such as fancy shawl dance for young ladies and fancy dance or grass dance for young men are popular for the athleticism they require. Powwows provide youngsters with a respite from the pressures and influences of mainstream life and the opportunity to be immersed in American Indian culture.

Powwows provide the public with an opportunity to learn more about American Indian culture. Spectators are invited into the dance circle for the round dance, a circular dance in which participants hold hands and alternate between moving clockwise and counterclockwise. Powwows also offer a variety of shopping. Food offered for sale varies by region and includes such delicacies as Indian tacos, corn soup, buffalo burgers, strawberry drink, and wild rice. Artists and craftspeople selling everything from jewelry, children's toys, and animal hides to beading supplies surround the dance arena.

The popularity of powwows grew tremendously in the mid-1970s and 1980s, and they continue to flourish. Today, one or more powwows are held within reasonable driving distance of almost any given location during the summertime. Indoor powwows take place during months of inclement weather. Powwows are held both on and off tribal land. Fairgrounds, farms, universities, and civic centers are all popular powwow venues. Tribes, organizations, or a combination of sponsors host powwows. Admission is charged at many events, especially those needing to raise the funds to cover overhead.

DANCE STYLES

American Indian powwow music, dance, and culture are divided into two styles based on region: northern style and southern style. Northern style comes from the region of the northern Great Plains and the Great Lakes, the northern United States, and all of Canada. Southern style comes from Oklahoma, Kansas, and the region that lies to the south of those states. Northern and southern style dance steps differ depending on the particular type of dance, such as women's traditional, and there are also differences in regalia. Perhaps the most perceptible difference between the two styles is the music. Northern style drummers sing in a high falsetto; southern style drummers use a lower vocal register.

Powwow music is inseparable from dance. Dance styles for men include men's traditional, including southern straight and men's northern traditional; men's fancy dance; and grass dance. Hoop dancing is a specialized dance originally performed by men. Today, women are hoop dancing too and have been successful in winning many hoop dance competitions, including the Hoop Dance World Championships. Common female dance styles include women's traditional, including southern traditional and northern traditional; fancy shawl; and jingle dress. For the purposes of competition, these categories are broken down even further. For example, women's traditional dancers with cloth dresses are separated from those wearing buckskin. There are also several age categories ranging from "tiny tots" to seniors. In the future, we may see the emergence of new dance styles for men and women and the necessary addition of competitive powwow categories. Performances by indigenous people from other regions, such as Aztec dancers, has been a rising trend over the past couple decades.

Clothing worn by powwow dancers is referred to as an outfit or regalia, never as a costume. Although most dance styles are represented across North America, regalia often incorporates symbols from tribal heritage and gifts received from friends and family.

At a number of powwows, a powwow princess is selected from a competitive pool of applicants to serve as a representative for her people. The powwow princess is not born into her position, and she does not secure it by heredity or beauty. She is chosen to serve as an ambassador for her nation because she demonstrates knowledge of her culture and is a good role model. She is expected to be well versed in her specific style of powwow dance and her culture, often including language and tribal history. The powwow princess dances behind the lead dancers of the powwow. She wears a crown and a sash that indicate her princess status and year of crowning. Her term generally lasts one year before the title is passed on to another young woman.

COMPETITION AND NONCOMPETITION POWWOWS

An important difference between powwows is whether they are a competition or noncompetition. Competition (or commercial) powwows, such as the Gathering of Nations in Albuquerque, New Mexico, not only attract thousands of people, but also offer thousands of dollars in prize money to singers and dancers. The Mashantucket Pequot nation's Schemitzun powwow in Hartford, Connecticut, offers over $1 million in prize money from its Foxwoods Casino's gambling revenue. The careful planning and construction of competition dance outfits is impressive. Dance regalia is becoming increasingly more expensive and more ornate. Serious dancers have several outfits that they change into during the course of the powwow.

Noncompetition powwows, also called noncontest or traditional powwows, are gaining in popularity and are more prevalent in certain states. Some dancers find that they have more fun without the pressure of dancing for competition, and they can spend more time socializing with family and friends. Some powwow committees have turned former competition powwows into noncompetition powwows because money to support dance prizes had become increasingly difficult to raise.

"TWO-SPIRIT" POWWOWS

Two-spirit is a term used in Indian country to refer to persons of "two spirits" that identify with both male and female essences. Many Native American people choose to use this expression in place of the imposed term *gay*. Two-spirit individuals may lean more toward one or the other essence in social, work, familial, and cultural aspects of their lives. Some two-spirit people feel alienated in their home communities. Others wish to make new two-spirit friends with whom they have ancestry and culture in common. Two-spirit societies have been founded in many urban areas. They have organized two-spirit powwows, private gatherings not advertised to the general public. Friends and family are sometimes invited and attend to show their support. These powwows give two-spirit individuals the opportunity to celebrate their culture, affirm their identity, and develop friendships.

PAN-INDIANISM

Pan-Indianism, also called pan-tribalism, refers to the contemporary musical and cultural trend across Native America of developing a universalized "Indian" culture. Pan-Indianism is described as an incorporation of old tribal traditions—mostly of Prairie-Plains derivation, "white" culture, and elements that are particularly pan-Indian themselves. Pan-Indian culture is criticized for privileging Prairie-Plains culture and for generalizing and melding American Indian music, culture, and social and spiritual values. The powwow is frequently identified as the central location of pan-Indianism. However, some believe labeling powwows as pan-Indian is inaccurate because there are significant musical and cultural distinctions present at powwows.

THE DRUM

A group of singers is referred to as a drum group, or "drum" for short. Small powwows may have one or two drums, while larger powwows, particularly those with drum competitions, may have dozens. Good drum groups attract good dancers who might attend a powwow specifically because their favorite drum group is playing there. Singers are vitally important to the success of the powwow, as they support the dancers and bring spectators to the circle. An excellent drum group gives dancers the opportunity to show off their finest dancing. Shawl dancers can seemingly float across the dance arena to a northern drum like Whitefish Jrs., and grass dancers can breeze across the circle to a southern drum like Southern Boyz.

The women's movement significantly affected American Indian culture, including powwows. In the 1960s, most women sang standing behind the men who sat at the drum, but American Indian women's roles are changing. Today, we see female chairpersons and tribal council members as well as women sitting behind the drum (Roberts 1998, 31, 114). While some native people are still apprehensive about all-female drum groups, these groups are respected and popular at many powwows. Seven Cedars is a well-liked group that has sung at powwows for many years in Pennsylvania and the surrounding region. As the role of women continues to evolve, changes will likely be reflected in the dance circle, with women serving in traditionally male roles such as powwow arena director, emcee, and flag bearer.

Mixed drum groups, where both men and women sit and beat the drum together, are in some cases more controversial than female drum groups because they mix the sexes. In some communities, mixed drumming happens frequently in informal settings. Mixed drums are becoming increasingly common on the powwow circuit. Drum groups such as the Kicking Woman Singers, which was founded by four brothers with the last name Kicking Woman in the early 1970s, has both male and female members and is well respected.

ECONOMIC CONCERNS

Powwows are susceptible to the rise and fall of the economy. Some vendors and dancers who used to make a living on the powwow trail can no longer afford to rely solely on the monies made through selling arts and crafts or prize money won in dance competitions because of increasing gas prices and the fact that spectators do not spend as much money at powwows in hard economic times. Vendors must make enough money to clear the cost of travel and their booth fee. Some powwow organizing committees have been overwhelmed by overhead such as increasing event insurance rates and venue rental costs, prompting them to shorten what were three or four day powwows to two or three days and in some cases just one day. Yet powwows continue to thrive, especially those funded by gaming tribes. New powwows continually spring up across the country. Growth in the number of powwows might threaten the viability of older powwows, especially when they are held on the same weekend. Powwows compete for the best dancers and vendors. Participants' decisions of which powwows to attend are influenced by location, prize money, host and guest drums, native celebrities who will be appearing, and where their friends and relatives are going.

CONTEMPORARY MUSIC

American Indian musicians entered into all genres of music by the 1990s with a worldwide audience, although only a small percentage were signed by record labels. Many of the artists popular to non-native as well as native audiences can be described broadly as contemporary artists. Their music ranges across every musical genre from New Age, folk, country, blues, and jazz to rock, rap, heavy metal, and opera. They are increasingly being asked to perform at music festivals, such as the Finger Lakes GrassRoots Festival of Music and Dance, which spotlights half a dozen American Indian performing groups every year, such as Keith Secola (Anishinabe) and the Wild Band of Indians, who are influenced by blues/folk/rock; Bear Fox (Mohawk), who weaves blues and folk influences into her music; and the punk-rock band Blackfire (Diné).

There are organizations that support contemporary musicians and award ceremonies that acknowledge their contributions. The Association for Native

Development in the Performing and Visual Arts (ANDPVA) is a nonprofit organization that provides support to Canadian indigenous artists in Ontario and around the world. One initiative of ANDPVA is the Indigenous Arts Network (IAN), which provides an interactive online atlas of indigenous artists across Canada with accompanying audio and video. The Native American Music Awards (NAMA), an awards show held annually in the United States beginning in 1998, honors American Indian musical artists in over 30 categories. The Canadian Aboriginal Music Awards, founded in the same year, takes place in conjunction with the four-day Canadian Aboriginal Festival, which includes education, arts and crafts, traditional food, a fashion show, and a powwow.

American Indian women have been successful in contemporary music, such as Oneida singer Joanne Shenandoah (Wolf clan), who has won numerous music awards, including a Grammy. Her music blends traditional Iroquois melodies with non-native influences and instrumentation. Pop artists like Lumbee Jana Mashonee have a following of young native fans.

Many contemporary Native American artists incorporate issues of Indian life into their lyrics. Some focus on political concerns and aim to reach a broader, non-native mainstream audience with their messages.

There is debate over whether certain contemporary artists break or reinforce stereotypes about American Indians. Some argue that certain performers evoke romantic depictions of American Indian people. Some elders and more conservative native people are concerned by what they consider to be inappropriate representations of American Indians, such as performers wearing skimpy clothing and dyed chicken feathers.

THE NATIVE AMERICAN FLUTE

Comanche Doc Tate Nevaquaya (1932–1996) was one of the most influential people in keeping the flute tradition alive. Since the mid-1970s, flute music has undergone a revival by artists such as R. Carlos Nakai (Diné-Ute) and Mary Youngblood (Aleut-Seminole), whose music has a wide audience and has educated audiences about the history of the flute. Because of its popularity, the Native American flute has also fallen victim to New Age enterprises that have exploited and romanticized it for commercial profit.

AUTHENTICITY

Issues of authenticity or "realness" of American Indian music are of concern to natives and non-natives, but usually for different reasons. Native Americans see stereotyping of music and culture as a real problem. Historically, portrayals of American Indian music in popular culture such as old Western movies have frequently been erroneous, inauthentic, and offensive to Native American people. Non-native audiences want to know what "real" American Indians look like and what "real" American Indian music sounds like, but they have been so misinformed by popular culture, the media, and even history books that they doubt the authenticity of real American Indians and real American Indian music when they encounter them. Native people are in a constant process of re-educating the public, work that is challenged by misappropriation of American Indian music by non-natives. It is hoped that through continuation of educational efforts, such as school programs and powwows, the public will develop a deeper understanding of who American Indian people are and why their music is so important to them.

REFERENCES

Canadian Aboriginal Music Awards. Available at http://www.canab.com/mainpages/events/musicawards.html

Diamond, Beverley. *Native American Music in Eastern North America: Experiencing Music, Expressing Culture*. New York: Oxford University Press, 2008.

Diamond, Beverley, M., Sam Cronk, and Franziska Von Rosen. *Visions of Sound: Musical Instruments of First Nations Communities in Northeastern America*. Chicago: University of Chicago Press, 1994.

Ellis, Clyde, Luke Eric Lassiter, and Gary H. Dunham. *Powwow*. Lincoln: University of Nebraska Press, 2005.

Gilley, Brian Joseph. "Two-Spirit Powwows and the Search for Social Acceptance in Indian Country." In Clyde Ellis, Luke Eric Lassiter, and Gary H. Dunham (Eds.), *Powwow*. Lincoln: University of Nebraska Press, 2005, 224–240.

Levine, Victoria Lindsay and Judith A. Gray. "Musical Interactions." In Ellen Koskoff (Ed.), Vol. 3 of *The Garland Encyclopedia of World Music: The United States and Canada*. New York: Garland Publishing, 2000, 480–490.

Native American Music Awards. Available at http://www.nativeamericanmusicawards.com/home.cfm

PowWows.com. Available at http://www.powwows.com.

Roberts, Chris. *Powwow Country: People of the Circle*. Missoula, MT: Meadowlark Publishing Company, 1998.

Wright-McLeod, Brian. *The Encyclopedia of Native Music*. Tucson: University of Arizona Press, 2005.

Print Media by Indians: Words and Ideas of American Indians

Robert E. Sanderson

While historians argue over who should be credited for saying that newspapers are the "first rough draft of history," we must note that much of that history, particularly about indigenous Americans, is fraught with distortions because of their ethnocentric—white only—bias in reporting. Until the arrival of Native American and Alaska Native journalists, all accounts of native life were collected, interpreted, and published by and for non-native readers. What was missing in these accounts was the native voice and the various perspectives that come only from the originators of the stories: the native peoples themselves. However, when Native Americans and Alaska Natives began printing their own words, the history of North America changed. These earlier and even contemporary native newspapers and periodicals challenged numerous distortions and often outright lies about indigenous peoples, and for the first time native as well as non-native people could read what indigenous Americans had to say about people, places, and events that helped shape the history of the United States and the tribal people living within its borders.

SEQUOYAH AND THE BIRTH OF THE INDIGENOUS AMERICAN PRESS

Although some oral historians contend that the Cherokee had a written language long before the 1820s, most modern scholars attribute Sequoyah with inventing the Cherokee syllabary, a written set of symbols that led Cherokees into literacy in their own language. Sequoyah's fascination with the written word that was used by the English-speaking Americans was perhaps the cornerstone of his development of the syllabary. According to Jim Parins, "Sequoyah at first thought that each letter [in English] stood for a word. Upon closer examination, however, he concluded that this could not be true, and that a better explanation was that each letter represented a sound. This idea, which came to him around 1809, was the seed from which the Cherokee syllabary grew" (Parins).

Sequoyah's basic premise was that letters stood for sounds, or syllables, in words spoken in Cherokee. He etched out a letter for each syllable spoken in Cherokee and combined his unique letters or symbols to form the Cherokee words in writing. Once he completed the syllabary, he had to convince his people of the practicability and importance of the written language. Of course, like anything new that requires change, Sequoyah met with some initial resistance. However, "once he had taught the system to some Cherokee youths, who were able to learn it quickly and easily, tribal leaders became enthusiastic. Sequoyah was hired as a teacher to help spread the syllabary's use, and in a short time, any Cherokee speaker who desired could read the language. Missionaries were enthusiastic, seeing a new way to help spread their message. With their help, the Cherokees were able to procure a set of type and set up their own printing operation. This led to the establishment of the *Cherokee Phoenix*, the first newspaper published by American. The Cherokee press also published Biblical passages, hymnals, and other tracts" (Parins).

The *Cherokee Phoenix* was first edited by Elias Boudinot, a man chosen by Principal Chief John Ross and the national council of the Cherokee nation. Boudinot and the Cherokee leadership foresaw the importance of the printed word in the future of Cherokee civilization. With the publication of the *Phoenix*, Cherokee could reap the benefits that their English-speaking neighbors had enjoyed for years. This new venue of communication could not only deliver to every Cherokee citizen that could read the news of the day the laws and public documents of the nation as well as articles on Cherokee arts and humanities, it could also preserve the culture and thoughts of the people for future Cherokee in a written form, one that promised to enhance the oral traditions of an indigenous people (Trahant 1995). The first edition of the *Phoenix* appeared on February 21, 1828, printed in both English and Cherokee. It consisted of four pages and included an article about the newspaper, the Cherokee constitution, the Cherokee syllabary, a translation of the Lord's Prayer from Cherokee into English, and other notices.

American native press has been producing newspapers, magazines, periodicals, and various other documents for public consumption for nearly 200 years. Since the publication of the first *Cherokee Phoenix*, Native Americans have experienced the full range of issues and problems that non-native journalists and publishers have in the turbulent world of print publication. Native press is not exempt or immune to the common difficulties that undermine any mass communication venture. The difficulties of censorship—the control or suppression of the publishing industry—and politicization have been some of the major problems that agents of social control have leveraged against the press in all modern societies, especially when the printed word holds so much power and has served as the primary vehicle of mass communication since the invention of the printing press. However, products of native press offer one distinct advantage over non-native press as chroniclers of history: "They make a significant statement about Indian or Alaska Native history because they present the Indian or native from various perspectives, the most important of which is his own" (Littlefield and Parins 1984, xi).

There exists considerable debate over what constitutes "native press," stemming largely over producer/publisher versus content. American Indians and Alaska Natives published newspapers and periodicals before the twentieth century, but much of the content of those publications was largely aimed at non-Indian readership with little mention of Indian affairs. With the advent of the *Cherokee Phoenix*, Native Americans began producing tribal newspapers and periodicals aimed at disseminating information by, for, and about native peoples. Prior to 1924, tribal newspapers were published by only three tribes, and they were owned, operated, or otherwise approved of by tribal authorities. The significance of these early publications was that they were a direct reaction to federal Indian policies and were giving tribes' perspectives on matters that affected their people. In the case of the *Phoenix*, the non-Indian reaction was to shut down the publication through intimidation, arrests of tribal leaders and white sympathizers, and ultimately confiscation of the printing plant (Littlefield and Parins 1984). The success of the *Phoenix* was that it was a powerful, native-produced propaganda tool that articulated the concerns of the Cherokee, their perspectives on removal, and their support for the Cherokee cause in their struggle to maintain their sovereignty in their homeland. Although the *Phoenix* was closed in Georgia, the newspaper re-emerged in the west in 1844 with the publication of the *Cherokee Advocate*, another publication that focused on reaffirming the dignity of the Cherokee people as "civilized" human beings and members of a sovereign nation. The *Advocate* remained in publication until 1853, but it was restarted in 1871 and continued printing until 1906, when the Cherokee government was dissolved.

Other tribes followed the example of the Cherokee publications and published their own newspapers in Indian Territory, largely focused on American Indian and tribal affairs in response to the continued encroachment upon Indian land by non-Indian populations. The Creek nation's *Indian Journal*, the Choctaw nation's *Choctaw News* and *Indian Champion*, and the Minnesota Chippewa nation's *Tomahawk*, were all published before 1924 and all followed the tribally published, pro-Indian format that began with the *Cherokee Phoenix*.

Tribal newspapers were essentially propaganda tools for tribal governments and were heavily biased toward the opinions and editorial slant of those in power.

Nontribal Indian newspapers, on the other hand, were owned and operated by professional native journalists who had a flair for the "business" of newspaper publishing. Nontribal newspapers were relatively freer in their editorial views and often wrote controversial articles that opposed "official" governmental positions on tribal affairs. Some nontribal papers and periodicals were published outside of native society and were read primarily by non-natives. However, the majority of nontribal publications were written, edited, and published in Indian country and enjoyed a native and non-native readership. The first of these nontribal newspapers was published by the Choctaws (*Choctaw Telegraph;* the *Choctaw Intelligencer*), the Chickasaws (*Chickasaw Intelligencer; Chickasaw and Choctaw Herald*), and the Cherokee—two Cherokee cousins, John Rollin Ridge and Elias C. Boudinot, were editors of several newspapers within and out of Indian Territory, and their publications reflected their differing political views (Littlefield and Parins 1984). Nontribal press continued to thrive in Indian Territory until around the turn of the twentieth century and the enactment of the Curtis Act of 1898. The Five Civilized Tribes of Indian Territory (Oklahoma) were among the last to undergo allotment and the dissolution of tribal governments, but this did not quell the enthusiasm and commitment to Indian journalism that had blossomed in the years leading up to the Curtis Act. The native press continued, and although nontribal press witnessed a decline in Oklahoma, it flourished in the Midwest, Great Lakes, and other areas with significant native populations. Littlefield and Parins (1984) summarize the importance of nontribal press, saying:

> The nontribal press, then, represents one of those familiar ironies in American and Alaska Native history. In the nineteenth century, the nontribal press contributed to the breakdown in tribal autonomy. It fed upon internal tribal conflicts, which contributed in large measure, either directly or indirectly, to its growth. The cause of these conflicts was usually federal Indian policy. That policy, especially as it related to education, contributed to the flourishing of the nontribal press in the early twentieth century. Ironically, it also led to the establishment of periodicals that were attempts at Indian unity and were voices for reform in Indian policy. (xviii)

PAN-INDIANISM AND THE PROLIFERATION OF THE INDIAN PRESS

In addition to tribal and nontribal press publications were Native American periodicals and intertribal publications that conveyed a pan-Indian perspective on events and issues that affected American Indians and Alaska Natives as a special interest group. These types of publications were usually "propagandistic or political in purpose" (Littlefield and Parins 1984, xviii). Largely twentieth-century newspapers and periodicals, they conveyed the responses of most Native Americans toward the federal Indian policies that had devastated tribes over the previous centuries, particularly policies such as Indian removal, allotment, and off-reservation boarding schools. Periodicals became increasingly important during this period because they articulated native concerns in a format that allowed an opportunity for reflection on topics of interest, whereas newspapers "have a greater effect on public opinion ... because of their immediacy" (Danky 1984, xvi) due to deadlines that have to be met in response to the developing events of a news story. Of course, the American Indian and Alaska Native press was reacting to white newspaper accounts of Native Americans that were decidedly negative, conveying Native American–white relations without the inclusion of the native voice. The white press of the late nineteenth and early twentieth centuries dominated any public discussion about Native Americans and Alaska Natives, and rarely did the American public become exposed to the native voice of that period. Andre Lopez produced a compilation of non-native newspaper accounts of Native Americans between 1885 and 1910 entitled *Pagans in Our Midst* (1980), which shows how Native Americans were referred to and treated by white journalists of the time. In response to the public opinion being formed around the turn of the twentieth century, Indian advocacy publications sought to address the many grievances that angered Indians, and reform organizations were being formed to garner support for Indian causes. The *Quarterly Journal of the Society of American Indians* (later the *American Indian Magazine*) was Indian owned and operated. The articles in the magazine reflected the sentiments of the reform movement and were often in support initiatives aimed at abdicating federal wardship responsibilities and further attempting the assimilation of the Native American population into mainstream America. Dr. Carlos Montezuma, dissatisfied with the "conservative" agenda of the Society of American Indians, left the organization and advocated for the elimination of the Bureau of Indian Affairs (BIA) in his own publication, *Wassaja* (Iverson 1982).

There were other pan-Indian or intertribal periodical and newspapers that voiced the concerns of a plethora of "progressive" American native movements and organizations, but a few focused on more localized or specific concerns, for example, *War-Whoop*, the *California Indian Herald*, and the *Alaska Fisherman*, all of which added their voices to the chorus of indigenous Americans advocating reform of the administration of Indian affairs by the federal government.

Another important contribution to Native American print media came from literary contributors in Indian country. A rich and enduring history of native writing has appeared in a variety of literary outlets, including weekly and monthly papers, school newsletters, and literary periodicals. The publication of the *Muzzinygun* marked the founding of Indian literary periodicals in 1826. Literary periodicals contained original stories, traditional stories, poetry, essays, and narratives by American Indians in the English language. Of particular interest were the writings of students attending off-reservation boarding schools, as they conveyed both the formal prose monitored and edited by school officials, and journal entries that often gave insight into the informal, yet disturbing daily life in these total institutions. For the most part, however, these literary products were clear demonstration of the effects of acculturation of native people into American life and their mastery of their non-native language, English. It was this period that produced some exceptional American Indian writers like Charles Alexander Eastman (Ohiyesa), who wrote *From the Deep Woods to Civilization* (1916), and Gertrude Simmons Bonnin (Zitkala Sa), author of *American Indian Stories* (1921). The two were schoolmates at Carlisle Indian Industrial School.

Assimilationists lauded the establishment of off-reservation boarding schools and the curriculum of the schools that came after the Indian school at Carlisle, Pennsylvania (established in 1879), and emphasized the complete transition to "English-only" language studies that concomitantly served as impetus for early influences in Indian "progressive" publications. *Eadle Keahtah Toh* and the *Carlisle Arrow and Red Man* were government-funded Indian school publications that advocated assimilationist federal Indian policy and were showpieces demonstrating the progress that "civilizing" efforts were making. Other Indian schools patterned their publications after the propagandistic model begun at Carlisle. *Talks and Thoughts of Hampton Indian Students*, the *Pipe and Peace*, the *Indian News*, and the *Chemawa American* were produced by Indian students before the end of the nineteenth century. The *Redskin*, the *Sherman Bulletin*, the *Indian School Journal*, the *Chilocco News*, the *Weekly Review*, the *Albuquerque Indian*, and the *Peace Pipe* were twentieth-century variants that served as instructional tools and public relations media while providing students and others with local news and subjects of interest (Littlefield and Parins 1984, xviii).

Although off-reservation boarding school printing presses turned out several newspapers, reservation school publications proved more successful as propaganda vehicles because they were more widely distributed to the Indian population and carried news of local interest to their readership. It is not certain whether these reservation and nonreservation school publications had an overall positive impact on the Indian population; however, they provided a means for Indians who would later write critical and insightful articles and books about American Indians and Alaska Natives to publish their early attempts at English poetry and prose. Simon J. Ortiz (poet), D'Arcy McNickle (writer and activist), Jim Northrup (syndicated columnist), and Tim Giago (journalist and publisher) are all boarding school graduates who have had successful careers as authors and journalists. Some wrote poems and narratives from their remembrances of Indian school, while others have woven images and feelings their experiences into the tapestry of their songs, for example, singer, songwriter, and actor Floyd Red Crow Westerman's *Boarding School Blues*. Regardless of the genre or medium, each aforementioned person alludes to the fact that Indian boarding school has had a profound impact on their lives.

Perhaps the most significant aspect of Native American print media in the twentieth century was that America's indigenous journalists and publishers had established themselves within the industry and continued to produce works that were distinctively American Indian or Alaska Native in content and style. At a time when most of the non-native population was willing to leave "the Indian" in the historical past, a relic of the nineteenth century, native press continued to publish newspapers, periodicals, poems, and literature about the contemporary lives of Native Americans. Indians and other natives were especially aware of the actions and repercussions of changes in federal Indian policy, and their reactions are well documented in native publications. Unlike publications of the nineteenth century with their overarching influence of the "civilizers," contemporary twentieth-century Indian and other native publications were generated, edited, and published for native peoples. It seems that Indian schools, churches, and other services (agencies) had an agenda aimed at fine-tuning the assimilation process with propaganda and reinforcement of mainstream American values, morality, and spirituality, and uncensored Indian publications were frowned upon in "official" circles.

In the late 1960s and early 1970s, a generation of Native Americans experienced a renaissance in the writings of articulate, well-educated, and serious native poets, journalists, and authors. Coined the Native American Renaissance by Kenneth Lincoln (1983), this was a period of revitalization by native writers in all genres of print media. Several outstanding writers from Indian country appeared at this time, including N. Scott Momaday, Leslie Marmon Silko, Simon J. Ortiz, and Louise Erdrich. Subsequently, in 1984 native writers witnessed the establishment of the American Indian Press Association (AIPA), which was the founding organization for what is today the Native American Journalists Association. The AIPA was not around long, but it was committed to the ethical and principled standards of a professional and free press association. Its first leader, Richard LaCourse, was considered by many to be the embodiment of all that is good in native journalism; he was highly principled and idealistic, and his journalistic standards were rigorous. It was not for lack of dedicated journalists that the association folded; rather, it was because of funding, which continues to plague native peoples in general, who are some of the poorest of America's poor. There are no publishing tycoons in Indian Country. However, most tribal newspapers and periodicals continue their work by the standards that were central to the AIPA.

Contemporary American Indian and Alaska Native contributors to print media owe tremendous gratitude to the forerunners of today's native writers, editors, and publishers. Today, there are hundreds of Indian and native publications: newspapers, periodicals, books, articles, and essays. Traditional styles have been passed from one generation to the next by the power of the printed word, and that power has become an important tool for native peoples who continue to thrive and prosper in spirit and intelligence because of their relationship to native media and their respect for the power of the written, as well as the spoken, word.

DIGITIZATION

Digital technology has already made a tremendous impact on the way we communicate in the twenty-first century. Traditional print media will continue to be produced; however, we are witnessing a significant shift in our patterns of information gathering, dissemination, and processing that increasingly limit the power that the printed word once enjoyed. Both native and non-native media outlets (newspapers and periodicals) have their online variants, and with advances in technology, many traditional printing operations have either closed, down-sized their operation, or transitioned to online publications that provide more up-to-the-minute information that people need to keep abreast of people, places, and events that impact their lives. Just as television revolutionized the entertainment industry in the 1950s, new technologies have revolutionized all forms of communication media. What was once the province of newsrooms and wire services is now interpersonal and available to anyone with a smart phone. No longer do people have to wait until an event is reported in the newspaper or broadcast on the nightly news—one simply has to tap an "app," and information in audio, video, or type format will appear on a tiny liquid crystal display (LCD) screen of any number of mobile devices. Ironically, although good for short-term use of information, digitized information presents a new series of storage and archiving problems that remain to be resolved.

Native publishers, constrained by budgets, often miss out on the benefits that advanced technology brings. Also, tribal communities represent some of America's poorest communities, where computers and personal digital assistants (PDAs) are too expensive to own or where Internet service may not exist. Such communities may depend almost entirely on weekly, biweekly, or monthly newspapers or newsletters to keep informed about local and native-specific events. It may be a long time before many tribal cultures incorporate digital paperless transactions and document storage.

Nonetheless, several Native American newspapers have transitioned to electronic format in their news delivery system while still producing paper-only versions for subscribers that require a printed version. For example, two national Native American publications, *Indian Country Today* and *News from Indian Country*, produce electronic versions of their newspapers, and several tribal weekly newspapers such as the *Navajo Times, Sho-Ban News, Char-Koosta News*, and *Lakota Country Times* have web-based news and information delivered over the Internet (NativeWeb Resources 2011).

The future of native print media is uncertain, but the Native American Journalists Association has been committed to promoting and mentoring young and aspiring native journalists since its founding in 1984 (Littlefield 2006). In addition, other organizations are involved in initiatives to ensure the survival of print and other forms of media that disseminate and preserve native thought far into the future. Wordcraft Circle of Native Writers and Storytellers—an outgrowth of the 1992 conference in Norman, Oklahoma, called Returning the Gift—has been an ongoing effort to give support to both emerging and professional Native American and indigenous writers throughout North and South America. Native Writers Circle of the Americas is another organization that awards Native American writers for their accomplishments in poetry, prose, and lifetime achievements. Contemporary magazines such as *SAY, Native Youth, Native Peoples*, and *Native Americas* are dedicated to providing American and Alaska Natives with news and information on contemporary social, political, and cultural issues in Indian country. In short, with the assistance of organizations like NAJA and others, American Indians and Alaska Natives are dedicated to preserving their past and ensuring their future by writing their stories and histories in newspapers, periodicals, and other printed materials, from a native perspective and in their own voice.

REFERENCES

Danky, James P. (Ed.). *Native American Periodicals and Newspapers, 1828–1982*, Westport, CT: Greenwood Press, 1984.

Francis, Lee. *Native Time: A Historical Time Line of Native America*. New York: St. Martin's, 1996.

Iverson, Peter. *Carlos Montezuma and the Changing World of American Indians*, Albuquerque: University of New Mexico Press, 1982.

Lincoln, Kenneth. *Native American Renaissance*. Berkeley and Los Angeles: University of California Press, 1983.

Littlefield, Daniel F., Jr. and James W. Parins. *American Indian and Alaskan Native Newspapers and Periodicals, 1826–1924*, Vol. 1. Westport, CT: Greenwood Press, 1984.

Littlefield, Daniel F., Jr. *Celebrating 178 Years of Native Journalism*. Panel discussion: Plenary Session at the annual meeting of the Native American Journalists Association, Tulsa, OK, August 10, 2006.

Lopez, Andre. *Pagans in Our Midst*, Rooseveltown, NY: Akwesasne Notes, 1980.

NativeWeb Resources. "Resources for Indigenous Cultures around the World," 2011. Retrieved from http://www.nativeweb.org/resources/news_media_television_radio/newspapers_native_indigenous/ on October 30, 2011.

Parins, James W. *Elias Cornelius Boudinot: A Life on the Cherokee Border*. Lincoln: University of Nebraska Press, 2005.

Parins, James W. *John Rollin Ridge: His Life and Works*. Lincoln: University of Nebraska Press, 1991.

Parins, Jim. "The Genius of Sequoyah." *ANPA Tribal Writers Digital Library*, July 2005. Retrieved from http://anpa.ualr.edu/digital_library/The%20Genius%20of%20Sequoyah.htm on September 29, 2011.

Trahant, Mark N. *Pictures of Our Nobler Selves*. Nashville: Freedom Forum First Amendment Center, 1995.

SECTION 9
ENVIRONMENT

American Indians and Solid Waste

Benjamin Lawson

"Ancient mariners told of the Flying Dutchman, a phantom ship eternally doomed to sail the waters around the Cape of Good Hope, never making port. In the Gulf of Mexico last week the real-life vessel *Mobro 4,000* seemed as damned as the Dutchman as it searched in vain for a friendly harbor. Southern ports had good reason for turning away the bereft barge: it was loaded with 3,168 tons of rancid, fly-infested trash from New York" (Lamar, Kane, and Kinsley 1987).

Reports of wandering trash barges, such as this one from *Time* in 1987, on New York's *Mobro*, brought waste management to the forefront of public consciousness across the United States in the late 1980s, but these barges' odyssey was emblematic of not just a moment in modern urban history, but of a long and complex policy debate over how to dispose of waste. This sense of impending waste crisis began in the large urban centers of the Northeast United States, but it soon spread across North America. After the mid-1990s, once the crisis mentality had subsided somewhat, Native American tribal lands became one of the focal points, or "problem areas," that remain in the ongoing debate over solid waste.

Indeed, the problems of inadequate solid waste disposal are among the most pressing issues currently facing many tribes. Waste disposal policy is extremely complex and is at once a social, political, economic, and environmental issue—finding a successful policy requires juggling economic considerations with political networks, and deflecting community resistance to siting disposal units nearby their homes. In particular, contemporary American Indian tribes face several issues. First, the inherent inadequacies of the United States' solid waste disposal policies limit the effectiveness of their application to tribal lands. Second, the federal government does not have authority to impose its regulations on tribal lands, yet

Tugboats haul garbage in New York Harbor south of the Verrazano-Narrows Bridge on May 17, 1987. The barge contains garbage from Islip, New York City, and Nassau County, New York. After eight weeks on the water, the New York City police gave their okay for the barge to moor in the harbor until a final determination for disposal was made. (AP Photo/David Bookstaver)

it seeks to obtain tribal compliance through other means. Sometimes tribes feel this relationship does not serve their interests well. Despite these two considerations, many tribes have opted to adopt federal waste disposal guidelines in order to obtain funding and technical assistance in cleaning up polluted dumps and establishing safer alternatives. Unsanctioned open dumps are of particular concern to many tribes; tribal leaders and the Environmental Protection Agency (EPA) have developed programs to combat illegal practices, but lack of economic resources and lack of education about the environmental hazards of illegal dumping or burning means that this practice remains widespread. In 1998, the Indian Health Service (IHS) reported that roughly 1,100 open dumps, of which 142 are "high-threat" sites, were on tribal land; for cleanup, the IHS estimated a cost of $126 million. Though federal agencies like the EPA provide assistance, the regulation of sanitary disposal and the cleanup of contaminated sites remains a huge issue.

A BRIEF HISTORY OF WASTE DISPOSAL

The history of waste disposal policy and breakthroughs in sanitary engineering provides insight into why solid waste disposal continues to pose significant problems for Indian tribes as well as the United States as a whole. The importance of developing effective waste disposal techniques was poorly understood until the nineteenth century—earlier, the relationship between inadequate disposal and the outbreak of disease was not understood. Nineteenth-century reformers viewed waste disposal primarily as a matter of human health. Although these reformers mistakenly attributed the outbreak of disease to the "miasma theory," which viewed filth and bad odors as the cause, they were correct in focusing on the removal of garbage from places where people would come into regular contact with it. Once scientists understood the role of germs, or bacteria, viruses and fungi, as the agents of infection, more efficient disposal techniques like the sanitary landfill and incineration became widespread.

After World War II, increased consumption rates, disposable packaging, and population growth led to innovative waste disposal techniques across the United States. Prior to the 1900s, nearly every community in the United States relied on open dumping on land or water as the primary method for solid waste disposal. Alternative technologies, such as the incinerator, were expensive, inefficient, and spewed noxious odors and chemicals. After World War II, most urban areas in the United States turned to the sanitary landfill, a dump where waste is compacted and covered daily to reduce odors and vermin such as rats and cockroaches, but many tribal communities, like many small towns until the early 1980s, continued to rely on open dumping. The 1976 Resource Conservation and Recovery Act (RCRA) outlawed open dumping in the United States; and the 1984 Hazardous Waste Act closed the remaining loopholes that had allowed some communities to sidestep RCRA at first. The move away from reliance on open dumping is highly significant in ecological and public health terms because sanitary landfills represent a huge environmental improvement over open dumping.

Today, the sanitary landfill is the most common method of waste disposal. Early experiments with improving open dumps occurred in 1904 in Champaign, Illinois, and in the 1910s in Seattle, Davenport, Iowa, and New Orleans. A similar method, controlled tipping, was also developed in England around the same time, where waste was put in lined trenches. Other cities, notably San Francisco and New York, developed variations of sanitary landfills in the 1930s. Jean Vincenz, the sanitary commissioner in Fresno, California, in the 1930s, was the innovator of the type of sanitary landfill that became widespread after it became the official U.S. Army policy in World War II, and in 1943, the U.S. Public Health Service recommended it for municipalities. What distinguished Vincenz's model was that he both covered waste daily with several inches of dirt to curb the threat of disease and noxious odors as well as to keep out rats, and he also divided the fill into compartments and compressed the waste before dumping. Although many sanitary experts understood that sanitary landfills were an environmental improvement to open dumps, most cities and towns in the United States decided not to implement them until forced to under RCRA.

Much of the existing accounts of tribal waste disposal stress the failures of tribes to keep pace with federal guidelines. But, as the brief summary of the history of waste management in the United States shows, it is important to remember that only recently did the federal government establish a clear and environmentally safe standard. In fact, since the nineteenth century, the moments of uncertainty outweigh the moments of clarity; improving waste disposal has been a process of trial and error as policymakers and engineers have sought to define and address the problems. Consequently, it is true that the EPA has focused on addressing the problems on tribal reservations in recent years, but that primarily reflects the EPA's awareness that it is in the interest of all to implement the relatively new environmental standards as much as possible throughout North America.

TRIBAL AUTHORITY AND FEDERAL POLICY

Federal policy has been the primary determinant of waste-disposal regulations, for tribes as well as for communities across the United States. Yet awareness of the environmental hazards of inadequate solid waste disposal did not garner much attention until the late 1960s, beginning with the 1965 Solid Waste Disposal Act, and has taken hold only with the regulatory and advisory efforts of the EPA since the late 1970s. Since then, rising public awareness, strict federal regulation, and well-publicized pollution of specific sites has led to widespread recognition that pollution due to poor disposal of solid waste is on par with air and water pollution.

One reason solid waste rapidly came to be seen a pressing issue in the 1960s was due to the rise of an activist environmental movement. This movement began, in part, due to influential exposés such as Rachel Carson's 1962 book *Silent Spring* about the negative effects of pesticides on ecosystems. Tragic examples of the health problems posed by unregulated dumps where toxic waste was buried, most famously at Love Canal near Buffalo, New York, in 1979, also played a part. Following these events, most U.S. policymakers and engineers finally recognized that solid waste posed an equally menacing pollution threat as unclean air or water. The increased environmental awareness concerning solid waste eventually influenced tribes as well; as one Native American stated in a 2002 EPA interview, "We never heard environmental messages growing up. We weren't aware of the dangers in our environment. I remember we sprayed our apple orchards with DDT and our cows with a substance to control flies. It wasn't until the creation of the various environmental agencies that we heard these things were dangerous" (EPA 2002, 3).

To address solid waste disposal problems nationwide, Congress passed a series of laws, beginning in earnest with the 1965 Solid Waste Act and the 1970 creation of the EPA as part of the Clean Air Act. Demonstrating the federal government's new level of commitment, between 1965 and 1970, the amount allocated for

> ## TRIBAL WASTE JOURNAL
>
> The *Tribal Waste Journal* is published by the Environmental Protection Agency (EPA) to help tribes with plans, policies, and implementation regarding sold waste. One section of Issue 8, from July 2011, dealt with open dumping on tribal lands. The section is reproduced in part here from the EPA website.
>
> > Open dumping continues to be a problem on tribal lands due to many factors including the lack of access to convenient, affordable disposal sites for: bulky materials, electronic waste (e-waste), tires, vehicles, and household hazardous waste. Other challenges include complex open dump sites that are difficult to clean, close, and maintain, as well as lack of funding for solid waste management alternatives to open dumping. In this issue of the Tribal Waste Journal, you will hear from tribal waste managers responsible for initiating, maintaining, and fostering support for new programs that provide ways to prevent open dumping....
> >
> > In this issue, you will find information on the many different types of waste you may find in open dumps. These include bulky items, old appliances, and hazardous waste (such as old paint or batteries) which are not collected along with other household waste. In many of the featured stories, special programs were initiated to focus on the collection and disposal of these along with other waste streams.
> >
> > It is important to have waste management programs in place before, or along with, efforts to clean up open dumps. Cleaning and closing open dumps may only solve part of the problem. If tribal members do not have another means of disposal, new open dumps may occur. To help you determine sustainable alternatives to open dumping, we have included information on different waste management strategies for your tribe. These include building a new transfer station or initiating a new collection service for tribal members.
> >
> > Based on the stories enclosed in this issue, we developed a list of six key elements of success. These key elements include: collaboration, support, education, sustainability, perseverance, and respect. Keep an eye out for these elements as you read through the issue.
>
> *Source*: Tribal Waste. U.S. EPA. Retrieved from http://www.epa.gov/epawaste/wyl/tribal/pdftxt/twj-8.pdf

research, training, demonstration projects (such as a model sanitary landfill to show how one should function), planning, and providing direct assistance was $59,274,000. In addition to providing federal money for state and local planning, the 1965 Solid Waste Act encouraged states and large urban areas to develop detailed future-oriented municipal solid waste (MSW) management plans. The federal government also sponsored conferences on MSW disposal, such as one held in St. Louis in September 1969 to consider the effects of the 1965 legislation for engineers and policymakers, which helped spread the word about what was, and was not, working. The most significant role of the 1965 Solid Waste Disposal Act was that it focused attention on existing disposal practices and highlighted their weaknesses.

State governments in particular felt the need to consolidate their authority at this time because, as a 1973 task force reported, "*most* local governments are presently incapable" of creating and managing a complicated MSW system (EPA 1973, ix). For example, California published a study related to statewide disposal in 1968, as part of its first comprehensive plan that was completed in 1970. This study found that due to the lack of a top-down plan, local disposal had "an inevitable lack of consistency" and was "deficient" on several counts. In fact, despite acceptance of sanitary landfills as the preferred method, the report lamented that only 10 percent of California's dumps could be classified as such, and that the state was facing an "impending crisis" (EPA 1971, v). By 1970, it was clear that most states were not up to the task of funding, regulating, and providing technical expertise; such a program required the direct involvement of the federal government in solid waste disposal planning and regulation, as well as providing funding to state and local agencies.

The most significant federal law for solid waste was the Resource Conservation and Recovery Act, first passed in 1976, of which Subtitle D dealt with MSW. Subtitle D gave states the authority to develop programs in accordance with federal guidelines for nonhazardous solid waste disposal. The EPA is the federal office in charge of establishing guidelines that states must follow. For Indian tribes, the authority of the EPA is more complex; federal and state regulations apply only under specific circumstances. In general, Subtitle D standards are not applicable to tribal land, but they may apply to a particular disposal site like a sanitary landfill on tribal land. To clarify the applicability of its regulations to tribal lands and demonstrate the benefits of compliance, the EPA has developed targeted funding incentives and educational programs specifically for tribal authorities.

Public health, preventing ecological destruction, and developing methods to "conserve material and energy" through re-use of materials, was the main stated goal of RCRA. These goals, in the words of one RCRA spokesperson at a public hearing held in Chicago on March 21, 1977, were "expected to be achieved through technical and financial assistance and through local government; prohibition of open dumping, conversion of existing dumps, and the regulation of hazardous waste" (EPA 1977, 33). To promote awareness of RCRA, the EPA held 10 public conferences in major cities in early 1977—significantly, the spokespeople readily acknowledged the federal government's past failures to effectively engage with the public, perhaps as a means to emphasize that increased federal regulation would not rob people of their political voice. Regardless, grassroots opposition to waste disposal policy—specifically the siting of facilities—remained strong.

In 1984, Congress passed the Hazardous and Solid Waste Act and strengthened the 1976 Resource Conservation and Recovery Act. This 1984 tweaking directly led to the widespread closure of existing landfill sites, and required state-of-the-art sanitary landfills with features like a base lining to prevent leakage of toxic chemicals, and strict rules outlawing the establishment of landfills in environmentally sensitive locations. For example, dumping in wetlands and salt marshes, once viewed as the perfect place for dumping waste, was outlawed. Based on these laws, the EPA also issued specific compliance requirements for landfills in 1979 and in 1993, which were sufficiently strict to force the closure of the majority of the existing landfills in the United States. This switch in attitude—the recognition that open dumping had serious health effects—is the foundation for ongoing efforts to combat open dumping on tribal lands.

Tribal landfills, however, were not directly subject to these laws and the EPA's requirements. In fact, the Supreme Court ruled against the EPA's attempts to force tribal compliance; so the EPA turned to offering tribes financial incentives to comply with its standards. For example, "EPA solid waste funds may pay for a new position, contractor support, the development and printing of public outreach materials, supplies, minor equipment purchases, and project-related travel" such as attending workshops to be educated on alternative options such as source reduction, or creating less waste in the first place, and on "green" disposal options such as recycling (EPA "Waste Management," n.d.).

Typically, the EPA awards solid waste grants to fund projects that clean up open dumps and draft plans for alternative disposal strategies. Much of the administration of EPA programs is done regionally though branch offices. For example, the EPA's Region 9, which includes the Pacific west, has its own solid waste program, which seeks to meet regional needs and partner with local government agencies and nonprofit organizations.

To promote compliance with its standards, the EPA has partnered with tribal communities to educate Native Americans about the inherent benefits of environmentally sound waste disposal. The use of media, such as the *Tribal Waste Journal*, is one way the EPA does this. In the *Tribal Waste Journal*, the EPA has published human-interest success stories from specific tribes and personal interviews of specific individuals to demonstrate how EPA-funded tribal policies have real-life impact on tribes. For example, in the May 2002 issue, it described the success of the Alabama-Coushatta tribe's successful EPA-funded new transfer station and how some tribal members "continued to use burn pits and other illegal disposal methods" until tribal leaders educated them about the benefits of the station as well as the health and environmental hazards of illegal dumping and burning.

Cleanup of old sites and developing new sanitary disposal sites remains a primary concern of tribal officials and the EPA. This is a serious issue for cities and towns across the United States, as well as on tribal lands. Nationwide, in a few cases, affluent cities strapped for green space are presently redeveloping their closed landfills into giant public parks. In other cases, little has been done except environmental cleanup. Historically, most tribes relied on open dumping, so the cleanup and redevelopment process for most tribes is to close the open dump or clear away the garbage heap, if necessary to take steps to minimize ongoing pollution and develop new disposal strategies.

One example of an EPA tribal success story, as reported in a March 2003 EPA newsletter entitled "Open Dump Cleanup Project Helps Tribes Fight Waste," is the Pueblo of Taos tribe's use of federal grants to close and cap its 5.4-acre open dump and develop a new plan for solid waste management. The open dump had been a health and environmental threat because it was located in proximity to residential homes and the tribe's water source, the Rio Pueblo. EPA grants also enabled post-closure maintenance and monitoring, such as the instillation of features to minimize continuing contamination of groundwater from the dump's leachate. Instead of constructing another local dump, for the short term, the tribe decided to contract with Waste Management, Inc. As a long-term solution, the tribe decided to construct its own local solid waste transfer station. Although tribal leaders were the most important policymakers, federal agencies played a significant role in terms of funding, providing technical assistance, and assisting with drafts of future disposal plans.

For the most part, tribal leaders have accepted the EPA's input. In 1986, for example, when Americans for Indian Opportunity (AIO) submitted a comprehensive survey of waste disposal practices on reservations, Ladonna Harris, the founder of AIO, praised the EPA: "EPA's Indian policy reflects principles in accordance with the goals and objectives of" Native American tribes (EPA 1986, preface, unnumbered document).

However, not all tribes were willing to work with AIO and the EPA—in the 1986 survey, of the 74 reservations of varying sizes that were sent surveys, only 51 (69 percent) took the time to respond. Of those tribes that did respond, however, many took the time to record detailed accounts of the self-assessed shortcomings of their reservations' waste disposal systems. Some noted violations of state standards, for example, the Cabazon reservation noted that there had been violations in 1984 and 1985 of California's bacteriological standards in groundwater, although there the tribe had been unable to locate the specific source of the water pollution.

Nationwide, citizen protest against the social inequalities embodied in waste disposal has long been a significant issue. In the nineteenth century, social reformers in cities such as New York and Chicago focused on cleaning up areas populated mainly by impoverished immigrants. Many of these immigrants survived as scavengers of open dumps, a form of recycling, or re-use of discarded materials. Then, as now, the wealthy create more waste, but the impoverished are the ones who live alongside it. Since the 1970s, grassroots social protests against the prevalence of unhealthful waste disposal sites in low-income or minority areas (environmental justice) have refocused attention on the implied power structure and health impact of waste disposal policy. The environmental justice movement began with minority groups speaking up against policies that force the impoverished and minorities to disproportionately live near waste treatment facilities such as landfills or transfer stations—places where garbage is deposited by trucks and compressed and loaded on more fuel-efficient trucks, trains, or barges for transfer to the landfill. Because minorities, like the impoverished, are more likely to live nearby where policymakers choose to site these facilities, many activist groups argue that 'environmental racism' is a better term.

Although tribal reservations tend to be separated from the urban areas where environmental justice protests have been most prominent, the larger issue of power relations and inequality does apply. One issue is that with the recent privatization of waste, the large regional landfills serving urban areas are now often located in rural areas, and hence waste from a large city like New York can affect communities thousands of miles away. Even more directly, however, is the cultural conflict of interest: some tribes feel their traditional way of life is threatened. For example, in 1990, the Yakima Indian Nation (YIN) in Washington State expressed concern to the EPA about that state's proposed policy revisions. The tribe cited its 1855 treaty with the United States, in which "it ceded land to the United States Government (land, which subsequently became 25.4% of the State of Washington), and the U.S. Government guaranteed the YIN certain rights (fishing, hunting, etc., at 'all usual and accustomed places')." Specifically, the Yakima Nation was concerned that the state's proposed project would "affect the Yakima way of life, its cultural resources, the freedom to practice religion on tribal and ceded lands, or the promises guaranteed in the Treaty of 1855" (EPA 1990, RO 13421). As this example shows, the relationship between tribes and state or federal government is tenuous, and although environmentalism, in terms of public and ecological health, is a common ground, tensions remain.

Like the environmental justice movement at large, tribal concerns make it clear that unequal power relations as well as political and economic assumptions underlie public works projects like solid waste management. Waste disposal is at once an engineering, political, economic, and social/cultural decision-making process. Waste barges brought awareness of a waste crisis to mainstream Americans in the 1980s, but the real problems and questions regarding waste disposal run much deeper than finding a new location or community willing to burn or bury our waste.

REFERENCES

Lamar, Jacob V. Jr, Joseph J. Kane, and Susan Kinsley, "Don't Be a Litterbarge." *Time*, May 4, 1987, 1–2.

Melosi, Martin. *Garbage in the Cities*. Pittsburgh: University of Pittsburgh Press, 1981 (revised 2005).

Melosi, Martin. *The Sanitary City*. Pittsburgh: University of Pittsburgh Press, 1991 (revised 2008).

U.S. Environmental Protection Agency (EPA). Initiating a National Effort to Improve Solid Waste Management. Washington: Government Printing Office, 1971.

U.S. Environmental Protection Agency (EPA). *Developing a State Resource Conservation and Recovery Program*. Washington: Government Printing Office, October 1979.

U.S. Environmental Protection Agency (EPA). *Survey of American Indian Environmental Protection Needs on Reservation Lands, 1986*. Submitted to the EPA by Americans for Indian Opportunity. Washington: Government Printing Office, September 1986.

U.S. Environmental Protection Agency (EPA). "YAKIAM [sic.] INDIAN NATION INVOLVEMENT IN RCRA ON TRIBAL AND CEDED LANDS," Note from Susan Absher to Sylvia Lowrance, Nov.5 1990 (RO 13421).

U.S. Environmental Protection Agency (EPA). "Safer Disposal for Solid Waste: The Federal Regulations for Landfills." Washington: Government Printing Office, March 1993.

U.S. Environmental Protection Agency (EPA). *Recycling Guide for Native American Nations*. Washington: Government Printing Office, June 1995. (EPA530-K-95-006).

U.S. Environmental Protection Agency (EPA). *Partnerships in Solid Waste Management*. Washington: Government Printing Office, December 1997. (EPA530-F-97-050).

U.S. Environmental Protection Agency (EPA). *Grant Resources for Solid Waste Activities in Indian Country*. Washington: Government Printing Office, August 1998. (EPA530-R-98-014).

U.S. Environmental Protection Agency (EPA). *Publications on Solid Waste Management in Indian Country*. Washington: Government Printing Office, August 1998. (EPA 530-B-98-004).

U.S. Environmental Protection Agency (EPA). *Training and Technical Assistance Directory for Tribal Solid Waste Managers*. Washington: Government Printing Office, March 1999. (EPA530-B-99-007).

U.S. Environmental Protection Agency (EPA). *Open Dump Cleanup Project Helps Tribes Fight Waste*. Washington: Government Printing Office, March 2003. (EPA530-F-03-005).

U.S. Environmental Protection Agency (EPA). *Tribal Decision-Makers Guide to Solid Waste Management*. Washington: Government Printing Office, November 2003. (EPA530-R-03-013€).

U.S. Environmental Protection Agency (EPA). *Catalog of Hazardous and Solid Waste Publications, Seventeenth Edition*. Washington: Government Printing Office, 2004.

U.S. Environmental Protection Agency (EPA). *Tribal Waste Journal*. Washington: Government Printing Office, May 2002 through September 2009. (EPA530-N-02-001 through EPA530-N-09-002).

U.S. Environmental Protection Agency (EPA) "RCRA Online." Retrieved from http://www.epa.gov/epawaste/inforesources/online/index.htm.

U.S. Environmental Protection Agency (EPA). "Waste Management in Indian Country." Retrieved from http://www.epa.gov/wastes/wyl/tribal/index.htm.

CLIMATE CHANGE

Chris Paci

Change over long periods is not readily noticed by most people, in particular for those of us removed from nature. Moreover, changes from one generation to the next can be forgotten. If no record is kept, it is easy to argue that the way we are today is the way we always were. One type of change that is being discussed a great deal in Native American communities, and elsewhere around the globe, is climate change. Most indigenous communities are uniquely sensitive and vulnerable to change, in particular those communities—or more precisely those segments of these communities—where people still practice traditions that place them in intimate contact with nature. How this is talked about is mostly based in cultural experience. For example, Bessa Blondin (Wandering Spirit 2005) outlined that the Sahtu Dené had prophecies passed down to her through oral tradition. Blondin was told that the Dené (literally, the people) would experience hardship starting in late 1900s to about 2025. There would be a lot of changes. Indigenous prophecies share in some ways the conclusions reached by climatologists: big change is coming, so be prepared. But what is climate change?

Climate change is from a scientific perspective—and by science we include both Western and indigenous knowledge—now accepted to mean that the earth's functions are being altered by human behavior, in particular by industrial development and population growth. Human activities are now at such a scale that the net result of these activities is influencing how natural systems function. Natural systems include the amount of rain and snow regions receive as well as the types of storms and their intensity and frequency. Human inputs to the environment are changing how these systems function. Most human impact comes from pollution and by-products of consumption. While nature can absorb a certain amount of human pollution, today's input is at such a scale that it now outstrips the natural capacity of these systems to absorb these inputs. It is argued that humans, collectively, are now changing the normal ecological balance of the planet, not just local ecological change from overfishing, deforestation, but system-wide changes in how the climate behaves.

Many aboriginal peoples, in particular elders, see climate change as a symptom of sickness. From a holistic perspective, everything is interconnected, that is, all living things, including rocks, water, and air. People are not removed from their environments; we are not superior to any other living thing in our world, and even rocks have life. All are part of nature, and all are connected to one another. This is no longer only a traditional perspective—it is the dominant mode of thinking that underlies ecological and environmental thinking. While some aboriginal peoples have turned their backs on this way of thinking, just like other parts of society, indigenous peoples are diverse; nature has not been removed from the equation.

While colonization has created radical changes to how indigenous peoples live in North America, some Americans and Canadians have adopted values that come from indigenous cosmologies, intentionally or not. By adopting a holistic perspective, many people have become aware that no matter how disconnected we may try to be from nature, we are only playing a dangerous game of isolationism. Beyond the material crisis that climate change represents, what remains unresolved for all cultures is an underlying conflict between our mode of production and way of life, with nature. It can be argued this is a spiritual and materialistic conflict, but it will be a conflict resolved only by becoming self-aware of our individual and collective contributions to the problem, addressing the problem by reducing our net contribution of greenhouse gases.

Climate is based on long-term measurement of meteorological phenomena in a given region. Information on climate patterns is based on data collected over the space of several decades, which provide information on seasonal variation in the atmosphere and on land and water, such as changes in temperature, humidity, precipitation, atmospheric pressure, the speed and direction of the winds, cloud cover, and sea surface temperatures. There is a certain degree of natural variation in climate, and seasonal variations are understood to be part of a stable pattern. Climate change, on the other hand, is indicated by variations beyond normal patterns and variation that can be attributed directly or indirectly to human behavior, in particular the release of greenhouse gases. These gases are primarily carbon dioxide and methane.

Al Gore, former vice president, observed that "what we do to nature we do to ourselves. The magnitude of environmental destruction is now on a scale few ever foresaw; the wounds no longer simply heal themselves" (2006, 161). He went on to argue that "by seizing the opportunity that is bound up in this crisis, we can unleash the creativity, innovation, and inspiration that are just as much a part of our human birthright as our vulnerability to greed and pettiness. The choice is ours. The responsibility is ours. The future is ours" (296). Gore and president of the Inuit

Circumpolar Conference, Sheila Watt-Cloutier, share the honor of having been recognized by the Nobel committee for their work raising public awareness about climate change. Watt-Cloutier's work focuses specifically on the Inuit and how climate change is a human rights issue. She was not awarded the Peace Prize, but Gore and the Intergovernmental Panel on Climate Change (IPCC) did. The extra dimension of this work is the mobilization of people, the awareness raising and education about the implications of what is an otherwise abstract and huge phenomenon. By making climate change impacts, drivers, and solutions easily comprehensible, these key figures have brought climate change to the dinner table, the classroom, and the floor of local, regional, and national governments. They have taken the scientific, international, and abstract and made it a neighborhood issue. They have unraveled the propaganda and spin of climate change deniers, which include a former U.S. president, and brought some semblance of sanity to the problem so that it can begin to be addressed.

Climate change is expressed in nature in many different ways, and communities adapting to change will follow a variety of strategies depending on both physical and social factors. Depending on a communities' altitude, proximity to bodies of water, or if it is in an arid environment, the impacts of climate change will be experienced differently. Adaptive responses will be subject to the relative behaviors and conditions of plants, birds, animals, and humans. Some will flourish whilst others will not. One thing that is certain for indigenous peoples the world over, in all of the change that has taken place since Europeans began to colonize traditional homelands, much has not changed for the better. By better we mean that the changes have improved spiritual and material conditions of life. Climate is now acting in a way that is far from predictable and bringing change that is not improving how vulnerable populations now live. Vulnerable populations include those who are sensitive to change, whose homes, infrastructure, food and fresh water supplies, and resiliency are subject to interruption. Poor communities lack the capacity to respond, adapt, and rebuild, and are most at risk.

Climate is driven by, and ultimately made up of, natural systems, including solar insulation, that is the amount of sunlight received by the surface of the earth. When discussing climate, most people talk about temperature, if it has rained or snowed, if these patterns match what we have known from the past, if it was what was forecasted. Outside the normal range, and people will get nervous. Most people listen to the weather forecast to know if they should put on a warm jacket or take an umbrella before they leave the house. This predictive ability is based on the forecasting of specialists, as we have lost much of our own ability to observe the complex feedback of nature to understand what is coming. It is more likely these days for us to watch colored cartoon-like images or satellite photos of time lapse wind and pressure systems on the evening news; most of us no longer look at clouds, stars, and the environment around us.

Today, we no longer exclusively relate climate to our immediate weather, through the successive patterns of the seasons for wherever we live. Climate is tied to the larger systems of hydrology and geography. In the past, these aspects of climate interacted with vegetation to produce largely predictable conditions that were relatively stable over long time periods, sometimes thousands or hundreds of thousands of years. Climate, to a great extent, continues to influence how we organize our societies, build our homes, and structure what we grow and produce. Climate is still driven by natural systems that inform one another, each influencing how the other systems function. The stability in climate, while relative and easily swayed by large-scale catastrophic events such as volcanoes and forest fires, meant that humans could grow settlements and adapt their means of production to best suit their environments. Human inputs to changes in climate were not much of a factor until the industrial revolution, and even then, not all people contributed negatively to the environment. It was the development of large urban centers and incredible advances in technology over the last 60 years as populations grew beyond historical carrying capacity. The change was slow and steady; not all cultures contributed to or understood change at the same pace. Some people were freed from meeting their basic survival needs, and the accumulation of wealth replaced the need to hunt or grow their own food. When people no longer needed to draw their own water or heat their homes with fuel they themselves gathered, and could live in large numbers in relative security, radical changes in nature were only a matter of time.

Commercial food production, municipal water systems, large-scale water diversion and hydro development, pipeline and refinery production of hydrocarbons—these are the basket of human ingenuity that have changed our natural environments. With minor exceptions, the small inputs of indigenous peoples have been relatively benign influences at the global scale. Large-scale system-wide change as a result of collective human activities was thought to be impossible until we entered the nuclear age. And to be frank, most of the change is a result of First World production and consumption of energy that has allowed a great deal of "improvement" in the human condition.

Indigenous peoples experience change differently depending on a number of variables. Adaptation is a function of how flexible we are, how we absorb shocks, and how able we are to mobilize resources to accommodate change. Not all change is bad, not all adaptations are good. In the 1990s, Wilfred Peltier (Anishnaabe), Elder in Residence at Carleton University, gave a seminar in which he talked about changes in nature. He talked about a meeting of community healers he had helped organize in the early 1980s, near Lake of the Woods. These medicine people came from all parts of North America to share their knowledge of plants. The main outcome of that meeting was the resounding agreement that everything was changing; medicines were not as strong, and many were harder to find than in the past. Many elders connected pollution and industrial impacts to the loss of strength of these plants. Overall, they argued that people were not respecting Mother Earth, and Mother Earth was responding.

The earth's climate has been radically altered by human activity, in particular through increasing urbanization and industrial development. Global warming, as climate change is being characterized, is the net result of our capacity to consume larger and larger quantities of fossil fuels, to heat our homes, to extend our lives, to produce our foods, to manufacture our products, to move us around the world in ways we never dreamed of 100 years ago. The problem with the term *global warming* is that climate change is not always being experienced as a warming; it is often experienced as a drying and wetting, a radical change in the intensity and frequency of storms, a cooling in some places, a gradual warming in others.

Consumption has been increasing with each generation and to all parts of the globe with little consideration for the costs or impacts it has on nature. This is not how indigenous peoples organize their economic activities, and historically all indigenous peoples had greater reverence and respect for nature. Despite this reverence, growth and technology of the larger society has become the norm for most people, including indigenous peoples. Modernization is difficult to resist, part in parcel with colonization, and both are changing indigenous worldviews. Most traditions are being lost to urbanization and modern life, our connections to nature fading or compartmentalized into vacations in parks. Until recently, it seemed there was no other way to live than to latch on to the flow of modernization, to build factories, to exploit natural resources, and thus to prosper along with the rest of society. The negative side effects to all this change are, however, giving all people cause to pause and to ask whether we are really on the right path.

Over the years, greenhouse gases released into the earth's atmosphere have accumulated and are building. Around 2002, a growing number of scientists, most of whom were climatologists, had been talking amongst themselves, mostly in an academic language that most people did not understand. These scientists began to openly discuss climate change—they still discussed the data and science at academic conferences, but they also translated their words into plain talk about greenhouse gases being trapped in the atmosphere. The media began to pick up on the otherwise convoluted message of climate change, leading to a more popular understanding of the increased risk that the accumulation of greenhouse gases was leading to irreversible changes in how our climate functioned. Problems like pollution, deforestation, and increased agricultural production were blamed as contributors to the problem. First World economies were blamed and poverty stricken Third World economies who sought a bigger slice of development were given a pass. Scientists warned that unlike the success of combatting long-range contaminants or fixing the ozone hole, climate change was irreversibly affecting the earth's atmosphere. Limiting the inputs that resulted in climate change would require society to make radical choices and large-scale decisions with herculean efforts.

For many indigenous peoples, in particular those who still practice traditions and harvest their own country food, the warning of change and solutions proposed to end the problem, resonated a great deal. It was nothing new, as many traditional peoples had been seeing changes in the health of animals and plants for generations. Often, indigenous people would say the earth was becoming unpredictable; they were witnessing a great deal of uncertainty and insecurity in their traditional territories, some of which was being prophesized.

It must be noted that the impacts of global climate change are being felt differently at different socioeconomic levels. Poor people experience climate change differently than the rich, just as poor countries experience climate change differently than developed countries. The unique cumulative impacts of climate change are being mitigated or ignored by a number of policy and resource modifications at the state, community, and household levels. The state ignores the impacts by arguing that it isn't real or isn't caused by human activity, or even if it is the economy is too fragile to do anything about it. One thing that is constant across all regions is that change is taking place.

Climate is one of those descriptive words that cover a lot of ground. It has always been part of the cosmologies and life ways of indigenous peoples. This essay discussed the relationship between climate change (global warming) and indigenous peoples. We started the essay by defining climate change. There have been efforts under the UN Framework Convention on Climate Change to reverse the changes. There are a number of significant regional climate assessment, such as the Arctic Climate Impact Assessment Report, that illustrate the kinds of work that can inform what is known today about climate change, its impacts, and what we can do to prepare and adapt to changes. In many aboriginal communities, people have been discussing the implications of climate change, both the prophecy and policy change that is required to adapt to change. Many traditional peoples are particular vulnerable and through risk management, they can begin to minimize these risks. Ultimately, halting global climate change will take the collective efforts of large national actors, industries, the First World, and the developing economies.

REFERENCES

Arctic Council. "The Changing Arctic: Indigenous Perspectives." In *Arctic Climate Impact Assessment*. New York: Cambridge University Press, 2005.

Gore, A. *An Inconvenient Truth: The Planetary Emergency of Global Warming and What We Can Do About It*. New York: Rodale Books. 2006.

Nuttall, Mark (Ed.). *Encyclopedia of the Arctic*. New York: Routledge, 2004.

Paci, C., C. Dickson, S. Nikels, H. M. Chan, and C. Furgal. "Food Security of Northern Indigenous Peoples in a Time of Uncertainty." In G. Duhaime and N. Bernard (Eds.), *Arctic Food Security*, Occasional publications 58. Edmonton: Canadian Circumpolar Institute Press, 2008.

Wandering Spirit, A. *The Dene in Denendeh: On the Top of the World*. Yellowknife, Northwest Territories, Canada: Dene Nation Production, 2005.

Environmental Racism

Patti Jo King

Devastating nineteenth-century Indian removal and reservation policies effectively reduced Indian lands to small islands within the American mainstream. The reservations set aside for tribes, primarily in the trans-Mississippi West, were largely remote tracts of land with seemingly little importance or economic worth. These lands, however, were later discovered to contain a variety of resources of immeasurable value. The monetary value of these resources is the most common factor behind all Native American environmental issues today. Land loss, location, and resource assessment, as well as the development or exploitation of those lands and resources almost always defines modern debates on environmental racism.

ECOCIDE

Assigned to these remnants of their former estates, native people eventually became the victims of a new kind of geopolitical racism that environmental scholars have called "ecocide" or "nuclear colonialism" (Hooks and Smith 2004). At the beginning of the twentieth century, the federal preoccupation with agriculture and grazing had already significantly changed the Indian landscape. In the high plains, Indians were encouraged to plow and repeatedly plant large fields of monoculture crops. Drought and the disastrous results of over cropping without rotation led to environmental catastrophes such as the Dust Bowl. Following World War II, these failures led the Indian Department to abandon its plans for long-term Indian agriculture. Furthermore, the adoption of domestic livestock brought about radical changes in landscape and biotic diversity of many reservation lands, particularly those in the Southwest. The government was unsuccessful in its attempts to solve the problems caused by overgrazing in these regions in the 1930s, and its sweeping programs of livestock reduction and reseeding, along with the introduction of new plant and animal species into already fragile ecosystems, only served to create bigger problems. As a consequence, the Southwestern tribes had to face a seemingly never-ending struggle with overgrazing, soil erosion, invasive noxious plants, and reclamation. Instead of creating a sustainable means of economic independence for tribes, these programs actually empowered the rise of greater Indian economic dependence on the federal government by largely ignoring native cultural ecological proclivities.

A number of reservations contained large, lush forests, making them likely targets for resource exploitation. Sales of government-managed timber industries among particular tribes in northern California, Oregon, Arizona, Minnesota, and Wisconsin, provided for them a new means of economic development. Gross and reckless mismanagement, such as clear-cutting and soil erosion, however, led to the unnecessary loss of thousands of acres of forest for almost all of these tribes. Lumbering operations that threatened sacred sites in areas such as the Black Hills of South Dakota and Taos Pueblo's Blue Lake region, created even further tension, mistrust, and anger between tribes and the federal government.

WATER POLITICS

Water has also been a central environmental issue in native lands, a scarce resource in the arid West that has pitted whites against tribes. In 1908, the Supreme Court issued a ruling in the pivotal case *Winters vs. the United States*. The case resulted from a situation at the Fort Belknap Reservation in Montana during which white settlers diverted water from the Milk River from the Fort Belknap community. The settlers were ordered to stop but argued that the Indians did not have prior appropriation use rights. The concept of prior appropriation is that the allocation of water of a particular stream is given to the first person to use it, or "first in time, first in right." The Winters decision states that when lands were first set aside as Indian reservations, Congress implied that the tribes who would live there would have first rights to the water for the purposes of agriculture and sustenance. As a result of this landmark decision, elaborate irrigation systems were constructed for just that purpose. While these systems did increase Indian self-sufficiency, they were often poorly constructed and maintained, leaving the tribes that depended on them open to further exploitation.

Reclamation, irrigation, and dam projects have also had unforeseen consequences for Native Americans. When in 1905 the government dammed the Truckee River for white irrigation as part of the Newlands Project, the Lahonan trout, a primary subsistence food of the Pyramid Paiutes, disappeared. The river's diversion also nearly killed Pyramid Lake. Since the 1930s, dams on the Columbia River and many of its tributaries have severely retarded the migration of salmon and other native fish species, and they ruined upstream spawning grounds. These projects have also destroyed native sacred sites. The Pick-Sloan Project on the Missouri River devastated the Standing Rock, Cheyenne River, Crow Creek, and Fort Berthold reservations, as the diverted water flooded their farmlands, villages, and sacred sites. The Eastern Cherokees and the Senecas were similarly affected by the building of the Kinzua and the Tellico Dams. But water diversion and diminished fish populations are not the only environmental side effects resulting from ill-conceived water politics.

CONTAMINATION AND TOXICITY

American Indians are also becoming increasingly concerned about the ill effects that toxic chemicals and waste products have on their environment, particularly since the mid-twentieth century. The ill effects of these substances have greatly increased in both intensity and magnitude over the past five decades. The danger of environmental contamination now threatens the relationship of tribes to the natural environment, and jeopardizes the health and well-being of native people themselves. This has created a need for new and better risk assessment and management procedures for use of government and tribal agencies in assessing the perils of toxicant exposure. Unfortunately, improved risk assessment and management procedures have been less than adequate in the past and as such, have not served American Indians well.

New assessment procedures must consider the social, cultural, and spiritual beliefs and practices that tie native people to the land and environment. Without these cultural considerations, assessment plans are inadequate for tribal communities. Therefore, over the past few decades, as environmental problems have continued to grow more complex, assessment and management have become high priorities for tribal administrators. For example, throughout the 1950s, the national challenge to harness inexpensive hydroelectric power resulted in the creation of dozens of dams on American rivers. Many tribes have been severely affected by the pollution of water, land, sediment, and air created by the increased industry that these new power sources attracted. The Akwesasne Mohawk nation is one of the best examples of this kind of contamination.

During the 1950s, several sites on the St. Lawrence River were selected for a series of locks and dams that would ultimately improve shipping in the Great Lakes region. Hundreds of manufacturers flocked to the area to take advantage of the new power source created by new hydroelectric plants. Three industry giants in particular, ALCOA, Reynolds, and General Motors, built their plants along the banks of the river. After months of discharging waste products by dumping them into the river, toxins accumulated in local fish and wildlife. Mohawk nation tribal members, especially women of childbearing age, experienced the ill effects of these toxins. The breast milk of nursing mothers who consumed locally caught fish was found to contain extremely high levels of toxins, posing a threat to their nursing infants.

URANIUM CONTAMINATION

Throughout the Cold War years, the federal government contracted with private companies to mine the uranium needed to sustain the nation's supply of nuclear weapons. Thousands of mines were excavated in the West and Southwest to harvest uranium-rich ore. Highgrade ore was sent to mills for processing and refinement, but low-grade ore was left among the tailings at mine sites along with waste water collection pools. When the Cold War ended and uranium was no longer needed, the mining companies simply walked away, leaving mines unsealed and radioactive wastes exposed. Contaminated mine sites constituted an extreme danger to anyone who came into contact with them. Although the government was well aware of the dangers associated with working with uranium or radium, more than 15,000 Navajos were hired during the Cold War years to work in processing mills or in mines with no safety measures in place and no instructions on how to protect themselves. Thousands of these miners have experienced health problems, yet they were refused compensation or the qualifications for being certified for compensation were so complicated that many were unable to meet them.

Furthermore, when the uranium boom ended, over 1,000 unsealed shafts, pits, and radioactive waste piles were abandoned on Navajo reservations in New Mexico, Arizona, and Utah. In many cases, Navajo families lived within a few hundred feet of these sites. The tribe's free-ranging livestock grazed among the waste piles and drank from the contaminated pools. Children played on the piles of dirt tailings, and families used the contaminated soil to build and repair their hogans. They also used contaminated rocks to heat their sweat lodges. It was not until 1988 that the Navajo Nation was awarded "Treatment as a State" status, giving the Environmental Protection Agency (EPA) the authority to treat a federally recognized tribe in the same manner as it would a state when implementing and managing environmental programs. This new status made it easier for these tribes to receive grant funds through the Superfund Memorandum of Agreement with the EPA. As an official Superfund site, the Navajo Nation can now be assured that adequate protective measures for public health, welfare, and the environment are being met. Superfund status also makes the Navajo nation eligible for recovery of cleanup costs from responsible parties (EPA.).

Mineral resources on reservation lands have also been both a blessing and a curse for native communities. For example, from the first discovery of oil on Osage lands in 1900, a new quest for nonrenewable resource development in

Indian country began. It was a devil's bargain, however, that on one hand offered a measure of economic relief for tribes, but on the other introduced incredible exploitation that threatened water, land, and air resources as well as damaged the health of native communities. Government mismanagement further compounded the problems. In the Southwest, coal and uranium mining devastated Navajo lands, water, and air. Additionally, a 273-mile-long slurry pipeline at the Peabody Coal Company's Black Mesa operation extracted 1.4 billion gallons of water annually from the aquifer, severely lowering the water table and depleting both Navajo and Hopi water supplies. The Navajo Generating Station at Page, Arizona, fueled by the coal from Black Mesa, compromised the air quality of the Grand Canyon and Four Corners region. After years of controversy, the Black Mesa mine closed in 2005 after a court settlement shut down the Mojave Generating Station in Laughlin, Nevada, for pollution violations. Then in December 2008, the U.S. Office of Surface Mining issued Peabody a new license but failed to provide a supplemental Draft Environmental Impact statement. The permit would have guaranteed Peabody's operations until the year 2026, but on January 5, 2010, Judge Robert G. Holt revoked the coal company's mining permit at Black Mesa.

In Alaska, the Alaskan Native Claims Settlement Act passed in 1971 and the North Slope energy boom, with its drilling sites, pipelines, and access roads, forever transformed the landscape and threatened mammals and waterfowl. The act provided Alaska Natives with 44 million acres of land and $962 million in compensation for ceded lands. It also established regional and village corporations, chartered under state laws that would manage the assets of the individual native shareholders in these corporations. Today, Native Alaskans place their faith in coalitions designed to sustain and rejuvenate. In 2011, the Alaska Conservation Foundation, partnered with the Alaska Native Steering Committee to establish the Alaska Native Fund to support efforts to preserve and protect Alaskan Native life ways and resources. The group has identified five issues as top priorities to be addressed. They are climate change, food security, sustainable economies, energy, and wellness. The foundation's mission is to build strategic leadership and support for Alaskan efforts to take care of wild lands, waters, and wildlife, which sustain diverse cultures, healthy communities, and prosperous economies.

The marginalization of native populations through environmental racism continues today. Whereas in the past it has taken the form of extermination of buffalo or eradication of native flora and fauna in exchange for domestic cattle and European grains, today the earth itself and its critical systems are being repressed. While all poor people are disadvantaged, Indian disadvantages are multiplied by the cultures and lifestyles that tie native people to the land. Because of their economic and political vulnerability, their lands have long been targeted by the federal government as well as large corporations for the dumping of the poisonous by-products of the dominant society. Yet today, with more economic power due to development, higher education, and incredible determination, American Indians are still resisting subjugation and are fighting back against environmental injustice.

REFERENCES

The Alaska Native Claims Settlement Act of 1971. 43 U.S.C. Chapter 33§ 1601-1629, PL 92-203. Available at http://www.lbblawyers.com/ancsa

Black Mesa Water Coalition. Available at http://www.blackmesawatercoalition.org/blackmesa.html.

Bullard, Robert D. and Benjamin Chavis, Jr. (Eds.). *Confronting Environmental Racism: Voices from the Grassroots.* Cambridge, MA: South End Press, 1999.

Cole, Luke and Sheila Foster. *From the Ground Up: Environmental Racism and the Rise of the Environmental Justice Movement.* New York: New York University Press, 2000.

Eichstaedt, Peter H. and Murrae Haynes. *If You Poison Us: Uranium and Native Americans.* New York: Red Crane Books, 1994.

Hooks, Gregory and Chad Smith. "The Treadmill of Destruction: National Sacrifice Areas and Native Americans" *American Sociological Review* 69, no. 4 (August 2004): 558–575.

Krech III, Shepard. *The Ecological Indian: Myth and History.* New York: W. W. Norton, 2000.

LaDuke, Winona. *All Our Relations: Native Struggles for Land and Life.* New York: South End Press, 1999.

Olson, Paul A. (Ed.). *The Struggle for the Land: Indigenous Insight and Industrial Empire in the Semiarid World.* Lincoln: University of Nebraska Press, 1990.

Sackman, Douglas. *Blackwell Companion to American Environmental History.* Malden, MA: Blackwell, 2010.

Shurts, John. *Indian Reserved Water Rights: The Winters Doctrine in Its Social and Legal Context.* Norman: University of Oklahoma Press, 2003.

U.S. Environmental Protection Agency (EPA). "Addressing Uranium Contamination in the Navajo Nation." Retrieved from http://www.epa.gov/region9/superfund/navajo-nation/ne-church-rock-mine.html.

Weaver, Jace (Ed.). *Defending Mother Earth: Native American Perspectives on Environmental Justice.* New York: Orbis Books, 1996.

Nuclear Waste

Thomas Maxwell Long

The accumulation of nuclear waste materials in the United States has been a growing concern for over five decades. Today, approximately 22 percent of all electricity comes from nuclear power facilities. Currently, storage of this incredibly hazardous material is deemed adequate by the Nuclear Regulatory Commission (NRC); however, the commission has advised that more storage facilities be built to accommodate the glut of waste. The American West is the region of the United States that, according to the commission, has the best physical environment for waste storage. The subregions include several sovereign Indian reservations, the use of a waste facilities upon which require Indian agreement.

The origin of atomic energy in the United States harkens back to World War II when President Franklin Roosevelt established the Manhattan Project for the construction of nuclear weapons. Following the successful conclusion of the war, President Harry Truman signed the Atomic Energy Act, which provided for the establishment of the Atomic Energy Commission (AEC). Perhaps the greatest significance of this congressional act was the removal of military control and the placement of oversight of atomic energy research and development in the civilian realm. However, the AEC did not immediately venture into the possibility of utilizing nuclear energy outside of bomb building until its second year.

The AEC then established the first nuclear reactor testing station dedicated to nuclear power for constructive purposes in Idaho in 1949. By the dawn of the 1950s, it was clear that the greater focus of the AEC was still the development of advanced nuclear weapons; a response in no small measure to the continued success of the Soviet Union to develop atomic bombs and thermonuclear devices in near parallel with the United States throughout the decade. Nuclear energy, though not abandoned, took a distant backseat to the bomb builders.

In 1955, the first nuclear power plant in the history of the world provided power to an entire city—Arco, Idaho, population 1,006. The atomic age came to Arco one year after the first nuclear powered submarine, USS *Nautilus*, was commissioned. In 1959, the first fully civilian–funded nuclear power station, the Dresden-1 in Illinois, went online and began to supply customers of Commonwealth Edison with electricity. The immediate success of Dresden-1 encouraged the development of nuclear power generators across the land over the next 15 years, and led President Lyndon Johnson to sign the Private Ownership of Special Nuclear Materials Act, which permitted nuclear power companies to own the radioactive fuel. Ironically, up to that point in history, the regulation of the spent fuel, or radioactive waste, had not been addressed beyond the requirements set forth by the AEC that all nuclear power stations maintain their waste in a controlled environment, without any specifications on how that should be done.

The National Academy of Sciences developed the concept of a deep geologic reservoir, effectively a sealed pit, in 1956, though full agreement on location, depth, and necessary geological makeup never came to fruition. By 1971, twenty-two nuclear power plants produced nearly 2.5 percent of the electricity consumed in the United States, and in 1973, U.S. utility companies launched the construction of 41 more nuclear power generator plants, though as of 1974, no unilateral regulation of nuclear waste by the AEC had been developed. However, Congress reacted to the AEC's apparently lackadaisical waste management by abolishing the agency and creating the NRC.

The charge given to the NRC was the protection of public health and safety. Ironically, the first known nuclear meltdown did not occur under the watch of the AEC, but rather under the allegedly watchful eyes of the NRC: Three Mile Island. On March 28, 1979, the Three Mile Island Nuclear Power Station, located in Pennsylvania, witnessed the meltdown of nearly 50 percent of its core due to an error in human judgment and for the first time, following the meltdown, the NRC did begin to focus on "human factors" as well as all things mechanical. Regulations concerning nuclear waste management remained static for nearly three years following the Three Mile Island incident.

In January 1983, Congress responded by officially recognizing the growing need for further nuclear power oversight, in particular nuclear waste management and passing a nuclear waste regulatory act. This landmark congressional act not only recognized the sovereignty of individual states to set standards for the development of nuclear waste storage facilities in accordance with the minimum standards set forth by the NRC and the Department of Energy (DOE), but it also recognized American Indian tribes as potential participants in this industry.

The passage of this act came at an important juncture in American history; by 1984, nuclear power generated more electricity in the United States than natural gas or hydropower, and only the burning of coal remained ahead of atomic energy in generating electricity. In 1981, President Ronald Reagan's first Secretary of the Interior, James G. Watt, first suggested the possibility of large-scale nuclear waste storage in the West, specifically in the Yucca Mountain in Nevada, as well as on various Indian reservations.

Following the tragedy at Chernobyl in the Soviet Union, the U.S. Congress stepped up the search for unified nuclear power and waste storage system in 1986. On December 22, 1987, the Nuclear Waste Policy Act of 1982 was amended to focus attention on the development of a permanent nuclear waste storage facility in the Yucca Mountain as well as permanent facilities within Indian tribal land in the West. The reservations of the Diné, Hopi, Apache, Pueblo, and Goshute, among others, were recognized for having the "proper qualities": location in the West, low population density, nonurban setting, and light precipitation.

The 1987 amendments to the Nuclear Waste Policy Act led to a heavy focus on the Yucca Mountain, one of the more geologically active locations in the Rocky Mountains, as well as other Native American lands as the only locations wherein permanent nuclear waste storage facilities could be constructed. Congress authorized billions of dollars in research grants for studies.

Examples of proposed nuclear waste storage facilities on Indian land are the Skull Valley Goshute Reservation and Mescalero Apache Reservation. The former first came to the attention of nuclear waste disposal corporations during the 1985 to 1989 cleanup of the decommissioned Vitro uranium mill outside of Salt Lake City, Utah. While assisting in the search for an acceptable site to temporarily store the hazardous materials collected at the uranium mill, the DOE reasoned that the Skull Valley reservation was a logical point due to its relatively close, yet removed, location from the mill site. During the 1994 to 1995 rush by nuclear power companies to form large associations in an effort to offset the costs of waste management facility development, the reservations of the Skull Valley Goshute along with the Mescalero Apache of New Mexico became the focus of possible waste storage sites, and both tribes were approached with business proposals.

In 1994, numerous proposals were made to the Mescalero-Apaches for using their vast reservation for storing nuclear waste. Within two years, after an intense series of political bouts within the tribe and with New Mexico Governor Bruce King and Senator Jeff Bingaman, the Mescalero halted any plans to develop a facility, which theoretically could have brought over $250 million to the tribe over the first 10 years of its existence. The Mescalero's neighbors to the north, the Skull Valley Goshute, began their discussions at nearly the same point in time, though the divide over allowing a nuclear waste facility in Utah went much deeper than in New Mexico.

The 122,085-acre reservation of the Skull Valley Goshute Indians is located an hour southwest of Salt Lake City. The land itself is rocky, and economic stability has eluded the tribe since they arrived at the reservation in 1863. However, the Skull Valley Goshute never surrendered their sovereignty when they signed the treaty with President Abraham Lincoln that established their tribal land boundaries and that guaranteed that the United States would recognize the Skull Valley Goshute as masters of their own destiny through self-governance.

When corporations first approached Skull Valley with proposals for nuclear waste storage facilities on the land, for which the Indians would be compensated hundreds of millions of dollars, all members of the tribe recognized the economic significance of the plans as well as related environmental concerns. No decisions were made immediately within the tribal leadership. Conflict did began immediately within the reservation as well as off the reservation as anti–nuclear waste activists and politicians attacked the Indians from all angles.

The Skull Valley Goshute first signed a cooperative agreement with the DOE on November 10, 1994, for the establishment of a study of the environmental impact of a storage facility that would house between 10,000 and 15,000 metric tons of spent nuclear fuel rods. As soon as the story hit the newswires, Utah Governor Mike Leavitt held a news conference and expressed his strong opposition, which was shared by many like-minded concerned citizens. In time, Senator Orrin Hatch also opposed the facility. The conflict within the Skull Valley tribe itself was even more intense.

A bullet-riddled Skull Valley nuclear waste sign stands along the highway leading to the Goshute Indian tribe reservation in Skull Valley, Utah, May 3, 2006. (AP Photo/Douglas C. Pizac)

Nuclear waste storage practices and proposed facility locations have not been consensus issues in the nation's history. Even though nuclear waste storage technology has come a long way over the past 50 years, there is still no guaranteed approach to safe containment of the nuclear waste. The facility on Goshute land would only be a "temporary" unit, aimed at a 40- to 50-year life span, which would be bound by much looser guidelines than a more permanent facility.

In 1989 when DOE approached the Indians with the concept, Leon Bear, then chairman of the Skull Valley band, along with several other leadership and non-leadership members, began researching the possibility of leasing a section of tribal land to a private concern for nuclear waste storage. From that moment through 1997, the conflict at Skull Valley was fairly minimal, as was the resistance from the Utah non–Native American population. The low-key atmosphere surrounding the proposed nuclear waste storage facility vanished in 1997 when the tribe signed a contract for a 44,000-metric-ton storage facility on 840 acres of land. Within a day, reporters began to flood into the Skull Valley band's office as well as the reservation. Tensions escalated on the reservation literally overnight. As the two sides on the reservation dug in and fought each other over the next nine years, all the pain and hardship they were experiencing made nearly daily headlines throughout the state. By 2000, the rift on the reservation had grown so wide that tribal leadership elections were routinely contested, and a series of lawsuits and court cases began to flood the courtrooms with cases ranging from fraud to embezzlement of tribal funds.

While the issues on the Goshute reservation continue, the proposed permanent nuclear waste storage facility in the Yucca Mountain has also come under scrutiny because the 1863 treaty between the Western Shoshone and the United States indicates that the site is actually under the jurisdiction of the Western Shoshone Indian Nation. Corbin Harney, a spiritual leader of the Western Shoshone, has repeatedly pointed out that his nation rejects the idea of their land being the largest nuclear dump site in the Americas. Furthermore, traditional Western Shoshone lands have long endured nuclear radiation issues as they have witnessed hundreds of nuclear bomb detonations, making their sovereign nation the most bombed on earth.

The challenge will continue in the coming years for sovereign Indian nations to maintain the integrity of their land at the same time as they consider the financial resources available to their people should they allow their lands to serve as nuclear waste disposal sites.

REFERENCES

"Comprehensive Nuclear Waste Plan Implemented." *Congressional Quarterly Almanac.* Washington D.C. Congressional Quarterly, Inc., 1982.

Energy Reorganization Act of 1974, section 201 (42 U.S.C. 5841).

The History of Nuclear Energy. Washington, DC: United States Department of Energy, Office of Nuclear Energy, 2006.

History of Nuclear Waste. Milwaukee, WI: Clean Wisconsin Organization, 2005.

Macfarlane, Allison M. and Rodney C. Ewing (Eds.). *Uncertainty Underground: Yucca Mountain and the Nation's High-Level Nuclear Waste.* Cambridge, MA: MIT Press, 2006.

Nuclear Waste Policy Act of 1982, Enacted Bill: 97 H.R. 3809, 96 Stat. 2201.

Nuclear Waste Policy Amendments Act of 1987, enacted Bill: 100 H.R. 3545, 101 Stat. 1330.

Vandenbosch, Robert and Susanne Vandenbosch. *Nuclear Waste Stalemate: Political and Scientific Controversies.* Salt Lake City, Utah: University of Utah Press, 2007.

POLLUTION

Patti Jo King

With well over 500 federally recognized tribes in the United States, including 229 Alaska Native communities, Indian country comprises about 53 million acres of land and contains much of the nation's remaining nonrenewable natural resources. Consequently, Indian tribes face a number of significant environmental problems. For centuries, Native Americans were called stewards of the earth, a romantic stereotype that often makes it difficult for the general public to accept or understand pollution on tribal lands. Yet basic issues such as solid waste disposal, underground storage tanks, trash disposal, and safe drinking water have been major ongoing environmental problems affecting the health and well-being of reservation communities for many years. Rural isolation, abject poverty, and lack of regulations have been the most prevalent underlying determinants of pollution on native lands, a phenomenon that has improved in many regions since the increase in economic development after 1990. Eighteen tribes to date have developed standards for surface water quality under the Clean Water Act (CWA); nevertheless, there are more divergent ecological concerns in Indian country that are creating such a demand for immediate intervention and remedial action, they have pushed these basic issues to the sidelines.

HAZARDOUS WASTE DUMPING

Many reservations, for example those located in rural areas, have been selected as or are located near hazardous waste sites. Chemical wastes emanating from these sites can contaminate water and food sources, decimate wildlife populations, and endanger the health of tribal community members. Solid, liquid, or hazardous wastes abandoned in open, unregulated areas have been a persistent problem on many reservations. The practice of hazardous waste dumping has created a state of environmental crisis for a number of tribes. Due to their federally recognized sovereign status, tribes have the authority to manage their environmental problems independently; however, many have limited sources of revenue and therefore are dependent on the federal government for help with environmental protection. Unfortunately, federally approved tribal regulatory programs are almost nonexistent, and as a result, enforcement responsibility frequently falls to the Environmental Protection Agency (EPA). Yet the EPA, perhaps due to limited resources, has often neglected its managerial and enforcement responsibilities on reservation lands.

TRIBAL ENVIRONMENTAL PROTECTION PROGRAMS

Ongoing development of tribal environmental protection programs, as well as tribal participation in direct implementation of federal environmental laws on native lands, is becoming increasingly important. The Navajo Nation, for example, recently enacted the first tribal superfund law. The 2005 Energy Policy Act, which creates tribal and industry opportunities for the development of tribal natural resources and chances for tribes and tribal enterprises to craft national energy policy, encourages tribes to take control of their own reservation resource development and management. In response, many tribes with increased economic resources from successful gaming activities are beginning to set their own environmental standards and are now creating, funding, and monitoring their own environmental protection programs. Tribes who can afford to do so, however, are still the exception rather than the rule.

The question of how to approach tribal environmental problems becomes more complicated when considering the enormous tracts of Indian land held in trust by the U.S. government. Although these lands do not include reservations, in many cases they lie adjacent to them. Most trust agreements were entered into by treaties negotiated in the 1850s and 1860s, when tribes routinely ceded control of their lands in exchange for federal protection from harassment and intrusion. Under the trust relationship, the government pledged to safeguard tribes and to protect their interests. In these agreements, tribes also retained rights of hunting, fishing, and enjoyment of their lands. The nature of the trust relationship, however, was shrouded in ambiguity, leaving the interpretation of trust responsibilities open to debate in ensuing years. In its pamphlet entitled *Working Effectively with Tribal Governments*, the EPA defines the federal trust responsibility as the need to meet "standards of good faith and due diligence, as well as protecting and managing Indian lands and natural resources" (EPA, Tribal Policies and Initiatives). Tribes, however, maintain that they should be able to continue to use these lands in the same ways their ancestors used them, and when these lands are contaminated, traditional subsistence lifestyles are rendered impossible (EPA, Tribal Policy and Initiatives). This debate is a major component of tribal consultations with the Department of Energy (DOE) concerning the cleanup of trust lands included on the Superfund National Priorities List. Many of these sites have been despoiled with plutonium, radionuclides, and other industrial chemical wastes such as heavy metals, organic solvents, and polychlorinated biphenyls commonly used in resource extraction. Tribes are often frustrated by what they believe to be exploitation of the rights and conditions set forth in these treaties. They believe their tribal members deserve and should be guaranteed safe use and enjoyment of these lands, and they demand that risk assessments be employed so that they can plan for the adequate cleanup of these lands. They also assert that risk assessment testing should be culturally sensitive, and include fish and game consumption hazards, rather than rely solely on the typical residential and industrial testing routinely done by the EPA. Because tribal standards are more demanding than those usually prescribed by federal agencies, these standards are a bone of contention between the DOE and tribes. One example is the Hanford nuclear site located in the state of Washington near the Yakama, Umatilla, and Nez Perce nations. The Hanford site, listed as one of the nation's most contaminated, is located on trust land ceded by treaties to the federal government. Contamination from this site has so thoroughly tainted the Columbia River salmon fishery, a resource of great cultural significance to these tribes, that the federal government may never be able to fulfill its treaty responsibilities to them.

In addition, the development of natural resources on native lands has been unduly manipulated, in part, through historic treaties between the paternalistic government and tribes. In past years, for instance, the Bureau of Indian Affairs (BIA) negotiated and managed coal development land leases, usually with little or no tribal input. Some tribes today, however, have taken over management of their own resources. A number of these tribes, such as the Northern Cheyenne, have also initiated legal actions in an effort to terminate early federally negotiated leases. Many Indian lands within the United States contain rich coal reserves and as a result have been targeted for coal extraction operations. Consequently, the native people who occupy these lands have long been subjected to the injurious environmental hazards of the coal industry. The rural nature of these tribes exacerbates the lack of economic development and subsequent poverty of many of these reservations. For this reason, economic hardship has often been a determining factor in tribal willingness to develop coal resources, even though such decisions often compromise the tribe's reverence for the land, create community divisions, foster resentment and resistance, and ultimately result in pollution. Furthermore, development often introduces a population of laborers from outside the area who are insensitive to the indigenous culture of the residents, causing further agitation within the community.

WASTE MANAGEMENT IN INDIAN COUNTRY

The Environmental Protection Agency's website provides information and guidelines regarding waste management in Indian Country. Some of this information is reproduced here.

BASIC INFORMATION

EPA's Tribal Solid Waste Management Program encourages municipal solid waste and hazardous waste management practices in Indian Country that are protective of human health and the environment. The information on this page provides a more in-depth look at our waste management program.

WHERE YOU LIVE

EPA tribal program contacts provide useful, up-to-date information about building waste management capacity, developing tribal infrastructure, realizing economic sustainability for tribal waste programs, and forging partnerships for waste management among tribes, states, local governments, and federal agencies.

GRANTS/FUNDING

To be successful, every solid waste management program needs funding. Unfortunately, especially in an era of tightening budgets, it may be difficult to find the needed resources. Remoteness, small community size, and lack of resources make this situation even more acute in Indian Country. The information on this page may help you locate the funding you need.

EDUCATION

Education can clarify the importance of good solid waste management to community members and to your tribal leadership, ensuring that your solid waste program will be supported as a high priority.

CASE STUDIES

The experience of other tribes, villages, and tribal consortia that have successful programs already in place or on the way is a valuable resource for tribes and Alaska native villages developing solid waste management programs. Officials of such organizations are often willing to share their expertise with others who

> are attempting similar programs. This page includes case studies from selected tribes.
>
> PUBLICATIONS
>
> Because of the unique challenges facing tribal waste managers, we have developed resource guides featuring in-depth information specific to Indian Country. Highlights include the *Tribal Decisionmaker's Guide to Solid Waste Management* and the *Tribal Waste Journal*.
>
> *Source*: Tribal Waste Management. Retrieved from http://www.epa.gov/wastes/wyl/tribal/index.htm

TRIBAL SUPPORT FOR WASTE STORAGE AND ENVIRONMENTAL OPPOSITION

Tribal support for the development of natural resources or hazardous waste storage on their lands has also sometimes led to conflict between tribes, non-Indian neighbors, and mainstream environmental groups. For example, in 1990, the Osage Nation of Oklahoma lobbied to stop a bill that would create Tallgrass Prairie National Park on the lucrative oil fields of their land. The revenues they reaped from the pumping of oil on their land created wealth for the Osage people and an abiding reluctance to abandon the industry. In the 1990s, waste disposal companies began approaching tribes to lease lands for trash and waste disposal dumps and landfills. A number of tribes, in need of an economic boost, agreed to these propositions, including the Campo Kumeyaay Nation of Mission Indians in southern California. The Campos signed a 20-year lease with the county of San Diego to use their lands as a dump site, much to the chagrin of their non-Indian neighbors, who complained about the potential for groundwater contamination. These dissenters asked the state to intervene and stop the tribe from the detrimental use of its lands. States, however, have no jurisdiction in Indian country; hence, the Campos went ahead with the deal, citing the need for employment opportunities for their tribal members. Other debates over potentially dangerous land use include tribes who have expressed interest in radioactive waste storage, such as the Tonkawa, Chickasaw, and Sac and Fox Tribes of Oklahoma; the Yakima in Washington; and the Mescalero Apaches in New Mexico. In response, environmental activists from some 50 tribes gathered at the Protecting Mother Earth Conference to raise awareness and try to end reservation storage of nuclear contaminants. In addition, the native consortium, the Council of Energy Resources Tribes, posited that tribes should strive to promote energy development and stimulate tribal economy through agreements that preserved tribal sovereignty and shun deals with companies that turn a blind eye to issues of contamination. Mainstream environmental organizations such as Greenpeace lent funding and organizational support to such tribal efforts.

ENVIRONMENTAL RACISM

The hazardous and exploitive side effects of resource extraction raise additional questions about environmental racism, justice, and native sovereignty. For instance, some two dozen Plains and Southwestern tribes have coal reserves on their lands. Some tribes, such as the Navajo, Hopi, and Crow, have long had ongoing mining operations on their lands; others, such as the Zuni, Ute, Ouray, and Uintah reservations, have been targeted for development. For over 20 years, uranium mining on Navajo lands compromised the health and safety of the tribe. The Vanadium Corporation of America and Kerr-McGee, principal owners of the mines, extracted from the Navajo nation over 4 million tons of uranium ore, much of which was used by the U.S. government to make weapons. Routinely exposed to radiation far in excess of safe levels and never informed of its dangers, Navajo miners began dying from mining-related illness within a few short years of working in the mines. To further complicate matters, radioactive tailings, or soil contaminated by toxic mine residue, was widely used in the construction of Navajo homes, spreading radioactivity throughout the community. Hundreds of families complained that their children were suffering from health problems, suspecting that radiation was to blame. After long and frustrating battles that stretched over 40 years, Congress finally passed the Radiation Exposure Compensation Act in 1990. The law required $100,000 in "compassion payments" to uranium miners diagnosed with cancer or other respiratory ailments; however, to qualify for compensation, a miner had to prove that he was suffering from one of the diseases identified for compensation. A grassroots organization, the Office of Navajo Uranium Miners, pressured the government to act responsibly when responding to its failure to warn the Navajos about the dangers and demanded compensation for damages. Nevertheless, compensation was complicated due to governmental guidelines and bureaucratic red tape.

THE DANGERS OF COAL EMISSIONS AND STRIP MINING

The Four Corners Steam Plant, located on the Navajo reservation in New Mexico, generates enough electricity to serve thousands of customers in the Four Corners region, an area that encompasses four states. While this is beneficial for the communities of the region, the plant has drawn much criticism because it is fueled by coal. According to Source Watch, a website devoted to environmental concerns, because the plant is one of largest coal-fired generating stations in the

> ## TRIBAL BROWNFIELDS AND RESPONSE PROGRAMS
>
> The Environmental Protection Agency has produced a report, "Tribal Brownfields and Response Programs," that describes how it is helping tribes deal with brownfields. Part of this report is reproduced here.
>
> Brownfields and other contaminated lands are found throughout the United States. Often legacies of an industrial past or bygone business, they dot the landscape of large and small communities.... They come in many forms and sizes. Brownfields can be the abandoned warehouse or corner gas station, the local mill site or abandoned mine. In Indian country they are as diverse as the communities in which they are found.
>
> To address environmental issues in Indian country, many tribes establish their own environmental protection and natural resource management offices. To clean up and reuse contaminated lands, many create brownfields programs or "Tribal Response Programs." However, tribal communities often lack funding to sustain environmental program capacity building and continue to need outside technical assistance and expertise. Additionally, many tribes seeking to address brownfields in their communities face problems that are found in many small or rural areas in the United States. Rural locations typically do not have the technical resources that many larger communities have, nor the economic drivers associated with more dense populations that might spur cleanup and reuse. Tribes may seek to return contaminated land to a non-economic reuse (e.g., returning land to a culturally beneficial reuse), which often must be funded by the public sector or tribal government and which may not attract the interest of those with private cleanup dollars.
>
> Despite the challenges, revitalization of contaminated lands is an environmental issue being addressed successfully across Indian country. With the assistance of grants and other resources available through EPA's Brownfields Program, tribes are making great strides in cleaning up and returning contaminated land back to productive use. By using the grants and tools available, tribes address their fundamental environmental and revitalization goals and enrich the health and welfare of their communities.
>
> *Source*: Tribal Brownfields. U.S. EPA. Retrieved from http://epa.gov/brownfields/state_tribal/tribalreport11.pdf

nation, it emits "157 million pounds of sulfur dioxide, 122 million pounds of nitrogen oxides, 8 million pounds of soot, and 2,000 pounds of mercury" each year. (Source Watch n.d.). The website also points out that the American Lung Association estimates that about 15 percent of the neighboring population is

Four Corners Power Plant is on Navajo land in northwest New Mexico. A new rule by federal regulators gives operators of power plants in the Southwest a choice of either trimming nitrogen oxide emissions by 87 percent or moving forward with plans to shutter three of the five plant's generating units, April 6, 2006. (AP Photo/Susan Montoya)

severely affected by respiratory diseases because of these toxic emissions. Source Watch also focuses attention on the San Juan generating station in nearby Farmington, New Mexico. This station has an annual emission rate of "100 million pounds of sulfur dioxide, 100 million pounds of nitrogen oxides, 6 million pounds of soot, and over 1000 pounds of mercury." (Source Watch n.d.). The organization also contends that the plant's toxic emissions of cadmium, selenium, and arsenic, as well as its contamination of local water supplies, have led to the death of livestock in the region (Source Watch n.d.).

In addition, two strip mines on Black Mesa, in operation since 1965 by the Peabody Western Coal Company, are the largest strip-mining operations in the United States. These mines supply coal for the Mohave Generating Station near Laughlin, Nevada, that ultimately provides electricity for southern California, Las Vegas, and parts of Arizona. Although the mines provide nearly 80 percent of the Hopi tribe's annual income and 60 percent of the Navajo's general fund, both tribes have voted to end Peabody's access to the Black Mesa aquifer, citing the company's creation of 40,000 tons of sulfur dioxide waste each year. Through the Navajo-Hopi Settlement Act of 1974, more than 12,000 Navajos have been relocated from their homes as a result of the mining, yet despite the urgency of the environmental crisis, remediation is still under debate. Debates weighing the economic benefits of coal mining against ecological concerns also take precedence regarding expansion of the Absaloka Mine near the Crow reservation and the effects of the Colstrip Steam Plant, as well as five strip mines which surround the Northern Cheyenne reservation, both in southeastern Montana. While substantial amounts of coal and power resources are generated in Indian country, these resources rarely benefit the tribes affected by the pollution their extraction creates. In the Black Mesa region, for example, only 20 percent of the Navajo community has running water, and only slightly more have electricity. For this reason, advocates of environmental justice who have studied the economic impact of fossil fuel extraction in Indian country hold that the human costs have far exceeded monetary value for tribes. They suggest that a portion of annual revenues from these operations should be invested in renewable energy projects on tribal lands.

FEDERAL RESPONSIBILITY AND PATERNALISM

Environmental racism, then, includes economic paternalism that stems from a lack of sufficient funding to support sustainable and environmentally friendly economic development. It also encompasses haphazard federal policies and practices that promote natural resource development on Indian lands that result in despoiled lands and fractured tribal communities. The lack of appropriate regulation and protection in Indian country can be attributed to careless federal regulatory measures, inadequate funding for safety and technical support for tribal programs, and failure to address and mandate the cleanup of hazardous waste sites in indigenous regions. The federal government has spent billions of dollars to support and subsidize state environmental programs in recent years but has spent far less on tribal efforts. Yet tribes, as low-income communities, are often more susceptible to the effects of contamination due to insufficient access to healthcare, poverty, and substandard living conditions. Moreover, tribal environmental issues cannot be separated from issues of tribal sovereignty, federal trust responsibilities, and treaty rights. Alaska Natives face even more challenges due to the special status of their lands. Environmental justice, which combines civil rights and the need for environmental protection, has become a much more important concern in the last few decades.

TRIBAL GREEN PROJECTS

With the national focus on more sustainable "green" resources recently, many tribes have taken an interest in renewable energy development. Although native lands have long played a pivotal role in U.S. energy resources, because of their tax-exempt status, Indian tribes are not eligible for federal tax incentives for such projects. This fact discourages companies working to develop renewable energy sources from partnering with tribes, yet a number of tribes have maintained their focus on green projects. Over 20 Plains tribes are living on lands that boast a wind power potential equal to or more than 50 percent of the installed electrical generation capacity in the entire United States. The Navajo Green Economy Coalition was established in 2007 to work with the Navajo Nation to develop tribal council and community support for green projects, and in 2009, the Navajos became the first tribal entity to pass green legislation. The Navajo Green Economy Commission, created by the new law, will eventually oversee funding and management of sustainable, low-pollution projects, and the Navajo Green Economy Fund will identify, obtain, and utilize federal, state, local, and private grants to support green projects. Other tribes are expected to follow in the Navajo footsteps. The final answer to many of the problems of pollution on tribal lands seems to lie in the continuing efforts of tribes to develop their own environmental standards and management programs. The ultimate success of these programs, however, will depend on continued dialogue and cooperation between tribes, states, and the federal government, with a commitment to devote funds that are adequate to get the job done, a willingness to gamble on tribal development of new technologies, and an empathetic understanding of cultural differences.

REFERENCES

Brugge, Doug. *The Navajo People and Uranium Mining*. Albuquerque: University of New Mexico Press, 2007.

Bryan, Susan Montoya. "Navajo Lawmakers Approve Superfund Bill to Cleanup Sites." *News from Indian Country*, March 2008. Retrieved from http://indiancountrynews.net/index.php?option=com_content&task=view&id=2730 on May 14, 2010.

Conant, Jeff. "Speaking Diné to Dirty Power: Navajo Challenge New Coal-Fired Plant." *CorpWatch: Holding Corporations Accountable*, April 3, 2007. Retrieved from http://www.corpwatch.org/article.php?id=14435 in June 2010.

Council of Energy Resource Tribes. *The Control and Reclamation of Surface Mining on Indian Lands*. Ann Arbor: University of Michigan Library, 1979.

Eichstaedt, Peter and Murrae Haynes. *If You Poison Us: Uranium and Native Americans*. New York: Red Crane Books, 1994.

EPA. Tribal Policies and Initiatives. Retrieved from http://www.epa.gov/owindian/wetg/training/EPA/common/data/text-only/Old/epa01c.htm.

Gallagher, Susan. "Proposal Would Move Mining onto Crow Reservation." *Helena Independent Record*, April 4, 2008. Retrieved from http://helenair.com/news/state-and-regional/proposal-would-move-mining-onto-crow-reservation/article_4479519e-386f-500b-bf0f-8b0dbe97ad89.html.

Grinde, Donald and Bruce Johansen. *Ecocide of Native America: Environmental Destruction of Indian Lands and Peoples*. New York: Clear Light Publishers, 1998.

Harkin, Michael E. and David Rich Lewis. *Native Americans and the Environment: Perspectives on the Ecological Indian*. Lincoln: University of Nebraska Press, 2007.

Hudson, Elizabeth. "Remnant Grassland Survives in Oklahoma." *High Country News*, March 7, 1994. Retrieved from http://www.hcn.org/issues/5/133 on June 10, 2010.

Indigenous Environmental Network. Available at http://www.ienearth.org/energy.html

Krech III, Shepard. *The Ecological Indian: Myth and History*. New York: Norton, 1999.

LaDuke, Winona. *All Our Relations: Native Struggles for Land and Life*. New York: South End Press, 1999.

Lewis, D. R. "Native Americans and the Environment: A Survey of Twentieth-Century Issues." *American Indian Quarterly* 19, no. 3 (1995): 423–477.

Monette, R. A. "Governing Private Property in Indian Country: The Double Edged Sword of the Trust Responsibility Arising out of Early Supreme Court Decisions and the General Allotment Act." *New Mexico Law Review* 25 (1995): 35, 39.

"Navajo Hopi Settlement Act of 1974," *Library of Congress*, H.R.10337. Retrieved from http://thomas.loc.gov/cgi-bin/bdquery/z?d093:HR10337:%7CTOM:/bss/d093query.html%7C in June 2010.

Nuclear Information and Resource Service. "Environmental Racism, Tribal Sovereignty, and Nuclear Waste." Retrieved from http://www.nirs.org/factsheets/pfsejfactsheet.htm on May 14, 2010.

Source Watch. "Coal Plants on Native American Lands." Retrieved from http://www.sourcewatch.org/index.php?title=Coal_and_Native_American_tribal_lands on November, 10, 2010.

U.S. Department of Energy. "Wind Power on Native American Lands: Opportunities, Challenges, and Status." Retrieved from http://www.nrel.gov/docs/fy07osti/41746.pdf on May 15, 2010.

U.S. Environmental Protection Agency (EPA). "Tribal Water Programs." Retrieved from http://www.epa.gov/region9/water/tribal/tribal-cwa.html on June 10, 2010.

Washington State Department of Health. "An Overview of Hanford and Radiation Health Effects." Retrieved from http://www.doh.wa.gov/hanford/publications/overview/overview.html on May 14, 2010.

Preserving Habitats

Ashley Corwyn Hall

Many Indian reservations in the United States are refuges for sensitive or endangered species. This fact reflects the reality that tribal governments tend to manage their lands in such a way that supports ecological integrity—in other words, tribes seek to preserve habitats that have supported both human communities and diverse plant and animal species for millennia, and which could potentially do so in the future. Tribal management goals in turn reflect traditional tribal insights regarding the interdependency of all life on earth.

The mutual dependence of the various components of ecosystems is sometimes compared to a spider's web in the sense that, just as cutting one strand of the web weakens it severely, eliminating even a single species from an ecosystem can have devastating consequences. Recognition and study of these interrelationships is also the cornerstone of the science of ecology. The further insight that earth's ecosystems are also interconnected leads to the realization that the diminishment of even one species in one ecosystem impoverishes all ecosystems and potentially endangers all species. Ultimately, this way of seeing the world also entails the understanding that human beings, like every part of creation, have a particular place in the world and particular roles to play as stewards, rather than masters, of their tribal territories and of the environment as a whole. Recognition of these facts is a central tenet of most tribal religious and philosophical traditions, carried forward through the generations in the rich oral traditions of America's tribal cultures.

Since the arrival of European settlers in the early seventeenth century, tribal nations in what is now the United States have witnessed destruction of habitats on a scale unprecedented in the continent's history. Conversion of lands that previously sustained animals, plants, and human beings alike into agricultural land supporting only a small handful of species began almost immediately with the arrival of Europeans. Mining, forestry, hydroelectric development, and urbanization are among the threats to North American habitats that emerged in the subsequent years.

In numerous cases across United States, tribes in the nineteenth and twentieth centuries, finding themselves in dire economic conditions, agreed to lease lands to non-Indian extractive industries like gold mining, oil, gas, and coal development; commercial, mono-crop agriculture; commercial timber harvesting; and others. In many of these cases, non-native corporations like Peabody Mining Company, Union Pacific, and many others misrepresented the ecological risks associated with their enterprises when negotiating leases with Indian tribes. They also typically failed to remunerate the tribes proportionately for the value of resources extracted from tribal lands. Today, American Indians control over 40 million acres of land in the lower 48 states. In most cases, land management decisions made by tribal governments support ecological diversity, but long-term damage caused by nineteenth- and twentieth-century industries also remain, sometimes almost entirely unremediated, within reservation lands.

Interrelated global ecological threats, like climate change, over fishing, urbanization, deforestation, and the drastic loss of biological diversity that is their corollary, are increasingly felt at the local level within tribal lands. In the face of longstanding and newly emerging threats, tribal people in the United States (along with indigenous communities throughout the Western Hemisphere) are taking the lead in environmental remediation and the preservation of threatened habitats within and around their current territories.

In fact, tribal governments are increasingly concerned with preserving habitats necessary to the survival of sensitive and endangered species. This is a cultural as well as strictly environmental concern for tribes because their traditional food sources, spiritual and ceremonial beliefs and practices, sociopolitical organization, and cultural identities are intimately connected to biological diversity and the continued vitality of ecosystems within their homelands and beyond. Therefore, in dealing with existing and emerging ecological threats, tribes tend to take an integrated, holistic approach to multifaceted ecological, cultural, social, and political problems, manifesting their fundamental and deeply held understanding of the interrelationships between the various facets of nature and culture. Tribal nations recognize the value of fragile and threatened ecosystems like prairies, wetlands, riparian (streamside) habitats, old-growth forests, deserts, alpine meadows, and others.

In many cases, successfully maintaining or reintroducing threatened species is linked to maintaining and revitalizing tribal cultures. Predators like wolves, coyotes, mountain lions, panthers, and others—often seen as threats or nuisances by non-native land managers—are viewed by many tribal nations as valuable members of the biotic community because they help regulate ecosystems by culling herds of herbivores, including deer, elk, antelope, and bison, that might otherwise overgraze and thereby threaten plants and other animals. Predators are also often especially important in Native American spiritual traditions. Salmon, trout, whales, bison, and other animals traditionally used by Native Americans as food, along with a variety of native plants, are also culturally important and have become subjects of tribal preservation efforts. Safeguarding predators and other animal species as well as native plant species requires preservation of the habitats they depend upon. Contemporary tribal nations are taking a wide range of actions aimed at preserving species and habitats, including consolidating and expanding tribal land holdings; cooperating with local, state, federal, and private entities to create conservation trusts; and revitalizing tribal hunting, fishing, forestry, agriculture, and other resource and land management practices based on Native American cultural attitudes toward the other-than-human world.

In some cases, Native American environmental goals are consistent with those of international, federal, state, and local agencies responsible for wildlife and environmental management, as well as the goals of environmental groups like the National Resources Defense Council (NRDC), World Wildlife Fund (WWF), Sierra Club, Greenpeace, EarthFirst!, and many others. However, while their overarching goals often coincide, there are many cases where the disparate underlying philosophies and approaches favored by these various groups bring them into conflict with each other. In addition, jurisdiction over land in Indian country containing sensitive ecosystems and species is extremely complex—a result of the history of territorial dispossession and fragmentation that often engenders additional conflicts. These factors, together with the inherent complexity of ecosystems and of tribal cultures, create an equally complex set of issues surrounding maintenance and preservation of habitats and native species.

PREDATORS

In Western cultures, most predators have long been regarded as competitors or enemies of humanity. Wolves, for instance, are often cast as villains in the Bible, as well as in European folk legends and fairy tales. In contrast, in many Native American cultures, wolves are traditionally valued as important members of ecosystems. Contemporary Native Americans, like the Northern Arapaho of the Wind River Reservation in Wyoming, welcome the presence of wolves and other predators, pointing out that wolves play a crucial role in protecting riparian ecosystems. The Northern Arapaho recognize that the presence of wolves makes wild herbivores and cattle wary about congregating for long periods of time around streams—particularly since they are especially vulnerable to ambushes by wolves in such areas. The Northern Arapaho also welcome bears, mountain lions, coyotes, and other predatory species, each of which has a unique and vital function within the ecosystem (Arapaho Ranch n.d.).

BISON

As noted in the essay on tribal land use in this encyclopedia, bison are a crucial material and spiritual component of many tribal cultures. The vast herds of bison, which once roamed the Great Plains and numbered between 50 and 200 million in the fifteenth century, had been decimated by the late nineteenth century. Now in the twenty-first century, several tribes are seeking to maintain or restore bison herds on their reservations.

Some tribes, like the Cheyenne River Sioux Tribe, Fort Belknap (Assiniboine/Nakota), Pine Ridge (Oglala Lakota), and others currently maintain bison herds on reservation land. These and several other tribes are in the process of collaborating with the environmental group Defenders of Wildlife to expand their herds. Others, including the Eastern Shoshone, who share the Wind River Reservation in Wyoming with the Northern Arapaho, are seeking to restore bison to their reservations.

The contemporary effort to restore bison to the Wind River Reservation is led by Jason Baldes (Eastern Shoshone), a graduate student in wildlife biology at the University of Montana. Baldes is working with tribal government and the Wildlife Conservation Society, attempting to establish a herd of about 1,000 bison at Wind River. He hopes that the reintroduced bison—to be made up of animals from Yellowstone National Park, the Henry Mountains (Utah), and Canada—will be able to share the 595,000-acre Northern Arapaho Ranch with the cattle currently residing there. The Eastern Shoshone and Northern Arapaho tribes passed a joint tribal resolution in September 2012 endorsing Baldes's proposal to return wild bison to the Wind River Reservation.

FISH

Tribes from the Great Lakes to the Northwest Coast have fished for salmon, cutthroat trout, sturgeon, whitefish, and other fish for millennia. However, starting in the 1800s, commercial overfishing, pollution from agriculture, mining, rapidly growing urban areas, and invasive species like the ocean lamprey (a kind of eel) severely reduced the numbers of fish in the Great Lakes region as well as in the Columbia Watershed.

Like peoples of the Northwest, many of the Anishinaabeg (also known as Chippewa or Ojibwa) peoples of the Great Lakes region secured off-reservation fishing rights in several of their many treaties with the United States over the years. Despite their treaty-protected rights to fish on- and off-reservation, the

Anishinaabeg people struggled throughout the twentieth century to exercise these rights due to local, state, and federal game laws as well as the drastic decline in native fisheries. For instance, the Keweenaw band of Chippewa in Michigan faced prosecution by state game officials in the 1950s and 1960s, even as they witnessed the continuing overharvesting of fish by commercial outfits and increasing pressure from sport fishermen.

Today, after a series of legal battles in which courts generally upheld Native American fishing rights, Great Lakes tribes, including the Keweenaw band of Chippewa (now known as the Keweenaw Bay Indian Community), are attempting to help restore native fisheries by establishing tribal fishing ordinances specifying the timing and duration of the fishing season and the number of fish tribal members are allowed to take, as well as through cooperative land and water management plans with local and state agencies, including protecting remaining wetlands vital to maintaining clean water and healthy fisheries. And while controversy over fishing rights continues, native peoples of the Great Lakes region hold events to educate the public about the cultural importance of fishing and the sustainable model of indigenous resource management.

EAGLES

The bald eagle is widely recognized as a symbol of the United States. Yet for centuries before the founding of the Republic, bald eagles and other raptors were culturally, spiritually, and symbolically important to many native peoples. After hunting, habitat destruction, and poisoning from pesticides like dichlorodiphenyltrichloroethane (DDT) decimated bald eagles and other birds in the late nineteenth century through the first half of the twentieth century, Native Americans found it increasingly difficult to obtain the birds whose feathers they prize for ceremonial purposes. In 1940, the federal government passed the Bald and Golden Eagle Protection Act (BGEPA), leading to prosecution of native and non-native individuals for the possession of eagle feathers. An amendment to the BGEPA passed in 1962 allowed Native Americans to possess eagle feathers for ceremonial purposes.

And while bald eagle populations have rebounded since the last quarter of the twentieth century—to the point where the species was removed from the Endangered Species list in 2007—Native Americans, along with some environmentalists, remain concerned about the bird's future viability given catastrophic losses of habitat. Some tribes, for example, the Zuni Pueblo of New Mexico, have decided to take an active role in protecting bald eagles and other raptors. In 1995, the Zuni began collaborating with the U.S. Fish and Wildlife Service and the New Mexico Department of Fish and Wildlife to establish an eagle sanctuary. The result, the Zuni Eagle Sanctuary, provides a home for injured eagles from the National Eagle Repository in Denver, Colorado, as well as ensures a source of feathers for the community's ceremonial needs. The first tribally operated avian sanctuary, the Zuni Eagle Sanctuary, has since won international recognition and has become a model for several tribal aviaries (Harvard University n.d.).

TREES AND PLANTS

In addition to the many sensitive and threatened animal species that are integral to tribal cultures, thousands of species of native trees and plants are crucial for traditional subsistence, ceremonial, and cultural reasons. For example, native people of California have utilized several species of oak for millennia. However, the rapid expansion of agriculture, industrial zones, and urban areas in California have led to a catastrophic decline in the oak woodlands that once dominated parts of the Central Valley and the foothills of the Sierra Nevada. Several California tribes are attempting to preserve, maintain, and expand on- and off-reservation oak woodlands through tribal initiatives and collaborations with state and private developers as well as conservation agencies. Tribal entities like the Graton Rancheria (Pomo/Coast Miwok) are in the process of obtaining additional tribally controlled lands and conservation easements to maintain and restore oak woodlands (Sarris 2011).

The Susanville Indian Rancheria, located in a relatively isolated, mountainous area of northeastern California, provides a good example of another route that California tribes can follow when seeking to achieve protection of cultural and ecological integrity in land use. Along with nearly 30 other California tribes, the Susanville Indian Rancheria operates a gaming establishment and hotel. Although the Rancheria's Diamond Mountain Casino is a much smaller and less lucrative endeavor than those near urban areas, it has helped the tribe purchase additional land for conservation and cultural uses. For instance, Susanville Rancheria bought a piece of land known as Cradle Valley Ranch in 2003. Consisting of 160 acres of forest and wetlands, parts of the property were being damaged by cattle. By purchasing the land and incorporating 65 acres of it into a Wetlands Reserve Project (WRP), Susanville Rancheria is protecting fragile wetlands, ensuring that birds and other animals that depend on such ecosystems are also protected (Middleton 2011, 219–222).

Many California Indian peoples have long and rich traditions of basket weaving. The Pomo, for instance, are world famous for their baskets, which are usually woven from grasslike native plants known as sedges and rushes that grow in riparian zones. Pomo baskets sometimes also incorporate feathers and abalone, as well as branches from redbud bushes and willow trees. Gathering materials for baskets is considered to be at least as important as weaving the basket itself. The catastrophic destruction of California's native ecosystems—especially riparian areas and wetlands, many of which lie outside contemporary California Indian reservations—has created great difficulty for many California Indian basket weavers, who find it increasingly difficult to gather necessary materials.

As part of an effort to maintain and revitalize Native American basket weaving across the state, California basket weavers from several tribes founded California Indian Basketweavers Association (CIBA) in the early 1990s. CIBA's vision statement outlines the group's priorities:

> establishing rapport and working with public agencies and other groups in order to provide a healthy physical, social, cultural, spiritual, and economic environment for the practice of California Indian basketry... increasing California Indian access to traditional cultural resources on public and tribal lands and traditional gathering sites, and encouraging the reintroduction of such resources and designation of gathering areas on such lands... raising awareness and providing education for Native Americans, the public, public agencies, arts, educational, and environmental groups or the artistry, practices and concerns of Native American Basketweavers [sic]... monitoring public and private land use and encouraging those management practices that protect and conserve traditional Native resources... [and] monitoring and discouraging pesticide use in traditional and potential gathering areas for the safety of weavers, gatherers, and others in tribal communities. (CIBA n.d.)

Along with many educational programs and basketry displays, CIBA collaborates with federal agencies like the Environmental Protection Agency (EPA), the Forest Service, the Bureau of Land Management, state agencies like California State Forestry, private land owners, and California tribal governments to meet their goals. Recently, CIBA held a meeting near Clear Lake, in Lake County, California, where a local non-Indian ranch owner agreed to suspend the use of pesticides in certain areas and to allow local California Indian basket weavers access to sites on his land where basket weaving materials are found. While land management issues are not always so easily resolved, CIBA's ongoing efforts to collaborate with various stakeholders and relevant agencies in order to conserve ecosystems used for gathering weaving materials promise to produce additional successes (Conner and Yamane 2010).

INTERTRIBAL CONSERVATION ORGANIZATIONS

The development of intertribal organizations with membership including people of diverse tribal affiliations has been a crucial component of Native American responses to the dynamic ecological, political, and economic conditions of the twentieth and twenty-first centuries. The National Congress of American Indians (NCAI), founded in 1946, is the oldest and most respected of such organizations. Along with addressing virtually every other issue affecting native peoples, the NCAI seeks to promote tribal control of trust lands by monitoring local, state, and federal activities that potentially impact tribal lands. The National Indian Youth Council (NIYC), founded in 1961, is another longstanding intertribal organization that works to support tribal land use policies. Both of these organizations have been active in advocacy at national and regional levels, and in litigation involving tribal land management and environmental issues. While both of these organizations contribute to the effort to ensure that tribal governments maintain control over decisions and activities directly affecting tribal land, they also address the full range of issues indirectly related to ecology and resources, including treaty rights, civil rights, and human rights (NCAI n.d.).

More recently, intertribal organizations focusing specifically on land use and conservation have emerged. For example, the Indian Country Conservancy (ICC) was incorporated as a federal nonprofit (501[c][3]) corporation in 2010. The principal goal of the ICC is to assist tribes in acquiring conservation lands (ICC n.d.). Other intertribal conservation organizations include the Indian Nation Conservation Alliance (INCA) and the Tribal Association of Conservation Districts (TACD).

REFERENCES

Arapaho Ranch. Available at http://www.arapahoranch.com/who.html.

Baldes, Jason. "Wind River Tribes Unite to Return Yellowstone Bison to Their Native Homeland." Retrieved from http://blog.nwf.org/2012/09/wind-river-tribes-unite-to-return-yellowstone-bison-to-their-native-homeland/.

Belone, Cecilia. "President's Statement." *National Indian Youth Council*. Retrieved from http://www.niyc-alb.org/president.htm in December 2011.

Benfield, Ken. "New HUD Grants Will Help Communities Pursue Sustainability." Retrieved from http://switchboard.nrdc.org/blogs/kbenfield/hud_answers_local_requests_wit.htm in November 2011.

Blakemore, Edward. "Native Americans Struggles in Reclaiming their Land: Annotated Bibliography." Retrieved from http://academic.udayton.edu/race/02rights/s98blak2.htm in October 2011.

Boswell, Evelyn. "Grad Student Plans to Reintroduce Bison on Reservation." *Indian Country Today*, December 5, 2011. Retrieved from http://indiancountrytodaymedianetwork.com/2011/12/05/grad-student-plans-to-reintroduce-buffalo-on-reservation-63333?utm_source=facebook&utm_medium=social&utm_content=grad-student-plans-to-reintroduce-buffalo-on-reservation-63333&utm_campaign=fb-posts.

California Indian Basketweavers Association (CIBA). "Keeping the Tradition Alive." Retrieved from http://www.ciba.org/vision.php.

Conner, Lois and Linda Yamane. "A Thousand Generation of Weavers." *News from Native California* 24, no. 1 (Fall 2010), 24–30.

Council of Energy Rich Tribes (CERT). Available at http://74.63.154.129/.

Davis, Thomas. *Sustaining the Forest, the People, and the Spirit*. New York: State University of New York (SUNY) Press, 2000.

Harvard University ASH Center for Democratic Governance and Innovation. "Zuni Eagle Sanctuary." Retrieved from http://www.innovations.harvard.edu/awards.html?id=6401.

Henson, Eric C. et al. *The State of the Native Nations: Conditions under U.S. Policies of Self-Determination: The Harvard Project on American Indian Economic Development*. Oxford: Oxford University Press, 2008.

Indian Country Conservancy (ICC). Available at http://www.indiancountryconservancy.org/newsupdates/.

Indigenous Peoples Issues and Resources Network. "United States: DOJ Request for Tribal Input on Two Issues Involving Eagle Feathers." Retrieved from http://indigenouspeoplesissues.com/index.php?option=com_content&view=article&id=12827%3Aunited-states-doj-request-for-tribal-input-on-two-issues-involving-eagle-feathers&catid=52%3Anorth-america-indigenous-peoples&Itemid=74&utm_source=feedburner&utm_medium=email&utm_campaign=Feed%3A+IndigenousPeoplesResources+%28Indigenous+Peoples+Issues+%26+Resources%29 in November 2011.

LaDuke, Winona. *Recovering the Sacred: The Power of Naming and Claiming*. Cambridge, MA: South End Press, (2005) 227–235.

Middleton, Beth Rose. *Trust in the Land: New Directions in Tribal Conservation*. Tucson: University of Arizona Press, 2011.

National Congress of American Indians (NCAI). "Land and Natural Resources." Retrieved from http://www.ncai.org/Land-Natural-Resources.24.0.html in October 2011.

Sarris, Greg (Graton Rancheria Tribal Chair). Personal Communication, October 21, 2011.

Weaver, Jace (Ed.). *Defending Mother Earth: Native American Perspectives on Environmental Justice*. New York: Orbis Books, 1995.

Wilkinson, Charles. *Blood Struggle: The Rise of Modern Indian Nations*. New York: W.W. Norton and Company, 2005.

Tribal Land Use

Ashley Corwyn Hall

Tribal nations today are in the process of exercising their intrinsic and federally recognized rights to sovereignty and self-determination. One of the most important ways they are doing this is by taking a principal and active role in regulating hunting, fishing, logging, water allocation, and agriculture on tribal lands. Along with engaging in coal, oil, gas, wind, solar, geothermal, hydroelectric energy development, and other kinds of development, tribal nations' increasingly prominent regulatory role can be seen as one of the means through which they seek to help create a sustainable economic basis for their own people and for the U.S. economy as a whole. Tribal nations face the challenge and opportunity of generating revenue while staying true to the traditional values that inform their relationships to their lands.

There are currently over 560 federally recognized American Indian tribes in the United States, and dozens more actively seeking federal acknowledgment. The members of present-day Native American tribal nations are the descendents of the original peoples of North America, many of whose oral traditions claim that they were created in their particular homeland on the continent. Some anthropologists assert that the ancestors of today's Native American people crossed a land bridge believed to have spanned the Bering Strait between Siberia and Alaska during the last Ice Age (more than 10,000 years ago). Native American origins are a controversial subject. Some, native and non-natives alike, support tribal explanations, while others promote competing stories, hypotheses, and theories. But regardless of how they view Native American origins, virtually everyone agrees that for thousands of years prior to European colonization, thousands of distinct peoples, the forerunners of today's tribal nations, occupied the lands that are now the United States of America and Canada.

Present-day tribal nations are sovereign, place-based entities that (aside from the unique case of Alaska) exercise control over approximately 45 million acres held in trust for them by the federal government. These lands comprise the 310 federal Indian reservations—land bases set aside for the exclusive benefit, use, and occupation of tribal peoples. Many of these areas were originally established through treaties and agreements between particular tribes and the federal government; others were created, diminished, augmented, or otherwise modified by statute or executive order.

In recent years, some tribal land bases have been consolidated or expanded through land purchases by tribal governments, individuals, and corporations. Many tribal nations have even begun to cooperate with non-native conservation groups, and private and public landowners to create cultural or conservation easements intended to limit development and safeguard important tribal locations and resources on lands not directly under tribal control.

Some federally recognized tribes hold restricted title to their lands, with stringent legal limitations on alienation, hypothecation, and encumbrance. An additional 10 million acres are held in trust by the federal government for individual tribal members in the lower 48 states, or are held by individual Native Americans, with legal restrictions against alienation or encumbrance. Restrictions against alienation generally preclude the sale, gift, or other devise of native land to non-native individuals or organizations; these restrictions are intended to help ensure that tribal territories cannot be fragmented or worse, eliminated entirely, by passing into private, non-native ownership. Restrictions on encumbrance of land to which tribes hold title are intended to obviate the possibility of individuals, banks, or other non-native entities taking possession of native lands through liens or other mechanisms.

While these restrictions are intended to protect tribal land bases (and they have largely been successful in this regard), they also place limits on how Native American communities and individuals may use their land—for instance, restrictions on encumbrance mean that tribes cannot use their land as security for private loans, a fact that sometimes hinders tribal economic development.

There are also state-designated reservations, controlled by state-recognized tribes; state-designated reservations tend to be much smaller than federal reservations and have a different legal history and status. Although not intended to diminish the importance of state-recognized tribal nations, the focus here is on federally recognized tribes and tribal lands.

The situation in Alaska is special. Lands held by Alaska Native corporations and villages amount to about 10 million acres, but there are no actual Indian reservations in Alaska, which became a state in 1959, long after the United States had ceased to make treaties or agreements with individual tribal nations. Instead, in 1971 the Alaska Federation of Natives (AFN), a coalition of dozens of native villages and tribal peoples, pressured Congress into passing the Alaska Native Claims Settlement Act (ANCSA), legislation that extinguished Alaska Native subsistence rights and aboriginal title to the vast majority of land in the state while providing a monetary award of almost $1 billion—the Alaska Native Fund—along with about 44 million acres of land as compensation. The ANCSA also stipulated the charter of the Alaska Native Corporations (ANCs), 12 regional tribal for-profit corporations (a thirteenth was subsequently added to allow Alaska Natives living outside the state to share in the settlement). The ANCs are owned entirely by Alaska Natives; each Alaska Native individual receives equal amounts of stock. The ANCs administer the Alaska Native Fund and hold title in fee simple to the 44 million acres of ANCSA land in Alaska. This type of title does not involve the restrictions on alienation and encumbrance that apply to lands held by tribes or individuals in the lower 48 states. However, the land is protected from alienation by an amendment to the ANCSA that precludes alienation of ANC stock. The ANCSA also established a process by which individual Alaska Native villages with populations of 25 or more can be chartered as for-profit corporations under Alaska state laws.

Although there are certain restrictions imposed by the federal government on the sale and disposition of trust lands, tribal nations exercise considerable control over land use policies affecting their land bases. In many cases, the philosophies governing tribal land use decisions have their origins in the distant past—they reflect the "attitudes, beliefs, and practices" developed by the native peoples who occupied North America long before invasion and colonization by Europeans and subsequent generations of Euro-Americans (Deloria 1996, 70). Despite warfare, disease epidemics, forced removal from homelands, the reservation system, allotment, forced acculturation, high rates of poverty, environmental degradation, the introduction of invasive plant and animal species, and other profound disruptions, many native nations continue to adhere to an environmental ethos established by their ancestors in the struggle to survive.

Modern tribal environmental and land use policies and practices are often extensions of aboriginal tribal cultures that tend to reflect their spiritual and philosophical traditions. These underlying values often reflect a sense of reverence for the natural world and acknowledge the interdependency of the human community, other living beings, and the lands they occupy. Tribal land use policies are expressions of sovereignty and self-determination complicated by the need to strike a difficult balance between ancestral principles of respect and reciprocity and the evolving environmental conditions and economic demands of the twenty-first century.

Given the facts of tribal and geographical diversity, it is helpful to take an approach to the study of current native land use that focuses on the following general regions: the Northeast, the Southeast, the Great Plains, the Southwest, the Great Basin, California, and the Northwest.

THE NORTHEAST

The Northeast includes the present-day states of Maine, New Hampshire, Vermont, Massachusetts, New York, Rhode Island, Connecticut, New Jersey, Pennsylvania, Delaware, Maryland, and parts of Virginia, as well as northern Kentucky and eastern Ohio. Prior to European colonization, the northeastern part of the United States was a heavily forested region, rich with deer, wild turkey, and other game animals. For hundreds of years, the area had been dominated by several large confederations of tribes—for example, the Haudenosaunee, the Algonquin, the Powhatan, and the Leni-Lenape—which often corresponded roughly with major language groups.

Despite the removal of many of their people to Oklahoma (Indian Territory) in the 1830s, the remaining Haudenosaunee, including the Cayuga and Seneca, have worked to maintain the aboriginal knowledge of their tribal agricultural traditions. The Cayuga, for instance, have recently engaged in a process of reacquiring land and revitalizing their agricultural and related cultural traditions. Thanks to the ceaseless efforts of tribal elders, both the knowledge of ancestral farming practices as well as actual native seed varieties were maintained and preserved even amidst aggressive efforts by non-natives to supplant them with Euro-American, mechanized, single-crop agriculture, hybrid, and most recently, genetically engineered plants. Like many other native peoples, the Haudenosaunee are currently in the process of mitigating the negative legacy of colonization by recovering their ancestral agricultural knowledge and practices.

The agricultural knowledge painstakingly safeguarded and maintained by generations of Cayuga tribal members is being put to use in Gakwiyo ("good food") Garden, a 100-acre plot of land where tribal members grow the Haudenosaunee Three Sisters (beans, corn, and squash) along with a variety of other plants and flowers. Produce from Gakwiyo Garden is distributed to more than 100 tribal households; surplus produce is sold at Cayuga Corners, a farm stand owned and operated by the Nation.

In addition to traditional Haudenosaunee cultivators, the Cayuga also plant over 200 acres with soybeans, a commercial crop produced for sale to local processing companies. The Cayuga are making slow but steady progress toward the goal of reacquiring land, recovering their agricultural traditions, and receiving the many ecological, health, and cultural benefits associated with their traditional land use practices. Hunting, fishing, and gathering are activities that have been more difficult to reestablish, given ecological changes throughout the region and the limited land base currently controlled by the Cayuga.

The Cayuga and Seneca also continue to engage in legal actions aimed at retrieving land ceded to the State of New York in fraudulent treaties, to seek monetary compensation for these and other wrongs, to maintain and revive traditional land use practices, and to develop new uses for their lands. Campgrounds, tax-free cigarette shops, convenience markets, and gaming establishments are a few novel uses to which the Cayuga, Seneca, and other Haudenosaunee peoples now put their lands.

THE SOUTHEAST

This region includes parts of the present-day state of Virginia, and encompasses West Virginia, North Carolina, South Carolina, Georgia, Florida, Alabama, Tennessee, Mississippi, and Louisiana, as well as parts of Kentucky, Ohio, Illinois, Missouri, and Arkansas. Like the peoples of the Northeast, peoples of the Southeast occupied their ancestral homelands for millennia before Europeans first arrived in North America. And, like the peoples of the Northeast, the peoples of the Southeast developed highly sophisticated land use practices long before the arrival of Europeans, including fortified permanent or semi-permanent towns and villages, fishing and hunting, shifting agriculture featuring the complementary combination of corn, beans, and squash, as well as tobacco—used both medicinally and ritually—and the gathering of wild plants for food and medicine.

There is archaeological evidence that the Southeastern peoples began practicing agriculture even earlier than those in the Northeast. Even before the introduction of corn, from Mexico, ancient peoples of the Southeast began cultivating indigenous plants, including a species of squash and sunflowers. The evidence shows that Native Americans of the Southeast were actively and selectively planting these and other plants in the rich, moist soil of river valleys and alluvial plains as long as 5,000 years ago, suggesting the Southeast was an independent center of agricultural innovation.

Over the course of millennia, Southeastern Native Americans engaged in a continual process of refining their horticultural knowledge and techniques, gradually incorporating new elements like corn and beans into their agricultural traditions. But, as in the Northeast, despite its great and growing importance, agriculture never entirely supplanted subsistence practices such as hunting, fishing, and foraging.

Yet another similarity between peoples of the Northeast and those of the Southeast is that they organized themselves into large confederations consisting of two or more tribal peoples. The Creek Confederacy, dominated by the Muskogee, a large group that was itself comprised of several different tribal groups, was one of the most powerful entities in the region. By the eighteenth century, the Creek Confederacy commanded a large land base within the present-day states of South Carolina, Georgia, Alabama, and Florida, within which each member tribe maintained political and cultural autonomy over both its central town and surrounding agricultural and hunting lands.

However, increasing pressure from Euro-American settlers in the late seventeenth through early nineteenth centuries threatened the customary life ways of Southeastern tribes. Despite efforts on the part of many of the Southeast's Native American peoples to accommodate colonial settlement by adopting Euro-American agricultural techniques as well as social, political, and religious models, by the early 1800s, Southeastern politicians and settlers were voicing their support for a plan to relocate all the indigenous nations of the region to Indian Territory. Ultimately, tens of thousands of Southeastern Native American tribal peoples—men, women, children, and elders—were forced to march more than 1,000 miles from their homelands in the fertile river valleys of their Southeastern homelands to the drastically different land and climate of Indian Territory (in present-day Oklahoma).

While environmental conditions were different in Indian Territory, the Mvskoke (Muskogee), often referred to as Creek, adapted rapidly to the new location, carrying on with their indigenous hunting, gathering and agricultural traditions, supplemented by the new crops like wheat, barley, and Asian cotton, and developing methods of animal husbandry centered on the cattle and pigs introduced by Euro-Americans. Blackberries and acorns, which had been important wild food sources in the Southeast, continued to feature prominently in the Mvskoke diet after the move to Indian Territory.

Despite these and many other attempts to adapt to their new circumstances, Mvskoke land tenure in Indian Territory faced ongoing threats throughout the nineteenth century, culminating in the unilateral decision on the part of the United States in 1871 to do away with the treaty-making process entirely. When coal and oil deposits were discovered in Indian Territory toward the end of the 1800s, many non-native speculators attempted to gain title to Mvskoke allotments.

Still, the Mvskoke held on to their tribal identity and to a small fraction of the original lands they had reserved by treaty in 1832. Throughout the first decades of the twentieth century, the Mvskoke continued their efforts to maintain their land base and life ways, though substantial advancements did not occur until the 1970s, when the first Mvskoke chief of the modern era, Claude Cox, was chosen. With renewed federal support, the Mvskoke began to recover some of the lands they had lost. Now, in the twenty-first century, the Mvskoke have consolidated their administrative jurisdiction over an area encompassing eight counties in east-central Oklahoma.

One recent success is the Mvskoke Food Sovereignty Initiative (MFSI). Founded in 2005, with headquarters in Okmulgee, Oklahoma, capital of the Mvskoke (Creek) Nation, the MFSI seeks to promote sustainable agriculture that will enable the Mvskoke people and other native and non-native residents in the Mvskoke

Tribal Administrative Jurisdiction to provide for their own health and nutritional needs. The MFSI currently operates two demonstration farms and assists dozens of households as they seek to cultivate family gardens. It has also established a seed bank—a repository for rare and endangered heirloom seed varieties, like *safke* corn, one of the varietals the Mvskoke have cultivated for hundreds or, in some cases, thousands, of years.

THE GREAT PLAINS

The Great Plains are a major ecosystem in the middle of the American continent, west of the Mississippi River and east of the Rocky Mountains. They consist of vast, mostly treeless grasslands and steppe and include parts of the present-day states of Minnesota, Iowa, Missouri, Kansas, Nebraska, Oklahoma, Texas, New Mexico, Colorado, Wyoming, North Dakota, South Dakota, and Montana. Archaeological evidence suggests that Native American peoples did not usually create permanent settlements in the plains themselves. Rather, they tended to live at the edges of the plains or in sheltered river or mountain valleys at the edges of the plains, where they were protected from the fierce, cold winds that blow across the open plains. Tribal peoples who utilized the Great Plains include the Nakota (Assiniboine), Dakota, Kansa, Osage, Quapaw, Caddo, Lipan Apache, Comanche, Kiowa, Arapaho, Cheyenne, Lakota, Arikara, Hidatsa, Mandan, Eastern Shoshone, Crow, and Blackfeet.

Prior to the arrival of Europeans, Native Americans who lived in the Great Plains region relied primarily on hunting among the vast herds of game animals, including deer, elk, antelope, and, especially bison, that roamed the open grasslands. The American bison (also known as American buffalo) was especially important to many of the tribes in the region—due both to their large numbers (estimates place the number of bison at around 50 to 200 million in the sixteenth century) and to the great amount of meat, hide, and other usable materials that a single animal could provide. Just as agriculture and other subsistence activities were integral parts of Northeastern and Southeastern native cultures, hunting bison was a profoundly important aspect of Plains material culture, and figured prominently in tribal ceremonial and spiritual life.

To undermine the indigenous Plains economy and force the people to surrender, the U.S. government unofficially sanctioned the destruction of the vast bison herds that formed the basis of Plains cultures. Together with commercial hunting—where often only the hides were taken and the rest of the animals were left to rot—increased pressure from Native American hunting, competition for grazing land from Euro-American cattle ranches and farms, the herds were decimated. By the 1880s, the American bison was virtually extinct.

Given its historical importance, it should come as no surprise that rescuing the bison from extinction has become an issue of great importance to contemporary

Plains tribes. In fact, the largest remaining bison herds are those living in Native American tribal territories. The Cheyenne River Sioux, for example, currently steward a herd of approximately 2,000 bison.

At the same time, Native American tribal peoples of the Great Plains have adapted to the market economy imposed by the dominant (U.S.) society and have become adept at catering to Euro-American tastes. For example, the Northern Arapaho, who share the Wind River Reservation in Wyoming with the Eastern Shoshone, began operating Arapaho Ranch in 1940 when the tribe faced grim economic conditions. Over time, the 595,000-acre ranch has become one of the most important facets of the Northern Arapaho economy, as well as a significant part of Wyoming's overall economy.

THE APSÁALOOKE (CROW)

Approximately 250 miles to the north of the Wind River Reservation lies the Crow Reservation, with headquarters in Crow Agency, Montana. The Crow, or Apsáalooke, raise cattle like the Northern Arapaho and grow a variety of commercial crops. However, they are also deeply involved in a different, and more controversial (though profitable) use of land—namely, coal mining and the extraction of oil and natural gas.

The Absaloka mine, for instance, has employed a significant number of Apsáalooke tribal members (around 70 percent of the mine's employees, or between 100 and 115 Apsáalooke individuals, on a seasonal basis as of 2002). Nontribal corporations operate over 100 oil and gas wells within the borders of the reservation, providing employment for tribal members and royalties to the tribe. In the meantime, the Crow continue to utilize other reservation resources, such as agriculture, timber, and—as a possible alternative to coal—the development of wind energy and construction of a new hydroelectric facility on the Bighorn River, downstream from an existing dam owned and operated by the tribe.

THE SOUTHWEST

The Southwest includes the present-day states of New Mexico and Arizona, as well as parts of Colorado, Texas, California, Nevada, and Utah. The region is ecologically and culturally diverse. It is home to a great number of tribal peoples like the 21 distinct Pueblo peoples and the Papago (Tohono O'odham), Havasupai, Hualapai, and Pima, who have lived in the region for thousands of years, as well as more recent arrivals, such as the Jicarilla Apache, Mescalero Apache, San Carlos Apache, and the Navajo (or Diné).

Pueblo peoples, who have lived in the region for millennia, developed dry-farming techniques that allowed them to create permanent settlements and to pursue the intensive cultivation of maize, beans, squash, melons, and chili peppers, as well as other crops. Dry farming requires no irrigation, depending entirely on atmospheric precipitation.

After taking possession of the region from its original Spanish colonizers, the United States followed the Spanish example of allowing many of the Pueblo peoples to maintain a high degree of cultural, political, and economic independence from the dominant society. Given their relative isolation, the Pueblos succeeded in maintaining their agricultural and other traditional land use practices like hunting and gathering throughout the nineteenth century and into the twentieth century with minimal disruption compared to most other tribal peoples. However, the twentieth and twenty-first centuries have brought new and serious threats to the Pueblo as well as to their neighbors, the Apache, Diné, and Tohono O'odham. Among these threats, environmental degradation caused by coal mining is particularly severe.

In response, the tribes have created the Black Mesa Water Coalition (BMWC) and collaborated with several environmental groups to develop the Just Transition, a plan intended to help them undertake the move from an economy heavily reliant on unsustainable resource extraction to one based on sustainable activities like farming and herding, as well as sustainable energy development, including solar and wind. More traditional land uses also continue, including the raising of sheep for meat and wool, farming, and hunting and gathering (Northern Arizona University n.d.).

Yet another type of land use in the Southwest is exemplified by the White Mountain Apache tribe of Arizona. After decades of leasing tribal forests to non-native timber companies—which often engaged in clear-cutting and other unsustainable practices—the White Mountain Apache decided to take a more active role in managing their forests. In the 1970s, the tribe expanded and modernized their timber mill, the Fort Apache Timber Company, and declined to renew their lease with Southwest Forest Industries. The White Mountain Apache replaced the practice of clear-cutting with selective logging to halt erosion and ensure the viability of their forests in perpetuity (Wilkinson 2005, 315–321).

INTERMOUNTAIN REGION

The Intermountain region comprises the area between the Rocky Mountains and the Sierra Nevada to the south, and the Cascade Mountains to the north. It includes the states of Utah and Nevada, as well as parts of Idaho, Arizona, Washington, Oregon, and California. The Intermountain region encompasses two primary topographic features or subregions: the Great Basin in the south and the Columbia Plateau in the north. While the flora and fauna found in each of these subregions varies, they share some features in common. Both are high in elevation, both tend to be arid or semiarid, and both include common topographical features like plateaus, basins, and ranges.

Native American peoples of the Great Basin are predominantly speakers of Numic (also known as Shoshonean) languages. Tribal peoples of the region include the Ute (Nuche), Southern Paiute, Western Shoshone (Newe), Mono, and Goshute. Archaeological evidence, together with tribal oral traditions, demonstrates that Native American peoples have lived in the Great Basin for thousands of years. Some of these inhabited semipermanent settlements were on the shores of lakes and on riverbanks, though the majority engaged in a cyclical pattern of seasonal migration to utilize various resources.

The Nuche (Utes), for instance, spent the winter months in lower elevations, conducting rabbit drives, hunting small game, fishing in streams and lakes, and gathering plants; in the spring and summer, they moved into higher elevations, where they hunted elk, bighorn sheep, and other animals. In the late summer and fall, as they prepared to return to lower elevations, they harvested nuts from the piñon pine, which grow best at elevations between 6,000 and 8,500 feet. Pine nuts were also a dietary staple of the Southern Paiute, the Newe, and other Great Basin peoples. American Indian peoples of the region continue to gather pine nuts to this day, valuing them for their flavor and high fat content.

Great Basin peoples developed sophisticated knowledge bases and land use practices that allowed them to adapt to some of the most inhospitable environmental conditions in North America. Traditional land use practices also took into account the fragility of Great Basin ecosystems. Except for certain ceremonies like the Shoshone, Paiute, and Ute Pine Nut Dance and the Ute Bear Dance, or in cases of subsistence activities requiring larger numbers—or at times of crisis—Great Basin people lived in small family groups for most of the year, allowing them to make sustainable use of the limited resources available in the region.

Currently, Great Basin peoples strive to maintain their traditional relationships to the region while adjusting to rapidly changing environmental, demographic, and economic conditions. Land management and environmental issues facing contemporary Great Basin tribal peoples include energy development, nuclear testing, urbanization, and perhaps most importantly, water use. For example, most water available in the Great Basin is presently diverted to burgeoning regional urban centers like Salt Lake City, Utah, and Las Vegas, Nevada, as well as a number of cities in southern California.

Despite having effectively lost control over large tracts of land, the Western Shoshone continue to assert their rights to the land under an 1863 Treaty (known as the Treaty of Ruby Valley) and currently raise livestock, plant a variety of crops, and hunt and gather, integrating ancient indigenous land use philosophy and practices with modern ranching and agriculture. Other Newe continue to use land falling within the borders of currently recognized Shoshone reservations at Duck

Valley and Ely (both in Nevada) for ranching, agriculture, and ceremonial purposes.

Given the scarcity of water in the region, which is necessary to the land use practices favored by the majority of Western Shoshone tribal members, and due to its vulnerability to potential pollution by nuclear testing and storage and from gold and silver mines in the area, the Western Shoshone Steering Committee and Western Shoshone tribal leaders initiated the Western Shoshone Defense Project (WSDP) in 1991. The WSDP has grown from a small, grassroots organization staffed by volunteers into one with a full-time, paid staff that collaborates with environmental groups and other parties interested in "...protecting, preserving, and restoring Newe rights and lands for present and future generations based on cultural and spiritual traditions" (Western Shoshone Defense Project n.d.). WSDP projects include educational activities like organizing community field trips, mapping cultural areas, and training Newe community members to become more effective advocates of culturally appropriate uses for disputed areas of their ancestral homeland, which they refer to as Newe Sogobia.

CALIFORNIA

The state of California is ecologically diverse. It includes alpine ecosystems in the Sierra Nevada and Cascades, arid ecosystems in the Mojave Desert, the large fertile Central Valley, oak woodlands in the foothills of the Sierra Nevada and Coast Ranges, and one of the longest and richest coastlines in the United States, as well as magnificent redwood forests. At the time the first Europeans entered the region, it was just as culturally diverse, with over 100 separate languages and several hundred distinct tribal groups. The many contemporary peoples of California include the Agua Caliente band of Cahuilla Indians, the Augustine band of Cahuilla Indians, the Sycuan band of the Kumeyaay Nation, Chemehuevi, the Santa Ynez band of Chumash Mission Indians of the Santa Ynez Reservation, the California Valley Miwok tribe, United Auburn Indian Community of the Auburn Rancheria, Federated Indians of Graton Rancheria (Coast Miwok and Pomo), Yurok, Hoopa, and Karuk.

California Indians traditionally pursued a wide range of land use strategies, depending on the location of their homelands. For instance, peoples of the valleys and foothills fished, hunted antelope, elk, deer, and other animals and harvested roots, plants, berries and nuts, including acorns—a crucial food source—while people in coastal regions emphasized fishing in California's rich coastal waters and estuaries, harvesting shellfish and kelp, and utilizing other marine resources.

In the wake of early Spanish colonization and the 1848 Gold Rush, contemporary California Indian peoples continue to struggle to hold onto their land bases—mostly small compared to those in other areas—and to protect them from ongoing mining, explosive urbanization, timber harvesting, farming and ranching, and other alien land uses introduced by Euro-Americans. While most California Indian reservations, or *rancherias*, as they are sometimes called, are very small (exceptions are Pomo, Hoopa, Yurok, and Karuk reservations in the north of the state), California tribes today are engaged in the process of developing ways to use their land that allow for economic development in the twenty-first century while still conforming to the sustainability and reciprocity of traditional native land use philosophies.

Agua Caliente Band of Cahuilla Indians

The most controversial new land use is the economic strategy of developing gaming establishments. The Agua Caliente band of Cahuilla Indians was among the first to pioneer this development strategy. Opponents of Indian gaming argue that it encourages alcohol and drug use, increases the likelihood of problem gambling, involves the risk of organized crime, leads to disputes over tribal enrollment, and creates other problems for tribal and non-native communities. A less well-known complaint against Indian gaming—raised by some tribal members and environmentally minded non-Indians—is that it is an inappropriate use of tribal land because it does not conform to traditional native land use attitudes, beliefs, or practices.

Tribal proponents of gaming, however, point to the dire economic conditions that have led them to pursue it as a form of development and to the fact that tribal peoples do enjoy a tradition of wagering on games of chance that long predates the emergence of casino-style gambling.

While some claim that casinos (and the related development of resort hotels, spas, and golf courses) appear to be inconsistent with tribal traditions of environmental stewardship and conservation, income from these projects has enabled the Agua Caliente band of Cahuilla Indians and other native nations to become financially independent—a critical condition necessary for the exercise of sovereignty. Revenue from gaming has also allowed the Agua Caliente people to contribute to programs like the federal government's Bureau of Land Management (BLM) California Desert Advisory Council.

THE NORTHWEST

The Columbia Plateau lies directly north of the Great Basin. Parts of the Columbia Plateau are also generally arid or semiarid. However, the region also includes more freshwater streams, rivers, and lakes, a greater number of wild animals, and more verdant vegetation than found in the Great Basin. Tribal peoples of the Columbia Plateau include the Nez Perce (Nimíipuu), Umatilla, Yakama, Okanogan, Coeur de'Alene, Cowlitz, Kalapuya, and many others who utilized the broad range of resources available within their territories. Like the peoples of the Great Basin, many of the Columbia Plateau peoples moved around from season to season, taking advantage of wild plant foods like camas root, service berry, and huckleberry, as well as hunting for animals like elk and deer, and, most important, fishing for salmon and other fish in the Columbia River and its many tributaries.

In the face of encroachment by Euro-American settlers, in 1855 territorial governor Isaac Ingalls Stevens proceeded to negotiate treaties with Columbia Plateau tribes including the Nez Perce, Yakama, and Umatilla. These treaties not only reserved to the tribes significant portions of their aboriginal territories, they also affirmed off-reservation gathering, hunting, and fishing rights to the tribes, who were to have unfettered access to all customary locations for these activities.

Nez Perce (Nimíipuu)

The Nimíipuu (Nez Perce) were among the tribal peoples who negotiated treaties with Governor Stevens. While their 1855 treaty reserved a territory of 8 million acres to the Nez Perce, a second treaty (1863) and allotment after 1887 further reduced and broke up Nez Perce lands. Left with a badly fragmented land base consisting of only about 11 percent of their reservation, they nevertheless reserved off-reservation land-use rights in the original 1855 treaty that remain in force today. Starting in the early twentieth century, the Army Corps of Engineers began building dams to impound water in the Columbia River system for agricultural, industrial, household, and hydroelectric use and to prevent flooding (Wilkinson 2005, 29–44).

Some of these dams, like Grand Coulee, on the main stem of the Columbia, were among the biggest in the world when they were built, and while they have greatly contributed to the growth of agriculture and of urban centers in the region, they have also contributed to a precipitous decline in salmon runs. Despite their treaty-guaranteed rights to use off-reservation traditional fishing sites, peoples like the Nimíipuu, Umatilla, Yakima, and others have found the quantity of salmon in their rivers drastically reduced. Since the mid-twentieth century, the Nimíipuu and allied tribes have engaged in a battle to assert their off-reservation fishing rights and to reverse the decline of the salmon runs. The Nimíipuu and others are also urging state fish hatcheries to release more salmon into the region's rivers and streams.

Recently, the Nimíipuu have begun using Geographical Information Systems (GIS) technology to document and map particular locations within their aboriginal territory that they can claim as traditional gathering, hunting, or fishing grounds or that have other significant cultural significance. Working with tribal elders and historical documents, tribal members and other volunteers are plotting important locations so that they can present irrefutable proof of the precise locations they currently claim among those where they reserve off-reservation fishing rights. The Nez

Perce mapping projects are also intended to lend weight to arguments concerning the economic and cultural damages they have suffered as a result of the thousands of dams on rivers in the Columbia Watershed. Already, in a limited number of cases, the government has agreed to remove dams or to install fish ladders with the hope that these measures will allow more salmon to reach their spawning areas and to increase their numbers.

Peoples of the Northwest Coastal region, located in present-day Oregon and Washington states, have also traditionally relied on salmon in the Columbia River system, as well as marine resources. Given the growth of non-native population centers on the Northwest Coast, Indian reservations tend to be much smaller in area than those of the Yakima, Umatilla, Nez Perce, Okanogan, and others further inland. Clear-cutting, agriculture, urbanization, overfishing, and other land uses introduced by Euro-Americans have all had deleterious effects on the salmon runs for coastal peoples like the Quinault, the Nisqually, the Puyallup, the Makah, and others. However, given their longstanding traditions of utilizing marine resources and their continued proximity to those resources, the coastal tribes of the Northwest have had distinct opportunities and unique problems.

THE MAKAH

For example, the Makah, a people who have lived in the Puget Sound area on the coast of present-day Washington State for millennia, have maintained a foothold in their aboriginal territory. Nevertheless, they encounter determined opposition to their decision to resume whale hunting, one of their most treasured traditional marine resource uses. Archaeological evidence from an ancient settlement, known as the Ozette Village Site, shows that the Makah engaged in whaling for at least 2,000 years before they voluntarily ceased the practice in the 1920s as a response to the decline in grey whale populations. When the grey whale was removed from the Endangered Species list in 1994, the Makah started planning their first whale hunt in over 70 years, which they conducted successfully in 1999.

While the Makah view their whale hunt as an integral part of their culture, a practice leading to many health and spiritual benefits, and as potentially sustainable—especially as compared to the commercial whaling that depleted whale herds in the first place—others, including environmental groups like the Sea Shepherd Society, are vehemently opposed to any and all whaling. Controversy is likely to continue, but for the present, the Makah have reached an agreement with the International Whaling Commission that affirms their right to take up to four grey whales annually. The federal government has also supported the Makah's whaling rights, noting that, like the Nez Perce and other Northwestern tribes, the Makah reserved their right to pursue traditional subsistence practices in traditional places on- and off-reservation in their 1855 treaty negotiated with Governor Isaac Stevens.

REFERENCES

Agua Caliente Band of Cahuilla Indians. "Tribal Council." Retrieved from http://www.aguacaliente.org/content/Tribal%20Council/.

Arapaho Ranch. Available at http://www.arapahoranch.com/index.php

Cayuga Nation. "Land Rights History." Retrieved from http://www.cayuganation-nsn.gov/LandRights/LandClaimHistory.

Corporation for Public Broadcasting. "American Buffalo: Spirit of a Nation." *Nature*. Retrieved from http://www.pbs.org/wnet/nature/episodes/american-buffalo-spirit-of-a-nation/introduction/2183/.

Coté, Charlotte. *Spirits of Our Whaling Ancestors: Revitalizing Makah and Nuu-chah-nulth Traditions*. Seattle: University of Washington Press, 2010.

Crow Indian Tribe. "Crow Natural, Socio-Economic and Cultural Resources Assessment and Conditions Report," April 15, 2002. Retrieved from http://www.blm.gov/pgdata/etc/medialib/blm/mt/field_offices/miles_city/og_eis/crow.Par.63678.File.dat/economy.pdf

Deloria, Vine, Jr. *God Is Red*. Boulder, CO: Fulcrum Publishing, 1996.

Deloria, Vine, Jr. and Clifford Lyttle. *The Nations Within: The Past and Future of American Indian Sovereignty*. Austin: University of Texas Press, 1998.

Foster, Pepper. *Native American Legal Update: Native American Land Use*. Retrieved from http://www.nativelegalupdate.com/articles/land-use/.

Henson, Eric C. et al. *The State of the Native Nations: Conditions under U.S. Policies of Self-Determination: The Harvard Project on American Indian Economic Development*. Oxford: Oxford University Press, 2008.

LaDuke, Winona. *Recovering the Sacred: The Power of Naming and Claiming*. Cambridge, MA: South End Press, 2005.

Middleton, Beth Rose. *Trust in the Land: New Directions in Tribal Conservation*. Albuquerque: University of Arizona Press, 2010.

Northern Arizona University. "Black Mesa, Arizona." *Land Use History of America (Colorado Plateau)*. Retrieved from http://cpluhna.nau.edu/Places/black_mesa.htm.

Russel, Scott (Secretary, Crow Nation's Executive Branch). "Tribal Development of Energy Resources and the Creation of Energy Jobs on Indian Lands." Congressional Testimony. Washington, D.C.: Government Printing Office, 2011. Retrieved from http://naturalresources.house.gov/uploadedfiles/russelltestimony04.01.11.pdf.

Scarry, Margaret C. and John F. Scarry. "Native American 'Garden Culture' in Southeastern North America." *World Archaeology* 37, no. 2 (June 2005) 259–274.

Treat, James. "Mvskoke Country: Sustainable Sovereignty." *Muscogee Nation News* 41, no. 15 (October 1, 2011). Retrieved from http://mvskokecountry.wordpress.com/tag/safke/.

Western Shoshone Defense Project. Available at http://www.wsdp.org/.

Wilkinson, Charles. *Blood Struggle: The Rise of Modern Indian Nations*. New York: W.W. Norton and Company, 2005.

Wilkinson, Charles. *The People Are Dancing Again: The History of the Siletz Tribe of Western Oregon*. Seattle: University of Washington Press, 2010.

SECTION 10
Canadian Indians and Other Aboriginal Peoples

Aboriginal Peoples and the Canadian Government

Chris Paci

According to the 2006 Canadian census, there were over 31 million Canadians, of which 1.2 million are aboriginal. The aboriginal population in Canada is made up of First Nation, Métis, and Inuit people living in over 1,000 communities. First Nations make up the majority of this population, at over 800,000. The second largest and fastest growing aboriginal population is the Métis, at around 300,000 people. The 100,000 Inuit inhabit mostly sub-Arctic and Arctic Canada. Aboriginal peoples are located throughout the country, from coast to coast, with many living in urban centers. Aboriginal peoples are not homogeneous; communities vary in size, culturally and linguistically, and by their historical development, political structures, economies, quality of life, and sustainability. Aboriginal peoples share a common historical struggle for equal rights and self-determination in Canada.

CONTEXT OF ABORIGINAL AND CANADIAN RELATIONS

All aboriginal nations have creation stories. Some speak of a giant spider, others of great migrations or falling from the sky. Still others speak of the formation of the land on the back of a turtle in a great sea of water. Some aboriginal origin stories speak of the people springing from the lands in which they now inhabit, and many people have names that speak of them coming from their land. The Dené are from Denendeh, for example. Many details about the specific cultural demographics, economies, mortality, quality of life, political structures, and so on are not well known by mainstream Canadians. This is surprising because Canadian policies were implemented in the past to assimilate aboriginal peoples, and more recently to address the problems these policies have caused.

From the mid-1500s until there was a country called Canada in 1867, the region was colonized by France and Britain. Prior to colonization, the area was inhabited by numerous First Nation peoples and Inuit. Métis were a result of colonial contact. Until about 1970, aboriginal relations with all levels of Canadian government can best be described as a state of resistance. Canadian governments mostly had a paternalistic view of aboriginal peoples. After 1970, a fundamental structural change culminated in the 1982 repatriation of the Canadian Constitution and the first steps in reconciliation of many longstanding aboriginal issues. Many small and large events have taken place over the years, and in this essay, we touch only on the highlights and key junctures of these relations.

Modern Canada is a multicultural social democracy, founded on a rich diversity of cultures, including aboriginal cultures. In 1982, the Canadian Constitution recognized three aboriginal peoples: "Indians, Métis and Inuit." It did not define who each of these peoples are other than to state that they have aboriginal rights and title. Treaties that had been signed with the Crown were recognized and affirmed. In Canada, federal legislation known as the Indian Act continued to control the lives of First Nations, and indirectly the Inuit and Métis. All aboriginal nations continue to receive marginal treatment and are poorly administered to by federal and provincial/territorial governments.

From time immemorial until about the late 1700s, First Nations and Inuit lived and flourished on the lands of their ancestors, along the oceans, lakes, and rivers in what became known today as Canada. Aboriginal societies developed complex systems of trade, political and economic alliances, complex cultures and traditions, and peace and war relations, which varied a great deal from one end of the country to the other and over time. The Métis people were born from the earliest interactions of First Nations and Europeans, starting in the mid-1600s. Over time, many Métis developed unique cultures, languages, and identities (in the United States, these people would be considered either Indians of the various tribes or more simply as Americans).

Before and as a result of sustained contact on the eastern Atlantic coast in the late 1400s, tremendous localized change occurred. This change swept over the land and affected the people differently depending on the timing and scale of change it brought. Disease and ideas were introduced that ultimately stressed aboriginal communities to the point of breaking. What is not known in detail can be partially reconstructed by archaeology and oral history research.

Canada as a nation grew with the trade in furs, and the 1600s and 1700s saw the establishment of forts and posts, which eventually grew into most of Canada's modern cities. Most fur trade posts attracted associated settlement and established at strategic locations along rivers and lakes of interior Canada. *Coeur de bois*, French men contracted in the fur trade, often took up life outside the forts with aboriginal women and many of their children formed historical Métis communities.

Métis communities evolved through a process of ethnogensis over the next few generations. Without exception, the earliest communities were established largely at pre-existing aboriginal villages, fishing sites, and so on. Up until 1815, in what became Canada, the relations between indigenous and newcomer was somewhat reciprocal. Samuel de Champlain feted the alliance with Wendat and Algonquin Chiefs stating that French sons and Indian daughters would marry to form a new nation. The English, in particular those who traded through the Hudson Bay, took a much more paternalistic view and forbid relations with Indian women. While this sanction was hard to enforce the general English attitude of superiority would later greatly shape colonial-aboriginal relations.

Aboriginal oral traditions continue to be embedded in diverse cultures and languages, expressed through storytelling art, craft, song, dance, and governance structures. Today in Canada, there continues to evolve many complex social organizations and forms of cultural expression—for example the Anishinaabe have clan systems and houses that support and govern political and economic relations, support trade with other nations, and establish peace alliances among nations (as well as outline the terms of warfare and retribution). These relations and their complexity were not respected after 1815 by foreign nations and not fully appreciated by Canadian authorities until recently. To say that all the richness and depth of aboriginal cultures was misunderstood and discounted by Europeans for political and economic reasons would be a gross oversimplification regardless of the accuracy of such a statement.

CONTACT: PEACE AND FRIENDSHIP, NO?

Canada was formed after European countries, in particular France in the late 1500s, made sustained and lasting contact with eastern Atlantic aboriginal peoples and those living along the St. Lawrence Seaway. The fur trade and military settlement were the main forces that drew settlement slowly west to the interior Great Lakes, Great Plains, and across the Rocky Mountains to the West Coast and north ward. Jacques Cartier visited the Iroquois village of Stradacona in 1535, and Samuel de Champlain established the first permanent French settlement at the site in 1608, which is today's Quebec City. Wendake village in Quebec City is one of the last remaining Wendat communities, a remnant of what was once a vast nation whose territories reached from Quebec to the Georgian Bay. Relations between the diversity of aboriginal peoples and the Canadian government after 1867 were shaped by 300 years of Crown relations and history.

Transformations to aboriginal societies over 400 years contributed to the establishment of Canada. Contact between Norse and Beothuks began on the Atlantic coast of present-day Newfoundland between 990 and 1050. Recent studies have found Beothuk DNA in a small number of Icelanders. The Beothuk were the first casualties of genocide. In contrast, sustained contact with coastal Inuit would not take place for 800 to 900 years after first contact. Whaling and Arctic exploration did not radically change Inuit life. In the 1950s, southern administrators sought to settle all Inuit into permanent settlements or relocate southern Inuit to the far north to establish Canadian sovereignty. The changes enacted in the 1950s radically stressed Inuit society.

By the late 1400s, seasonal European fishing posts were established in present-day Atlantic Canada, and small annual trade missions from France began exploring the New World. Between the 1530s and the mid-1600s, the economy shifted from fish to furs, and permanent settlements followed. Forts were established in New France, a region that encompassed a large swath of North America from the Atlantic coast, along the St. Lawrence River and Great Lakes, down the Mississippi and Ohio Valleys to the territories of New Spain, present-day coastal Florida and Texas. The English colonies also began taking hold during this period, and their populations flourished on the eastern seaboard. The total English population in New England and New York eclipsed the French in Quebec. Interior Canada was primarily indigenous and sparsely populated.

Much of modern Canada was called Rupert's Land. Established through royal charter to the Hudson Bay Company in 1670, the charter gave the company of adventurers in London the right to monopolize trade in all the lands that drained into Hudson Bay, that is, most of present-day Canada. Rupert's Land was sold by the Hudson's Bay Company to the government of Canada in 1869 without a single discussion with aboriginal peoples. The response was two-fold, a rejection by the Métis living mostly in Red River Settlement and an organized resistance to the imposition of Canadian rule. The push for those living in Rupert's Land was recognition of existing land rights. In Red River the tiny settlement had aspirations to enter confederation as a province and not as an unorganized territory. The push by First Nations was for Treaties throughout the region.

While European nations were establishing themselves in North America for both trade and military purposes, aboriginal nations on the eastern seaboard were also allying themselves to various growing settlements. Religious conversion and a general attitude by Europeans superiority meant that reciprocal relations could not last. Throughout the early formative period, competition between French and English for furs, as well as growing settlement pressures, ultimately lead to conflict, war, and displacement. In some instances, peace and friendship treaties were signed; however, over time, aboriginal populations were pushed to the margins and relations soured.

Modern North America was transformed by increasing pressures of settlement, in-migration of European influences, and industrial development and urbanization. Competition for resources and lack of local say in the direction of economic development how resources ought to be developed increasingly saw conflict as the hallmark of colonization. By the time of the British defeat of the French in Quebec City at the Plains of Abraham in 1759, the Boston Tea Party in 1773 and the American Revolution of 1776, a more focused colonial project began to emerge on both sides of the border. The Royal Proclamation of 1763 set in law that Indian title could be ceded through the authority of the British Crown. Following the War of 1812, United Empire Loyalists flooded north, and the Canadian-American border was cemented. The 1800s saw expansion west, on both sides of the border, which included successive waves of contact between aboriginal peoples, traders, missionaries, settlers, and government. The Métis people, who over generations developed their own aboriginal identity, ultimately came into conflict with the British views of Canada in the late 1800s at Red River and later at Batoche.

ABORIGINAL RELATIONS WITH CANADA TODAY

Within 100 years of Canada becoming a British colony, it petitioned the Crown to become a dominion within the commonwealth. The modern state continues to embrace the monarchy. The British North America Act of 1867 spelled out areas of exclusive powers for federal and provincial governments that remained unchanged by the 1982 Constitution Act. The establishment of a House of Commons and provincial legislatures with exclusive areas of jurisdiction largely shut out aboriginal peoples, who did not have the right to vote until 1960. Until recently, there was little aboriginal influence over the political development of the country. As Canada began to form, it developed a policy of assimilation, instituted state-sponsored and church-run residential schools, and established the *Indian Act* to manage "Indians" as wards of the state.

Canada has a decentralized democratic government. The federal government is centralized in Ottawa, and each Province acts like a state and has a legislative assembly or house. As well there are now three territorial governments in Canada's north, which operate under legislative authority of the government of Canada. The federal government is elected with members of Parliament representing all parts of the country. A second house, the Senate, provides sober second thought to legislation passed by Parliament, and its members are appointed for life by the Prime Minister. The head of state of Canada is the Governor General, the Queen's representative. However, the Prime Minister is the elected head of government and the Prime Minister recommends the Governor General every four or five years to the Queen. While the Governor General is now largely symbolic, the Prime Minister's office has grown increasingly powerful over the years. Throughout Canada's history as a nation, the government has sought to deny aboriginal peoples' basic human rights and to find ways to reconcile this legacy.

Aboriginal people are a federal responsibility. First Nations and their lands, as well as Inuit issues and concerns, are handled by the Minister of Aboriginal

Affairs and Northern Development, previously known as Indian Affairs and Northern Development Canada. The Minister also serves as the interlocutor of Métis and non-status Indians. Some social issues are handled by programs and services under the authority of the Minister of Human Resources and Skills Development while other aspects are under the authority of Environment Canada, Department of Fisheries and Oceans, Natural Resources Canada, and the Department of National Defense. Provincial governments have no jurisdiction over aboriginal lands; however, many areas of jurisdiction such as education are a provincial responsibility and has a direct bearing on them.

Canada has 10 provincial governments (Newfoundland, Nova Scotia, New Brunswick, Prince Edward Island, Quebec, Ontario, Manitoba, Saskatchewan, Alberta, British Columbia) and three relatively dependent territorial governments (Yukon, Northwest Territories, and Nunavut). Provincial and territorial governments have historically had a poor relationship with aboriginal peoples. This is odd as, for example, Manitoba was formed in 1870 because the Métis took a stand to establish the province. Also, in northern Canada, the majority of the population in two of the three territories is aboriginal. Until 1982, there was little interest in anything more than assimilating aboriginal peoples; in 1969 the federal government developed a "white paper" to absorb aboriginal peoples into the body politic. The move was one response to underdevelopment of reserve communities and poor urban aboriginal populations, both of which are a prominent feature of modern aboriginal-state relations. The aboriginal response to the white paper was mobilization and organization of aboriginal peoples to articulate their desire for recognition and fulfillment of Treaty promises, and ultimately recognition and protection with the Constitution of Canada in 1982. Today, most provinces have ministers with some authority and responsibility for aboriginal issues who try to address social issues that impact aboriginal poverty.

Most of the total Canadian population is located in nine major cities (Toronto, Montreal, Vancouver, Ottawa-Gatineau, Edmonton, Calgary, Quebec, Winnipeg, Hamilton), and with the exception of Edmonton, most are located along the southern boundary of the country, within 200 kilometers of the United States. In all cases urban populations continue to grow. The three northern territories and the northern parts of most of the provinces outside of the Atlantic Provinces are sparsely populated and have a greater density and aboriginal demographic profile than southern Canadian urban and rural centers. Looking at total population numbers, the northern regions of Canada face a more dynamic demographic ebb and flow associated with the boom and bust of resource development. Aboriginal populations continue to grow faster than the Canadian average and exhibit greater degrees of poverty during ebb flows and bust cycles of development. While some aboriginal households are able to return or practice to a larger degree their traditional economic activities, others are not so adaptive

> # CANADIAN CONSTITUTION ACT OF 1982
>
> The Canadian Constitution Act of 1982 established Canada's constitution and includes a statement of rights and freedoms, including the rights and freedoms of Canada's First Nations.
>
> Canadian Constitution Act of 1982 Section 35
> Rights of the Aboriginal Peoples of Canada
> 35(1) The existing aboriginal and treaty rights of the aboriginal peoples of Canada are hereby recognized and affirmed.
> (2) In this Act, "aboriginal peoples of Canada" includes the Indian, Inuit and Métis peoples of Canada.
> (3) For greater certainty, in subsection (1) "treaty rights" includes rights that now exist by way of land claims agreements or may be so acquired.
> (4) Notwithstanding any other provision of this Act, the aboriginal and treaty rights referred to in subsection (1) are guaranteed equally to male and female persons.
>
> *Source*: Canadian Constitution Act of 1982. Retrieved from http://laws-lois.justice.gc.ca/eng/Const/Const_index.html

and there exist high levels of suicide, substance abuse, and other associated negative social issues.

WORDS

Native, aboriginal, and *indigenous* are terms used in Canada with meanings that vary depending on context and one's point of view. There are social, political, and legal dimensions to these terms. Each aboriginal nation has their own names as nations, that is, known mostly by the people themselves. So the Métis or Wet'suwet'en are examples of aboriginal peoples who are indigenous to different parts of Canada. The specific names and cultures of people were largely known only by a small group of people who either administered their affairs or studied or worked with them. The majority of Canadians, in particular new Canadians, are relatively ignorant of the history and diversity of aboriginal peoples in Canada; it was not taught as part of the mainstream education system.

To be native is to come from a place, to be of a land, to share a common understanding and history of these relationships. Native Studies as a subject developed in Canadian universities, first at Trent University in the 1980s, followed closely by the University of Manitoba, Saskatchewan, and then across the county. These departments were places for serious scholarly thought about all things native, from art and literature to politics and economic development, and all things in between.

Aboriginal is the term most widely used throughout Canada, particularly since 1982, and it describes the three founding people: First Nation, Métis, and Inuit. People have names for themselves: Algonquin, Anishnabe, Cree, Haudenesaune, Wendat, Nisga'a, Blackfoot, Sioux, Tlicho, Gwich'in, Inuvialuit, Métis, and so on.

FIRST NATIONS

The Assembly of First Nations (AFN) is the national chiefs organization in Canada. Each province and territory has an AFN representative, vice chief, and First Nations are organized by tribal chiefs and councils. *First Nation* is the preferred term to replace *Indian*. A reserve is a small portion of land, set aside by treaty, that was part of the original territory of Indians and that is held in trust by the Minister of Aboriginal Affairs and Northern Development (unless otherwise stated in a land claim or self-government agreement). As such, the term *First Nation* describes both the band and the larger political and social organization of similar peoples. For example, the Cree are comprised of many communities with three dialects, whose territories stretch across the boreal forest. Today, First Nations are approximately 630 reserve communities and a multitude of off-reserve communities. According to linguists, there are 10 First Nation language families in Canada (Algonquin, Athapaskan, Haida, Iroquoian, Kootenayan, Salishan, Siouan, Tlingit, Tsimshian, and Wakashan). These categories represent at least 54 different First Nations. First Nations also have formed community charter communities and are unorganized. Many have intact cultures and languages that date to before contact. Most, however, are maladapted by outside influences of the Indian Act and control by colonial authorities. Few communities number more than 5,000, with the majority being less than 1,000.

MÉTIS

Today, the Métis are organized formally in Ontario, Manitoba, Saskatchewan, Alberta, and British Columbia. At the national level, they have formed the Metis National Council. It is likely the Métis living in the Northwest Territories, Quebec, and the Atlantic provinces, will seek some form of recognition; however, they may organize themselves somewhat different from what is already established. Even within the current Métis nation, there is a great deal of diversity. For example, in Ontario, there are more than 33 community councils and in northern Alberta, Métis have established collective landholdings since the 1930s. In 1869 in Manitoba and in 1885 in Saskatchewan, Canada negatively responded to Métis resistance, eventually hanging the Métis leader Louis Riel on November 16, 1885.

> ## ABORIGINAL AFFAIRS AND NORTHERN DEVELOPMENT CANADA AND THE MÉTIS PEOPLE
>
> The *Royal Commission Report on Aboriginal Peoples* includes a discussion of the Métis people, which is reproduced here.
>
> Aboriginal Affairs and Northern Development Canada's (AANDC's) responsibilities and its partnerships with First Nation people and communities range from negotiating land claim and self-government agreements to providing social services, education and economic development. These activities support AANDC's vision, and help to maintain and strengthen the relationship between the Government of Canada and First Nations people. . . .
>
> Métis are one of three recognized Aboriginal peoples in Canada, along with the Indians (or First Nations) and Inuit.
>
> Approximately one third of all Aboriginal people in Canada identify themselves as Métis. Census data from 2006 shows Métis as the Aboriginal group that experienced the highest growth at 91%, reaching 389,785 people.
>
> Between 1996 and 2006, important political and legal milestones may have encouraged individuals to identify themselves as Métis. The Métis received significant recognition in the final report of the Royal Commission on Aboriginal Peoples (1996) and in recent years they have won one important supreme court case related to the recognition of hunting rights (R. vs. Powely).
>
> The Office of the Federal Interlocutor provides funding to support representative Métis, non-status Indian and off-reserve Aboriginal organizations, so they can better represent their constituents, become more accountable, develop partnerships and develop and train their personnel. In addition, the Federal Interlocutor is the Minister responsible for federal participation in tripartite negotiation processes between Métis or off-reserve Aboriginal organizations, provinces and the Federal Government. These processes focus on discussing mutually agreeable priority issues.
>
> *Source*: Aboriginal Affairs and Northern Development. Retrieved from http://www.aadnc-aandc.gc.ca/eng/1307458586498

Métis speak several languages, depending on the cultural heritage of the community. Michif is the language formally documented for people in Saskatchewan, Manitoba and North Dakota, and work is underway to document Michif in Ontario. The Métis continue to struggle for recognition and reconciliation with Canada.

INUIT

The Inuvialuit, one of four Inuit peoples in Canada, were one of the first aboriginal peoples to successfully negotiate a modern land claim agreement in the 1990s and they continue to be part of the Northwest Territories. In addition, the Inuit are the only aboriginal people in Canada to have formed their own territorial government, Nunavut, which includes non-aboriginal representation. Similar in form and shape to the legislature of the Northwest Territories, Nunavut was partitioned from the western Arctic in 1999 and continues to evolve as a territorial government. From the capital Iqaluit, the Nunavut government provides the Inuit living there with a greater degree of autonomy and decision-making authority. However, as a territory they remain under the administration of the Minister of

The town of Iqaluit, Nunavut Territory, is located about 200 miles south of the Arctic Circle in Canada. Iqaluit is the capital of Canada's newest province, Nunavut Territory, which was carved out of the Northwest Territories to become a semi-autonomous region in 1999. There are some 7,000 people in Iqaluit, most of whom are Inuit, nomadic hunters who have lived in the frozen climes of Canada, Alaska, Russia, and Greenland for thousands of years. The Inuit are the first people on earth to experience the impact of global warming and claim the United States is violating their human rights by being the world's largest emitter of greenhouse gases. (AP Photo/Beth Duff-Brown)

Aboriginal Affairs and Northern Development, and have established their own land corporations and other representative organizations. The Inuit are an international people, represented by the Inuit Circumpolar Conference. They are found in Arctic Canada (Nunavut, Northwest Territories, northern Quebec, and Labrador), the United States (Alaska), and Greenland.

In Canada, Inuit were historically known as Eskimo. Aleut is still their linguistic designation, but the linguistic term represents at least four distinct dialects. The Inuit are a diverse people, with urban populations in Toronto, Montreal, Ottawa, Winnipeg, and Edmonton. Many of the traditional hunting cultural values still have a role in today's society, such as patience and perseverance, and the Inuit struggle with issues that are unique to their place in the world.

CONCLUSION

Until 1969, Canada's Indian policy was largely a force for aboriginal assimilation and deculturation. Through the establishment of such measures as criminalizing peoples' movement, taking away their liberty to organize, providing minimal services, creating dependency, and setting up industrial and residential schools, Canada sought to "civilize" and remake aboriginal peoples into British subjects. The impacts of these flawed policies continue to be felt today. Since the 1970s, aboriginal-Canadian relations have begun the long slow process of reconciliation. Constitutional protection in 1982 resulted in many changes, but many challenges also surfaced. For instance, in 1990 at Kahnesetake, Oka, community members were in a standoff with the Canadian army over the expansion of a golf course into disputed territory. Similarly, the death of Dudley George at Ipperwash led to an inquiry that uncovered in 2007 racism and political interference of police by then Premier Mike Harris in Ontario. That same year, Prime Minister Harper stood up in the House of Commons and apologized for the treatment of aboriginal students in residential schools. In 2010, Canada said it would sign the United Nations Framework on the Rights of Indigenous Peoples, and the Province of Ontario declared it the Year of the Métis.

REFERENCES

Assembly of First Nations. Available at www.afn.ca
Deloria, P. and N. Salisbury (Eds.). *A Companion to American Indian History*. Hoboken, NJ: Blackwell, 2004.
Indian and Northern Affairs Canada. Available at www.ainc-inac.gc.ca
Inuit Tapiriit Kanatami. Available at www.itk.ca
Métis National Council. Available at www.metisnation.ca
Métis Nation of Ontario. Available at www.metisnation.org
Paci, Chris. "The Métis." In M. Nuttall (Ed.), *Encyclopedia of the Arctic*. London: Routledge, 2006.

Biocolonialism: Genetic Science and Aboriginal Peoples

Amy L. Fletcher

Biocolonialism is a broad term that refers to controversial issues embedded in the relationship between Western biotechnology and indigenous cultures. Current research projects in molecular biology, such as studying the use of human stem cells for tissue regeneration or studying the links between genes, lifestyles, and disease to develop "personalized medicine," promise major advances in the treatment of human disease and suffering. However, genetic research also poses many challenges to indigenous communities, who must develop mechanisms for ensuring both individual and community consent to such research projects, and for protecting indigenous knowledge and belief systems. Against the background of Western economic and political colonialism dating from the fifteenth century to the present, Native Americans must weigh the possible benefits of biotechnologies and genomics against the potential costs to native communities, tribes, and customs. Issues within the broad category of biocolonialism include individual versus community forms of consent, the ethical requirements of informed consent, the ownership of genetic samples and information, and the political and cultural implications of population-based genetic research for traditional knowledge and spirituality.

GENETICS

In April 1953, scientists James Watson (American) and Francis Crick (British) published an article in the journal *Nature* that described the double helical structure of deoxyribonucleic acid (DNA). DNA is, in lay terms, the chemical "code" of heredity, containing the basic "instruction manual" for the development of all living things. While Watson and Crick's article is written for other professional scientists, the mainstream press and society soon realized that by offering a strong theory of how DNA is arranged in cells, Watson and Crick made a crucial step in the understanding—and potential application—of molecular biology. Indeed, James Watson, Francis Crick, and (colleague) Maurice Wilkins won the 1962 Nobel Prize in Physiology or Medicine for their work on the structure and composition of DNA. Several related research fields such as chemistry, genetics, and molecular biology continued to advance from this insight throughout the Cold War. By the mid-1970s, techniques of genetic modification led to the first related human health treatment used routinely in medicine—recombinant DNA (rDNA) in the synthesis of human insulin, offered as a superior alternative to the then-common practice of using purified pig insulin to treat diabetes. The emergence of rDNA technology also resulted in the now-famous Asilomar Conference on Recombinant DNA in February 1975, wherein scientists debated the ethical and regulatory challenges inherent in the ability to modify and transfer genes between species.

Research in genetics exploded both publicly and commercially in the 1980s and 1990s. For example, in 1994, the Flavr Savr tomato—a tomato genetically modified with an antisense gene to delay the ripening process—was the first genetically engineered product determined to be safe for human consumption by the U.S. Food and Drug Administration (FDA). While certified as being "as safe as conventionally grown tomatoes," the product experienced both production and distribution difficulties, as well as a degree of public resistance, and the company (Calgene) ceased production of it in 1997. Nevertheless, the widespread planting of genetically modified (GM) commercial crops such as soybeans continued, as did research into the human health applications of genomics and genetic modification. Perhaps the most visible international project, launched in 1990 with significant financial contributions from the United States, was the Human Genome Project (HGP). An international HGP consortium set itself the tasks of identifying every gene in the human genome (now estimated to be approximately 22,000) and mapping these genes to the chromosomes in the human body. Establishing this reference genome—taken from a mixture of several anonymous human blood samples—would be a major scientific achievement that also enabled much more sophisticated research in such areas as gene therapy, preimplantation genetic diagnosis, genetic testing, and pharmacogenomics (the study of how genes, heredity, and lifestyle interact to produce human diseases).

The completion of the Human Genome Project in 2003 was heralded internationally in the press by governmental officials, corporations, and scientists. Advocates of advanced genetic research promoted the agricultural and medical innovations, as well as consequential economic benefits, that could flow through to society from applications of genetic modification in microbes, plants, animals and humans. However, controversies arose in civil society about both the speed and the potential consequences of scientific tampering with nature. Environmental activists, in particular, began to actively protest projects such as the Monsanto Corporation's "terminator gene" (which would have rendered Monsanto's seeds sterile after one breeding season, thus preventing subsistence farmers from using traditional seed-cultivation methods). They also increasingly expressed resistance to both field trials and commercial planting of GM crops, arguing that the potential for contamination of natural crops and plants was too high, and urging the adoption of the precautionary principle due to the alleged unproven and unknown risks of GM crops both to agricultural and human health.

INDIGENOUS CONCERNS

It is within the context of environmental concerns that global indigenous groups, including many Native American organizations and tribes, began to express cultural objections to both the point and the pace of genetic modification and transgenics. Indigenous groups were, and remain, especially concerned about the race to patent—and thus lock down ownership rights to—genes. Tribes noted that, for example, their knowledge systems often had recognized the medicinal properties of particular plants for centuries, and that this knowledge was passed to subsequent generations via oral and community traditions. Western science and law, however, rewarded only those individuals or groups who had successfully filed a patent to claim private ownership of a gene. Not only did the rush to patent genes offend Native American spirituality and a cultural tradition that saw nature as the common heritage of humanity (a view shared by many non-native groups, as well), but it also introduced a new form of colonialism—biopiracy—that often used traditional knowledge to identify the best plants for medical research, while bypassing any sort of monetary reward for, or even acknowledgement of, traditional knowledge and customs. For example, India had to spend years and a substantial amount of money to achieve the revocation of patents originally granted by the U.S. Patent and Trademark Office for turmeric and basmati, and by the European Patent Office for a neem-tree antifungal product (all three substances had been used for thousands of years in traditional Indian society).

Many Native American tribes attended the first International Conference on the Cultural and Intellectual Property Rights of Indigenous Peoples, held in New Zealand in 1993. The resulting Mataatua Declaration is a milestone in the recognition of indigenous cultural property rights and asserts that the established right of tribal self-determination includes an inherent right for indigenous tribes to be recognized as the "exclusive owners of their culture and intellectual property." Issues surrounding biopiracy, patents, and cultural ownership remained controversial following the 1993 conference, often resulting in protracted litigation between tribes and scientists and/or corporations and Western research institutes.

Fears about biopiracy and biocolonialism extended from plants to humans, as genetic research continued to accelerate in the 1990s. Many indigenous groups around the world took note of a 1991 research project conducted in Tristan da Cunha (the most remote island in the world) by researchers with Mt. Sinai Hospital in Toronto. The indigenous population of Tristan da Cunha exhibits unusually high levels of hereditary asthma, and studying the group to identify a possible asthma gene was how researchers initially presented the project to the inhabitants, who agreed to participate in the interests of medical research and human health. The researchers took 272 blood samples from a total population of 295 people. What the inhabitants found out only after the researchers left the island is that Sequanna Therapeutics (a biotechnology company that collaborated with Mt. Sinai Hospital in the project) eventually sold its asthma research, including cell lines derived from the Tristan da Cunha blood samples, to a German pharmaceutical company for $70 million, with none of the money going back to the island. Sequanna responded to vehement global criticism by offering to build a youth basketball court for the community.

HUMAN GENOME DIVERSITY PROJECT

Based on this and other controversial cases—such as the patent granted (and later revoked) by the U.S. Patent Office to a cell line derived from a Hagahai tribal member in Papua New Guinea—indigenous tribes and activist organizations began to focus on the potential threats of human health–related and population-based genomic research. The Native American community generally opposed the proposed Human Genome Diversity Project (HGDP), a collective stance shared with indigenous tribes and groups globally. The HGDP—not a part of the HGP—was first proposed by Stanford geneticist Luigi Luca Cavilli-Sforza in 1991. In a letter to the prestigious journal *Genomics*, Cavilli-Sforza and colleagues proposed a systematic study of the whole range of human genetic diversity. They highlighted, in particular, the perceived scientific imperative to collect and preserve blood samples from isolated indigenous tribes, many of which were described in HGDP-related forums as being on the verge of extinction and/or at risk of genetic "contamination" from encroaching urban populations.

The scientists and backers of the HGDP were surprised when the project's goals almost immediately began to be contested by angry indigenous groups. Many of the tribes identified as "isolated" either objected vehemently to the notion that they were "going extinct" or noted that, if they were in fact in danger of being lost to human history, this was often the inevitable consequence of past experiences with Western colonialism and exploitation. Tribes and affiliated activist groups also expressed resentment at the lack of community consultation prior to the announcement of the project and argued that while genomics may represent cutting-edge

Medical anthropologist Carol Jenkins examines members of the isolated Hagahai tribe of Papua New Guinea in this undated photo. Blood cells from one tribesman, potentially useful for medical research, have been patented by the U.S. government. (AP Photo/Travis Jenkins)

twenty-first-century research, the inherent notion of indigenous tribes as being "primitive" and worthy of being studied only as anthropological "relics" was a familiar and insulting continuation of Western science as practiced in the eighteenth and nineteenth centuries. Finally, tribes noted that the HGDP as planned would require a serious expenditure of funds, while appropriations for the basic health needs of indigenous adults and children often fell woefully short of meeting tribal needs. Following the second HGDP planning meeting in 1992, which led to increased tensions between the project's backers and indigenous groups, the World Council of Indigenous Peoples began to refer to the HGDP as the Vampire Project, arguing that it preyed secretly on the blood of others.

The HGDP raised significant cultural issues for indigenous groups, including many Native American tribes. HGDP proponents originally estimated that over 5,000 distinct human populations exist on earth. Yet many anthropologists, indigenous groups, and activists began to question how this estimate was made, and how the scientists defined populations. They noted that references to "genetically pure tribes" harkened back, however unintentionally, to the divisive and often racist rhetoric of the eugenics period (late nineteenth to mid-twentieth centuries). Moreover, the designation of "purity" often seemed to fluctuate depending on whether it helped or hurt tribal political interests. For example, in 1993, the Yuchi Community in Sapulpa, Oklahoma, was the first Native American group to be contacted directly by a scientist (and University of Florida anthropology professor) associated with the HGDP. The Yuchi initially responded positively to the potential health benefits, including flexible funding for community health needs, which were promised in return for participation in the project. However, in addition to ongoing concerns about the ownership of data and processes for obtaining community consent to the project, some critics noted that the Yuchi were then in the middle of an (ultimately) unsuccessful petition to the Branch of Acknowledgement and Recognition of the Bureau of Indian Affairs (BIA) seeking federal recognition of the Yuchi people as an independent and sovereign tribe. The scientific designation of the Yuchi language as an "isolate" and the stated anthropological interest in blood samples from Yuchi "fullbloods" arguably provided strong scientific support of the Yuchi claim for tribal recognition. Yet the tribe noted that while science recognized their distinctiveness, and even sought to profit from it, the federal government did not, raising important questions about exactly when and why science is used to justify particular decisions.

The relationship between population genetics and traditional tribal knowledge is extraordinarily complicated. While the Yuchi arguably should have benefitted from the scientific interest in them as "anthropologically distinct," the more common threat is that research into human identity and migration patterns undermines traditional and ancient Native American creation narratives. Indeed, many Native American tribes began to suspect that the ostensibly "neutral" and health-related research goals of the HGDP (and similar population-based projects) actually threatened to reopen or complicate legal claims to land and treaty rights, and potentially to call into question both tribal identities and the post-1492 designation of Native Americans as the indigenous peoples of the United States. (Similar issues have been raised by indigenous peoples in Canada, Australia, and New Zealand, among other countries.) For example, the Skull Valley band of Goshutes and the Northwest band of the Shoshone sponsored a day of lectures and discussion at an Indian walk-in center in January 2003 in Utah titled "The Evils of Biocolonialism: mtDNA Research and its Threat to Native Americans." (mtDNA is the abbreviation for mitochondrial DNA, which is inherited strictly from the mother. It is not found in the cell nucleus, like other DNA, but instead in organelles called mitochondria.) At that time, Jackie Swift, the Nevada-based program director of the Indigenous Peoples' Council on Biocolonialism, stated: "For us, the concept of biocolonialism is an extension of the colonialism process. They still exploit the land and the people, only at a microscopic level" (Sullivan 2003).

Designation as a federally recognized tribe is crucially important for indigenous peoples in the United States because tribal governments have sovereign authority and can protect the collectively held rights of the tribe. A landmark case in this regard was *Santa Clara Pueblo vs. Martinez* (1978). The case was brought against Santa Clara Pueblo (a tribe that dates to at least the fifteenth century) by Julia Martinez (a full-blooded member of the tribe) and her daughter. They were seeking to end the traditional practice by which Santa Clara Pueblo denied tribal membership to the children of female (but not male) members who married outside the tribe. The plaintiffs argued that this practice violated the Indian Civil Rights Act of 1968. However, the U.S. Supreme Court decided in favor of the defense, arguing that the principle of tribal common-law sovereign immunity protected the tribe from this sort of lawsuit. In effect, the case strengthened tribal rights to determine their own membership. This is important in the context of contemporary population genomics, which typically seeks to find genetic patterns of inheritance, thus equating identity with biology. Yet in many cases, the determination of Native American tribal identity is a question of history, politics, and culture, and the assignment of membership is a solemn privilege and right that tribes seek to retain. Critics of population-based research on indigenous groups also note that, as in any other human group across deep time, Native American tribes have experienced war and rape, migration, marriage outside the community, and the blending of previously antagonistic tribes into new social groupings. To define Native American identity solely through genetic inheritance arguably reduces the complexity of Native American history, undermines tribal rights to determine membership, and reintroduces a type of genetic "essentialism" that can produce both racism and discrimination. These issues arose recently (2011) with respect to the Cornell University Genetic Ancestry Project. Citing lack of consultation and of informed consent, as well as expressing concerns over the cultural impact of population-based genomic research, the American Indian Program at Cornell, as well as the National Congress of American Indians (NCAI) and the UN Permanent Forum on Indigenous Issues, formally oppose the project in its current form.

The tension between indigenous communities and genomics will likely remain a salient issue in the United States as the ability to isolate, extract, and manipulate genes increases apace. The examples noted herein represent only a small portion of cases wherein Native American consent, traditions, knowledge, and ownership rights have been exploited in the name of science. However, it is also crucial to remember that tribes can benefit tremendously from biological research, when it is done ethically and in line with tribal norms of community consent. Reconciling traditional knowledge with modern methods of molecular biology and genetic engineering also holds the potential for immense cultural, medical, and economic benefit to Native American communities. For example, in March 2011, at a meeting co-convened by the UN World Intellectual Property Organization (WIPO) and India's Council of Scientific and Industrial Research (CSIR), representatives from 35 countries discussed the possibility of scaling-up India's highly successful

Traditional Knowledge Digital Library (TKDL) to protect other countries and groups facing exploitation of their traditional knowledge.

In the area of human health, results from a recent study by St. Jude's Children's research Hospital and Children's Oncology Group, published in the journal *Nature Genetics*, established that a genetic variation known as PDE4B helps to explain why children and young adults of Native American ancestry experience a significantly higher risk of relapse and cancer recurrence when being treated for acute lymphoblastic leukemia (ALL), the most common childhood cancer. The study was based on the use of genomics to define ancestry, rather than self-declared patient status. Investigators hope that doctors can begin to treat ALL patients of Native American ancestry with additional chemotherapy, a protocol that represents significant progress toward personalized cancer care. In a policy brief on Native Americans and human genetic research prepared for the NCAI, Puneet Chawla Sahota notes that the Salt River Pima-Maricopa Indian Community (SRPMIC) formed a partnership with the Translational Genomics Research Institute to conduct medical genetics research on diabetes and other diseases. SRPMIC contributed $5 million to the project and is an active partner. As we live through the often-cited Century of the Gene, what these examples suggest is that the relationship between tribal knowledge and Western science is not (and never has been) a simple juxtaposition of "traditional" and "modern," but rather a complex and potentially mutually beneficial relationship whose positive effects depend both on the strength of the ethical and consultative procedures developed by tribes, and the degree to which scientists and corporations respect the specific complexities of biological research within Native American communities.

REFERENCES

Grounds, Richard A. "The Yuchi Community and the Human Genome Diversity Project." *Genes, People and Property* 20, no. 2 (Summer 1996). Retrieved from http://www.culturalsurvival.org/publications/cultural-survival-quarterly/united-states/yuchi-community-and-human-genome-diversity-pr on May 27, 2011.

Indigenous Peoples Council on Biocolonialism. Available at http://www.ipcb.org

The International Treaty of Plant Genetic Resources for Food and Agriculture. Available at http://www.planttreaty.org/access_en.htm

Jaffe, Sam. "Groundwork for Genetic Studies." *Scientist* 16, no. 23 (2002): 51. Retrieved from http://classic.the-scientist.com/?articles.view/articleNo/14384/ on September 22, 2012.

The Mataatua Declaration. Available at http://www.wipo.int/export/sites/www/tk/en/folklore/creative_heritage/docs/mataatua.pdf

National Congress of American Indians, Policy Research Center. Available at http://www.ncaiprc.org/

Reardon, Jenny. "The Human Genome Diversity Project: A Case Study in Coproduction." *Social Studies of Science* 31, no. 3 (June 2001): 357–388.

Sahota, Puneet Chawla. "Genetics Research and American Indian/Alaska Native Communities: Research Regulation Toolkit," 2009. Retrieved from http://www.ncaiprc.org/files/Genetics%20Research%20and%20AIAN%20Communities.pdf on May 27, 2011.

Shelton, Brett Lee. "Consent and Consultation in Genetic Research on American Indians and Alaska Natives." Indigenous Peoples Council on Biocolonialism. Retrieved from http://www.ipcb.org/publications/briefing_papers/files/consent.html on May 27, 2011.

Sullivan, Tim. "American Indians Wary of DNA Tests." *Salt Lake Tribune*, January 27, 2003. Retrieved from http://www.nathpo.org/News/NAGPRA/News-NAGPRA27.htm on May 27, 2011.

Whitt, Laurelyn. *Science, Colonialism, and Indigenous Peoples: The Cultural Politics of Law and Knowledge*. Cambridge: Cambridge University Press, 2009.

Contemporary Issues of Aboriginal People in Canada

David Walsh

Native peoples in Canada have faced many issues that are similar to those that Indians in the United States have experienced. They share a similar historical relationship with their nation's government, similar policies toward education and boarding schools, and a shared regulation of religious rituals. As in the United States, Canadian Indians have engaged in sovereignty movements, struggled with poor conditions on reserves (such as poverty, lack of jobs and education, alcoholism, domestic violence, and gang violence), and engaged in contemporary movements to maintain, reclaim, and revitalize their languages and cultures. The following essay provides an overview of the various issues facing Canada's Indian population today.

By some accounts, Canadian aboriginals have had a harder time then Native Americans in the United States. The UN Human Development Index, which rates countries based on markers of health, education, and a decent standard of living, determined in 2001 that while Canada as a whole ranked eighth in the world, Canadian aboriginals ranked thirty-second, barely behind American Indians in the United States, who came in at thirtieth. That same year, the Canadian Royal Commission on Aboriginal Peoples found that aboriginal peoples' living standards have improved over the last 50 years but still lag behind the general population. Life expectancy is 8.1 years less for aboriginal men, and 5.5 years less for aboriginal women. The rate of premature mortality is almost four and a half times higher than the general population (death before the age of 75 due to suicide or unintentional injury).

Canadian aboriginals have acquired a presence in Canadian consciousness that Native Americans have not been able to achieve in the United States. A particular milestone was the inclusion of aboriginal groups in the Canadian Constitution Act of 1982: "35(1) The existing aboriginal and treaty rights of the aboriginal peoples of Canada are hereby recognized and affirmed. 35(2) In this Act, 'aboriginal peoples of Canada' includes the Indian, Inuit, and Métis peoples of Canada."

There are three different groups of indigenous peoples recognized in the Canadian Constitution. First are the First Nations (or "Indian"), which is equivalent to Native Americans in the United States and comprises the largest and most diverse segment of aboriginal peoples in Canada. Second are the Inuit (previously referred to as Eskimo), a distinct ethnic group who live in the Arctic areas of Canada, as well as Greenland, northern Alaska, and northeast Russia. And third are the Métis, the descendants of predominantly French fur trappers and native women. As a cultural distinction, the Métis are a unique aboriginal group living mostly in Alberta, but this demarcation is problematic because many Quebecois and descendants of Anglican trappers and aboriginal women also claim an ethnic rather than cultural Métis status. It was considered a major victory for the Métis, sometimes referred to as the "forgotten people," to be included in the constitutional definition of aboriginal people.

Constitutional recognition was a political milestone for Canadian aboriginals engaged in a long history of struggle. For contemporary aboriginal people of Canada, land rights, education, religious rights, and the plight of aboriginal women are four major concerns. All of these issues depend on native peoples' representation in the Canadian political sphere.

POLITICAL REPRESENTATION

In addition to three ethnically distinct indigenous groups, there are also three different classifications for native peoples' relationship to the Canadian government. The first governmental classification is status. "Status Indians" are registered under the Indian act of 1876. This relationship was established for descendants of those who signed treaties with the British crown or the Canadian government. The second classification is non-status Indians. This encompasses native peoples of Canada who are not recognized under the Indian Act and are denied the rights and benefits granted to status Indians but are nonetheless recognized as ethnically Indian. The third classification is treaty Indians, who are aboriginal peoples who acquired treaties after the Indian Act of 1876. The largest group of treaty Indians are the Métis.

The existence of three different groupings of aboriginal peoples, and three different classifications for aboriginal peoples, complicates aboriginal politics. As such, multiple organizations have developed to represent these various groups. Historically, the Office of Indian and Northern Affairs (roughly equivalent to the Bureau of Indian Affairs [BIA] in the United States) has been the major governmental organization working with native peoples in Canada. But since the early 1980s, various aboriginal-lead organizations have developed to represent native peoples. The largest such organization is the Assembly of First Nations, which represents most First Nations people in Canada (over 700,000 people). The assembly is comprised of all 633 First Nations bands. Their counterpart organization is the Native Council of Canada, which was formed to include all nonstatus First Nations people. The Inuit Tapirisat of Canada represents the Inuit peoples of Canada's Arctic regions, which is about one third of Canada's territory. The Métis National Council represents both ethnic and cultural Métis people. There are a few major aboriginal women's organizations as well, for example, Pauktuutit (serving Inuit women), the Native Women's Association of Canada (serving status Indians), and the Women of the Métis Nation.

These and other aboriginal political organizations were formed during the late 1960s and early 1970s. Until 1953, it was illegal for status Indians in Canada to raise funds to form political organizations. And it was only in 1959 that status Indians acquired the right to vote in the Canadian Parliament. In the 1970s, the Canadian government resumed the practice of signing treaties with indigenous peoples. Referred to as comprehensive claims agreements, these new treaties allowed the First Nations whose territory was not previously covered by treaty to negotiate with the federal government, thus the classification treaty Indian.

While aboriginal peoples were demanding political voices in the United States and Canada, the Canadian government was also taking new interest in native peoples, specifically in regards to land use and natural resource extraction. World War II increased interest in natural resources; mines and hydroelectric plants were opened across Canada's north, while oil and gas exploration likewise spread over lands that were previously inconsequential to the federal government.

With renewed interest in native lands came renewed interest in native peoples as citizens. The 1969 White Paper on Indian Policy seemed to present a solution to both problems, that is, integrating indigenous peoples into Canadian society and freeing up land for natural resource extraction. The paper proposed an abolition of special rights for Indians in Canada, including reserve land, and instead advocated strong measures promoting indigenous peoples' assimilation into the Canadian mainstream. Put forth by then Minister of Indian Affairs Jean Chrétien, under the Liberal Party and Prime Minister Pierre Trudeau, the paper was met with outrage by native peoples. This led to increased aboriginal political activism and a general outcry among native peoples against the White Paper. A response was issued titled "Citizens Plus" but referred to popularly as the "Red Paper." The response argued in favor of special legal status on the grounds of aboriginal and treaty rights.

The government backed off of the White Paper in 1973, but the newly formed aboriginal political organizations did not stop there. Riding the momentum of defeating the White Paper, these groups turned their struggle toward land rights.

> ## INUIT CIRCUMPOLAR CONFERENCE
>
> The Inuit Circumpolar Conference is an organization representing and advocating the unity and rights of Inuit people throughout the Arctic. Its website describes the organization. Part of the description is reproduced here.
>
>> The Inuit Circumpolar Council (ICC) is an international Indigenous Peoples' Organization representing approximately 160.000 Inuit living in the Arctic regions of Alaska, Canada, Greenland and Chukotka, Russia.
>> The principal goals of ICC are:
>>
>> - To strengthen unity among Inuit of the Circumpolar region
>> - To promote Inuit rights and interests on the international level
>> - To ensure and further develop Inuit culture and society for both the present and future generations
>> - To seek full and active participation in the political, economic, and social development in our homelands
>> - To develop and encourage long-term policies which safeguard the Arctic environment
>> - To work for international recognition of the human rights of all Indigenous Peoples
>>
>> Inuit Circumpolar Council is also involved in different international fora.
>
> *Source*: Inuit Circumpolar Conference. Retrieved from http://www.inuit.org/. Used by permission.

This prompted the federal government to establish claims process and policy under which the parties could negotiate land entitlements. Since the 1970s, land rights (hunting rights, trade and economic conditions, self-government, and sovereignty) have been a major issues concerning aboriginal peoples in Canada.

JURISDICTION OVER LAND

A UN report on indigenous peoples declared in 2009 that "the restrictions put on Aboriginal peoples' ability to protect, meaningfully benefit from and freely dispose of their land and resources constitute the main obstacle to real economic development among First Nations, Métis and Inuit" (United Nations 2009, 24). The Royal Commission on Aboriginal People's reported that since the 1867 confederation of colonies into Canada, "Two-thirds of land possessed by aboriginal peoples has been 'whittled away' through appropriation, theft, encroachment and the environmental consequences of policies and activities imposed on indigenous peoples without their consent" (UN 2009, 25). Land rights have been a major issue for indigenous groups across Canada. Some of the more influential struggles have included groups as diverse as the Mohawk and the Restigouche in Quebec, the Lubicon Lake Cree, the Saalequun, and the Inuit.

In 1990 confrontation over land between the Kanesatake Mohawk and Canadian government in Oka, southern Quebec, led to military action. Kanesatake protestors set up blockades to prevent the development of a golf course on land traditionally claimed by the tribe. During the protest, one police officer was killed, resulting in the Canadian armed forces being called in to remove the barriers. To diffuse the situation, the federal government purchased the disputed land and offered it to the Kanesatake tribe. Yet tension still persists in the relationship between the federal government and the Mohawk.

More recently, in June of 2009, Akwesasne Mohawk leadership protested and effectively shut down an international border crossing with the United States that lies on the Mohawk reserve. The protest was in response to a decision to arm Canadian border patrol on the reserve. In September 2009, the issue was resolved in part with the creation of a tribal passport, a "secure certificate of Indian status" identity card that Akwesasne tribal members may use to cross the border on their reserve.

Unlike other provinces, Quebec does not have a history of treaties to override provincial laws. In 1981, Indian resistance to regulation of hunting and fishing led to a particularly volatile confrontation with Quebec police. Four hundred armed police raided the Restigouche reserve community with bulldozers, helicopters, and tear gas. The police blocked a bridge leading out of the reserve, and in response, tribal members blocked the four roads leading into the reserve. After the police were called out of the area, an agreement on hunting and fishing rights was reached.

In 1965 in British Columbia, the question of treaty rights toward land use was upheld in the landmark *Regina v. White and Bob* Supreme Court case. The Saalequun tribe on Vancouver Island had ceded land to Governor Sir James Douglas in 1854 but had reserved hunting rights. In 1964, tribal members were charged with possession of six deer outside of hunting season. The Supreme Court upheld the tribe's rights, ruling that treaty rights overruled provincial game laws. First Nations in other provinces soon followed in their own pursuits of treaty rights. Although a win for tribal hunting rights, the Supreme Court decision rested on upholding treaties and did not mention aboriginal rights specifically. Federal game laws, however, have been held to prevail over treaties.

While hunting is an issue of aboriginal right to land use, another issue involves the use of aboriginal land by non-native businesses, especially in regards to natural resources. The Lubicon Lake Cree of northern Alberta, for example, blockaded access to nearly 10,000 square kilometers of oil- and timber-rich land, threatening the resource extraction industry in the area, as a means to settle their 40-year-old land claim. They were in a stalemate with the federal government from 1989 to 1993. The Lubicon members, along with the other Alberta Indians who had joined forces and formed the Woodland Cree band, eventually received a settlement including a 143-square-kilometer reserve and $19 million for economic development.

The Inuit live in the only area of Canada where aboriginal people are the majority. Like the First Nations, the Inuit have been pursing more self-determination and sovereignty.

The Inuit do not have historical treaties with Canada, and they did not enter into land claims negotiations until 1973. The Inuit were first brought into a direct relationship with the government in 1939. Around this time, they were introduced to fur trapping by the Hudson Bay Company, and many were persuaded to take up the occupation. The collapse of the fur trade in the 1940s had a devastating impact on their communities.

In the 1950s, Canada's federal government took notice of their plight and began offering aid to those without food, as they were doing for First Nations people. The Inuit were encouraged to relocate around the Hudson Bay trading posts, which nearly all of them did, giving up their traditional way of life to settle in small northern villages. At this time, the government also relocated a group of Inuit from northern Quebec to two villages in the high Arctic, one of the motivating factors being to strengthen Canada's land claims to that area.

The 1960s campaigns against seal hunting, although originally aimed at non-native commercial kills of newly born harp seals, had a devastating effect on the Inuit and their traditional hunt for mature ringed seals. By 1982, the European community had boycotted all seal product imports, a serious blow to the Inuit economy.

Currently, the major land issue affecting the Inuit and all of Canada's aboriginal groups is climate change. Climate change poses numerous threats to all Canadians; however, aboriginals are most vulnerable to environmental changes. Indigenous communities, especially in the Arctic and sub-Arctic, are already experiencing a decline in traditional food sources, prompting indigenous communities to become more dependent on federal aid. Some communities are forced to relocate as the thawing of permafrost damages buildings and destroys winter roads, which provide access to communities only during the coldest months.

The threat of climate change has led to new partnerships between indigenous communities and environmental scientists. Climate change scientists in the Canadian Arctic and sub-Arctic have combined their methods with "traditional knowledge," that is, the knowledge held by elders and hunters of communities, which is acquired through personal relationships to, and traditional understandings of, the land and natural environment in which they live. The Northwest Territories passing of the Traditional Knowledge Policy in 1993 mandated that scientists in the territory work with traditional knowledge holders, effectively creating a new relevancy in contemporary Canadian society for indigenous life ways. The

2009 UN report on indigenous peoples states that traditional knowledge is "directly linked to the concept of self-determination in the sense that indigenous peoples have the right to manage their own heritage, knowledge and biodiversity and, in order to do so, their rights to their territories and resources must be fully recognized and protected" (United Nations 2009, 65). It appears that traditional knowledge will be a major issue for Canadian aboriginal peoples in the years to come.

EDUCATION

In the 1880s, inspired by U.S. policy, Canada adopted a system of aboriginal boarding schools, termed simply residential schools. These schools forced assimilation into mainstream Euro-Canadian society. Young children were taken from their homes and enrolled in Christian boarding schools where the strategy of education was, as the superintendent of the first boarding school in the United States, Captain Richard Pratt put it, "Kill the Indian, save the man." Students were not allowed to wear traditional clothing, practice traditional religion or customs, or speak in their native languages. Boys were forced to cut their hair. Assimilation through the erasure of Indian culture and the regulation of native bodies reached an extreme in Alberta in 1928 when legislation was passed allowing for the forced sterilization of girls in boarding schools. British Columbia passed similar legislation in 1933.

While the United States officially dropped the boarding school policy following the Meriam Report in 1928, Canada maintained its residential school system into the 1970s. The last federally run residential school, the Gordon Residential School in Saskatchewan, was closed in 1996. Both countries share a history of boarding school atrocities, although abuses have been better documented in Canada.

The Truth Commission into Genocide in Canada found in 2001 that the Roman Catholic Church, the United Church of Canada, the Anglican Church of Canada, and the federal government were collectively responsible for the deaths of more than 50,000 aboriginal children in residential schools. The Truth Commission documents the deaths of children through beating, exposure to below freezing temperatures, and medical experimentation. Others lived through physical, sexual, and psychological abuse at the hands of their teachers and caretakers, only to commit suicide as adults or find solace in alcohol and drugs. The legacy of the boarding schools can be found in contemporary problems of alcoholism, drug abuse, and domestic violence among aboriginal communities.

Although residential schools existed far longer in Canada than in the United States, Canada has been more active in reconciliation. Since the 1990s, thousands of lawsuits have been filed against churches and the government, with settlements costing over $1 billion. Many Canadian churches have created reconciliation programs, unlike in the United States. And in June 2008, Prime Minister Stephen Harper issued an official apology to aboriginal peoples for the boarding school legacy.

Since the boarding school system was abandoned, education has been looking up for Canadian Indian youth. In 1969, only 10 percent of Indian children began their last year of high school, with far fewer graduating. In 1989, forty percent had continued onto their senior year, and the number has been steadily climbing. However, education for aboriginal youth still has a long way to go. The Canadian Royal Commission on Aboriginal Peoples found in 2001 that about 70 percent of aboriginal students living on reserves do not graduate from high school, with graduation rates around 30 percent annually. Many rural communities do not have facilities for secondary education, so often the only option for students wishing to attend high school is traveling to a school outside their community.

CHALLENGES OF ABORIGINAL EDUCATION IN CANADA

Russell Lawson

Canadian secondary schools, on- and off-reservation, are not preparing students for higher education, according to Devon Fiddler of the University of Saskatchewan, vice-president of aboriginal relations for the Indigenous Students' Council. As a result, the number of First Nations students who matriculate at colleges and universities is low. "Despite the fact that they are the fastest-growing population in Canada, only eight per cent of Aboriginal youth achieve post-secondary qualifications. Among First Nations youth, only four per cent of students finish post-secondary education." Why? According to Fiddler, secondary students at off-reservation schools face stereotyping and discrimination, which limits their educational experience. "On-reserve high schools are not always much better, though staff and faculty better understand the challenges their students face." One of the problems facing First Nations students is the lack of financial support, which groups such as Indspire (formerly National Aboriginal Achievement Foundation) are trying to correct. According to its website, Indspire is a "Charitable organization that is dedicated to raising funds to deliver programs that provide the necessary tools for Indigenous peoples, especially youth to achieve their potential. To date Indspire, through its Education Program has awarded more than $42.7-million in scholarships and bursaries to more than 11,500 First Nations, Inuit and Métis students nationwide." To people like Indspire's director, Roberta Jamieson, Canadian provinces such as Saskatchewan, which has a predominance of aboriginal students, must encourage First Nations students to attend college to help alleviate unemployment and social problems.

Source: Yelland, Tannara. "Aboriginal Education Should Be a Priority." *Canadian University Press Newswire*. Retrieved from http://cupwire.ca/articles/37570

ABORIGINAL WOMEN

It was not until the 1980s that the Indian Act recognized aboriginal women's rights. In 1982, bands were given the power to decide whether a woman would lose her Indian status by marrying a non-Indian. In 1985, the act was again revised, granting women the right to retain their status when marrying a non-Indian and to pass status on to their children. This revision also reinstated status to aboriginal people who had lost or forfeited their status through other means (such as enfranchisement or attending college).

At the time of the changes to the act, 20 percent of the estimated 50,000 eligible nonstatus Indians were expected to apply. By 1986, 42,000 non-status Indians, 84 percent, had applied for their status to be reinstated. By 1991, status had been successfully regained by 69,593 people. This does not mean, however, that people who regained their status were welcomed into bands. The federal government was then moved to create another distinction, this time between those who are members of bands and those who are registered federally.

A widespread problem in Canada has been the murder and disappearance of native women. Over 520 aboriginal women have gone missing or been murdered in Canada since the 1970s. More than half of these cases have occurred since 2000, with British Columbia having the highest number. Of great concern to the families and communities of these women is the lack of attention this issue has garnered. In 2008, the UN Committee on the Elimination of Discrimination against Women issued a statement saying, "Hundreds of cases involving aboriginal women who have gone missing or been murdered in the past two decades have neither been fully investigated nor attracted priority attention" (UN 2008).

The reasons for this phenomenon are unclear; however, there may be a few contributing factors. Many aboriginal women come from backgrounds of poverty, little education, little employment opportunities, and oftentimes histories of alcoholism and physical abuse. Women in these situations may turn to prostitution as a viable means of employment. Lack of opportunities may also be a convincing factor for staying in abusive relationships. Or an alternative to these options may be living on the streets, where women are more vulnerable to sexual assault and abduction.

RELIGION

The assimilation strategies that led to the boarding school system also led to the banning of native religious practices found to be offensive to Euro-Canadian sensibilities. A 1914 ban on "give away" ceremonies was designed to stop the potlatch rituals of native peoples along the Pacific seaboard from Washington to British Columbia and into southern Alaska. Potlatches, with their elaborate gifting ceremonies that sometimes culminated in the destruction of wealth, were seen as antithetical to the newly developed economic principles of both the United States and Canada. The strict crackdown along both sides of the border involved prosecution of potlatch participants and confiscation of the goods being gifted (such as elaborately carved canoes, masks, and religious paraphernalia). The confiscated goods were often dispersed to museums in the United States and Canada, frequently crossing the border from where they were taken.

Plains Indians too faced religious persecution. The Métis's 1869 Red River Rebellion in Manitoba and 1885 Saskatchewan rebellions, followed by the Ghost Dance movements of the Sioux in the 1890s, increased the desire of both Canadian and U.S. governments to restrict indigenous sovereignty. Like the potlatch ceremonies, Plains dances were outlawed.

In the 1920s, the ban was enforced with rigor, along with a crackdown on the Sun Dance ceremony of Plains tribes. Piercing the chest with large hooks during the Sun Dance was seen as uncivilized and un-Christian. The 1920s regulation against these practices was encouraged by Christian missionaries who were outraged to find the practice persisting in secret. It was not until the 1951 reworking of the Indian Act that these ceremonies were legalized.

Today, repatriation efforts have recovered much of the confiscated potlatch materials. It has been, however, a long and tedious process. Many museums in the United States refuse to repatriate goods to First Nations in Canada, stating that they were purchased in good faith. Although museums are held to the Native American Graves and Repatriation Act in the United States, there are no legal ramifications if museums refuse to return goods across the border.

CONCLUSION

Even though Canada has come a long way from the extreme assimilative policies of early confederation, assimilation as the answer keeps rearing its ugly head. Beginning with the regulation of religious practices and a boarding school system that strove for full religious and cultural conversions, assimilation was violently enforced. It was not until the 1900s that religious rights were reinstated and the boarding school system was shut down. Prime Minister Stephen Harper's public apology to aboriginal people for the boarding school system acknowledged in the present the errors of Canada's assimilationist agenda, apparently bringing it to an end. Yet assimilation as an answer to contemporary First Nations issues is still being articulated, demonstrating that the ideology of cultural superiority at the heart of assimilation strategies remains strong. Although First Nations, Inuit, and Métis people have made great strides over the last 50 years to better the situations of aboriginal peoples, and their position in Canadian culture, clearly much work remains to be done.

REFERENCES

Dickason, Olive and David T. McNab. *Canada's First Nations: A History of Founding Peoples from Earliest Times*. New York: Oxford University Press, 2008.

Guimond, Eric, Gail Valaskakis, and Madeleine Dion Sout (Eds.). *Restoring the Balance: First Nations Women, Community, and Culture*. Winnipeg: University of Manitoba Press: 2009.

Human Development Report. *Making New Technologies Work for Human Development*. UN Development Programme, 2001.

Milly, John Sheridan. *A National Crime: The Canadian Government and the Residential School System, 1879 to 1986*. Winnipeg: University of Manitoba Press, 1999.

Ray, Arthur J. *An Illustrated History of Canada's Native People: I Have Lived Here since the World Began*. Montreal: McGill-Queens University Press, 2011.

Royal Commission on Aboriginal Peoples. *Report of the Royal Commission on Aboriginal Peoples*. Ottawa: Canada Communications Group, 2001.

United Nations. *Committee on the Elimination of All Forms of Discrimination against Women*, CEDAW/C/CAN/CO/7. 7 November 2008. http://daccess-dds-ny.un.org/doc/UNDOC/GEN/N08/602/42/PDF/N0860242.pdf

Human Rights of Indigenous People Worldwide

Yuka Mizutani

Issues related to the human rights of indigenous people have come into focus worldwide in the past couple of decades. The problems each indigenous group faces differ, depending on historical background, as well as the laws and policies of nation-states. However, some aspects are shared. Common issues include rights of land tenure, fishing, and hunting; revitalization of language and culture; improvement of socioeconomic status; and opportunities for education. The International Fund for Agricultural Development (IFAD) points out the following facts: indigenous peoples make up 5 percent of the world population, but they constitute 15 percent of the world's poor; one third of the world's extremely poor rural people are indigenous people; and only 6 percent of the land of the entire world is legally owned by indigenous people (IFAD n.d.).

Especially under the leadership of the United Nations, the world has recently paid more attention to indigenous human rights. According to the UN Declaration on the Rights of Indigenous Peoples in 2007, indigenous people "have suffered from historic injustices as a result of, inter alia, their colonization and dispossession of their lands, territories and resources" (United Nations 2007, 2). As a result, indigenous people have often been deprived of the privilege of developing according to their own needs. A census by the United Nations indicates there are around 370 million indigenous people in 90 countries (Department of Economic and Social Affairs 2009, 1). The definition of *indigenous* depends on each nation-state or region. For instance, in the United States, each indigenous nation is responsible for determining who is a member. Many use indigenous blood quantum, or the fraction that is Indian, to determine membership. Also, in the U.S. census, citizens voluntarily declare whether they are indigenous. On the other hand, the Mexican government has used knowledge of an indigenous language to determine whether people are considered indigenous. Therefore, it is almost impossible to count the exact number of indigenous people in the world. Roughly 4,000 indigenous languages exist. Also, 7,000 indigenous groups live in more than 70 countries. Seventy percent of indigenous people live in Asia. In some countries, indigenous people are not the ethnic minority. For instance, Bolivia and Guatemala's populations are more than half indigenous (IFAD n.d.).

Although problems regarding human rights of indigenous peoples worldwide have long been one of its biggest concerns, the United Nations started working harder to solve them in 1993, when the Working Group completed a Draft Declaration of the Rights of Indigenous Peoples in cooperation with indigenous peoples. That year was also proclaimed the International Year of the World's Indigenous People. From 1995, revisions were made by the Working Group of the Commission on Human Rights (which later became the Human Rights Council), along with various indigenous representatives. The United Nations declared years from 1995 to 2004 the International Decade of the World's Indigenous People. This was renewed for the Second International Decade of the World's Indigenous People from 2005 to 2015. On September 13, 2007, the UN General Assembly adopted the declaration. After adoption of the declaration, the Working Group on indigenous populations became the Expert Mechanism on the Rights of Indigenous Peoples, part of the Office of the United Nations High Commissioner for Human Rights. The Expert Mechanism works to solve issues related to indigenous peoples. Also, the International Labour Organization (ILO) has been working on this issue for a long time. ILO Conventions No. 107 (in 1957) and No. 169 (in 1989) both apply to situations regarding the human rights of indigenous people. The Permanent Forum on Indigenous Issues (UNPFII) was established in 2000 to discuss various issues, including human rights.

However, the situation of indigenous people in the world does not instantly improve with discussions and the adoption of declarations at the level of international politics. Each nation-state has its own policies to determine who indigenous people are and how to treat them. Therefore, the type and degree of the problems each indigenous group faces vary. Yet common problems are seen—for example, discrimination, violence, and poverty—that threaten the well-being, both physical and psychological, of indigenous people. In addition, indirect issues, including environmental destruction and climate change, endanger the existence of indigenous people. Besides the ILO, other sections of the United Nations work with indigenous people, such as the High Commissioner for Refugees (UNHCR); the World Health Organization (WHO); the United Nations Educational, Scientific and Cultural Organization (UNESCO); the United Nations Children's Fund (UNICEF); and the United Nations Human Settlements Programme (UN-HABITAT). The Inter-Agency Support Group (IASG) was established to help all

> ## UNITED NATIONS DECLARATION ON THE RIGHTS OF INDIGENOUS PEOPLE
>
> The UN Declaration on the Rights of Indigenous People was adopted in 2007. The text in part is reproduced here.
>
> Recognizing that respect for indigenous knowledge, cultures and traditional practices contributes to sustainable and equitable development and proper management of the environment.
>
> *Article 29*
> 1. Indigenous peoples have the right to the conservation and protection of the environment and the productive capacity of their lands or territories and resources. States shall establish and implement assistance programmes for indigenous peoples for such conservation and protection, without discrimination.
>
> *Source*: United National Declaration of Rights. Retrieved from http://www.un.org/esa/socdev/unpfii/documents/DRIPS_en.pdf /

these UN divisions work collaboratively. Currently, 31 organizations are participating in IASG (United Nations Permanent Forum on Indigenous Issues).

INDIGENOUS PEOPLE IN CANADA

In Canada, indigenous people are called aboriginal, including the First Nations, Inuit, and Métis people. Recognition of indigenous rights by the Canadian government happened later than it did in the United States. In 1968, the National Indian Brotherhood of Canada (currently the Assembly of First Nations) was established. This organization played a key role in changing Canadian indigenous policy. The Canadian government attempted to change the Canadian Constitution in 1978, primarily to respond to French-Canadian issues. Yet the National Indian Brotherhood of Canada successfully got the federal government to add issues relating to indigenous rights to this discussion. As a result, the Canadian government promised to incorporate treaty rights and to include indigenous peoples' participation in Canadian politics related to indigenous issues. The agency of the Canadian government in charge of indigenous issues is Indian and Northern Affairs Canada. Today, indigenous peoples in Canada have reserves or lands that the Canadian government intended to be used for agricultural purposes.

As so many Canadian indigenous people live in the northern part of the country close to the Arctic, there are concerns that global warming will affect their traditional and modern life ways. Also, there are other problems, such as a lower rate of aboriginal students in higher education than other ethnicities. The Council of Ministers of Education started to work on this problem in 2004. In the Aboriginal Education Action Plan, the council suggested improving education for aboriginal students to meet the demands of aboriginal communities. Also, the council suggested making an effort to develop a better framework for teacher training, to prepare aboriginal and nonaboriginal teachers to work with aboriginal students of different levels. Another concern is mental health. According to Canadian government statistics, suicide rates among Inuit youth are 11 times higher than the national average. Therefore, the Canadian government, nongovernmental organizations, schools, and clinics are working to build better prevention programs (Getches, Wilkinson, and Williams 2005, 949–952).

INDIGENOUS PEOPLE IN MEXICO

In Mexico, CDI (Comisión Nacional para el Desarrollo de los Pueblos Indígenas; the National Commission for the Development of Indigenous Peoples) was established in 2003. Before its establishment, INI (Instituto Nacional Indigenista; the National Indigenous Institute) was in charge of indigenous issues since 1948. Activities of CDI vary from cultural protection and tourism to legal assistance and improvement of infrastructure (Comisión Nacional n.d.). Still, many Mexican indigenous people insist that their human rights are not protected enough. One way they express their frustration is to involve themselves in antigovernmental political activities such as EZLN (Ejército Zapatista de Liberación Nacional; the Zapatista Army of National Liberation), widely called Zapatista. This organization is based in Chiapas, in southern Mexico, where the majority of residents are indigenous people. Zapatistas felt their lives were threatened when NAFTA (North American Free Trade Agreement) went into effect in 1994 because the free trade of goods with other countries can lower their incomes. A statistic shows that 80.6 percent of the indigenous people in Mexico are facing poverty; during the 1990s, the economic gap between indigenous and nonindigenous peoples in selected countries in Latin America grew wider than in previous periods (IFAD n.d.). Since the income of people in Chiapas has historically been lower than in other parts of Mexico, NAFTA was a big threat to indigenous people there. Therefore, some indigenous people in Chiapas declared their intention to act against the Mexican government. However, it must be emphasized that not all indigenous people in Mexico take part in activities with force.

Mexico, unlike the United States, has not set aside lands only for the use of indigenous people, such as reservations. The only exception is the Indigenous

Members of the Zapatista National Liberation Army (EZLN) stand guard at a meeting with supporters in Morelia, in Mexico's Chiapas state, July 23, 2007. The rebels have pledged to move away from armed struggle and toward politics but have not clearly defined their new political role more than a decade after seizing several towns in southern Chiapas state in a short-lived revolt for Indian rights and socialism. (AP Photo/Moyses Zuniga)

Zone provided for the Yaqui people in northern Mexico by President Cardenas in the 1930s. Yet even the Yaqui people lack a nation-to-nation relationship with the federal government of Mexico.

INDIGENOUS PEOPLE IN NEW ZEALAND

In New Zealand, the Ministry of Maori Development works with the Maori people. In 1840, the Treaty of Waitangi was signed between Britain and the Maori people. The text of this treaty was written in both English and Maori, but the contents of the two versions differed slightly, particularly in the part about land property. The Maori version of the treaty was written as if land property would be protected even after the arrival of settlers. Yet British settlers took land away from Maori by force and via the Native Land Act of 1865.

During the 1970s, the Maori people started to become more active in pursuing their human rights. As a result, the Treaty of Waitangi Act was established in 1975. By this act, Maori people were given the right to report violations of the 1840 Treaty of Waitangi to a court called the Waitangi Tribunal. Land rights of the Maori people are still under discussion, as well as other problems such as health problems, a higher crime rate, and poverty (Naito 2005, 115–129). At the same time, some improvements have been made. The Maori language is taught as a part of mandatory education to both Maori and non-Maori students. Moreover, some higher education courses are taught in the Maori language to facilitate the understanding of Maori culture and society. Now, Maori culture is understood in a more positive way than previously. In the tourism industry, it is one of the biggest appeals to international travelers.

INDIGENOUS PEOPLE IN AUSTRALIA

In Australia, the Department of Families, Housing, Community Services and Indigenous Affairs is responsible for issues related to aboriginal and Torres Strait Islander peoples. The aboriginal and Torres Strait Islander peoples have been suppressed just as indigenous peoples in other countries have. For example, International Fund for Agricultural Development (IFAD) statistics show that life expectancy for aboriginal men in Australia is 18 years shorter than for Australian men of other ethnicities (IFAD n.d.). Also, 500 aboriginal languages were lost after the arrival of European settlers. Even so, the situation has started to improve. In December 2010, the Australian government announced that they would consider amending the Australian Constitution to acknowledge the special place of aboriginal and Torres Strait Islander peoples. As a result, the government appointed an expert panel to discuss constitutional change during 2011. The decision was made based on the UN Declaration on the Rights of Indigenous Peoples of 2007. The Australian government aims to establish a new national indigenous representative body, as well as to fund grassroots initiatives to provide opportunities for Australian first peoples to address colonialist acts of the national government. Also, the Australian government is willing to work on improving aboriginal and Torres Strait Islander peoples' health, education, and employment situation (Commonwealth of Australia 2012). In addition to political actions, aboriginal people are rediscovering and recognizing their identity and dignity through art and crafts. Pieces of both traditional and contemporary aboriginal art are traded at relatively high prices between aboriginal and nonaboriginal people. Recognition of aboriginal art in the national and international markets is helping the aboriginal people recover from historical trauma and strengthen their ethnic identity. At the same time, the art and craft industry is becoming a way to bring cash income to aboriginal communities.

INDIGENOUS PEOPLE IN EUROPE

Indigenous people exist in Europe, too. For instance, the Sami (formerly called Lapp) people reside in an area close to the Arctic, which is now a part of Russia,

Finland, Sweden, and Norway. There are several different dialects and cultures among the Sami people. However, they share a common ethnic identity. Many factors have endangered Sami life and culture. One of these is the existence of the international borders, which have restricted the Sami people's geographical mobility. Also, nonindigenous people became interested in the natural resources on Sami land, including fish, trees, and minerals. These factors have caused tremendous negative effects on Sami traditional customs, particularly on reindeer grazing. As a result, many Sami people have had to relocate to urban areas to make a living from wage labor.

However, a political movement and attempts at cultural revitalization started in the twentieth century. Initially the activity was regional, asking for land rights for reindeer grazing. Later, many organizations were established on the national level. In 1953, the first meeting of the Nordic Sami conference was held. Sami people across the international borders participated in this conference. Then the Sami Council was established in 1956. The Sami Council is an organization that unites various Sami organizations in Russia, Finland, Sweden, and Norway. In the 1990s, the Sami language was recognized as an official language within Sami land in Norway, Finland, and Sweden. In Sami communities in these countries, primary education is offered in the Sami language. The Sami people are on the way to revitalizing their ethnic identity and language, which had been damaged by colonization (Shoji 2005, 58–75).

INDIGENOUS PEOPLE IN JAPAN

Issues and problems related to indigenous people exist outside of Western countries. One of many countries in which indigenous issues are actively discussed is Japan. Japan has been considered an ethnically homogeneous country, on both national and international levels. However, the Ainu people have lived in the northern part of Japan, mainly in Hokkaido, the most northern island of the Japanese archipelago, from time immemorial. The Ainu people have their own language and culture distinct from the mainstream Japanese people. They resided in a part of current Russian territory as well, where Russia and Japan set the international border. (Later, the Japanese government removed these Ainu people in Russia to Hokkaido.) In about the fifteenth century, mainstream Japanese people started to colonize Hokkaido. The Ainu people were called Former Aborigines (*Kyu Dojin*) and were forced to assimilate into mainstream Japanese society.

The situation surrounding the Ainu people greatly changed after the Japanese government's recognition of the Ainu as an indigenous people in June 2008, following the UN Declaration on the Rights of Indigenous Peoples of 2007. But political issues related to the Ainu began to gradually change from the 1990s on. The Hokkaido Former Aborigines Protection Act, which had been active since 1899, was terminated. Concurrently, the Law for the Promotion of Ainu Culture and the Dissemination and Advocacy of Knowledge was enacted. This law aimed to protect and revitalize Ainu language, culture, and traditional environment (Ainu Association of Hokkaido). An Ainu person, Shigeru Kayano, became the first member of the House of Representatives in 1994. Still, Ainu living conditions need further improvement. According to a 2006 census, 1.6 times more Ainu people than mainstream Japanese people were living on welfare. Also, 17.4 percent of Ainu people received higher education, while 38.5 percent of mainstream Japanese people do (Hokkaido Prefecture Office n.d.). A survey conducted in 2008 by the Center for the Ainu and Indigenous Studies at Hokkaido University also shows some aspects of the modern life of the Ainu people in Hokkaido. According to the survey, only 10 percent of respondents are constantly aware of their ethnic heritage (Onai 2010, 122). Rates of smoking, drinking, and gambling are higher than the national average (Onai 2010, 124). These numbers indicate the Ainu people hold problems common to indigenous people in other countries, such as handing down ethnic consciousness and maintaining wellness.

There are many Ainu people living outside of Hokkaido prefecture, too. From 2010 to 2011, the Japanese government and the Ainu Association of Hokkaido called for Ainu people outside of Hokkaido to voluntarily participate in their survey in order to find out about their life conditions. According to the results, the number of people living on the welfare is three times more than the national average. Nine out of 142 people work in an industry related to the Ainu culture. Thirty-one point one percent received higher education, which is about 10 percent higher than the Ainu people in Hokkaido, though it is 13 percent lower than the national average. Eleven point nine percent participate in activities related to the Ainu culture, which is 7.5 percent less than the Ainu people in Hokkaido. Thirty-seven point six percent have never told their neighbors and friends about their ethnicity, and 34.8 percent have not told their children that they are Ainu. The survey concludes that the Ainu people outside of Hokkaido are facing difficulties, just like the Ainu people in Hokkaido (Prime Minister of Japan and His Cabinet, 10, 13, 18, 23, 26).

INDIGENOUS PEOPLE IN TAIWAN

The Taiwanese government has recognized 14 indigenous groups. The Taiwanese Council of Indigenous Peoples was established in 1996 to take care of indigenous issues. Indigenous peoples in Taiwan went through colonization by Holland, China, Japan, and Taiwan, as this island has been occupied by these various nation-states. In Taiwan, indigenous people live in the mountains. As nonindigenous people developed the land from the plains toward the mountainous part of the island, Taiwanese indigenous cultures and societies were faced with ruination. The indigenous political movement in Taiwan was started in 1983 by indigenous university students. In 1984, the Alliance of Taiwan Aborigines was founded to speak out against problems related to indigenous peoples and their communities. This movement had many goals: recovering land rights, eliminating from textbooks a story called the Wu Feng Myth that insulted indigenous peoples, rescuing indigenous teenagers from the sex industry, cancelling the building of a facility for nuclear waste on indigenous land, preserving indigenous languages, using indigenous names rather than Chinese names, abolishing the term *mountain compatriots* to denote indigenous people in Taiwan, ending the stereotyping of indigenous culture through tourism, and establishing autonomous land for indigenous peoples. Although some of these goals have been accomplished, problems still remain. Currently, political and legal conditions surrounding the Taiwanese indigenous peoples are rapidly changing (Takebayashi 1995a, 633; Takebayashi 1995b, 634).

INDIGENOUS PEOPLE ELSEWHERE IN THE WORLD

Although too numerous to mention in this essay, there are indigenous peoples in other parts of the world, too, including the Middle East, Africa, South Asia, South America, and Pacific islands. As globalization continues and human rights in general come to be increasingly protected, groups of people who have been hiding their ethnic identities will no doubt start identify themselves as indigenous people.

Today, many indigenous nations and organizations communicate and collaborate nationally and internationally to discuss various problems. Numerous international conferences, meetings, and symposia are held about indigenous peoples worldwide. Some annual events are the UNPFII (UN Permanent Forum on Indigenous Issues) annual meeting, the Indigenous World Film Festival (hosted by the Alaska Native Heritage Center), and the International Indian Treaty Council Conference. Examples of occasional events held in 2012 were the World Indigenous Lawyers' Conference, the World Indigenous Television Broadcasters Conference, and the World Indigenous Housing Conference. Through these events, indigenous people are sharing information and building networks among themselves.

However, language barriers can prevent indigenous peoples in non-English-speaking countries from participating in discussions on the international level. Most events are held in English, and participants tend to be from English-speaking countries. This seems to be deeply related to the lack of educational opportunities for indigenous people. English is taught as a part of compulsory education and higher education in many non-English-speaking countries, but many indigenous people cannot gain access to education. Therefore, they cannot receive information shared in the international indigenous community. Additionally, since many indigenous peoples face economic inequality, they cannot afford to attend such events.

These are some of the obstacles for indigenous people to attain human rights. Yet compared with past centuries, human rights for indigenous people worldwide are generally improving. Many indigenous and nonindigenous people are eagerly working on this issue.

REFERENCES

Anaya, S. James. *International Human Rights and Indigenous Peoples*. New York: Aspen Publishers, 2009.

Comisión Nacional para el Desarrollo de los Pueblos Indígenas (National Comission for the Development of the Indigenous Peoples). Available at http://www.cdi.gob.mx/

Commonwealth of Australia. "Recognising Aboriginal and Torres Strait Islander Peoples in the Constitution: Report of the Expert Panel," January 2012. Retrieved from http://www.youmeunity.org.au/uploads/assets/3446%20FaHCSIA%20ICR%20report_text_Bookmarked%20PDF%2012%20Jan%20v4.pdf

Department of Economic and Social Affairs, Division for Social Policy and Development, Secretariat of the Permanent Forum on Indigenous Issues, United Nations. *State of the World's Indigenous Peoples*. New York: United Nations Publications, 2009.

Getches, David H., Charles F. Wilkinson, and Robert A. Williams, Jr. *Cases and Materials on Federal Indian Law* (5th ed.). St. Paul, MN: West, 2005.

Hokkaido Prefecture Office. "Seikatsu Jittai Chousa" (Survey of Actual Life). Retrieved from http://www.pref.hokkaido.lg.jp/ks/ass/jittai.htm (in Japanese) on January 31, 2011.

Indian and Northern Affairs Canada. Available at http://www.ainc-inac.gc.ca/index-eng.asp

International Fund for Agricultural Development (IFAD). "Statistics." *Rural Poverty Portal*. Retrieved from http://www.ruralpovertyportal.org/web/rural-poverty-portal/topic/statistics/tags/indigenous_peoples on September 11, 2012.

Ivison, Duncan, Paul Patton, and Will Sanders (Eds.). *Political Theory and the Rights of Indigenous Peoples*. New York: Cambridge University Press, 2000.

Naito, Akiko. "Daichi No Mana No Yukue: Maori No Tochi Ken Mondai" (Destination of Mana of Land: Problems of the Land Rights of Maori). In Tsuneo Ayabe, Keiji Maegawa, and Satoshi Tanahashi (Eds.), *The First Peoples of Oceania*. Tokyo: Akashi Shoten, 2005.

Onai, Toru. *Living Conditions and Consciousness of Present-day Ainu; Report on the 2008 Hokkaido Ainu Living Conditions Survey*. Sapporo: Center for Ainu & Indigenous Studies, Hokkaido University, 2010.

Prime Minister of Japan and His Cabinet, Council for Ainu Policy Promotion, Working Group on Research on Living Conditions of Ainu People outside Hokkaido. ""Hokkaidougai Ainu No Seikatsu Jittai Chousa Sagyoubukai" Houkoku" (Report of "Working Group on Research on Living Conditions of Ainu People outside Hokkaido"). Retrieved from http://www.kantei.go.jp/jp/singi/ainusuishin/dai3/siryou3_3.pdf (in Japanese) June, 2011.

Pritchard, Sarah (Ed.). *Indigenous Peoples, the United Nations and Human Rights*. London: Zed Books, 1998.

Shoji, Hiroshi, "Sami: Senjumin Ken Wo Motomete" (Sami: In Search of Indigenous Rights). In Sadao Umesao, Kiyoshi Hara, and Hiroshi Shoji (Eds.), *The First Peoples of Europe*. Tokyo: Akashi Shoten, 2005.

Takebayashi, Masahiro. "Taiwan." In Sadao Umesao and Masaki Matsubara (Eds.), *Sekai Minzoku Mondai Jiten* (Encyclopedia of Nations and Ethnic Relations). Tokyo: Heibonsha, 1995a.

Takebayashi, Masahiro. "Taiwan Genjumin Undou" (Taiwan Indigenous Movement). In Sadao Umesao and Masaki Matsubara (Eds.), *Sekai Minzoku Mondai Jiten* (Encyclopedia of Nations and Ethnic Relations). Tokyo: Heibonsha, 1995b.

United Nations. *Declaration on the Rights of Indigenous Peoples*, 2007. Retrieved from http://www.un.org/esa/socdev/unpfii/documents/DRIPS_en.pdf on September 10, 2012.

United Nations Permanent Forum on Indigenous Issues. "Inter-Agency Support Group on Indigenous Issues." Retrieved from http://social.un.org/index/IndigenousPeoples/InterAgencySupportGroup.aspx

Missionaries to Canada's First Nations

Joyce Martin

European explorers who came to North America brought a desire to conquer and control but to convert to Christianity as well. Along with soldiers were Catholic and Protestant missionaries who believed that Christ called upon Christians to spread the message of Christianity to all peoples throughout the world, including North America. Missionary work in North America was simultaneously benevolent and controlling, trying to convert people for the benefit of their souls but exercising undue power and control in the process. The effects of the centuries of missionary activities in Canada are still felt today.

NEW FRANCE

Canada's First Nations saw two waves of Christian missionaries, Roman Catholic during French colonization and Protestant during British colonization. During the early history of Canada, France was the dominant European colonial power, and Roman Catholic was the dominant religion. Canada was often referred to as New France during this period of French rule. New France was a commercial colony initially based largely on the fur trade instead of widespread settlement, unlike the United States or Mexico.

From 1608 to 1663, New France functioned as a private colony with certain companies having a monopoly on trade, exchanging European items such as clothing, guns, and blankets for North American furs. Missionaries were part of the North American fur trade, accompanying traders, trappers, and settlers as they met and traded with the First Nations people.

Members of both the Iroquois and Huron confederacies participated in the fur trade. In 1570, the Mohawks, Oneidas, Onondagas, Cayugas, and Senecas formed the Iroquois League of Five Nations. The Huron confederation, located around the Georgian Bay, included the Deer, Rock, Bear, and Cord. The Iroquois and the Huron were often at odds with each other. The Huron oversaw a large agricultural and commercial network and participated in the fur trade with French traders. Jesuit missionaries settled in close proximity to them.

Huron willingness to convert to Christianity during this early period of the fur trade may have been influenced by the economics of the fur trade. While overall only 15 percent of Huron identified as Christian, 50 percent of Huron in the fur trade identified as Christian. This discrepancy could be explained by the fact that once an individual converted, he was considered French and therefore he was paid more for his furs than non-French traders.

While missionaries and traders occasionally worked at cross-purposes with the native population, it was often through trading companies that missionaries gained entry to a native community. The trading companies engaged the missionaries to encourage the First Nations to continue work in the fur trade. For example, traders encouraged Jesuit missionaries to ask Huron to leave their children in settlements for religious training while they travelled to find furs. The Huron were thriving until Europeans introduced smallpox into the area. The disease was devastating. By 1641, half of the Huron population had perished due to smallpox. This left the Huron vulnerable to their rivals the Iroquois. Once the Iroquois defeated the Huron, they went on to control an increasing share of the fur trade.

SAMUEL DE CHAMPLAIN

Samuel de Champlain, called the Father of New France, established a post in Quebec (originally a Huron village called Stadacona) in 1608. Champlain wanted to see Quebec serve as a center for missions to the First Nations. Unlike England, which dominated colonies with large numbers of settlers, France had a small population in Canada. Given the relatively small numbers of French in Canada and the limited resources France gave to the colonies, it was necessary for them to work together with the First Nations in exploration, trade, and war. Therefore, the French forged alliances through cooperation, trade, and mutually beneficial military alliances. Missionaries like Champlain allied with the colonial officials in their belief that the First Nations people would want to convert to the Roman Catholic Church and would ultimately want to become French subjects, which would benefit both the missionaries and France as a colonial power.

The French traders initially had good relationships with both the Huron and Iroquois, but in 1609, Samuel de Champlain sided with the Huron during an attack on the Iroquois. In response to the French siding with their rival, after the attack, many Iroquois considered the French their enemy.

JEAN DE BREBEUF

Jesuit priest Jean de Brebeuf (1593–1649) was another early missionary to New France. In 1632, the monarchy gave a monopoly of religious services in central Canada to the Jesuits. The Jesuits initially focused on the Algonquin people and attempted to transform them into farmers. Then the Jesuits began a mission in the Huron territory near Georgian Bay. The Huron were fur traders and allies of the French. Jesuits often accompanied explorers as they began to travel to First Nations communities, and the early Jesuits attempted to live like the indigenous communities around them. The Jesuit publication *Relations*, published from 1632 to 1673, included thrilling tales of the missionaries and served to increase donations and motivate others to take up missionary work in New France. Jean de Brébeuf authored the 1635 and 1636 editions of *Relations*, writing about the Huron missions.

The Huron may have accepted Jean de Brebeuf into their community to a certain degree since they gave him the name Echon, meaning a tree with medicinal properties. The Huron also named him a chief in 1638. Jean de Brébeuf translated the fundamentals of Catholic doctrine into their language and composed the country's first Christmas carol, "Jesus is Born" (*Jesous Ahatonhia*).

The Huron experienced increased dependence on the French given the rising pressures from the Iroquois and contagious diseases. In 1649, the Five Nations Iroquois, the Huron rival, killed Brebeuf and other missionaries. The 1640s brought increased violence, and the number of Jesuits working in Canada dwindled, as did the number of conversions. During peace negotiations in 1653, the Iroquois invited priests to come and live with them, which increased Jesuit presence again.

FRANCOIS XAVIER DE MONTMORENCY LAVAL

Jesuit priest Francois Xavier de Montmorency Laval was the chief religious authority in New France from 1659 to 1684. He worked to restrict the trade of alcohol with First Nations. Laval asserted the church's control over education in the colony and set up a seminary in Quebec to train clergy. The Catholic Church named Francois Xavier de Montmorency Laval the first bishop of Quebec, over 100 years before there was a Catholic bishop living in what is now the United States. Francois Laval moved the point of influence for the Catholic Church in Canada from the King of France to the Pope in Rome.

FEMALE MISSIONARIES

Canada had many female missionaries in the seventeenth century, despite opposition from their families, state, and church officials. In 1635, Jesuit Pére Paul le Jeune commented in *Relations* about the large number of nuns who wanted to emigrate to work with Indigenous women and children. Officials in France seemed to want to limit the number of nuns arriving in New France, preferring women who were eligible to marry. The large number of women interested in missionary work in Canada can be viewed against the backdrop of the Counter Reformation happening in Europe, with many upper class women becoming involved in religious callings. Even with officials reluctant to support female missionaries, Canada became a place where noncloistered nuns could be active and unmarried lay women could serve the church.

Marie Guyart

Marie Guyart, or Marie de l'Incarnation, was the superior of the first Ursuline community in Quebec, a teaching order. Marie de l'Incarnation learned the Algonquin, Iroquoian, and Huron languages and wrote dictionaries in Algonquian and Iroquois. She also translated catechisms into Huron and Algonquian. The Ursuline convent in Canada started a missionary school that taught Iroquois, Algonquian, and French girls.

SEBASTIAN RALE

During the transition period between French and British rule, the church and missionary presence in Canada was in decline. During the growing number of conflicts between France and England in North America, the church increasingly became an arm of the French state. France considered French-sponsored missions and new colonies to be military posts. Often, military garrisons were built on missions or missionaries were posted at military posts. During this period, there was an even greater shortage of missionary volunteers.

The life of Sebastian Rale exemplifies the tension between the French and the British during this time of transition. Rale was a Jesuit missionary to indigenous people in Quebec and Acadia. He was a preacher and linguist, and he helped to develop written forms for two indigenous languages. But the British perceived him to be an agitator among First Nations who opposed Britain. He was killed in 1724 during a time of particularly high tension between the French and the British, and some believe the British placed a price on his head.

The time of transition came to an end in 1763 when the Treaty of Paris ceded Canada and most of New France to Britain after the Seven Years' War, also known as the French and Indian War.

BRITISH RULE 1763–1867

France ceded control of Canada to the British in 1763 at the end of the French and Indian War. The indigenous population that had been allied with the French missions created a coalition called the Federation of Seven Tribes or Seven Nations of Canada to resist British rule, but it dissolved after the U.S. Revolutionary War. A traditional religious revival led by Neolin (Lenni Lenape) protested the British occupation and advocated a return to traditional religions. The British partially acknowledged indigenous peoples' land rights in upper Canada in the Proclamation of 1763, although treaties ceding First Nations land to the British began in 1764 and continued thereafter. In the 1800s, British colonial powers sought to "civilize" the indigenous population of Canada through education, and educational efforts were undertaken by missionaries. The money needed to accomplish this mission work was often raised by Britain through the sale of lands taken from the indigenous people.

MORAVIAN MISSIONARIES

Prior to British control, the French Catholic church had a monopoly on missions in Canada. After this point, the denominations became more diverse. Moravian missionaries established commercial trade interests in Canada and competed with the Hudson Bay Company.

David Zeisberger, a missionary for the Church of the United Brethren or Moravians, established mission towns among the Algonquin people following the French and Indian War. He moved farther west, building a church west of the Ohio River. In 1782, while Zeisberger was traveling, American troops killed 100 Christian American Indians. Zeisberger went to Canada with the surviving refuges, and he founded Fairfield in Ontario in 1792.

METHODIST MISSIONARIES

Mississauga Chippewa and Welsh, Peter Jones (or Kahkewaquonaby, Sacred Feathers) was a Methodist minister, tribal leader, and writer. Jones established a Methodist farming village in 1825. He translated religious texts into Algonquian and wrote *Life and Journals of Kah-ke-wa-quona-by* (1860) and *History of the Ojebway Indians: With Especial Reference to Their Christianity* (1861). Jones fought for quality education and a stable land base for his people.

Methodist minister William Case mentored Peter Jones prior to their falling out when Case asked a non-native missionary to retranslate works already translated by Jones. Case worked among the Mississauga on the shore of Lake Ontario. Two years after Jones established his Methodist farming village, William Case established a Methodist village that at its highest point had a population of 200.

In addition to working with Case, Jones also helped Alvin Torry, the first Methodist missionary in the Grand River area in Ontario. Torry was not successful in winning converts to Christianity until he began to work with Jones. Torry organized a Methodist Indian society, and he and the members built a church and school.

Torry converted Jones's cousin David Sawyer (Kezhegowinninne). Torry baptized Sawyer into the Methodist Episcopal Church in 1825. Sawyer began teaching at the Lake Simco mission in Ontario in 1829, and later worked with the Matchedash band on Georgian Bay. Sawyer preached in Ojibwa and acted as an interpreter. David Sawyer moved to the New Credit Reserve near Brantford, Ontario, in 1861 and when his father died, he was named chief. He served in this position for 25 years.

TRADITIONAL RELIGIOUS MOVEMENT

Jones and other First Nations missionaries had one response to the colonial pressures. Another response was the rise of Midewiwin or Grand Medicine Society rooted in traditional Ojibwa religious practices (Hirschfelder and Molin 2000, 138–139). The society combined knowledge of plants and healing with a moral code. Its goal was to promote a long and healthy life. Midewiwin was considered a gift from the Creator. Initiates had to undergo extensive instruction in origin traditions, herbs, prayers and songs, and moral teachings.

WOMAN'S MISSIONARY SOCIETY

Missionaries continued their work in Canada into the late 1800s. In 1880, the Methodist Church of Canada started the Woman's Missionary Society, its first mission society. The Methodist Church of Canada was not a particularly wealthy organization. They did not, for example, have enough money to send representatives overseas as other religious organizations were doing at this time. But the women who ran the Woman's Missionary Society were often well connected with spare time to devote to their cause, and they proved to be excellent fundraisers. The national organization Woman's Missionary Society had branches in many small towns, and these smaller branches became part of their local congregations and local communities. This missionary society provided a national leadership stage for women, and the organization remained powerful for 45 years.

ANGLICAN MISSIONARIES

The Church Missionary Society, an Anglican missionary society founded in 1799, sponsored missionary work around the world, including Canada. In 1820, the Church Missionary Society sent John West to the Red River region in northwest Canada at Fort Garry (present-day Winnipeg, Manitoba) (Murphy 1996, 153). West established the first Protestant mission in the Canadian northwest. He began a campaign to promote a sedentary agricultural way of life among the French-speaking Métis people in the area. West worked as both a Hudson Bay chaplain and a Church Missionary Society representative, and he preached to both native and non-native people. He hoped to establish a mission school and took on pupils, including a young Cree child named Sakacewescam (Henry Budd).

HENRY BUDD

Budd became the first North American Indian to be ordained in the Church of England (Anglican Church). John West named Sakacewescam after his former rector, the Reverend Henry Budd. Twelve years after completing attendance at West's Church Missionary School, Budd became school director at another mission school in the Red River area. In 1840, he became involved in missionary work, traveling to Cumberland Lake and W'passkwayaw (later known as The Pas, Manitoba). Budd worked with Cree and Ojibway people and acted as an interpreter. In 1853, he was ordained a priest in the Anglican Church and often preached in the Cree language.

By the mid-1800s, the disappearance of game and the rampant spread of disease brought by European colonists, fur traders, and missionaries challenged the unity and self-sufficiency of the First Nations. Missionaries believed that assimilation through Christianity was the best way to help the First Nations. The colonial government, happy to shift the perceived burden off the state, encouraged the church's increased missionary efforts. Many cooperative efforts between the First Nations and the churches broke down around 1840s as the church used coercive and assimilationist methods in reaction to native resistance.

MISSIONARIES AND THE CANADIAN EDUCATION SYSTEM

In 1841, Canada was united once again as the Province of Canada. Canada remained a British colony until the British North America Act of 1867 created the Dominion of Canada.

There is a long history of missionaries in Canada founding and administering schools to educate First Nations children, starting as early as 1600 with missionaries such as Marie Guyart. From approximately 1860 to 1960, with the federal government's cooperation, both Protestant and Catholic missionaries funded and/or ran residential schools for indigenous children. Nonindigenous institutions assumed control over the education of indigenous children. Within this education system, children were separated from their parents, and the schools were used as a means to assimilate indigenous children, moving them away from their communities, language, clothing, and traditional lifestyles.

This missionary- and government-run system of residential schools led to many acts of emotional, physical, and sexual abuse against the native students. Complaints against the schools and school officials were highlighted in the *Report of the Royal Commission on Aboriginal Peoples*, which was published in Canada in 1996. By 1998, four of the churches involved in residential schools had issued apologies to the First Nations, as did the Canadian government. Residential school attendees who were victims of abuse continue to seek reparations and justice through the court system.

The government- and missionary-run education system's suppression of indigenous language use also has had a lasting negative effect on Canada's First Nations people. Currently, 50 of Canada's 53 indigenous languages are in danger of extinction. In 1972, the National Indian Brotherhood created a document entitled *Indian Control of Indian Education*, which proposed that indigenous educators take charge of educating indigenous people. While this has not yet been fully realized, First Nations people continue to develop initiatives to deliver culturally relevant education.

REFERENCES

Allaire, Gratien. "From 'Nouvelle-France' to 'Francophonie Canadienne': A Historical Survey." *International Journal of the Sociology of Language* 2007, 185 (2007): 25–52.

Choquette, Leslie. " 'Ces Amazones du Grand Dieu': Women and Mission in Seventeenth-Century Canada." *French Historical Studies* 17, no. 3 (1992): 627–655.

Clarke, Brian. "English-Speaking Canada from 1854." In *A Concise History of Christianity in Canada*. Edited by Terrance Murphy. Oxford: Oxford University Press, 1996.

Crowley, Terry. "The French Regime to 1760." In *A Concise History of Christianity in Canada*. Edited by Terrance Murphy. Oxford: Oxford University Press, 1996.

Dickson, Olive. *Canada's First Nations: A History of Founding Peoples from Earliest Times*. Norman: University of Oklahoma Press, 1992.

Haig-Brown, Celia. *Taking Control: Power and Contradiction in First Nations Adult Education*. Vancouver: University of British Columbia Press, 1995.

Hirschfelder, Arlene and Paulette Molin. *Encyclopedia of Native American Religions* (2nd ed.). New York: Facts on File, 2000.

Miller, J. R. "Troubled Legacy: A History of Native Residential Schools." *Saskatchewan Law Review* 66 (2003): 357–382.

Murphy, Terrance. "The English Speaking Colonies to 1854." In *A Concise History of Christianity in Canada*. Edited by Terrance Murphy. Oxford: Oxford University Press, 1996.

Neegan, Erica. "Excuse Me: Who Are the First Peoples of Canada? A Historical Analysis of Aboriginal Education in Canada Then and Now." *International Journal of Inclusive Education* 9, no. 1 (2005): 3–15.

Noll, Mark. *A History of Christianity in the United States and Canada.* Grand Rapids, MI: Wm. B. Eerdmans, 2003.

O'Connor, Pamela. "Squaring the Circle: How Canada Is Dealing with the Legacy of Its Indian Residential Schools Experiment." *International Journal of Legal Information* 28, no. 2 (2000): 232–265.

Robertson, Roland. *Rotting Face: Smallpox and the American Indian.* Caldwell, ID: Caxton Press, 2001.

Waldman, Carl. *Biographical Dictionary of American Indian History to 1900* (rev. ed.). New York: Facts on File, 2000.

Worldwide Indigenous Activism

Lindsey Hanson

Indigenous activism takes place not just in North America, but throughout the world, in particular in countries that were once colonies of European imperialists. Indigenous people in these countries face social ills similar to that of American Indians, and often focus their efforts on land claims, the need for economic equality, and access to education and political power.

According to the UN Forum on Indigenous Issues, there are over 370 million indigenous people in approximately 70 countries. These indigenous groups have experienced social problems and injustices as a result of colonization. Many of these indigenous peoples have engaged in activism to remedy these problems. This essay will discuss indigenous activism in a few countries, as well as organized indigenous activism on an international level.

INDIGENOUS ACTIVISM IN AUSTRALIA

One indigenous group that has garnered international attention is the aboriginal people of Australia. The term *aboriginal* actually refers to different indigenous groups in Australia. Additionally, Australia is home to the Torres Strait Islanders, an indigenous people group that does not fall under the umbrella category of "aboriginal." Like their American Indian counterparts, the indigenous peoples of Australia are more likely than members of the majority to be unemployed, to have poor health, and to spend time in jail. Also like their American Indian counterparts, many were removed from their homes and placed in church missions for schooling as late as the 1970s.

Indigenous activism in Australia peaked during the 1960s and 1970s. However, some of the first political organizations, like the Australian Aborignes' Protection Association, the Association for the Protection of the Native Races of Australia and Polynesia, and the Aboriginal Union, had their genesis in the 1920s. Other well-known organizations include the Australian Aborigines' League and the Aborigines Progressive Association. These groups have fought for land and civil rights for the indigenous peoples of Australia.

Like African American civil rights activists, indigenous activists in Australia organized freedom rides, or bus tours, to highlight inequities in the areas of education and housing, and to address segregation and discrimination. Indigenous activists also fought for equal wages and social benefits, and in the late 1960s were successful in removing negative references to aboriginals in the Australian Constitution. In the early 1970s, activists won repeal of an act that required "assisted" aboriginal Queenslanders (aboriginal Queenslanders who were found not to be able to manage their own finances) to have their wages paid into a trust fund controlled by local police. The fight for compensation for past wages paid into these trusts is an ongoing battle waged by activists today. Contemporary activists also continue to fight for land rights and social and economic equality for the indigenous peoples of Australia.

INDIGENOUS ACTIVISM IN CANADA

Despite the 1927 Indian Act that prohibited indigenous Canadians from practicing their traditional culture and language, and from forming political organizations, the indigenous peoples of Canada have organized to protect and enhance their rights. Organizations like the American Indian Movement (AIM) have garnered some support in Canada and have played a role in Canadian activist efforts aimed at gaining tribal sovereignty and the right to organize across tribes. Other influential groups include the League of Indians of Canada, which was formed to address land and hunting rights, as well as economic inequality and inequalities in education, health, and housing.

In 1951, the Indian Act was revised. The revised act no longer forced assimilation, but it included no protections for indigenous culture, did not grant the right to vote in federal elections, and continued to prohibit indigenous people from drinking alcohol on their own land. It was not until 1960 that activists secured the right of indigenous peoples to vote in federal elections without giving up their treaty rights. In 1969, the Indian Act was finally abolished, and native governments were given more control over their own affairs. Current indigenous activism in Canada is largely focused on land claims and increasing sovereignty for indigenous governments.

INDIGENOUS ACTIVISM IN MEXICO AND LATIN AMERICAN

As in the United States, indigenous movements in Mexico became more prominent during the 1970s. Like other indigenous movements, the Mexican movements emphasized the importance of land claims, the protection of natural resources and culture, and political participation. Well-known national organizations include the National Council of Indigenous Peoples, National Union of Autonomous Regional Peasant Organizations, and Indigenous Peoples Independent Front. Indigenous enterprises in the areas of forestry and coffee production also play an important role in strengthening indigenous organizations and identity.

Although many other countries in Latin America are home to groups and organizations advocating for indigenous rights, perhaps one of the best-known Latin American activists is Rigoberta Menchu. Menchu, who was born in rural Guatemala, is the 1992 winner of the Nobel Peace Prize. She participated in various land reform and other activist movements. She eventually moved to France because of the dangers she faced in Guatemala. The activist faced a great deal of criticism after reports that an autobiography that was ghost-written for her entitled *I, Rigoberta Menchu* contained numerous fabrications and exaggerations. However, she remains active in indigenous rights movements worldwide.

Guatemala's Nobel Prize laureate Rigoberta Menchu waves to students during a conference in Mexico City, October 2, 2007. (AP Photo/Marco Ugarte)

ORGANIZED INTERNATIONAL INDIGENOUS ACTIVISM

Claims to land and natural resources as well as cries for social and economic equality are common to indigenous groups worldwide. As a result, there have been efforts to organize indigenous groups internationally and to address some of the common issues indigenous peoples face on an international level. One such effort was the World Council of Indigenous Peoples (WCIP), a Canadian-based organization formed in the 1970s. The

WCIP dissolved in 1996 but formerly had observer status in the United Nations. Current organizations addressing indigenous rights internationally include the Center for World Indigenous Studies, which is dedicated to research and education related to indigenous issues worldwide. The International Work Group for Indigenous Affairs (IWGIA) was founded in 1968. The group supports various indigenous rights groups throughout the world and encourages these groups to engage with international human rights organizations. Survival International provides legal and public relations support for indigenous people groups, and engages in public education campaigns for these groups. The organization has offices throughout the world as well as has consultative status with the United Nations.

The United Nations itself has declared August 9 the International Day of the World's Indigenous Peoples. In September 2007, after almost 20 years of debate, the General Assembly adopted the Declaration on the Rights of Indigenous Peoples. The declaration is a nonbinding agreement that lays out indigenous peoples' rights to language, health, employment, education, culture, and identity. The declaration promotes the participation of indigenous peoples in matters that impact them and prohibits discrimination against indigenous peoples. The United States, Canada, Australia, and New Zealand were the only countries to vote against the declaration. However, in December 2010, the Obama administration announced the United States' support for the declaration. Canada, Australia, and New Zealand had already endorsed the treaty.

Despite these gains, indigenous activists throughout the world remain active in an effort to secure social and economic equality for indigenous groups that have long been subject to inequality and majority government suppression. The UN Declaration on the Rights of Indigenous Peoples is one new tool for these activists to call upon.

REFERENCES

Center for World Indigenous Studies. Available at http://cwis.org
Clark, Jennifer. *Aborigines & Activism: Race, Aborigines & the Coming of the Sixties to Australia*. Crawley: University of Western Australia Press, 2008.
International Work Group for Indigenous Affairs. Available at www.iwgia.org
Menchu, Rigoberta. *I, Rigoberta Menchu* (2nd ed.). Brooklyn, NY: Verso, 2010.
National Museum of Australia. *Collaborating for Indigenous Rights 1957–1973*. Retrieved from http://www.indigenousrights.net.au/ on February 26, 2011.
Purich, Donald. *Our Land: Native Rights in Canada*. Davidson, NC: Lorimer, 1986.
United Nations. *United Nations Declaration on the Rights of Indigenous Peoples*. Retrieved from http://www.un.org/esa/socdev/unpfii/documents/DRIPS_en.pdf
Weinberg, Bill. *Homage to Chiapas: The New Indigenous Struggles in Mexico*. Brooklyn, NY: Verso, 2002.

About the Editor and Contributors

THE EDITOR

Russell M. Lawson, Ph.D., is professor of history at Bacone College in Muskogee, Oklahoma. His published works include two previous encyclopedia published by ABC-Clio, *Poverty in America: An Encyclopedia* (cowritten with Ben Lawson) and *Science in the Ancient World: An Encyclopedia*. In 2010, Lawson was Visiting Fulbright Research Chair in Transnational Studies at Brock University in Ontario. He holds a doctorate in history from the University of New Hampshire.

THE CONTRIBUTORS

Terry Ahlstedt, Ph.D. Candidate, Department of History, University of Nebraska–Lincoln

John H. Barnhill, Independent Scholar, Houston, Texas

Debra Buchholtz, Lecturer, Department of Geography and Anthropology, California State Polytechnic University

Amy L. Fletcher, Senior Lecturer, Political Science Programme, University of Canterbury, Christchurch, New Zealand

Brian Gillis, Ph.D. Candidate, Department of English, University of California at Berkeley

C. Steven Hager, Director of Litigation at Oklahoma Indian Legal Services; Justice on the Supreme Court for the Kaw Nation of Oklahoma; Chief Judge for the Kickapoo Tribe in Kansas

Iris Hahn-Santoro, Ph.D. Candidate, American Studies, University of Heidelberg

Ashley Corwyn Hall, Lecturer, Native American Studies, University of California at Davis, and Sonoma State University

Lindsey Hanson, Staff Attorney, Anishinabe Legal Services, Cass Lake, Minnesota

Ralph Hartsock, Senior Music Cataloger, University of North Texas Libraries

Wendell Johnson, Social Sciences Librarian, University Libraries, Northern Illinois University

Patti Jo King, Assistant Professor, American Indian Studies, University of North Dakota

William P. Kladky, Adjunct Lecturer, Department of Sociology, College of Notre Dame, Maryland

Bill Kte'pi, Independent Scholar, Nashua, New Hampshire

Benjamin Lawson, Ph.D. Candidate, Department of History, University of Iowa

Thomas Maxwell Long, Associate Professor of History, California State University at San Bernardino

Joyce Martin, Curator, Labriola National American Indian Data Center, Arizona State University Libraries

Dylan A. T. Miner, Assistant Professor of Transcultural Studies, Residential College in the Arts and Humanities, Michigan State University

Yuka Mizutani, Assistant Professor, School of Sociology, Toyo University, Japan

Courtney Elkin Mohler, Assistant Professor, Theatre and Dance, Santa Clara University

Chris Paci, Manager, Education and Training, The Métis Nation of Ontario

Claire Palmiste, Crillash (research center), University of the French West Indies and Guiana

Steven J. Peach, Ph.D. Candidate, History, University of North Carolina at Greensboro

Susan M. Taffe Reed, Postdoctoral Research Associate, Music, University of North Carolina at Chapel Hill

Darren R. Reid, Tutor, History, University of Dundee

Melissa A. Rinehart, Independent Scholar, Fort Wayne, Indiana

Claudette Robertson, Independent Historian and Grants Consultant and Adjunct Professor, History, College of the Muscogee Nation, Oklahoma City Community College, Oklahoma State University

Robert E. Sanderson, Professor, and Associate Director of the Sequoyah National Research Center, University of Arkansas at Little Rock

Mary Scriver, Independent Scholar, Valier, Montana

Rodney G. Thomas, Independent Scholar, Spanaway, Washington

Anne Uhlig, Independent Scholar, Leipzig, Germany

David Walsh, Ph.D. Candidate, Religious Studies, Arizona State University

Linda Sue Warner, Special Assistant to the President on Tribal Affairs, Northeastern A&M Junior College, Miami, Oklahoma

Renae Watchman, Assistant Professor, Department of English, Mount Royal University

Stan C. Weeber, Associate Professor of Sociology, McNeese State University

Abby Wightman, Assistant Professor of Anthropology, Mary Baldwin College

G. Lola Worthington, Ph.D. Candidate, University of California at Los Angeles, American Indian Studies

Index

ABC Wide World of Sports, 407
Abenaki people, 516
Aboriginal Curatorial Collective, 645, 647
Aboriginal Education Action Plan, 803
Aboriginal People's Television Network (APTN), 660, 661–62
Aboriginal Tourism Association of British Columbia, 97
Aboriginal Union, 821
Aborigines Progressive Association, 821
Abramoff, Jack, 89–90
Absaloka Mine, 740, 759
Academy Awards, 665
Access to Recovery Program, 257
Acculturation theory, 351–52
Ackerman, William V., 100
Acknowledgement process, 441–43
Activism. *See also* American Indian Movement (AIM); Environmental issues
    Alcatraz Island, occupation of, 546, 548–49, 574, 601–3, 617–18, 619–20
    American Indian Chicago Conference, 441, 603, 617
    in Australia, 820–21
    in Canada, 821
    climate change, 714–15
    Congress and, 574–76
    contemporary, 550–52
    cultural revitalization, 598
    documentary film as, 670
    federal recognition, 600–601
    fish-ins, 599–600, 617
    Indian centers and, 21
    individuals, 545–46
    introduction to, 597–98
    in Mexico and Latin America, 822
    National Indian Youth Council, 51, 547, 551, 603–4, 615, 616–17, 623–24
    organized international activism, 822–23
    women and, 50–53
    after World War II, 547–48
    before World War II, 543–45
    worldwide, 820–23
Act Relative to Employment for Certain Adult Indians On or Near Indian Reservations, 120
Adams, David Wallace, 349, 351
Addison, Stanford, 670
Adena culture, 319
Adequate Yearly Progress (AYP), 174
Adolescents. *See* Youth
Adoma Indians, 606
Adoption, 215–17
Adoption and Foster Care Analysis and Reporting System, 191–92
Adoption and Safe Families Act of 1997 (ASFA), 192, 226
Adoption Assistance and Child Welfare Act of 1980, 192, 226
Adult Vocational Training Program, 39
Advertising and Indian identity
    Federal Indian Arts and Crafts Act of 1990, 59–60
    introduction to, 57–58, 60
    mythic Indian, 61–63
    stereotypes used to market American tobacco, 64–66

Advisory Council on Historic Preservation (ACHP), 277, 295
Advocacy for Women and Kids in Emergency (AWAKE), 193
African Americans, 41, 57, 115–16, 487, 547
After the Mayflower, 667
Agriculture, 109–10, 349, 720–21, 755–57, 759–60
Agriculture, Department of (USDA), 206
Agua Caliente band of Cahuilla Indians, 763
Ahtone, Heather, 645
Ainu people, 806–7
Air pollution, 276
Akaka, Daniel, 576
Akwesasne Cultural Gathering for the Deaf, 164
Akwesasne Mohawks, 722–23, 793
Akwesasne reservation, 638
Alabama, 513
Alabama Indian Affairs Commission, 514
Alaska Conservation Foundation, 724
Alaska Federation of Natives (AFN), 754
Alaska Native Claims Settlement Act, 431, 754
Alaska Native Corporations (ANCs), 754
Alaska Native Fund, 724
Alaska Native Games, 414
Alaska Native Knowledge Network, 144
Alaska Natives, 149, 235, 251–52, 740, 753–54
Alaska Native Steering Committee, 724
Alaskan Native Claims Settlement Act, 724
Albo, Frank, 670
Alcatraz Island, occupation of, 546, 548–49, 574, 601–3, 617–18, 619–20
The Alcatraz Proclamation to the Great White Father and his People, 549
Alcatraz-Red Power Movement (ARPM), 550–51
ALCOA, 722
Alcohol, 23–24, 193, 233, 251–52, 493, 612, 631. *See also* Substance abuse
Aleiss, Angela, 658
Alexander Hamilton U.S. Custom House, 354, 359
Alexie, Sherman, 659, 666, 669
Algonquian language, 182, 336–37, 814
Algonquian people, 337
Algonquian Peoples of the Chesapeake exhibit, 358–59
Alienation, 753
Allegheny Reservation, 603
Allen, Paula Gunn, 194
Allen v. Cherokee Nation Tribal Council, 630
Alliance of Taiwan Aborigines, 808
All Tribes Inc., 602
Always Becoming (Naranjo-Morse), 358

American Anthropological Association, 677
American Bible Society, 338, 341, 342
American Board of Commissioners for Foreign Missions (ABCFM), 338
American Civil Liberties Union (ACLU), 459–60, 600
"American Community: American Indians and Alaska Natives American Community Survey," 8
American Community Survey, 8–9, 11, 12
American Experience series, 667
American Folklife Center (AFC), 683
American Friends Service Committee, 600
American Greeting Corporation, 110
American Indian Alaska Native Tourism Association, 96–97
American Indian Arts and Crafts Act (AIACA), 324
American Indian Chicago Conference, 441, 603, 617
American Indian Christian Circle, 371
American Indian College Committee, 134
American Indian College Fund, 135
American Indian Committee on Alcohol and Drug Abuse, 551
American Indian Defense Association, 203
American Indian English. *See* Red English
American Indian Ethnic Renewal (Nagel), 624
American Indian Federation, 616
American Indian Film Festival, 662, 671
American Indian Film Institute (AIFI), 665, 671
American Indian Grafitti: This Thing Life, 667
American Indian Higher Education Consortium (AIHEC), 135, 143, 594–95
American Indian Holocaust and Survival (Thornton), 29
The American Indian in Urban Society (Waddell and Watson), 70–71
American Indian Leadership Program, 593
American Indian Movement (AIM). *See also* Activism; Red Power
  Alcatraz Island, occupation of, 546, 548–49, 574, 601–3, 617–18, 619–20
  as beginning of Native American rights movement, 224
  in Canada, 821
  creation of, 618–19
  mascots and, 308, 495
  occupation of the BIA building, 431, 622, 623
  overview of, 604
  Red Power, 615, 618–19
  Wounded Knee incident, 224, 469, 545–46, 551, 604, 621, 622, 623
American Indian Pidgin English. *See* Red English

American Indian Policy Review Commission, 204
American Indian Relief Council (AIRC), 159
American Indian Religious Freedom Act, 367, 458, 620
American Indian Repertory theater, 654
American Indians and Crime, 191, 609
American Indian Science and Engineering Society (AISES), 389–90
American Indian Self Determination Act of 1975, 118
American Indian Sign Language, 164–66
American Indian Studies Program, 134
American Indian Theater Ensemble (AITE), 653
American Indian Trust Fund Management Reform Act of 1994, 563–64
American Lung Association, 738–39
American Memory Project, 280
American Museum of Natural History, 280, 377
American Presbyterian Mission, 342
American Psychological Association (APA), 230, 302
American Psychological Association Statement on American Indian Mascots, 306
American Revolutionary War, 521–22
Americans for Indian Opportunity (AIO), 710
American Sign Language (ASL), 162
American SPIRITual History to Identify American Indians or Alaska Natives Using Traditional Indian Medicine, 266
Amnesty International, 546
Anasazi people, 274, 320–21, 642
Ancient Society, or the Researches in Lines of Human Progress from Savagery, through Barbarism to Civilization (Morgan), 347
Anderson, David W., 431
Anglican Church of Canada, 795
Anglican missionaries, 816–17
Anglo orphanages, 219
Anishinaabe Coalition for Peace and Justice, 501
Anishinaabeg, 746–47
Ansson, Richard, 110–11
Antimeth campaign, 253–54
Antiquities Act of 1906, 274, 277
Anxiety disorders, 234
Anzaldúa, Gloria, 6–7
Apache Wars, 607
Apess, William, 366
Apo, Peter, 595
Apology, Canadian, 795, 798
Apology, congressional, 573–74, 576
Appalachian Mountains, 5
Apsáalooke (Crow), 759

Aquash, Annie Mae, 546, 584
Arapaho people, 544
Archaeological Resources Protection Act of 1979, 274
Archambault, JoAllyn, 644
Archeological Resources Protection Act, 432
Architecture, 384–85, 643
Arica, Battle of, 360
Arizona, 585
Arkansas State University, 304
Army, U.S., 199
Army Corps of Engineers, 275, 330–31, 334, 381–82
Army Medical Museum, 377
Art. *See also* Fraudulent Indian art
  East, 639–40
  history, theory, and methods of, 644–45
  introduction to, 637–38
  Mesoamerica, 643
  modern and contemporary, 645–47
  North, 638–39
  Northwest coast, 640
  Southwest, 641–43
  stereotypes in, 395
  West, 640–41
Articles of Confederation, 477, 569–70
Artman, Carl J., 431
Asah, Spencer, 646
Asatru Folk Assembly (AFA), 333–34
Asch, Moses, 278–79
Ashevak, Kenojuak, 639
Assembly of First Nations (AFN), 776, 791
Assimilation. *See also* Boarding school movement
  Act Relative to Employment for Certain Adult Indians On or Near Indian Reservations, 120
  Bureau of Indian Affairs, 428–29
  Canada, 779
  Congress and, 570
  domestic abuse and, 194
  early Indian education, 130
  education and, 350
  identity and, 73–74
  institutional racism and, 498
  laws, 350
  marriage and, 13
  private property, 350
  resistance to, 4–6
  sovereignty and, 467
  through sports, 404
  women and, 49
Assimilative Crimes Act, 579
Assiniboine people, 262, 266
Assinins, Michigan, 223

Association for Native Development in the Performing and Visual Arts (ANDPVA), 688–89
Association for Recorded Sound Collections, 276
Association for the Protection of the Native Races of Australia and Polynesia, 821
Atanarjuat: The Fast Runner, 659
Athlete of the Century, 407
Athletes. *See also specific athletes*
   20th century, 405–13
   baseball players, 406, 408–12, 508, 509
   boarding schools, 403–5
   college athletics and reservations, 503–10
   discrimination, 410–12
   historical background, 404–5
   introduction to, 403
   other events, 412–13
   recent notable athletes, 413–14
   reservations and college athletics, 503–10
Atlanta Braves, 307
Atomic Energy Act, 726
Atomic Energy Commission (AEC), 726–27
Auchiah, James, 646
Audio Engineering Society, 276
Augsbug College, 303
Australia, indigenous people in, 805, 820–21
Australian Aborigines' League, 821
Australian Aborigines' Protection Association, 821
Australian Constitution, 821
Australian Creole language, 343
Authentic assessment, 140
Authenticity, 100–102, 689–90. *See also* Fake Indians
Aztecas del Norte (Forbes), 7
Azure, Mark Henry, 163

Babbit, Bruce, 332, 334
Bacone, Almon C., 172
Baffin Island, 639
Baird, Jessie Little Doe, 343
Bald and Golden Eagle Protection Act (BFEPA), 747
Bald eagle, 747–48
Baldes, Jason, 746
Baltimore Terrapins, 410
Banks, Dennis, 546, 670
Bannock tribe, 366
Baptists, 366
Barkan, Elazar, 540
Barnes, Joseph, 377
Barron v. Baltimore, 478
Barrus, Timothy, 288
Baseball Hall of Fame, 408–9, 410, 509

Baseball players, 406, 408–12, 508, 509
Basketball players, 509
Basketry, 641, 748–49
Bauer, Yehuda, 535, 538, 541
B. Dreams, 668
Beadwork, 639, 641
Bear, Leon, 730
Bear Fox, 688
Beatty, Willard, 133
Beckwourth, James, 246
Begay, Fred, 388, 391
Begay, Harrison, 646
Begay, Theresa Tully, 210
Behavioral health, 229
Behay, Notah, 509
Behind the Door of a Secret Girl, 668
Belaney, Archibald, 286, 288
Bellecourt, Clyde, 546, 547
Bell Water and Housing Project, 52
Beloved Woman, 48
Bemidji, Minnesota, 489–90, 496, 501
Bemidji Area Race Relations Council, 501
Benally, Klee, 661
Bench, Johnny, 413
Bender, Charles Albert, 409–10, 412, 508–9
Beneficiaries, rights of, 562–63
Benefiel, John, 373
Bennett, Robert Lafollette, 132, 430
Beothuks, 771–72
Berdaches. *See* Two-spirits
Berlo, Janet C., 646
Bestiality, 242–43
Better Schools for Arizona, 153–54
Between the Lions, 156–57
Between Two Worlds (Wohaw), 641
Beynon, William, 278
Bible Society, 338
Bible translations into indigenous languages. *See also* Christianity and Native spirituality
   Bible Society era, 338
   Boudinot, 15, 338, 420–21, 692, 694
   Evans, 338–39, 343
   federal Indian policy, 340
   historical background, 336–37
   Horden, 339
   Jones, P., 339–40, 815–16
   modern era, 341–42
   Navajo Bible, 342
   professionalized translation, 341
   results of, 342–43
   Wycliffe Bible Translators, 340–41, 342, 343
Bigpond, Negiel, 370, 373
Bilateral descent, 10
Bilingual education, 430
Bill of Rights, 454, 476, 478–80, 555, 570
Bingaman, Jeff, 728

Bin Laden, Osama, 486
Biocolonialism
  genetics, 780–82
  Human Genome Diversity Project, 551, 783–87
  indigenous concerns, 782–83
Biopiracy, 782–83
Bison, 746, 758
"Bitter Earth," 195–96
Blackbird, John, 661
Blackburn, Elizabeth, 267
Black Coyote, 164
Black Elk, 316
Black English, 183
Black English (Dillard), 182
Blackfire, 688
Blackfoot people, 262
Blackfoot Reservation, 79
Black Hills, 619, 721
Black Mesa Community School, 177
Black Mesa mining site, 724, 739, 740
Black Mesa Water Coalition (BMWC), 760
Black Power, 548, 621
Blazer, Arthur, 593
Blondin, Bessa, 713
Bloodthirsty Savage stereotype, 103
Blue Bay Healing Center, 256
Blue Canyon Day School, 203
Blue Lake region, 721
Boarding school movement
  athletics and, 403–5
  in Canada, 795, 817–18
  civilizing mission, 194
  curriculum, 232, 387–88, 391
  establishment of, 428
  health and, 202–3
  language and, 184–85
  overview of, 169–72
Board of Indian Commissioners, 340, 427, 577
Boas, Franz, 645
Bobb, Johnnie, 500
Bodmer, Karl, 674
Body Indian (Gieogamah), 653
Boldt Decision, 224
Bonnichsen v. United States, 330, 333–34
Bonnin, Gertrude Simmons, 184
Books-a-Go Go, 157–58
Borderlands, 3–7
Borderlands/La Frontera (Anzaldúa), 6–7
Borrego Springs Bank, 110
Boston Tea Party, 284
Boudinot, Elias, 15, 338, 420–21, 692, 694
Bowl Championship Series, 304
Bowman, Arlene, 667, 669–70
Boys and Girls Club of America, 207
Boy Scouts, 677

BP, 565
Bradford, Kent, 414
Bradford, Sam, 413–14
Bradford, William, 62
Branch of Acknowledgement and Research (BAR), 441
Brando, Marlon, 600, 665
Braveheart, Maria Yellow Horse, 237
Brebeuf, Jean de, 813
Breuninger, August, 133
British and Foreign Bible Society, 338
British Columbia, 793
British Museum, 644
British North America Act of 1867, 773, 817
British Proclamation Act, 445
Brock, Isaac, 523
Broken Arrow, Oklahoma, 93
Brown, Anna, 584
Brown, Eddie F., 431
Brown, Lester, 244
Brownback, Sam, 373, 576
Browner, Tara, 683
Brownfields, 738
Bruce, Louis, 410, 431
Bruce-Scott, Jean, 654
Budd, Henry, 817
"Buffalo Bill's Wild West Show," 63, 651
Buffalo Dance, 658
Buhl Woman skeleton, 329–30
Bureau of Indian Affairs (BIA). *See also* Dawes Act; Relocation program
  assimilation, 428–29
  Bennett and, 132
  boarding school movement and, 171
  conversion to Christianity as federal policy, 340
  corruption in, 544
  dominance of in tribal affairs, 325
  economic development, 117–18
  education and, 73, 133
  establishment of, 426–27, 544
  federal recognition, 512
  gaming and casinos, 93
  healthcare and, 199, 204
  Indian representation, era of, 430–32
  introduction to, 426–28
  Johnson O'Malley program, 138–39, 155, 173–74
  jurisdiction, 580
  land ownership, 82–83
  land use, 599
  New Deal and, 429–30
  occupation of, 431, 622, 623
  political activism, 620
  relocation programs, 616
  reservations, 444, 446

sovereignty and, 469–70, 473, 624
termination and, 326
trust lands, 564, 734
unemployment statistics, 115
Bureau of Indian Education (BIE), 140–42, 171, 174–75, 177, 428
Bureau of Justice Statistics, 191, 487, 613
Bureau of Labor Statistics, 115
Burial remains, 275
Burke Act of 1906, 429, 562
Burkhart, Ernest, 584
Bury My Heart at Wounded Knee, 31
Buscombe, Edward, 663
Bush, George H. W., 381
Bush, George W., 121, 177, 442
The Business of Fancydancing, 669
Butler, Alec, 248
Byler, William, 224–25

Cabazon reservation, 710
Caddos, 380
Cahokia, 320
Cahuilla Indians, 763
Cakchiquel Indians, 341
Calhoun, John C., 426, 544
California, 513, 515, 578, 585, 601, 641, 708, 748–49, 762–63
California Indian Basketweavers Association (CIBA), 749
California State–San Marcos, 154
California State University system, 154
Campbell, Ben Nighthorse, 355, 506
Camp Fire Girls, 677
Campo Kumeyaay Nation of Mission Indians, 736
Canadian Aboriginal Music Awards, 689
Canadian Constitution Act of 1982, 770, 773, 775, 790
Canadian Indians and aboriginal peoples
  activism, 821
  biocolonialism, 780–88
  boarding school movement in, 795, 817–18
  Canadian Constitution Act of 1982, 770, 773, 775, 790
  Canadian government and, 769–79
  communal property in, 32
  conclusion, 779
  contact, 771–73
  contemporary issues of, 789–99
  contemporary relations, 773–75
  context of relations, 769–71
  education and, 795–96
  First Nations, 33, 96–97, 98, 770, 776, 790
  governmental system of Canada, 773–74
  human rights, 802–3
  indigenous film outlets and resources, 661–62
  Inuit, 770, 772, 778–79, 790, 794
  Inuit Circumpolar Conference, 792
  land, jurisdiction over, 792–95
  Métis, 220, 638, 639, 641, 770–73, 776–77, 790
  missionaries, 811–19
  political representation, 790–92
  religion, 797–98
  Royal Commission Report on Aboriginal Peoples, 777, 789, 791–92, 795, 818
  terms, 775–76
  women, 797
Cancer, 205, 261
Cangleska, 195
Canyon de Chelley National Monument, 103, 321
Capital punishment, 613
Carcieri, Dan, 457
Cardinal, Douglas, 357
Cardiovascular disease, 23, 80
Carewe, Edwin, 658, 667
Carlisle Indian Industrial School
  Bender and, 409, 508
  creation of, 148, 170–71, 428
  language and, 184
  mascot, 398
  military recruitment, 525
  Thorpe and, 406, 506
Carpentiria, California, 495
Carson, Rachel, 706
Carter, Asa Earl (Forrest), 285–86, 289
Carter, Jimmy, 135, 620
Cartesian system of inquiry, 386–87
Cartier, Jacque, 771
Case, William, 339, 815
Cash crops, 417
Casinos. *See* Gaming and casinos
Castaneda, Carlos, 288–89
Catawba people, 439
Catholic Church, 147, 223, 366, 370, 795, 811–14
Catlin, George, 395, 674
Cavilli-Sforza, Luigi Luca, 783
Cayuga people, 755–56, 812
Cayuse people, 330
Cedar Bough, 237
Cellulose, 277
Censorship, 692
Census Bureau, U.S., 8–9, 11, 12, 30, 31
Center for United States Indian Police Training and Research, 582
Centers for Disease Control and Prevention (CDC), 23, 191
Central Arizona Water Project, 448

Central New York Consortium on Native American Studies, 303–4
Ceramics, 642
Ceremonial worlds, 314–17
Cervical cancer, 261
Chamberlain, Joba, 509
Champagne, Duane, 632
Champions of Change, 594
Champlain, Samuel de, 14, 771, 812–13
Changes, 668
Chants, 265
Chaput, Charles, 370
Cheney, Jim, 314–15
Cheramie, Steve, 369
Chernobyl nuclear incident, 728
Cherokee Advocate, 693
Cherokee constitution, 630
Cherokee Female Seminary, 298
Cherokee Freedmen controversy, 629–30
Cherokee Heritage Center, 298–99
Cherokee Historical Association, 280
Cherokee Insane Asylum, 223
Cherokee National Historical Society, 298
Cherokee National Museum, 280
Cherokee Nation v. Georgia, 199, 466–67, 478, 514, 554
Cherokee Night (Riggs), 652
Cherokee Orphan Asylum, 221, 223–24
Cherokee Phoenix, 338, 420, 630, 692–93
Cherokee Phoenix and Indian Advocate, 338
Cherokees
  agriculture, 349
  Bible translation, 338
  Cherokee Night, 652
  Civil War and, 523
  confederacy, 321
  dam projects, 722
  diabetes, 265
  intermarriage, 15
  language, 691–92
  option to become a state, 445
  orphans and, 221–24
  publications, 691–94
  schools, 142
  on state recognition, 517
  substance abuse, 250
  Supreme Court on, 445, 590 (*see also* *Cherokee Nation v. Georgia*)
  tobacco and, 419–20
  treaties, 569
  tribal membership, 33–34
  tribal museum, 298–99
  Women's Council, 48
Cherokee Tobacco Case, 421
Cherokee Treaty of 1866, 419
Cherokee Tribal Child Protective Services, 250

Cheyenne people, 340, 544, 641
Cheyenne River Sioux, 746, 759
Chiapas state, 803–4
Chicago, 20, 69–70, 274
Chicago Daily News, 280, 409
Chicago Indian Center, 20
Chickasaws, 220, 523, 694, 736
Chief Big Heart, 413
Chief Joseph, 63
Chief Osceola, 304, 305–6
Chief Plenty Coups State Park, 99
Chief Wahoo, 301, 304, 486, 495
Child abuse, 190, 226. *See also* Domestic abuse
Child Abuse Prevention and Treatment Act, 190, 191, 192
Child custody proceedings, 211–12
"Child Maltreatment 2008" report, 191
Child protection system, 25
Children. *See also* Boarding school movement; Indian Child Welfare Act (ICWA); Orphans
  forcible removal of, 224–25
  health of, 205–6
  infant mortality, 206
  poverty and, 115–16
  urban living and, 25–26
Child Welfare League of America, 224
"Child Welfare Outcome 2003" report, 192
Chinook people, 439
Chippewa people, 277, 369, 440, 619, 693, 746–47
Chiricahua Apaches, 607
Chivington, John Milton, 544
Choctaw Code Talkers, 670
Choctaw News, 693
Choctaws, 110, 142, 220, 265, 523, 693–94
Chrétien, Jean, 791
Christianity and Native spirituality. *See also* Bible translations into indigenous languages; Spiritual practices
  American Indian Christian Circle, 371
  American Indian Religious Freedom Act, 367, 458, 620
  contemporary Native American Christians, 369–70
  contemporary Native American churches, 368–69
  controversies, 370–72
  conversion as federal policy, 340
  differences, 372
  early Native American religions and, 365–67
  faith healing, 265
  historical background, 364
  identity and, 372
  Iroquois and Huron confederacies and, 812

legislation and, 367–68
Oklevueha Native American Church, 365
reconciliation, 372–73
sovereignty and, 466
two-spirits, 247
Christmas in the Clouds, 671
Chrystos, 248
Chunky, 404
Churchill, Ward, 537–38, 539, 540
Church Missionary Society, 339, 816–17
Citizenship, 34, 407, 456, 477, 525, 629–30
City life. *See* Urban living/urbanization
City of Boerne v. Flores, 458
Civil disobedience, 549, 599–600, 619. *See also* Activism
Civilization and Indians
 early American civilizations, 319–21
 European contact, 323–24
 introduction to, 318–19
 sophisticated societies, 321–23
 20th-century society, 324–27
Civilization Fund, 348
Civilization program, 348–49
"Civilizing agent," 58, 348–49
Civil rights. *See also* Activism; Discrimination; Red Power
 citizenship, 456
 competing jurisdictions, 456–58
 cultural and religious rights, 458
 education and, 459–60
 historical background, 454–55
 remaining challenges, 461–63
 stereotypical symbols, 457, 460–61
Civil War, American, 523–24, 607
Claims Distribution Act of 2004, 499
Clans, 10–11
Clark, Geoffrey A., 381–82
Clarke, Ron, 408, 505
Clean Air Act, 706
Clean Water Act, 732
Clements, Marie, 650, 654
Cleveland Indians, 301, 304, 411, 486
Cleveland Spiders, 408–9, 508
Cliff Palace, 321
Climate change
 activism, 714–15
 adaptations, 716–17
 consumption and, 717
 definition of, 714
 expressions of in nature, 715
 impact of, 716, 718, 794
 scientific perspective, 713–14
 as a symptom of sickness, 714
Clinton, Bill, 132–33, 442, 458, 473, 499
Clovis-first theory, 332
Club Native: How Thick Is Your Blood? 661

Clum, John, 578
Coal emissions, 737–40
Coalition Against Racism in Education (CARE), 495–96
Cobell, Elouise, 564, 575
Cobell v. Salazar, 564–65, 567, 575
Cocaine, 253. *See also* Substance abuse
Cockenoe, 337
Code of Federal Regulations (CFR), 556, 579
Code of Indian Tribal Offenses, 581
Code talkers, 526–27
Cody, Iron Eyes, 286–87
Cody, Radmilla, 669
Cody, Spencer, 372
Collective trauma, 231
College athletics and reservations, 503–10. *See also* Athletes
College Football Hall of Fame, 406
Colleges and universities. *See also* College athletics and reservations
 early Indian education, 130
 in the era of self-determination, 132–33
 federal boarding schools, 130–31
 Johnson and, 131–32
 Meriam Report, 131
 Native American studies, 135–36
 progress in higher education, 136–37
 tribal college movement, 133–35
Collier, John, 172, 200, 233, 324–25, 429–30, 526, 572, 598, 624
Collier Commission, 581
Colliflower v. Garland, 479
Colonialism, 336, 394–95, 397, 426. *See also* Biocolonialism
Colorado Rockies, 509
Colstrip Steam Plant, 740
Columbus, Christopher, 58, 534
Colville people, 275, 330
Commerce Clause, 477, 514, 553–54, 578
Committee of One Hundred Citizens, 172
Committee on Indian Affairs, 426
Commonwealth Edison, 727
Communal vs. individualistic culture, 68–69
Competition powwows, 686
Comprehensive Employment and Training Act, 123
Confederated Salish and Kootenai tribes (CSKT), 106–7, 110, 111, 256
Confederated Tribes of the Umatilla Indian Reservation (CTUIR), 330, 334
Confederated Tribes of the Warm Springs Reservation, 296
Confederations, 322–23
Congregationalists, 366
Congress, U.S.
 in the 20th century, 571–73

activism, 574–76
Dawes Act, 570–72
First Congress, 570
formal apology, 373, 573–74
historical background, 569–71
Conklin, Martha, 342
Connecticut, 513, 515
Conservation organizations, intertribal, 749–50
Constitution, U.S. *See also* Supreme Court, U.S.
application of to American Indian nations, 478–79
Constitutional Convention, 570
Indian Child Welfare Act and, 210–11
Indian Civil Rights Act of 1968 and, 479–82
Iroquois constitution and, 476–77
references to American Indians in, 477–78, 514, 553–54
sovereignty and, 466
tribal constitutions as model for, 476–77
Constitutional Convention, 569–70
Constructivist epistemology, 312–13
Consumption, 717
Contamination and toxicity, 722–23
Continental Congress, 426, 569, 577
Controlled tipping, 705
Cooke, Wequash, 181
Cook-Lynn, Elizabeth, 135
Cooper, James Fenimore, 182, 395, 650–51, 676
Cordero, Eli, 495
Cornell University Genetic Ancestry Project, 786
Corruption, 91–93, 544
Cortez, Colorado, 496–97
Cotton Petroleum Corp. v. New Mexico, 471
Council of Energy Resource Tribes (CERT), 631, 736–37
Council of Scientific and Industrial Research (CSIR), 786
Counterintelligence Program (COINTELPRO), 622
Country Money, 417
Courts. *See also* Supreme Court, U.S.
civil cases, 559–60
tribal, 556–59, 581
tribes and the federal government, 553–55
Courts of Indian Offense, 13, 350, 556, 581
Coville language, 180–81
Cow Creek tribe, 108–9
Cowlitz people, 439
Cox, Claude, 757
Crab Nebula, 274
Cradle Valley Ranch, 748
Crania collections, 377–78

"Credo for American Indian Theater" (New), 653
Creek Confederacy, 756–58
Creek Council House Museum, 280
Creek people, 93, 523, 693
Creek war, 522
Cree language, 339
Cree people, 262, 338–39, 776, 817
Crick, Francis, 780–81
Crime. *See also* Prisons
against American Indians, 25, 486–88, 611–12
American Indians and, 611–12
hate crimes, 24–25
within Indian country, 584–85
statistics, 609
Crittenden, Joe, 630
Cromwell, James, 286
Crosby, Maria, 644
Cross deputization, 580–81
Crotan Normal School, 172
Crow Creek South Dakota School, 203
Crow Dog, 556, 607
Crow Dog, Ex Parte, 607–8
Crow people, 96, 243, 246, 624, 737, 740
Crow Reservation, 99, 759
"Crying Indian," 286–87
Culin, Stewart, 275, 645
Cult of Domesticity, 46–47, 222
Cultural and heritage centers and museums, 297–98
Cultural and religious rights, 458
Cultural appropriation, tourism and, 100–102
Cultural constructivism, 312–13
Cultural depictions of American Indians, 485–86. *See also* Stereotypes
Cultural discontinuity theorists, 154–55
Cultural exploitation, 380. *See also* Repatriation
Cultural genocide, 535
Cultural preservation. *See also* Historical preservation
issues in, 274–76
laws to aid in, 277
places for, 280
preservation and cultural resource management, 273–74
preservationists, 278–79
specific materials, preservation of, 276–77
Cultural Resource Center (CRC), 354, 360–61
Cultural resource management, 273–74
Cultural revitalization, 598
Cultural trauma, 230–34

Culture. *See also* National Museum of the American Indian (NMAI); Spiritual practices
   acculturation theory, 351–52
   contemporary, 351–52
   definitions and assumptions, 345–46
   images of American Indians, 346–48
   modernization of, 345–53
   science and scientists, 384–92
Current Population Survey, 115
Curriculum, 143–44, 397. *See also* Education
Curtis, Edwin S., 63
Curtis Act of 1898, 223, 694
Cushing, Franklin Hamilton, 645
Cusick, Dennis, 646
Custalow, Linwood, 388
Custer Died for Your Sins (Deloria), 377, 598

Dakota Commemorative March, 238
Dakota people, 289–90, 607
Daly, Shirley, 600–601
Dam projects, 108–9, 603, 616, 721–22, 764
Dances, 276, 685–86
Dances with Wolves, 284
Dancing on the Moon, 668
Dandurnd, Joseph A., 654
Dartmouth College, 410
Dartmouth University, 304
Daugherty, Rob, 380
Davis, Jeffrey, 165
Dawes, Henry, 232, 428, 570
Dawes Act (General Allotment Act)
   assimilation and, 428–29
   Congress and, 570–72
   kinship patterns, 12
   land allotment, 32, 69, 232–33, 350, 446, 494, 555, 562
   orphanages and, 223
   reversal of, 468
Dawson, John, 372
The Dead Can't Dance, 668, 671
Dead River, 667
Deaf and hearing-impaired people
   American Indian Sign Language, 165–66
   education of, 162
   historical background, 164–65
   identity and, 162–63, 165–66
   introduction to, 161–63
   organizations for, 163–64
Death rituals, 319
DeBerg, Renee, 141
Declaration of Independence, U.S., 484
Declaration of Indian Purpose, 617
Declaration of War Against Exploiters of Lakota Spirituality, 289–90
Decorah, Kennedi, 76

Deer, Ada, 50, 51, 52, 431, 600–601
Deer, Tracey, 660, 661
Deere, Phillip, 372
Defenders of Wildlife, 746
Deganeweda-Quezalquotl University, 172
Delaware (state), 513, 515
Delaware people, 321, 445, 569
Deloria, Vine, Jr., 135, 315–17, 377, 470, 547, 548, 598
DeMille, Cecil B., 396, 658
Democratic Party, 469
Demographics, Indian. *See also* Census Bureau, U.S.
   current information, 30–31
   earliest information, 29–30
   future studies, 34–35
   North American differences, 32
   politics, 33–34
   pre-European contact populations, measurement of, 32–33
   reasons for, 28–29
   secrecy, 33
   tribal membership, issues in, 34
Dennis, Darrell, 654
Densmore, Frances, 683
Denver, 485, 594
Department of Labor Employment and Training Administration (DOLETA), 123
Depression, 23, 80, 234
Descartes, Rene, 386
Descent, rules of, 9–10, 48
Desert Archaic Culture, 419–20
Determination of Rights and Unity for Menominee Shareholders (DRUMS), 51, 600–601
Devereaux, Minnie, 660
Devils Lake Sioux, 448
Devil's Tower National Monument, 103
Diabetes, 80, 205–6, 260–61, 264–66
Diagnostic and Statistical Manual of Mental Disorders (DSM), 236
Diamond, Beverly, 683
Diamond, Neil, 659
Diamond Mountain Casino, 748
Dickinson College, 409, 508
Dickson, Don, 380
Dickson Indian Mounds, 380
Dillard, J. L., 182, 183
Dime novels, 663
Diné. *See* Navajo people
Diné College, 134–35
Direct Employment Assistance program, 39
Discrimination. *See also* Civil rights; Racism
   in athletics, 410–12
   in education, 459–60, 489–90
   in employment, 489

in healthcare, 490
in housing, 24, 489
in law enforcement, 490
urban living and, 24–25
Diseases, 233, 260–61. *See also* Healthcare; Traditional healing and modern medicine
Disenrollment crisis, 91–92
Dively, Valerie, 162
Division of Law and Order, Research and Statistical Unit, 582
Divorce, 13
DNA, 780–81
DNA testing, 334
Dobyn, Henry, 536
Documentary film, 670
The Doe Boy, 661, 666
Dolley, Jeff, 303
Dolores, Juan, 278
Domestic abuse
    causes of, 193–95
    complexity of, 192–93
    extent of in Native communities, 190–92
    introduction to, 189–90
    jurisdictional complexities, 194–95
    prevention and protection, 195–97
    statistics, 190–91
"Domestic Violence Is Not a Lakota/Dakota Tradition," 195
Don't Get Sick after June: American Indian Healthcare, 670
Doolittle Report, 544
Dorgan, Bryron, 575, 585
Douglas, James, 793
Drama. *See* Theater and performance
Dreamcatchers, 289
Dreams, 370
Dreamspeakers, 662
Dropout factories, 152
Dropouts, 152–55
Drug abuse. *See* Substance abuse
Drug Abuse Control Act, 458
Drug Enforcement Agency (DEA), 472–73
Drug-Free Communities Support Program, 257
Drug-Free Schools and Communities Program, 256
Drums, 687–88
Due process, 480
Dunn, Dorothy, 646
Duran, Eduardo, 237
Durham, Jimmie, 647
Duro v. Reina, 608
Duwamish people, 439, 442
Dvořák, Antonín, 278

Eagles, 747–48
Early childhood education, 151–52
EarthFirst! 745
East, American Indian art of, 639–40
East Bay Asian Local Development Corporation, 41
Eastern Arctic Inuit language, 336
Eastern Navajo people, 501
Eastern Shoshone, 746, 759
Eastlake, Charles, 776
Eastman, Charles, 184, 367, 388, 392, 598
Eastwood, Clint, 659
Eaves, Charles, 380
Echo Hawk, Larry, 431
Echo Hawk, Walter, 380
Echo-Hawk Theater Ensemble, 654
Ecocide, 720–21
Ecological genocide, 535
Economic development, 117–19, 507–8. *See also* Economy and work; Gaming and casinos
Economic Opportunity Act, 200
Economic Policy Institute, 115, 123
Economic Research Service, 115
Economy and work. *See also* Gaming and casinos
    advertising and Indian identity, 57–66
    leadership in, 593
    poverty in urban areas, 67–74
    poverty on reservations, 75–84
    smoke shops, 416–25
    tourism, 96–104
    tribal economic diversification, 105–13
    unemployment, 114–25
Edge of America, 666
Edgerton, Faye, 342
Edison, Thomas, 658
Education. *See also* Boarding school movement; Colleges and universities; Public education
    of Alaska Natives, 149
    assimilation and, 350
    attainment, 114
    Bureau of Indian Affairs, 73, 133
    Bureau of Indian Education, 140–42, 171, 174–75, 177, 428
    Canadian Indians and aboriginal peoples, 795–96
    Canadian missionaries and, 817–18
    civil rights, 459–60
    current issues and legislation in public education, 169–79
    curriculum, 143–44, 397
    deaf and hearing-impaired people, 161–68
    discrimination in, 459–60, 489–90
    dropouts, 152–55

early childhood education, 151–52
early Indian education, 130
  in the era of self-determination, 132–33
  federal boarding schools, 130–31
  federal reservation schools, 147–49
  higher education, 73, 172
  Indian colleges and universities, 129–37
  Indian Education Act of 1972, 132, 139, 155, 173, 174, 621
  Indian Education: A National Tragedy, 176
  Indian Head Start, 157
  Indian schools, 138–50
  Johnson and, 131–32
  language and culture, 145–46
  legislation and Native American public education, 172–74
  literacy and illiteracy, 151–60
  Meriam Report on, 131
  mission schools, 147, 427–28
  of Native American Deaf, 162
  Native American language immersion, 144
  Native American studies, 135–36
  No Child Left Behind Act, 141, 174–76
  Office of Indian Education (OIE), 132–33, 139
  postsecondary schools, 143
  poverty and, 80
  progress in higher education, 136–37
  science and, 387–88
  technology, 146
  tribal college movement, 133–35
  tribally contracted schools, 142–43
  unemployment and, 119
  urban living and, 21–22
Education, Department of, 133, 136, 138, 176–77
The Education of Little Tree (Carter), 285–86, 289
Education rights, 451
Edwards, Beth, 668
Eisenhower, Dwight, 600
Elementary and Secondary Education Act of 1965, 131
Eliot, John, 182, 336–37
Ellers, Flo, 369
Ellsbury, Jacoby, 509
Emerson, Haven, 203
Emotional problems. *See* Psychological and emotional problems
Employment discrimination, 489
Employment Division of Oregon v. Smith, 458
Empty land doctrine, 494
Encumbrance, 753
Endangered species, 744–45, 747–48

Energy, Department of (DOE), 727, 728–30, 734
Energy, tribal economic diversification and, 108–9
Energy Policy Act, 733
English as a second language (ESL), 143
English-only policy, 184–85
Enrollment, 212
Environmental genocide, 535
Environmental issues
  climate change, 713–19, 794
  habitat preservation, 743–51
  nuclear waste, 726–31
  pollution, 732–42
  solid waste, 703–12
  tribal environmental protection programs, 733–34
  tribal land use, 599, 752–66
Environmental justice movement, 711, 740
Environmental Protection Agency (EPA), 704, 706–11, 723, 733, 735–36, 738
Environmental racism
  contamination and toxicity, 722–23
  ecocide, 720–21
  overview of, 498–501
  pollution and, 737
  poverty and, 711
  uranium contamination, 723–25
  water rights, 721–22
Episcopalians, 366
Epistemology. *See* Ways of knowing, Indian
Equal Opportunity Act, 131
Eskimo. *See* Inuit
Espinoza, Greybuck, 668
Ethnic identity, 397. *See also* Identity, Indian
Ethnocentrism, 398–99
Ethnocide, 535
Ethnographers, 63
Ethnographic present, 346–47
Ethnography, 346–48
Ettawageshik, Frank, 442
Europe, indigenous people in, 805–6
European contact, 323–24, 466
European science, 386–87
European Western films, 663
Evangelical Lutheran Church of America (ELCA), 369
Evans, James, 338–39, 343
Evans-Pritchard, Deirdre, 101
Evers, Medgar, 547
Eve's Fund, 157–58
"The Evils of Biocolonialism: mtDNA Research and its Threat to Native Americans," 785
Exclusion, historic, 292–94
The Exiles, 658
Exogamy, 10–11

Expansionism, 61
Ex Parte Crow Dog, 607–8
Expert Mechanism on the Rights of Indigenous Peoples, 801
Eyre, Chris, 65–66, 659, 661, 662–63, 665, 666–68, 669

Fake Indians, 285–88. *See also* Identity, Indian
Families First Domestic Violence Collaboration Project, 193
Family, 8–9. *See also* Kinship
Family Preservation Services Program, 226
Faraday, Michael, 276
Farmer's Market program, 206
Farmington, New Mexico, 461–62, 488–89, 739
Farwell, Arthur, 278
Fasthorse, Larissa, 654
Federal Acknowledgement Process, 441–43
Federal Acknowledgement Task Force, 442
Federal boarding schools. *See* Boarding school movement
Federal Bureau of Investigation (FBI), 457, 469, 488, 497, 545, 549, 580, 622
Federal Cylinder Project, 683
Federal Indian Arts and Crafts Act of 1990, 59–60
Federal Law Enforcement Training Center (FLETC), 582
Federal recognition
  acknowledgement process, 441–43
  benefits of, 435–37
  introduction to, 434–35
  political activism, 600–601
  Shinnecock tribe, 438
  state recognition and, 512
  termination and, 438–41
Federal reservations. *See* Reservations
Federation of Seven Tribes, 815
Fetal alcohol syndrome, 252
Fewkes, Jesse Walter, 683
Fiddler, Devon, 796
Field Museum of Natural History, 377
Fifteenth Amendment, 456
Fifth Amendment, 210–11, 478, 479
The 5th World, 661, 668
Film about Indians
  contemporary state of, 660–62
  future outlook, 662–63
  Indians in popular imagination, 284
  introduction to, 657–59
  key figures, 659–60
  stereotypes, 396–97
Film by Indians
  documentary film as activism and history telling, 670

as entertainment, 671
Eyre and his predecessors, 65–66, 659, 661, 662–63, 665, 666–68, 669
festivals and groups, 671–72
introduction to, 665–66
portraits of Native American lives, 669–70
reservation life in, 668–69
Finger Lakes GrassRoots Festival of Music and Dance, 688
Finland, 806
First Amendment, 58, 371, 458, 460–61, 478–79
First National Conference for Native Americans with Mental Illness, 238
First Nations, 33, 96–97, 98, 770, 776, 790. *See also* Canadian Indians and aboriginal peoples
First Nations Film and Video Festival, 671
Fish, habitat and, 746–47
Fisher Robe, 675–76
Fishing. *See* Hunting and fishing rights
Fish-ins, 599–600, 617
Five Civilized Tribes, 221, 223, 305–6, 523, 554–55, 694
Fixico, Donald L., 41, 68, 73
Flandreau Indian School, 134
Flandreau Santee Sioux, 100
Flathead Indian community, 238
Fletcher, Alice Cunningham, 278, 280, 428–29
Florence Development Partners, 93
Florida, 513
Florida State University, 304, 305–6
Flower Beadwork People, 639–40
Flute, Native American, 682, 689
Foghorn (Gieogamah), 653
Folkways Records, 278–79
Food and Drug Administration (FDA), 781
Food Distribution program, 206
Football players, 406, 413–14
Forbes, Jack, 7, 134, 135
Ford, John, 658, 663
Forest County Potawatomi community, 108, 109
Forest Grove Indian Industrial and Training School, 170
Forest Service, 458
Formal apology, Canadian, 795, 798
Formal apology, congressional, 573–74, 576
Forrest, Edwin, 651
Fort Apache Timber Company, 760
Fort Belknap Reservation, 721, 746
Fort Garry, 817
Fort Hall Reservation, 366
Fort Harker, 377
Fort Peck Indian Reservation, 91
49 (Gieogamah), 653

Foster, Waawaatte, 248
Foster care, 215–16, 221–22
Four Corners Steam Plant, 737–39
Four Fires LLC, 108, 110
Four Sheets to the Wind, 669
Fourteenth Amendment, 454, 456, 477, 478
Fox, Kit, 412–13
Fox tribe, 736
Foxwoods Casino, 686
Fraher, Diane, 669
Frank, Billy, Jr., 600
Frank, L., 248
Franklin, Benjamin, 426, 476
Fraschilla, Fran, 510
Fraudulent Indian art, 673–79
Fredericks, Thomas W., 431
Freedmen controversy, 629–30
Freedom of Information Act, 549
Freeman, Michael, 540
Freisen, J. D., 592
French and Indian War, 814
Friends of America's Past, 333
Fry, Aaron, 645
Fry Bread Babes, 661
Fur trade, 15–16, 417, 770, 812

Gakwiyo Garden, 755
Gallagher, Clarence, 411
Gaming and casinos
  conflict between tribes, 88–90
  conflict within tribes, 90–93
  criticism of, 633
  economic development, 507–8
  economic diversification and, 105
  federal recognition and, 437
  local debates over, 93–94
  as the new buffalo, 85, 87–88, 105
  role of in poverty on reservations, 81, 87
  sovereignty and, 473–74
  tourism-oriented expansion, 105–7
  tribal government and, 633
Gaming World International, 91
Gammoudi, Mohammed, 408
Gasquet-Orleans (GO) Road, 368
Gathering of Nations, 686
Gawboy, Robert, 509
Geiogamah, Hanay, 650
Gender/gender roles, 46–47, 243–44, 349. *See also* Women
General Allotment Act. *See* Dawes Act
General Crimes Act, 579, 607
General Motors, 722
Genetically modified (GM) commercial crops, 781–82
Genetics. *See* Biocolonialism

Genocide
  cultural, 232
  debate over, 538–40
  definitions and clarifications, 535–38
  stakes of debate, 541
  terminology, struggle over, 534–35
  UN convention on, 535, 536, 537
Genomics, 783
Geographical Information Systems (GIS), 764–65
George, Dudley, 779
George Gustav Heye Center, 354, 359–60
Georgia, 513, 515, 590
Gerard, Forrest, 431
German Enigma code, 526
Geronimo, 63, 486, 607, 619
Geronimo (film), 667
Ghost Dance, 366, 367, 524, 798
Ghost sickness, 236
Gieogamah, Hanay, 653
Gieschenatsi, 597
Gila Cliff Dwellings, 277
Gila River Department of Corrections and Rehabilitation, 608
Gipp, Gerald, 380
Glancy, Diane, 654
Global warming, 717. *See also* Climate change
Gnadenhutten massacre, 283
The Godfather, 665
The Golden Woman (Mattina), 181
Golfers, 509
Gomez, Terry, 653, 654
A Good Day to Die, 670
Goodland Academy, 220
Goodland Indian Orphanage, 220
Goodman, Nelson, 313–14
Gordon, Joe, 411
Gordon Residential School, 795
Gore, Al, 714–15
Goshute reservation, 498
Gourneau, Roxanne, 231
Gover, Kevin, 431
Governance, vs. leadership, 591
Government assistance, 621
Government orphanages, 223–24
Graham, John, 546
A Grammar of a Massachusetts Indian (Eliot), 182
Grand Coulee Dam, 764
Grandfather Rocks, 358
Grand Medicine Society, 816
Grant, Dorothy, 640
Grant, Ulysses S., 427, 446, 523–24, 577
Grassroots politics. *See* Activism
Graton Racheria, 748
Great Basin, 760–62

Great Britain, 521–22, 815
Great Circle of Life, 262
Great Depression, 673
The Greatest Canadians, 523
Great Falls, Montana, 219
Great Lakes region, 5, 10, 369, 445, 476, 639, 746–47
Great Law of Peace, 476
Great Plains, 385, 758–59
Green Corn ceremonies, 222
Green Grows the Lilacs (Riggs), 652
Greenhouse gases, 717
Green Party, 546
Greenpeace, 737, 745
Grey Owl, 286, 288
Grint, K., 595
Gros Ventres community, 351, 479
Gustav V, King, 406
Guyart, Marie, 814, 817
Gwich'in language, 336

Habitat for Humanity, 265
Habitat preservation
  bison, 746
  fish, 746–47
  intertribal conservation organizations, 749–50
  introduction to, 743–45
  predators, 745–46
Hagahai tribe, 784
Ha Ha, Minnie, 660
Haida people, 384
Halcyon Days (Catlin), 675
Hale, William K., 584
Hall, Robert, 182, 183
Hall, Tex, 373
Hallett, William E., 431
Hamilton, Alexander, 570
Hamilton, Samuel S., 426–27
Hammond, Sue Anne, 162
Hampton Institute, 148
Hampton Normal and Agricultural School, 170, 184
Hampton Virginia Boarding School, 203
"Handbook on Child Sexual Abuse," 195
Handsome Lake, 366
"Hand Talk," 165
Haney, Mike, 380
Hanford nuclear site, 734
Hannahville Indian Community, 225
Hanson, Lindsey, 545–46, 620, 623
Happy Birthday, Grandma, 668
Hard Rock Hotels and Casinos, 106, 107
Harjo, Joy, 654
Harney, Corbin, 730
Harper, Stephen, 795, 798

Harris, Ladonna, 710
Harris, Mike, 779
Harrison, Bob, 509
Harrison, William Henry, 522
Harvard Project on American Indian Economic Development, 111
Harvey, Kiara, 584–85
Haskell Indian Junior College, 133
Haskell Indian Nations University, 134, 143, 380, 594, 653–54
Haskell Indian School, 203
Haskell Institute, 133, 349, 407, 505, 506
Hassell, Jerry, 163
Hatch, Orrin, 729
Hate crimes, 24–25
Haudenosaunee people, 755–56
Hawaii, 513
Hayt, Ezra, 170, 578
Hazardous and Solid Waste Act, 709
Hazardous Waste Act, 705
Hazardous waste dumping, 732–33
Head Start program, 156–57
Healing. *See* Traditional healing and modern medicine
Health. *See also* Healthcare; Psychological and emotional problems
  assessment of, 202–3
  behavioral health, 229
  boarding school movement and, 202–3
  domestic abuse, 189–98
  Indian Child Welfare Act, 209–18
  infant mortality, 206, 249
  leadership in, 594
  in Meriam Report, 204
  orphans, 219–27
  poverty and, 80
  preventive care, 206–7
  psychological and emotional problems, 228–41
  sexual issues, 242–48
  substance abuse, 249–59
  suicide, 230, 231, 235, 252, 493
  Together Raising Awareness for Indian Life, 206, 207
  traditional healing and modern medicine, 260–69
  Tribal Self-Governance Demonstration Project, 201, 202
  urban living and, 23–24
  of women and children, 205–6
  World War II and, 204
Health and Human Services, Department of (DHHS), 191, 230, 430
Healthcare. *See also* Traditional healing and modern medicine
  of American Indians, 199–208

Bureau of Indian Affairs and, 199, 204
discrimination in, 490
mental health treatment, 235–39
poverty and, 74, 76–77
self-determination, 201
in urban areas, 23–24
Hearing Radmilla, 669
Heart-break syndrome, 236
Heart disease, 205
Heart of the Earth Survival School, 26
Heisman Trophy, 414
Hemp, 472–73
Herring, Elbert, 427
Herzog, George, 683
Heterarchies, 590
Heye, George Gustav, 355, 357, 362
Hickel, Walter Joseph, 602
Hicks, Leonard, 338
Hide Away, 667
Hierarchies, 589–90
Higher Education Reauthorization Act, 143
Highway, Tompson, 650
Hill, Asa Thomas, 380–81
Hill, Lillie Rosa-Minoka, 388
Hill 57, 219–20
Hispanic Americans, 115–16
Historical preservation. *See also* Cultural preservation
  funding of, 296
  historic exclusion, 292–94
  Indian ownership, control, and cultural sovereignty, 299
  Indians as federal consultants, 294–96
  National American Indian Heritage Week, 295
  National Historic Preservation Act, 293
  Native cultures, definition of, 298–99
  Native inclusion, 294
  repatriation, 361–62, 376–83, 458, 798
  tourism and, 297
  tribally owned cultural and heritage centers and museums, 297–98
Historical trauma, 230–34
"History of the American Indian Deaf" (Kelley), 161
History of the Ojebway Indians (Jones), 815
Hobsbawm, Eric, 299
Ho-Chunk Incorporated, 111–12
Ho Chunk Nation casino, 81
Hohokam culture, 321, 642
Hokeah, Jack, 646
Hokkaido, 806–7
Hokkaido Former Aborigines Protection Act, 806–7
Hokkaido University, 807
Hollow, Walt, 266

Holm, Tom, 135
Holm Bill, 640
Holocaust, use of term, 534–41
Holt, Robert G., 724
Holy Family Orphans' Home, 223
Homelessness, 43–44
Homophobia, 247
Homosexual experimentation, 242–43
Homosexuality, 245. *See also* Two-spirits
Honey Moccasin (Niro), 660
Hoopa Valley reservation, 580
Hoop dancing, 685
Hootch, Molly, 149
Hoover, Herbert, 429
Hopewell culture, 319, 639
Hopi Rehabilitation Center, 608
Hopis, 102, 320–21, 371–72, 384, 404, 724, 737, 739
Horden, John, 339
Houma people, 435, 440
House, Donna, 358
House Committee on Indian Affairs, 133–34
Houser, Allen, 646
House Resolution 698, 325–26. *See also* Termination and recognition
Housing, 22, 24, 489, 634. *See also* Architecture
Housing and Urban Development (HUD), 24
Houston, James, 639
Howard, O. O., 578
Howe, Oscar, 646, 647
"How it Began" podcast, 358
Hoxie, Frederick, 598
Hudson Bay Company, 32, 772, 794, 815
Human Genome Diversity Project (HGDP), 551, 783–87
Human Genome Project (HGP), 781
Human remains, 361–62. *See also* Kennewick Man; Repatriation
Human Rights Council, 801
Human rights of indigenous people worldwide
  in Australia, 805
  in Canada, 802–3
  elsewhere, 808–9
  in Europe, 805–6
  introduction to, 800–803
  in Japan, 806–7
  in Mexico, 803–4
  in New Zealand, 804–5
  in Taiwan, 807–8
Hunt, George, 278
Hunting, women and, 47–48
Hunting and fishing rights, 452, 456–57, 599, 764, 765, 793
Hunting economy, 758–59

Huron confederation, 812–13
Huron language, 814
Hurons, 418
Hypothecation, 753

I, Rigoberta Menchu (Menchu), 822
Iba, Hank, 411
Ickes, Harold L., 429
Idaho's Forgotten War, 670
Identity, Indian
   advertising and, 57–66
   assimilation, 73–74
   Christianity and, 372
   civilization and Indians, 318–27
   commandeering Indian spiritual practices, 288–90
   contemporary Native American identity, 283–91
   cultural preservation, 273–82
   fake Indians, 285–88
   historical background, 283–84
   historical preservation, 292–300
   Indian mascots, 284, 301–10
   Indian ways of knowing, 311–17
   literacy and, 159
   of Native American Deaf, 162–63, 165–66
   ownership of Indian remains, 328–35
   stereotypes, 393–99
   urban living and, 26, 70–71
   what is an Indian question, 285
If I Can Read, I Can Do Anything program, 156
ImagineNative, 662
Imagining Indians, 661
Imprint, 661, 666
Improving Indian Education Initiative, 174
"Improving Tribal Consultation in the Next Administration," 296
Incarceration rate, 610–11
Incest, 243
Independent Living Program, 226
India, 786–87
"Indian," representation of, 650–52
Indian Act, 770, 773, 790, 797, 821
Indian and Native American Program, 123
Indian Appropriation Act, 421, 446
Indian Arts and Crafts Act of 1990, 58, 59–60, 513, 647, 673–74
Indian Arts and Crafts Board (IACB), 673
Indian Arts and Crafts Board and Act of 1935, 673
Indian Arts and Crafts Sales Act (New Mexico), 101
Indiana Territory, 522
Indian awareness, 619–20
Indian Bill of Rights, 455. *See also* Indian Civil Rights Act of 1968

Indian Burial Pit (Kansas), 380
Indian Champion, 693
Indian Child Welfare Act (ICWA)
   appealing decisions, 215
   Constitution, U.S. and, 210–11
   constitutionality of, 210–11
   courts and, 557
   definitions of, 211–12
   domestic abuse and, 192, 196
   forcible removal of Indian children, 225
   government assistance, 621
   jurisdiction and transfer under, 212–13
   juvenile detention, 612
   need for, 209–10
   orphans and, 221
   other protections of, 217
   placement preferences and tribal control, 215–16
   protections of, 213–15
   text of opening, 216–17
   urban living and, 21, 25
   voluntary actions, 215
Indian Citizenship Act, 446, 477, 525, 555, 571
Indian Civil Rights Act of 1968, 194, 448, 450, 455, 457, 476, 479–82, 557–58, 786
Indian Claims Commission, 233, 430, 446, 601
Indian Claims Commission Act, 430
Indian Commerce Clause, 211
Indian Control of Indian Education, 818
Indian Country, 63, 427, 448. *See also* Indian Territory
Indian Country Conservancy (ICC), 750
Indian Country Today, 302
Indian Crimes Act of 1976, 579
Indian Desk, 368
Indian Education Act of 1972, 132, 139, 155, 173, 174, 621
Indian Education: A National Tragedy—A National Challenge, 132, 173, 176
Indianer, 661
Indianer Inuit, 662
Indian Financing Act, 431
Indian Gaming Regulatory Act (IGRA), 85, 86, 469, 474, 633
Indian Grammar Begun (Eliot), 182
Indian Head Start program, 156–57
Indian Health Care Act, 513, 621
Indian Health Care Improvement Act, 200–201
Indian Health Care Resource Center, 236–37
Indian Health Services (IHS)
   behavioral health, 229
   country jails, 610
   establishment of, 200
   historical trauma, 230
   leadership in, 594
   mental health treatment, 235

in Meriam Report, 204
physicians and services, 262
on solid waste, 704
statistics, 260
substance abuse, 251
transfer to Public Health Service, 430
uranium contamination, 74
urban living and, 21, 24
Indian Health Services (IHS) National Patient Information Reporting System, 80
Indian Historical Society, 547, 618
Indian Human Resources Center, 121
Indian Intercourse Act, 561
Indian Journal, 185, 693
Indian Life Readers, 430
Indian Liquor Act of 1897, 429
"Indian maiden," 486
Indian mascots
  American Psychological Association Statement on American Indian Mascots, 306
  as a civil rights issue, 457, 460–61
  conclusion, 308–9
  elimination, reasons for, 302–3
  "good" vs. "bad," 307–8
  introduction to, 301–2
  movement to abandon, 303–6
  pseudo Indian identities and, 284
  racism and, 486, 495
  reasons to keep, 307
  stereotypes, 398
Indian Metropolis (LaGrand), 68, 71
Indian Nation Conservation Alliance (INCA), 750
Indian Nations at Risk, 152
Indian New Deal. *See* Indian Reorganization Act (IRA)
Indian Nonintercourse Act of 1790, 514
Indian Plays, 651
Indian Relocation Act, 39
Indian Removal Act, 61–62, 69, 232, 427, 445
Indian Reorganization Act (IRA)
  allotment policy, 562
  Bureau of Indian Affairs and, 431
  Congress and, 572
  constitutions and, 555
  education and, 172
  effects of, 233, 429–30
  law and order, 579
  leadership in, 592
  overview of, 324–26
  passage of, 598
  recognition and, 439
  reservations and, 446, 448
  self-government and, 624

  sovereignty and, 467–68
  tribal leadership, 589
  urbanization and, 69
Indian representation, era of at the BIA, 430–32
Indian Rights Association, 429
"Indian rolling," 461–62
Indian Room, 677, 678
Indian Self-Determination and Education Assistance Act of 1975, 429, 431, 447, 450–51, 507, 621, 624, 632
Indian Sign Language. *See* American Indian Sign Language
Indians of All Tribes, 618
Indian Story and Song from North America (Fletcher), 278
Indian Territory, 5, 693–94, 757. *See also* Indian Country
Indian Time Theater, 654
Indian Tourism Seminar, 98
Indian Trade and Intercourse Act, 348
Indian tribal courts. *See* Courts
Indian trust land. *See* Trust lands
Indian University, 172
Indian University of Pennsylvania, 305
Indigenous Action Media, 661
Indigenous Arts Network, 689
Indigenous Games, 414
Indigenous People's Council on Biocolonialism, 785
Indigenous Peoples Independent Front, 822
Indigenous Screen Cultures in Canada, 661
Indigenous Women's Network (IWN), 51
Indigenous World Film Festival, 808
Individual Indian Money (IIM) accounts, 563
Industrial hemp, 472–73
Industrial Training School. *See* Carlisle Indian Industrial School
Infant mortality, 206, 249
Infinity of Nations: Art and History in the Collections of the National Museum of the American Indian exhibit, 359–60
"Injuns!" Native Americans in the Movies (Buscombe), 663
Insects, preservation and, 277
Institute for Development of Indian Law, 470
Institute of American Indian Arts (IAIA), 647, 653
Institutional racism, 497–98
Inter-Agency Support Group (IASG), 801–2
Inter-American Commission on Human Rights, 499
Inter Caetera, 466
Intercessory prayer, 369

Interfaith Center for Corporate Responsibility, 304
Intergovernmental Panel on Climate Change, 715
Interior, Department of the. *See also* Bureau of Indian Affairs (BIA)
   education, 133, 174
   healthcare, 199–200
   repatriation, 330–31, 334, 382
   schools, 138, 140
   trust lands, 561
   trust reform, 565
Interior Salishian language, 180–81
Intermarriage, 14–16, 41
Intermountain region, land use, 760–62
Internal Order of Red Men, 677
International Association of Sound and Audiovisual Archives, 276
International Conference on the Cultural and Intellectual Property Rights of Indigenous Peoples, 782
International Day of the World's Indigenous Peoples, 823
International Decade of the World's Indigenous People, 801
International Fund for Agricultural Development (IFAD), 800, 805
International Indian Treaty Council (IITC), 604, 808
International Labour Organization (ILO), 801
International Reconciliation Coalition, 372
International Work Group for Indigenous Affairs (IWGIA), 823
International Year of the World's Indigenous People, 801
Internet, 44, 146, 674
Internship at Cultural Resource Center, 360
Intertribal Deaf Council (IDC), 161, 163
Intertribal Friendship House, 20–21
Intoxication in Indian Country Act of 1892, 429
Inuit, 659, 770, 772, 778–79, 790, 794. *See also* Canadian Indians and aboriginal peoples
Inuit Broadcasting Corporation (IBC), 661–62
Inuit Circumpolar Conference (ICC), 779, 792
Inuit Tapirisat of Canada, 791
Inuvialuit, 778
Iqaluit, 778
Iron River, Michigan, 496
Iroquois Confederacy, 322–23, 476–77, 521–22, 526, 569, 682
Iroquois League, 616, 812–13
Iroquois people, 416–17, 418
Irrealism, 313–14
Irving, Washington, 650
Ishi, 458
Isleta Pueblo, 278

Isuma TV, 662
Itam Hakim, Hopiit, 667

Jackson, Andrew, 61–62, 232, 427, 445
Jackson, Jason, 683
Jacob, Tvli, 665, 667
Jacobson, Oscar B., 646
Jails in Indian country, 608–9, 610. *See also* Prisons
"Jails in Indian Country, 2009," 191
Jaimes, M. Annette, 541
Jamestown, Virginia, 61
Jamieson, Roberta, 796
Japan, indigenous people in, 806–7
Jaspersen, Otto, 182
Jefferson, Thomas, 338, 348, 445
Jelderks, John, 334
Jenkins, Carol, 784
Jenkins Act of 1949, 421–22
Jennings, Hughie, 409
Jesuits, 813
Jeune, Pére Paul le, 814
Jewish people. *See* Holocaust, use of term
Jim Thorpe Classic, 509
Jobaa'ii, Asdzáán, 263–64, 268
John Carter of Mars, 663
John Paul II, Pope, 370
Johnson, Lyndon, 70, 129, 131–32, 200, 430, 727
Johnson O'Malley program, 138–39, 155, 173–74
Johnson v. McIntosh, 466, 514, 554, 561
Johnston, J. Younger, 658
Johnston, Philip, 527
Jones, Augustus, 339
Jones, Johnpaul, 357
Jones, Margaret B., 288
Jones, Peter, 339–40, 815–16
Jones, William, 203
Judd, Steve, 665, 667
Jump Starting Literacy Program, 158
Jurisdiction, 212–13, 580–81
Justice, Department of, 194, 583, 585, 609
Just Transition, 760
Juvenile detention, 612

Kahnawake Mohawks, 266
Kahnawake Schools Diabetes Prevention Program (KSDPP), 266
Kananga, Mariano Flores, 360
Kanesatake Mohawks, 793
Kansas, 513
Kansas University, 505
Karuk people, 243
Katz, Stephen, 539–40, 541
Kayano, Shigeru, 807

Keams, Geraldine, 653
Kelley, Walter, 161–62, 163, 164
Kenekuk, 366
Kennedy, Edward, 132
Kennedy Report, 132
Kennewick Man, 275, 328–35, 378, 381–82, 575
Kentucky, 513
Kerr-McGee, 737
Keweenaw Bay Indian Community, 747
A Key into the Language of America (Williams), 181, 182
Keyser, Louisa, 641
Kialegee Tribe, 93–94
Kicking Woman Singers, 688
Kidnapping, 225
Kidwell, Clara Sue, 135
Killing the Indian Maiden (Marubbio), 660
King, Bruce, 653, 654, 728
King, Martin Luther, Jr., 547
King, Randy, 435
Kingdom of Hawaii, 575
King Philip's War, 284, 337, 607, 651
Kinship
    intermarriage, 14–16, 41
    lineages and clans, 10–11
    marriage, 12–13
    patterns, changes in, 12
    rules of descent, 9–10, 48
    traditional kinship, 8–18
Kinzua Dam, 603, 616, 722
Kiowa Five, 646
Kiowa people, 641
Kissed by Lightening, 661
Klah, Hosteen, 245
Klain, Bennie, 661
Klamath people, 439
Klamath Termination Act, 430
Knowledge, Indian. *See* Ways of knowing, Indian
Knox, Henry, 146, 348, 426
Kohler, Jack, 668
Kootenai people. *See* Confederated Salish and Kootenai tribes (CSKT)
Korean War, 528–29
Kriol language, 343
Kroeber, Alfred, 40
Kuhn, Thomas, 315
Kunuk, Zacharias, 659
Kurok people, 419–20
Kwakiutl people, 384

Lac Court Orieles Ojibwa, 550
Lacrosse, 404
LaDuke, Winona, 546
LaFavor, Carole S., 248
La Flesche, Francis, 278, 280, 388
La Flesche, Joseph, 278
La Flesche, Susan, 388
LaGrand, James B., 41, 68, 73
Lake Mohonk Conference, 203
Lake Simco mission, 816
Lakota people, 237, 246, 257, 289–90, 419
Land allotments, 32, 69, 232–33, 350, 446, 494, 555, 562
Land O'Lakes butter, 307
Land rights, 448–49
Land use
    Agua Caliente band of Cahuilla Indians, 763
    Apsáalooke (Crow), 759
    California, 762–63
    Canada, 792–95
    environmental issues, 599
    freedom of, 461
    Great Plains, 758–59
    intermountain region, 760–62
    introduction to, 752–55
    Makah, 765
    Nez Perce (Nimíipuu), 764–65
    Northeast, 755–56
    Northwest, 763–65
    Southeast, 756–58
    Southwest, 759–60
Language. *See also* Bible translations into indigenous languages
    Algonquian language, 336–37, 814
    American Indian Sign Language, 164–66
    American Sign Language, 162
    Australian Creole language, 343
    as a barrier at the international level, 808–9
    as a barrier to academic achievement, 153–54
    boarding school movement and, 184–85
    Carlisle Indian Industrial School, 184
    Cherokees, 691–92
    Coville language, 180–81
    Cree language, 339
    and culture in Indian schools, 145
    Eastern Arctic Inuit language, 336
    English as a second language (ESL), 143
    English-only policy, 184–85
    Gwich'in language, 336
    Huron language, 814
    Kriol language, 343
    Literacy and illiteracy and, 153–54, 155
    Native American language immersion, 144
    Native American Languages Act, 145–46
    Native language immersion programs, 177
    Navajo language, 336
    Red English, 180–86
    Santee Dakota language, 336

Wampanoag language, 343
Western Cree language, 336
Wôpanâak Language Reclamation Project, 343
Lapp people, 805–6
Large-scale crests, 640
The Last of the Mohicans (Cooper), 395, 650–51
Latin America, indigenous people in, 822
Laubin, Gladys, 677
Laubin, Reginald, 677
Laval, François Xavier de Montmorency, 813
Law, sovereignty and, 450–51, 470–72
Law and order rights, 450–51
Law enforcement in Indian country. *See also* Crime; Prisons
 conclusion, 585–86
 Courts of Indian Offense, 13, 350, 556, 581
 crimes within Indian country, 584–85
 discrimination in, 490
 federal status and self-governance, 579
 funding in 2010, 585
 historical background, 577–78
 jurisdiction and cross-deputization, 580–81
 law and order rights, 450–51
 obstacles to, 582–83
 operations, 581–82
 statistics, 583–84
 tribal courts, 556–59, 581
 Tribal Law and Order Act, 586
Law for the Promotion of Ainu Culture and the Dissemination and Advocacy of Knowledge, 807
Lawson, Russell, 629–30
Laxson, Joan D., 102–3
Leadership
 in economics, 593
 vs. governance, 591
 in health and social welfare, 594
 historical background, 590–92
 introduction to, 589–90
 sacred place and, 595
 styles, 592–93
 for youth, 594–95
The League of the Ho-de-sau-nee, or Iroquois (Morgan), 346
Leap, William, 182, 183–84, 185
Leatherwork, 641
Leavitt, Mike, 729
Leclerc, Laurent, 164–65
Lee, Hugh, 559
Lee, Thornton, 509
Leech Lake Reservation, 452, 489, 501, 562
Leechman, Douglass, 182, 183

"Legal incidence test," 471
The Legend of Secret Pass, 668–69
Lelawi Theater, 359
Lemhi tribe, 366
Lemkin, Rafaël, 537
Lenape, Lenni, 815
l'Epée, Abbé de, 165
Let the Healing Begin camp meeting, 369
Levant, Ronald F., 303
Levine, Victoria Lindsay, 683
Lew, Alan, 97–98
Lewis, David, Jr., 263, 265, 267
Lewis and Clark expedition, 396
Library of Congress, 155, 280, 658, 683
Liddle, Ralph, 670
Life and Journals of Kah-ke-wa-quona-by (Jones), 815
Life expectancy, 228, 249
Lightfoot, Thomas, 578
Liliuokalani, Queen, 366–67
Lincoln, Abraham, 607, 729
Lind, Jane, 653
Lindgren, Gerry, 408
Lineages, 10–11
Linton, Ralph, 351
Literacy and illiteracy. *See also* Education
 attempts to improve, 155–59
 dropouts, 152–55
 early Indian education, 151–52
 language and, 153–54, 155
Literature, 6–7, 144, 159, 650. *See also* Art; Music
Little Bighorn, Battle of, 446
Little Bighorn battlefield, 99–100
Little Bighorn Battlefield National Monument, 103
Little Black Sambo, 57, 301, 486
Littlefeather, Sacheen, 665
Littlefield, Daniel F., Jr., 694
Little Shell Chippewa, 220
Little Wound School, 177
Lobbying, 89–90
Locke, John, 286
Lone Wolf v. Hitchcock, 554
Long, Sylvester, 287–88
Longest Walk, 604, 619, 620
Longfellow, Henry Wadsworth, 62
Long Lance, Buffalo Child, 287–88
Looking Cloud, Arlo, 546, 584
Los Angeles Board of Education, 304
Louisiana, 513, 515
Louisiana Purchase, 445
Love and Consequences (Jones), 288
Lowe, Blackhorse, 661, 668
Lubicon Lake Cree, 793–94
Lujan, James, 654

Lujan, Tony, 133
Lumbee people, 435, 440
Lummis, Charles Fletcher, 278
Lund, Karen C., 658
Lurie, Nancy, 603
Luther, Billy, 660
Lutherans, 369
Lyng v. Northwest Indian Cemetery Protective Association, 368, 458
Lynn, L. C., 592

Mack, Connie, 410
MacKenzie, Kent, 658
Madison, James, 543, 570
Maidu people, 245
Maine State Prison, 613–14
Main Poc, 366
Major Crimes Act of 1885, 194, 556, 579, 608
Makah, 765
Making the White Man's Indian (Aleiss), 658
Mala, Ray, 660
Mandaree Day School, 177
Manhattan Project, 726
Manifest Destiny, 61
Manitou Api, Where the Sun Rises, 670
Mankiller, Wilma, 40, 50, 51–53, 547, 630
Manshantucket Pequots, 686
Manypenny, George W., 427
Maori people, 804–5
Maracle, Ross, 369
Marijuana, 253
Marquette, Michigan, 223
Marquette University, 305
Marriage, 12–16, 41
Marriott Residence Inn, 108
Marshall, George Preston, 307
Marshall, John, 466–67, 471, 514
Marshall Trilogy decisions, 445
Martin, Brenda M., 97, 98
Martin, Geronimo, 342
Martin, Peter, 388
Martinez, Julia, 786
Martínez, Julián, 642
Martínez, María, 642
Martinez, Tobias, 266
Marubbio, M. Elise, 660
Maryland, 513
Masayesva, Victor, Jr., 661, 667
Mascots. *See* Indian mascots
Mashonee, Jana, 689
Mason, John, 181
Massachusetts, 513, 515
Mataatua Declaration, 782
Matheson, Don, 600
Matrilineal descent, 10, 15, 48, 221
Mattina, Anthony, 180–81

Matus, Don Juan, 288
May, Karl, 663
Maya people, 643
Mayflower protest, 549, 619
Mayo, Lisa, 654
Mayo Clinic, 267
McCain, John, 82, 575
McCaleb, Neal, 431
McCarren Amendment, 450
McCloud, Janet, 50, 604
McDermott, Jim, 576
McGurk, Leroy, 413
McKenney, Thomas L., 426
McNickle, D'Arcy, 184
Means, Lorelei DeCora, 604
Means, Russell, 546
Medicaid, 24
Medicine Horse, Susan Stewart, 99
Medicine Lodge religion, 369
Meiners, Linda Hagar, 162
Meinholz, Rolland, 653
Melody, Pat, 653
Memorandum of Agreement on Indian Substance Abuse Prevention, 255
Memorandums of understanding (MOU), 580–81
Menchu, Rigoberta, 822
Mending the Sacred Hoop, 195
Menominee Indians, 51, 52, 233, 427, 439, 572–73, 600–601
Menominee Restoration Act, 430, 431, 573, 601
Menominee Termination Act, 430, 600
Menominee Tribal Jail, 608
Menominee Tribe v. United States, 456–57
Menomonee schools, 147
Meriam, Lewis, 429
Meriam Report, 129, 131, 172–73, 204, 429–30, 446, 545, 572, 598
Mescalero Apache reservation, 498, 728
Mescalero Apaches, 736
Mesoamerica, 643
El Mesquite (O'Shea), 6
Mestizos, 6–7
Metacom, 394
Metacom's War. *See* King Philip's War
Metamora, or the Last of the Wampanoags (Stone), 284, 651
Methamphetamine, 193, 252–55. *See also* Substance abuse
Methodist Church of Canada, 816
Methodist Episcopal Church, 339
Methodist missionaries, 366, 815–16
Métis, 220, 638, 639, 641, 770–73, 776–77, 790. *See also* Canadian Indians and aboriginal peoples

Métis National Council, 776, 791
Metlakatla Indian Community, 580
Metz, Betty, 158
Mexico, indigenous people in, 32, 803–4, 822
Meyers, John Tortes, 410, 412
Miami people, 590
Miasma theory, 705
Michigan, 513
Michigan State University, 661
Middle East, wars of the, 530–31
Middle Woodland Period, 639
Midewiwin, 816
Midthunder, Angelique, 670
Miguel, Gloria, 654
Miguel, Muriel, 654
Military
   American Revolutionary War, 521–22
   citizenship and, 34
   Civil War, American, 523–24, 607
   code talkers, 526–27
   Korean War, 528–29
   Vietnam War, 529–30
   War of 1812, 366, 445, 522–23
   wars of the Middle East, 530–31
   women, 53, 525, 528
   World War I, 58, 524–25
   World War II, 204, 325, 525–27, 547, 572
Mille Lacs Band of Chippewa Indians, 555
Mille Lacs Band of Ojibwe, 96, 437, 440–41
Miller, Jeff, 510
Mills, Billy, 404, 407–8, 413, 505
Mimbres Indians, 274, 321, 642
Mineral resources, 723–24
Mining, 724, 737–40, 744
Minneapolis, 22, 549, 619
Minneapolis American Indian Center, 196
Minnesota Uprising, 607
Minto people, 251
Mirabel, Eva, 646
Missionaries to Canada's First Nations
   Anglican, 816–17
   Brebeuf, 813
   during British rule, 815
   Budd, 817
   Canadian education system, 817–18
   Champlain, 812–13
   Laval, 813
   Methodist, 815–16
   Moravian, 815
   New France, 811–12
   Rale, 814
   traditional religious movement, 816
   women, 814, 816
Missions, 4, 219–20, 337, 394–95
Mission schools, 147, 427–28

Mississaugas, 339, 815
Mississippian culture, 319–20, 639
Mississippi Band of Choctaw Indians v. Holyfield, 211, 213
Mississippi Valley, 319–20
Miss Navajo (Luther), 660
Miss Navajo Nation, 669
Missouri, 513
Mitsitam Café, 358
Mixtec people, 643
Mobility rates, 22
Mobro, 703
Modern, definition of, 345–46
Modernization of American Indian culture
   becoming modern, 348–51
   contemporary, 351–52
   definition of, 346
   definitions and assumptions, 345–46
   images of American Indians, 346–48
Modern medicine. *See* Traditional healing and modern medicine
Mohave Generating Station, 739
Mohawk Girls, 660
Mohawks, 90, 266, 476, 812
Mohican people, 440
Mollhausen, Baldiun, 675
Momaday, N. Scott, 184
A Momentary Lapse of Brilliance, 668
Monk's Mound, 320
Monophony, 682
Monroe, James, 338
Monsanto Corporation, 782
Montana, 97, 513, 515
Montana Blackfoot people, 249
Montana v. United States, 194
Monte Albán, 643
Montezuma, Carlos, 388
Montezuma Castle, 277
Montgomery, Kate, 671
Monument Valley, 663
Mooney, James, 63, 535
Moorehead, Warren K., 319
Mopope, Stephen, 646
Morales, Mauro, 264
Moravian missionaries, 815
Morgan, J. P., 63
Morgan, Lewis Henry, 346–48, 650
Morongo Casino, Resort & Spa, 88
Morongo Indian Reservation, 88
Morrison, Kelsey, 584
Morrison, Marion. *See* Wayne, John
El Morro, 277
Morton, Rogers, 52, 431
Mound-building cultures, 319–20, 639
Moundville, Alabama, 320
Mountain Apache Police Department, 608

Mount Edgecumbe High School, 149
Mount Pleasant, Franklin P., 508
Mount Rushmore, 619
Movement, freedom of, 461
Mueller, David, 670
Multicultural literature, 159
Multi-Ethnic Placement Act, 226
Multiple-migration theory, 332
Murie, James, 278, 388
Muscogee Creek people, 262, 263, 580
Museum at Warm Springs, 280
Museum of Contemporary Native Art, 646
Museum of the American Indian, 357
Museum of the Cherokee Indian, 280
Museums, 280, 297–98, 354–63, 646
Music
   academic scholarship, institutions, and repatriation, 683–84
   authenticity, 689–90
   competition and noncompetition powwows, 686
   contemporary, 688–89
   dance styles, 276, 685–86
   drum, 687–88
   economic concerns, 688
   elements of, 681–83
   Native American flute, 682, 689
   pan-Indianism, 687
   powwows, 684–87
   Two-spirit powwows, 686–87
Muskogee people, 756–57
Mutual masturbation, 242–43
Muwekma-Ohlone, 40
Mvskoke Food Sovereignty Initiative (MFSI), 757–58
Mvskoke people, 757
Mvskoke Tribal Administration Jurisdiction, 757–58
Myer, Dillon S., 38
Mythic Indian, 61–63
Myths, 314–15

Nagel, Joane, 624
Nahua tribe, 643
Nakai, Raymond, 134
Nakai, R. Carlos, 689
Nakota people, 289–90
Naranjo-Morses, Nora, 358
Narcomey, 305
Narragansett Indian Smoke Shop, 422
Narragansett people, 416, 440
Nasdijj, 288
Nash, Philleo, 431
Natchez nation, 322
National Academy of Sciences, 727

National Advisory Council on Indian Education (NACIE), 129, 131
National American Cultural Preservation Act, 277
National American Indian Heritage Week, 295
National Assessment of Adult Literacy, 151
National Assessment of Educational Progress (NAEP), 139
National Association for Mental Illness (NAMI), 230
National Association for the Advancement of Colored People (NAACP), 600, 616
National Association of the Native American Deaf, 163
National Book Festival, 155
National Center for American Indian Enterprise Development, 112
National Center for Educational Statistics, 151
National Child Abuses and Neglect Data System, 191
National Coalition on Racism in Sports and Media (NCRSM), 303, 304–5, 308, 546, 604
National Collegiate Athletic Association (NCAA), 303, 304–5
National Commission for the Development of Indigenous Peoples, 803
National Congress of American Indians (NCAI)
   activism, 547, 623–24
   biocolonialism, 786
   conservation, 749–50
   domestic abuse, 193
   establishment of, 616
   federal acknowledgement, 442
   health, 206–7
   historic preservation, 295–96
   language, 145
   leadership and, 594
   on mascots, 303
   trust reform, 566–67
   unemployment, 123
National Council of American Indians (NCAI), 254
National Council of Indigenous Peoples, 822
National Council on Indian Opportunity (NCIO), 132
National Council on Indian Work, 551
National Crime Victimization Survey, 611
National Environmental Policy Act, 432
National Film Board of Canada (NFB), 662
National Gallery (London), 276
National Historic Preservation Act, 274, 277, 292, 293, 294, 295–96, 432
National Household Survey on Drug Abuse, 250
National Indian Brotherhood, 551

National Indian Brotherhood of Canada, 802, 818
National Indian Child Welfare Association (NICWA), 193, 196
National Indian Education Association (NIEA), 130, 174–75, 459
National Indian Education Study, 139, 177
National Indian Gaming Association (NIGA), 87
National Indian Gaming Commission, 633
National Indian Hall of Fame, 407
National Indian Health Board, 594
National Indian Leadership Training, 551
National Indian Management Service of America (NIMS), 152–53
National Indian School Board Association, 145
National Indian Youth Council (NIYC), 51, 547, 551, 603–4, 615–17, 623–24, 750
National Indigenous Institute, 803
National Institute for Literacy, 151
National Institute of Justice, 585
National Institute of Mental Health, 230
National Interagency Fire Center (NIFC), 432
Nationality Act of 1940, 456
National Museum for Natural History, 280, 361
National Museum of the American Indian (NMAI)
 collection of, 355, 357
 cultural preservation, 277, 280
 Cultural Resource Center, 354, 360–61
 George Gustav Heye Center, 354, 359–60
 introduction to, 354–55
 on the National Mall, 357–59
 National Museum of the American Indian Act, 356
 Native Networks, 662
 repatriation, 361–62
 tribal museums, 298
National Museum of the American Indian Act, 277, 354–55, 356
National Organization for Women (NOW), 54
National Park Service (NPS), 99–100, 103, 294, 330–31, 382
National Register of Historic Places, 292
National Resources Defense Council (NRDC), 745
National Survey on Drug Use and Health, 256
National Track and Field Hall of Fame, 407, 408
National Trust for Historic Preservation, 297
National Union of Autonomous Regional Peasant Organizations, 822
National Unity Task Force, 133
Native American and Indigenous Studies Association, 645
Native American Art Studies Association, 645
Native American Church (NAC), 263, 265, 365, 368–69, 370–71, 458, 478–79
Native American Church v. Navajo Tribal Council, 478–79
Native American Circle of Prayer and Spirit Wind, 370
Native American Deaf. *See* Deaf and hearing-impaired people
Native American Education Program (NAEP), 158–59
Native American Employment Training Council, 121
Native American Film + Video Festival, 671
Native American Graves Protection and Repatriation Act (NAGPRA)
 academic scholarship, institutions, and repatriation, 683
 activism, 551, 574–75
 funding, 296
 implementation of, 432
 interpretations and intent of the law, 379
 Kennewick Man, 275, 328–31, 332–34
 passage of, 277
 repatriation, 377–78
 text of, 378–79
Native American Health Center, 41
Native American Housing and Self-Determination Act (NAHASDA), 634
"Native American Language Immersion: Innovative Native Education for Children and Families," 144
Native American Languages Act, 145–46
Native American Music Awards, 689
Native American orphanages, 221–23
Native American Prison Support, 614
Native American Producers Alliance, 671
Native American Program of the Sundance Institute, 671
Native American Project of Theology, 369
Native American Public Telecommunications, 662, 665, 671
Native American Rights Fund (NARF), 452, 462–63, 501, 551, 564, 617–18
Native American Serving Non-Tribal Institutions (NASNTI), 143
Native Americans for Community Action, Inc., 237
Native American Sports Council (NASC), 414
Native American studies, 135–36
Native American Theater Ensemble (NATE), 653
Native American Tribal Conference, 123
Native Arts Circle, 671
Native Christian Fellowship, 369
Native Council of Canada, 791

Native Hawaiian Government Reorganization Act, 575–76
Native Hawaiians, 575
Native Land Act of 1865, 804
Native language immersion programs, 177
Native Networks, 661, 662
Native Studies, 775–76
Native Tourism Alliance, 97
Native Voices: A Festival of Native Plays, 654
Native Voices at the Autry Museum of the Southwest, 654–55
Native ways of knowing (NWK). *See* Ways of knowing, Indian
Native Women's Association of Canada, 791
Native Youth Media Makers, 662
Natural rights doctrine, 466
Nature, 286
Nature Genetics, 787
Nautilus, USS, 727
Navajo Bible, 342
Navajo Bible Training School, 342
Navajo Code Talkers, 527
Navajo Community College, 134–35, 172
Navajo Generating Station, 724
Navajo Green Economy Coalition, 741
Navajo-Hopi Settlement Act of 1974, 739
Navajo language, 336
Navajo Nation Reservation, 444
Navajo Peacemaking Program, 555
Navajo people
    art of, 642–43
    boarding schools, 210
    Christianity, 370
    crime and, 584
    education and, 459
    education rights, 451
    federal recognition, 440
    military participation, 526–27
    mining, 724, 737, 739–40
    orphans, 225
    pollution and, 733
    Rough Rock Demonstration school, 142
    smallpox, 203
    substance abuse, 252
    tourism, 103
    traditional healing, 263, 265
    uranium contamination, 723
    violence against, 461–62, 488–89
Navajo reservation, 103, 510, 615
Navajo Talking Pictures, 667, 669–70
Navajo Times, 134
Navajo Tribal Council, 371
Navajo Tribal Court, 555
Nebraska State Historical Society, 381
Necessary and Proper Clause, 578
Neconish, Ernest, 52

Neconish, Jane, 52
Nelson, Gaylord, 52
Nelson, Mary Alice, 660
Neolin, 815
Nesutan, Job, 337
Neuroscience, 313
Nevada v. Hicks, 582–83
Nevaquaya, Doc Tate, 689
New, Lloyd Kiva, 653
New Age beliefs, 289
New Buffalo, 85, 87–88, 105
New Credit Reserve, 816
New Deal, 200, 429–30, 467–68
Newfoundland, 771–72
New France, 811–12
New Jersey, 513, 515
Newlands Project, 721
New Left, 621
New Mexico, 101, 156–57, 617
Newton, Isaac, 523
New York (state), 513, 515–16
New York Giants, 410
New York Post, 301
New York Times, 286
New York Yankees, 411
New Zealand, indigenous people in, 804–5
Nez Perce (Nimíipuu), 275, 330, 428, 734, 764–65
Nibley, Lydia, 670
Nichol, Fred, 551
Nida, Eugene, 341
Nike, Inc., 65, 207
Niro, Shelley, 660, 661
Nixon, Richard, 132, 200, 550, 601, 620
Nobel Peace Prize, 715, 822
Noble Savage concept, 60, 62, 63, 103, 286, 651–52, 676
No Child Left Behind Act (NCLB), 141, 174–76
Noncompetition powwows, 686
Nonstandard English. *See* Red English
Norse, 771
North, American Indian art of, 638–39
North American Free Trade Agreement (NAFTA), 803
North Carolina, 513, 516
North Carolina–Pembroke, 304
Northeast, land use in, 755–56
Northern Arapaho, 745–46, 759
Northern Arapaho Ranch, 746, 759
Northern Cheyenne, 734, 740
North States Power Company, 550
Northwest coast
    American Indian art of, 640
    architecture of, 384

hunting and fishing rights, 452, 599–600, 746–47
land use, 763–65
rules of descent, 10
Northwest Coast Indian Art (Holm), 640
Northwest Native American reading curriculum, 158
Northwest Ordinance, 570
Northwest Territory, 445, 794
Norway, 806
Nuche people, 761
Nuclear colonialism, 720–21
Nuclear power plants, 727–28
Nuclear Regulatory Commission (NRC), 499, 726–27
"Nuclear sacrifice zones," 498
Nuclear waste, 726–31. *See also* Uranium contamination
Nuclear Waste Policy Act, 728
Nunavut, 778

Oakes, Richard, 51, 601
Obama, Barack, 123, 565, 575, 576
Objectivism, 312
Obomsawin, Alanis, 661
Oenga, Andrew, 565
Offering Smoke (Paper), 419
Office of Equal Opportunity, 620
Office of Facilities, Environmental and Cultural Resources (OFECR), 432
Office of Facilities Management and Construction, 432
Office of Federal Acknowledgement, 434–35, 436
Office of Indian Affairs, 427–28, 430, 572, 581
Office of Indian and Northern Affairs, 790–91
Office of Indian Education (OIE), 132–33, 139
Office of Indian Education Program (OIEP), 139
Office of Indian Water Rights, 550
Office of National Drug Control Policy (ONDCP), 254, 256–57
Office of Navajo Uranium Miners, 737
Office of Technical Assistance and Training, 582
Office of the Nuclear Waste Negotiator, 498
Office of the Special Trustee for American Indians (OST), 563–64, 566–67
Ogalala Lakota College, 172
Oglala Lakota people, 245
Oglala reservation, 469
Oglala Sioux Tribe, 472
Ohio, 513, 515
Ohio River Valley, 5, 319–20, 445, 639
Ojibwa language, 221
Ojibway people, 746–47, 816–17

Oklahoma, 513
Oklahoma! 652
Oklahoma Agriculture and Mechanical College, 411
Oklahoma Hall of Fame, 407
Oklahoma Tax Commission v. Chickasaw, 471
Oklahoma Tax Commission v. Citizen Band Potawatomi Indian Tribe, 470
Oklevueha Native American Church (ONAC), 365
Old Oraibi, New Mexico, 321
Oliphant, Mark David, 557, 582
Oliphant v. Suquamish Tribe, 194, 557, 582, 583, 608
Olson, John, 71
Olympic athletes, 406, 407–8, 505, 508
Olympic Hall of Fame, 408
Omaha people, 278, 428
One Bull, 677
Oneida people, 108, 238, 476, 812
One-migration theory, 332
One Sky Center, 236
Onondagas, 624, 812
Oorang Indians, 406
"Open Dump Cleanup Project Helps Tribes Fight Waste," 710
Opler, Morris, 13
Oral tradition, 238, 276, 332–33, 771
Oravetz, Ladine, 110–11
Oregon, 599
Oregon Trail, 591
Oregon v. Smith, 458
Organizational theorists, 154
Organization of American States (OAS), 499
Orphans
 Anglo orphanages, 219
 forcible removal of Indian children, 224–25
 government orphanages, 223–24
 missions and, 219–20
 Native American orphanages, 221–23
 postorphanage Indian children, 224–26
Ortiz, Alfonso, 388
Osage Nation, 736
Osage people, 584, 723
Osage Tribal Museum, 280
Osceola, Max B., Jr., 107
Osceola, William, 107
O'Shea, Elena Zamora, 6
Ottawa people, 277
Ouray people, 737
Our Lives: Contemporary Life and Identities exhibit, 359
"Outing system," 170
Outta Your Backpack Media, 661

Owens, Jayhawk, 509
Ownership of Indian remains, 328–35
Ozette Village Site, 765

Paatuwaqatsi: Water, Land & Life, 667
Pacific Islanders in Communications, 671
Pacific Northwest. *See* Northwest coast
Painted manuscripts, 643
Paiute people, 451, 459
Pan-Indianism, 687, 694–97
Paper, Jordan, 419
Pappan, Dawena, 92
Parins, Jim, 691–92, 694
Paris, Damara Goff, 161
Parker, Arthur C., 133
Parker, Ely Samuel, 427, 430, 523–24
Parochial schools, 147
Partnership for a Drug-Free America, 254
Passamaquoddy Tribe, 109, 621
Paternalism, 740, 770
Patrilineal descent, 10, 48
Pauktuutit, 791
Pawnee nation, 377–78, 380–81
Paxton Boys, 283
Peabody Coal Company, 724
Peabody Mining Company, 744
Peabody Museum of American Archaeology and Ethnology, 278, 377, 644
Peabody Western Coal Company, 739
Peacemaking Circles, 555
Peace Policy, 427, 446
Peach Springs Detention Center, 608
Peltier, Leonard, 545–46, 549–50
Peltier, Wilfred, 716–17
Pennsylvania Hall of Fame, 407
Pennsylvania State University, 593
Penobscots, 621
Pentecostals, 369–70
Pequots, 181
Pequot War, 540, 606
Perdue, Theda, 15, 348–49
Perez, Santiago, 141
Perkel, Samuel F., 57
Personal jurisdiction, 213
Peyote, 257–58, 264, 365, 368, 371, 458, 478–79. *See also* Spiritual practices
Phenomenalists, 314
Philadelphia Athletics, 409–10, 508–9
Phillips, Ruth B., 646
Phinney, Archie, 388
Phoenix Indian Center, 20–21, 37
Photographers, 63
Phratries, 11
Physicalists, 314
Piaget, Jean, 313

Pickard, Cindy, 670
Pick-Sloan Project, 722
Picout-Aquash, Anna Mae, 584
Pidgin English. *See* Red English
Pierce, Franklin, 427
Pierson-Little Thunder, Julie, 654
Piestewa, Lori Ann, 53
Pike, Zebulon, 380
Pima Indians, 261
Pine Leaf, 246
Pine Ridge Correctional Facility, 608
Pine Ridge Reservation. *See also* Wounded Knee incident
  Aquash murder, 546, 584
  bison on, 746
  FBI confrontation, 549
  Mills and, 407
  Peltier and, 545
  poverty, 75–76, 78, 452
  racism, 496
  sovereignty and, 472–73
Pipe-smoking, 418–20
Pit River tribe, 444
Plains Apache, 350
Plains Indian Sign Language. *See* American Indian Sign Language
Plenty Chief, Wesley, 380
Plymouth Rock, 549, 619
Pocahontas, 14, 64, 396, 660
Pocowatchit, Rodrick, 665, 668, 671
Police corruption, 92–93
Police officers, Native, 462
Political activism. *See* Activism
Political representation of Canadian aboriginal peoples, 790–92
Pollution. *See also* Environmental racism; Solid waste
  coal emissions and strip mining, 737–40
  federal responsibility and paternalism, 740
  hazardous waste dumping, 732–33
  Tribal Brownfields and Response Program, 738
  tribal environmental protection programs, 733–34
  tribal green projects, 740–41
  waste management in Indian country, 735–36
  waste storage, 736–37
Polygyny, 13
Polyphony, 682
Pommersheim, Frank, 467
Pomo people, 641, 748–49
Ponca people, 147
Pontifex, Romanus, 466
Poodry v. Tonawanda Band of Seneca Indians, 481–82

Poor Bear, Myrtle, 545–46
Poor People's Campaign, 604
Poplar, Montana, 231
Popular imagination, Indians in, 284
Portal of the Palace of Governors, 101
Port Madison Reservation, 582
Posey, Alexander Lawrence, 184, 185
Postorphanage Indian children, 224–26
Postsecondary schools, 143
Posttraumatic stress disorder (PTSD), 234
Potawatomi people, 427, 470–71
Potlatches, 797–98
Potomac atrium, 358
Pottery, 642
Poverty. See also Poverty on reservations
   assimilation and identity, 73–74
   children and, 115–16
   education and, 80
   gaming and casinos, 81, 87
   health and, 80
   healthcare and, 74, 76–77
   institutional racism and, 498
   rural, 78
   statistics, 72–73, 75–77
   substance abuse, 249
   tribal government and, 631
   unemployment and, 114, 115–16
   in urban areas, 67–74
   urban Indian experience, definition of, 68–71
   urban life, adaptation to, 71–74
   welfare, 73
Poverty on reservations
   collateral impacts of, 80
   examples of, 77–79
   Indian gaming, role of, 81
   overview of, 75–77
   persistence of, 81–83
   unemployment and, 79
Powwows, 70, 684–87
Pratt, Richard Henry, 130, 133, 170–71, 209, 428, 524–25, 795
Praying Indians, 337, 394
Praying Towns, 337, 394
Predators, habitat and, 745–46
Pre-European contact populations, measurement of, 32–33
Premarital sex, 242–43
Presbyterians, 220, 366
Present trauma, 231
Preservation. See Cultural preservation
Presidential Medal of Freedom, 53
President's Race Commission, 485
Press. See Print media by Indians
Prevent All Cigarette Trafficking Act (PACT Act), 422–23
Preventive healthcare, 206–7

Primogeniture, 48
Princesses and squaws, 395–97
Print media by Indians
   digitization, 698–99
   Indian press, proliferation of, 694–97
   indigenous American press, 691–94
   Pan-Indianism, 694–97
   Sequoyah, 691–94
Prisons. See also Crime; Law enforcement in Indian country
   alcohol and, 612
   American Indians under correction, 610–11
   capital punishment, 613
   challenges, 613–14
   crime and American Indians, 611–12
   crime statistics, 609
   introduction to, 606–7
   jails in Indian country, 608–9
   juvenile detention, 612
   legislation and, 607–8
   medical facilities, 610
   other programs, 610
   recidivism, 613
   spiritual practices, 613–14
Private Fuel Storage, 498–99
Private Ownership of Special Nuclear Materials Act, 727
The Problem of Indian Administration. See Meriam Report
Procedural knowledge, 311
Professional Football Hall of Fame, 407
Property Clause, 578
The Prophet, 522. See also Tenskwatawa
"Proposal to Create an American Indian University" (Forbes), 134
Propositional knowledge, 311
Protecting Mother Earth Conference, 736
Pruitt, Scott, 93
Psychological and emotional problems. See also Healthcare
   behavioral health, 229
   historical trauma, 230–34
   introduction to, 228–29
   research, 234–35
   suicide, 230, 231, 235, 252, 493
   symptomology, 228–29
   treatment, 235–39
Public Broadcasting System (PBS), 156, 662
Public education, 171–78. See also Boarding school movement; Education
Public Health, Department of, 200
Public Health Service, 199, 430, 705
Public Law 83–280, 579–81
Public Law 280, 556, 599, 608
Pueblo Bonito complex, 321
Pueblo Cultural Center, 280

Pueblo of Taos tribe, 710, 721
Pueblos, 102, 278, 320–21, 384, 404, 624, 759–60
Purdue University, 509
Puritans, 336–37
Pyramid Lake reservation, 91, 721

Quakers, 366
Quebec, 793, 812–13
Quetzalcoatl, Dekanawida, 134
Quicwa, 196
Quil Ceda Village, 107–8
Quillwork, 639, 641
Quyawayma, Al, 388

Race relations
 in Bemidji, Minnesota, 489–90, 496, 501
 crimes against American Indians, 486–88
 cultural depictions of American Indians, 485–86
 in Farmington, New Mexico, 488–89
 improvement of, 490–91
 introduction to, 484–85
 invisibility of, 485
Racism
 domestic abuse and, 194
 environmental, 498–501
 fighting against, 501–2
 historical background, 283, 494
 institutional, 497–98
 introduction to, 493–94
 stereotypes and slurs, 495–96
 violence, 496–97
Radiation Exposure Compensation Act, 737
Radical constructivism, 313
Radicalism, 621–22
"Radio Free Alcatraz," 602–3
Raheja, Michelle H., 657, 658, 659
Rainbow Bridge National Monument, 103
Rale, Sebastian, 814
Ramirez, Renya K., 40
Ramsey, John, 584
Rasmuson Theater, 358
Reagan, Ronald, 573
Real estate, tribal economic diversification and, 107–8
The Reawakening, 669
Recidivism, 613
Recognition. *See* Federal recognition; State recognition
Recombinant DNA (rDNA), 781
Recording mediums, 276
Recordings, preservation of, 278–79
Recreational vehicle (RV) resorts, 106
Red Bird, Stanley, 134
Red Clay Casino, 93

Red Cloud, Nebraska, 380
Red English
 in federal Indian schools, 184–85
 origins and evolution of, 182–83
 sound, form, and meaning, 183–84
 in translation, 180–82
Redfacing, 659
Red Feather, 531
Red Horse, John, 135
Red-Horse, Valerie, 670
Red Lake reservation, 489, 501
Red Power. *See also* Activism; Civil rights
 Alcatraz Island, occupation of, 617–18
 American Indian Movement, 615, 618–19
 decline of, 622–24
 government assistance, 621
 Indian awareness, 619–20
 Longest Walk, 620
 National Indian Youth Council, 616–17
 Native American studies, 136
 origins of, 547
 precursors, 615–16
 radicalism, 621–22
 repatriation and, 379
 Trail of Broken Treaties, 623
 women, 49–50
 Wounded Knee incident, 623
Red River Rebellion, 798
Red River Settlement, 772
Redroad, Randy, 661
The Red Road Project, 158
Red Wing, Princess, 396–97, 660
Reel Injun (Diamond), 659
Regina v. White and Bob, 793
Regional Indian Youth Council (RIYC), 617
Rehnquist, William, 470
Reifel, Benjamin, 431
Reilly, Julie, 279
Reinecke, John, 182
Reinholz, Randy, 654
Relations, 813, 814
Religion. *See* Christianity and Native spirituality; Spiritual practices
Religious freedom, 458
Religious Freedom Restoration Act (RFRA), 368, 458
Religious orphanages, 223
Relocation program. *See also* Urban living/urbanization
 Act Relative to Employment for Certain Adult Indians On or Near Indian Reservations, 120
 communal vs. individualistic culture, 68–69
 education and, 133
 history of, 19–20, 38–39
 psychological effects of, 233
 urbanization before, 37–38

Removal policy, 554
Renal failure, 206
Rendon, Marcie, 654
Repatriation. *See also* Native American Graves Protection and Repatriation Act (NAGPRA)
   in Canada, 798
   history and influential class, 379–81
   Indian music and, 683–84
   interpretations and intent of the law, 379
   introduction to, 376–78
   Ishi, 458
   National Museum of the American Indian (NMAI), 361–62
   opposition to, 381–82
Republican Party, 469
Reservation Economic Summit (RES), 112
Reservation Reelism (Raheja), 657, 658
Reservations. *See also* Dawes Act; Poverty on reservations
   college athletics and, 503–10
   education rights, 451
   in films by Indians, 668–69
   fishing and hunting rights, 452
   governance, 448–49
   historical background, 445–47
   in Indian Child Welfare Act, 212
   introduction to, 444–45
   land rights, 448–49
   law and order rights, 450–51
   life on, 114, 447
   sovereign immunity, 448
   water rights, 449–50
Reservation schools, 147–49
Reserved Rights Doctrine, 452
Residence Inn Capitol by Marriott, 108
Resistance, in borderlands, 4–6
Resource Conservation and Recovery Act (RCRA), 705, 708–9
Restigouche reserve community, 793
Reuters, 630
Revenue Act, 421
Reynolds, 722
Reynolds, Allie Pierce, 410–11, 412
Reynor, Dianne Yeahquo, 654
Rez Life (Treuer), 447
Rhoades, Everett, 388, 392
Rhoads, Charles J., 429
Rhoads, James E., 429
Richie, Chip, 670
Ridge, John, 15, 338, 523, 590, 694
Riding In, James, 135
Riel, Louis, 776
Riggs, Lynn, 652
Right of occupancy, 470
Riparian water system right, 448–49

Risling, Dave, 134, 135
Ritual Clowns, 667
Roanoke Museum store, 358
Roberts, Selena, 509
Robinson, Tahnee, 509
Rocks at Whiskey Trench, 661
Rolfe, John, 14
Romero, Diego, 642
Roosevelt, Franklin, 200, 429, 467–68, 726
Roosevelt, Theodore, 277
Rosaldo, Renato, 644
Rosales, Jon, 423
Rosario, Sonya, 670
Rosebud, South Dakota, 265
Rosebud Sioux Reservation, 77, 96, 225, 556
Rosebud Sioux Tribe Law Enforcement, 608
Ross, John, 523, 590, 692
Ross, Mary, 388
Rough Rock Demonstration school, 142
Rousseau, Jean-Jacques, 60
Roy, Loriene, 155–56
Royal Commission Report on Aboriginal Peoples, 777, 789, 791–92, 795, 818
Royal Proclamation of 1763, 773, 815
Running Brave for American Indian Youth, 76
Running Strong for American Indian Youth, 408
Rupert's Land, 772
Rushing, W. Jackson, 646
Russia, 805–6
Ruthless Savage concept, 651–52

S&K Aerospace, 110
S&K Global Solutions, 110
Saalequun tribe, 793
Sacagawea, 396
Sacred Circle, 163–64
The Sacred Hoop (Allen), 194
Sacred pipe, 418–20
Sacred place, leadership and, 595
Sac tribe, 736
Sahota, Chawla, 787
Sainte-Marie, Buffy, 547
Sakacewescam, 817
Sakiestewa, Ramona, 357
Salish people. *See* Confederated Salish and Kootenai tribes (CSKT)
Salt, Lynn, 670
Salt River Department of Corrections, 608
Salt River Pima-Maricopa Indian Community (SRPMIC), 787
Sami Council, 806
Sami people, 805–6
Sampling, 30
Sand Creek Massacre, 372, 541, 544
San Diego, 121

San Diego State University, 154
Sand paintings, 642
Sandy Lake band, 440–41
San Francisco, 618, 620
Sanitary landfills, 705
San Juan Paiutes, 440
San Manuel band, 108
San Manuel Miner, 134
Santa Clara Pueblo v. Martinez, 481, 786
Santa Fe, New Mexico, 641–42, 646, 647
Santa Fe Indian Market, 642
Santa Fe Indian School, 646
Santee Dakota language, 336
Saskatchewan rebellions, 798
Satiacum, Robert, 599–600
Saulte Ste. Marie Chippewa Tribe, 81
Sawyer, David, 816
Scalp Dance, 367
Scanlon, Michael, 90
Scholder, Fritz, 647
Schoolcraft, Henry Rowe, 62
Schools, Indian
　Alaska Native education, 149
　Bureau of Indian Education, 140–42
　curriculum, 143–44
　early federal reservation schools, 147–49
　early history of, 146–47
　introduction to, 138–40
　language and culture, 145–46
　mission schools, 147
　Native American language immersion, 144
　Office of Indian Education, 139
　postsecondary schools, 143
　Red English, 184–85
　technology, 146
　tribally contracted schools, 142–43
Schools, parochial, 147
Science and scientists
　American Indian Science and Engineering Society (AISES), 389–90
　education and, 387–88
　European science, 386–87
　Indian scientists, 388–89
　life, science of, 384–86
　tribal involvement, 390–92
Screen Actors Guild, 661
The Searchers, 663
Seattle, 37–38
Seaweed, Willie, 360
Secola, Keith, 688
Second Continental Congress, 570
Second Powhatan War, 606
Secrecy, demographics and, 33
Segar, Grace, 342
Self-Determination
　Congress and, 575
　education and, 132–33
　gaining, 324–25
　healthcare and, 200, 201
　under international law, 464
　Nixon and, 550
Self-governance, law enforcement and, 579
Sells, Cato, 524
Seminoles, 106, 107, 222, 305, 523
Senate Indian Affairs Committee, 90
Senecas, 221, 321, 387, 476, 521–22, 523, 603, 722, 755–56, 812
Senior Citizen Nutrition program, 206
Sentencing Circles, 555
Seowtewa, Alex, 371
Sequanna Therapeutics, 783
Sequoyah, 691–92
Sequoyah Orphan Training School, 224
The Sermon and Speeches of the Rev. Peter Jones (Jones), 339–40
Serrano Indians, 108
Seven Years' War, 814
Sexual division of labor, 46–47
Sexual issues
　American Indian gender, 243–44
　contemporary two-spirits, 247–48
　historical two-spirits, 244–47
　introduction to, 242–43
Sexual taboos, 243
Seymour, Peter, 180
Shaker Church, 368–69
Shakopee Mdewakanton Sioux, 471–72
Sharmoot, Mustafa, 413
Shawnee people, 427, 569, 590
Shenandoah, Joanne, 689
Shinnecock tribe, 434, 438
Shoshone-Bannock tribes, 329–30
Shoshone tribe, 366
Shotridge, Louis, 278
Shouting Secrets, 667
Sierra Club, 745
The Silent Enemy (film), 660
The Silent Enemy (Long Lance), 287–88
Silent Spring (Carson), 706
Silent Thunder, 670
"Silent Witness National Initiative" exhibit, 195
Silko, Leslie Marmon, 184
Silverheels, Jay, 660
Silversmith, Dorothy, 342
Simon, Herbert, 313
Sioux, 221, 278, 549, 591–92, 601, 621, 675
Sioux Ghost Dance, 658
Sioux War, 446
Sisseton-Wahpeton Sioux, 225
Sitka, Alaska, 149
Sitting Bull, 63, 677

Sixkiller, Sonny, 414
Skins, 659, 666
Skinwalkers, 659, 666
Sklallam reservation, 158
Skull Valley band, 498–99
Skull Valley Goshute Reservation, 728–30, 785
Sleepdancer, 668
Smallpox, 812
Smallpox vaccinations, 199–200, 427
Smith, Caleb B., 427
Smith, Chad, 630
Smith, Edward P., 170
Smith, Harold J., 660
Smith, John, 396
Smith, John Q., 578
Smith, Kenneth L., 431
Smithsonian Folkways, 279
Smithsonian Institution, 275, 279, 354, 361–62, 377, 574, 644, 677
Smoke shops
  early Native American economies, 416–17
  medicinal, ceremonial, and ritual use of tobacco, 417–20
  tobacco entrepreneurship, 420–21
  tribal sovereignty, 421–24
Smoke Signals, 65–66, 659, 666, 669
Smoke Signals (newsletter), 432
Smokey, Lois, 646
Smoki Dance, 102
Snake Dance, 102
Snoqualmie people, 457
Snyder Act. *See* Indian Citizenship Act
Snyder Act of 1921, 429
Social constructivism, 312
Social evolution, 347
Society of American Indians (SAI), 133, 616
Sockalexis, Louis Francis, 408–9, 411–12, 413, 508
Soldier Blue, 284
Solid waste
  history of waste disposal, 704–6
  introduction to, 703–4
  tribal authority and federal policy, 706–11
  Tribal Waste Journal, 707, 709, 736
  waste management in Indian country, 735–36
Solid Waste Act, 707–8
Solid Waste Disposal Act, 706
Solix–Southern Ute, 109
Sombero, Solon, 133
The Song of Hiawatha (Longfellow), 62
A Son of the Forest (Apess), 366
Sorkin, Alan, 71
Souers, Jerome, 510
The Soul of the Indian (Eastman), 367
Source Watch, 737–39

South Carolina, 513, 516
South Dakota, 226, 457, 497, 621
Southeast
  American Indian art of, 640
  as a borderland, 5
  intermarriage, 15
  land use, 756–58
  rules of descent, 10
Southern Plains War, 170
Southern Ute Alternative Energy LLC, 109
Southern Ute Indian tribe, 109
South K, 585
Southwest
  American Indian art of, 641–43
  architecture of, 384
  ecocide, 720–21
  land use, 759–60
  long distance running for communication, 404
  mining, 724
  nuclear sacrifice zones, 498
  rules of descent, 10
Southwestern Indian Polytechnic Institute (SIPI), 143
Southwest Intertribal Voices (SWIV), 497
Sovereign immunity, 448, 470, 786
Sovereignty. *See also* Federal recognition; Tribal sovereignty
  activism, 548, 551
  competing jurisdictions, 456–58
  conclusion, 474–75
  erosion of, 466–70
  gaming, 473–74
  historical background, 464, 466
  Indian Reorganization Act, 468
  Justice Department statement on, 465
  Justice Department statement on tribal sovereignty, 465
  land rights, 448–49
  law and, 450–51, 470–72
  overview of, 445
  Pine Ridge Reservation, 472–73
  smoke shops and, 421–24
  tax issues, 420–24
Special Supplemental Nutrition Program for Women, Infants, and Children. *See* Women Infants and Children (WIC)
Speck, Frank, 683
Spiderwoman Theater, 653, 654
Spirit Alive Victory Camp Meeting, 369
Spirit Lake Reservation, 264, 370
Spirit of the Wind, 670
Spiritual genocide, 535
Spiritual practices. *See also* Christianity and Native spirituality; Missionaries to Canada's First Nations

Bible translations into indigenous languages, 336–44
Canadian Indians and aboriginal peoples, 797–98
civil rights and, 458
commandeering, 288–90
cultural and religious rights, 458
disease, 263–65
mental health, 236
military participation and, 531
mission efforts and, 232
Native spirituality and Christianity, 364–75
pipe-smoking, 418–20
in prisons, 613–14
two-spirits, 245
Spivey, Towana, 388
Sporting News, 307
Sport magazine, 407
Sports Illustrated, 308
Spotted Elk, Molly, 660
Spotted Tail, 556, 607
The Squaw Man, 396
Squaws and princesses, 395–97, 486, 495, 652. *See also* Stereotypes
Standing Bear, Luther, 170–71, 660
Standing Bear v. Crook, 555
Standing Rock reservation, 91
Standing Silent Nation, 473
Stanford University, 304, 305
Stanford University School of Medicine, 265
Stannard, David, 539, 540
Star, Aragon, 654
Starkey, Janessa, 668
State governments, 89, 420–24, 470–71
State recognition. *See also* Federal recognition
controversies, 517–18
economic development, 112
federally recognized tribes, 512
historical roles of federal and state governments, 514
introduction to, 511
overview of, 513
rights of, 514–17
survey of, 514–17
State's Racial Integrity Act of 1924, 512
St. Cyr, Lillian, 396–97, 660
Stereotypes. *See also* Indian mascots
colonial, 394–95
Indians, the classroom, and xenophobia, 397–99
introduction to, 393
of Native American youth, 504–5
19th-century art and literature, 395
precursors of white progress, 397
princesses and squaws, 395–97, 486, 495, 652
racism and, 495–96
symbols, 460–61
tobacco marketing, 64–66
tourism and, 102–3
Stevens, Charles "Charlie," 660
Stevens, Isaac Ingalls, 764, 765
Stevens, John Paul, 470
Stewart, Ellen, 653
Stillday, Tom, 373
St. John's University, 305
St. Jude's Children's Research Hospital and Children's Oncology Group, 787
St. Louis Rams, 413–14
Stoic Indian stereotype, 103
Stone, John Augustus, 651
Stonecut, 639
St. Regis Mohawk tribe, 238
Strip mining, 737–40
Strongheart, Nipo T., 660
Structure of Scientific Revolutions (Kuhn), 315
St. Thomas Orphan's Home, 220
Student Nonviolent Coordinating Committee, 621
Students for a Democratic Society, 621
"A Study of Omaha Indian Music" (Fletcher and La Flesche), 278
Subject matter jurisdiction, 213
Substance abuse
alcohol, 23–24, 193, 233, 251–52, 493, 612, 631
community solutions, 256–57
domestic abuse and, 193
drugs, 252–55
institutional support, 250–51
introduction to, 249–50
magnitude of, 250
Memorandum of Agreement on Indian Substance Abuse Prevention, 255
peyote as an alternative, 257–58
prevention of, 255
racism and, 493
unemployment and, 119
Substance Abuse and Mental Health Services Administration, 250
Sudden infant death syndrome (SIDS), 206
Suicide, 230, 231, 235, 252, 493
Sullivan, John, 93
Sullivan Expedition, 522
Summer Institute of Linguistics (SIL), 341, 342
Sun, Moon and Feather, 654
Sun Dance, 366, 367, 369, 458, 798
Sundance Film Festival, 666
Superfund sites, 723, 733–34
Supremacy Clause, 578

Supreme Court, Canadian, 793
Supreme Court, U.S.
  on the Cherokee nation, 445
  on civil cases, 559
  on criminal law, 607–8
  domestic abuse and, 194
  environmental racism and, 499
  federal government relationship with American Indians, 514, 554
  fishing and hunting rights, 452
  government responsibility for Indians, 199, 427
  Indian Child Welfare Act, 211
  Indian Civil Rights Act and, 481–82
  Indian lands, 561
  Indian tribal courts, 557
  law enforcement and, 582
  religious freedom, 458
  solid waste management, 709
  sovereign immunity, 786
  sovereignty and, 446, 466–67, 470–71, 478, 621
  spiritual practices, 368
  tax issues, 421, 423
  water rights, 450, 721
Survival of American Indians Association (SAIA), 50, 600, 617
Survival schools, 25–26
Susanville Indian Rancheria, 748
Sustainable Nations Development Project, 123
Suttle, Steffany, 661
Svingen, Orlan, 381
Swallow, Jay, 370, 373
Sweden, 806
Sweet, Jill D., 102
Swentzell, Roxanne, 642
Swift, Jackie, 785
Swimmer, Ross, 52, 431
Swimmers, 509
Swinomish Indian Tribal Community, 106
Syncretism, 232, 247, 371

Table Mountain Racheria, 91–92
Tahdooahnippah Leadership Variables, 595
Taiwan, indigenous people in, 807–8
Taiwanese Council of Indigenous Peoples, 807
Talk of the Nation, 447
Tallgrass Prairie National Park, 736
Talton, Bob, 478
Talton v. Mayes, 478, 479
Taos, New Mexico, 321
Tax, Sol, 603
Tax Commission v. Citizen Band Potawatomi Indian Tribe of Oklahoma, 423
Tax issues, 420–24, 470–71
Taylor, Drew Haden, 654

Teacher's Institute, 222
The Teachings of Don Juan (Castaneda), 288–89
Tecumseh, 522–23
Tecumseh's Vision, 667
Teens. *See* Youth
Tejanos, 4
Tekakwitha Orphanage, 226
Teller, Henry M., 13, 367
Tellico Dam, 722
Tenacity, 666
Tennessee, 513
Tenochtitlan, 32
Tenskwatawa, 366, 522
Tenth Amendment, 210–11, 480, 514
Teotihuacan, 643
Termination and recognition
  Congress and, 572
  effects of, 430, 438–41, 447
  overview of, 325–26
  political activism, 600
  relocation programs, 616
  urban living and, 26
Texas, 4, 368
Texas Indian Wars, 607
Textiles, 276–77, 643
Thanksgiving Day protest, 549, 619
Theater and performance
  from the 1930s to the present, 652–55
  genre, definition of, 648–49
  "Indian," representation of, 650–52
  native worldview in, 650
  survival of traditions, 649
  trickster character, 649–50
Thief of Time, 666
Third Amendment, 480
Third-genders, 13
Third World Liberation Front, 619–20
Thirteenth Amendment, 629
Thom, Mel, 603
Thomas, Dale, 380
Thomas, David Hurst, 348
Thomas, Robert, 135
Thomas, Sachem Matthew, 422
Thompson, Morris, 431
Thompson, Stephen, 412
Thornton, Russell, 29, 535, 538–39, 540
Thorpe, Jim, 405–7, 412, 413, 506, 508
A Thousand Roads, 666
Three Affiliated Tribes, 92
Three Fires, 108, 110
Three Mile Island Nuclear Power Station, 727
Three Tales of Choices, 668
Thum, Pam, 369
Thunderbird Theater, 653–54
Thunderhawk, Madonna, 604

Tiller Research, 112
Time magazine, 703
Tippecanoe, Battle of, 522–23
Tobacco. *See also* Smoke shops
   entrepreneurship, 420–21
   growing of, 61
   medicinal, ceremonial, and ritual use of, 417–20
   stereotypes used to market, 64–66
   use of in early trading, 417
Tobacco notes, 417
Tobeluk v. Lind, 149
Together Raising Awareness for Indian Life (T.R.A.I.L.), 206, 207
Tohono O'odham Detention Center, 608
Tohono O'odham reservation, 638
Tokyo Joe, 413
Toledo, Francisco, 643
Tomahawk, 693
Tonawanda Senecas, 624
Tonkawa people, 736
Tonto, 277, 495
Torry, Alvin, 816
Totem poles, 640
Tourism
   authenticity and cultural appropriation, 100–102
   economic costs, benefits, and competition, 97–100
   historic preservation and, 297
   introduction to, 96–97
   National Park Service, 103
   stereotypes, 102–3
   tribal economic diversification, 105–7
Townsend, William Cameron, 341
Track and field, 406, 407–8, 505, 508
Trade Commission Act, 58
Trademark Trial and Appeal Board, 308
Traders, intermarriage and, 15–16
Traditional healing and modern medicine
   diagnosis, 262–63
   disease and medicine in Native America, 260–61
   efficacy and the healed, 267–68
   etiological explanations, 263–65
   living in the cosmos, 261–62
   theories and methods of healing, 265–67
Traditional kinship. *See* Kinship
Traditional Knowledge Digital Library (TKDL), 787
Traditional Knowledge Policy, 794
Traditional religious movement, 816
Trail of Broken Treaties, 224, 431, 546, 551, 604, 621, 622, 623
Trail of Tears, 298–99, 590
Trail of Tears (film), 667

Transfer Act, 200
Transformers, 663
Transgender, 244
Translational Genomics Research Institute, 787
Trash barges, 703–4
Trauma, cultural, 230–34
Treaty of Canandaigua, 603
Treaty of Ft. Laramie, 472–73, 549, 601
Treaty of New Echota, 523, 590
Treaty of Paris, 814
Treaty of Ruby Valley, 499, 761
Treaty of Smoky Hill, 380
Treaty of Tordesillas, 494
Treaty of Waitangi, 804
Trees and plants, habitat and, 748–49
Trenbirth, Steve, 668–69
Trent University, 775
Treuer, David, 447
Tribal Alliance of Sovereign Indian Nations (TASIN), 89
Tribal Association of Conservation Districts (TACD), 750
"Tribal Brownfields and Response Program," 738
Tribal college movement, 133–35
Tribal constitutions, 476–77
Tribal Decisionmaker's Guide to Solid Waste Management, 736
Tribal economic diversification
   energy, 108–9
   other expansions, 109–10
   potential remedies, 111–12
   problems of, 110–11
   real estate, 107–8
   tourism, 105–7
Tribal Economic Vitality Initiative (TEVI), 112
Tribal Education Department National Assembly (TEDNA), 142
Tribal education departments (TEDs), 177–78
Tribal employment rights officers (TEROs), 119
Tribal environmental protection programs, 733–34
Tribal government
   conclusion, 633–34
   Freedmen controversy, 629–30
   history, 626–28
   issues in, 631–33
   structure and function of, 628–29
Tribal Government Gaming and Economic Self-Sufficiency Act of 1998, 92
Tribal green projects, 740–41
Tribal Historic Preservation Office, 294, 298
Tribal identity, 785–86
Tribal Law and Order Act, 123, 480–81, 585–86
Tribal Law and Policy Institute, 196

Tribal Law Enforcement Summit, 583
Tribally contracted schools, 142–43
Tribally Controlled Community College Assistance Act, 135, 143
Tribally Controlled School Act, 142
Tribal membership, demographics and, 34
Tribal Self-Governance Demonstration Project, 201, 202
Tribal Solid Waste Management Program, 735
Tribal sovereignty. *See* Sovereignty
Tribal Waste Journal, 707, 709, 736
Trickster character, 649–50
Tristan da Cunha, 783
Trudeau, Pierre, 791
Truman, Harry, 726
Trustees, duties of, 562–63
Trust Funds Accounting System (TFAS), 566–67
Trust lands
  American Indian Trust Fund Management Reform Act of 1994, 563–64
  Congress and, 575
  environmental protection programs, 733–34
  history of, 561–62
  mismanagement, accusations of, 564–65
  reform, 565–68
  workings of, 562–63
Truth Commission into Genocide in Canada, 795
Tsakoke, Monroe, 646
Tsehoosoi Dine Bi olta I Navajo K–6 Immersion School, 145
Tuba City, Arizona, 510
Tuhbenahneequay, 339
Tulalip Resort Casino, 108
Tulalip Tribes, 107–8
Turtle Mountain Reservation, 370
Tutu, Desmond, 546
20-Point Position Paper, 551
Twiss, Richard, 370
Two Rivers Native American Training Center, 370
Two Spirit People (Brown), 244
Two-spirit powwows, 686–87
Two-spirits, 13, 244–48
Two Spirits, 670
Tyendinaga Indian Reserve, 369

Udall, Stewart, 430
Uintah people, 737
Umatilla people, 275, 330, 332–33, 734
Umatilla Reservation, 330
Uncas (fictional character), 395
UN Committee on the Elimination of Discrimination against Women, 797
UN Convention on Genocide, 535, 536, 537

UN Declaration on the Rights of Indigenous Peoples, 800, 805, 806, 823
Unemployment
  Act Relative to Employment for Certain Adult Indians On or Near Indian Reservations, 120
  causes of, 116–17
  drug abuse, 119
  education, lack of, 119
  federal government and, 120–21
  gaming and casinos, 87
  insufficient economic development, 117–19
  introduction to, 114–15
  poverty and, 79–80, 114, 115–16
  poverty on reservations, 79
  psychological effects of, 233
  recent developments, 123–24
  statistics, 115–16
  substance abuse, 249
  tourism and, 96
  women and, 116–17
  Workforce Investment Act, 121–22
UN Forum on Indigenous issues, 820
UN Framework Convention on Climate Change, 718
UN Framework on the Rights of Indigenous Peoples, 779
UN High Commissioner for Refugees (UNHCR), 801
UN Human Development Index, 789
Uniform Commercial Code, 110–11
Unilineal descent, 10
UN Independent Committee on the Elimination of Racial Discrimination, 499
Union Pacific, 744
Unitarians, 366
United Bible Societies, 341
United Church of Canada, 795
United Indians of All Tribes, 549
United National Indian Tribe Youth (UNITY), 594
United Nations, 469, 499, 800–801, 823
United Nations Children's Fund (UNICEF), 801
United Nations Convention on Genocide, 536
United Nations Convention on the Rights of the Child, 159
United Nations Declaration on the Rights of Indigenous People, 802
United Nations Educational, Scientific and Cultural Organization (UNESCO), 801
United Nations Human Settlements Programme (UN-HABITAT), 801
United States v. Blackfeet Tribe, 469
United States v. Dennis Banks and Russell Means, 551

United States v. Kagama, 427, 446
United States v. Wadena, 482
United States v. Wheeler, 558
United States v. Winans, 452, 457
Unity Healing Center, 237
University of California–Davis, 134
University of Illinois, 304
University of Kansas, 407
University of Manitoba, Saskatchewan, 775
University of North Dakota, 303, 304
University of Oklahoma, 305, 414, 646
University of Washington–Seattle, 266
Unmarked Human Burial Sites and Skeletal Remains Protection Act, 381
UN Permanent Forum on Indigenous Issues, 786, 801, 808
UN World Intellectual Property Organization (WIPO), 786
Upham, Hiram, 369
Uranium contamination, 723–25. *See also* Nuclear waste
The Urban American Indian (Sorkin), 71
The Urban Experience in America (Fixico), 68
Urban Indian Child Welfare Centers, 25
Urban Indian Housing Program (UIHP), 22, 24
Urban Indian Relocation Program, 133, 201, 601
Urban living/urbanization
 children, 25–26
 contemporary, 41, 43
 discrimination, 24–25
 education, 21–22
 future of, 43–44
 hate crimes, 24–25
 health, 23–24
 history of, 19–20
 housing, 22
 impact of, 36–45
 Indian and non-Indian interaction, 40–41
 Indian experience, definition of, 68–71
 Indian facts, 42
 Indian identity, 26, 70–71
 institutions of, 20–21
 interaction among Indian people, 39–40
 Phoenix Indian Center, 37
 poverty and adaptation to urban life, 71–74
 poverty in, 67–74
 before the relocation program, 37–38
 relocation program history, 38–39
 tribal government and, 632–33
U.S. Code, 579
U.S. Commission on Civil Rights, 83, 303, 308, 450, 459, 460, 488, 631
U.S. Court system. *See* Courts
U.S. Department of Energy, 109

U.S. Economic Development Agency, 98
U.S. Fish and Wildlife Service, 747
U.S. Holocaust Memorial Museum, 538
U.S. Indian Police Academy, 581
Ute people, 737, 761

Vaccinations, 199–200, 427
Valentine, Rick, 413
Value-neutral truths, 315
Vanadium Corporation of America, 737
Vanishing American, Indians as, 395, 534, 658, 674
Velarde, Pablita, 646
Vermont, 513, 516
Viejas band, 108, 110, 111, 112
Vietnam War, 529–30
Vincenz, Jean, 705
Violence. *See also* Domestic abuse
 American Indian Movement and, 622
 against Navajos, 461–62
 racism and, 496–97
 against women, 54, 797
Violence against Women Act, 190, 192, 585
Virginia, 512, 513, 516–17
Vision Project, 647
Vizenor, Gerald, 63, 546
Vocational Training Act of 1957, 73
Voting rights, 462
Voting Rights Act of 1965, 456

Waddell, Jack, 70–71
Wagnon v. Prairie Band, 470–71
Wahpeton, 388
Waitangi Tribunal, 804–5
Walker Art Center, 671
Walla Walla people, 330
Walt Disney Pictures, 663
Wampanoag language, 343
Wampanoag people, 619, 651
Wampum, 416–17
Wanapums, 275, 330
War Dancing, 350
Warm Springs Apaches, 607
Warm Springs Detention Center, 608
Warm Springs Museum, 296
Warner, L. S., 595
War of 1812, 366, 445, 522–23
War on Poverty, 70, 73
War on Terrorism, 530–31
Warpath tobacco, 64
War Relocation Authority, 38
Warren, Alvin, 254
Warrior, Clyde, 603, 617
Warrior, Robert Allen, 372
Wars of the Middle East, 530–31
Washington, 112, 585, 599, 617

Washington, George, 522, 577
Washington Redskins, 307, 308, 461, 486
Washoe people, 641
Waste disposal. *See* Solid waste
Waste Management, Inc., 710
Waste storage, 736–37
Water rights, 449–50, 721–22
Watie, Buck, 338
Watie, Stand, 420–21, 523
Watkins, Joe, 382
Watson, James, 780–81
Watson, O., 70–71
Watt, James G., 728
Watt-Cloutier, Sheila, 715
Wa-Wan Press, 278
Wayne, John, 658
Ways of knowing, Indian
   ceremonial worlds, 314–17
   constructivist epistemology, 312–13
   irrealism, 313–14
   radical constructivism, 313
   types of knowledge, 311–12
Weasel, Elvin, 369
Weaving, 642–43
Weaving Worlds, 661
Webb, Angela, 669
Weber, Laura, 388
Welch, James, 184
Welfare, 73
Welsh Bible, 338
We Shall Remain, 667
West, American Indian art of, 640–41
West, John, 817
Western Cree language, 336
Western Shoshone Defense Project, 762
Western Shoshone people, 499–500, 730, 761–62
We Talk, You Listen (Deloria), 548
"We the People: American Indians and Alaska Natives in the United States," 30–31
Wetlands Reserve Project (WRP), 748
WGBH productions, 156
Whale hunt, 765
Wheeler, Anthony Robert, 558
Wheeler-Howard Act. *See* Indian Reorganization Act (IRA)
Wheelock, Ezra, 169
Whiskey Indian stereotype, 103
White, James, 600–601
White, Laurence, 203
White Buffalo Calf Woman Society, 196
White Earth Reservation, 79, 91, 489, 501, 546
White House Tribal Nations Summit, 567
Whiteley, Peter, 102
White Mountain Apache, 760
White Mountain Apache Tribe v. Bracker, 471

White Paper on Indian Policy, 791
White Plume, Alex, 472–73
Wiconi International, 370
Wilbur, Silvia, 600–601
Wild Band of Indians, 688
Wildcat, Daniel, 380
Wildlife Conservation Society, 746
Wild West Shows, 651
Wilkins, Maurice, 781
Williams, Paul, 559
Williams, Roger, 181, 182
Williams v. Lee, 471, 559
Wilson, Alex, 247
Wilson, Debra American Horse, 531
Wilson, Jack, 366
Window on Collections, 359
Wind River Reservation, 77–78, 456, 745–46, 759
Winnebagos, 111–12, 369, 427, 428
Winner, South Dakota, 459–60
Winnetou, 663
Winters v. United States, 450, 721
Witt, Shirley Hill, 50, 51, 388, 603
W. K. Kellogg Foundation, 144
Wohaw, 641
Wolves, 745
Woman of Compassion, 263–64, 268
Woman's Missionary Society, 816
Women
   activism and, 50–53
   assimilation and, 49
   athletics and, 403
   Canadian Indians and aboriginal peoples, 797
   Cult of Domesticity, 46–47, 222
   diminished power, 49–50
   drums playing, 687–88
   early political power, 48–49
   expanded political role, 53
   health of, 205–6
   hunting women, 47–48
   introduction to, 46–47
   military participation, 53, 525, 528
   missionaries, 814, 816
   specific women, 50–53
   stereotypes of, 395–97, 660
   two-spirits, 246
   unemployment and, 116–17
   violence against, 54
Women Infants and Children (WIC), 24, 206
Women of All Red Nations (WARN), 49–50, 604
Women of the Métis Nation, 791
Women's Council, 48
Woodland Cree band, 794
Wôpanâak Language Reclamation Project, 343

Worcester, Samuel, 338, 554
Worcester v. Georgia, 338, 467, 471, 514, 554
Workforce Investment Act (WIA), 121–22
Working Effectively with Tribal Governments, 733
Working Group of the Commission on Human Rights, 801
World Council of Indigenous Peoples (WCIP), 784, 822–23
World Health Organization (WHO), 801
World's Columbians Exposition, 274
World War I, 58, 524–25
World War II, 204, 325, 525–27, 547, 572
World Wildlife Fund (WWF), 745
Wounded Knee (film), 667
Wounded Knee, Battle at, 164
Wounded Knee incident, 224, 469, 545–46, 551, 604, 621, 622, 623
Wounded Knee Massacre, 367
Wounded spirit, 236
Wovoka, 366
Wrestling, 412–13
Wu Feng Myth, 808
Wycliffe, John, 341
Wycliffe Bible Translators, 340–41, 342, 343

Xenophobia, 397–99

Yackeschi, Videll, 370
Yahi Indians, 458
Yakama people, 275, 330, 734
Yakima Indian Nation (YIN), 711
Yakima people, 624, 736
Yakima Reservation, 147
Yaquai people, 592
Yazzie, Isabel, 210
Yellowrobe, William S., 654
Young, Phyllis, 604
Youngblood, Mary, 689
Young Deer, James, 396–97, 658, 667
Youth, 249–50, 594–95. *See also* National Indian Youth Council (NIYC)
Youth Anti-Drug Media Campaign, 256
Youth Risk Behavioral Surveillance System Survey, 235
Yucca Mountain, 499–500, 728, 730
Yuchi Community, 785
Yuki people, 245
The Yup'ik Way, 668

Zapatista Army of National Liberation, 803–4
Zeisberger, David, 815
Zuni culture, 244
Zuni Eagle Sanctuary, 747–48
Zuni people, 245, 275, 737, 747–48